Hinduism

To

Nandita Kothari Sarma

My daughter
Born on August 1, 2007
(amidst editing the proofs and compiling
the index for this book!)

vakratuṇḍamahākāya-
sūryakoṭisamaprabhā
nirvighnaṃ kuru me deva
sarvakāryeṣu sarvadā

May Lord Gaṇeśa remove
all obstacles in your path.

Hinduism

A Reader

Edited by
Deepak Sarma

BLACKWELL PUBLISHING
350 Main Street, Malden, MA 02148-5020, USA
9600 Garsington Road, Oxford OX4 2DQ, UK
550 Swanston Street, Carlton, Victoria 3053, Australia

First published 2008 by Blackwell Publishing Ltd

1 2008

Library of Congress Cataloging-in-Publication Data

Hinduism : a reader / edited by Deepak Sarma.
p. cm.
Includes bibliographical references and index.
ISBN 978-1-4051-4989-1 (hardcover : alk. paper)—ISBN 978-1-4051-4990-7 (pbk. : alk. paper)
1. Hinduism. I. Sarma, Deepak, 1969–

BL1107.3.H55 2008
294.5—dc22

2007013898

A catalogue record for this title is available from the British Library.

Set in 9.5/12pt Galliard
by SPi Publisher Services, Pondicherry, India.
Printed and bound in Singapore
by C.O.S. Printers Pte Ltd

The publisher's policy is to use permanent paper from mills that operate a sustainable forestry policy, and which has been manufactured from pulp processed using acid-free and elementary chlorine-free practices. Furthermore, the publisher ensures that the text paper and cover board used have met acceptable environmental accreditation standards.

For further information on
Blackwell Publishing, visit our website at
www.blackwellpublishing.com

Contents

Acknowledgments

I am grateful to Gavin Flood for helping me to conceive of this project. In fact, it was my search for a useful *Reader* to accompany his various introductory texts that led me to propose this one. I am thankful to Arti Dhand for her suggestions about texts to include. I wish to thank Patrick Olivelle and Michael Witzel whose prompt and informative answers to my queries helped enormously. Many thanks to the readers of my proposal for their suggestions about texts to include and exclude. My greatest thanks goes to the translators of the texts that I have used here. Their work makes my work possible.

Copyright Acknowledgments

The editor and publisher gratefully acknowledge the permission granted to reproduce the copyright material in this book:

1 Excerpts from Wendy Doniger O'Flaherty (tr.), *The Rig Veda*. Harmondsworth: Penguin Books, 1986, pp. 25–31, 33–4, 61–4, 87–92, 99–100, 121–3, 128–30, 148–51, 160–2, 224–5, 247–9, 252–7, 267–71, 288–92. Reproduced by permission of Penguin Books Ltd.
2 Excerpts from Patrick Olivelle (tr.), *Upaniṣads*. Oxford: Oxford University Press, 1996, pp. 7–17, 40–52, 64–7, 72–3, 98–101, 116–17, 122, 130–7, 140–3, 148–56, 231–47, 252–65, 288–90. By permission of Oxford University Press.
3 Excerpts from W. Caland (tr.), *The Jaiminigṛhyasūtra*. Delhi: Motilal Banarsidass, 1984, pp. 10–23, 28–56. Reprinted by permission of Motilal Banarsidass Publishers (P) Ltd.
4 Excerpts from J.A.B. van Buitenen (tr.), *The Mahābhārata* (Books 2, 3, 4, and 5). Chicago: University of Chicago Press, 1975 (Phoenix ed. 1981), pp. 134–55, 444–61, 796–807. Reprinted by permission of the publisher, University of Chicago Press.
5 Excerpts from Barbara Stoler Miller (tr.), *The Bhagavad-Gītā*. New York: Bantam Books, 1986, pp. 21–7, 29–39, 44–9, 56–9, 82–7, 97–109, 110–13, 143–54. Copyright © 1986 by Barbara Stoler Miller. Used by permission of Bantam Books, a division of Random House, Inc.

6 Excerpts from Robert Goldman (tr.), *The Rāmāyaṇa of Vālmīki*, Vol. 1. Princeton, NJ: Princeton University Press, 1984 (first Princeton pb. edn., without annotation, 1990), pp. 121–7, 248–53. © 1985 Princeton University Press, 1990 Paperback edition. Reprinted by permission of Princeton University Press.
Excerpts from Sheldon Pollock (tr.), *The Rāmāyaṇa of Vālmīki*, Vol. 3. Princeton, NJ: Princeton University Press, 1990, pp. 123–7, 150–63, 169–91. © 1991 Princeton University Press. Reprinted by permission of Princeton University Press.

7 Excerpts from Cornelia Dimmitt and J.A.B. van Buitenen (eds.), *Classical Hindu Mythology: A Reader in the Sanskrit Purāṇas*. Philadelphia: Temple University Press, 1978, pp. 35–43, 55, 58, 66–9, 76–9, 85–99, 106–13, 116–17, 157–88, 215–18, 237–40, 312–20. Used by permission of Temple University Press. © 1978 by Temple University. All rights reserved.

8 Excerpts from Edwin Bryant (tr.), *Krishna: The Beautiful Legend of God*. Harmondsworth: Penguin Books, 2003, pp. 81–9, 111–18, 125–37, 338–45, 416–19. Reproduced by permission of Penguin Books Ltd.

9 Excerpts from Patrick Olivelle (tr.), *The Law Code of Manu*. Oxford: Oxford University Press, 2004, pp. 15–20, 23–53, 65–9, 76–7, 80–1, 87–107, 148–57, 170–3, 178–210. By permission of Oxford University Press.

10 Excerpts from House of Commons, *Papers Relating to East India Affairs viz. Hindoo Widows and Voluntary Immolations*. London: House of Commons, 1821, pp. 23–9, 111–19. Parliamentary material is reproduced with the permission of the Controller of HMSO on behalf of Parliament.

11 Excerpts from Bruce C. Robertson (ed.), *The Essential Writings of Raja Rammohan Ray*. Delhi: Oxford University Press, 1999, pp. 69–79, 113–22. Reproduced by permission of Oxford University Press India, New Delhi.

12 Excerpts from Valerian Rodrigues, *The Essential Writings of B.R. Ambedkar*. Delhi: Oxford University Press, 2002, pp. 95–105, 263–303. Reproduced by permission of Oxford University Press India, New Delhi.

14 Excerpts from Kancha Ilaiah, *Why I Am Not a Hindu: A Sudra Critique of Hindutva Philosophy, Culture and Political Economy*. Calcutta: Samya, 2005 (2nd edn.), pp. x–xii, 1–19. © 2007 Kancha Ilaiah, Calcutta: Samya, 2007. Reproduced by kind permission.

15 Excerpts from V. D. Savarkar, *Hindutva*. Bombay: S. S. Savarkar, 1969 (5th edn.), pp. 102–41.

16 Excerpts from The Constitution of India. Article 15 published with the kind permission of EBC Publishing Pvt. Ltd., 4 Lalbagh, Lucknow, India.

Every effort has been made to trace copyright holders and to obtain their permission for the use of copyright material. The publisher apologizes for any errors or omissions in the above list and would be grateful if notified of any corrections that should be incorporated in future reprints or editions of this book.

Introduction

This *Reader in Hinduism* seeks to merge two very different yet intimately related worlds of Hinduism. On the one hand, it includes texts in "Classical" Hinduism, which were originally in Sanskrit and whose audience was largely *brāhmaṇas*, members of the priestly class. On the other hand, this reader also includes texts written by people who were either vehemently opposed to the worldview described in these Classical texts or were grappling with how to interpret them for a modernized Hindu and Indian society. These thought provoking and controversial texts should not be read independently of their Classical counterparts since they are integral to them. Read together, they provide an extraordinary perspective on both the Classical world and in the worlds which rejected them or were struggling with them.

By definition, no reader can be comprehensive. After all, if it were, then it would contain the entire corpus of texts, rather than a select few. The texts and passages that I have chosen in both sections are integral to both the world of Hinduism and its modern *avatāras*, incarnations, and adversaries. To this end I have included selections from the *Vedas* and the *Upaniṣads*, the *Mahābhārata*, the *Bhagavad Gītā*, and the *Rāmāyaṇa*, the *Purāṇas* and the *Bhāgavāta Purāṇa*, and *Jaiminigṛhyasūtra* and *Mānavadharmaśāstra*. Though these are the tips of an enormous iceberg, they seem to be the most foundational for the Hindu world developed by the *brāhmaṇas*. The selections that concern issues of modernity include selections from the *British Parliamentary Papers Relating to East India Affairs* (specifically the "problem" of *satī*) and Rāja Rammohan Ray's contemporaneous responses, challenges to the *varṇa* system put forth by Dr Ambedkar, their parallels in the Indian Constitution and the work of Dr Kancha Ilaiah, a twenty-first century social activist of the Dalitbahujan (the "Untouchables"), and finally, concerns about the nature of Hinduism itself as described in *The Hindu Marriage Act* and in V. D. Savarkar's *Hindutva*. These too are the tips of icebergs that have been largely ignored by scholars of Hinduism until only recently.

The selections are self-contained and include brief introductions as well as suggestions for further reading for those interested. These introductions are meant to point students in the right direction, rather than to be comprehensive monographs. The *Reader* trampolines to much larger projects and readings.

The selections here also point towards some significant challenges that have faced and continue to face the Hindu community as a whole. The question revolves around making the Classical texts meaningful for students and practitioners of Hinduism who have been exposed to or brought up amidst Enlightenment ideals of equality. The provocative texts that I have included here are attempts to answer these challenges. In fact, juxtaposing the texts as I have done in this *Reader* may assist others in offering their own answers.

A note about transliteration

There is some inconsistency in the texts included here in the way that Sanskrit words are transliterated. The disparities are most obvious when one examines the ways that these translators have presented the term *bråhmåa*, the priestly class. Some used the anglicized "Brahmin" while others used brahmana or even Brahmun. Given the length of these texts it has not been possible to edit them to be consistent. In my introductory sections, however, I have used the term *bråhmåa*. In general I have tried to use the International Alphabet of Sanskrit Transliteration, a method that was first adopted by the International Congress of Orientalists at Athens in 1912. So if readers see inconsistencies in the ways that some words are presented this should not be a cause for alarm. Rather, it should point towards the history of the transliteration of Sanskrit.

Part I

Classical Texts

Chapter 1

The *Vedas*

The *Vedas* ("wisdom" texts) are a body of orally transmitted texts that originated around 1500 BCE.[1] Their origins are ambiguous and a matter of great controversy as some scholars attribute them to the Indus-Valley civilization and others to the Indo-European "Aryans" ("noble-ones" in Sanskrit) who migrated into the Indus valley and either destroyed or merged with the inhabitants of the Indus Valley.[2] Historicity aside, the *Vedas* are held by some Hindus to be *apauruṣeya*, not of human authorship, and to have been received by *ṛṣi*, seers, whose number vary from seven, the so-called *saptaṛṣis*, to ten. The language of the revelation was Sanskrit, the "perfect" ("*saṃskṛta*") language of the universe. According to some Hindus, their non-human origins makes these indisputably true texts the foundations for Hindu epistemology. Given their oral origins, they are also known as *śruti* (the "heard" texts). Often times, then, Hindu use the terms *śruti* and *Vedas* interchangeably.

The *Vedas* are largely concerned with rituals and *yajñas*, sacrifices (also known as *homas*), to propitiate *devas*, gods and goddesses, which were performed by *brāhmaṇas*, members of the priestly class. The *Vedas* include descriptions of *devas*, such as Indra, to whom sacrifices are to be made. The *homas*, sacrifices, were often of animals such as the horse and the bull, though milk, ghee (clarified butter) and the plant *soma*, were also offered into *agni* (the sacrifical fire). The *yajamāna* (patron of the sacrifice) paid for elaborate rituals that were enjoined in the *Vedas* to be performed by ritual virtuosos. They concurrently chanted Sanskrit *mantras* (liturgical verses) also found in the *śruti*. In some cases the rituals were homologies and linked the body and the universe with the sacrifice.

The *Vedas* are comprised of four traditions, *Ṛg*, *Yajur*, *Sāma*, and *Atharva*. These are each further divided into four categories of texts: the *Saṃhitās*, *Brāhmaṇas*,[3] *Āraṇyakas*, and *Upaniṣads*. This ordering, from *Saṃhitā* to *Upaniṣad*, also reflects the order in which they were composed. While the *Saṃhitās* were composed by about 1500 BCE, the *Upaniṣads* were not completed until about 400 BCE.[4] *The Ṛg Veda Saṃhitā* is the oldest of these and is comprised of ten *maṇḍalas* (books) and 1,028 hymns. The *Ṛg Saṃhitā* is filled with metrical *mantras*, characterizations of, and myths about, *devas*, invocations to the gods, rituals, and verses (*ṛc*) that pertain to the envisioned social world of the *Vedas*. The *Sāman Saṃhitā* is comprised of songs (*sāmans*) based on the *Ṛg Veda* with rules for proper recitation (*gaṇa*). Given the centrality of Sanskrit, instruction was required to ensure that the texts were recited and chanted properly. If they were not, then there could be unwanted consequences or, for that matter, none and all. The *Yajur Saṃhitā* contains ritual instructions and the accompanying *mantras (yajus)*. The fourth *Samhitā*, the *Atharva*, is a collection of magical spells of the Atharvans and Aṅgiras.[5] In it one finds a wide variety of incantations, from those that prevent disease, to those that cause one's enemy to become diseased, and from those that attract lovers, to those that cause ill to befall rival lovers.

The texts that follow the *Saṃhitās* are increasingly more abstract and reflective about the *Saṃhitās*. While *Brāhamaṇas* are texts that largely concern ritual exegesis and the rules and regulations for performing a proper *yajña*, the *Āraṇyakas* are texts about the interpretation of the ritual. The *Upaniṣads* continue the interpretive trajectory that began with the *Āraṇyakas* and offer interpretations that tie the rituals with cosmological and metaphysical matters. Taken as a whole, the *Vedas* helped to define the social, political, and religious world of early Hinduism. Though not accepted by all identified as Hindus, the *Vedas* nonetheless are an orientation point for them.

The passages included here are from the *Ṛg Veda*. Many of the hymns from the *Ṛg Veda* "were intended to be recited at the yearly Soma ritual, celebrated at the time of the New Year."[6] The first few myths are creation myths. *Nāsadīya* 10.129, is filled with enigmatic paradoxes and concludes with a playful skepticism or humility. *The Unknown God, the Golden Embryo* 10.121, mixes a speculative creation myth with sacrificial obligation.

Puruṣa-Sūkta 10.90, arguably the most important hymn in all of the *Vedas*, is a theological justification for the entire Vedic social system. In it, the sacrificial world of the *Vedas* is described as born from a *yajña* of *puruṣa*, the "primal" man. The entire universe as well as the social system of the *Vedas* – namely, the four-fold *varṇa*, class system, of the *brāhmaṇas*, priestly class, *kṣatriyas*, warrior class, *vaiśyas*, merchant class, and *śūdras*, laboring class – is born from this cosmic sacrifice.

The theme of the creation of the *yajña* continues with hymn 10.130, *The Creation of the Sacrifice*, in which the one finds the universe characterized as a weaving loom. *Cosmic Heat*, hymn 10.190 is about the creation of *ṛta*, order, from *tapas*, heat generated from asceticism.

As already mentioned, the *Vedas* were composed in Sanskrit, regarded as the archetypal language. To this end, the next two hymns are both to *vāc*, speech or language, itself. *Vāc* is invoked as a goddess in 10.71, and in 10.125 praised and then characterized as the deity who is the mother of the universe.

The next set of passages provides examples of ritual hymns. *Rājasūya*, the *Royal Consecration*, 10.173 is indicative of the relationships between the *Vedas* and political power while hymns 1.162 and 1.163 concern *aśvamedha*, the horse sacrifice. The *aśvamedha* found here is a glorification of the horse, which was the vehicle of the Vedic people and may have been the means by which the Indo-Aryans entered South Asia.[7] Following these hymns are a number of invocations and myths about *devas* and *devis* of the *Vedas* including Agni, the sacrificial fire, *soma*, the psychotropic drug (possibly *psilocybin* mushrooms)[8] consumed by both sacrificers and *devas* of the *Vedas*, Indra, god of the thunderstorm, the *soma*-drinking, dragon-killing, *deva*-hero.

In *The Killing of Vṛtra* 1.32, Indra symbolically kills the dragon Vṛtra and with its body creates the world. Rudra, who has been speculated to be the precursor of the god Śiva is the subject of *Have Mercy on Us, Rudra* 1.114, and 10.10 *Yama and Yamī*, is another speculative creation myth centered upon incest.

Purūravas and Urvaśī 10.95 is a myth about the water nymph Urvaśī and her lover Purūravas. Continuing this theme of lovers, *The Marriage of Sūryā* 10.85 is the prototype of human marriages and a hymn of the marriage of Sūryā, the daughter of Sūrya, the sun, and *Soma*.

Sleeping Spell 7.55, *Against Rival Wives* 10.145, *The Triumphant Wife* 10.159, and *For a Safe Pregnancy and Birth* 10.184, are each spells from the *Ṛg Veda* which, when chanted properly, were believed to bring about the desired effect. *To Protect the Embryo* 10.162 has been interpreted by some as a *Vedic* prohibition of abortion.

While these hymns are the mere tip of a proverbial iceberg they exemplify *Vedic* ritual, sacrifice, invocations, and spells.

Notes

1 Michael Witzel, "*Vedas* and *Upaniṣads*" in G. Flood (ed.), *A Blackwell Companion to Hinduism*. Oxford: Blackwell Publishing, 2003.

2 See Edwin Bryant and Laurie Patton (eds.), *The Indo-Aryan Controversy.* London: Routledge, 2005; and Edwin Bryant, *The Quest for the Origins of Vedic Culture: The Indo-Aryan Migration Debate*. Oxford: Oxford University Press, 2001.

3 The text is spelled identically with the name of the class. I differentiate between the two by capitalizing the name of the text.

4 Witzel, "*Vedas* and *Upaniṣads*", p. 68.

5 Axel Michaels, *Hinduism Past and Present*. Princeton, NJ: Princeton University Press, 2004, p. 56.

6 Witzel, "*Vedas* and *Upaniṣads*", p. 69.

7 Wendy Doniger O'Flaherty, *The Rig Veda*. London: Penguin Books, 1981, p. 85.

8 See R. Gordon Wasson, *Soma: Divine Mushroom of Immortality*. New York: Harcourt Brace Jovanovich, 1971.

Further reading

Bryant, Edwin and Laurie Patton (eds.), *The Indo-Aryan Controversy.* London: Routledge, 2005.

Bryant, Edwin, *The Quest for the Origins of Vedic Culture: The Indo-Aryan Migration Debate*. Oxford: Oxford University Press, 2001.

Flood, Gavin, *An Introduction to Hinduism*. Cambridge: Cambridge University Press, 1999.

Gonda, Jan, *Vedic Literature*. Wiesbaden: Harrassowitz, 1975.

Jamison, Stephanie, *The Ravenous Hyenas and the Wounded Son: Myth and Ritual in Ancient India*. Ithaca, NY: Cornell University Press, 1991.

Mahony, William K., *The Artful Universe: An Introduction to the Vedic Religious Imagination*. Albany, NY: State University of New York Press, 1998.

Michaels, Axel, *Hinduism Past and Present*. Princeton, NJ: Princeton University Press, 2004.
O'Flaherty, Wendy Doniger, *The Rig Veda*. London: Penguin Books, 1981.
Patton, Laurie, *Authority, Anxiety, and Canon: Essays in Vedic Interpretation*. Albany, NY: State University of New York Press, 1994.
Wasson, R. Gordon, *Soma: Divine Mushroom of Immortality*. New York: Harcourt Brace Jovanovich, 1971.
Witzel, Michael, "*Vedas* and *Upaniṣads*" in G. Flood (ed.), *A Blackwell Companion to Hinduism*. Oxford: Blackwell Publishing, 2003.

The Rig Veda

10.129 Creation Hymn (Nāsadīya)

1. There was neither non-existence nor existence then; there was neither the realm of space nor the sky which is beyond. What stirred? Where? In whose protection? Was there water, bottomlessly deep?

2. There was neither death nor immortality then. There was no distinguishing sign of night nor of day. That one breathed, windless, by its own impulse. Other than that there was nothing beyond.

3. Darkness was hidden by darkness in the beginning; with no distinguishing sign, all this was water. The life force that was covered with emptiness, that one arose through the power of heat.

4. Desire came upon that one in the beginning; that was the first seed of mind. Poets seeking in their heart with wisdom found the bond of existence in non-existence.

5. Their cord was extended across. Was there below? Was there above? There were seed-placers; there were powers. There was impulse beneath; there was giving-forth above.

6. Who really knows? Who will here proclaim it? Whence was it produced? Whence is this creation? The gods came afterwards, with the creation of this universe. Who then knows whence it has arisen?

7. Whence this creation has arisen – perhaps it formed itself, or perhaps it did not – the one who looks down on it, in the highest heaven, only he knows – or perhaps he does not know.

10.121 The Unknown God, the Golden Embryo

1. In the beginning the Golden Embryo arose. Once he was born, he was the one lord of creation. He held in place the earth and this sky. Who is the god whom we should worship with the oblation?

2. He who gives life, who gives strength, whose command all the gods, his own, obey; his shadow is immortality – and death. Who is the god whom we should worship with the oblation?

3. He who by his greatness became the one king of the world that breathes and blinks, who rules over his two-footed and four-footed creatures – who is the god whom we should worship with the oblation?

4. He who through his power owns these snowy mountains, and the ocean together with the river Rasā, they say; who has the quarters of the sky as his two arms – who is the god whom we should worship with the oblation?

5. He by whom the awesome sky and the earth were made firm, by whom the dome of the sky was propped up, and the sun, who measured out the middle realm of space – who is the god whom we should worship with the oblation?

6. He to whom the two opposed masses looked with trembling in their hearts, supported by his help, on whom the rising sun shines down – who is the god whom we should worship with the oblation?

7. When the high waters came, pregnant with the embryo that is everything, bringing forth fire, he arose from that as the one life's breath of the gods. Who is the god whom we should worship with the oblation?

8. He who in his greatness looked over the waters, which were pregnant with Dakṣa, bringing forth the sacrifice, he who was the one god among all the gods – who is the god whom we should worship with the oblation?

9. Let him not harm us, he who fathered the earth and created the sky, whose laws are true, who created the high, shining waters. Who is the god whom we should worship with the oblation?

Excerpts from Wendy Doniger O'Flaherty (tr.), *The Rig Veda*. Harmondsworth: Penguin Books, 1986.

10. O Prajāpati, lord of progeny, no one but you embraces all these creatures. Grant us the desires for which we offer you oblation. Let us be lords of riches.

10.90 Puruṣa-Sūkta, or The Hymn of Man

1. The Man has a thousand heads, a thousand eyes, a thousand feet. He pervaded the earth on all sides and extended beyond it as far as ten fingers.

2. It is the Man who is all this, whatever has been and whatever is to be. He is the ruler of immortality, when he grows beyond everything through food.

3. Such is his greatness, and the Man is yet more than this. All creatures are a quarter of him; three quarters are what is immortal in heaven.

4. With three quarters the Man rose upwards, and one quarter of him still remains here. From this he spread out in all directions, into that which eats and that which does not eat.

5. From him Virāj was born, and from Virāj came the Man. When he was born, he ranged beyond the earth behind and before.

6. When the gods spread the sacrifice with the Man as the offering, spring was the clarified butter, summer the fuel, autumn the oblation.

7. They anointed the Man, the sacrifice born at the beginning, upon the sacred grass. With him the gods, Sādhyas, and sages sacrificed.

8. From that sacrifice in which everything was offered, the melted fat was collected, and he made it into those beasts who live in the air, in the forest, and in villages.

9. From that sacrifice in which everything was offered, the verses and chants were born, the metres were born from it, and from it the formulas were born.

10. Horses were born from it, and those other animals that have two rows of teeth; cows were born from it, and from it goats and sheep were born.

11. When they divided the Man, into how many parts did they apportion him? What do they call his mouth, his two arms and thighs and feet?

12. His mouth became the Brahmin; his arms were made into the Warrior, his thighs the People, and from his feet the Servants were born.

13. The moon was born from his mind; from his eye the sun was born. Indra and Agni came from his mouth, and from his vital breath the Wind was born.

14. From his navel the middle realm of space arose; from his head the sky evolved. From his two feet came the earth, and the quarters of the sky from his ear. Thus they set the worlds in order.

15. There were seven enclosing-sticks for him, and thrice seven fuel-sticks, when the gods, spreading the sacrifice, bound the Man as the sacrificial beast.

16. With the sacrifice the gods sacrificed to the sacrifice. These were the first ritual laws. These very powers reached the dome of the sky where dwell the Sādhyas, the ancient gods.

10.130 The Creation of the Sacrifice

1. The sacrifice that is spread out with threads on all sides, drawn tight with a hundred and one divine acts, is woven by these fathers as they come near: 'Weave forward, weave backward,' they say as they sit by the loom that is stretched tight.

2. The Man stretches the warp and draws the weft; the Man has spread it out upon this dome of the sky. These are the pegs, that are fastened in place; they made the melodies into the shuttles for weaving.

3. What was the original model, and what was the copy, and what was the connection between them? What was the butter, and what the enclosing wood? What was the metre, what was the invocation, and the chant, when all the gods sacrificed the god?

4. The Gāyatrī metre was the yoke-mate of Agni; Savitṛ joined with the Uṣṇi metre, and with the Anuṣṭubh metre was Soma that

reverberates with the chants. The Bṛhatī metre resonated in the voice of Bṛhaspati.

5. The Virāj metre was the privilege of Mitra and Varuṇa; the Triṣṭubh metre was part of the day of Indra. The Jagatī entered into all the gods. That was the model for the human sages.

6. That was the model for the human sages, our fathers, when the primeval sacrifice was born. With the eye that is mind, in thought I see those who were the first to offer this sacrifice.

7. The ritual repetitions harmonized with the chants and with the metres; the seven divine sages harmonized with the original models. When the wise men looked back along the path of those who went before, they took up the reins like charioteers.

10.190 Cosmic Heat

1. Order and truth were born from heat as it blazed up. From that was born night; from that heat was born the billowy ocean.

2. From the billowy ocean was born the year, that arranges days and nights, ruling over all that blinks its eyes.

3. The Arranger has set in their proper place the sun and moon, the sky and the earth, the middle realm of space, and finally the sunlight.

10.71 The Origins of Sacred Speech

1. Bṛhaspati! When they set in motion the first beginning of speech, giving names, their most pure and perfectly guarded secret was revealed through love.

2. When the wise ones fashioned speech with their thought, sifting it as grain is sifted through a sieve, then friends recognized their friendships. A good sign was placed on their speech.

3. Through the sacrifice they traced the path of speech and found it inside the sages. They held it and portioned it out to many; together the seven singers praised it.

4. One who looked did not see speech, and another who listens does not hear it. It reveals itself to someone as a loving wife, beautifully dressed, reveals her body to her husband.

5. One person, they said, has grown awkward and heavy in this friendship; they no longer urge him forward in the contests. He lives with falsehood like a milkless cow, for the speech that he has heard has no fruit no flower.

6. A man that abandons a friend who has learned with him no longer has a share in speech. What he does hear he hears in vain, for he does not know the path of good action.

7. Friends have eyes and ears, but their flashes of insight are not equal. Some are like ponds that reach only to the mouth or shoulder; others are like ponds that one could bathe in.

8. When the intuitions of the mind are shaped in the heart, when Brahmins perform sacrifices together as friends, some are left behind for lack of knowledge, while others surpass them with the power to praise.

9. Those who move neither near nor far, who are not real Brahmins nor pressers of the Soma; using speech in a bad way, they weave on a weft of rags, without understanding.

10. All his friends rejoice in the friend who emerges with fame and victory in the contest. He saves them from error and gives them food. He is worthy to be pushed forward to win the prize.

11. One sits bringing to blossom the flower of the verses. Another sings a song in the Śakvarī metre. One, the Brahmin, proclaims the knowledge of the ancient ways. Another lays out the measure of the sacrifice.

10.125 Speech

1. I move with the Rudras, with the Vasus, with the Ādityas and all the gods. I carry both Mitra and Varuṇa, both Indra and Agni, and both of the Aśvins.

2. I carry the swelling Soma, and Tvaṣṭṛ, and Pūṣan and Bhaga. I bestow wealth on the pious sacrificer who presses the Soma and offers the oblation.

3. I am the queen, the confluence of riches, the skilful one who is first among

those worthy of sacrifice. The gods divided me up into various parts, for I dwell in many places and enter into many forms.

4. The one who eats food, who truly sees, who breathes, who hears what is said, does so through me. Though they do not realize it, they dwell in me. Listen, you whom they have heard: what I tell you should be heeded.

5. I am the one who says, by myself, what gives joy to gods and men. Whom I love I make awesome; I make him a sage, a wise man, a Brahmin.

6. I stretch the bow for Rudra so that his arrow will strike down the hater of prayer. I incite the contest among the people. I have pervaded sky and earth.

7. I gave birth to the father on the head of this world. My womb is in the waters, within the ocean. From there I spread out over all creatures and touch the very sky with the crown of my head.

8. I am the one who blows like the wind, embracing all creatures. Beyond the sky, beyond this earth, so much have I become in my greatness.

10.173 Royal Consecration

1. I have brought you here; remain among us. Stay steadfast and unwavering. Let all the people want you, and let the kingship never fall away from you.

2. Stay right here – do not slip away, but stay unwavering, like a mountain. Stand steadfast here, like Indra, and here uphold the kingdom.

3. Indra has supported him firmly with a firm oblation. Let Soma – and Brahmaṇaspati also – speak up for him.

4. Firm is the sky and firm the earth, and firm are these mountains. Firm is all this world, and firm is this king of all the people.

5. Steadfast let King Varuṇa, steadfast the god Bṛhaspati, steadfast let Indra and Agni maintain your steadfast kingship.

6. With a firm oblation we touch the firm Soma. Thus let Indra make all the people who bring tribute yours alone.

1.163 Hymn to the Horse

1. When you whinnied for the first time, as you were born coming forth from the ocean or from the celestial source, with the wings of an eagle and the forelegs of an antelope – that, Swift Runner, was your great and awesome birth.

2. Yama gave him and Trita harnessed him; Indra was the first to mount him, and the Gandharva grasped his reins. You gods fashioned the horse out of the sun.

3. Swift Runner, you are Yama; you are Āditya; you are Trita, through the hidden design. You are like and not like Soma. They say you have three bonds in the sky.

4. They say you have three bonds in the sky, three in the waters, and three within the ocean. And to me you appear, Swift Runner, like Varuṇa, that is said to be your highest birth.

5. These are the places where they rubbed you down when you were victorious; here are the marks where you put down your hooves. Here I saw your lucky reins, which the Guardians of the Order keep safely.

6. From afar, in my heart I recognized your soul, the bird flying below the sky. I saw your winged head snorting on the dustless paths easy to travel.

7. Here I saw your highest form eager for nourishment in the place of the cow. As soon as a mortal gets the food that you enjoy, the great devourer of plants awakens him.

8. The chariot follows you, Swift Runner; the young man follows, the cow follows, the love of young girls follows. The troops follow your friendship. The gods entrusted virile power to you.

9. His mane is golden; his feet are bronze. He is swift as thought, faster than Indra. The gods have come to eat the oblation of the one who was the first to mount the swift runner.

10. The celestial coursers, revelling in their strength, fly in a line like wild geese, the ends held back while the middle surges forward, when the horses reach the racecourse of the sky.

11. Your body flies, Swift Runner; your spirit rushes like wind. Your mane, spread in many directions, flickers and jumps about in the forests.

12. The racehorse has come to the slaughter, pondering with his heart turned to the gods. The goat, his kin, is led in front; behind come the poets, the singers.

13. The swift runner has come to the highest dwelling-place, to his father and mother. May he go to the gods today and be most welcome, and then ask for the things that the worshipper wishes for.

1.162 The Sacrifice of the Horse

1. Mitra, Varuṇa, Aryaman the Active, Indra the ruler of the Ṛbhus, and the Maruts – let them not fail to heed us when we proclaim in the assembly the heroic deeds of the racehorse who was born of the gods.

2. When they lead the firmly grasped offering in front of the horse that is covered with cloths and heirlooms, the dappled goat goes bleating straight to the dear dwelling of Indra and Pūṣan.

3. This goat for all the gods is led forward with the racehorse as the share for Pūṣan. When they lead forth the welcome offering with the charger, Tvaṣṭṛ urges him on to great fame.

4. When, as the ritual law ordains, the men circle three times, leading the horse that is to be the oblation on the path to the gods, the goat who is the share for Pūṣan goes first, announcing the sacrifice to the gods.

5. The Invoker, the officiating priest, the atoner, the fire-kindler, the holder of the pressing-stones, the reciter, the priest who prays – fill your bellies with this well-prepared, well-sacrificed sacrifice.

6. The hewers of the sacrificial stake and those who carry it, and those who carve the knob for the horse's sacrificial stake, and those who gather together the things to cook the charger – let their approval encourage us.

7. The horse with his smooth back went forth into the fields of the gods, just when I made my prayer. The inspired sages exult in him. We have made him a welcome companion at the banquet of the gods.

8. The charger's rope and halter, the reins and bridle on his head, and even the grass that has been brought up to his mouth – let all of that stay with you even among the gods.

9. Whatever of the horse's flesh the fly has eaten, or whatever stays stuck to the stake or the axe, or to the hands or nails of the slaughterer – let all of that stay with you even among the gods.

10. Whatever food remains in his stomach, sending forth gas, or whatever smell there is from his raw flesh – let the slaughterers make that well done; let them cook the sacrificial animal until he is perfectly cooked.

11. Whatever runs off your body when it has been placed on the spit and roasted by the fire, let it not lie there in the earth or on the grass, but let it be given to the gods who long for it.

12. Those who see that the racehorse is cooked, who say, 'It smells good! Take it away!', and who wait for the doling out of the flesh of the charger – let their approval encourage us.

13. The testing fork for the cauldron that cooks the flesh, the pots for pouring the broth, the cover of the bowls to keep it warm, the hooks, the dishes – all these attend the horse.

14. The place where he walks, where he rests, where he rolls, and the fetters on the horse's feet, and what he has drunk and the fodder he has eaten – let all of that stay with you even among the gods.

15. Let not the fire that reeks of smoke darken you, nor the red-hot cauldron split into pieces. The gods receive the horse who has been sacrificed, worshipped, consecrated, and sanctified with the cry of 'Vaṣat!'

16. The cloth that they spread beneath the horse, the upper covering, the golden trappings on him, the halter and the fetters on his feet – let these things that are his own bind the horse among the gods.

17. If someone riding you has struck you too hard with heel or whip when you

shied, I make all these things well again for you with prayer, as they do with the oblation's ladle in sacrifices.

18. The axe cuts through the thirty-four ribs of the racehorse who is the companion of the gods. Keep the limbs undamaged and place them in the proper pattern. Cut them apart, calling out piece by piece.

19. One is the slaughterer of the horse of Tvaṣṭṛ; two restrain him. This is the rule. As many of your limbs as I set out, according to the rules, so many balls I offer into the fire.

20. Let not your dear soul burn you as you go away. Let not the axe do lasting harm to your body. Let no greedy, clumsy slaughterer hack in the wrong place and damage your limbs with his knife.

21. You do not really die through this, nor are you harmed. You go to the gods on paths pleasant to go on. The two bay stallions, the two roan mares are now your chariot mates. The racehorse has been set in the donkey's yoke.

22. Let this racehorse bring us good cattle and good horses, male children and all-nourishing wealth. Let Aditi make us free from sin. Let the horse with our offerings achieve sovereign power for us.

1.1 I Pray to Agni

1. I pray to Agni, the household priest who is the god of the sacrifice, the one who chants and invokes and brings most treasure.

2. Agni earned the prayers of the ancient sages, and of those of the present, too; he will bring the gods here.

3. Through Agni one may win wealth, and growth from day to day, glorious and most abounding in heroic sons.

4. Agni, the sacrificial ritual that you encompass on all sides – only that one goes to the gods.

5. Agni, the priest with the sharp sight of a poet, the true and most brilliant, the god will come with the gods.

6. Whatever good you wish to do for the one who worships you, Agni, through you, O Angiras, that comes true.

7. To you, Agni, who shine upon darkness, we come day after day, bringing our thoughts and homage

8. to you, the king over sacrifices, the shining guardian of the Order, growing in your own house.

9. Be easy for us to reach, like a father to his son. Abide with us, Agni, for our happiness.

1.26 Agni and the Gods

1. Now get dressed in your robes, lord of powers and master of the sacrificial food, and offer this sacrifice for us.

2. Young Agni, take your place as our favourite priest with inspirations and shining speech.

3. The father sacrifices for his son, the comrade for his comrade, the favourite friend for his friend.

4. May Varuṇa, Mitra and Aryaman, proud of their powers, sit upon our sacred grass, as upon Manu's.

5. You who were the first to invoke, rejoice in our friendship and hear only these songs.

6. When we offer sacrifice to this god or that god, in the full line of order, it is to you alone that the oblation is offered.

7. Let him be a beloved lord of tribes for us, a favourite, kindly invoker; let us have a good fire and be beloved.

8. For when the gods have a good fire, they bring us what we wish for. Let us pray with a good fire.

9. So let praises flow back and forth between the two, between us who are mortals and you, the immortal.

10. Agni, young spawn of strength, with all the fires take pleasure in this sacrifice and in this speech.

8.79 This Restless Soma

1. This restless Soma – you try to grab him but he breaks away and overpowers everything. He is a sage and a seer inspired by poetry.

2. He covers the naked and heals all who are sick. The blind man sees; the lame man steps forth.

3. Soma, you are a broad defence against those who hate us, both enemies we have made ourselves and those made by others.

4. Through your knowledge and skills, rushing forward you drive out of the sky and the earth the evil deed of the enemy.

5. Let those who seek find what they seek: let them receive the treasure given by the generous and stop the greedy from getting what they want.

6. Let him find what was lost before; let him push forward the man of truth. Let him stretch out the life-span that has not yet crossed its span.

7. Be kind and merciful to us, Soma; be good to our heart, without confusing our powers in your whirlwind.

8. King Soma, do not enrage us; do not terrify us; do not wound our heart with dazzling light.

9. Give help, when you see the evil plans of the gods in your own house. Generous king, keep away hatreds, keep away failures.

9.74 Soma Pressed in the Bowls

1. Like a new-born child he bellows in the wood, the tawny racehorse straining to win the sun. He unites with the sky's seed that grows great with milk. With kind thoughts we pray to him for far-reaching shelter.

2. He who is the pillar of the sky, the well-adorned support, the full stalk that encircles all around, he is the one who by tradition sacrifices to these two great world-halves. The poet holds together the conjoined pair, and the refreshing foods.

3. The honey of Soma is a great feast; the wide pasture of Aditi is for the man who follows the right way. Child of dawn, the bull who rules over the rain here, leader of the waters, worthy of hymns, he is the one who brings help here.

4. Butter and milk are milked from the living cloud; the navel of Order, the ambrosia is born. Together those who bring fine gifts satisfy him; the swollen men piss down the fluid set in motion.

5. The stalk roared as it united with the wave; for man he swells the skin that attracts the gods. He places in the lap of Aditi the seed by which we win sons and grandsons.

6. Relentlessly they flow down into the filter of a thousand streams; let them have offspring in the third realm of the world. Four hidden springs pouring forth butter carry down from the sky the ambrosia that is the oblation.

7. He takes on a white colour when he strains to win; Soma, the generous Asura, knows the whole world. He clings to inspired thought and ritual action as he goes forth; let him hurl down from the sky the cask full of water.

8. Now he has gone to the white pot coated by cows; the racehorse has reached the winning line and has won a hundred cows for Kakṣīvat, the man of a hundred winters. Longing for the gods in their heart, they hasten forth.

9. Clarifying Soma, when you are sated with waters your juice runs through the sieve made of wool. Polished by the poets, Soma who brings supreme ecstasy, be sweet for Indra to drink.

4.26–7 Soma and Indra and the Eagle

4.26

1. [*Indra:*] 'I was Manu and I was the Sun; I am Kakṣīvat, the wise sage. I surpassed Kutsa the son of Arjuna; I am the inspired Uśanas – look at me!

2. 'I gave the earth to the Āryan; I gave rain to the mortal who made an offering. I led forth the roaring water; the gods followed after my wish.

3. 'Ecstatic with Soma I shattered the nine and ninety fortresses of Śambara all at once, finishing off the inhabitant as the hundredth, as I gave aid to Divodāsa Atithigva.

4. 'O Maruts, the bird shall be supreme above all birds, the swift-flying eagle above all eagles, since by his own driving power that needs no chariot wheels, with his powerful wings he brought to man the oblation loved by the gods.'

5. Fluttering as he brought it down, the bird swift as thought shot forth on the wide path; swiftly the eagle came with the honey of Soma and won fame for that.

6. Stretching out in flight, holding the stem, the eagle brought the exhilarating and intoxicating drink from the distance. Accompanied by the gods, the bird clutched the Soma tightly after he took it from that highest heaven.

7. When the eagle had taken the Soma, he brought it for a thousand and ten thousand pressings at once. The bringer of abundance left his enemies behind there; ecstatic with Soma, the wise one left the fools.

4.27

1. [*The eagle:*] 'While still in the womb, I knew all the generations of these gods. A hundred iron fortresses guarded me, but I, the eagle, swiftly flew away.'

2. [*Soma:*] 'He did not drag me out against my will, for I surpassed him in energy and manly strength. In a flash, the bringer of abundance left his enemies behind as he outran the winds, swelling with power.'

3. As the eagle came shrieking down from heaven, and as they led the bringer of abundance down from there like the wind, as the archer Kṛśānu, reacting quickly, aimed down at him and let loose his bowstring,

4. the eagle bearing Indra brought him down like Bhujyu from the summits of heaven, stretching out in swift flight. Then a wing feather fell in mid-air from the bird as he swooped on the path of flight.

5. The white goblet overflowing with cows' milk, the finest honey, the clear juice offered by the priests – now let the generous Indra raise it to drink until ecstatic with Soma; let the hero raise it to drink until ecstatic with Soma.

1.32 The Killing of Vṛtra

1. Let me now sing the heroic deeds of Indra, the first that the thunderbolt-wielder performed. He killed the dragon and pierced an opening for the waters; he split open the bellies of mountains.

2. He killed the dragon who lay upon the mountain; Tvaṣṭṛ fashioned the roaring thunderbolt for him. Like lowing cows, the flowing waters rushed straight down to the sea.

3. Wildly excited like a bull, he took the Soma for himself and drank the extract from the three bowls in the three-day Soma ceremony. Indra the Generous seized his thunderbolt to hurl it as a weapon; he killed the first-born of dragons.

4. Indra, when you killed the first-born of dragons and overcame by your own magic the magic of the magicians, at that very moment you brought forth the sun, the sky, and dawn. Since then you have found no enemy to conquer you.

5. With his great weapon, the thunderbolt, Indra killed the shoulderless Vṛtra, his greatest enemy. Like the trunk of a tree whose branches have been lopped off by an axe, the dragon lies flat upon the ground.

6. For, muddled by drunkenness like one who is no soldier, Vṛtra challenged the great hero who had overcome the mighty and who drank Soma to the dregs. Unable to withstand the onslaught of his weapons, he found Indra an enemy to conquer him and was shattered, his nose crushed.

7. Without feet or hands he fought against Indra, who struck him on the nape of the neck with his thunderbolt. The steer who wished to become the equal of the bull bursting with seed, Vṛtra lay broken in many places.

8. Over him as he lay there like a broken reed the swelling waters flowed for man. Those waters that Vṛtra had enclosed with his power – the dragon now lay at their feet.

9. The vital energy of Vṛtra's mother ebbed away, for Indra had hurled his deadly weapon at her. Above was the mother, below was the son; Dānu lay down like a cow with her calf.

10. In the midst of the channels of the waters which never stood still or rested, the body was hidden. The waters flow over Vṛtra's

secret place; he who found Indra an enemy to conquer him sank into long darkness.

11. The waters who had the Dāsa for their husband, the dragon for their protector, were imprisoned like the cows imprisoned by the Paṇis. When he killed Vṛtra he split open the outlet of the waters that had been closed.

12. Indra, you became a hair of a horse's tail when Vṛtra struck you on the corner of the mouth. You, the one god, the brave one, you won the cows; you won the Soma; you released the seven streams so that they could flow.

13. No use was the lightning and thunder, fog and hail that he had scattered about, when the dragon and Indra fought. Indra the Generous remained victorious for all time to come.

14. What avenger of the dragon did you see, Indra, that fear entered your heart when you had killed him? Then you crossed the ninety-nine streams like the frightened eagle crossing the realms of earth and air.

15. Indra, who wields the thunderbolt in his hand, is the king of that which moves and that which rests, of the tame and of the horned. He rules the people as their king, encircling all this as a rim encircles spokes.

2.12 'Who is Indra?'

1. The god who had insight the moment he was born, the first who protected the gods with his power of thought, before whose hot breath the two world-halves tremble at the greatness of his manly powers – he, my people, is Indra.

2. He who made fast the tottering earth, who made still the quaking mountains, who measured out and extended the expanse of the air, who propped up the sky – he, my people, is Indra.

3. He who killed the serpent and loosed the seven rivers, who drove out the cows that had been pent up by Vala, who gave birth to fire between two stones, the winner of booty in combats – he, my people, is Indra.

4. He by whom all these changes were rung, who drove the race of Dāsas down into obscurity, who took away the flourishing wealth of the enemy as a winning gambler takes the stake – he, my people, is Indra.

5. He about whom they ask, 'Where is he?', or they say of him, the terrible one, 'He does not exist', he who diminishes the flourishing wealth of the enemy as gambling does – believe in him! He, my people, is Indra.

6. He who encourages the weary and the sick, and the poor priest who is in need, who helps the man who harnesses the stones to press Soma, he who has lips fine for drinking – he, my people, is Indra.

7. He under whose command are horses and cows and villages and all chariots, who gave birth to the sun and the dawn and led out the waters, he, my people, is Indra.

8. He who is invoked by both of two armies, enemies locked in combat, on this side and that side, he who is even invoked separately by each of two men standing on the very same chariot, he, my people, is Indra.

9. He without whom people do not conquer, he whom they call on for help when they are fighting, who became the image of everything, who shakes the unshakeable – he, my people, is Indra.

10. He who killed with his weapon all those who had committed a great sin, even when they did not know it, he who does not pardon the arrogant man for his arrogance, who is the slayer of the Dasyus, he, my people, is Indra.

11. He who in the fortieth autumn discovered Śambara living in the mountains, who killed the violent serpent, the Dānu, as he lay there, he, my people, is Indra.

12. He, the mighty bull who with his seven reins let loose the seven rivers to flow, who with his thunderbolt in his hand hurled down Rauhiṇa as he was climbing up to the sky, he, my people, is Indra.

13. Even the sky and the earth bow low before him, and the mountains are terrified of his hot breath; he who is known as the Soma-drinker, with the thunderbolt in his hand, with the thunderbolt in his palm, he, my people, is Indra.

14. He who helps with his favour the one who presses and the one who cooks, the

praiser and the preparer, he for whom prayer is nourishment, for whom Soma is the special gift, he, my people, is Indra.

15. You who furiously grasp the prize for the one who presses and the one who cooks, you are truly real. Let us be dear to you, Indra, all our days, and let us speak as men of power in the sacrificial gathering.

1.114 Have Mercy on Us, Rudra

1. We bring these thoughts to the mighty Rudra, the god with braided hair, who rules over heroes, so that it will be well with our two-footed and four-footed creatures, and in this village all will flourish unharmed.

2. Have mercy on us, Rudra, and give us life-force. We wish to bow low in service to you who rule over heroes. Whatever happiness and health Manu the father won by sacrifice, we wish to gain that with you to lead us forth.

3. We wish to gain your kindness, Rudra, through sacrifice to the gods, for you are generous. O ruler over heroes, come to our families with kindness. Let us offer the oblation to you with our heroes free from injury.

4. We call down for help the dreaded Rudra who completes the sacrifice, the sage who flies. Let him repel far from us the anger of the gods; it is his kindness that we choose to have.

5. Tawny boar of the sky, dreaded form with braided hair, we call you down and we bow low. Holding in his hand the healing medicines that we long for, let him grant us protection, shelter, refuge.

6. These words are spoken for Rudra, the father of the Maruts, words sweeter than sweet, to strengthen him. And grant us, O immortal, the food for mortals. Have mercy on us, and on our children and grandchildren.

7. Do not slaughter the great one among us or the small one among us, nor the growing or the grown. Rudra, do not kill our father or our mother, nor harm the bodies dear to us.

8. Do not harm us in our children or grandchildren, nor in our life-span, nor in our cows or in our horses. Rudra, do not in fury slaughter our heroes. With oblations we call you here for ever.

9. I have driven these praises to you as the herdsman drives his cattle. Grant us kindness, father of the Maruts, for your kindness brings blessings most merciful, and so it is your help that we choose to have.

10. Keep far away from us your cow-killing and man-killing power, O ruler of heroes. Have mercy on us and speak for us, O god, and grant us double protection.

11. Seeking help, we have spoken in homage to him. Let Rudra with the Maruts hear our call. Let Mitra, Varuṇa, Aditi, Sindhu, Earth and Sky grant this to us.

10.10 Yama and Yamī

1. [*Yamī:*] 'Would that I might draw my friend into intimate friendship, now that he has gone far across the ocean. A man of foresight should receive a grandson from the father, thinking of what lies ahead on earth.'

2. [*Yama:*] 'Your friend does not desire this friendship, in which a woman of his kind would behave like a stranger. The heroes, the sons of the great spirit, supporters of the sky, see far and wide.'

3. [*Yamī:*] 'The immortals desire this, that offspring should be left by the one mortal. Let your mind unite with my mind; as a husband, enter the body of your wife.'

4. [*Yama:*] 'Shall we do now what we have not done before? Shall we who spoke truth out loud now whisper falsehood? The divine youth in the waters and the woman of the waters – such is our source, our highest birth.'

5. [*Yamī:*] 'The god Tvaṣṭṛ, the creator and impeller, shaper of all forms, made us man and wife even when we were still in the womb. No one disobeys his commands; earth and sky are our witnesses for this.'

6. [*Yama:*] 'Who was witness of that first day? Who has seen it? Who can proclaim it here? The law of Mitra and Varuṇa is high. Yet what will you say to men, wanton woman, to seduce them?'

7. [*Yamī:*] 'Desire for Yama has come upon me, Yamī, the desire to lie with him upon the same bed. Let me open my body to him as a wife to her husband. Let us roll about together like the two wheels of a chariot.'

8. [*Yama:*] 'These spies of the gods, who wander about here below, do not stand still, nor do they blink their eyes. Wanton woman, go away fast with another man, not with me. Roll about with him like the two wheels of a chariot.'

9. [*Yamī:*] 'She would do what he wished in the nights and in the days; she would deceive the eye of the sun for the instant of the blink of an eye. We twins are related in the same way as sky and earth. Let Yamī behave toward Yama as if she were not his sister.'

10. [*Yama:*] 'Later ages will come, indeed, when blood relatives will act as if they were not related. Make a pillow of your arm for some bull of a man. Seek another husband, lovely lady, not me.'

11. [*Yamī:*] 'What good is a brother, when there is no protector? What good is a sister, when destruction breaks out? Overcome with desire, I whisper this again and again: mingle your body with my body.'

12. [*Yama:*] 'Never will I mingle my body with your body. They call a man who unites with his sister a sinner. Arrange your lustful pleasures with some other man, not with me, lovely lady. Your brother does not want this.'

13. [*Yamī:*] 'Dammit, Yama, how feeble you are. I have not been able to find any mind or heart in you. Some other woman will surely embrace you like a girth embracing a harnessed stallion or a creeper embracing a tree.'

14. [*Yama:*] 'You too, Yamī, will surely embrace another man, and he will embrace you, as a creeper embraces a tree. Seek *his* mind, and let him seek yours. Join with him in proper harmony.'

10.95 Purūravas and Urvaśī

1. [*Purūravas:*] 'My wife, turn your heart and mind to me. Stay here, dangerous woman, and let us exchange words. If we do not speak out these thoughts of ours they will bring us no joy, even on the most distant day.'

2. [*Urvaśī:*] 'What use to me are these words of yours? I have left you, like the first of the dawns. Go home again, Purūravas. I am hard to catch and hold, like the wind . . . '

3. [*Purūravas:*] ' . . . or like an arrow shot from the quiver for a prize, or like a racehorse that wins cattle, that wins hundreds. As if there was no man with power there, they made the lightning flash and in their frenzy thought to bleat like sheep.

4. 'She brought to her husband's father nourishing riches, and whenever her lover desired her she came to his home across from her dwelling-place and took her pleasure in him, pierced by his rod day and night.'

5. [*Urvaśī:*] 'Indeed, you pierced me with your rod three times a day, and filled me even when I had no desire. I followed your will, Purūravas; you were my man, king of my body.'

6. [*Purūravas:*] 'Sujūrṇi, Śreṇi, Sumnaāpi, and Hradecakṣus, Granthinī, Caraṇyu – they have all slipped away like the red colours of dawn, lowing one louder than the other, like milk cows.'

7. [*Urvaśī:*] 'When he was born, the goddesses encircled him and the rivers that sing their own praises raised him, since the gods raised you, Purūravas, for the great battle, for the killing of enemies.'

8. [*Purūravas:*] 'When I, a mortal man, courted these immortal women who had laid aside their veils, they shied away from me like excited gazelles, like horses grazed by the chariot.'

9. [*Urvaśī:*] 'When a mortal man, wooing these immortal women, unites with their group as they wish, make your bodies beautiful, like water birds, like horses biting in their love-play.'

10. [*Purūravas:*] 'She of the waters flashed lightning like a falling lightning-bolt and brought me the pleasures of love. From the water was born a noble, manly son. Let Urvaśī lengthen the span of his life.'

11. [*Urvaśī:*] 'You who were born to protect, Purūravas, have turned that force against me. I warned you on that very day, for I knew, but you did not listen to me. Why do you talk in vain?'

12. [*Purūravas:*] 'When will the son born of me seek his father? He will shed tears, sobbing, when he learns. Who would separate a man and wife who are of one heart, when the fire still blazes in the house of the husband's parents?'

13. [*Urvaśī:*] 'I will answer: he will shed tears, crying, sobbing, longing for tender care. I will send you what I have of yours. Go home; you will never have me, you fool.'

14. [*Purūravas:*] 'What if your lover should vanish today, never to return, going to the farthest distance? Or if he should lie in the lap of Destruction, or if the ferocious wolves should eat him?'

15. [*Urvaśī:*] 'Purūravas, do not die; do not vanish; do not let the vicious wolves eat you. There are no friendships with women; they have the hearts of jackals.

16. 'When I wandered among mortals in another form, and spent the nights with you for four years, once each day I swallowed a drop of butter, and even now I am sated with that.'

17. [*Purūravas:*] 'I, the lover of Urvaśī, long to draw her to me, though she fills the air and measures the middle realm of space. Return and reap the reward for a good deed. Fire consumes my heart.'

18. [*The poet:*] This is what these gods say to you, son of Iḷā: 'Since you are a kinsman of death, your descendants will sacrifice to the gods with the oblation, but you shall taste joy in heaven.'

10.85 The Marriage of Sūryā

1. The earth is propped up by truth; the sky is propped up by the sun. Through the Law the Ādityas stand firm and Soma is placed in the sky.

2. Through Soma the Ādityas are mighty; through Soma the earth is great. And in the lap of these constellations Soma has been set.

3. One thinks he has drunk Soma when they press the plant. But the Soma that the Brahmins know – no one ever eats that.

4. Hidden by those charged with veiling you, protected by those who live on high, O Soma, you stand listening to the pressing-stones. No earthling eats you.

5. When they drink you who are a god, then you are filled up again. Vāyu is the guardian of Soma; the moon is the one that shapes the years.

6. The Raibhī metre was the woman who gave her away; the Nārāśāṃśī metre was the girl who accompanied her. The fine dress of Sūryā was adorned by the songs.

7. Intelligence was the pillow; sight was the balm. Heaven and Earth were the hope-chest when Sūryā went to her husband.

8. The hymns of praise were the shafts and metre was the diadem and coiffure. The Aśvins were the suitors of Sūryā, and Agni was the one who went in front.

9. Soma became the bridegroom and the two Aśvins were the suitors, as Savitṛ gave Sūryā to her husband and she said 'Yes' in her heart.

10. Thought was her chariot and the sky was its canopy. The two luminaries were the two carriage animals when Sūryā went to the house.

11. Your two cattle, yoked with the verse and the chant, went with the same accord. You had hearing for your two wheels. In the sky the path stretched on and on.

12. The two luminaries were your wheels as you journeyed; the outward breath was made into the axle. Sūryā mounted a chariot made of thought as she went to her husband.

13. The wedding procession of Sūryā went forward as Savitṛ sent it off. When the sun is in Aghā they kill the cattle, and when it is in Arjunī she is brought home.

14. When you Aśvins came to the wedding in your three-wheeled chariot, asking for Sūryā for yourselves, all the gods gave you their consent, and Pūṣan, the son, chose you as his two fathers.

15. When you two husbands of beauty came as suitors for Sūryā, where was your single wheel? Where did you two stand to point the way?

16. Your two wheels, Sūryā, the Brahmins know in their measured rounds. But the one wheel that is hidden, only the inspired know that.

17. To Sūryā, to the gods, to Mitra and Varuṇa, who are provident for all creation, to them I have bowed down.

18. These two change places through their power of illusion, now forward, now backward. Like two children at play they circle the sacrificial ground. The one gazes upon all creatures, and the other is born again and again marking the order of the seasons.

19. He becomes new and again new as he is born, going in front of the dawns as the banner of the days. As he arrives he apportions to the gods their share. The moon stretches out the long span of life.

20. Mount the world of immortality, O Sūryā, that is adorned with red flowers and made of fragrant wood, carved with many forms and painted with gold, rolling smoothly on its fine wheels. Prepare an exquisite wedding voyage for your husband.

21. 'Go away from here! For this woman has a husband.' Thus I implore Viśvāvasu with words of praise as I bow to him. 'Look for another girl who is ripe and still lives in her father's house. That is your birthright; find it.

22. 'Go away from here, Viśvāvasu, we implore you as we bow. Look for another girl, willing and ready. Leave the wife to unite with her husband.'

23. May the roads be straight and thornless on which our friends go courting. May Aryaman and Bhaga united lead us together. O Gods, may the united household be easy to manage.

24. I free you from Varuṇa's snare, with which the gentle Savitṛ bound you. In the seat of the Law, in the world of good action, I place you unharmed with your husband.

25. I free her from here, but not from there. I have bound her firmly there, so that through the grace of Indra she will have fine sons and be fortunate in her husband's love.

26. Let Pūṣan lead you from here, taking you by the hand; let the Aśvins carry you in their chariot. Go home to be mistress of the house with the right to speak commands to the gathered people.

27. May happiness be fated for you here through your progeny. Watch over this house as mistress of the house. Mingle your body with that of your husband, and even when you are grey with age you will have the right to speak to the gathered people.

28. The purple and red appears, a magic spirit; the stain is imprinted. Her family prospers, and her husband is bound in the bonds.

29. Throw away the gown, and distribute wealth to the priests. It becomes a magic spirit walking on feet, and like the wife it draws near the husband.

30. The body becomes ugly and sinisterly pale, if the husband with evil desire covers his sexual limb with his wife's robe.

31. The diseases that come from her own people and follow after the glorious bridal procession, may the gods who receive sacrifices lead them back whence they have come.

32. Let no highwaymen, lying in ambush, fall upon the wedding couple. Let the two of them on good paths avoid the dangerous path. Let all demonic powers run away.

33. This bride has auspicious signs; come and look at her. Wish her the good fortune of her husband's love, and depart, each to your own house.

34. It burns, it bites, and it has claws, as dangerous as poison is to eat. Only the priest who knows the Sūryā hymn is able to receive the bridal gown.

35. Cutting, carving, and chopping into pieces – see the colours of Sūryā, which the priest alone purifies.

36. I take your hand for good fortune, so that with me as your husband you will attain a ripe old age. Bhaga, Aryaman, Savitṛ, Purandhi – the gods have given you to me to be mistress of the house.

37. Pūṣan, rouse her to be most eager to please, the woman in whom men sow their seed, so that she will spread her thighs in her desire for us and we, in our desire, will plant our penis in her.

38. To you first of all they led Sūryā, circling with the bridal procession. Give her back to her husbands, Agni, now as a wife with progeny.

39. Agni has given the wife back again, together with long life and beauty. Let her have a long life-span, and let her husband live for a hundred autumns.

40. Soma first possessed her, and the Gandharva possessed her second. Agni was your third husband, and the fourth was the son of a man.

41. Soma gave her to the Gandharva, and the Gandharva gave her to Agni. Agni gave me wealth and sons – and her.

42. Stay here and do not separate. Enjoy your whole life-span playing with sons and grandsons and rejoicing in your own home.

43. Let Prajāpati create progeny for us; let Aryaman anoint us into old age. Free from evil signs, enter the world of your husband. Be good luck for our two-legged creatures and good luck for our four-legged creatures.

44. Have no evil eye; do not be a husband-killer. Be friendly to animals, good-tempered and glowing with beauty. Bringing forth strong sons, prosper as one beloved of the gods and eager to please. Be good luck for our two-legged creatures and good luck for our four-legged creatures.

45. Generous Indra, give this woman fine sons and the good fortune of her husband's love. Place ten sons in her and make her husband the eleventh.

46. Be an empress over your husband's father, an empress over your husband's mother; be an empress over your husband's sister and an empress over your husband's brothers.

47. Let all the gods and the waters together anoint our two hearts together. Let Mātariśvan together with the Creator and together with her who shows the way join the two of us together.

7.55 Sleeping Spell

1. Lord of the House, you who drive away diseases and permeate all forms, be a gentle friend to us.

2. White and tawny son of Saramā, when you bare your teeth they gleam like spears in your snapping jaws. Fall fast asleep!

3. Bark at the thief or at the marauder, as you run up and back again, O son of Saramā. But you are barking at those who sing Indra's praises; why do you threaten us? Fall fast asleep!

4. Tear apart the wild boar, for he would tear you apart. But you are barking at those who sing Indra's praises; why do you threaten us? Fall fast asleep!

5. Let the mother sleep; let the father sleep; let the dog sleep; let the master of the house sleep. Let all the kinsmen sleep; let our people all around sleep.

6. The one who rests and the one who moves, and whoever sees us – we close their eyes tightly as we close up this house.

7. The bull with a thousand horns, who rises up out of the sea – with the help of that powerful one we put the people to sleep.

8. The women lying on benches or lying in chairs or lying in beds, the wives who smell good – we put all of them to sleep.

10.145 Against Rival Wives

1. I dig up this plant, the most powerful thing that grows, with which one drives out the rival wife and wins the husband entirely for oneself.

2. Broad-leaved plant sent by the gods to bring happiness and the power to triumph, blow my rival wife away and make my husband mine alone.

3. O highest one, I am the highest one, higher than all the highest women, and my rival wife is lower than the lowest women.

4. I will not even take her name into my mouth; he takes no pleasure in this person. Far, far into the distance we make the rival wife go.

5. I have emerged triumphant, and you also have triumphed. The two of us, full of the power to triumph, will triumph over my rival wife.

6. I have placed the plant of triumph on you, and grasped you with my power to triumph. Let your heart run after me like a cow after a calf, like water running in its own bed.

10.159 The Triumphant Wife

1. There the sun has risen, and here my good fortune has risen. Being a clever woman, and able to triumph, I have triumphed over my husband.

2. I am the banner; I am the head. I am the formidable one who has the deciding word. My husband will obey my will alone, as I emerge triumphant.

3. My sons kill their enemies and my daughter is an empress, and I am completely victorious. My voice is supreme in my husband's ears.

4. The oblation that Indra made and so became glorious and supreme, this is what I have made for you, O gods. I have become truly without rival wives.

5. Without rival wives, killer of rival wives, victorious and pre-eminent, I have grabbed for myself the attraction of the other women as if it were the wealth of flighty women.

6. I have conquered and become pre-eminent over these rival wives, so that I may rule as empress over this hero and over the people.

10.184 For a Safe Pregnancy and Birth

1. Let Viṣṇu prepare the womb; let Tvaṣṭṛ shape the forms. Let Prajāpati shed the seed; let Dhātṛ place the embryo in you.

2. Place the embryo, Sinīvalī; place the embryo, Sarasvatī. Let the twin Aśvins, the lotus-garlanded gods, place the embryo in you.

3. With golden kindling woods the Aśvins churn out fire. We invoke that embryo for you to bring forth in the tenth month.

10.162 To Protect the Embryo

1. Let Agni the killer of demons unite with this prayer and expel from here the one whose name is evil, who lies with disease upon your embryo, your womb.

2. The one whose name is evil, who lies with disease upon your embryo, your womb, the flesh-eater – Agni has driven him away with prayer.

3. The one who kills the embryo as it settles, as it rests, as it stirs, who wishes to kill it when it is born – we will drive him away from here.

4. The one who spreads apart your two thighs, who lies between the married pair, who licks the inside of your womb – we will drive him away from here.

5. The one who by changing into your brother, or your husband, or your lover lies with you, who wishes to kill your offspring – we will drive him away from here.

6. The one who bewitches you with sleep or darkness and lies with you – we will drive him away from here.

Chapter 2

The *Upaniṣads*

The *Upaniṣads* are the fourth and last *genre* of texts that form the *Vedic* corpus, each located in one of the four branches of the *Vedas*, namely the *Ṛg*, *Sāma*, *Yajur*, and *Atharva*. Composed between about the seventh and third centuries BCE by many different authors, they were taught orally as esoteric doctrine from teacher to student as secret lore. For this reason they are called the *Upaniṣads* (*upa*, near to, *niṣad*, to sit down) in reference to the ways that the texts were taught. These texts were further reinterpretations of the rituals central to and described in the *Saṃhitās* and that were interpreted as systems of homologies in the *Brāhmaṇas*.[1] While ritual was dominant in the earlier *Vedas, jñāna*, knowledge, and esoteric philosophical teachings eclipsed ritual and became central in the *Upaniṣads.*

The *Upaniṣads* were largely concerned with the internalization of the sacrifice and with laying the foundations for the theological system that was to supplant the ritual world of the *Vedas.*[2] Though all the *Upaniṣads* shared this purpose, this does not mean that they offered a unified philosophical position. Beginning in the eighth century, scholars of Vedānta, such as Śaµkarācārya, viewed the *Upaniṣads* as the culmination and essence of *Vedic* thought and sought to unify these disparate texts through elaborate hermeneutics and, as a result, to put forth several coherent (and conflicting) philosophical positions. The *Upaniṣads* moved the center of attention from the sacrifice to reflections about the nature of the *ātman*, self, and new ways to conceive of the components of the sacrifice as parts and mechanisms of the body and as knowledge about the nature of the universe itself. The *aśvamedha* sacrifice, a public horse sacrifice that was connected with the expansion of parameters of one's kingdom, that is described in *Śatapatha Brāhmaṇa* was reinterpreted as having cosmological significance where the horse's head now represented the dawn, its eye the sun, and so on. The external sacrifice is morphed into an internal meditation. The external sacrifice, for example, becomes a sacrifice of the *prāña*, breath. These correlations, of course, are taught *upanṣad*, in secret and at the feet of a teacher.

The *Upaniṣads* are the origins of much of the language and theology typically associated with Hinduism and Hindu philosophy. One finds speculative verses about the *ātman*, self, and characterizations of the mechanism of birth and rebirth in *saṃsāra*, mundane reality, which became central to the post-sacrificial world of Hinduism. It is in the *Upaniṣads* that one finds the first Hindu presentations of the mechanism of *karma*, the cycle of cause and effect that plays a role in events in one's current and future life, *puṇya*, good *karma*, and *pāpa*, bad *karma*. *Mokṣa*, liberation from the cycle of birth and rebirth, is also described in the *Upaniṣads*. *Jñāna*, as the method by which one achieves *mokṣa*, is proposed as an alternative to the *Vedic* world of ritual.

The concept of *Brahman*, an impersonal absolute that is identified with the essence of the self, the ritual, and the cosmos, is first developed in the *Upaniṣads*. Again, though these concepts are found in the *Upaniṣads*, it would be an error (or a theological judgment) to assume or to conclude that the *Upaniṣads* propose a unified position. It is also incorrect to suppose that they offer a consistent position on the nature of the *ātman*, its relationship with *Brahman*, and the precise knowledge needed to obtain *mokṣa*. In this connection, the most popular interpretation of the *Upaniṣads* is an impersonalist monism that equates *Brahman* with *ātman* argued vehemently by Śaṃkarācārya, the founder of the Advaita, non-dual, School of Vedānta and his followers. Though there certainly are places in the *Upaniṣads* that corroborate his position, there are other places where Śaṃkarācārya was forced to offer controversial interpretations. In contrast, Madhvācārya, a thirteenth-century scholar of Vedānta, held that the Upaniṣads confirmed that *Brahman* and each *ātman* were different from one another. Like his counterpart, Madhvācārya too had to offer controversial interpretations of passages. Given this diversity, it is not possible to reduce the *Upaniṣads* to Śaṃkarācārya's, or any other thinkers, interpretation.[3]

The *Upaniṣads* were composed by many authors though several stand out including Yājñavalkya (*Bṛhadāraṇyaka*), Uddālaka Āruṇi (*Chāndogya*), Satyakāma Jābāla among others. Though some of these teachers are *brāhmaṇas*, some are *kṣatriyas*. Both Jainism and Buddhism, which originated at the same time as the *Upaniṣads*, also had teachers, namely the Buddha and the Mahavīra, who were both from *kṣatriya* backgrounds. The inclusion of *kṣatriyas* has led some scholars to draw conclusions about the multi-faceted relationships that were developing between *brāhamaṇas* and *kṣatriyas* at this time. In addition, several women, Gārgī Vācaknavi (BU 3.6.8) and Maitryi are also presented as teachers. The number and variety of authors lead scholars to conclude that the texts were edited as anthologies of independent texts.

The selections here have been taken from five *Upaniṣads*, three in their entirety. As already mentioned, all five are primarily concerned with esoteric teachings about the nature of the sacrifice, about the nature of the *ātman* and *Brahman*, their relationship with one another, as well as the mechanism of *karma* and rebirth in *saṃsāra*. The first set of passages (1.1 and 1.2) are from the *Bṛhadāraṇyaka* and are reinterpretations of the *aśvamedha*, horse, sacrifice. In them the universe and the horse are identified with one another. The subsequent two passages, 1.3 and 1.4 are focused on the importance of *prāṇa*, the breath, and creation as it pertains to the *ātman*, and the *Brahman*. 3.6 is a debate between a female ascetic, Gārgī, and Yājñavalkya and echoes some of the skeptical and humorous sentiment of *Nāsadīya* 10.129 from the *Ṛg Veda Saṃhitā*. 3.7–3.9 are also debates about the nature of the universe and about the variety of gods. The next passage is from 4.4 and explains what happens after death. The last excerpt from the *Bṛhadāraṇyaka* is 5.1. It is a characterization of *Brahman*. Contemporary Hindus frequently chant the opening verse in 5.1.

The first passage of the *Chāndogya Upaniṣad* is connected with the *Udgītha*, the *Vedic* High Chant that is paramount in the *Sāma Veda*. In 1.1–1.4 the *Udgītha* is reinterpreted and then identified with the sound *Oṃ*. In 2.23 the passage juxtaposes *dharma*, law, *Brahman*, and *Oṃ*. 3.12 is in reference to the Gāyātrī *mantra*, a hymn to the sun that is central to the initiation rites for *brāhmaṇas* as described in the *Vedas*, and equates the *mantra* with the entire universe. 4.4–4.9 is the story of Satyakāma Jābāla and his effort to become a *Vedic* student while 4.10–4.15 is the story of Upakosala Kāmalāyana, another student of the *Vedas*. 4.16 and 4.17 concerns the sacrifice and how to make up for errors.

Chāndogya 5.3–5.10 are a dialogue between Śvetaketu, a student who received teachings from his father, and Pravāhaṇa Jaivali, who corrects the errors in his thinking. Perhaps the most well-known passages from the *Chāndogya* can be found in 6.1–6.16. In this section Śvetaketu is questioned and taught by his father Uddālaka Āruṇi about the nature of the relationship between the *ātman* and the *Brahman*, each time concluding with the phrase *tat tvam asi*, "that's how you are." The correct interpretation of these passages and this particular phrase has been the greatest matter of dispute among the schools of Vedānta. As mentioned earlier, the Advaita school founded by Śaṃkarācārya reads them as proof of identity between the *ātman* and the *Brahman* while the interpretation offered by Madhvācārya, founder of the Mādhva School of Vedānta, argues the exact opposite.

The *Kaṭha Upaniṣad*, here in its entirety, is a conversation between Naciketas and Yama, the God of Death. The conversation is the result of being given to Death by his father, Uśan, who spoke impatiently and angrily to his son. After going to the abode of death and not receiving a proper welcome, Naciketas is granted three boons by Death, one of which is to learn about the nature of death. The *Kaṭha* is an account of this dialogue.

The *Śvetāśvatara Upaniṣad* is quite different from other *Upaniṣads* as it offers a clearly theistic analysis of the universe. In it, the god Rudra is characterized as a supreme being who plays a vital part in the granting of *mokṣa*. In addition it includes references to the mechanism of *karma* as well as to *yoga*, and echoes concepts and ideas from the Sāṃkhyā and Yoga traditions of Indian philosophy.

The *Māṇḍūkya Upaniṣad* is a brief etymological analysis of the syllable *Oṃ*. The Sanskrit etymology ties the syllable with the world, *Brahman*, and the *ātman* as well as with three distinct states of being and knowing, waking, dreaming, and deep sleep.

Notes

1 Michael Witzel, "*Vedas* and *Upaniṣads*" in G. Flood (ed.), *A Blackwell Companion to Hinduism*. Oxford: Blackwell Publishing, 2003.

2 Though the *Upaniṣads* are part of the *Vedas*, they are often referred to as in oppositon with them. This is because of the radically different vision of the world that they put forth compared to the earlier *Vedic* texts.

3 Joel Brereton, "*Tat tvam asi* in Context." *Zeitschrift der Deutschenladischen Gesellschaft* 1313, 1981: 172–91.

Further reading

Brereton, Joel, "*Tat tvam asi* in Context." *Zeitschrift der Deutschenladischen Gesellschaft* 1313, 1981: 172–91.

Olivelle, Patrick, *Upaniṣads*. Oxford: Oxford University Press, 1996.

Witzel, Michael, "*Vedas* and *Upaniṣads*" in G. Flood (ed.), *A Blackwell Companion to Hinduism*. Oxford: Blackwell Publishing, 2003.

The *Upaniṣads*

Bṛhadāraṇyak *Upaniṣad*

Chapter 1

1 The head of the sacrificial horse, clearly, is the dawn – its sight is the sun; its breath is the wind; and its gaping mouth is the fire common to all men. The body (*ātman*) of the sacrificial horse is the year – its back is the sky; its abdomen is the intermediate region; its underbelly is the earth; its flanks are the quarters; its ribs are the intermediate quarters; its limbs are the seasons; its joints are the months and fortnights; its feet are the days and nights; its bones are the stars; its flesh is the clouds; its stomach contents are the sand; its intestines are the rivers; its liver and lungs are the hills; its body hairs are the plants and trees; its forequarter is the rising sun; and its hindquarter is the setting sun. When it yawns, lightning flashes; when it shakes itself, it thunders; and when it urinates, it rains. Its neighing is speech itself.

[2] The day, clearly, was born afterwards to be the sacrificial cup placed in front of the horse, and its womb is in the eastern sea. The night was born afterwards to be the sacrificial cup placed behind the horse, and its womb is in the western sea. These two came into being to be the sacrificial cups placed in front of and behind the horse. It became a racer and carried the gods. It became a charger and carried the Gandharvas. It became a courser and carried the demons. It became a horse and carried the humans. The sea, indeed, is its counterpart; the sea is its womb.

2 In the beginning there was nothing here at all. Death alone covered this completely, as did hunger; for what is hunger but death? Then death made up his mind: 'Let me equip myself with a body (*ātman*).' So he undertook a liturgical recitation (*arc*), and as he was engaged in liturgical recitation water sprang from him. And he thought: 'While I was engaged in liturgical recitation (*arc*), water (*ka*) sprang up for me.' This is what gave the name to and discloses the true nature of recitation (*arka*). Water undoubtedly springs for him who knows the name and nature of recitation in this way. [2] So, recitation is water.

Then the foam that had gathered on the water solidified and became the earth. Death toiled upon her. When he had become worn out by toil and hot with exertion, his heat – his essence – turned into fire.

[3] He divided this body (*ātman*) of his into three – one third became the sun and another the wind. He is also breath divided into three. His head is the eastern quarter, and his two forequarters are the south-east and the north-east. His tail is the west, and his two hindquarters are the south-west and the north-west. His flanks are the south and the north. His back is the sky; his abdomen is the intermediate region; and his chest is this earth. He stands firm in the waters. A man who knows this will stand firm wherever he may go.

[4] Then death had this desire: 'Would that a second body (*ātman*) were born for me!' So, by means of his mind, he copulated with speech, death copulated with hunger. Then the semen he emitted became the year. The year simply did not exist before this. He carried him for as long as a year, at the end of which he gave birth to him. As he was born, death opened its mouth to swallow him. He cried out, '*Bhāṇ*!' That is what became speech.

[5] Death reflected: 'If I kill him, I will only reduce my supply of food.' So, with that speech and that body (*ātman*) he gave birth to this whole world, to everything that is here – Ṛgvedic verses, Yajurvedic formulas, Sāmavedic chants, metres, sacrifices, people, and animals. He began to eat whatever he gave birth to. 'He eats (*ad*) all' – it is this that gave the name to and discloses the true nature

---

Excerpts from Patrick Olivelle (tr.), *Upaniṣads*. Oxford: Oxford University Press, 1996.

of Aditi. When someone comes to know the name and nature of Aditi in this way, he becomes the eater of this whole world, and the whole world here becomes his food.

[6] Then death had this desire: 'Let me make an offering once more, this time with a bigger sacrifice.' So he strenuously toiled and fiercely exerted himself. When he had become worn out by toil and hot with exertion, his splendour – his vigour – departed from him. Now, splendour – vigour – consists of the vital breaths. So, when his vital breaths had departed, his corpse began to bloat. His mind, however, still remained within his corpse.

[7] Then he had this desire: 'I wish that this corpse of mine would become fit to be sacrificed so I could get myself a living body (*ātman*)!' Then that corpse became a horse. 'Because it bloated (*aśvat*), it became fit to be sacrificed (*medhya*)' – that is what gave the name to and discloses the true nature of the horse sacrifice (*aśvamedha*). Only a man who knows the horse sacrifice in this way truly understands it.

Death believed that the horse was not to be confined in any way. At the end of one year, he immolated it as a sacrifice to himself, while he assigned the other animals to the gods. That is why people, when they immolate the horse consecrated to Prajāpati, regard it as an offering to all the gods.

The sun that shines up there, clearly, is a horse sacrifice; the year is its body (*ātman*). The fire that burns down here is the ritual fire; these worlds are its body. Now, there are these two: the horse sacrifice and the ritual fire (*arka*). Yet they constitute in reality a single deity – they are simply death. [Whoever knows this] averts repeated death – death is unable to seize him, death becomes his very body (*ātman*), and he becomes one of these deities.

3 Now, Prajāpati's offspring were of two kinds: gods and demons. Indeed, the gods were the younger of his offspring, while the demons were the older; and they were competing for these worlds. So the gods said to themselves: 'Come, let us overcome the demons during a sacrifice by means of the High Chant.'

[2] They then told speech: 'Sing the High Chant for us.' Speech said 'Very well', and sang the High Chant for them. It procured for them by that singing whatever useful there is in speech; it keeps for itself (*ātman*) whatever is pleasant in what it says. The demons thought: 'With this as their Udgātr, they are sure to overcome us.' So they rushed at it and riddled it with evil. That evil is the disagreeable things a person says – they are that very evil.

[3] Then the gods told breath: 'Sing the High Chant for us.' Breath said, 'Very well', and sang the High Chant for them. It procured for them by that singing whatever useful there is in breath; it keeps for itself whatever is pleasant in what it smells. The demons thought: 'With this as their Udgātṛ, they are sure to overcome us.' So they rushed at it and riddled it with evil. That evil is the disagreeable things a person smells – they are that very evil.

[4] Then the gods told sight: 'Sing the High Chant for us.' Sight said, 'Very well', and sang the High Chant for them. It procured for them by that singing whatever useful there is in sight; it keeps for itself whatever is pleasant in what it sees. The demons thought: 'With this as their Udgātr, they are sure to overcome us.' So they rushed at it and riddled it with evil. That evil is the disagreeable things a person sees – they are that very evil.

[5] Then the gods told hearing: 'Sing the High Chant for us.' Hearing said, 'Very well', and sang the High Chant for them. It procured for them by that singing whatever useful there is in hearing; it keeps for itself whatever is pleasant in what it hears. The demons thought: 'With this as their Udgātr, they are sure to overcome us.' So they rushed at it and riddled it with evil. That evil is the disagreeable things a person hears – they are that very evil.

[6] Then the gods told mind: 'Sing the High Chant for us.' Mind said, 'Very well', and sang the High Chant for them. It procured for them by that singing whatever useful there is in the mind; it keeps for itself whatever is pleasant in what it thinks. The demons thought: 'With this as their Udgātṛ, they are sure to

overcome us.' So they rushed at it and riddled it with evil. That evil is the disagreeable things a person thinks – they are that very evil.

In this way they assaulted these deities with evil and riddled them with evil.

[7] Then the gods told the breath within the mouth: 'Sing the High Chant for us.' This breath said, 'Very well', and sang the High Chant for them. The demons thought: 'With this as their Udgātṛ, they are sure to overcome us.' So they rushed at it and tried to riddle it with evil. But, like a clod of earth hurled against a rock, they were smashed to bits flying in all directions and perished. As a result, the gods prospered, while the demons came to ruin. When someone knows this, he himself will prosper, while an enemy who hates him will come to ruin.

[8] The gods then asked: 'Where has he gone who stood by us like that?'

'Here within the mouth.'

This is Ayāsya, the Āṅgirasa, for it is the essence of the bodily parts.

[9] Now, this same deity is called Dur, because death keeps far (*dūra*) from it. And death likewise keeps far from a man who knows this. [10] This same deity drove out from the other deities the evil that is death and chased it to the very ends of the earth. There it threw their evils down. Therefore, one should never visit foreigners or travel to frontier regions lest one run into evil and death.

[11] This same deity, after it had driven out from the other deities the evil that is death, carried them beyond the reach of death. [12] Speech was the first one that it carried. And when speech was freed from death, it became fire. So, having gone beyond death, the fire now blazes here. [13] Then it carried breath. And when breath was freed from death, it became wind. So, having gone beyond death, the wind now blows here. [14] Then it carried sight. And when sight was freed from death, it became the sun. So, having gone beyond death, the sun now glows up there. [15] Then it carried hearing. And when hearing was freed from death, it became the quarters. These quarters have gone beyond death. [16] Then it carried the mind. And when the mind was freed from death, it became the moon. So, having gone beyond death, the moon now shines up there. In the same way, this deity carries beyond the reach of death anyone who knows this.

[17] Then the breath within the mouth procured a supply of food for itself by singing, for it alone eats whatever food is eaten and stands firm in this world. [18] But the other deities said to it: 'This whole world is nothing but food! And you have procured it for yourself by singing. Give us a share of that food.' It told them, 'Come and gather around me.' They said, 'Very well', and gathered around it on all sides. Therefore, whatever food one eats through it satisfies also these others. When someone comes to know this, his people will gather around him in the same way; he will become their patron, their chief, and their leader; he will become an eater of food and a sovereign. And if anyone among his people tries to become a rival of someone who knows this, that man will be incapable of supporting even his own dependants. On the other hand, anyone who follows him, as well as anyone who, while following him, wishes to support his own dependants, becomes capable of supporting them.

[19] This breath is Ayāsya, the Āṅgirasa, for it is the essence of the bodily parts. Now, the essence of the bodily parts is breath, for it is very clear – the essence of the bodily parts is breath. Therefore, any part of the body from which breath departs is sure to wither, for it is the very essence of the bodily parts.

[20] And it is also Bṛhaspati. Bṛhatī, after all, is speech, and it is the lord (*pati*) of speech. So it is Bṛhaspati. [21] And it is also Brahmaṇaspati. *Brahman*, after all, is speech, and it is the lord (*pati*) of speech. So it is Brahmaṇaspati. [22] And it is also the Sāman. The Sāman, after all, is Speech. 'It is both she (*sā*) and he (*ama*)' – this gave the name to and discloses the true nature of the Sāman. Or maybe it is called Sāman because it is equal in size (*sama*) to a gnat or a mosquito, on the one hand, and to an elephant, to these three worlds, or even to the entire universe, on the other. When anyone comes to know the Sāman in this way,

he obtains union with and residence in the same world as the Sāman. [23] And it is also the High Chant (*udgītha*). The 'high' (*ut*) is, after all, breath, for this whole world is held up (*uttabdha*) by breath. And 'chant' (*gītha*) is simply speech. Since it is high (*ut*) and it is chant (*gītha*), it is the High Chant (*udgītha*).

[24] This same point was made by Brahmadatta Caikitāneya while he was drinking King Soma: 'May this King make my head shatter apart if Ayāsya Āṅgirasa sang the High Chant by any other means, for by speech and breath alone did he sing it.'

[25] When someone knows the wealth of this Sāman, he comes to possess wealth. Now, the Sāman's wealth (*sva*) is the tone (*svara*) itself. For this reason, when someone is about to carry out priestly functions, he hopes for a rich tone in his voice so he can perform his priestly functions with a voice rich in tone. And for the same reason, people always try to find a priest with a rich tone for a sacrifice, that is, one who possesses that wealth. A man undoubtedly comes to possess wealth, when he knows in this way the wealth of the Sāman.

[26] When someone knows the gold of this Sāman, he comes to possess gold. Now the Sāman's gold (*suvarṇa*) is the tone (*svara*) itself. A man undoubtedly comes to possess gold, when he knows in this way the gold of the Sāman.

[27] When someone knows the basis of this Sāman, he comes to possess a solid basis. Now, the Sāman's basis is speech itself, for, basing itself on speech, the breath sings it. Some, however, take food to be its basis.

[28] Next comes the chanting of the purificatory lauds. The Prastotṛ priest sings the Introductory Praise of the Sāman, and, as he is singing the Introductory Praise, the patron of the sacrifice should silently recite:

> From the unreal
> lead me to the real!
> From the darkness
> lead me to the light!
> From death
> lead me to immortality!'

The unreal is death, and the real is immortality – so, when he says, 'From the unreal lead me to the real', what he is really saying is: 'From death lead me to immortality'; in other words, 'Make me immortal.' Darkness is death, and light is immortality – so, when he says, 'From the darkness lead me to the light', what he is really saying is: 'From death lead me to immortality'; in other words, 'Make me immortal.' In the statement, 'From death lead me to immortality', there is nothing obscure.

He may, further, procure a supply of food for himself by singing the remaining lauds. When he is singing them, therefore, he should choose as a reward anything he may desire. An Udgātṛ priest who has this knowledge is able to procure by his singing whatever he desires, either for himself or for the patron of the sacrifice. Now this is true world conquest. When a man knows that Sāman in this way, there is no fear of his being left without a world.

4 In the beginning this world was just a single body (*ātman*) shaped like a man. He looked around and saw nothing but himself. The first thing he said was, 'Here I am!' and from that the name 'I' came into being. Therefore, even today when you call someone, he first says, 'It's I', and then states whatever other name he may have. That first being received the name 'man' (*puruṣa*), because ahead (*pūrva*) of all this he burnt up (*uṣ*) all evils. When someone knows this, he burns up anyone who may try to get ahead of him.

[2] That first being became afraid; therefore, one becomes afraid when one is alone. Then he thought to himself: 'Of what should I be afraid, when there is no one but me?' So his fear left him, for what was he going to be afraid of? One is, after all, afraid of another.

[3] He found no pleasure at all; so one finds no pleasure when one is alone. He wanted to have a companion. Now he was as large as a man and a woman in close embrace. So he split (*pat*) his body into two, giving rise to husband (*pati*) and wife (*patnī*). Surely this is why Yājñavalkya used to say: 'The two of us are

like two halves of a block.' The space here, therefore, is completely filled by the woman.

He copulated with her, and from their union human beings were born. [4] She then thought to herself: 'After begetting me from his own body (*ātman*), how could he copulate with me? I know – I'll hide myself.' So she became a cow. But he became a bull and copulated with her. From their union cattle were born. Then she became a mare, and he a stallion; she became a female donkey, and he, a male donkey. And again he copulated with her, and from their union one-hoofed animals were born. Then she became a female goat, and he, a male goat; she became a ewe, and he, a ram. And again he copulated with her, and from their union goats and sheep were born. In this way he created every male and female pair that exists, down to the very ants.

[5] It then occurred to him: 'I alone am the creation, for I created all this.' From this 'creation' came into being. Anyone who knows this prospers in this creation of his.

[6] Then he churned like this and, using his hands, produced fire from his mouth as from a vagina. As a result the inner sides of both these – the hands and the mouth – are without hair, for the inside of the vagina is without hair. 'Sacrifice to this god. Sacrifice to that god' – people do say these things, but in reality each of these gods is his own creation, for he himself is all these gods. From his semen, then, he created all that is moist here, which is really Soma. Food and eater – that is the extent of this whole world. Food is simply Soma, and the eater is fire.

This is *brahman*'s super-creation. It is a super-creation because he created the gods, who are superior to him, and, being a mortal himself, he created the immortals. Anyone who knows this stands within this super-creation of his.

[7] At that time this world was without real distinctions; it was distinguished simply in terms of name and visible appearance – 'He is so and so by name and has this sort of an appearance.' So even today this world is distinguished simply in terms of name and visible appearance, as when we say, 'He is so and so by name and has this sort of an appearance.'

Penetrating this body up to the very nail-tips, he remains there like a razor within a case or a termite within a termite-hill. People do not see him, for he is incomplete as he comes to be called breath when he is breathing, speech when he is speaking, sight when he is seeing, hearing when he is hearing, and mind when he is thinking. These are only the names of his various activities. A man who considers him to be any one of these does not understand him, for he is incomplete within any one of these. One should consider them as simply his self (*ātman*), for in it all these become one. This same self (*atman*) is the trail to this entire world, for by following it one comes to know this entire world, just as by following their tracks one finds [the cattle]. Whoever knows this finds fame and glory.

[8] This innermost thing, this self (*ātman*) – it is dearer than a son, it is dearer than wealth, it is dearer than everything else. If a man claims that something other than his self is dear to him, and someone were to tell him that he will lose what he holds dear, that is liable to happen. So a man should regard only his self as dear to him. When a man regards only his self as dear to him, what he holds dear will never perish.

[9] Now, the question is raised: 'Since people think that they will be come the Whole by knowing *brahman*, what did *brahman* know that enabled it to become the Whole?'

[10] In the beginning this world was only *brahman*, and it knew only itself (*ātman*), thinking: 'I am *brahman*.' As a result, it became the Whole. Among the gods, likewise, whosoever realized this, only they became the Whole. It was the same also among the seers and among humans. Upon seeing this very point, the seer Vāmadeva proclaimed: 'I was Manu, and I was the sun.' This is true even now. If a man knows 'I am *brahman*' in this way, he becomes this whole world. Not even the gods are able to prevent it, for he becomes their very self (*ātman*). So when a man venerates another deity, thinking, 'He is one, and

I am another', he does not understand. As livestock is for men, so is he for the gods. As having a lot of livestock is useful to a man, so each man proves useful to the gods. The loss of even a single head of livestock is painful; how much more if many are lost. The gods, therefore, are not pleased at the prospect of men coming to understand this.

[11] In the beginning this world was only *brahman*, only one. Because it was only one, *brahman* had not fully developed. It then created the ruling power, a form superior to and surpassing itself, that is, the ruling powers among the gods – Indra, Varuṇa, Soma, Rudra, Parjanya, Yama, Mṛtyu, and Īśāna. Hence there is nothing higher than the ruling power. Accordingly, at a royal anointing a Brahmin pays homage to a Kṣatriya by prostrating himself. He extends this honour only to the ruling power. Now, the priestly power (*brahman*) is the womb of the ruling power. Therefore, even if a king should rise to the summit of power, it is to the priestly power that he returns in the end as to his own womb. So, one who hurts the latter harms his own womb and becomes so much the worse for harming someone better than him.

[12] *Brahman* still did not become fully developed. So it created the Vaiśya class, that is, the types of gods who are listed in groups – Vasus, Rudras, Ādityas, All-gods, and Maruts.

[13] It still did not become fully developed. So it created the Śūdra class, that is, Pūṣan. Now, Pūṣan is this very earth, for it nourishes this whole world, it nourishes all that exists.

[14] It still did not become fully developed. So it created the Law (*dharma*), a form superior to and surpassing itself. And the Law is here the ruling power standing above the ruling power. Hence there is nothing higher than the Law. Therefore, a weaker man makes demands of a stronger man by appealing to the Law, just as one does by appealing to a king. Now, the Law is nothing but the truth. Therefore, when a man speaks the truth, people say that he speaks the Law; and when a man speaks the Law, people say that he speaks the truth. They are really the same thing.

[15] So there came to be the priestly power, the ruling power, the Vaiśya class, and the Śūdra class. Among the gods the priestly power (*brahman*) came into being only in the form of fire, and among humans as a Brahmin; it further became a Kṣatriya in the form of a Kṣatriya, a Vaiśya in the form of a Vaiśya, and a Śūdra in the form of a Śūdra. In the fire, therefore, people seek to find a world for themselves among the gods, and in the Brahmin a world among humans, for *brahman* came into being in these two forms.

If someone were to depart from this world without perceiving his own world, it will be of no use to him as it remains unknown to him, just like the Veda that is not recited or a rite that is left undone. If a man who does not know this performs even a grand and holy rite, it is sure to fade away after his death. It is his self (*ātman*) alone that a man should venerate as his world. And if someone venerates his self alone as his world, that rite of his will never fade away, because from his very self he will produce whatever he desires.

[16] Now, this self (*ātman*) is a world for all beings. So, when he makes offerings and sacrifices, he becomes thereby a world for the gods. When he recites the Vedas, he becomes thereby a world for the seers. When he offers libations to his ancestors and seeks to father offspring, he becomes thereby a world for his ancestors. When he provides food and shelter to human beings, he becomes thereby a world for human beings. When he procures fodder and water for livestock, he becomes thereby a world for livestock. When creatures, from wild animals and birds down to the very ants, find shelter in his houses, he becomes thereby a world for them. Just as a man desires the well-being of his own world, so all beings desire the well-being of anyone who knows this. All this is known and has been thoroughly examined.

[17] In the beginning this world was only the self (*ātman*), only one. He had this desire: 'I wish I had a wife so I could father offspring. I wish I had wealth so I could perform rites.' That is the full extent of desire; one does not get anything more, even if one desires it. So

even today when one is single, one has the desire: 'I wish I had a wife so I could father offspring. I wish I had wealth so I could perform rites.' As long as someone has not obtained either of these, he considers himself to be utterly incomplete. Now, this is his completeness – his mind is himself (*ātman*); his speech is his wife; his breath is his offspring; his sight is his human wealth, for people find wealth with their sight, while his hearing is his divine wealth, for people hear about it with their hearing; and his body (*ātman*) is his rites, for one performs rites with one's body. This is the five-fold sacrifice – the sacrificial animal is fivefold, the human being is fivefold, and this whole world, whatever there is, is fivefold. Anyone who knows this obtains this whole world.

[. . .]

Chapter 3

[. . .]

6 Then Gārgī Vācaknavī began to question him. 'Yājñavalkya,' she said, 'tell me – since this whole world is woven back and forth on water, on what, then, is water woven back and forth?'

'On air, Gārgī.'

'On what, then, is air woven back and forth?'

'On the worlds of the intermediate region, Gārgī.'

'On what, then, are the worlds of the intermediate region woven back and forth?'

'On the worlds of the Gandharvas, Gārgī.'

'On what, then, are the worlds of the Gandharvas woven back and forth?'

'On the worlds of the sun, Gārgī.'

'On what, then, are the worlds of the sun woven back and forth?'

'On the worlds of the moon, Gārgī.'

'On what, then, are the worlds of the moon woven back and forth?'

'On the worlds of the stars, Gārgī.'

'On what, then, are the worlds of the stars woven back and forth?'

'On the worlds of the gods, Gārgī.'

'On what, then, are the worlds of the gods woven back and forth?'

'On the worlds of Indra, Gārgī.'

'On what, then, are the worlds of Indra woven back and forth?'

'On the worlds of Prajāpati, Gārgī.'

'On what, then, are the worlds of Prajāpati woven back and forth?'

'On the worlds of *brahman*, Gārgī.'

'On what, then, are the worlds of *brahman* woven back and forth?'

At this point Yājñavalkya told her: 'Don't ask too many questions, Gārgī, or your head will shatter apart! You are asking too many questions about a deity about whom one should not ask too many questions. So, Gārgī, don't ask too many questions!'

Thereupon, Gārgī Vācaknavī fell silent.

7 Then Uddālaka Āruṇi began to question him. 'Yājñavalkya,' he said, 'once we were living in the land of the Madras learning about the sacrifice in the house of Patañcala Kāpya. He had a wife possessed by a Gandharva. We asked him who he was, and the Gandharva said that he was Kabandha Ātharvaṇa. He then asked Patañcala Kāpya and the students there who were learning about the sacrifice: "Tell me, Kāpya – do you know the string on which this world and the next, as well as all beings, are strung together?" "That, my lord, I do not know," replied Patañcala Kāpya. He then asked Patañcala Kāpya and the students there who were learning about the sacrifice: "Tell me, Kāpya – do you know the inner controller of this world and the next, as well as of all beings, who controls them from within?" "That, my lord, I do not know," replied Patañcala Kāpya. He then told Patañcala Kāpya and the students there who were learning about the sacrifice: "Clearly, Kāpya, if a man knows what that string is and who that inner controller is – he knows *brahman*; he knows the worlds; he knows the gods; he knows the Vedas; he knows the spirits; he knows the self; he knows all."

'And I know it. So, if you drive away the cows meant for the Brahmins, Yājñavalkya, without knowing what that string is and who that inner controller is, your head will shatter apart!'

'Gautama, I do know what that string is and who that inner controller is.'

'Of course, anyone can say, "I know! I know!" Tell us what precisely you know.'

[2] Yājñavalkya told him: 'Clearly, Gautama, that string is the wind. It is on the string of wind, Gautama, that this world and the next, as well as all beings, are strung together. That is why people say of a dead man, "His bodily parts have come unstrung", for they are strung together, Gautama, on the string of wind.'

'Quite right, Yājñavalkya. Now tell us who the inner controller is.'

[3] 'This self (*ātman*) of yours who is present within but is different from the earth, whom the earth does not know, whose body is the earth, and who controls the earth from within – he is the inner controller, the immortal.

[4] 'This self of yours who is present within but is different from the waters, whom the waters do not know, whose body is the waters, and who controls the waters from within – he is the inner controller, the immortal.

[5] 'This self of yours who is present within but is different from the fire, whom the fire does not know, whose body is the fire, and who controls the fire from within – he is the inner controller, the immortal.

[6] 'This self of yours who is present within but is different from the intermediate region, whom the intermediate region does not know, whose body is the intermediate region, and who controls the intermediate region from within – he is the inner controller, the immortal.

[7] 'This self of yours who is present within but is different from the wind, whom the wind does not know, whose body is the wind, and who controls the wind from within – he is the inner controller, the immortal.

[8] 'This self of yours who is present within but is different from the sky, whom the sky does not know, whose body is the sky, and who controls the sky from within – he is the inner controller, the immortal.

[9] 'This self of yours who is present within but is different from the sun, whom the sun does not know, whose body is the sun, and who controls the sun from within – he is the inner controller, the immortal.

[10] 'This self of yours who is present within but is different from the quarters, whom the quarters do not know, whose body is the quarters, and who controls the quarters from within – he is the inner controller, the immortal.

[11] 'This self of yours who is present within but is different from the moon and the stars, whom the moon and the stars do not know, whose body is the moon and the stars, and who controls the moon and the stars from within – he is the inner controller, the immortal.

[12] 'This self of yours who is present within but is different from space, whom space does not know, whose body is space, and who controls space from within – he is the inner controller, the immortal.

[13] 'This self of yours who is present within but is different from darkness, whom darkness does not know, whose body is darkness, and who controls darkness from within – he is the inner controller, the immortal.

[14] 'This self of yours who is present within but is different from light, whom light does not know, whose body is light, and who controls light from within – he is the inner controller, the immortal.'

That was with respect to the divine sphere. [15] What follows is with respect to beings.

'This self of yours who is present within but is different from all beings, whom all beings do not know, whose body is all beings, and who controls all beings from within – he is the inner controller, the immortal.'

That was with respect to beings. [16] What follows is with respect to the body (*ātman*).

'This self of yours who is present within but is different from the breath, whom the breath does not know, whose body is the breath, and who controls the breath from within – he is the inner controller, the immortal.

[17] 'This self of yours who is present within but is different from speech, whom speech does not know, whose body is speech, and who controls speech from within – he is the inner controller, the immortal.

[18] 'This self of yours who is present within but is different from sight, whom sight does not know, whose body is sight, and who controls sight from within – he is the inner controller, the immortal.

[19] 'This self of yours who is present within but is different from hearing, whom hearing does not know, whose body is hearing, and who controls hearing from within – he is the inner controller, the immortal.

[20] 'This self of yours who is present within but is different from the mind, whom the mind does not know, whose body is the mind, and who controls the mind from within – he is the inner controller, the immortal.

[21] 'This self of yours who is present within but is different from the skin, whom the skin does not know, whose body is the skin, and who controls the skin from within – he is the inner controller, the immortal.

[22] 'This self of yours who is present within but is different from perception, whom perception does not know, whose body is perception, and who controls perception from within – he is the inner controller, the immortal.

[23] 'This self of yours who is present within but is different from the semen, whom the semen does not know, whose body is the semen, and who controls the semen from within – he is the inner controller, the immortal.

'He sees, but he can't be seen; he hears, but he can't be heard; he thinks, but he can't be thought of; he perceives, but he can't be perceived. Besides him, there is no one who sees, no one who hears, no one who thinks, and no one who perceives. It is this self of yours who is the inner controller, the immortal. All besides this is grief.'

Thereupon, Uddālaka Āruṇi fell silent.

8 Then (Gārgī) Vācaknavī spoke. 'Distinguished Brahmins!' she said. 'I am going to ask this man two questions. If he can give me the answers to them, none of you will be able to defeat him in a theological debate.'

'Ask, Gārgī.'

[2] She said: 'I rise to challenge you, Yājñavalkya, with two questions, much as a fierce warrior of Kāśi or Videha, stringing his unstrung bow and taking two deadly arrows in his hand, would rise to challenge an enemy. Give me the answers to them!'

'Ask, Gārgī.'

[3] She said: 'The things above the sky, the things below the earth, and the things between the earth and the sky, as well as all those things people here refer to as past, present, and future – on what, Yājñavalkya, are all these woven back and forth?'

[4] He replied: 'The things above the sky, the things below the earth, and the things between the earth and the sky, as well as all those things people here refer to as past, present, and future – on space, Gārgī, are all these woven back and forth.'

[5] She responded: 'All honour to you, Yājñavalkya. You really cleared that up for me! Get ready for the second.'

'Ask, Gārgī.'

[6] She said: 'The things above the sky, the things below the earth, and the things between the earth and the sky, as well as all those things people here refer to as past, present, and future – on what, Yājñavalkya, are all these woven back and forth?'

[7] He replied: 'The things above the sky, the things below the earth, and the things between the earth and the sky, as well as all those things people here refer to as past, present, and future – on space, Gārgī, are all these woven back and forth.'

'On what, then, is space woven back and forth?'

[8] He replied: 'That, Gārgī, is the imperishable, and Brahmins refer to it like this – it is neither coarse nor fine; it is neither short nor long; it has neither blood nor fat; it is without shadow or darkness; it is without air or space; it is without contact; it has no taste or smell; it is without sight or hearing; it is without speech or mind; it is without energy, breath, or mouth; it is beyond measure; it has nothing within it or outside of it; it does not eat anything; and no one eats it.

[9] 'This is the imperishable, Gārgī, at whose command the sun and the moon stand apart.

This is the imperishable, Gārgī, at whose command the earth and the sky stand apart. This is the imperishable, Gārgī, at whose command seconds and hours, days and nights, fortnights and months, seasons and years stand apart. This is the imperishable, Gārgī, at whose command rivers flow from the snowy mountains in their respective directions, some to the east and others to the west. This is the imperishable, Gārgī, at whose command people flatter donors, and gods are dependent on patrons of sacrifices, and forefathers, on ancestral offerings.

[10] 'Without knowing this imperishable, Gārgī, even if a man were to make offerings, to offer sacrifices, and to perform austerities in this world for many thousands of years, all that would come to naught. Pitiful is the man, Gārgī, who departs from this world without knowing this imperishable. But a man who departs from this world after he has come to know this imperishable – he, Gārgī, is a Brahmin.

[11] 'This is the imperishable, Gārgī, which sees but can't be seen; which hears but can't be heard; which thinks but can't be thought of; which perceives but can't be perceived. Besides this imperishable, there is no one that sees, no one that hears, no one that thinks, and no one that perceives.

'On this very imperishable, Gārgī, space is woven back and forth.'

[12] 'Distinguished Brahmins!' said Gārgī. 'You should consider yourself lucky if you escape from this man by merely paying him your respects. None of you will ever defeat him in a theological debate.'

Thereupon, Vācaknavī fell silent.

9 Then Vidagdha Śākalya began to question him. 'Tell me, Yājñavalkya – how many gods are there?' Saying, 'As many as are mentioned in the ritual invocation within the laud to the All-gods', he answered in accordance with this very ritual invocation: 'Three and three hundred, and three and three thousand.'

'Yes, of course,' he said, 'but really, Yājñavalkya, how many gods are there?'

'Thirty-three.'

'Yes, of course,' he said, 'but really, Yājñavalkya, how many gods are there?'

'Six.'

'Yes, of course,' he said, 'but really, Yājñavalkya, how many gods are there?'

'Three.'

'Yes, of course,' he said, 'but really, Yājñavalkya, how many gods are there?'

'Two.'

'Yes, of course,' he said, 'but really, Yājñavalkya, how many gods are there?'

'One and a half.'

'Yes, of course,' he said, 'but really, Yājñavalkya, how many gods are there?'

'One.'

'Yes, of course,' he said, 'but then who are those three and three hundred, and those three and three thousand?'

[2] 'They are only the powers of the gods,' Yājñavalkya replied. 'There are only thirty-three gods.'

'Who are those thirty-three?'

'The eight Vasus, the eleven Rudras, and the twelve Ādityas – that makes thirty-one. Then there are Indra and Prajāpati, making a total of thirty-three.'

[3] 'Who are the Vasus?'

'The Vasus are fire, earth, wind, the intermediate region, sun, sky, moon, and stars. They are called Vasus because this whole treasure (*vasu*) is entrusted to them.'

[4] 'Who are the Rudras?'

'The ten vital functions (*prāṇa*) in a man, with the self (*ātman*) as the eleventh. They make people weep when they depart from this mortal body. They are called Rudras because they make people weep (*rud-*).'

[5] 'Who are the Ādityas?'

'The Ādityas are the twelve months of the year, for they carry off this whole world as they proceed. They are called Ādityas because they carry off (*ādadānāḥ*) this whole world as they proceed (*yanti*).'

[6] 'Who is Indra? And who is Prajāpati?'

'Indra is just the thunder, and Prajāpati is the sacrifice.'

'What is thunder?'

'The thunderbolt.'

'What is the sacrifice?'

'The sacrificial animals.'

[7] 'Who are the six?'

'The six are fire and earth, wind and the intermediate region, sun and sky – for these six are this whole world.'

[8] 'Who are the three gods?'

'Just these three worlds, for all the gods live in them.'

'Who are the two gods?'

'Food and breath.'

'Who are the one and a half?'

'The purifying wind that is blowing here. [9] Now, some may ask: "But the purifying wind here blows as one only. So how can he be one and a half?" He is one and a half (*adhyardha*) because in him this whole world increases (*adhyardh-*).'

'Who is the one god?'

'Breath. He is called "Brahman" and "Tyad".'

[10] 'The person whose abode is the earth, whose world is fire, and whose light is the mind – should someone know that person, the final goal of every self (*ātman*), he would be a man who truly knows, Yājñavalkya.'

'I know that person, the final goal of every self, of whom you speak. He is none other than this bodily person. But tell me, Śākalya – who is his god?'

'The immortal,' Śākalya replied.

[11] 'The person whose abode is passion, whose world is the heart, and whose light is the mind – should someone know that person, the final goal of every self, he would be a man who truly knows, Yājñavalkya.'

'I know that person, the final goal of every self, of whom you speak. He is none other than this person immersed in passion. But tell me, Śākalya – who is his god?'

'Women,' Śākalya replied.

[12] 'The person whose abode is visible appearances, whose world is sight, and whose light is the mind – should someone know that person, the final goal of every self, he would be a man who truly knows, Yājñavalkya.'

'I know that person, the final goal of every self, of whom you speak. He is none other than that person up there in the sun. But tell me, Śākalya – who is his god?'

'Truth,' Śākalya replied.

[13] 'The person whose abode is space, whose world is hearing, and whose light is the mind – should someone know that person, the final goal of every self, he would be a man who truly knows, Yājñavalkya.'

'I know that person, the final goal of every self, of whom you speak. He is none other than this person connected with hearing and echo. But tell me, Śākalya – who is his god?'

'The quarters,' Śākalya replied.

[14] 'The person whose abode is darkness, whose world is the heart, and whose light is the mind – should someone know that person, the final goal of every self, he would be a man who truly knows, Yājñavalkya.'

'I know that person, the final goal of every self, of whom you speak. He is none other than this person consisting of shadow. But tell me, Śākalya – who is his god?'

'Death,' Śākalya replied.

[15] 'The person whose abode is visible appearances, whose world is sight, and whose light is the mind – should someone know that person, the final goal of every self, he would be a man who truly knows, Yājñavalkya.'

'I know that person, the final goal of every self, of whom you speak. He is none other than this person here in a mirror. But tell me, Śākalya – who is his god?'

'Life,' Śākalya replied.

[16] 'The person whose abode is the waters, whose world is the heart, and whose light is the mind – should someone know that person, the final goal of every self, he would be a man who truly knows, Yājñavalkya.'

'I know that person, the final goal of every self, of whom you speak. He is none other than this person here in the waters. But tell me, Śākalya – who is his god?'

'Varuṇa,' Śākalya replied.

[17] 'The person whose abode is semen, whose world is the heart, and whose light is the mind – should someone know that person, the final goal of every self, he would be a man who truly knows, Yājñavalkya.'

'I know that person, the final goal of every self, of whom you speak. He is none other than this person associated with a son. But tell me, Śākalya – who is his god?'

'Prajāpati,' Śākalya replied.

[18] At this point Yājñavalkya exclaimed: 'Poor Śākalya! I'm afraid these Brahmins have made you their cat's-paw.'

[19] Śākalya said: 'Tell me, Yājñavalkya – what is the formulation of truth (*brahman*) you know that has enabled you here to out-talk these Brahmins of Kuru and Pañcāla?'

'I know the quarters together with their gods and foundations.'

'Since you say that you know the quarters together with their gods and foundations, [20] according to you, who is the god of the eastern quarter?'

'The sun.'

'On what is the sun founded?'

'On sight.'

'On what is sight founded?'

'On visible appearances, for one sees visible appearances with one's sight.'

'On what are visible appearances founded?'

'On the heart, for one recognizes visible appearances with the heart. So visible appearances are founded on the heart.'

'You're absolutely right, Yājñavalkya! [21] According to you, who is the god of the southern quarter?'

'Yama.'

'On what is Yama founded?'

'On the sacrifice.'

'On what is the sacrifice founded?'

'On the sacrificial gift.'

'On what is the sacrificial gift founded?'

'On faith, for a man gives a sacrificial gift only when he has faith. So the sacrificial gift is founded on faith.'

'On what is faith founded?'

'On the heart, for one recognizes faith with the heart. So faith is founded on the heart.'

'You're absolutely right, Yājñavalkya! [22] According to you, who is the god of the western quarter?'

'Varuṇa.'

'On what is Varuṇa founded?'

'On water.'

'On what is water founded?'

'On semen.'

'On what is semen founded?'

'On the heart. For that very reason, when someone has a son who is a picture of him, people say: "He's dropped right out of his heart! He's carved from his very heart!" So semen is founded on the heart.'

'You're absolutely right, Yājñavalkya! [23] According to you, who is the god of the northern quarter?'

'The moon.'

'On what is the moon founded?'

'On the sacrificial consecration.'

'On what is the sacrificial consecration founded?'

'On truth. For that very reason, they instruct a man consecrated for sacrifice: "Speak the truth." So the sacrificial consecration is founded on truth.'

'On what is truth founded?'

'On the heart, for one recognizes truth with the heart. So truth is founded on the heart.'

'You're absolutely right, Yājñavalkya! [24] According to you, who is the god of the zenith, the fixed quarter?'

'Fire.'

'On what is fire founded?'

'On speech.'

'On what is speech founded?'

'On the heart.'

'On what is the heart founded?'

[25] At this Yājñavalkya exploded: 'What an imbecile you are to think that it could be founded anywhere other than ourselves! If it were anywhere other than ourselves, dogs would eat it, or birds would tear it up.'

[26] 'On what are you and your self (*ātman*) founded?'

'On the out-breath.'

'On what is the out-breath founded?'

'On the in-breath.'

'On what is the in-breath founded?'

'On the inter-breath.'

'On what is the inter-breath founded?'

'On the up-breath.'

'On what is the up-breath founded?'

'On the link-breath. About this self (*ātman*), one can only say "not ——, not —— ". He is ungraspable, for he cannot be grasped. He is undecaying, for he is not subject to decay. He has nothing sticking to him, for he does not stick to anything. He is not bound; yet he neither trembles in fear nor suffers injury. Now, those are the eight abodes, the eight worlds, the eight gods, and the eight persons. I ask you about that person providing the hidden connection (*upaniṣad*) – the one who carries off these other persons, brings them back, and rises above them? If you will not tell me that, your head will shatter apart.'

Śākalya did not know him, and his head did, indeed, shatter apart. Robbers, moreover, stole his bones, mistaking them for something else.

[27] Yājñavalkya then spoke: 'Distinguished Brahmins! If any one of you would like to question me, he may do so; or, if you prefer, all of you may question me together. Or else, if any one of you would like me to, I will question him; or, if you prefer, I will question all of you together.' But those Brahmins did not dare.

[28] So he questioned them with these verses:

Man is like a mighty tree –
that's the truth.
His body hairs are its leaves,
His skin is its outer bark.
Blood flows from his skin,
As sap from the bark of a tree.
Blood flows when the skin is pricked,
As sap, when the bark is slit.

His flesh is the sapwood;
His sinews are the fibres –
that's certain.
His bones are the heartwood;
And his marrow resembles the pith.

A tree when it's cut down,
Grows anew from its root;
From what root does a mortal man grow,
When he is cut down by death?

Do not say, 'From the seed';
For it's produced from him
while he is still alive;
And like a tree
sprouting from a seed,
It takes birth at once,
even before he dies.

A tree, when it's uprooted,
Will not sprout out again;
From what root does a mortal man grow,
When he is cut down by death?

Once he's born,
he can't be born again.
Who, I ask,
will beget him again?

Perception, bliss, *brahman*,
The gift of those who give,
The highest good –
awaits those who know this
and stand firm.

Chapter 4

[...]

4 'Now, as this self (*ātman*) grows steadily weaker and begins to lose consciousness, these vital functions (*prāṇa*) throng around him. Taking into himself these particles of light, he descends back into the heart. When the person connected with sight turns back, the man loses his ability to perceive visible forms. [2] So people say: "He's sinking; he can't see!" – "He's sinking; he can't smell!" – "He's sinking; he can't taste!" – "He's sinking; he can't speak!" – "He's sinking; he can't hear!" – "He's sinking; he can't think!" – "He's sinking; he can't feel a touch!" – "He's sinking; he can't perceive!" Then the top of his heart lights up, and with that light the self exits through the eye or the head or some other part of the body. As he is departing, his lifebreath (*prāṇa*) departs with him. And as his lifebreath departs, all his vital functions (*prāṇa*) depart with it.

'He then descends into a state of mere awareness and develops into one who is thus endowed with perception. Then learning and rites, as well as memory, take hold of him.

[3] 'It is like this. As a caterpillar, when it comes to the tip of a blade of grass, reaches out to a new foothold and draws itself onto it, so the self (*ātman*), after it has knocked

down this body and rendered it unconscious, reaches out to a new foothold and draws itself onto it.

[4] 'It is like this. As a weaver, after she has removed the coloured yarn, weaves a different design that is newer and more attractive, so the self, after it has knocked down this body and rendered it unconscious, makes for himself a different figure that is newer and more attractive – the figure of a forefather, or of a Gandharva, or of a god, or of Prajāpati, or of *brahman*, or else the figure of some other being.

[5] 'Clearly, this self is *brahman* – this self that is made of perception, made of mind, made of sight, made of breath, made of hearing, made of earth, made of water, made of wind, made of space, made of light and the lightless, made of desire and the desireless, made of anger and the angerless, made of the righteous and the unrighteous; this self that is made of everything. Hence there is this saying: "He's made of this. He's made of that." What a man turns out to be depends on how he acts and on how he conducts himself. If his actions are good, he will turn into something good. If his actions are bad, he will turn into something bad. A man turns into something good by good action and into something bad by bad action. And so people say: "A person here consists simply of desire." A man resolves in accordance with his desire, acts in accordance with his resolve, and turns out to be in accordance with his action. [6] On this point there is the following verse:

A man who's attached goes with his action,
to that very place to which
his mind and character cling.
Reaching the end of his action,
of whatever he has done in this world –
From that world he returns
back to this world,
back to action.

'That is the course of a man who desires.

'Now, a man who does not desire – who is without desires, who is freed from desires, whose desires are fulfilled, whose only desire is his self – his vital functions (*prāṇa*) do not depart. *Brahman* he is, and to *brahman* he goes. [7] On this point there is the following verse:

When they are all banished,
those desires lurking in one's heart;
Then a mortal becomes immortal,
and attains *brahman* in this world.

'It is like this. As a snake's slough, lifeless and discarded, lies on an anthill, so lies this corpse. But this non-corporeal and immortal lifebreath (*prāṇa*) is nothing but *brahman*, nothing but light.'

'Here, sir, I'll give you a thousand cows!' said Janaka, the king of Videha.

[8] 'On this point there are the following verses:

There is an ancient path
extremely fine and extending far;
It has touched me, I've discovered it!
By it they go up to the heavenly world
released from here,
wise men, knowers of *brahman*.

[9] In it are the white and the blue, they say,
the orange, green, and red.
By *brahman* was this path discovered;
By it goes the knower of *brahman*,
the doer of good, the man of light.

[10] Into blind darkness they enter,
people who worship ignorance;
And into still blinder darkness,
people who delight in learning.

[11] 'Joyless' are those regions called,
in blind darkness they are cloaked;
Into them after death they go,
men who are not learned or wise.

[12] If a person truly perceives the self,
knowing 'I am he';
What possibly could he want,
Whom possibly could he love,
that he should worry about his body?

[13] The self has entered this body, this dense jumble.
If a man finds him,
Recognizes him,
He's the maker of everything – the author of all!
The world is his – he's the world itself!

[14] While we are still here, we have come to know it.
If you've not known it, great is your destruction.
Those who have known it – they become immortal.
As for the rest – only suffering awaits them.

[15] When a man clearly sees this self as god,
the lord of what was
and of what will be,
He will not seek to hide from him.

[16] Beneath which the year revolves
together with its days,
That the gods venerate
as the light of lights,
as life immortal.

[17] In which are established
the various groups of five,
together with space;
I take that to be the self –
I who have the knowledge,
I who am immortal,
I take that to be –
the *brahman*,
the immortal.

[18] The breathing behind breathing, the sight behind sight, the hearing behind hearing, the thinking behind thinking –
Those who know this perceive *brahman*,
the first,
the ancient.

[19] With the mind alone must one behold it –
there is here nothing diverse at all!
From death to death he goes, who sees
here any kind of diversity.

[20] As just singular must one behold it –
immeasurable and immovable.
The self is spotless and beyond space,
unborn, immense, immovable.

[21] By knowing that very one a wise Brahmin
should obtain insight for himself.
Let him not ponder over a lot of words;
it just tires the voice!

[22] 'This immense, unborn self is none other than the one consisting of perception here among the vital functions (*prāṇa*). There, in that space within the heart, he lies – the controller of all, the lord of all, the ruler of all! He does not become more by good actions or in any way less by bad actions. He is the lord of all! He is the ruler of creatures! He is the guardian of creatures! He is the dike separating these worlds so they would not mingle with each other. It is he that Brahmins seek to know by means of vedic recitation, sacrifice, gift-giving, austerity, and fasting. It is he, on knowing whom, a man becomes a sage. It is when they desire him as their world that wandering ascetics undertake the ascetic life of wandering.
[. . .]

Chapter 5

1 The world there is full;
The world here is full;
Fullness from fullness proceeds.
After taking fully from the full,
It still remains completely full.

'*Brahman* is space. The primeval one is space. Space is windy.' This was what the son of Kauravyāyaṇī used to say. This is the Veda. Brahmins know it. And by this I know whatever one must know.
[. . .]

Chāndogya *Upaniṣad*

Chapter 1

1 OṂ – one should venerate the High Chant as this syllable, for one begins the High Chant with OṂ. Here is a further explanation of that syllable.

[2] The essence of these beings here is the earth; the essence of the earth is the waters; the essence of the waters is plants; the essence of plants is man; the essence of man is speech; the essence of speech is the Ṛg verse; the essence of the Ṛg verse is the Sāman chant; the essence of the Sāman chant is the High Chant. [3] This High Chant is the quintessence of all essences; it is the highest, the ultimate, the eighth.

[4] What ultimately is the Ṛg verse? What ultimately is the Sāman chant? What ultimately is the High Chant? These questions have been the subject of critical enquiry.

[5] The Ṛg is nothing but speech; the Sāman is breath; and the High Chant is this syllable OṂ. Speech and breath, the Ṛg and the Sāman – each of these sets, clearly, is a pair in coitus.

[6] This pair in coitus unites in the syllable OṂ, and when a pair unites in coitus, they satisfy each other's desire. [7] So, when someone knows this and venerates the High Chant as this syllable, he will surely become a man who satisfies desires.

[8] Clearly, this syllable signifies assent, for one says 'OṂ' when one assents to something. And assent is nothing but fulfilment. So, when someone knows this and venerates the High Chant as this syllable, he will surely become a man who fulfils desires.

[9] It is by means of this syllable that the triple Veda continues – the Adhvaryu priest says 'OṂ' before he issues a call; the Hotṛ says 'OṂ' before he makes an invocation; and the Udgātṛ says 'OṂ' before he sings the High Chant. They do so to honour this very syllable, because of its greatness and because it is the essence.

[10] Those who know this and those who do not both perform these rites using this syllable. But knowledge and ignorance are two very different things. Only what is performed with knowledge, with faith, and with an awareness of the hidden connections (*upaniṣad*) becomes truly potent.

Now, then – that was a further explanation of this very syllable.

2 Once, when the gods and the demons, both children of Prajāpati, arrayed themselves against each other, the gods got hold of the High Chant. 'With this we will overpower them', they thought.

[2] So they venerated the High Chant as the breath within the nostrils. The demons riddled it with evil. As a result, one smells with it both good and bad odours, for it is riddled with evil.

[3] Then they venerated the High Chant as speech. The demons riddled it with evil. As a result, one speaks with it both what is true and what is false, for it is riddled with evil.

[4] Then they venerated the High Chant as sight. The demons riddled it with evil. As a result one sees with it both what is good to see and what is not, for it is riddled with evil.

[5] Then they venerated the High Chant as hearing. The demons riddled it with evil. As a result, one hears with it both what is good to hear and what is not, for it is riddled with evil.

[6] Then they venerated the High Chant as the mind. The demons riddled it with evil. As a result, one envisages with it both what is good to envisage and what is not, for it is riddled with evil.

[7] Finally, they venerated the High Chant as just this breath here within the mouth. And when the demons hurled themselves at it, they were smashed to bits like a clod of earth hurled against a target that is a rock. [8] And if anyone contemplates evil against or hurts a person who knows this, he will be smashed to bits like a clod hurled against a target that is a rock. That person is a rock target. [9] One never recognizes with this breath either good or bad odours, for it is free from evil. Therefore, whenever one eats or drinks, one nourishes thereby the other vital functions (*prāṇa*). When, at the end, one fails to find it, one departs; indeed, at the end one leaves the mouth wide open.

[10] Aṅgiras venerated the High Chant as that breath. People consider Aṅgiras to be just that, because it is the essence (*rasa*) of the bodily parts (*aṅga*). [11] Bṛhaspati venerated the High Chant as that breath. People consider Bṛhaspati to be just that, because speech is great (*bṛhatī*) and it is the lord (*pati*) of speech. [12] Ayāsya venerated the High Chant as that breath. People consider Ayāsya to be just that, because it proceeds (*ayate*) from the mouth (*āsya*). [13] Then Baka Dālbhya came to know that. He became the Udgātṛ priest of the people of Naimiṣa and secured their desires for them through his singing. [14] And, indeed, when someone knows this and venerates the High Chant as this syllable, he too will become a man who secures desires through singing.

All that was with respect to the body (*ātman*).

3 What follows is with respect to the divine sphere. One should venerate the High Chant as the sun up there that gives warmth. As it rises (*udyan*), it sings the High Chant (*udgāyati*) for the creatures. As it rises, it dispels darkness and fear. Anyone who knows this is sure to become a man who dispels fear and darkness.

[2] This breath in here and that sun up there are exactly the same. This is warm, and so is that. People call this sound (*svara*), and they call that shine (*svara*) and shining back (*pratyāsvara*). Therefore, one should venerate the High Chant as both this here and that up there.

[3] Now, then, one should venerate the High Chant as just the inter-breath. When one breathes out, it is the out-breath; when one breathes in, it is the in-breath. And the inter-breath is where the out-breath and the in-breath meet. The inter-breath is the same as speech. One speaks, therefore, without breathing out or in. [4] Speech is the same as the Ṛg verse. One recites a Ṛg verse, therefore, without breathing out or in. The Ṛg verse is the same as the Sāman chant. One sings a Sāman chant, therefore, without breathing out or in. The Sāman chant is the same as the High Chant. One sings the High Chant, therefore, without breathing out or in. [5] Even activities other than these, activities that require strength, such as churning a fire, running a race, and stretching a strong bow, are performed without breathing out or in. For this reason, one should venerate the High Chant as just the inter-breath.

[6] Now, then, one should venerate the syllables of the word *udgītha* – High Chant – namely *ud*, *gī*, and *tha*. The syllable *ud* is simply breath, for people rise up (*ud-sthā*) by means of breath; the syllable *gī* is speech, for speech utterances are called words (*gir*); and the syllable *tha* is food, for this whole world rests (*sthita*) on food. [7] The syllable *ud*, likewise, is the sky, *gī* is the intermediate region, and *tha* is the earth. And again, the syllable *ud* is the sun, *gī* is the wind, and *tha* is the fire. So also, the syllable *ud* is the Sāmaveda, *gī* is the Yajurveda, and *tha* is the Ṛgveda. When someone knows them in this way and venerates these syllables of the High Chant, namely, *ud*, *gī*, and *tha* – speech will yield for him the milk which is the very milk of speech, and he will come to own and to eat his own food.

[8] Now, then, this is how wishes are fulfilled. One should venerate the following as things to turn to. A man should repair to the Sāman chant which he is about to use in a liturgical praise, [9] to the Ṛg verse which supplies the lyrics of that chant, and to the seer who composed that verse. A man should repair to the deity whom he is about to praise with that chant. [10] A man should repair to the metre of the chant which he is about to use in his praise. A man should repair to the arrangement of the chant which he is about to use in his praise. [11] A man should repair to the direction to which he addresses his praise. [12] Turning to himself (*ātman*), finally, he should sing the hymn of praise, focusing his mind completely on his wish. He can certainly expect that the wish he had as he sang the praise will be fulfilled.

4 OṂ – one should venerate the High Chant as this syllable, for one begins the High Chant with OṂ. Here is a further explanation of that syllable.

[2] When the gods feared death, what they did was to enter the triple Veda. They covered it with the metres. The fact that the gods covered (*chad*) it with them gave the name to and discloses the true nature of the metres (*chandas*). [3] But death saw the gods there in the Ṛg verses, in the Sāman chants, and in the Yajus formulas, just as one sees a fish in water. When the gods discovered this, they emerged from the Ṛg, Sāman, and Yajus, and entered into the very sound. [4] So, when one finishes a Ṛg verse, or a Sāman chant, or a Yajus formula, one makes the sound OṂ. This syllable – the immortal and the fearless – is that very sound. Upon entering that syllable, the gods became immortal and free from fear.

[5] A man who utters this syllable with that knowledge enters this very syllable, the sound that is immortal and free from fear. As the gods became immortal by entering it, so will he.

[. . .]

Chapter 2

[. . .]

23 There are three types of persons whose torso is the Law (*dharma*).

The first is one who pursues sacrifice, vedic recitation, and gift-giving.

The second is one who is devoted solely to austerity.

The third is a celibate student of the Veda living at his teacher's house; that is, a student who settles himself permanently at his teacher's house.

All these gain worlds earned by merit.

A person who is steadfast in *brahman* reaches immortality.

[2] Prajāpati incubated the worlds, and, when they had been incubated, the triple Veda sprang from them. He incubated the triple Veda, and, when it had been incubated, these syllables *'bhūr, bhuvaḥ, svar'* sprang from it. [3] He incubated these syllables, and, when they had been incubated, the syllable OṂ sprang from them. As all the leaves are bored through by a pin, so all words are bored through by OṂ. This whole world is nothing but OṂ.

[. . .]

Chapter 3

[. . .]

12 Whatever there is, this entire creation – clearly, all that is the Gāyatrī. And the Gāyatrī is speech, for speech sings (*gāyati*) and protects (*trāyati*) this entire creation.

[2] Now, take this Gāyatrī – clearly, it is just the same as this earth here, for this entire creation rests upon the earth and never extends beyond its limits.

[3] And take this earth – clearly, it is just the same as this body of a person here, for these vital functions (*prāṇa*) rest within the body and never extend beyond its limits.

[4] And take this body of a person here – clearly, it is just the same as this heart here within a person, for these vital functions rest within the heart and never extend beyond its limits.

[5] This is the Gāyatrī that consists of four quarters and six types. This is declared in a Ṛg verse:

> [6] Such is his greatness –
> Even greater than that is that person.
> One quarter of him are all creatures,
> Three quarters the immortal in heaven.

[7] And take what people call *'brahman'* – clearly, it is nothing but this space here outside a person. And this space here outside a person – [8] clearly, it is the same as this space here within a person. [9] And this space here within a person – clearly, it is the same as this space here within the heart; it is full and non-depleting. Anyone who knows this obtains full and non-depleting prosperity.

[. . .]

Chapter 4

[. . .]

4 One day Satyakāma Jābāla said to his mother Jabālā: 'Mother, I want to become a vedic student. So tell me what my lineage is.' [2] She replied: 'Son, I don't know what your lineage is. I was young when I had you. I was a maid then and had a lot of relationships. As such, it is impossible for me to say what your lineage is. But my name is Jabālā, and your name is Satyakāma. So you should simply say that you are Satyakāma Jābāla.'

[3] He went to Hāridrumata Gautama then and said: 'Sir, I want to live under you as a vedic student. I come to you, sir, as your student.'

[4] Hāridrumata asked him: 'Son, what is your lineage?' And he replied: 'Sir, I don't know what my lineage is. When I asked my mother, she replied: "I was young when I had you. I was a maid then and had a lot of relationships. As such, it is impossible for me to say what your lineage is. But my name is Jabālā, and your name is Satyakāma." So I am Satyakāma Jābāla, sir.'

[5] Hāridrumata then told him: 'Who but a Brahmin could speak like that! Fetch some

firewood, son. I will perform your initiation. You have not strayed from the truth.' So he initiated the boy and, picking out four hundred of the most skinny and feeble cows, told him: 'Son, look after these.' As he was driving them away, Satyakāma answered back: 'I will not return without a thousand!' He lived away for a number of years, and when the cows had increased to a thousand this is what happened.

5 The bull called out to him: 'Satyakāma!' He responded: 'Sir?' The bull said: 'Son, we have reached a thousand. Take us back to the teacher's house, [2] and I will tell you one quarter of *brahman*.'

'Please tell me, sir.'

And the bull told him: 'One-sixteenth of it is the eastern quarter; one-sixteenth is the western quarter; one-sixteenth is the southern quarter; and one-sixteenth is the northern quarter. Consisting of these four-sixteenths, this quarter of *brahman* is named Far-flung, my son.

[3] 'When someone knows this and venerates this quarter of *brahman* consisting of four-sixteenths as Far-flung, he will become far-flung in this world. A man will win far-flung worlds, when he knows this and venerates this quarter of *brahman* consisting of four-sixteenths as Far-flung.'

6 The bull continued: 'The fire will tell you another quarter.' The next morning Satyakāma drove the cows on, and at the spot where they happened to be around sunset he built a fire, corralled the cows, fed the fire with wood, and sat down behind the fire facing the east.

[2] The fire then called out to him: 'Satyakāma!' He responded: 'Sir?'

[3] 'Son, I will tell you a quarter of *brahman*.'

'Please tell me, sir.'

And the fire told him: 'One-sixteenth of it is the earth; one-sixteenth is the intermediate region; one-sixteenth is the sky; and one-sixteenth is the ocean. Consisting of these four-sixteenths, this quarter of *brahman* is named Limitless, my son.

[4] 'When someone knows this and venerates the quarter of *brahman* consisting of these four-sixteenths as Limitless, there will be no limits for him in this world. A man will win limitless worlds, when he knows this and venerates the quarter of *brahman* consisting of these four-sixteenths as Limitless.'

7 The fire continued: 'A wild goose will tell you another quarter.' The next morning Satyakāma drove the cows on, and at the spot where they happened to be around sunset he built a fire, corralled the cows, fed the fire with wood, and sat down behind the fire facing the east.

[2] A wild goose then flew down and called out to him: 'Satyakāma!' He responded: 'Sir?'

[3] 'Son, I will tell you a quarter of *brahman*.'

'Please tell me, sir.'

And the wild goose told him: 'One-sixteenth of it is the fire; one-sixteenth is the sun; one-sixteenth is the moon; and one-sixteenth is lightning. Consisting of these four-sixteenths, this quarter of *brahman* is named Radiant, my son.

[4] 'When someone knows this and venerates the quarter of *brahman* consisting of these four-sixteenths as Radiant, he will become radiant in this world. A man will win radiant worlds, when he knows this and venerates the quarter of *brahman* consisting of these four-sixteenths as Radiant.'

8 The wild goose continued: 'A water-bird will tell you another quarter.' The next morning Satyakāma drove the cows on, and at the spot where they happened to be around sunset he built a fire, corralled the cows, fed the fire with wood, and sat down behind the fire facing the east.

[2] A water-bird then flew down and called out to him: 'Satyakāma!' He responded: 'Sir?'

[3] 'Son, I will tell you a quarter of *brahman*.'

'Please tell me, sir.'

And the water-bird told him: 'One-sixteenth of it is breath; one-sixteenth is sight; one-sixteenth is hearing; and one-sixteenth is the mind. Consisting of these four-sixteenths, this quarter of *brahman* is named Abode-possessing, my son.

[4] 'When someone knows this and venerates the quarter of *brahman* consisting of these four-sixteenths as Abode-possessing, he will have an abode in this world. A man will win worlds possessing abodes, when he knows this and venerates the quarter of *brahman* consisting of these four-sixteenths as Abode-possessing.'

9 Finally he reached his teacher's house. The teacher called out to him: 'Satyakāma!' He responded: 'Sir?'

[2] 'Son, you have the glow of a man who knows *brahman*! Tell me – who taught you?'

'Other than human beings,' he acknowledged. 'But, if it pleases you, sir, you should teach it to me yourself, [3] for I have heard from people of your eminence that knowledge leads one most securely to the goal only when it is learnt from a teacher.' So he explained it to him, and, indeed, he did so without leaving anything out.

10 Upakosala Kāmalāyana once lived as a vedic student under Satyakāma Jābāla and tended his fires for twelve years. Now, Satyakāma, although he permitted other students of his to return home, did not permit Upakosala to do so. [2] His wife then told him: 'The student has performed his austerities and faithfully tended the fires. Teach him before the fires beat you to it.' But Satyakāma went on a journey without ever teaching him.

[3] Now, Upakosala became so afflicted that he stopped eating. His teacher's wife told him: 'Come on, student, eat. Why have you stopped eating?' He told her: 'The desires that lurk within this man are many and bring various dangers. I am overwhelmed by afflictions, and I will not eat.'

[4] The fires then said to each other: 'The student has performed his austerities and faithfully tended us. So come, let us teach him.' And they told him: '*Brahman* is breath. *Brahman* is joy (*ka*). *Brahman* is space (*kha*).'

[5] He replied: 'I can understand that *brahman* is breath. But I don't understand how it can be joy or space.'

'Joy is the same as space,' they replied, 'and space is the same as joy.' And they explained to him both breath and space.

11 Thereupon, the householder's fire instructed him: 'Earth, fire, food, and sun – I am the person one sees in the sun; so I am all those.'

[2] 'When someone knows this and venerates him in this way – he rids himself of bad actions; he provides himself with a world; he lives long and reaches the full span of his life; and the line of his descendants will not die out. We will serve him in this world and the next – when someone knows this and venerates him in this way.'

12 Then the southern fire instructed him: 'The waters, the quarters, the stars, and the moon – I am the person one sees in the moon; so I am all those.'

[2] 'When someone knows this and venerates him in this way – he rids himself of bad actions; he provides himself with a world; he lives long and reaches the full span of his life; and the line of his descendants will not die out. We will serve him in this world and the next – when someone knows this and venerates him in this way.'

13 Finally, the offertorial fire instructed him: 'Breath, space, sky, and lightning – I am the person one sees in lightning; so I am all those.'

[2] 'When someone knows this and venerates him in this way – he rids himself of bad actions; he provides himself with a world; he lives long and reaches the full span of his life; and the line of his descendants will not die out. We will serve him in this world and the next – when someone knows this and venerates him in this way.'

14 Then the fires told him: 'Upakosala! Son, now you have this knowledge both of ourselves and of the self (*ātman*). Your teacher, however, will point out the goal to you.'

His teacher finally returned. The teacher called out to him, 'Upakosala!' [2] He responded: 'Sir?'

'Son, your face glows like that of a man who knows *brahman*. Tell me – who taught you?'

'Who could possibly have taught me, sir?' – in so saying, he denies it in a way. And alluding to the fires, he continued: 'These look like this now, but they were different.'

'What did they tell you, son?'

[3] 'This,' he acknowledged.

'They just told you about the worlds, son. But I will tell you that about which it is said: "When someone knows it bad actions do not stick to him, just as water does not stick to a lotus leaf."'

'Sir, please teach me that.'

And this is what he told him.

15 'The person you see here in the eye – he is the self (*ātman*),' he told him. 'He is the immortal free from fear; he is *brahman*. So, even if someone pours water or ghee in that eye, it just runs to the two borders.

[2] 'They call him "Lovely-uniting" (*saṃyadvāma*), for all lovely things (*vāma*) come in concert (*abhisaṃyanti*) to him. All lovely things come in concert also to anyone who knows this.

[3] 'He is also 'Lovely-leading' (*vāmanī*), for he leads (*nī*) all lovely things (*vāma*). Anyone who knows this also leads all lovely things.

[4] 'He is also 'Shining' (*bhāmanī*), for he shines in all the worlds. Anyone who knows this also shines in all the worlds.

[5] 'Now, whether they perform a cremation for such a person or not, people like him pass into the flame, from the flame into the day, from the day into the fortnight of the waxing moon, from the fortnight of the waxing moon into the six months when the sun moves north, from these months into the year, from the year into the sun, from the sun into the moon, and from the moon into the lightning. Then a person who is not human – he leads them to *brahman*. This is the path to the gods, the path to *brahman*. Those who proceed along this path do not return to this human condition.'

16 The wind that purifies – that is the sacrifice. The wind, as it moves, purifies this whole world. Because it purifies this whole world as it moves (*yan*), it is the sacrifice (*yajña*).

Its two tracks are mind and speech. [2] One of those the Brahman priest constructs with his mind, while the Hotṛ, Adhvaryu, and Udgātṛ priests construct the other with their speech.

If it happens that the Brahman priest breaks in and speaks after the start of the morning litany and before its concluding verse, [3] he constructs only one of the tracks, while the other is left out. So his sacrifice founders, just like a one-legged man, when he walks, or a cart, when it moves on just one wheel. And when the sacrifice founders, the patron of that sacrifice also founders. He becomes a pauper after offering the sacrifice.

[4] If, on the other hand, the Brahman priest does not break in and speak after the start of the morning litany and before its concluding verse, the priests construct both the tracks, and neither is left out. [5] So his sacrifice becomes steady, just like a man walking with both feet, or a cart moving on both wheels. And when the sacrifice becomes steady, the patron of the sacrifice also becomes steady. He becomes a rich man after offering the sacrifice.

17 Prajāpati incubated the worlds. And as they were being incubated, he extracted their essences – the fire from the earth, the wind from the intermediate region, and the sun from the sky.

[2] He incubated these three deities. And as they were being incubated, he extracted their essences – the Ṛg verses from the fire, the Yajus formulas from the wind, and the Sāman chants from the sun.

[3] He incubated this triple Veda. And as they were being incubated, he extracted their essences – the word *bhūḥ* from the Ṛg verses, the word *bhuvaḥ* from the Yajus formulas, and the word *svaḥ* from the Sāman chants.

[4] So, if the sacrifice suffers an injury on account of a Ṛg verse, he should make an offering in the householder's fire with the words '*bhūḥ svāhā*!' This way he binds any injury suffered by the Ṛg verses and the

sacrifice, using the very essence and power of the Ṛg verses.

[5] And if the sacrifice suffers an injury on account of a Yajus formula, he should make an offering in the southern fire with the words '*bhuvaḥ svāhā*!' This way he binds any injury suffered by the Yajus formulas and the sacrifice, using the very essence and power of the Yajus formulas.

[6] And if the sacrifice suffers an injury on account of a Sāman chant, he should make an offering in the offertorial fire with the words '*svaḥ svāhā*!' This way he binds any injury suffered by the Sāman chants and the sacrifice, using the very essence and power of the Sāman chants.

[7] Just as one binds gold with salt, silver with gold, tin with silver, lead with tin, copper with lead, wood with copper, and leather with wood, [8] so by the power of these worlds and of these deities and of this triple Veda he binds an injury done to a sacrifice. When one who knows this becomes the Brahman priest, that sacrifice is equipped with healing medicine. [9–10] And when one who knows this becomes the Brahman priest, that sacrifice inclines towards the north. There is this verse about the Brahman priest who knows this:

> Wherever it turns,
> there a human goes.
> Alone among the priests,
> the Brahman protects,
> Like a mare, the men of Kuru.

A Brahman priest who knows this protects the sacrifice, the patron of the sacrifice, and all the priests. Therefore, a man should select as his Brahman priest only someone who knows this, and never someone who is ignorant of this.

Chapter 5

[. . .]

3 Śvetaketu, the son of Āruṇi, came one day into the assembly of the land of Pañcāla. Pravāhaṇa Jaivali asked him: 'Son, did your father teach you?' Śvetaketu replied: 'Yes indeed, my lord.'

[2] 'Do you know where people go from here when they die?'

'No, my lord.'

'Do you know how they return again?'

'No, my lord.'

'Do you know how the two paths – the path to the gods and the path to the fathers – take different turns?'

'No, my lord.'

[3] 'Do you know how that world up there is not filled up?'

'No, my lord.'

'Do you know how at the fifth offering the water takes on a human voice?'

'No, my lord.'

[4] 'Did you not say that you had been educated? Without knowing these things how can anyone call himself educated?'

Deeply hurt, Śvetaketu returned to his father's house and told him: 'Without actually teaching me, sir, you told me that you had taught me! [5] That excuse for a prince asked me five questions, and I couldn't answer a single one of them.'

The father said: 'As you report them to me, son, I do not know the answer to even one of them. If I had known them, how could I have not taught them to you?'

[6] Gautama then came to the king's place. When he arrived, the king received him with respect. In the morning Gautama went into the assembly hall, and the king said to him: 'Gautama, sir, choose a gift of human riches.' Gautama responded: 'Keep your human riches, Your Majesty. Tell me exactly what you told my boy.'

The king became worried [7] and ordered him to stay a while longer. Finally he told him: 'As to what you have asked me, Gautama, let me tell you that before you this knowledge had never reached the Brahmins. As a result in all the worlds government has belonged exclusively to royalty.' The king then told him:

4 'A fire – that's what the region up there is, Gautama. Its fire-wood is the sun; its smoke is the sunbeams; its flame is the day; its embers are the moon; and its sparks are the constellations. [2] In that very fire gods offer faith, and from that offering springs King Soma.

5 'A fire – that's what a rain-cloud is, Gautama. Its firewood is the wind; its smoke is the thunder-cloud; its flame is lightning; its embers are thunder; and its sparks are hail. [2] In that very fire gods offer King Soma, and from that offering springs rain.

6 'A fire – that's what the earth is, Gautama. Its firewood is the year; its smoke is space; its flame is the night; its embers are the quarters; and its sparks are the intermediate quarters. [2] In that very fire gods offer rain, and from that offering springs food.

7 'A fire – that's what a man is, Gautama. His firewood is speech; his smoke is breath; his flame is the tongue; his embers are sight; and his sparks are hearing. [2] In that very fire gods offer food, and from that offering springs semen.

8 'A fire – that's what a woman is, Gautama. Her firewood is the vulva; when she is asked to come close, that is her smoke; her flame is the vagina; when one penetrates her, that is her embers; and her sparks are the climax. In that very fire gods offer semen, and from that offering springs the foetus.

9 'Therefore it is said: "at the fifth offering the waters take on a human voice." Covered by the placenta, the foetus lies inside the womb for nine or ten months or thereabouts and is then born. [2] Once he is born, he lives his allotted life span. When he has departed, when he has reached his appointed time – they take him to the very fire from which he came, from which he sprang.

10 'Now, the people who know this, and the people here in the wilderness who venerate thus: "Austerity is faith" – they pass into the flame, from the flame into the day, from the day into the fortnight of the waxing moon, from the fortnight of the waxing moon into the six months when the sun moves north, [2] from these months into the year, from the year into the sun, from the sun into the moon, and from the moon into lightning. Then a person who is not human – he leads them to *brahman*. This is the path leading to the gods.

[3] 'The people here in villages, on the other hand, who venerate thus: "Gift-giving is offerings to gods and to priests" – they pass into the smoke, from the smoke into the night, from the night into the fortnight of the waning moon, and from the fortnight of the waning moon into the six months when the sun moves south. These do not reach the year [4] but from these months pass into the world of the fathers, and from the world of the fathers into space, and from space into the moon. This is King Soma, the food of the gods, and the gods eat it. [5] They remain there as long as there is a residue, and then they return by the same path they went – first to space, and from space to the wind. After the wind has formed, it turns into smoke; after the smoke has formed, it turns into a thunder-cloud; [6] after the thunder-cloud has formed, it turns into a rain-cloud; and after a rain-cloud has formed, it rains down. On earth they spring up as rice and barley, plants and trees, sesame and beans, from which it is extremely difficult to get out. When someone eats that food and deposits the semen, from him one comes into being again.

[7] 'Now, people here whose behaviour is pleasant can expect to enter a pleasant womb, like that of a woman of the Brahmin, the Kṣatriya, or the Vaiśya class. But people of foul behaviour can expect to enter a foul womb, like that of a dog, a pig, or an outcaste woman.

[8] 'Then there are those proceeding on neither of these two paths – they become the tiny creatures revolving here ceaselessly. "Be born! Die!" – that is a third state.

'As a result, that world up there is not filled up.

'A man should seek to protect himself from that. On this point there is this verse:

[9] A man who steals gold, drinks liquor,
and kills a Brahmin;

A man who fornicates with his teacher's wife – these four will fall.
As also the fifth – he who consorts with them.

[10] 'A man who knows these five fires in this way, however, is not tainted with evil even if he associates with such people. Anyone who knows this becomes pure and clean and attains a good world.'
[...]

Chapter 6

1 There was one Śvetaketu, the son of Āruṇi. One day his father told him: 'Śvetaketu, take up the celibate life of a student, for there is no one in our family, my son, who has not studied and is the kind of Brahmin who is so only because of birth.'

[2] So he went away to become a student at the age of 12 and, after learning all the Vedas, returned when he was 24, swell-headed, thinking himself to be learned, and arrogant. [3] His father then said to him: 'Śvetaketu, here you are, my son, swell-headed, thinking yourself to be learned, and arrogant; so you must have surely asked about that rule of substitution by which one hears what has not been heard of before, thinks of what has not been thought of before, and perceives what has not been perceived before?'

[4] 'How indeed does that rule of substitution work, sir?'

'It is like this, son. By means of just one lump of clay one would perceive everything made of clay – the transformation is a verbal handle, a name – while the reality is just this: "It's clay."

[5] 'It is like this, son. By means of just one copper trinket one would perceive everything made of copper – the transformation is a verbal handle, a name – while the reality is just this: "It's copper."

[6] 'It is like this, son. By means of just one nail-cutter one would perceive everything made of iron – the transformation is a verbal handle, a name – while the reality is just this: "It's iron."

'That, son, is how this rule of substitution works.'

[7] 'Surely, those illustrious men did not know this, for had they known, how could they have not told it to me? So, why don't you, sir, tell me yourself?'

'All right, son,' he replied.

2 'In the beginning, son, this world was simply what is existent – one only, without a second. Now, on this point some do say: "In the beginning this world was simply what is non-existent – one only, without a second. And from what is non-existent was born what is existent."

[2] 'But, son, how can that possibly be?' he continued. 'How can what is existent be born from what is non-existent? On the contrary, son, in the beginning this world was simply what is existent – one only, without a second.

[3] 'And it thought to itself: "Let me become many. Let me propagate myself." It emitted heat. The heat thought to itself: "Let me become many. Let me propagate myself." It emitted water. Whenever it is hot, therefore, a man surely perspires; and thus it is from heat that water is produced. [4] The water thought to itself: "Let me become many. Let me propagate myself." It emitted food. Whenever it rains, therefore, food becomes abundant; and thus it is from water that foodstuffs are produced.

3 'There are, as you can see, only three sources from which these creatures here originate: they are born from eggs, from living individuals, or from sprouts.

[2] 'Then that same deity thought to itself: "Come now, why don't I establish the distinctions of name and appearance by entering these three deities here with this living self (*ātman*), [3] and make each of them threefold." So, that deity established the distinctions of name and appearance by entering these three deities here with this living self (*ātman*), [4] and made each of them threefold.

'Learn from me, my son, how each of these three deities becomes threefold.

4 'The red appearance of a fire is, in fact, the appearance of heat, the white, that of water, and the black, that of food. So vanishes from the fire the character of fire – the transformation is a verbal handle, a name – while the reality is just, "It's the three appearances."

[2] 'The red appearance of the sun is, in fact, the appearance of heat, the white, that of water, and the black, that of food. So vanishes from the sun the character of sun – the transformation is a verbal handle, a name – while the reality is just, "It's the three appearances."

[3] 'The red appearance of the moon is, in fact, the appearance of heat, the white, that of water, and the black, that of food. So vanishes from the moon the character of moon – the transformation is a verbal handle, a name – while the reality is just, "It's the three appearances."

[4] 'The red appearance of lightning is, in fact, the appearance of heat, the white, that of water, and the black, that of food. So vanishes from lightning the character of lightning – the transformation is a verbal handle, a name – while the reality is just, "It's the three appearances."

[5] 'It was, indeed, this that they knew, those extremely wealthy and immensely learned householders of old, when they said: "Now no one will be able to spring something upon us that we have not heard of or thought of or understood before." For they derived that knowledge from these three – [6] when they noticed anything that was reddish, they knew: "That is the appearance of heat"; when they noticed anything that was whitish, they knew: "That is the appearance of water"; when they noticed anything that was blackish, they knew: "That is the appearance of food"; [7] and when they noticed anything that was somehow indistinct, they knew: "That is a combination of these same three deities".

'Learn from me, son, how, when they enter a man, each of these three deities become threefold.

5 'When one eats food it breaks down into three parts. The densest becomes faeces, the medium becomes flesh, and the finest becomes mind. [2] When one drinks water it breaks down into three parts. The densest becomes urine, the medium becomes blood, and the finest becomes breath. [3] When one eats heat it breaks down into three parts. The densest becomes bones, the medium becomes marrow, and the finest becomes speech. [4] For the mind is made up of food, son; breath, of water; and speech, of heat.'

'Sir, teach me more.'

'Very well, son.'

6 'When one churns curd, its finest part rises to the top and becomes butter. [2] In the same way, son, when one eats food its finest part rises to the top and becomes mind; [3] when one drinks water its finest part rises to the top and becomes breath; [4] and when one eats heat its finest part rises to the top and becomes speech. [5] For the mind is made up of food, son; breath, of water; and speech, of heat.'

'Sir, teach me more.'

'Very well, son.

7 'A man, my son, consists of sixteen parts. Do not eat for fifteen days, but drink water at will. Breath is made of water; so it will not be cut off if one drinks.'

[2] Śvetaketu did not eat for fifteen days. Then he came back to his father and said: 'What shall I recite, sir?'

'The Ṛg verses, the Yajus formulas, and the Sāman chants.'

'Sir, I just can't remember them,' he replied. [3] And his father said to him:

'It is like this, son. Out of a huge fire that one has built, if there is left only a single ember the size of a firefly – by means of that the fire thereafter would not burn all that much. Likewise, son, you are left with only one of your sixteen parts; by means of that at present you don't remember the Vedas.

'Eat, and then you will learn from me.'

[4] He ate and then came back to his father. And he answered everything that his father asked. [5] And the father said to him:

'It is like this, son. Out of a huge fire that one has built, if there is left only a single ember the size of a firefly and if one were to cover it with straw and set it ablaze – by means of that, the fire thereafter would burn very much. [6] Likewise, son, you were left with only one of your sixteen parts, and when you covered it with food, it was set ablaze – by means of that you now remember the Vedas, for the mind, son, is made up of food; breath, of water; and speech, of heat.'

And he did, indeed, learn it from him.

8 Uddalāka Āruṇi said to his son, Śvetaketu: 'Son, learn from me the nature of sleep. When one says here: "The man is sleeping", son, then he is united with the existent; into himself (*sva*) he has entered (*apīta*). Therefore, people say with reference to him: "He is sleeping" (*svapiti*), for then he has entered into himself.

[2] 'It is like this. Take a bird that is tied with a string. It will fly off in every direction and, when it cannot find a resting-place anywhere else, it will alight back upon the very thing to which it is tied. Similarly, son, the mind flies off in every direction and, when it cannot find a resting-place anywhere else, it alights back upon the breath itself; for the mind, my son, is tied to the breath.

[3] 'Son, learn from me about hunger and thirst. When one says here: "The man is hungry", then the water drives away with what he has eaten. So, just as one calls someone a "cattle-driver", or a "horse-driver", or a "man-driver", similarly one calls water "hunger" – the "food-driver".

'With regard to this, son, you should recognize this as a bud that has come out. It cannot be without a root, [4] and what could its root be if not food? Likewise, son, with food as the bud, look to water as the root; with water as the bud, look to heat as the root; and with heat as the bud, look to the existent as the root. The existent, my son, is the root of all these creatures – the existent is their resting-place, the existent is their foundation.

[5] 'When, moreover, one says here: "The man is thirsty", then the heat drives away with what he has drunk. So, just as one calls someone a "cattle-driver", or a "horse-driver", or a "man-driver", similarly one calls heat "thirst" – the "water-driver".

'With regard to this, son, you should recognize this as a bud that has come out. It cannot be without a root, [6] and what could its root be if not water? Likewise, son, with water as the bud, look to heat as the root; and with heat as the bud, look to the existent as the root. The existent, my son, is the root of all these creatures – the existent is their resting-place, the existent is their foundation.

'I have already explained to you, son, how, when they enter a man, each of these three deities become threefold.

'When a man is dying, my son, his speech merges into his mind; his mind, into his breath; his breath, into heat; and heat, into the highest deity.

[7] 'The finest essence here – that constitutes the self of this whole world; that is the truth; that is the self (*ātman*). And that's how you are, Śvetaketu.'

'Sir, teach me more.'

'Very well, son.

9 'Now, take the bees, son. They prepare the honey by gathering nectar from a variety of trees and by reducing that nectar to a homogeneous whole. [2] In that state the nectar from each different tree is not able to differentiate: "I am the nectar of that tree", and "I am the nectar of this tree". In exactly the same way, son, when all these creatures merge into the existent, they are not aware that: "We are merging into the existent." [3] No matter what they are in this world – whether it is a tiger, a lion, a wolf, a boar, a worm, a moth, a gnat, or a mosquito – they all merge into that.

[4] 'The finest essence here – that constitutes the self of this whole world; that is the truth; that is the self (*ātman*). And that's how you are, Śvetaketu.'

'Sir, teach me more.'

'Very well, son.

10 'Now, take these rivers, son. The easterly ones flow towards the east, and the westerly ones flow towards the west. From the ocean, they merge into the very ocean; they become just the ocean. In that state they are not aware that: "I am that river", and "I am this river". [2] In exactly the same way, son, when all these creatures reach the existent, they are not aware that: "We are reaching the existent". No matter what they are in this world – whether it is a tiger, a lion, a wolf, a boar, a worm, a moth, a gnat, or a mosquito – they all merge into that.

[3] 'The finest essence here – that constitutes the self of this whole world; that is the truth; that is the self (*ātman*). And that's how you are, Śvetaketu.'

'Sir, teach me more.'

'Very well, son.

11 'Now, take this huge tree here, son. If someone were to hack it at the bottom, its living sap would flow. Likewise, if someone were to hack it in the middle, its living sap would flow; and if someone were to hack it at the top, its living sap would flow. Pervaded by the living (*jīva*) essence (*ātman*), this tree stands here ceaselessly drinking water and flourishing. [2] When, however, life (*jīva*) leaves one of its branches, that branch withers away. When it leaves a second branch, that likewise withers away, and when it leaves a third branch, that also withers away. When it leaves the entire tree, the whole tree withers away.

[3] 'In exactly the same way,' he continued, 'know that this, of course, dies when it is bereft of life (*jīva*); but life itself does not die.

'The finest essence here – that constitutes the self of this whole world; that is the truth; that is the self (*ātman*). And that's how you are, Śvetaketu.'

'Sir, teach me more.'

'Very well, son.

12 'Bring a banyan fruit.'

'Here it is, sir.'

'Cut it up.'

'I've cut it up, sir.'

'What do you see there?'

'These quite tiny seeds, sir.'

'Now, take one of them and cut it up.'

'I've cut one up, sir.'

'What do you see there?'

'Nothing, sir.'

[2] Then he told him: 'This finest essence here, son, that you can't even see – look how on account of that finest essence this huge banyan tree stands here.

'Believe, my son: [3] the finest essence here – that constitutes the self of this whole world; that is the truth; that is the self (*ātman*). And that's how you are, Śvetaketu.'

'Sir, teach me more.'

'Very well, son.

13 'Put this chunk of salt in a container of water and come back tomorrow.' The son did as he was told, and the father said to him: 'The chunk of salt you put in the water last evening – bring it here.' He groped for it but could not find it, [2] as it had dissolved completely.

'Now, take a sip from this corner,' said the father. 'How does it taste?'

'Salty.'

'Take a sip from the centre. – How does it taste?'

'Salty.'

'Take a sip from that corner. – How does it taste?'

'Salty.'

'Throw it out and come back later.' He did as he was told and found that the salt was always there. The father told him: 'You, of course, did not see it there, son; yet it was always right there.

[3] 'The finest essence here – that constitutes the self of this whole world; that is the truth; that is the self (*ātman*). And that's how you are, Śvetaketu.'

'Sir, teach me more.'

'Very well, son.

14 'Take, for example, son, a man who is brought here blindfolded from the land of Gandhāra and then left in a deserted region. As he was brought blindfolded and left there blindfolded, he would drift about there towards the east, or the north, or the south. [2] Now, if someone were to free him from his blindfold and tell him, "Go that way; the land of Gandhāra is in that direction", being a learned and wise man, he would go from village to village asking for directions and finally arrive in the land of Gandhāra. In exactly the same way in this world when a man has a teacher, he knows: "There is a delay for me here only until I am freed; but then I will arrive!"

[3] 'The finest essence here – that constitutes the self of this whole world; that is the truth; that is the self (*ātman*). And that's how you are, Śvetaketu.'

'Sir, teach me more.'

'Very well, son.

15 'Take, for example, son, a man gravely ill. His relatives gather around him and ask: "Do you recognize me?" "Do you recognize me?" As long as his voice does not merge into his mind; his mind, into his breath; his breath, into heat; and heat, into the highest deity, he recognizes them. [2] When, however, his voice merges into his mind; his mind, into his breath: his breath, into heat; and heat, into the highest deity, then he no longer recognizes them.

[3] 'The finest essence here – that constitutes the self of this whole world; that is the truth; that is the self (*ātman*). And that's how you are, Śvetaketu.'

'Sir, teach me more.'

'Very well, son.

16 'Take, for example, son, a manacled man brought here by people shouting: "He's a thief! He has committed a theft! Heat an axe for him!" Now, if he is guilty of the crime, then he turns himself into a lie; uttering a falsehood and covering himself in falsehood, he takes hold of the axe and gets burnt, upon which he is executed. [2] If, on the other hand, he is innocent of the crime, then he turns himself into the truth; uttering the truth and covering himself with the truth, he takes hold of the axe and is not burnt, upon which he is released.

[3] 'What on that occasion prevents him from being burnt – that constitutes the self of this whole world; that is the truth; that is the self (*ātman*). And that's how you are, Śvetaketu.'

And he did, indeed, learn it from him.

[...]

Kaṭha *Upaniṣad*
Chapter 1

UŚAN, the son of Vājaśravas, once gave away all his possessions. He had a son named Naciketas. [2] Young as he was, faith took hold of him while the cows presented as sacrificial gifts were being led away, and he reflected:

[3] 'They've drunk all their water, eaten all their fodder,
They have been milked dry, they are totally barren –
"Joyless" are those worlds called,
to which a man goes
who gives them as gifts.'

[4] So he asked his father: 'Father, to whom will you give me?' He repeated it for a second time, and again for a third time. His father yelled at him: 'I'll give you to Death!'

[5] [NACIKETAS *reflects*.] I go as the very first of many.
I go as the middlemost of many.
What's it that Yama must do,
That he will do with me today?

[6] [A VOICE.] Look ahead! See how they have gone,
those who have gone before us!
Look back! So will they go,
those who will come after us.
A mortal man ripens like grain,
And like grain he is born again.

[7] A Brahmin guest enters a house
as the fire in all men.
Bring water, O Vaivasvata,
that is how they appease him.

[8] Hopes and expectations, fellowship and goodwill,
Children and livestock, rites and gifts –
all these a Brahmin wrests from the foolish man,
in whose house he resides without any food.

[DEATH.] [9] Three nights, O Brahmin, you stayed in my house,
a guest worthy of homage, without any food;
Three wishes, therefore, deign to make in return.
So homage to you, O Brahmin!
And may I fare well!

[NACIKETAS] [10] That with his temper cooled,
his anger subdued,
Gautama, O Death, be to me well-disposed.
That he greet me with joy, when by you I'm dismissed –
this is the first of my three wishes.

[DEATH.] [11] He'll be affable in the future, just as before;
Auddālaka Āruṇi, I have dismissed you.
He'll have restful nights, his anger subdued,
seeing you released from the jaws of Death.

[NACIKETAS.] [12] In the world of heaven there is no fear;
there one has no fear of old age or you.
Transcending both these – both hunger and thirst,
beyond all sorrows, one rejoices in heaven.

[13] You, O Death, are studying,
the fire-altar that leads to heaven;
Explain that to me, a man who has faith;
People who are in heaven enjoy th'immortal state –
It is this I choose with my second wish.

[DEATH.] [14] I shall explain to you –
and heed this teaching of mine,
O Naciketas, you who understand –
the fire-altar that leads to heaven,
to the attainment of an endless world,
and is its very foundation.
Know that it lies hidden,
In the cave of the heart.

[NARRATOR.] [15] He described to him that fire-altar –
the beginning of the world –
What type the bricks, how many; and how they are to be laid.
And he repeated it exactly as described.
Delighted at him, then, Death said to him again;

[16] Well-pleased, the large-hearted one said to him:
[DEATH.] Here I grant you another wish today.
This fire-altar will bear your very name.
Take also this glittering disk of gold.

[17] This is a three-Nāciketa man –
Uniting with the three, performing the triple rite,
he crosses over birth and death.
Perceiving the *brahman* that is being born,
as the god who is to be adored,
recognizing this disk of gold to be that,
he attains unending peace.

[18] This is a three-Nāciketa man –
Knowing these three, and, with that knowledge,
Piling the altar of Naciketas,
he shoves aside the fetters of death before him,
passes beyond sorrow,
and rejoices in heaven.

[19] This, Naciketas, is your fire that leads to heaven,
which you chose with your second wish.
People will proclaim this your very own fire.
Choose your third wish, O Naciketas.

[NACIKETAS.] [20] There is this doubt about a man who is dead.
'He exists,' say some; others, 'He exists not.'
I want to know this, so please teach me.
This is the third of my three wishes.

[DEATH.] [21] As to this even the gods of old had doubts,
for it's hard to understand, it's a subtle doctrine.
Make, Naciketas, another wish.
Do not press me! Release me from this.

[NACIKETAS.] [22] As to this, we're told, even the gods had doubts;
and you say, O Death, it's hard to understand.
But another like you I can't find to explain it;
and there's no other wish that is equal to it.

[DEATH.] [23] Choose sons and grandsons who'd live a hundred years!
Plenty of livestock and elephants, horses and gold!
Choose as your domain a wide expanse of earth!
And you yourself live as many autumns as you wish!

[24] And if you would think this is an equal wish –
You may choose wealth together with a long life;
Achieve prominence, Naciketas, in this wide world;
And I will make you enjoy your desires at will.

[25] You may ask freely for all those desires,
hard to obtain in this mortal world;
Look at these lovely girls, with chariots and lutes,
girls of this sort are unobtainable by men –
I'll give them to you; you'll have them wait on you;
but about death don't ask me, Naciketas.

[NACIKETAS.] [26] Since the passing days of a mortal, O Death,
sap here the energy of all the senses;
And even a full life is but a trifle;
so keep your horses, your songs and dances!

[27] With wealth you cannot make a man content;
Will we get to keep wealth, when we have seen you?
And we get to live only as long as you will allow!
So, this alone is the wish that I'd like to choose.

[28] What mortal man with insight,
who has met those that do not die or grow old,
himself growing old in this wretched and lowly place,
looking at its beauties, its pleasures and joys,
would delight in a long life?

[29] The point on which they have great doubts –
what happens at that great transit –
tell me that, O Death!
This is my wish, probing the mystery deep.
Naciketas wishes for nothing other than that.

Chapter 2

[DEATH.] [1] The good is one thing, the gratifying is quite another;
their goals are different, both bind a man.
Good things await him who picks the good;
by choosing the gratifying, one misses one's goal.

[2] Both the good and the gratifying
present themselves to a man;
The wise assess them, note their difference;
and choose the good over the gratifying;
But the fool chooses the gratifying
rather than what is beneficial.

[3] You have looked at and rejected, Naciketas,
things people desire, lovely and lovely to look at;
This disk of gold, where many a man founders,
you have not accepted as a thing of wealth.

[4] Far apart and widely different are these two:
ignorance and what's known as knowledge.
I take Naciketas as one yearning for knowledge;
the many desires do not confound you.

[5] Wallowing in ignorance, but calling themselves wise,
thinking themselves learned, the fools go around,
staggering about like a group of blind men,
led by a man who is himself blind.

[6] This transit lies hidden from a careless fool,
who is deluded by the delusion of wealth.
Thinking 'This is the world; there is no other',
he falls into my power again and again.

[7] Many do not get to hear of that transit;
and even when they hear,
many don't comprehend it.
Rare is the man who teaches it,
lucky is the man who grasps it;
Rare is the man who knows it,
lucky is the man who's taught it.

[8] Though one may think a lot, it is difficult to grasp,
when it is taught by an inferior man.
Yet one cannot gain access to it,
unless someone else teaches it.
For it is smaller than the size of an atom,
a thing beyond the realm of reason.

[9] One can't grasp this notion by argumentation;
Yet it's easy to grasp when taught by another.
You're truly steadfast, dear boy,
you have grasped it!
Would that we have, Naciketas,
one like you to question us!

[10] What you call a treasure, I know to be transient;
for by fleeting things one cannot gain the perennial.
Therefore I have built the fire-altar of Naciketas,
and by fleeting things I have gained the eternal.

[11] Satisfying desires is the foundation of the world;
Uninterrupted rites bring ultimate security;
Great and widespread praise is the foundation –
These you have seen, wise Naciketas,
And having seen, firmly rejected.

[12] The primeval one who is hard to perceive,
wrapped in mystery, hidden in the cave,
residing within th'impenetrable depth –
Regarding him as god, an insight
gained by inner contemplation,
both sorrow and joy the wise abandon.

[13] When a mortal has heard it, understood it;
when he has drawn it out,
and grasped this subtle point of doctrine;
He rejoices, for he has found
something in which he could rejoice.
To him I consider my house
to be open Naciketas.

[NACIKETAS?] [14] Tell me what you see as –
Different from the right doctrine and from the wrong;
Different from what's done here and what's left undone;
Different from what has been and what's yet to be.'

[DEATH?] [15] The word that all the Vedas disclose;
The word that all austerities proclaim;
Seeking which people live student lives;
That word now I will tell you in brief –
It is OṂ!

[16] For this alone is the syllable that's *brahman*!
For this alone is the syllable that's supreme!
When, indeed, one knows this syllable,
he obtains his every wish.

[17] This is the support that's best!
This is the support supreme!
And when one knows this support,
he rejoices in *brahman*'s world.

[DEATH] [18] The wise one –
he is not born, he does not die;
he has not come from anywhere;
he has not become anyone.
He is unborn and eternal, primeval and everlasting.
And he is not killed, when the body is killed.

[The dialogue between Naciketas and Death ends here.]

[19] If the killer thinks that he kills;
If the killed thinks that he is killed;
Both of them fail to understand.
He neither kills, nor is he killed.

[20] Finer than the finest, larger than the largest,
is the self (*ātman*) that lies here hidden
in the heart of a living being.
Without desires and free from sorrow,
a man perceives by the creator's grace
the grandeur of the self.

[21] Sitting down, he roams afar.
Lying down, he goes everywhere.
The god ceaselessly exulting –
Who, besides me, is able to know?

[22] When he perceives this immense, all-pervading self,
as bodiless within bodies,
as stable within unstable beings –
A wise man ceases to grieve.

[23] This self cannot be grasped,
by teachings or by intelligence,
or even by great learning.
Only the man he chooses can grasp him,
whose body this self chooses as his own.

[24] Not a man who has not quit his evil ways;
Nor a man who is not calm or composed;
Nor even a man who is without a tranquil mind;
Could ever secure it by his mere wit.

[25] For whom the Brahmin and the Kṣatriya
are both like a dish of boiled rice;
and death is like the sprinkled sauce;
Who truly knows where he is?

Chapter 3

Knowers of *brahman*, men with five fires,
and with the three fire-altars of Naciketas,
They call these two 'Shadow' and 'Light',
the two who have entered –
the one into the cave of the heart,
the other into the highest region beyond,
both drinking the truth
in the world of rites rightly performed.

[2] May we master the fire-altar of Naciketas,
a dike
for those who have sacrificed;
the imperishable, the highest *brahman*,
the farther shore
for those who wish to cross the danger.

[3] Know the self as a rider in a chariot,
and the body, as simply the chariot.
Know the intellect as the charioteer,
and the mind, as simply the reins.

[4] The senses, they say, are the horses,
and sense objects are the paths around them;
He who is linked to the body (*ātman*), senses,
and mind,
the wise proclaim as the one who enjoys.

[5] When a man lacks understanding,
and his mind is never controlled;
His senses do not obey him,
as bad horses, a charioteer.

[6] But when a man has understanding,
and his mind is ever controlled;
His senses do obey him,
as good horses, a charioteer.

[7] When a man lacks understanding,
is unmindful and always impure;
He does not reach that final step,
but gets on the round of rebirth.

[8] But when a man has understanding,
is mindful and always pure;
He does reach that final step,
from which he is not reborn again.

[9] When a man's mind is his reins,
intellect, his charioteer;
He reaches the end of the road,
that highest step of Viṣṇu.

[10] Higher than the senses are their objects;
Higher than sense objects is the mind;
Higher than the mind is the intellect;
Higher than the intellect is the immense self;

[11] Higher than the immense self is the unmanifest;
Higher than the unmanifest is the person;
Higher than the person there's nothing at all.
That is the goal, that's the highest state.

[12] Hidden in all the beings,
this self is not visibly displayed.
Yet, people of keen vision see him,
with eminent and sharp minds.

[13] A wise man should curb his speech and mind,
control them within th'intelligent self;
He should control intelligence within the immense self,
and the latter, within the tranquil self.

[14] Arise! Awake! Pay attention,
when you've obtained your wishes!
A razor's sharp edge is hard to cross –
that, poets say, is the difficulty of the path.

[15] It has no sound or touch,
no appearance, taste, or smell;
It is without beginning or end,
undecaying and eternal;
When a man perceives it,
fixed and beyond the immense,
He is freed from the jaws of death.

[16] The wise man who hears or tells
the tale of Naciketas,
an ancient tale told by Death,
will rejoice in *brahman*'s world.

[17] If a man, pure and devout, proclaims this great secret
in a gathering of Brahmins,
or during a meal for the dead,
it will lead him to eternal life!

Chapter 4

The Self-existent One pierced the apertures outward,
therefore, one looks out, and not into oneself.
A certain wise man in search of immortality,
turned his sight inward and saw the self within.

[2] Fools pursue outward desires,
and enter the trap of death spread wide.
But the wise know what constitutes th'immortal,
and in unstable things here do not seek the stable.

[3] Appearance and taste, smell and sounds,
touches and sexual acts –
That by which one experiences these,
by the same one understands –
what then is here left behind?

So, indeed, is that!

[4] That by which one perceives both
the states of sleep and of being awake;
Knowing that it's th'immense, all-pervading self,
a wise man does not grieve.

[5] When a man perceives close at hand
this living, honey-eating self,
The lord of what was and what will be –
it does not seek to hide from him.

So, indeed, is that!

[6] He who was born before heat,
who before the waters was born,
who has seen through living beings –
Entering the cave of the heart,
[one sees] him abiding there.

So, indeed, is that!

[7] She who comes into being with breath,
Aditi, who embodies divinity,
who was born through living beings –
Entering the cave of the heart,
[one sees] her abiding there.

So, indeed, is that!

[8] Jātavedas is hidden within the two fire-drills,
fostered, as a fetus by women with child;
With offering should men as they awake,
worship the fire each and every day.

So, indeed, is that!

[9] From which the sun rises,
and into which it sets;
In it are fixed all the gods;
beyond it no one can ever pass.

So, indeed, is that!

[10] Whatever is down here, the same is over there;
and what is over there is replicated down here.
From death to death he goes, who sees
here any kind of diversity.

So, indeed, is that!

[11] With your mind alone you must understand it –
there is here no diversity at all!
From death to death he goes, who sees
here any kind of diversity.

So, indeed, is that!

[12] A person the size of a thumb
resides within the body (*ātman*);
The lord of what was and what will be –
from him he does not hide himself.

So, indeed, is that!

[13] The person the size of a thumb
is like a fire free of smoke;
The lord of what was and what'will be;
the same today and tomorrow.

So, indeed, is that!

[14] As the rain that falls on rugged terrain,
runs hither and thither along the mountain slopes;
So a man who regards the laws as distinct,
runs hither and thither after those very laws.

[15] As pure water poured into pure water
becomes the very same;
So does the self of a discerning sage
become, O Gautama.

Chapter 5

The unborn one, free of crooked thoughts,
has a fort with eleven gates;
One who attends to it will not grieve,
but, freed from it, he will be set free.

So, indeed, is that!

[2] The goose seated in the light, the Vasu seated in the sky;
The Hotṛ seated at the altar, the guest seated in the house;
Seated in men, seated in the wide expanse,
Seated in the truth, seated in heaven;
Born from water, born from cows,
Born from the truth, born from rocks;
The great truth!

[3] The out-breath he conducts upward,
the in-breath he drives backward;
All the gods worship him,
the Dwarf seated in the middle.

[4] When this embodied self dwelling in the body
comes unglued and is freed from the body –
what then is here left behind?

So, indeed, is that!

[5] Not by the out-breath, not by the in-breath;
does any mortal live;
By another do people live, on which those two depend.

[6] Come, I'll tell you this secret and eternal
formulation of truth (brahman);
And what happens to the self (*ātman*), Gautama,
when it encounters death.

[7] Some enter a womb by which
an embodied self obtains a body,
Others pass into a stationary thing –
according to what they have done,
according to what they have learned.

[8] This person, creating every desire,
who lies awake within those who sleep;
That alone is the Pure! That is *brahman*!
That alone is called the Immortal!
On it all the worlds rest;
beyond it no one can ever pass.

So, indeed, is that!

[9] As the single fire, entering living beings,
adapts its appearance to match that of each;
So the single self within every being,
adapts its appearance to match that of each,
yet remains quite distinct.

[10] As the single wind, entering living beings,
adapts its appearance to match that of each;
So the single self within every being,
adapts its appearance to match that of each,
yet remains quite distinct.

[11] As the sun, the eye of the whole world,
is not stained by visual faults external to it;
So the single self within every being,
is not stained by the suffering of the world,
being quite distinct from it.

[12] The one controller, the self within every being,
who makes manifold his single appearance;
The wise who perceive him as abiding within themselves,
they alone, not others, enjoy eternal happiness.

[13] The changeless, among the changing,
the intelligent, among intelligent beings,
the one, who despenses desires among the many;
The wise who perceive him within themselves;
they alone, not others, enjoy unending bliss.

[14] 'This is that' – so they think, although
the highest bliss can't be described.
But how should I perceive it?
Does it shine?
Or does it radiate?

[15] There the sun does not shine,
nor the moon and stars;
There lightning does not shine,
of this common fire need we speak!
Him alone, as he shines, do all things reflect;
this whole world radiates with his light.

Chapter 6

Its roots above, its branches below,
this is the eternal banyan tree.
That alone is the Bright! That is *brahman*!
That alone is called the Immortal!
On it all the worlds rest;
beyond it no one can ever pass.

So, indeed, is that!

[2] All that is here, whatever that lives,
having arisen, moves within the breath;
Great is the fear, the bolt is raised up;
those who know it become immortal.

[3] The fear of it makes the fire burn;
The fear of it makes the sun shine;
The fear of it makes them run –
Indra and Wind,
and Death, the fifth.

[4] If one were able to realize it here,
before his body dissolves;
It will serve him to obtain a body
within the created worlds.

[5] As in a mirror, so in the body (*ātman*);
As in a dream, so in the fathers' world;
As in water a thing becomes somewhat visible,
so in the Gandharva world;
Somewhat as in shadows and light,
so in *brahman*'s world.

[6] The separate nature of the senses;
Their rise and fall as they come
Separately into being –
when a wise man knows this,
he does not grieve.

[7] Higher than the senses is the mind;
Higher than the mind is the essence;
Higher than the essence is the immense self;
Higher than the immense is the unmanifest.

[8] Higher than the unmanifest is the person,
pervading all and without any marks.
Knowing him, a man is freed,
and attains immortality.

[9] His appearance is beyond the range of sight;
no one can see him with his sight;
With the heart, with insight, with thought,
has he been contemplated –
Those who know this become immortal.

[10] When the five perceptions are stilled,
together with the mind,
And not even reason bestirs itself;
they call it the highest state.

[11] When senses are firmly reined in,
that is Yoga, so people think.
From distractions a man is then free,
for Yoga is the coming-into-being,
as well as the ceasing-to-be.

[12] Not by speech, not by the mind,
not by sight can he be grasped.
How else can that be perceived,
other than by saying 'He is!'

[13] In just two ways can he be perceived:
by saying that 'He is',
by affirming he's the real.
To one who perceives him as 'He is',
it becomes clear that he is real.

[14] When they are all banished,
those desires lurking in one's heart;
Then a mortal becomes immortal,
and attains *brahman* in this world.

[15] When the knots are all cut,
that bind one's heart on earth;

Then a mortal becomes immortal –
For such is the teaching.

[16] One hundred and one, the veins of the heart.
One of them runs up to the crown of the head.
Going up by it, he reaches the immortal.
The rest, in their ascent, spread out in all directions.

[17] A person the size of a thumb in the body (*ātman*), always resides within the hearts of men;
One should draw him out of the body with determination,
like a reed from the grass sheath;
One should know him
as immortal and bright.
One should know him
as immortal and bright.

[18] Then, after Naciketas received this body of knowledge.
and the entire set of yogic rules taught by Death,
He attained *brahman*; he became free from aging and death;
so will others who know this teaching about the self.

Śvetāśvatara *Upaniṣad*

Chapter 1

PEOPLE who make enquiries about *brahman* say:

What is the cause of *brahman*? Why were we born? By what do we live? On what are we established? Governed by whom, O you who know *brahman*, do we live in pleasure and in pain, each in our respective situation?

[2] Should we regard it as time, as inherent nature, as necessity, as chance, as the elements, as the source of birth, or as the Person? Or is it a combination of these? But that can't be, because there is the self (*ātman*). Even the self is not in control, because it is itself subject to pleasure and pain.

[3] Those who follow the discipline of meditation have seen God, the self, and the power, all hidden by their own qualities. One alone is he who governs all those causes, from 'time' to 'self.'

[4–5] We study it –

as a wheel that is one-rimmed and threefold, with sixteen tips, fifty spokes, twenty counter-spokes, and six sets of eight, whose single rope is of many forms; that divides itself into three different paths; and whose delusion regarding the one springs from two causes.

as a river whose waters are the five sense organs; whose fierce crocodiles are the five sources of birth; whose waves are the five breaths; whose primal source is the five types of perception; which has five whirlpools; whose rapid current is the five types of sorrow; which divides itself in fifty ways; and which has five sections.

[6] Within this vast wheel of *brahman*, on which all subsist and which abides in all, a goose keeps moving around. When he perceives himself (*ātman*) as distinct from the impeller, delighted by that knowledge he goes from there to immortality.

[7] This highest *brahman*, however, has been extolled thus: There is a triad in it – oneself, the foundation, and the imperishable. When those who know *brahman* have come to know the distinction between them, they become absorbed in and totally intent on *brahman* and are freed from the womb.

[8] This whole world is the perishable and the imperishable, the manifest and the unmanifest joined together – and the Lord bears it, while the self (*ātman*), who is not the Lord, remains bound, because he is the enjoyer. When he comes to know God, he is freed from all fetters.

[9] There are two unborn males – the one knows and the other is ignorant; the one is Lord and the other is not the Lord. There is just one unborn female, who is joined to the enjoyer and the objects of enjoyment. And then there is the self (*ātman*), limitless and displaying every form, not engaged in any activity. When someone finds these three, he finds this *brahman*.

[10] The primal source is perishable, while Hara is immortal and imperishable. The one God rules over both the perishable and the self

(*ātman*). By meditating on him, by striving towards him, and, further, in the end by becoming the same reality as him, all illusion disappears.

[11] When one has known God, all the fetters fall off; by the eradication of the blemishes, birth and death come to an end; by meditating on him, one obtains, at the dissolution of the body, a third – sovereignty over all; and in the absolute one's desires are fulfilled.

[12] This can be known, for it abides always within one's body (*ātman*). Higher than that there is nothing to be known. When the enjoyer discerns the object of enjoyment and the impeller – everything has been taught. That is the threefold *brahman*.

[13] When a fire is contained within its womb, one cannot see its visible form and yet its essential character is not extinguished; one can grasp the fire once again from its womb by means of tinder. In just the same way, one can grasp both within the body by means of the syllable OṂ.

[14] When one makes one's own body the bottom slab and the syllable OṂ the upper drill, by twirling it constantly through meditation one would see God, just as one would the hidden thing.

[15–16] Like oil in sesame seeds and butter in curds, like water in the river-bed and fire in the fire-drills, so, when one seeks it with truth and austerity, one grasps that self (*ātman*) in the body (*ātman*) – that all-pervading self, which is contained [in the body], like butter in milk.

That is *brahman*, the highest object of the teachings on hidden connections (*upaniṣad*), an object rooted in austerity and the knowledge of the self.

Chapter 2

Yoking first his mind, and extending then his thoughts, Savitṛ, having recognized the fire as the light, brought it here from the earth.

[2] With minds yoked, we [make the offering] under the stimulus of the god Savitṛ for the strength to go to heaven.

[3] Yoking the gods, as they go to heaven with their mind and to the firmament with their thought, may Savitṛ stimulate them to create the lofty light.

[4] They yoke their minds, they yoke their thoughts, those inspired poets of the lofty poet. That one alone who knows the patterns has apportioned the offerings. Resounding is the praise of the god Savitṛ.

[5] I yoke with adorations the ancient formulation (*brahman*) of you two. The praises spread wide, like the suns on their course. All the sons of the immortal hear them, when they have reached the heavenly abodes.

[6] Where the fire is churned, where the wind wafts, where the Soma juice flows over – there the mind is born.

[7] By means of Savitṛ and his stimulus let a man take delight in that ancient formulation (*brahman*). Make there a source of birth for yourself. And the gifts you have given, not even an iota [would fall] from you [to someone else's lot].

[8] When he keeps his body straight, with the three sections erect, and draws the senses together with the mind into his heart, a wise man shall cross all the frightful rivers with the boat consisting of that formulation (*brahman*).

[9] Compressing his breaths in here and curbing his movements, a man should exhale through one nostril when his breath is exhausted. A wise man should keep his mind vigilantly under control, just as he would that wagon yoked to unruly horses.

[10] Level and clean; free of gravel, fire, and sand; near noiseless running waters and the like; pleasing to the mind but not offensive to the eye; provided with a cave or a nook sheltered from the wind – in such a spot should one engage in yogic practice.

[11] Mist, smoke, sun, wind, fire, fireflies, lightning, crystal, moon – these are the apparitions that, within yogic practice, precede and pave the way to the full manifestation in *brahman*.

[12] When earth, water, fire, air, and ether have arisen together, and the body made up of these five becomes equipped with the

attribute of yoga, that man, obtaining a body tempered by the fire of yoga, will no longer experience sickness, old age, or suffering.

[13] Lightness, health, the absence of greed, a bright complexion, a pleasant voice, a sweet smell, and very little faeces and urine – that, they say, is the first working of yogic practice.

[14] Just as a disk smeared with clay, once it is cleaned well, shines brightly, so also an embodied person, once he has perceived the true nature of the self, becomes solitary, his goal attained, and free from sorrow.

[15] When, by means of the true nature of the self, which resembles a lamp, a man practising yogic restraint sees here the true nature of *brahman*, he is freed from all fetters, because he has known God, unborn, unchanging, and unsullied by all objects.

[16] This God does pervade all quarters. He was born the first, yet he remains within the womb. He it is, who was born; he, who will be born. His face everywhere, he stands turning west towards men.

[17] He who abides as God in the fire; who abides in the waters; who has entered every being; who abides in the plants; who abides in the trees – to that God adoration! Adoration!

Chapter 3

Who alone, wielding the net, reigns by his sovereign powers, reigns over all worlds by his sovereign powers; who also alone is present at their rise and birth – those who know this become immortal.

[2] There is only one Rudra; he has not tolerated a second who would reign over these worlds by his sovereign powers. After drawing in all beings, he stands as the protector at the end of time turning west towards men.

[3] Eyes everywhere and face everywhere, arms everywhere and feet everywhere, he forges with his two hands, he forges with the wings, producing the heaven and earth, the one God.

[4] Who, as the source and origin of the gods and the ruler over them all, as the god Rudra, and as the great seer, in the beginning created Hiraṇyagarbha – may he furnish us with lucid intelligence.

[5] That form of yours, O Rudra, which is benign and not terrifying, which is not sinister-looking – with that most auspicious form of yours, O Mountain-dweller, look upon us.

[6] The arrow, O Mountain-dweller, that you hold in your hand to shoot – make it benign, O Mountain-protector; hurt not man or beast.

[7] Who is higher than that, higher than *brahman*, the immense one hidden in all beings, in each according to its kind, and who alone encompasses the whole universe – when people know him as the Lord, they become immortal.

[8] I know that immense Person, having the colour of the sun and beyond darkness. Only when a man knows him does he pass beyond death; there is no other path for getting there.

[9] This whole world is filled by that Person, beyond whom there is nothing; beneath whom there is nothing; smaller than whom there is nothing; larger than whom there is nothing; and who stands like a tree planted firmly in heaven.

[10] What is higher than that is without visible appearance and free from affliction. Those who know it become immortal; as for the rest, only suffering awaits them.

[11] Who is the face, head, and neck of all, who resides deep in the heart of all beings, and who pervades everything – he is the Blessed One. Therefore, the Benign One is present everywhere.

[12] The Person, clearly, is the immense Lord. He is the one who sets in motion the real. The Imperishable One rules over the light, this totally flawless attainment.

[13] The Person the size of a thumb abiding within the body (*ātman*) always resides within the hearts of people. With the heart, with insight, with thought has he been contemplated. Those who know this become immortal.

[14] The Person had a thousand heads, a thousand eyes, and a thousand feet. Having encompassed the earth on all sides, he extended ten fingers' breadth beyond it.

[15] This whole world is just the Person, whatever there was and whatever there will be. Even over immortality he rules, when he rises above [the world] through food.

[16] With hands and feet everywhere, with eyes, heads, and faces everywhere, and with ears everywhere, that remains encompassing everything in the world –

[17] That, which appears to possess the powers of all the senses but is devoid of every sense, which is the lord, the ruler of the whole world, the vast refuge of the whole world.

[18] Within the fort with nine gates, the embodied one flutters to the outside like a goose; it is the master of the whole world, of both the immobile and the mobile.

[19] He moves swiftly, but he has no feet; he grasps, but he has no hands; he sees, but he has no eyes; he hears, but he has no ears. He knows what is there to know, but there is no one who knows him. They call him the first and immense Person.

[20] Finer than the finest, larger than the largest, is the self that lies here hidden in the heart of a living being. A man who, by the creator's grace, sees that desireless one as the majesty and as the Lord will be free from sorrow.

[21] I know that unageing and ancient one as the self in all beings, as present in all because of his pervasiveness; the one, about whom those who enquire after *brahman* proclaim – he always brings about the cessation of birth.

Chapter 4

Who alone, himself without colour, wielding his power creates variously countless colours, and in whom the universe comes together at the beginning and dissolves in the end – may he furnish us with lucid intelligence.

[2] The fire is simply that; the sun is that; the wind is that; and the moon is also that! The bright one is simply that; *brahman* is that; the waters are that; and Prajāpati is that!

[3] You are a woman; you are a man; you are a boy or also a girl. As an old man, you totter along with a walking-stick. As you are born, you turn your face in every direction.

[4] You are the dark blue bird, the green one with red eyes, the rain-cloud, the seasons, and the oceans. You live as one without a beginning because of your pervasiveness, you, from whom all beings have been born.

[5] One unborn male [billy-goat], burning with passion, covers one unborn female [nanny-goat] coloured red, white, and black, and giving birth to numerous offspring with the same colours as hers, while another unborn male leaves her after he has finished enjoying her pleasures.

[6] Two birds, who are companions and friends, nestle on the very same tree. One of them eats a tasty fig; the other, not eating, looks on.

[7] Stuck on the very same tree, one person grieves, deluded by her who is not the Lord. But when he sees the other, the contented Lord – and the Lord's majesty – his grief disappears.

[8] The syllable amidst the Ṛg, the syllable upon which all the gods are seated in the highest heaven – when a man does not know it, what will he do with a Ṛg. Seated here together are people who do know it!

[9] Metres, sacrifices, rites, religious observances, the past, the future, and what the Vedas proclaim – from that the illusionist creates this whole world, and in it the other remains confined by the illusory power.

[10] One should recognize the illusory power as primal matter, and the illusionist, as the great Lord. This whole living world is thus pervaded by things that are parts of him.

[11] Who alone presides over womb after womb; in whom this whole world comes together and dissolves – when someone recognizes that Lord who fulfils wishes as the God who is to be adored, he attains this unending peace.

[12] Who, as the source and origin of the gods and the ruler over them all, as the god Rudra, and as the great seer, looked on as Hiraṇyagarbha was being born – may he furnish us with lucid intelligence.

[13] Who is the Supreme Lord of the gods; on whom the worlds rest; who rules over the

bipeds and the quadrupeds here – to what god shall we offer oblations?

[14] Who is finer than the finest, in the midst of disorder; who is the creator of the universe displaying various forms; who, alone, encompasses the universe – when someone recognizes him as the Benign One, he attains unending peace.

[15] It is he who protects the world at the right time, the lord of the universe hidden in all beings. When someone thus knows him, after whom seers and gods strive, he severs the fetters of death.

[16] When someone knows the one who is extremely fine, like the spume on top of the ghee, as the Benign One hidden in all beings; when someone recognizes him, who alone encompasses the universe, as God – he is freed from all fetters.

[17] That God, the maker of all, the immense self (*ātman*), is always residing in the hearts of people. With the heart, with insight, with thought has he been contemplated. Those who know this become immortal.

[18] When there was darkness, then there was neither day nor night, neither the existent nor the non-existent – the Benign One alone was there. He was the imperishable, he was 'the excellent [glory] of Savitṛ', and from him has come forth the ancient wisdom.

[19] No one will catch hold of him from above, from across, or in the middle. There is no likeness of him, whose name is Immense Glory.

[20] His appearance is beyond the range of sight; no one can see him with his sight. Those who know him thus with their hearts – him, who abides in their hearts – and with insight become immortal.

[21] 'He is the Unborn One! – so some man, filled with awe, takes refuge with Rudra – Protect me always with that kindly face of yours!'

[22] 'Do not hurt us in our offspring or descendants, in our life, in our cattle or horses. Do not slay in anger, O Rudra, our valiant men. Oblations in hand, we invite you to your seat.'

Chapter 5

Two things, knowledge and ignorance, are set down in the imperishable and infinite fort of *brahman*, where they lie hidden. Now, ignorance is the perishable and knowledge is the immortal. But the one who rules over both knowledge and ignorance is another –

[2] who alone presides over womb after womb, and thus over all visible forms and all the sources of birth; who in the beginning carried this Kapila born of the seer together with his body of knowledge and would look on him as he was being born.

[3] Spreading out one net after another in diverse ways within this world, this God gathers them in. After creating it once again, the Lord likewise tears it down. The immense self (*ātman*) exercises his sovereignty over the whole world.

[4] As the draught-ox shines, lighting up all the quarters, above, below, and across, so this God, blessed and adorable, alone rules over wombs and inherent natures.

[5] Who, as the womb of all, not only ripens by his inherent nature, but also would bring all those in need of ripening to full development, and who would apportion all the qualities – he alone rules over this whole universe.

[6] It is hidden in the secret Upaniṣads of the Veda. Recognize it, O Brahmins, as the womb of *brahman*. The gods of old and the seers who knew it became of one essence with it and so came to be immortal.

[7] The one who, in association with the qualities, performs fruitful actions also enjoys the fruits of that very act. Displaying every form, endowed with the three qualities, and along three paths he roams about as the lord of vital breaths together with his own actions.

[8] He is as large as a thumb and equal in appearance to the sun when he is equipped with the faculties of imagination and self-consciousness. But one sees also another no larger than the tip of an awl who is equipped only with the quality of intelligence and the quality of the body (*ātman*).

[9] When the tip of a hair is split into a hundred parts, and one of those parts further into a hundred parts – the individual soul (*jīva*), on the one hand, is the size of one such part, and, on the other, it partakes of infinity.

[10] It is neither a woman nor a man, nor even a hermaphrodite; it is ruled over by whichever body it obtains.

[11] The birth and growth of the body (*ātman*) takes place through the offerings of intention, touch, and sight, and by means of food, drink, and impregnation; whereas the embodied self assumes successively in different situations the physical appearances that correspond to its actions.

[12] The embodied self assumes numerous physical appearances, both large and small, in accordance with its qualities. One sees also another cause of their union in accordance with the qualities of the actions and the body (*ātman*).

[13] Who is without beginning or end, in the midst of disorder; who is the creator of the universe displaying various forms; who, alone, encompasses the universe – when someone recognizes him as God, he is freed from all fetters.

[14] Who is to be grasped with one's heart, who is called 'Without-a-Lord', who brings about existence and non-existence, who is the Benign One, and who produces both the creation and its constituent parts – those who know him as God have cast aside their bodies.

Chapter 6

Some wise men say it is inherent nature, while others say it is time – all totally deluded. It is rather the greatness of God present in the world by means of which this wheel of *brahman* goes around.

[2] Who always encompasses this whole world – the knower, the architect of time, the one without qualities, and the all-knowing one – it is at his command that the work of creation, to be conceived of as earth, water, fire, air, and space, unfolds itself.

[3] After completing that work and drawing it back again; after joining himself with the realities one after another – with one, with two, with three, or with eight, as well as with time and with the subtle qualities of the body (*ātman*);

[4] and after undertaking the works endowed with the qualities; *he* who would apportion all the modes of existence – when they are no more, the work he has produced is destroyed – *he* carries on, when the work is dissolved, as someone other than those realities.

[5–6] One sees him as the beginning, as the basis and cause of the joining, as beyond the three times, and also as without parts. He, from whom the unfolding of the world has come forth, is higher than and different from the time-confined forms of the tree.

After we have first venerated that adorable God displaying every form, the source of all beings, as residing within one's heart, and then recognized him as the one who bestows righteousness and removes evil, as the Lord of prosperity, as abiding within ourselves (*ātman*), as the Immortal residing in all beings –

[7] we will find this highest Great-Lord among lords, the highest God among gods, the highest master among masters, the God beyond the highest as the adorable Lord of the universe.

[8] One cannot find in him either an obligation to act or an organ with which to act; neither can one see anyone equal to him, let alone someone who surpasses him. One hears about his highest and truly diverse power, which is part of his very nature and is the working of his knowledge and strength.

[9] There is no one in the world who is his master, nor anyone who rules over him. He has no distinguishing mark. He is the cause, the Overlord over the overlords of the sense organs, and he has neither parent nor overlord.

[10] The one God who covers himself with things issuing from the primal source, from his own inherent nature, as a spider, with the threads – may he procure us dissolution in *brahman*.

[11] The one God hidden in all beings, pervading the universe, the inner self of all beings, the overseer of the work, dwelling in all beings, the witness, the spectator, alone, devoid of qualities,

[12] the one controller of the many who are inactive, who makes the single seed manifold – the wise who perceive him as abiding within themselves (*ātman*), they alone, not others, enjoy eternal happiness.

[13] The changeless, among the changing, the intelligent, among intelligent beings, the one, who dispenses desires among the many – when a man knows that cause, which is to be comprehended through the application of Sāṃkhya, as God, he is freed from all fetters.

[14] There the sun does not shine, nor the moon and stars; there lightning does not shine, of this common fire need we speak! Him alone, as he shines, do all things reflect; this whole world radiates with his light.

[15] He is the one goose in the middle of this universe. He himself resides as fire within the ocean. Only when a man knows him does he pass beyond death; there is no other path for getting there.

[16] He is the creator of all; the knower of all; his own source of birth; the knower; the architect of time; the one without qualities; the one with all knowledge; the Lord of both the primal source and of individual souls; the ruler over the qualities; and the cause of liberation from remaining within, and bondage to the rebirth cycle.

[17] He who is one with him, immortal, abiding as the Lord, the knower, present everywhere, and the protector of this universe – he rules this living world eternally. There is no other cause to becoming the Lord.

[18] Who at first created the *brahman* and delivered to him the Vedas; who manifests himself by his own intelligence – in that God do I, desirous of liberation, seek refuge –

[19] in him, who, like a fire whose fuel is spent, is without parts, inactive, tranquil, unblemished, spotless, and the highest dike to immortality.

[20] Only when people will be able to roll up the sky like a piece of leather will suffering come to an end, without first knowing God.

[21] By the power of his austerities and by the grace of God, the wise Śvetāśvatara first came to know *brahman* and then proclaimed it to those who had passed beyond their order of life as the highest means of purification that bring delight to the company of seers.

[22] This supreme secret was proclaimed during a former age in the Vedānta. One should never disclose it to a person who is not of a tranquil disposition, or who is not one's son or pupil.

[23] Only in a man who has the deepest love for God, and who shows the same love towards his teacher as towards God, do these points declared by the Noble One shine forth.

Māṇḍūkya *Upaniṣad*

OṂ – this whole world is that syllable! Here is a further explanation of it. The past, the present, and the future – all that is simply OṂ; and whatever else that is beyond the three times, that also is simply OṂ – [2] for this *brahman* is the Whole. *Brahman* is this self (*ātman*); that [*brahman*] is this self (*ātman*) consisting of four quarters.

[3] The first quarter is Vaiśvānara – the Universal One – situated in the waking state, perceiving what is outside, possessing seven limbs and nineteen mouths, and enjoying gross things.

[4] The second quarter is Taijasa – the Brilliant One – situated in the state of dream, perceiving what is inside, possessing seven limbs and nineteen mouths, and enjoying refined things.

[5] The third quarter is Prājña – the Intelligent One – situated in the state of deep sleep – deep sleep is when a sleeping man entertains no desires or sees no dreams –; become one, and thus being a single mass of perception; consisting of bliss, and thus enjoying bliss; and having thought as his mouth. [6] He is the Lord of all; he is the knower of all; he is the inner controller; he is the womb of all – for he is the origin and the dissolution of beings.

[7] They consider the fourth quarter as perceiving neither what is inside nor what is outside, nor even both together; not as a mass of perception, neither as perceiving

nor as not perceiving; as unseen; as beyond the reach of ordinary transaction; as ungraspable; as without distinguishing marks; as unthinkable; as indescribable; as one whose essence is the perception of itself alone; as the cessation of the visible world; as tranquil; as auspicious; as without a second. That is the self (*ātman*), and it is that which should be perceived.

[8] With respect to syllables, OṂ is this very self (*ātman*); whereas with respect to the constituent phonemes of a syllable, it is as follows. The constituent phonemes are the quarters, and the quarters are the constituent phonemes, namely, 'a', 'u', and 'm'.

[9] The first constituent phoneme – 'a' – is Vaiśvānara situated in the waking state, so designated either because of obtaining (*āpti*) or because of being first (*ādimattva*). Anyone who knows this is sure to obtain all his desires and to become the first.

[10] The second constituent phoneme – 'u' – is Taijasa situated in the state of dream, so designated either because of heightening (*utkarṣa*) or because of being intermediate (*ubhayatva*). Anyone who knows this is sure to heighten the continuity of knowledge and to become common; and a man without the knowledge of *brahman* will not be born in his lineage.

[11] The third constituent phoneme – 'm' – is Prājña situated in the state of deep sleep, so designated either because of construction (*miti*) or because of destruction (*apīti*). Anyone who knows this is sure to construct this whole world and to become also its destruction.

[12] The fourth, on the other hand, is without constituent phonemes; beyond the reach of ordinary transaction; the cessation of the visible world; auspicious; and unique.

Accordingly, the very self (*ātman*) is OṂ. Anyone who knows this enters the self (*ātman*) by himself (*ātman*).

Chapter 3

The *Jaiminigṛhyasūtra*

The *Jaiminigṛhyasūtra*, *Jaimini's Treatise on Domestic Ritual*, is a *Gṛhya Sūtras* from the *Sāmaveda* branch of the *Vedas*. The *Gṛhya Sūtras* are a *genre* of literature devoted exclusively to domestic *yajñas*, sacrifices, to be performed at home and required "the service of only a single priest."[1] Along with the *Śrauta Sūtras* which concerned public rituals and the *Dharma Sūtras*, which concerned law and social mores, the *Gṛhya Sūtras* were classified as *Kalpa Sūtras*. The *Kalpa Sūtras*, furthermore, were held to be a *vedāṅga*, limb of the *Vedas*, and broadly construed, concerned the correct performance of the ritual, thus linking them with the foundational *Vedic* texts. These texts are estimated to have been composed between the sixth and fourth century BCE.

The *Gṛhya Sūtras*, though enjoined for all *dvijas*, twice borns, eventually became *brāhamaṇa*-oriented. They thus contained rites that pertained to household matters including rituals for maintaining purity, rites of passage pertaining to birth, puberty, marriage, and death.

The passages from the *Jaiminigṛhyasūtra* included here concern pre-natal rituals (1.5 and 1.7) and birth and infancy rites of passage (1.8–1.11). Rites enjoining the *upanayana*, investiture with the sacred thread, and initiation into *Vedic* learning (1.12), and rites that are to be performed as a *Vedic* student (1.13), as well as the rituals performed at the end of this student life (1.18 and 1.19) are also found among the passages selected from the *Jaiminigṛhyasūtra*. 1.20–1.22 are about the *vivāha*, wedding, and those immediately following (1.23–1.24) are about rites performed as a married householder. Passages 2.1–2.5 involve the *śraddha*, funeral, and ancestral ceremonies. The last passage included here (2.6) is a description of a rite ensuring the purity of one's house.

Many of the rituals described in the *Jaiminigṛhyasūtra* and other *gṛhyasūtras* still play a significant role in Hindu practices today. Contemporary *brāhamaṇa* families perform the *upanayana* ceremony in India and in the diaspora. The *śraddha* outlined in the *Jaiminigṛhyasūtra* is also used as a template for many Hindus.

Note

1 Ludo Rocher, "The Dharmaśāstras" in G. Flood (ed.), *A Blackwell Companion to Hinduism*. Oxford: Blackwell Publishing, 2003.

Further reading

Apte, V. M., *Social and Religious Life in the Grihya Sutras.* Bombay: Popular Book Depot, 1954.
Dange, Sindhu, *Hindu Domestic Rituals: A Critical Glance.* Delhi: Ajanta, 1985.
Gonda, Jan, *The Ritual Sūtras.* Wiesbaden: Otto Harrassowitz, 1977.
Olivelle, Patrick, *Dharmasūtras: The Laws Codes of Ancient India.* New York: Oxford University Press, 1999.
Pandey, Rajbali, *Hindu Saṁskāras: Socio-Religious Study of the Hindu Sacraments.* Delhi: Motilal Banarsidass Publishers, 1969.
Rocher, Ludo, "The *Dharmaśāstras*" in G. Flood (ed.), *A Blackwell Companion to Hinduism.* Oxford: Blackwell Publishing, 2003.

Jaiminigṛhyasūtra

I. 5

The ceremony to secure the birth of a male child

The ceremony to secure the birth of a male child takes place in the third month (of the pregnancy), except in the case of a woman who has a child.

Having boiled a mess of rice in *ghee*, or having consecrated by the sacrificial formula, as is done with a *sthâlî pāka*, a portion of ghee mixed with coagulated milk, he should offer it with the *puruṣasūkta*.

Having shaped two beans and a barley corn into the male organ of procreation, he should give it her to eat together with a drop of sour milk with the formula (which should be muttered by the pregnant woman): "Prajāpati, the male, the overlord, may he give me a long living glorious son. May I together with my husband bring forth living children."

Then having fastened a *nyagrodha* shoot, which has fruits, with two threads, one white, one red, she should bear it on her throat.

This they, say, is a sure means to get a son.

A garment is the sacrificial fee.

I. 6

The Śraddha *preceding every sacrament*

Now we shall explain the *śrāddha* which on the day previous (to any festivity) must be performed in honour of the glad-faced Fathers (the Manes).

It finds place in the fortnight of the waxing moon, under a propitious *nakṣatra*.

On the preceding day or on the day itself having dressed food he invites clean and learned *brāhmins*.

Being clean, and having put on a white, not wet garment, wearing his uppergarment above the left shoulder and beneath the right arm-pit, having sipped water, he offers bali-offerings consisting of four white substances: thick sour milk, unhusked rice, perfume, white flowers, having spread *darbha* grass on the fire place with the tips to the east, saying: "To Agni obeisance! To Soma, obeisance! To Prajāpati, obeisance! To the allgods, obeisance! To the seers, obeisance! To the Bhûtas, obeisance! To the Manes, obeisance! To all the gods, obeisance!" To the *brāhmins* he gives food fit for offering, together with thick sour milk, or, according to another view, together with food and eatables such as beans, fish, flesh. Then he takes the following four substances: rice, barley, flowers and mustard, and together with these a jar filled with water, saying to the brāhmins: "Compose your mind, be propitious," and then with the syllable *om*: "Let the glad-faced Manes be pleased." In the same way the others should answer, conformably to each wish.

I. 7

The parting of the hair

The parting of the pregnant wife's hair he should perform in the 4th., 6th. or 8th. month, during the bright half of the moon, under an auspicious *nakṣatra*, when the moon stands in conjunction with *hasta* or with a subsequent nakṣatra.

After he has boiled a *sthālīpāka* (a mess of rice) mixed with sesamum and *mudga* beans, he should sacrifice, while she standing behind lays her hand on his shoulder, with the "great words" and with the verse addressed to Prajāpati. After he has made her sit down to the west of the fire on a splendid seat or on a mattress of *erakā* grass covered over with a new garment, he should by means of the white-spotted part of a porcupine's quill that has three white spots, part her hair right over

Excerpts from W. Caland (tr.), *The Jaiminigṛhyasūtra*. Delhi: Motilal Banarsidass, 1984.

the nose up to the head (i. e. beginning at the forehead and ending at the top of the head) with the formula: "For outbreathing thee; for inbreathing thee; for throughbreathing thee." Having adorned the tips of her hair on the right side with wreath and in the same way on the left side, he should fill a vessel of white brass with water mixed with gold dust, and, while causing her to look at this water, ask her: "Him, Bhûḥ, bhuvaḥ, svah! What do you see?" The other answers: "Children, cattle and good luck for me, long life for my husband." A garment or a piece of gold is the sacrificial fee.

During ten days he should sacrifice into a fire mustard seed mixed with rice husks, with the two verses: "To Ṣaṇḍa, to Marka, to Upavîra. Let Ṣauṇḍikera, Ulûkhala, Malimluca, Duṇâṣi, Cyavana vanish hence. Svâhâ. – Let Âlikhat, Vilikhat, Animiṣ, Kimvadanta, Upaśruti, Kumbhin, the foe of Aryaman, Pâtrapâṇi, Nipuṇahan, Antrîmukha, Sarṣapâruṇa vanish hence. Svâhâ."

During a period of ten days husband and wife are impure on account of the childbirth. At the end of this period after having bathed she rises (from the childbed).

I. 8

The ceremony for the new born child

When a boy has been born the ceremony of the new born child takes place. Before the sucking he should grind to powder some rice and barley by means of a piece of gold and cause the child to eat (of this powder) with the formula: "Here is food, here sap, here nectar together with breath; thy mother is the earth, thy father the sky." Live a hundred autumns, look a hundred autumns." Then he speaks over him the verse: "From limb to limb thou art produced, out of the heart thou art born. Thou, verily, art the self, called son, so live a hundred autumns, see a hundred autumns. He then consigns him: "To the day I consign thee; let the day consign thee to the night; let the night consign thee to day and night together; let day and night consign thee to the half-months; let the half months consign thee to the months; let the months consign thee to the seasons; let the seasons consign thee to the year; let the year consign thee to old age, to death." – Then he says: "Who art thou? Who of many art thou?" (and): "Enter upon the month that belongs to the Lord of days, N. N." Then he gives him the secret name with the formula: "Veda art thou", he then kisses him on the head with the formula: "Be a stone, be an axe, be insuperable gold; with the cattle's *himkâra* I kiss thee." In the same way he kisses the head of his sons after returning from a journey.

I. 9

The giving of the name

Next the giving of the name. It takes place in the first half of the month under an auspicious nakṣatra, or on the twelfth day. The father or the teacher (*âcârya*) should give the name. The father should sit down with the child on his lap, after having wrapped it in a new garment. He should give him a two- or three- or foursyllabic name, beginning with a sonant, with a semivowel in it, derived from the name of the nakṣatra (with which the birth has coincided) of the deity (which presides over this nakṣatra), (or) derived from the (i. e. the father's) name, containing no *taddhita* (suffix), ending in ā for a female child; or the name may be appropriate. – (On this occasion) and on all occasions when a sacrifice on behalf of the boy is performed, he sacrifices to the *naksatra*, to the deity of the nakṣatra and to the weekday (of the birth). Moreover he sacrifices to the following eight deities: to Agni, to Dhanvantari, to Prajāpati, to Indra, to the Vasus, to the Rudras, to the Ādityas, to the Allgods. If these are well honored with sacrifice, all the deities are propitious.

I. 10

The first feeding with solid food

Now the (first) feeding with solid food. Having fed in the first half of the month under an auspicious nakṣatra a number of brahmins, he should cause the child to partake of food fit for sacrifices, whilst muttering the verse: "Lord of food, give us food painless and strong, bring forward the giver, bestow vigour on us: on men and animals.

I. 11

The tonsure of the child's head

In the third year (after the day of the birth) he should shape the twisted hair (of his son) (i. e. he should perform the *cūḍākarman*), according to some authorities in the third year reckoned from the beginning of pregnancy. During the northern course of the sun, in the first half the month, under an auspicious *nakṣatra* having caused a number of *brahmins* to pronounce their blessing, he should in the afternoon carry forward the fire and put down to the south of the fire four vessels: two filled with rice and barley on both sides (i. e. the vessel with rice to the west, the one filled with barley to the east), between these two other vessels, one filled with sesamum, one filled with beans.

While the boy, who has sipped water, touches him from behind, he should sacrifice (four times *ghee*) with the "great words" and a fifth time with the Virūpākṣa formula (see I. 2).

They pour out the water decocted from the various kinds of herbs – the rice, barley, sesamum and beans (above mentioned) are the "various kinds of herbs." – Then he takes up the razor with the verse: "Hither has come Savitṛ with the razor, approved of by the All-gods, by the Maruts; may he, Viśvakarman, be propitious unto us; do ye protect us ever with prosperity." He takes the water with the verse: "Come, Vāyu, with the hot water; may Aditi shave the hair." With the verse: "May the waters moisten thee for life, for old age, for splendour" he should moisten the hair near the right ear. In this (hair) he puts three *darbha* blades or a single one. He should hold (the hair and the blade in his left hand) with the verse: "Prajāpati hold again and again, for good shaving." Having touched with a mirror thrice (the hairs and the grass blades) in upward direction, he should shave off (some hair together with parts of the blades) by means of the razor, muttering (the three mantras): "With the razor, wherewith the creator has shaved (the head) of Bṛhaspati, of Agni, of Indra, for the sake of long life, therewith I shave thy (head), for the sake of long life, of glory, and of welfare." – With the razor, wherewith Prajāpati has shaved (the head) for the Maruts householders, therewith I shave thy (head) for the sake of long life, of glory, and of welfare. – With the razor wherewith this one may go about further, and may long see the sun, therewith I shave thy (head) for the sake of long life, of glory, and of welfare." In the same way the back and the left side of the head. At each *mantra* he should deposit the hair and the rest of the darbha blades on bull's dung, which should not be put on the bare ground; if the boy belongs to the *brahmin* caste, this bull's dung should be put to the east, if he belongs to the two other castes, behind. He then should hand over the razor to the barber with the mantra: "When thou shearest with the... razor, O barber, make the limbs clean; do not injure the life, the splendour, O barber." (The barber then shaves the hair) according to the custom of the *Gotra* or family (of the boy).

After the boy has been washed, he (i. e. the father or the *ācārya*) should perform the *prāyaścitta* offerings. By the...... act, and without *mantras* the ritual is performed for a female child. If it is performed with the *mantras*, the sacrifice (of the principal oblations) should be performed afterwards.

Then he takes hold of his (i. e. the boy's) head and mutters the verse: "The threefold age of Kaśyapa, Jamadagni's threefold age, the threefold age that belongs to the gods, may that threefold age belong to thee."

The hair he should bury in a cornfield or in a cowshed. The person who arranges the hair should take the full vessels. A cow constitutes the sacrificial fee.

I. 12

The initiation of the student

In the 7th year he should initiate a *brahmin* – in the 5th, one that is desirous of spiritual lustre, in the 9th, one that is desirous of attaining long life-, in the 11th a *kśatriya*, in the 12th a *vaiśya*. He should not perform the initiation after he has passed his 16th year. "For (in this case) he becomes of shattered testicles, equal to a śûdra" it is said in holy tradition).

Then (viz. when he has reached this age) they bring him (to his spiritual teacher) after he has bathed, has been adorned, his eyes have been anointed, and the barber has made his toilette.

He should put on him a new garment with one of the three following verses, according to his caste: "We clothe, O Soma, this (boy) with the holy word, for the sake of great learning, so that it (i. e. the garment) may lead him to old age and he may long watch over learning. Live thou a hundred autumns, see thou a hundred autumns, – We clothe, O Indra, this (boy) with the holy word, for the sake of great power, so that it may lead him to old age and he may long watch over power. Live thou a hundred autumns, see thou a hundred autumns. – We clothe, O Posa, this (boy) with the holy word, for the sake of great wealth, so that it may lead him to old age and he may long watch over wealth. Live thou a hundred autumns, see thou a hundred autumns."

Now the teacher, having made him sit down to the west of the fire with his face directed toward the east, and wearing his upper garment above the left shoulder and beneath the right arm-pit, makes him rinse his mouth. Then he makes him stand up, strews northward pointed *darbha* grass to the north of the fire, puts on this grass an unbroken stone, and causes him to step with his right foot on this stone with the verse: "Mount here on the stone, like the stone be thou firm; press away thy enemy, but let not thy enemy slay thee."

Now the teacher causes him to sit down to the west of the fire with his face turned to the east, and himself sits to the left (of the boy) and sacrifices, whilst the boy takes hold of him, with the "great words" and the oblations to the Vedas, pouring after each formula the dregs of each oblation into the mouth of the boy: "Bhûh, the Ṛk-verses. Svāhā! Bhuvaḥ. the Yajus-formulae, Svāhā! Svaḥ, the Sāman-chaunts. Svāhā!"

When the boy has swallowed the dregs and rinsed his mouth, the teacher causes him to stand up, and leads him around the fire, turning his right side to it, with the formula: "Obeisance to the Wind, obeisance be made to Agni, obeisance to Earth, obeisance to the Plants, obeisance I make to you, to the unseen Great One" (and he addresses the boy with the words): "Study thou, who art going to study" (to which the boy answers): "Imparter, So-and so, impart to So-and-so the Veda."

Now the teacher causes him to stand to the west of the fire with his face turned toward the east, whilst he himself stands before him with his face turned toward the west. Then they join their open hands together, the teacher holding his own above those of the boy. The hands of the teacher are now filled by some other person with water, so that the water trickling down, fills the hands of the other (i. e. the boy). He (i. e. the boy) directs him: "I have come hither for studentship; initiate me." "Who by name art thou?" Answering: "So-and-so" he (the boy) should mention his own name. Now the teacher mutters: "Him! Bhûḥ, bhuvaḥ, svah! With him who comes hither we have come together. Drive ye thoroughly away death. May we walk unhurt; may this one walk in bliss." He then seizes with his right hand his (i. e. the boy's) right hand, with the formula: "Indra has seized thy hand, Dhātṛ has seized thy hand, Pūṣan has seized thy hand, Savitṛ has seized thy hand, Aryaman has seized thy hand. Thou art Mitra by rights; Agni is thy teacher." Having touched (the place of) his navel, he mutters: "Thou art the knot of the breaths; do not loosen thyself; make not an opening to death, thou that art free from (premature) death." Having gradually passed with his hand along his right shoulder, he mutters, whilst touching (the place of) his heart: "In my will be thy heart; after my will shall thy will follow; in my word thou shalt rejoice with all thy will; let Bṛhaspati join thee to me."

He now consigns him: "To Agni I consign thee. To Vāyu I consign thee. To god Savitr I consign thee. To the Waters I consign thee. To the Plants I consign thee. To all the Gods I consign thee. To all the Beings I consign thee, for the sake of security."

Now he directs him: "A student art thou. Put fuel on (the fire). Drink water (as thy only beverage). Do the service. Do not sleep in the day-time."

He (i. e. the student) puts pieces of fuel anointed with ghee on the fire with the following mantras, one after each svāhā: "To Agni, to the great Jātavedas, I have brought a piece of wood. As thou, Agni, art inflamed through the piece of wood, thus may I prosper through long life, splendour, vigour, gift, insight, wisdom, offspring, cattle, holy lustre, the enjoyment of food, and riches. Svāhā. – The insight that dwells with the Apsaras, the mind that dwells with the Gandharvas, the divine insight and that which is born from men: May that insight, the fragrant one, rejoice me. Svāhā. – Bhûḥ, svāhā. – Bhuvah, svāhā. – Svaḥ, svāhā. – Bhûḥ, bhuvaḥ, svaḥ, Svāhā."

He (i. e. the student) ties a girdle round himself with the verses: "Here protecting me from evil words, purifying my kind as a purifier, bringing strength to exhalation and inhalation, has come to me the sisterly goddess, this blessed girdle. – A protector of right, a defender of mortification, slaying the goblins, overpowering the foes: do thou, O blessed girdle, surround me from all sides; may we, that wear thee, not perish." The girdle consists of *muñja*-grass for a *brahmin*, of *mûrvā*-grass for a *kṣatriya*, of *tāmala*-bark mixed with *muñja*-grass for a *vaiṣya*, or for all of *muñja*-grass.

Now as for the garments: the undergarment consists (for all) of linen or hemp; the uppergarment for a *brahmin* is made of the skin of an antelope, for a kṣatriya of the ruru-deer, for a *Vaiṣya* of a goat, or for all of the antelope.

With the formula: "Evil averting art thou" he should give the staff, reaching up to the nose, of *palāśa*-wood for a *brahmin*, of *bilva*-wood for one who is desirous of spiritual lustre, of nyagrodha-wood for a *kṣatriya*, of *udumbara*-wood for a *Vaiśya*, or for all of *palāśa*-wood.

He should beg food first of his mother, then of other friendly disposed women. He should beg, if he is a *brahmin*, with the word 'Lady' at the beginning: "Lady, give alms"; with this word in the middle, if he is a Kṣatriya: "Give, Lady, alms"; with this word at the end, if he is a Vaiśya: "Give alms, Lady" not emphasizing (i. e. speaking nearly inaudibly) the last syllable of the word bhikṣam (alms) and of the word "give" (dehi). Or all may beg with the word "Lady" at the beginning.

When something abnormal (something to be atoned for) occurs between the act of assuming the garment and of begging alms), he should cause him to sip water with the formula: "You are living, bestow life on him. Waters are ye by name, immortal ones are ye by name; *svadhā* are ye be name; of you, being such, may I partake; receive me into favour; be auspicious to me. Obeisance to you, do not hurt me."

The begged food is brought to the teacher.

After three days, or on the same day, he (i. e. the teacher) should recite to the student the verse addressed to Savitṛ, to the west of the fire: first by verse quarters, then by verse-halves, then entire. When the pupil has learned the verse and has (by learning the first verse of the *Ṛgveda*, the first chaunt of the *Sāmaveda*, the first formula of the *Yajurveda*) begun the (study of the) *Vedas*, he puts on the fire sticks of wood anointed with ghee, with the formula: "Agni, lord of the observances, I shall keep the observance, may I be equal to it, may I succeed in it. Svāhā! Vāyu, lord of the observances etc . . . Svāhā! Âditya, lord of the observances etc . . . Svāhā! Lord of the observances, ruling over the observances, etc . . . Svāhā!" This instruction in the performance of the observances is everywhere practised (where an occasion presents itself). At the close of the period during which the observances are kept, he should alter the formula, so as to say (in stead of: "I shall keep, . . . may I be equal, . . . may I succeed): "I have kept, . . . I have been equal, . . . I have succeeded."

Then he instructs him (i. e. the student): "Be a student of the *Veda*, subject to the teacher, subdued, lying on the ground, bearing the staff, the girdle, the antelope-hide, the matted hair abstaining from women, falsehood, honey, meat, perfume, garlands." During three days he eats no pungent or saline food.

After the lapse of the three days he should leave the village in eastern or northern direction, go to a *palāṣa* tree, anoint it with "the great words," sacrifice a mess of boiled rice (at the foot of the tree), throw away his sacred thread, his staff, etc., and return (to the village). The sacrificial fee consists of a cow.

I. 13

The twilight devotion

In the evening and the morning he should, being pure, at the brink of the water (i. e. on a shore, a bank) with a purifier (i. e. a grass stalk) in his hand, wash himself with water with the three verses, beginning: "You, waters, are", with the four verses, beginning: "May this gladdening one cross"; the vāmadevya chaunt (comes) at the end. Sitting on a pure spot on *darbha* grass, holding *darbha* grass in his hand, directed toward the west, restraining his speech, he should meditate on the evening twilight until the appearance of the stars. When the stars have appeared, he should, after having thrice restrained his breath, repeat the verse addressed to Savitṛ a thousand times or a hundred times, (but) at least ten times. He then addresses to the fire the verse beginning: "Agni, be thou our nearest"; to Varuṇa the verse beginning: "Thou art Varuṇa and Mitra." In the same way in the morning, but now directed toward the east, and he addresses to the Sun the verse beginning: "Out of the darkness" and to Mitra the verse beginning: "To Mitra, to Aryaman." If the sun should rise or set while he is sleeping, he should repeat mentally the verse addressed to Savitṛ during the rest of that (day or night). This is the atonement in this case.

[. . .]

I. 18

The study of the *Veda* lasts twelve years; reckoned from the birth onward, according to some authorities (in which case, if he is a brahmin, the study is extended over six years only); or until he has learnt the *Veda*. Constantly he has to add fuel to the fire in the evening, and to go out seeking alms evening and morning. He should avoid two three-stringed objects: a three-stringed amulet and three-stringed shoes.

In the sixteenth year the *godāna* (finds place), that means: "the cutting of the beard." The *mantras* are the same as those used for the tonsure (I.11). The undertaking of the observances is the same as that of the initiation (I.12). Here, however, no new garment is prescribed. He causes to shave off all the hair of his body and to cut his nails, according to Audgāhamani with the exception of his toplock. When he has been shaved, he should bathe. With the formula: "Thou art the skin (the bark) of the trees. O cleansing one, cleanse me. I bring thee near for the sake of long life, of lustre" he rubs himself with paste prepared from (the bark of) trees. With the formula: "Thou art the perfume of the trees. O sweet-scented one, make me sweet-scented among gods and men. I bring thee near for the sake of long life, of lustre" he rubs, after having bathed, his body with ointment. With the formula: "Thou art the flower of the trees. O sweet-scented one, make me (etc. as above)", he fastens a garland on (his head). With the formula: "Thou art a mirror (*ādarśa*); may both gods and men look (*ādṛśyāsan*, sic !) at me. Thou art shining, may I shine among gods and men" he should look at himself in the mirror. Having taken away the wreath he (i. e. the teacher) should give him directions (to put fuel on the fire etc.). The ordinances (to which the student is subjected) during the years (of the study following after the godāna) are treated. A cow is the fee.

I. 19

The bath taken at the end of studentship

After he has studied the Veda and observed the observances, a *brāhmin*, being about to take the (absolving) bath, gets ready the (following) requisites: a new garment, a mat of *erakā*-grass, paste for the bath, ointment, flowers, collyrium, a mirror, two new garments, a three-stringed amulet, a bamboo staff and two white shoes. A fully equipped barber stands near on the north side.

Having spread out the mat of erakā grass and covered it with the new garment with the fringe toward the north, he (the teacher) should cause him (i. e. the student) to sit down with his face directed toward the east and should throw his staff into the water with the formula: "Thou art the thunderbolt destined for the enemies." The girdle he should make him loosen with the verse beginning: "Unloose the highest." The girdle also he should throw into the water. The mantras (for the shaving) are the same as those of the shaving (I.18); the shaving also takes place. He shaves (on this occasion) first his head, then his beard, then his other limbs successively; he (the student or the teacher?) should bury the hair of his head, the hair of his beard and his nail-clippings at the root of an aśvattha or *udumbara*-tree. With luke-warm water, holding a piece of gold between (the water and the body) he (i. e. the teacher) should bathe him with the verse: "Be thou propitious and most favourable to us, and gracious, O Sarasvatī; let us not be separated from sight of thee."

He should take the bath under the nakṣatra Rohiṇi, this *nakṣatra* belongs to Prajāpati, if he wishes to get offspring. He should take the bath under the *nakṣhatra* Mṛgaśiras, this nakṣatra belongs to Soma, if he wishes that a Soma-sacrifice may fall to his share. He should take the bath under the *nakṣatra* Tishya, this *nakṣatra* belongs to Bṛhaspati, and Bṛhaspati is the *Brahman* (the holy Word, the *Veda*), if he wishes to get spiritual lustre. He should take the bath under the *nakṣatra* Hasta, this nakṣatra belongs to Savitṛ, if he wishes to be impelled by Savitr. He should take the bath under the *nakṣatra* Anūrādhās, this *nakṣatra* belongs to Mitra, if he wishes to be dear to his friends (mitra). He should take the bath under the *nakṣatra* Śravaṇa, this nakṣatra belongs to Viṣṇu, and Viṣṇu is the sacrifice, if he wishes that a sacrifice may fall to his share.

He (i. e. the teacher) should invest him with the new garment with the verse: "We clothe, O Soma this boy" etc. Then he should salve his eyes, first the left and then the right, with the verse beginning: "With glory me."

The three-stringed amulet, which must be made of *palāśa*-wood if he is desirous of averting evil, he (i. e. the student) fastens to his neck with the formula: "Thou art the one averting evil", of *bilva*-wood, if he is desirous of spiritual lustre with the formula: "May I become possessed of spiritual lustre," of *arka*-wood, if he is desirous of getting food with the formula: "May I eat food."

With the formula: "Thou art the Gandharva Viśvāvasu; protect thou me, guard thou me" he takes the bamboo staff.

He should put on the two shoes with the formula: "You are the leaders, lead me." First he fastens on the right one.

The observances for him are the following: he should not wish for sport with a girl that has not reached the age of puberty, he should not run while it is raining, nor take his shoes in his own hand, nor gather fruits of the trees himself, nor go toward evening to another village, neither go alone nor together with *Śûdras*, not look into a well, not climb a tree nor a bridge, nor be seated without inteposing (something between himself and the ground), not eat food which has been brought in at the western door; nor (prepared) food that has turned sour, nor food which has been cooked twice (i. e. has been warmed) or which has been kept over for the night, except such as is prepared of vegetables, meat, barley, rice, flour, parched rice, juice of sugarcane, coagulated milk, honey, and ghee. He should not laugh if there is no cause for mirth, not bathe naked, not speak harsh words, avoid scandal and quarrels.

According to Âruṇi Gautama there are three kinds of Snātakas: the Snātaka by knowledge, the Snātaka by the completion of his observances, and the Snātaka by knowledge **and** by the completion of his observances. Of these the last ranks foremost, the first two are equal (to each-other).

(The Arghya reception on *Madhuparka*)

When he has taken the (absolving) bath (and has become a "Snātaka') he should address his teacher: "Your honour should bring me the *madhuparka*" (i. e. the mixture of ghee, curds, and honey). He or another person, competent to replace the teacher should bring to him, who is seated with his face turned toward the east, the *madhuparka*: the bed of grass (to sit down upon), the water for washing the feet, the *arghya* water, and the water for sipping, each separately. He seats himself on the bed of grass. He washes his feet with the water destined for this use with the formula: "In me may fortune rest": when it is a *śûdra* who washes his feet, the left foot should be washed first; then the right foot with the formula: "In me may rest the *pādyā virāj*." With the verse beginning: "In me may lustre" he should accept the arghya water; the water offered him for sipping he should sip. Underneath the wooden vessel (in which the *madhuparka* is now to be given), a bushel of grass is held; the two bushels of grass (viz. this one and the other one, mentioned in the following sentence) are (beforehand) tied together at their topparts; one bushel of grass lies above the vessel; between these two bushels curds and honey are put together in the vessel. If he adds curds, the madhuparka is a *dadhimantha*, if water: a *udamantha*, if milk: a *payasya*. This *madhuparka* he should accept with the formula: "On the impulse of god Savitṛ (I accept thee with the arms of the Aṣvins with the hands of Pûṣan)". Having put it down on the ground and having mixed the contents with his thumb and ring-finger, he should thrice eat of it with the formula: "For the sake of glory, of fortune, of food, of holy lustre (I take) thee to me."

The rest of it he should give to a *brahmin*, having seized the vessel at the left side, or to a non-*brahmin*, but then after first having sprinkled it with water, or he may bury (the remains) in a hole. Any other person then holding a knife in his hand, speaks, looking at the cow, (which now is brought near): "The cow, the cow, the cow!" To this (cow) he addresses the formula: "The cow will become a milch-cow" (and the verse): "The mother of the Rudras, the daughter of the Vasus, the sister of the Âdityas, the navel of immortality – to the people who understand me I will say: do not kill the guiltless cow, which is Aditi. – Let it drink water, let it eat grass." Immediately after this verse he should say: "Om! Let it loose", but if it is to be killed: "Slaughter it."

Now there are six persons, to whom the arghya reception is due: an officiating priest at a Vedic sacrifice, a teacher, a Snātaka, a King who has received the royal consecration, a dear friend, and a learned brahmin. For these he should kill the guest cow. He should sprinkle her with water with the formula: "For the guest (I sprinkle thee)."

I. 20

The wedding (I. 20–22)

Having taken the (absolving) bath he (should return home and) attend upon his parents, being subject to them. With their permission he should take for his wife a girl, who has reached the age of puberty, who is his equal in birth, who should belong to a different gotra (from her husband's), who should not be related to his mother in the seventh degree, who should be younger than himself who is older.

The messenger (who is to ask the girl in his name) he dismisses with the verse: "May be free from thorns, and straight, the paths by which our friends go a wooing for us; may Aryaman, may Bhaga lead us all, may our domestic state be well regulated, ye gods!"

On the fire, when it is being brought near on the occasion of the taking of the hand i. e. at the wedding proper, he speaks the verse: "May Agni come hither the first of the deities; may he release the offspring of this (woman) from the fetter of death. May this king Varuṇa grant, that this woman shall not weep over distress (falling to her lot) through her sons." To the fire, when it has been kindled, he addresses, standing before it and looking at it, the verse: "May Agni *gārhapatya* protect this woman, may he lead her offspring to long life. With fertile womb may she be the mother of living children; may she experience delight in her sons."

Before the fire a *brahmin*, restraining his speech, should stand turned to the west, holding a vessel filled with water; to the south of the fire the mother (of the bride) should stand holding in a winnowing basket roasted grain mixed with śamî leaves, in the absence of the mother any female person who can replace her (i. e. the mother's sister or the mother's mother). To the west of the fire he should put down a mat of *erakâ* reed, or a bundle of grass, or something else of that kind, after having rolled it up, so that, when (at the moment the bridegroom and the bride are going to take their seat upon it) it is pushed forward, it reaches up to the western part of the grass strewn (around the fire).

Now he gives her the two garments after having sprinkled them and having spoken over them the verse: "The goddesses, who spun, who wove, who spread out and who drew out the end on both sides, may these goddesses clothe thee with long life. Put this grament on, living long."

Then he should address her: "Strike on this *erakâ* mat with your right foot (so that the mat lies as indicated above). (The bride does so) with the formula: "May the path leading to the husband be successful for me." If she should not mutter, he (the groom) himself should mutter, changing it: "for her" (instead of "for me"). On the southern (i. e. right) part of the mat he causes the bride to sit down, the bridegroom himself takes place on the northern (left) part. They should touch one another (putting, for a moment, their hand on each other's shoulder). He himself (sitting on the mat) should offer the following burnt oblations speaking loudly, whilst the bride takes hold of him. Having sacrificed with "the great words" (i. e. bhûḥ, svâhâ! bhuvaḥ, svâhâ! svaḥ, svâhâ; bhūr bhuvaḥ svaḥ, svâhâ!) he sacrifices seven offerings, pouring the residue of the ghee after the oblation with the first verse on the head of the bride: "Thou who liest down athwart, thinking: "it is I who keep all things asunder", thee with a stream of *ghee* we propitiate completely. To samrādhā, Svāhā! (1). May no lament arise at night in thy house, may the weeping (females) take their abode apart from thee, mayest thou not beat thy breast with loose hair, mayest thou, with thy husband living, shine in thy husband's world, beholding thy offspring, with well-willing mind. Svāhā! (2). May Anumati approve today our sacrifice among the gods, and may Agni the oblation-carrier bring this about; may he prosper. Svāhā! (3). May heaven protect thy back, Vāyu thy thighs, and the two Aśvins thy breast, may Savitṛ protect thy suckling sons. Until the garment is put on (thy sons) may Bṛhaspati guard (them) and the All-gods afterwards. Svāhā! (4). Taking childlessness, death of sons, evil, and distress (from thee) as a wreath from the head, I fasten it to thy foes as a fetter. Svāhā! (5). Whichever evil was in all thy limbs, that I have removed by the offerings made with a ladle full of *ghee*. Svāhā! (6) (and the last or seventh) with the verse beginning: "O Prajāpati."

I. 21

Now he seizes with his right hand her right hand – her open hand with the fingers extended, if he wishes male, her fingers (only), if he wishes female children, her hand together with the thumb, if he wishes both – with the verses: "I seize thy hand that we may be blessed with good-fortunes, that with me as a husband thou mayest live to old age. Bhaga, Aryaman, Savitṛ, Purandhi, the gods, have given thee to me that we may rule our house. – Soma gave her to the Gandharva; the Gandharva gave her to Agni; Agni gave welfare and riches and this one to me. – Soma acquired thee first as his wife, after him the Gandharva acquired thee. Thy third husband is Agni, the fourth am I, (thy) human (husband)."

Then he should make her step upon a stone after the manner described in the chapter on initiation (I.8), changing the masculine gender into the feminine.

Whilst being regarded by the bride on the north-eastern part of the fire he murmurs the verses: "Be not of evil eye, not bringing death to me, thy husband; bring luck to the cattle, be kindly disposed and full of lustre. Give birth to living children, love the gods, be friendly. Bring luck to our two- and four-footed ones. – May Prajāpati generate progeny for us, may Aryaman unite us to reach old age, enter, not ill-omened, the world of thy husband. Bring luck to our two- and four-footed ones. – Lead her, O Pūṣan, to us, the highly blessed one, into whom men pour their sperm, her, who may willingly part her thighs, into whom we willingly may introduce the member. – Yonder am I, this one art thou; the Sāman am I, the Ṛc art thou; the mind am I, the word art thou, the Heaven am I, the Earth art thou. Come, let us join together, let us unite our sperm to generate a male child. Be devoted to me, occupy one couch with me, thou So-and-so." Here he should instead of "So-and-so" put in her name.

Thereupon the pair should walk around the fire, whilst the bridegroom mutters the formula: "Thou art food, strength by name is thy mother; come thou to me with progeny, with wealth."

After the circumambulation her brother or another person who is a friend of hers should pour with his joined hands out of the winnowing basket into her joined hands roasted grain sprinkled with *ghee*, "picking out" again and again (i. e. not all the grain at once, but at several times). Having "spread under" and poured over (the roasted grain) some ghee, the other one (i. e. the bride) should sacrifice it in the fire with the three verses: "This young girl going from her parents to the world of her husband, has sacrificed away her *dīkṣa*. Svāhā. – This woman, strewing grains into the fire, prays: "May my husband live long, may my relations be prosperous." Svāhā. – To the god Aryaman the girl has sacrificed, to Agni; may he, the god Aryaman, loosen her from here, not from thence. Svāhā! After each oblation he mutters, four times (i. e. after each of these three, and after the fourth one, mentioned beneath) the verse: "May we find our way with thee through all hostile powers, as through streams of water." Without mantra the person who holds the roasted grain (the mother etc. cp. I.20) should pour out as a fourth oblation (the rest of the grain in the winnowing basket) for (the obtaining of) a (special) wish (i. e. in order that the bride may see fulfilled any wish, on which she has to fix her thought). The right neb of the winnowing basket they call "the wish."

On the north-eastern part of the fire he causes her to step forward seven steps, each with one of the following formulae: "One for sap; may Viṣṇu go after thee. – Two for juice; may Viṣṇu go after thee. – Three for prosperity; may Viṣṇu go after thee. – Four for comfort; may Viṣṇu go after thee. – Five for progeny; may Viṣṇu go after thee. – Six for the seasons; may Viṣṇu go after thee. – Be a friend of seven steps."

At the seventh (step), having caused her to stand directed to the east, they should sprinkle her out of the vessel filled with water with the three verses, beginning: "Ye waters are beneficent."

The lookers-on he addresses with the verse: "This woman wears auspicious ornaments. Come up to her and behold her. Having brought luck to her, go away back to your houses."

Then he should make her look on the pole-star, the star *arundhatī* (i. e. *alkor* of *ursa major*), and the seven seers (*ursa major*), when she declares: "Let me see (them)." To the pole-star she addresses looking at it, the formula: "Thou art the pole-star (*dhruva*, firm), may I become firm (i. e. fixed) in the house of my husband So-and-so", uttering the name of her husband (instead of "So-and-so"), and at the end of the formula her own name in the nominative case. On *arundhatī* she looks with the formula: "Arundhatī, may I be held fast by my husband So-and-so," uttering the name of her husband and at the end of the formula her own name.

I. 22

When she departs (to the house of her husband), he speaks over her the verse; "May Pūṣan lead thee thence, grasping thy hand; may the Aśvins carry thee forth in a chariot; go to the house, that thou mayest be a housewife; having control thou shalt speak unto the council."

When she has reached her own house, (some women) of good disposition, that possess beautiful progeny and have reached old age together (with their respective husbands), make her descend with the verse: "May here succeed for thee by progeny what is dear (to you). Watch thou over this house for housewife-ship; unite yourself with this one, your husband; then, being not deficient, thou shalt speak to the council."

Thereupon he makes her sit down on a bull's hide with the hairy side turned upwards, with the verse: "Here may cows sit down, here horses, here men. Here may also Pūṣan with a thousand sacrificial gifts sit down." Having placed a boy in her lap he should throw sweetmeats or fruits (in its hands). Having removed the boy he should, whilst the wife holds on to him from behind, sacrifice with the following eight formulae, each concluded with the word Svāhā!: "Here is steadiness. Here is independant steadiness. Here is delight. Here take delight. In me the steadiness. In me the independent steadiness. In me the joy. In me rejoice."

During a period of three days and nights they should abstain from saline or pungent food and from sexual intercourse, sleeping on the ground and lying together without approaching one another. After the lapse of the three days they should cohabit. In the night (following on the three-day period) (begins) the ritual work of the married pair. He should sacrifice the expiatory oblations with the formulae: "Expiating Agni! Thou art the expiation of the gods. I, a *brahmin*, entreat thee, desirous of protection. The substance, which dwells in her that brings death to progeny, reṃove from her. Svāhā. – Expiatory Vāyu! Thou art the expiation of the gods. I, a brahmin, entreat thee, desirous of protection. The substance, which dwells in her that brings death to cattle, remove from her. Svāhā. – Expiatory Sûrya! Thou art the expiation of the gods. I, a *brahmin*, entreat thee, desirous of protection. The substance, which dwells in her that brings death to the husband, remove from her. Svāhā. – Expiatory Candra! Thou art the expiation of the gods. I, a *brahmin*, entreat thee, desirous of protection. The substance, which dwells in her that brings destruction to the house, remove from her. Svāhā. – Expiatory Agni, Vāyu, Sûrya, Candra, you are the expiation of the gods. I, a brahmin, entreat you, desirous of protection. The substance, which dwells in her that brings destruction to fame, remove ye from her. Svāhā."

Having sacrificed from a *sthālīpāka* to Agni and Prajāpati and having poured together into a wooden vessel the remnants of each oblation, he should address her with the words: "Anoint thy vital canals." First (she anoints) the navel, then the organs of sense which are above (viz. eyes, nose, ears, mouth), then those beneath (the navel).

After the three days have passed, the cohabitation takes place, after the husband has muttered the three following verses: "May

Viṣṇu make the womb ready; may Tvaṣṭṛ frame the shape (of the child), may Prajāpati pour forth the sperm, may Dhātṛ give thee conception. – Give conception, Sinīvālī, give conception, Sarasvatī; may the two Aśvins, the gods wreathed with lotus, give conception to thee. – The embryo, which the Aśvins with golden fire-drill produce: that embryo I put into thee, for giving birth in the tenth month."

The cohabitation takes place in this manner after each menstrual period.

After the burnt oblations he should give a cow to his teacher, in default of the teacher he should give a cow to (some) *brahmins.*

I. 23

The regular evening and morning sacrifices

At the evening and morning-sacrifice he offers first an oblation of *ghee* to Agni, a second to Prajāpati; thus also in the morning, but then instead of Agni: to Sûrya.

The Vaiśvadeva

Of his evening and morning-food he puts aside two great portions destined for the bali-offerings, and sacrifices into the fire from the foremost portion: "To Agni. Svāhā! To Soma. Svāhā! To Dhanvantari. Svāhā! To Heaven and Earth. Svāhā! To the All-gods. Svāhā! To all the Deities. Svāhā! To Prajāpati. Svāhā!" The last one only mentally (i. e. he thinks only: "To Prajāpati. Svāhā").

Then to the north of the fire he offers (on the ground) a bali-sacrifice with the verse: "The gladdening, trembling, increase-bringing ones, that follow on the track of the wind: to these I, desirous of food, offer a bali-sacrifice. May much nutritive food fall to my share." In the same way if (someone) hungers.

On the place where he collects his revenues (his rice, barley, etc.) he offers a bali-sacrifice with the formula: "To Death's abode." Of the rest bali-offerings are made sun-wise, with the formula: "To the house-deities I offer a bali; may they accept this from me, may they protect me, may they guard me, may they preserve me. To these obeisance, to these Svāhā," first near the water-jar, then in the middle of the house, in the north-eastern part, near the bed, on the threshold, near the enclosure, and near the place where the Brahman has his seat. The remains he should pour out for Dhanvantari.

At all the house-rites a benediction must be said (by one or more *brahmins* who must then be entertained with food). This (benediction) is called the great means of appeasement (i. e. of averting evil).

I. 24

The sacrifice of the first fruits

When he is about to undertake the sacrifice of the first fruits, he should first perform a sacrifice with the old fruits to Agni, Dhanvantari, Prajāpati and Indra, they offer three oblations of the first fruits, in autumn of rice, in spring of barley, in the rainy season of millet. On these occasions a mess of the corns boiled whole, is offered successively to Indra and Agni, to the Allgods, to Heaven and Earth. Or one mess only is offered. The "spreading-under" and the sprinkling of ghee have been dealt with (and should take place here). Twice he cuts off a fragment from the sacrificial substance, then he should partake of it after having muttered the verse: "From the good ye have led us to the better, ye gods! Through thee, the nourishment, may we obtain thee. Thus enter into us, O Potion, being refreshment, for the good of our children and ourselves, pleasant." Of the barley he should partake with the verse: "This barley, mixed with honey, they have ploughed through Sarasvatī under Manu. Indra was lord of the plough, the hundredfold wise one; ploughers were the Maruts, the exuberant givers." Of the millet he should partake with the verse: "May Agni partake first, for he knows how the sacrificial substance is; may he, the friend of all human tribes, make the herbs blessed for us."

II. 1

The śrâddha *(II. 1–2)*

When thy are going to perform a *śrāddha*, they should bathe, put on clean garments, strew the house with sesamum, and prepare the food, sprinkling it with "substances fit for oblation"; during all the acts they should use the left hand, wear the sacred thread (or the upper garment) on the right shoulder and beneath the left arm-pit. All that he gives, he should give after sprinkling it with "substances fit for oblation." The expression: "substances fit for oblation" means: sesamum.

Having brought tooth sticks, water and unguents proper for bathing, water for washing the feet, which has been drawn first of all, he causes to sit down (some, at least three) *brahmins*, spotless in three respects (i. e. knowledge, birth, and behaviour) with the verse: "May my Fathers come to their share, called by the Virāj, from the oceanic water. Live ye upon this undiminished (share), delight ye at free will in that which is given by me." Then he should give to the brahmins *darbha* grass cut off near the root, having made (from this grass) layers wound from right to left, with the formula: "Here, Father, So-and-so is a seat for thee and for those who come here with thee; for these also is the seat." In the same way for his grandfather and great grandfather. Then he should give them water mixed with sesamum (pouring it out) through a strainer, perfumes and flowers.

Having cut off a portion of the food and having sprinkled it with ghee, he takes the grass for strewing around the fire etc., asks the *brahmins*' permission to sacrifice into the fire, carries it forward in south-eastern direction and strews the grass shaking it around the fire three times from left to right, wearing his sacred thread (or his upper-garment) on his right shoulder and beneath his left arm-pit. He should sprinkle water around the fire three times from left to right and three times from right to left. The fuel and the enclosing pegs are of *udumbara*-wood, as also the ladle. Having made and consecrated by mantras the two purifyers, and having "purified" with them the food, he throws the purifyers into the fire and sacrifices by means of the ladle (from the food): "To Agni, who carries the oblation to the Manes. Svadhā! Obeisance! Svāhā! – To soma, who is accompanied by the Fathers. Svadhā! Obeisance! Svāhā." Then having shifted his sacred thread (or his upper-garment) to the left shoulder, and having touched water, he throws the ladle into the fire with the formula: "To Yama, who is accompanied by the Angiras. Svāhā!" Having performed the namaskāra according to the deities, he should sprinkle (again) water around the fire in the same way as before.

Then he puts a big portion of food with condiments in (different) vessels and pours milk or ghee upon it with the verse: "In the raw ones (i. e. the cows) the boiled nectar has entered; delight ye at free will in that which is given by me." The big portions he assigns with the verses: "This, ye Fathers, is your share, given in the vessels, the nectar, full of svadhā. Live ye upon this undiminished (share), delight at free will in that which is given by me. – The immortal Word, the immortal Waters, the (immortal) Food: this is the threefold, one-law-ed immortality of the Word. Delight ye at free will in these three given by me; may here, ye gods, be weal for us. – This sacrifice to the Fathers is the highest: what is given in the vessels, what is destined for the Fathers, O Agni. Word and Mind, ye Fathers, are your offering. Delight ye at free will in what has been given by the Aśvins. – The Fathers here on the earth, those in the atmosphere, and those of the ocean, those that have reached the Word, that have become immortal, may these all delight in this sacrificial substance. – Here is strength (food) for you and here Svadhā, eat ye and drink it, and may this (portion) not be diminished for you. Take with you the Svadhā: the spring of nectar; enjoy the Svadhā, ye Fathers, that is here. – The strength (food) and the deity that is here, ye Fathers, upon that may we live a hundred years. Make ye my life full of light and devoid of old age." There upon he puts these (vessels with food) down near the brahmins and assigns them with his thumb, muttering: "To So-and-so. Svadhā. To So-and-so. Svadhā."

While thy eat he speaks over them the verse: What by me (is bestowed) against or with my will, on an imperfect brahmin or on a non-*brahmin*, what food drops into terrific Nirṛti, by which our Fathers and the deities are gladdened – may Vāyu purify all that; by it, being purified, may the deities rejoice, in it may the Fathers rejoice."

Having chanted the Âśvasāman, composed on the verse beginning: "The ocean roared," and having asked if (their meal) is finished, he should, wearing his sacred thread (or his uppergarment) upon his left shoulder, make them rinse their mouths. Then he says: "May you be pleased", circumambulates them, turning his right side toward them, and while they depart, mutters over them the verse: "What a black bird and a beast of prey, what an unclean person, have eaten of the food prepared by me with *mantras*, may Savitṛ Vaiśvānara purify that; by it, being purified may the deities rejoice; in it may the Fathers rejoice themselves."

II. 2

Having begged for the rest (of the food, to do with it as he pleases) he should return (from the spot to where he has accompanied the departing *brahmins*). He smears with bull's dung a quadrangular spot, directed toward the southeast, and in the middle of it by means of a piece of wood scratches a line with the formula: "Driven away are the *asuras*, the *rākṣasas*, the *piśācas*, who dwell among the Fathers", and lays down to the south of this square a firebrand with the verse: "Whatsoever asuras roam about at will assuming various shapes, being large-bodied or small-bodied (?), may Agni expel them from this space." Having strewn *darbha* grass along the line, he makes him (i. e. his father) rinse his mouth by means of a vessel filled with water (from which he pours out some quantity): "Father So-and-so, rinse thy mouth, and may these that accompany thee here also rinse their mouths." In the same way for his grandfather and great-grandfather. On these places (where he has poured out the water, for each of the three ancestors a little more to the south) he lays down little balls of boiled rice, addressing each of his ancestors by his name, with that part of the hand which is sacred to the Manes, with the formula: "This is for thee, Father So-and-so, and for those who accompany thee. Svadhā. Obeisance." In the same way for his grandfather and great-grandfather. If he does not know their names, then with the formulae: "Father, this is for thee. Grandfather, this is for thee. Great-grandfather, this is for thee." If he does not know his kinsmen (nor their names), then with the formulae: "This is for the Fathers, who dwell on the earth. This is for the Grandfathers who dwell in the atmosphere. This is for the Great-grandfathers who dwell in the heaven." With the formula: "Here, ye Fathers, regale yourselves; like bulls come hither, each to your own share" he should turn round to the north and sit down, holding his breath as long as possible. Then he (turns back and) having muttered the formula: "The Fathers have regaled themselves; like bulls they are come hither, each to his own share", he makes them rinse their mouths in the same way as described above, he loosens the tuck of his garment, performs obeisance to each of the deities, and assigns garments to them: a knot of wool or a cloth consisting of the fringe of his garment, with the formulae: "Here is a garment for you, O Fathers; give ye a house to us, O Fathers; give fruit to the womb, O Fathers: a boy wreathed with lotus, that here may be a male child." He gives ointment and collyrium with the formula: "Anoint thee, So and-so!" and "Anoint thy eyes. So-and-so!" He should give perfumes and flowers. He then addresses them with the following six formulae of obeisance: "Obeisance to your sap, ye Fathers! Obeisance to your lustre, ye Fathers! Obeisance to your life, ye Fathers! Obeisance to your terror, ye Fathers! Obeisance to your strength, ye Fathers! Obeisance to your wrath, ye Fathers! and to your Svadhā. Obeisance to you, ye Fathers!" With the verse: "Ye waters, who carry food, nectar, *ghee*, milk, *kīlāla* and *parisrut*, are Svadhā; satiate my Fathers" he pours out water, and speaks over it the verse: "May it not diminish for me; may great liberality fall to my share; may the *Brahmins* delight in the food I offer repeatedly. May what I give (to the Brahmins) become for me in the highest abode Nectar-water of a thousand streams. – May Gods and Fathers subsist here upon this liberality of mine. Live ye upon this undiminished (share), delight at free will in that which is given by me." He then circumambulates, turning toward it his right side, (the spot where the ancestors have been regaled) with the verse: "They who are common and benevolent, the living amongst the living, mine: may their prosperity fall to my lot in this world through a hundred years."

The rice balls may be eaten by a sick person, by one who is desirous of food, or they may be thrown into the fire or the water, or given to a goat, a cow, or a *brahmin*. Of the rest (i. e. either the rice from which the rice balls have been taken, or the rest of the food eaten by the *brahmins*) he may eat, but he should not eat his fill.

II. 3

The Aṣṭakás

On each of the three dark halves of the months following on the Âgrahayaṇī-fullmoonday fall the Aṣṭakās: the Aṣṭakā of vegetables, the Aṣṭakā of meat, and the Aṣṭakā of flour-cakes. The sacrificial substance is vegetables, flesh, flour-cakes, and (for all) a mess of boiled rice. Of these substances he should sacrifice into the fire in the manner prescribed for a *sthālīpāka*, with the formulae: "To the Aṣṭakā. Svāhā! To the Aṣṭakā par excellence. Svāhā! To the favourable Aṣṭakā. Svāhā! To the Samvatsara, to the Parivatsara, to the Idāvatsara, to the Idvatsara, to the Âvatsara make ye (the offering) with obeisance. Through thee may we, undecayed, unbeaten, long enjoy the favour of these (years), which are worthy of sacrifice. Svāhā!". Having poured out the burnt-oblations, he should respectfully address (the fire?) with the formula: "Come, thou good Fortune (or: "O Bhaga); come, thou good Fortune; come, thou good Fortune."

At the middle Aṣṭakā he should have a cow slaughtered. He should sprinkle her with the formula: "To the Aṣṭakā agreeable I sprinkle thee." Of this (cow) he should take out the left flank, the left *apaghanī* and the left buttock.

On the next day he performs the *anvaṣṭakya-śrāddha* (i. e. the *śrāddha* on the day after the *aṣṭakā*), or it may take place on the same day. Having made sit down (some) *Brahmins* (at least three), who are worthy to partake of the sacrificial substances, he should satiate them, carry forward to the south (out of this fire) six fires, and dig near each of these fires one trench, a span long, three fingers broad, one finger deep. In these trenches he deposits the balls of boiled rice, addressing his ancestors each with his name, with that part of the hand which is sacred to the Manes. The marrow he lays down for the male ascendants, the ribs (etc.) for the female ones.

Some *adhvaryus* teach about this subject, that the middle rice ball (offered at the *anvaṣṭakya-śrāddha*) should be eaten by the wife of one who is desirous of offspring; thus also (the middle rice ball) of an (ordinary) *śrāddha*, or the *sthālīpāka*.

II. 4

The funeral ceremonies (II. 4–5)

When the corpse of one who had consecrated and during his lifetime maintained the three sacred fires has gone lost, he (viz. the son) should fetch 360 *palāśa*-stems and shape these on the skin of a black antelope into a human frame: for the head he lays down 40, for the neck 10, for the two arms 100, for the fingers again 10, for the breast 30, for the belly 20, for the thighs 100, for the organ of generation 10, for the knees and the legs 30, for the toes 10. "So many are the bones of a man", says the sacred tradition.

If the corpse has not gone lost, they should shave the hair, pare the nails, wash it and raise it on a pyre; here they pile also his sacrificial utensils in the way described in the chapter of the *brāhmaṇa* which begins: "on it they place him; on his nostrils he should put down the two *sruvaladles*". Having previously taken four ladle-fuls of *ghee*, according to the prescripts of the chapter in the *brāhmaṇa* beginning: "He who knows thus, if he should fall ill", (and then having made an oblation with this ghee in the fire) he puts, if possible, a piece of gold on the mouth of the corpse, propels the fires to the pyre and addresses it respectfully with the chaunts: with the one composed on the verse beginning: "The eagle flying in the vault", according to the *grāmageya*; when the smoke has risen upwards, with the one composed on the verse beginning: "Thy sparkling smoke arises" and when the fire has risen, with one of the two composed on the verse beginning: "Agni, be gracious; thou art great". The Sāmans should be chanted right off ("without returning" i. e. without repetition): "without returning in yonder World" so says a *brāhmaṇa*.

II. 5

If the wife of one who has consecrated his three sacred fires, comes to die before him, he should cremate her with a fire produced from the fire-drill or with a *sāntapana* fire.

Having selected as burial ground a spot, which by its nature is not saline, and whence the water flows down from right to left tortuously, or a spot, where herbs grow, and here having cremated the corpse, they go away without looking back in order to bring the libation of water to the deceased; this they do not perform in streaming water. The libation should be poured out so that always the youngest among them pours it out before the elder one; at the brink of the water; and if there is no brink, after having dug a well. With the nameless finger (i. e. the ringfinger) of the left hand he throws once some water forward, uttering the name of the deceased. If (the libation is made) in streaming water, they should first loosen the hair on the head, they plunge into the water and having poured out the water-libation out of the hollow of the two open hands held together, they should tie up the hair and each of them should touch the fire of a firebrand with the formula: "O Agni *śukāhi* (?), drive ye away my evil." He should touch a *śamī*-branch with the formula: "Thou art a *śamī*, remove (śamaya) my evil", a stone, with the formula: "A stone art thou; hard (steady) art thou; may I be steady"; then without any formula, a piece of bull's dung.

When he has poured out the libation of water he should sit down with his face directed toward the south, and those who have accompanied him should sit down near him. Another one addresses to them edifying words. At sunset they enter the village.

During this (day and the following) night they subsist on one single bean, or in complete indifference to all worldly enjoyments (i. e. eating nothing at all).

On the next day he mixes milk and water (goes to the spot of cremation) and besprinkles the bones (with this mixture) by means of a goatshorn, a cow-horn or an earthen pail.

On the third day he should mix perfumes with herbs in water sprinkle the bones by means of a śamī or palāśa-branch and put them into an urn without making a noise (i. e. so that no grating sound is made by the bones touching one another). If the deceased was a woman, then in an earthen water-jar. Passing a crossway, a great arbour or a stream, he should bury (the urn) in the stair of a landing place of a stream.

On the third day after the decease they make them (i. e. the participants) bathe with *apāmārga*-plants, clay and cowdung.

Having washed their clothes they remain idle during a period of ten days. From the fourth day on they should subsist on food begged (from the neighbours). From this (begged food) the offering into the fire has been demonstrated (and should in the well-known way take place during these ten days), and with this begged food they should pass along together the time they expect.

After the lapse of the period of the ten days they should perform a *śrāddha*. Until they perform this *śrāddha* they should not give (alms). The restrictions for the nakṣatras are: (this *śrāddha* should take place) under (i. e. when the moon stands in conjunction with) the maghās, under *nakṣatras* consisting of one single star, under *bharaṇī*, and of the double nakṣatras under the former; not under the fixed ones, viz. *rohiṇī* and under the later star of a double *nakṣatra*. Having made (some) brahmins sit down who are worthy to partake of sacrificial substances, and having satiated these, he should give one single ball of boiled rice, (changing the plural of all the *mantras* with which it is offered) into the singular, and leaving out the addition: "and to those who accompany thee" (II. 2). He should satisfy all their (i. e. the brahmins') desires. Having accompanied them and having begged for the rest of the food, to do with it as he pleases (cp. II. 2, beg), he should return. The rest he should not partake of; only after having made the *brahmins* pronounce their blessing he may partake of it.

II. 6

The rite of the house

Now follows (the description) of the rite of the house. If he wishes that his house may flourish he should every month, every season or every year in the first half of the month under an auspicious nakṣatra undertake the rite for averting evil from his house. Having by means of indra *vallī*-creepers tied together *apāmārga*, *palāśa*, *śirīṣa*, *arka udumbara*, *sadābhadra* and *amṛtatṛṇa*, and (with this kind of broom) having cleansed and swept his house, having be sprinkled it with water, having sprinkled it all over by means of a handful of *darbha*-grass with the five products of the cow, having strewn about white mustard seed, he should in the middle of the house perform the *bali*-offerings to the house and sacrifice oblations of ghee to Vāstoṣpati and then a thousand times sacrifice *ghee* with the verse addressed to Savitṛ. This same sacrifice then takes place in the south-eastern, then in the south-western, then in the north-eastern and then in the north-western part of the house; or in the middle (only). The sacrificial fee consists of a cow, a garment or a piece of gold. Then he should regale (some) *brahmins* with food and make them pronounce their benedictions.

Thus performing he enjoys endless and great prosperity, he gets many sons, who do not die young, the fire burns not his house, no biting animals will devour him, no thieves, rivals, demons or devils annoy him.

If his cows grow sick he should in the midst of his cows sacrifice a thousand *ghee*-offerings in the same way (viz. with the verse addressed to Savitṛ). The same holds good of the sickness of horses, camels, asses, goats and sheep, buffaloes, elephants and any of his bipeds or quadrupeds.

[. . .]

Chapter 4

The *Mahābhārata*

The *Mahābhārata*, the "Great History of the descendants of Bharata," is the longest epic poem in the world. Over 100,000 verses, the *Mahābhārata* is a story of the birth of a war between two cousinly groups, the Pāṇḍava brothers and Kaurava brothers. Chiefly about *kṣatriya dharma*, the basic text was composed between 100 BCE and 100 CE. As they were orally transmitted bardic poems they continued to change up until the fourth century CE. The centrality of *kṣatriya dharma*, the duty of the warrior, placed in both the *Mahābhārata* and the *Rāmāyaṇa* (another Hindu epic tale) reveals the links between the political and the theological. Both also play essential roles in the development and popularization of Hindu theism, specifically Vaiṣṇava theism.

The story concerns a dispute about the succession of rule over the kingdom first begun by Vicitravīrya. Vicitravīrya had two sons, Pāṇḍu and Dhṛtarāṣṭra. Dhṛtarāṣṭra, born blind, was unable to assume the throne and so Pāṇḍu does. After Pāṇḍu dies Dhṛtarāṣṭra reclaims the throne and the five sons of Pāṇḍu,[1] known collectively as the Pāṇḍavas – namely Yudhiṣṭhira, Bhīma, Arjuna, Nakula, and Sahadeva – are raised along with their 100 cousins, the sons of Dhṛtarāṣṭra, known collectively as the Kauravas. Problems arise when Duryodhana, the oldest son of Dhṛtarāṣṭra, claims to be the legitimate heir to the throne and begins a dispute with his cousins. Although Dhṛtarāṣṭra divides the kingdom in two, the conflict persists and Yudhiṣṭhira (ironically, the son of *Dharma*) loses his half of the kingdom to his Kaurava cousins in a fixed dice game. In the process, Draupadī, the common wife of all five brothers, is also gambled and lost by Yudhiṣṭhira, and subsequently humiliated by her Kaurava relatives. The dice play continues and Yudhiṣṭhira once again loses though the consequence is that the Pāṇḍavas are to be exiled from the kingdom for 12 years, and must spend the thirteenth year undetected and undercover. In the fourteenth year the Pāṇḍavas return and the battle for the kingdom begins. With Kṛṣṇa on their side they prepare for a war that is to last for 18 days. Just as the war is about to begin, when both the Pāṇḍava and Kaurava armies are arrayed on the battle field of the Kurus, Arjuna, dejected, speaks to Kṛṣṇa, who is both an *avatāra* of Viṣṇu and Arjuna's charioteer, about the *dharma* of battling one's relatives. This dialogue that ensues is the *Bhagavad Gītā*. The war is dreadful and all of the Kauravas are killed. Despite winning, Yudhiṣṭhira abdicates and leaves for Indra's heaven along with his brothers and their wife Draupadī. All die in transit other than Yudhiṣṭhira who is followed by a lone dog. When invited to go to heaven, Yudhiṣṭhira stipulates that he would accept, though only if accompanied by the dog who has been a *bhakta*, devotee. The dog, surprisingly, is *Dharma* himself. Although his brothers achieved heaven given that they have followed their *dharma* as *kṣatriyas*, it is denied to Yudhiṣṭhira who has been affectionate towards the dog, and thus attached to earthly and mundane matters.

The *Mahābhārata* is a frame story and is filled with other embedded stories that are well known in the South Asian context. These include the story of the *apsara* Śakuntala that was also told by the poet Kalidāsa as one of his most well-known plays. These narratives, as well as the larger narrative of the cousinly conflict, are popular in India and are the sources for plays and oral recitations.[2] The *Mahābhārata*, like the *Rāmāyaṇa*, was an immensely popular 94-episode TV series directed by B. R. Chopra that was shown from 1988 to 1990. Additionally, Director Peter Brook filmed a version of the *Mahābhārata* in 1989 with an international set of actors and actresses.

The first section, 2.27.58–2.27.64, included is from *Sabhāparvan, The Book of the Assembly Hall.* Here the dicing game between Śakuni, uncle of Duryodhana, and Yudhiṣṭhira is described. In the later half of 2.27.58 Yudhiṣṭhira loses everything including himself and, soon after, loses Draupadī. In 2.27.59 Duryodhana insults Draupadī and orders her to be brought before the Kauravas, for whom she is now a slave. She refuses (2.27.60) and debates whether Yudhiṣṭhira even had the right to gamble her, given that he had lost himself first. This motif, about the legitimacy of the bet itself, echoes throughout these sections. In 2.27.61 Duryodhana humiliates Draupadī by forcing her to disrobe, despite the fact that she is menstruating. During the disrobing she miraculously remains clothed. At this time Bhīma vows to drink Duryodhana's blood to avenge her. Draupadī again voices her condemnation of the bet itself in 2.27.62 and in the sections that follow, 2.27.63–65, Dhṛtarāṣṭra offers her boons that she uses to obtain the freedom of her husbands. This is the crucial moment in the plot that sets the Pāṇḍavas and Kauravas hurtling towards battle.

The second section called "The Drilling Woods" (3.44.295–3.44.299) is from the *Āraṇyakaparvan, The Book of the Forest.* In the first portion of this account (3.44.295–3.44.297), the Pāṇḍavas, other than Yudhiṣṭhira, are each poisoned by a *yakṣa*, a spirit. The *yakṣa* poisons them when they ignore his requirement that they answer a series of riddles before drinking the water from a lake. Crazed with thirst, each of the brothers disregards the warning of the *yakṣa*, and faces the fatal consequences. Yudhiṣṭhira does not follow their fate and answers the *yakṣa*'s clever puzzles (3.44.297) just as does Sophocles' Oedipus when he answers the riddle of the Sphinx. After answering all of the questions successfully he is granted a wish to revive one brother and Yudhiṣṭhira chooses Nakula. The *yakṣa* then reveals itself to be the god *Dharma* to Yudhiṣṭhira.

The last selection, "The Temptation of Karṇa" (5.55.138–148) from the *Mahābhārata* included here is from the *Udyogaparvan, The Book of the Effort.* The story centers upon Karṇa, the first son of Kuntī (mother of the Pāṇḍavas). Karṇa was born from the union of Kuntī and the god Sūrya. After giving birth to him, the unmarried Kuntī abandons Karṇa and has her virginity restored to her by Sūrya. Karṇa is later adopted by Adhiratha, a charioteer, and Rādhā, his wife, and raised with no knowledge of his *kṣatriya* heritage. He is later befriended by the Kauravas and takes their side in the battle with the Pāṇḍavas.

In an emotional conversation, Karṇa learns of his birth from Kṛṣṇa who advises him to embrace his Pāṇḍava past and relinquish his Kaurava identity (5.55.138). Karṇa replies that his loyalties lie with the Kauravas rather than the Pāṇḍavas since his mother Kuntī abandoned him (5.55.139). Kṛṣṇa and Karṇa then talk about the terrible war that is about to ensue (5.55.140–5.55.141). The scene changes and now Kuntī decides to confront Karṇa with the truth of his birth in order to prevent the imminent bloodshed (5.55.142). In this poignant and agonizing scene, she meets Karṇa and asks him to accept and to embrace his brothers. He refuses but promises to kill no brother other than his chief rival Arjuna (5.55.143–5.55.144). Sections 5.55.145–5.55.147 are discussions among the Kauravas about the looming war and conversations about the dynasty itself.

Notes

1 His sons are actually fathered by gods.

2 Joyce Burkhalter Flueckiger and Laurie J. Sears (eds.), *Boundaries of the Text: Epic Performances in South and Southeast Asia*. Ann Arbor, MI: University of Michigan Press, 1991.

Further reading

Brockington, John, *The Sanskrit Epics*. Leiden: Brill, 1998.

Brockington, John, "The Sanskrit Epics" in G. Flood (ed.), *A Blackwell Companion to Hinduism*. Oxford: Blackwell Publishing, 2003.

Flueckiger, Joyce Burkhalter and Laurie J. Sears (eds.), *Boundaries of the Text: Epic Performances in South and Southeast Asia*. Ann Arbor, MI: University of Michigan Press, 1991.

Goldman, Robert P., *Gods, Priests, and Warrior: The Bhṛgus of the Mahābhārata*. New York: Columbia University Press, 1977.

Hiltebeitel, Alf, *The Cult of Draupadī*. Chicago: University of Chicago Press, 1988.

Hiltebeitel, Alf, *The Ritual of Battle: Krishna in the Mahābhārata*. Albany, NY: State University of New York Press, 1990.

Hiltebeitel, Alf, Rethinking the *Mahābhārata: A Reader's Guide to the Education of the Dharma King*. Chicago: University of Chicago Press, 2001.

Hopkins, Edward Washburn, *The Great Epic of India: Its Character and Origin*. New Haven: Yale University Press, 1920.

Katz, Ruth Cecily, *Arjuna in the Mahabharata: Where Krishna Is, There Is Victory.* Delhi: Motilal Banarsidass, 1990.

McGrath, Kevin, *The Sanskrit Hero: Karna in Epic Mahābhārata*. Leiden: Brill, 2004.

Sharma, Arvind (ed.), *Essays on the Mahābhārata*. Leiden: E. J. Brill, 1991.

Woods, Julian F., *Destiny and Human Initiative in the Mahābhārata*. Albany, NY: State University of New York Press, 2001.

The *Mahābhārata*

The Dicing

Śakuni said:

58.1 You have lost vast wealth of the Pāṇḍavas, Yudhiṣṭhira. Tell me what wealth you have left, Kaunteya, what you have not yet lost!

Yudhiṣṭhira said:

I know of untold riches that I possess, Saubala. But, Śakuni, pray, why do you ask about my wealth? Myriad, ton, million, crore, a hundred million, a billion, a hundred thousand crores, an ocean count of drops I can stake! That is my stake, king, play me for it!

Vaiśaṃpāyana said:

At these words Śakuni decided, tricked, and cried "Won!" at Yudhiṣṭhira.

Yudhiṣṭhira said:

5 I have countless cattle and horses and milch cows and sheep and goats, whatever belongs to our color of people east of the Indus, Saubala. That is my stake, king, I play you for it!

Vaiśaṃpāyana said:

At these words Śakuni decided, tricked, and cried "Won!" at Yudhiṣṭhira.

Yudhiṣṭhira said:

My city, my country, the wealth of all my people, excepting brahmins, all my people themselves, excepting brahmins, are the wealth I have left, king. That is my stake, king, I play you for it!

Vaiśaṃpāyana said:

At these words Śakuni decided, tricked, and cried "Won!" at Yudhiṣṭhira.

Yudhiṣṭhira said:

Here are the ornaments with which the princes glitter, the earrings and breastplates and all the adornment of their bodies. That is my stake, king, I play you for it!

Vaiśaṃpāyana said:

10 At these words Śakuni decided, tricked, and cried "Won!" at Yudhiṣṭhira.

Yudhiṣṭhira said:

This dark youth with the bloodshot eyes and the lion shoulders and the large arms, this Nakula and all he owns shall be one throw.

Śakuni said:

But Prince Nakula is dear to you, King Yudhiṣṭhira! If we win this stake, what more do you have to gamble?

Vaiśaṃpāyana said:

Having said this, Śakuni addressed those dice and cried "Won!" at Yudhiṣṭhira.

Yudhiṣṭhira said:

This Sahadeva preaches the Laws,
And has in the world earned the name of a scholar:
For this loving prince who does not deserve it,
I play with you like an enemy!

Vaiśaṃpāyana said:

15 At these words Śakuni decided, tricked, and cried "Won!" at Yudhiṣṭhira.

Śakuni said:

I have now won, king, these two dear sons of Mādrī. Yet methinks Bhīmasena and Arjuna are dearer to you.

Yudhiṣṭhira said:

Surely this is an Unlaw that you are perpetrating, without looking to propriety! You want to pluck us like flowers!

Śakuni said:

A drunk falls into a hole, a distracted man walks into a tree trunk, you are our elder and better, king – farewell to you, bull of the Bharatas! When gamblers play, Yudhiṣṭhira, they prattle like madmen of things they have not seen asleep or awake!

Yudhiṣṭhira said:

20 Like a ferry he carried us over in battle,
Defeater of foes, a prince of vigor;
For this world hero who does not deserve it,
For Phalguna I play you, Śakuni!

Excerpts from J. A. B. van Buitenen (tr.), *The Mahābhārata* (Books 2, 3, 4, and 5). Chicago: University of Chicago Press, 1975.

Vaiśaṃpāyana said:
At these words Śakuni decided, tricked, and cried "Won!" at Yudhiṣṭhira.

Śakuni said:

Here I have won the Pāṇḍavas' bowman,
The left-handed archer, of Pāṇḍu the son!
Now gamble, O king, your beloved Bhīma,
If that's what you, Pāṇḍava, have left to throw!

Yudhiṣṭhira said:

Who led us, who guided us to the battle,
Like the Thunderbolt-wielder the Dānavas' foe,
Looking down, great-spirited, knitting his brow,
With a lion's shoulders and lasting wrath.

Whose equal in might is nowhere to be found,
The first of club warriors, enemy-killer –
For this good prince who does not deserve it
I play you, king, for Bhīmasena!

Vaiśaṃpāyana said:
25 At these words Śakuni decided, tricked, and cried "Won!" at Yudhiṣṭhira.
Śakuni said:
You have lost great wealth, you have lost your brothers, your horses and elephants. Now tell me, Kaunteya, if you have anything left to stake!
Yudhiṣṭhira said:
I myself am left, dearly loved by all my brothers. When won, we shall slave for you to our perdition.
Vaiśaṃpāyana said:
At these words Śakuni decided, tricked, and cried "Won!" at Yudhiṣṭhira.
Śakuni said:
This is the worst you could have done, losing yourself! If there is something left to stake, it is evil to stake oneself!
Vaiśaṃpāyana said:
30 Thus spoke the man so dexterous at dicing, who had won in the gaming all those brothers arrayed there, the champions of the world, each with one throw.
Śakuni said:
Yet there is your precious queen, and one throw is yet unwon. Stake Kṛṣṇā of Pāñcāla, and win yourself back with her!
Yudhiṣṭhira said:
35 She is not too short or too tall, not too black or too red, and her eyes are red with love – I play you for her! Eyes like the petals of autumn lotuses, a fragrance as of autumn lotuses, a beauty that waits on autumn lotuses – the peer of the Goddess of Fortune! Yes, for her lack of cruelty, for the fullness of her body, for the straightness of her character does a man desire a woman. Last she lies down who was the first to wake up, who knows what was done or left undone, down to the cowherds and goatherds. Her sweaty lotuslike face shines like a lotus. Her waist shaped like an altar, hair long, eyes the color of copper, not too much body hair ... such is the woman, king, such is the slender-waisted Pāñcālī, for whom I now throw, the beautiful Draupadī! Come on, Saubala!
Vaiśaṃpāyana said:
40 When the King Dharma had spoken this word, Bhārata, the voices that were raised by the elders spelled of "Woe! Woe!" The hall itself shook, king, and talk started among the kings. Bhiṣma, Droṇa, Kṛpa, and others broke out in sweat. Vidura buried his face in his hands and looked as though he had fainted; he sat, head down, brooding, wheezing like a snake. But Dhṛtarāṣṭra, exhilarated, kept asking, "Has he won, has he won?" for he did not keep his composure. Karṇa, Duḥśāsana, and their cronies were mightily pleased, but of others in the hall the tears flowed freely. But Saubala, without hesitation, with the glow of the winner and high with passion, again addressed the dice and cried, "We have won!"

Duryodhana said:

59.1 All right, you Steward, bring Draupadī,
The beloved wife whom the Pāṇḍavas honor,
Let her sweep the house and run on our errands –
What a joy to watch! – with the serving wenches!

Vidura said:

The incredible happens through people like you,
You don't know it, nitwit, you are tied in a noose!
You hang over a chasm and do not grasp it,
You dumb deer to anger tigers!

You are carrying poisonous snakes on your head, their pouches full of venom! Don't infuriate them, fool, lest you go to Yama! Kṛṣṇā is not a slave yet, Bhārata! I think she was staked when the king was no longer his own master.

5 Dhṛtarāṣṭra's son the prince bears fruit,
Like the bamboo, only to kill himself:
He is ripe for death, but he fails to see
That dicing leads to a dangerous feud.

Be never hurtful or speak cruelly,
Nor extort the last from a penniless man,
Nor speak the wounding, hell-earning words
That when voiced hurt another man.

Those words beyond need fly from the mouth,
And the one they hurt grieves day and night:
Those words that strike where the other hurts
No wise man will loose on another man.

For this goat, they say, dug up a knife,
When a knife was missing, by pawing the ground.
It became a means to cut its own throat:
So dig up no feud with Pāṇḍu's sons!

They don't speak either good or ill
Of the forest-dweller or householder,
But of the ascetic of mature wisdom,
The same people bark like the curs they are.

10 This dreadful crooked door tilts toward hell
You know it not, Dhṛtarāṣṭra's son;
There are many will follow you down that road,
Now the game has been won, with Duḥśasana!

The gourds will sink and the rocks will float,
And the ships will forever be lost on the seas.
Before the fool prince, Dhṛtarāṣṭra's son,
Will lend his ear to my apt words!

For this to be sure spells the end of the Kurus,
A grisly end, the perdition of all.
The words of the sage, so apt, and his friends
Are no longer heard, and greed just grows!

Vaiśaṃpāyana said:

60.1 "A plague on the Steward," he said and rose,
Maddened with pride, Dhṛtarāṣṭra's son,
And he looked at his usher in the hall
And to him he spoke amidst those grandees,

"Go, usher, and bring me Draupadī here!
You have nothing to fear from the Pāṇḍavas.
The Steward is timid and speaks against it,
But never did he wish that *we* should prosper!"

The usher, a bard, at his master's word
Went quickly out upon hearing the king,
And he entered, a dog in a lion's den,
Crawling up to the Queen of the Pāṇḍavas.

The usher said:

Yudhiṣṭhira, crazed by the dicing game,
Has lost you to Duryodhana, Draupadī.
Come enter the house of Dhṛtarāṣṭra,
To your chores I must lead you, Yājñasenī!

Draupadī said:

5 How dare you speak so, an usher, to me?
What son of a king would hazard his wife?
The king is befooled and crazed by the game –
Was there nothing left for him to stake?

The usher said:

When nothing was left for him to stake,
Ajātaśatru wagered you.
Already the king had thrown for his brothers,
And then for himself – then, Princess, for you.

Draupadī said:
Then go to the game and, son of a bard, ask in the assembly, "Bhārata, whom did you lose first, yourself or me?" When you have found out, come and take me, son of a bard!

Vaiśaṃpāyana said:
He went to the hall and asked Draupadī's question. "As the owner of whom did you lose us?" so queries Draupadī. "Whom did you lose first, yourself or me?" But Yudhiṣṭhira did not stir, as though he had lost consciousness, and made no reply to the bard, whether good or ill.

Duryodhana said:

10 Let Kṛṣṇā of the Pāñcālas come here and ask the question herself. All the people here shall hear what she or he has to say.

Vaiśaṃpāyana said:

As he was in Duryodhana's service, the usher, who was the son of a bard, went to the king's lodgings and, as though shuddering, said to Draupadī,

The men in the hall are summoning, Princess!
Methinks that the fall of the Kurus has come.
That fool will not protect our fortunes
If *you* have to come to the hall, O Princess.

Draupadī said:

That is how he disposes, the All-Disposer,
Both touches touch the sage and the fool:
He said, "In this world only Law is supreme":
He shall bring us peace when the Law is obeyed!

Vaiśaṃpāyana said:

15 But Yudhiṣṭhira, on hearing what Duryodhana wanted to do, sent an acceptable messenger to Draupadī, O bull of the Bhāratas. In her one garment, knotted below, weeping and in her courses, she went to the hall, the Pāñcāla princess, and stood before her father-in-law.

Watching the courtiers' faces, the Prince
Duryodhana said gleefully to the bard,
"Bring her here, good usher, right here on this spot,
So the Kauravas may speak up to her face!"

So the *sūta* who was in Duryodhana's service,
But afraid of the wrath of the Drupada Princess,
Shed all his pride and asked the assembled,
"Who am I to speak to a Draupadī?"

Duryodhana said:

Duḥśāsana, he is a fool, this bard's son,
He is terrified of the Wolf-Belly!
Fetch and bring yourself Yajñasena's daughter,
How can our powerless rivals prevent you?

Vaiśaṃpāyana said:

Thereupon the son of the king rose up,
On hearing his brother, eyes reddened with wrath,
And entered the dwelling of those great warriors,
And he said to Draupadī, daughter of kings,

20 "All right now, come, Pāñcālī, you're won!
Look upon Duryodhana, without shame!
You shall now love the Kurus, long-lotus-eyed one,
You've been won under Law, come along to the hall!"

In bleak spirits did she rise,
And wiped with her hand her pallid face.
In despair she ran where the women sat
Of the aged king, the bull of the Kurus.

And quickly the angry Duḥśāsana
Came rushing to her with a thunderous roar;
By the long-tressed black and flowing hair
Duḥśāsana grabbed the wife of a king.

The hair that at the concluding bath
Of the king's consecration had been sprinkled
With pure-spelled water, Dhṛtarāṣṭra's son
Now caressed with force, unmanning the Pāṇḍus.

Duḥśāsana, stroking her, led her and brought her,
That Kṛṣṇā of deep black hair, to the hall,
As though unprotected amidst her protectors,
And tossed her as wind tosses a plantain tree.

25 And as she was dragged, she bent her body
And whispered softly, "It is now my month!
This is my sole garment, man of slow wit,
You cannot take me to the hall, you churl!"

But using his strength and holding her down,
By her deep black locks, he said to Kṛṣṇā,
"To Kṛṣṇa and Jiṣṇu, to Hari and Nara,
Cry out for help! I shall take you yet!

"Sure, you be in your month, Yajñasena's daughter,
Or wear a lone cloth, or go without one!
You've been won at the game and been made a slave,
And one lechers with slaves as the fancy befalls!"

Her hair disheveled, her half skirt drooping,
Shaken about by Duhśāsana,
Ashamed and burning with indignation,
She whispered again, and Kṛṣṇā said,

"In the hall are men who have studied the books,
All follow the rites and are like unto Indras.

They are all my *gurus* or act for them:
Before their eyes I cannot stand thus!

30 "You ignoble fool of cruel feats,
Don't render me nude, do not debase me!
These sons of kings will not condone you,
Were Indra and Gods to be your helpmates!

"The king, son of Dharma, abides by the Law,
And the Law is subtle, for the wise to find
out:
But even at his behest I would not
Give the least offense and abandon my virtue.

"It is *base* that amidst the Kaurava heroes
You drag me inside while I am in my month;
There is no one here to honor you for it,
Though surely they do not mind your plan.

"Damnation! Lost to the Bhāratas
Is their Law and the ways of sagacious barons,
When all these Kauravas in their hall
Watch the Kuru Law's limits overstridden!

"There is no mettle in Droṇa and Bhīṣma,
Nor to be sure in this good man;
The chiefs of the elders amongst the Kurus
Ignore this dread Unlaw of this king."

35 As she piteously spoke the slim-waisted queen
Threw a scornful glance at her furious
husbands
And inflamed with the fall of her sidelong
glances,
The Pāṇḍavas, wrapped with wrath in their
limbs.

Not the kingdom lost, nor the riches looted,
Nor the precious jewels plundered did hurt
As hurt that sidelong glance of Kṛṣṇā,
That glance of Kṛṣṇā sent in fury.

Duḥśāsana, though, watched only Kṛṣṇā
Who was looking down on her wretched lords,
And shaking her wildly – she was close to
fainting –
Cried cruelly "Slave!" and laughed aloud.

And Karṇa applauded his word to the full
And heartily laughing acknowledged it,
And Subala's son, king of Gāndhāra,
Likewise cheered on Duḥśāsana.

Apart from these two and Duryodhana,
All other men who sat in the hall,
On seeing Kṛṣṇā dragged into the hall,
Were filled with misery beyond measure.

Bhīṣma said:

40 As the Law is subtle, my dear, I fail
To resolve your riddle the proper way:
A man without property cannot stake
another's –
But given that wives are the husband's chattels?

Yudhiṣṭhira may give up all earth
With her riches, before he'd give up the truth.
The Pāṇḍava said, "I have been won,"
Therefore I cannot resolve this doubt.

No man is Śakuni's peer at the dice,
And he left Yudhiṣṭhira his own choice.
The great-spirited man does not think he was
cheating,
Therefore I cannot speak to the riddle.

Draupadī said:

In the meeting hall he was challenged, the
king,
By cunning, ignoble, and evil tricksters
Who love to game; he had never much tried it.
Why then do you say he was left a choice?

Pure, the best of Kurus and Pāṇḍavas,
He did not wake up to the playing of tricks,
He attended the session and when he'd
lost all,
Only then he agreed to hazard me.

45 They stand here, the Kurus, they stand in
their hall,
Proud owners of sons and daughters-in-law:
Examine ye all this word of mine,
And resolve my riddle the proper way!

Vaiśampāyana said:

So she piteously spoke and flowing with
tears
Kept looking at those who were her
husbands;
Meanwhile Duḥśāsana said many words
That were bitter and mean and none that were
gentle.

The Wolf-Belly looked and watched how she
Was dragged, in her courses, with upper cloth
drooping,
Who so little deserved it, in desperate pain;
He looked at his brother and gave voice to
his rage.

Bhīma said:

61.1 There are a lot of whores in the country of gamblers, Yudhiṣṭhira, but they never throw for them, for they have pity even for women of that stripe. The tribute that the king of the Kāśis brought and all our vast wealth, the gems that the other kings of the earth brought in, the mounts and prizes, the armor and weaponry, the kingdom, yourself and we have all been staked and lost to others. This I didn't mind much, for you are the master of all we possess. But you went too far, I think, when you staked Draupadī. She did not deserve this! After she had won Pāṇḍavas as a girl, she is now because of you plagued by Kauravas, mean and cruel tricksters! It is because of her that I hurl my fury at you! I shall burn off your arms! Sahadeva! Bring the fire!

Arjuna said:

5 Never before have you said words like these, Bhīmasena! Surely your respect for the Law has been destroyed by our harsh enemies! Don't fall in with the enemy's plans, obey your highest Law: no one may overreach his eldest brother by Law. The king was challenged by his foes, and, remembering the baronial Law, he played at the enemy's wish. *That* is our great glory!

Bhīmasena said:

10 If I'd thought he'd done it for his own glorification, I'd have forced his arms together and burned them in the blazing fire, Dhanaṃjaya!

Vaiśaṃpāyana said:

15 Hereupon, seeing the grief of the Pāṇḍavas and the torment of Pāñcāli, Vikarṇa, a son of Dhṛtarāṣṭra's, spoke out: "Ye kings! Answer the question that Yajñasena's daughter has asked! We must decide or we shall go to hell! Bhīṣma and Dhṛtarāṣṭra are the eldest of the Kurus; they are here but say nought, nor does the sagacious Vidura. Droṇa Bhāradvāja is here, the teacher of us all, and so is Kṛpa, yet even they, most eminent of brahmins, do not speak to the question! All the other kings, assembled here from every horizon, should shed all partisan feelings and speak up as they think. Consider the question that the beautiful Draupadī has raised repeatedly, kings, and whatever your side, make your answer!"

20 Thus did he speak many times to all the men who were sitting in the hall, but none of the kings said aught, whether good or bad. Vikarṇa spoke again and again to all those kings, and sighing, kneading his hands, he finally said, "Make your answer, kings, or do not. But I shall tell you, Kaurava, what I think is right in this matter. Ye best of men, they recount four vices that are the curse of a king: hunting, drinking, dicing, and fornicating. A man with those addictions abandons the Law, and the world does not condone his immoderate deeds. The Pāṇḍava was under the sway of his vice when the gamblers challenged him and he staked Draupadī. The innocent woman is held in common by all the Pāṇḍavas, and the Pāṇḍava staked her when he already had gambled away his own freedom. It was Saubala who mentioned Kṛṣṇā when he wanted a stake. Considering all this I do not think she has been won."

25–30 When they heard this, there was a loud outcry from the men in the hall as they praised Vikarṇa and condemned Saubala. When the noise died down, the son of Rādhā, fairly fainting with fury, grasped his shining arm and said, "Are there not many mockeries of the truth found in Vikarṇa? As the fire burns the block from which it was drilled, so the fire he generates will lead to his perdition! All these men here have failed to reply despite Kṛṣṇā's urging. I hold that Draupadī has been won, and so do they hold. You are torn to pieces by your own folly, Dhārtarāṣṭra, for, still a child, you announce in the assembly what should be said by your elders. A younger brother of Duryodhana's, you do not know the true facts of the Law, if you stupidly maintain that Kṛṣṇā, who has been won, has not in fact been won. How, son of Dhṛarāṣṭra, can you hold that Kṛṣṇā has not been won when the eldest Pāṇḍava staked all he owned in the assembly hall? Draupadī is part of all he owns, bull of the Bharatas, then how can you hold that Kṛṣṇā, won by Law, has not been won? Draupadī was mentioned by name and the

Pāṇḍavas allowed her to be staked – then by what reasoning do you hold that she has not been won?

35 "Or if you think that it was against the Law to bring her into the hall clad in one piece of clothing, listen to what I have to say in reply to that. The Gods have laid down that a woman shall have one husband, scion of Kuru. *She* submits to many men and assuredly is a whore! Thus there is, I think, nothing strange about taking her into the hall, or to have her in one piece of clothing, or for that matter naked! She, the Pāṇḍava's wealth, and the Pāṇḍavas themselves have all been won by Saubala here according to the Law.

"Duḥśāsana, this Vikarṇa is only a child, blabbing of wisdom! Strip the clothes from the Pāṇḍavas and Draupadī!"

40–45 Hearing this, all the Pāṇḍavas shed their upper clothes and sat down in the assembly hall. Then Duḥśāsana forcibly laid hold of Draupadī's robe, O king, and in the midst of the assembly began to undress her. But when her skirt was being stripped off, lord of the people, another similar skirt appeared every time. A terrible roar went up from all the kings, a shout of approval, as they watched that greatest wonder on earth. And in the midst of the kings Bhīma, lips trembling with rage, kneading hand in hand, pronounced a curse in a mighty voice: "Take to heart this word of mine, ye barons that live on this earth, a word such as never has been spoken before nor any one shall ever speak hereafter! May I forfeit my journey to all my ancestors, if I do not carry out what I say, if I not tear open in battle the chest of this misbegotten fiend, this outcaste of the Bharatas, and drink his blood!"

50 When they heard this curse, which exhilarated all the world, they offered him much homage and reviled Dhṛtarāṣṭra's son. A pile of clothes was heaped up in the middle of the hall, when Duḥśāsana, tired and ashamed, at last desisted and sat down. The gods among men in the hall raised the hair-raising cry of "Fie!" as they watched the sons of Kuntī. The people shouted, "The Kauravyas refuse to answer the question," and condemned Dhṛtarāṣṭra.

Thereupon, raising his arms and stopping the crowd in the hall, Vidura, who knew all the Laws, made his speech.

Vidura said:

55 Draupadī, having raised the question, now weeps piteously as though she has none left to protect her. If you do not resolve it, men in this hall, the Law will be offended. The man who comes to the hall with a grievance is like a blazing fire: the men in the hall must appease him with true Law. If a man comes with a grievance and raises a question of Law with the men in the hall, they must resolve the question and shed all partiality. Vikarṇa has answered the question according to his lights, kings of men; you too must speak to the question according to yours. If a person sits in the hall and fails to answer a question, although he sees the Law, he incurs half the guilt that accrues if the answer is false. And he who has gone to the hall, knows the Law, yet resolves it falsely, certainly incurs the full guilt of the falsehood. On this they quote this ancient story, the exchange between Prahlāda and the Hermit, Angiras' son.

60 Prahlāda, you know, was the king of the Daityas; his son was Virocana, who ran into Sudhanvan Āngirasa over a girl. Their desire for the girl made each aver that he was the better man, and, so we have heard, they made a wager and staked their lives. They argued the question and asked Prahlāda, "Which of us is the better man? Resolve the question and do not speak falsely!" Frightened by the quarrel, he looked at Sudhanvan, and Sudhanvan furiously said to him, burning as Brahmā's staff, "If you speak falsely, Prahlāda, or if you fail to speak, the Thunderbolt-wielder shall blow your head to a hundred pieces with his bolt!" At Sudhanvan's words the Daitya trembled like an *aśvattha* leaf, and he went to Kaśyapa to question that most august sage.

65 *Prahlāda said:*

You are wise in the Law, both in that of the Gods and that of the Asuras. Now listen, great sage, to a question of brahmin Law. Tell me at my bidding what worlds hereafter may that man expect who fails to decide a question of Law or gives the wrong answer?

Kaśyapa said:

70–75 He who knows the answer but either from love, anger, or fear fails to resolve the question lets loose on himself a thousand of Varuṇa's nooses; and for every noose to be loosened takes a year. Therefore say the truth straightaway, if you know the truth! Where a Law comes to the hall pierced by Unlaw and they do not pull out the thorn, there it will pierce the men in the hall. The leader takes half, the culprit has a quarter, and the last quarter goes to those in the hall who do not condemn the culprit. The leader is guiltless, the men in the hall are freed, and the blame goes to the culprit, if the culprit is condemned. But they who explain the Law falsely, Prahlāda, to the one who brings the question, kill their own offerings and oblations for seven generations upward and downward. The grievance of the man whose property has been stolen, of the man whose son has been killed, of a man against a debtor, of one who has been mulcted by a king, of a wife deserted by her husband, of a man dropped from a caravan, of a bigamist's wife or a man beaten before witnesses, these grievances, so the lords the Thirty Gods say, are equal. And all these grievances a man incurs who judges falsely. As a witness is held to be the one who sees or hears a misdeed in his presence, a witness who speaks the truth is not hurt in his Law or his Profit.

Vidura said:

Having heard Kaśyapa's word, Prahlāda said to his son, "Sudhanvan is better than you, as Angiras is better than I. Sudhanvan's mother is better than yours, Virocana. Sudhanvan is now the master of your life."

Sudhanvan said:

You relinquish your love for your son to stand firm on the Law – set free your son, may he live for a hundred years!

Vidura said:

80 Thus you have heard the ultimate Law, ye all who are sitting in the hall. Now ponder what should be done in response to Kṛṣṇā's question!

Vaiśaṃpāyana said:

Even upon hearing Vidura's words the kings failed to speak. But Karṇa said to Duḥśāsana, "Take this slave wench Kṛṣṇā to the house!" Duḥśāsana, in the hall, dragged away the trembling and ashamed woman who miserably complained to the Pāṇḍavas.

Draupadī said:

62.1 I have a duty that is more pressing, which I could not perform before, confused as I was by this strong man who dragged me about forcibly. I must greet my betters in the assembly of the Kurus! Let it not be my fault, if I did not do this before!

Vaiśaṃpāyana said:

He dragged her onward, and, wretched with misery, she fell to the ground. Unused to such treatment she lamented in the assembly –

Draupadī said:

5–10 I on whom the assembled kings set eye in the arena at my Bridegroom Choice, but never before or after, I am now brought into the hall! I whom neither wind nor sun have seen before in my house, I am now seen in the middle of the hall in the assembly of the Kurus. I whom the Pāṇḍavas did not suffer to be touched by the wind in my house before, they now allow to be touched by this miscreant. The Kurus allow – and methinks that Time is out of joint – their innocent daughter and daughter-in-law to be molested! What greater humiliation than that I, a woman of virtue and beauty, now must invade the men's hall? What is left of the Law of the kings? From of old, we have heard, they do *not* bring law-minded women into their hall. This ancient eternal Law is lost among the Kauravas. How can I, wife of the Pāṇḍus, sister of Dhṛṣṭadyumna Pārṣata, and friend of Vāsudeva, enter the hall of the kings? Is the wife of the King Dharma whose birth matches his a slave or free? Speak, Kauravas. I shall abide by your answer. For this foul man, disgrace of the Kauravas, is molesting me, and I cannot bear it any longer, Kauravas! Whatever the kings think, whether I have been won or not, I want it answered, and I shall abide by the answer, Kauravas.

Bhīṣma said:

15–20 I have said, good woman, that the course of the Law is sovereign. Great-spirited brahmins on earth fail to encompass it. What a powerful man views as Law in the world, that do others call the Law at a time when Law is in question. I cannot answer the question decisively, because the matter is subtle and mysterious as well as grave. Surely the end of this lineage is in sight, for all the Kurus have become so enslaved by greed and folly. Those born in high lineages, do not, good woman, stray from the path of the Law, however beset by disaster, just as you who stand here as our bride. Such is the conduct that you yourself practice, princess of the Pāñcālas, for though you have come to grief, you still look to the Law. Droṇa and the other elders who are wise in the Law sit bent over as though spiritless with empty bodies. But Yudhiṣṭhira, I think, is the authority on this question: let he himself speak out and say whether you have been won or not.

Vaiśaṃpāyana said:

> Upon witnessing all those many events
> And Draupadī screeching, a winged osprey,
> The kings said nought, neither good nor bad,
> For they feared for Dhṛtarāṣṭra's son.
>
> And seeing the sons and grandsons of kings
> Keep silent, the son of Dhṛtarāṣṭra
> Began to smile and said this word
> To the daughter of the Pāñcāla king:
>
> "Let the question now rest with the mettlesome Bhīma,
> With Arjuna and with Sahadeva,
> And your husband Nakula, Draupadī:
> Let them speak the word that you have begotten.
>
> **25** "In the midst of these nobles they must declare
> For thy sake that Yudhiṣṭhira's not thy master,
> And thus they must make King Dharma a liar,
> Pāñcālī, so you escape servitude!
>
> "King Dharma, great-spirited, firm in the Law,
> The peer of Indra, himself must declare
> Whether he owns you or does not own you;
> At his word you must choose, the one or the other.
>
> "For all the Kauravas in the assembly
> Are caught inside your misery:
> They cannot resolve it, the noble-hearted,
> And they look to your unfortunate masters."
>
> The men in the hall all loudly approved
> The word that the king of the Kurus had spoken;
> There were those who cheeringly waved their clothes,
> But also cries of "Woe!" were heard.
> And all the kings in cheerful spirits
> Applauded the Law of the first of the Kurus.

30 All the kings looked at Yudhiṣṭhira, their faces turned sideways: "What will the law-wise prince say? What will the Terrifier say, the Pāṇḍava undefeated in battle? And Bhīmasena and the twins?" thus they wondered, greatly curious. When the noise had died down, Bhīmasena spoke, grasping his broad, sandal-scented arm.

35 "Had Yudhiṣṭhira the King Dharma not been our own *guru* and lord of our family we should never have suffered this! He owns our merit and our austerities, he commands our lives. If he holds himself defeated, so are we defeated. No mortal who walks the earth would have escaped me with his life, for touching the hair of Pāñcālī! Look at my arms, long and round like iron-studded bludgeons: once caught in them not the God of the Hundred Sacrifices could escape from them! But now, like this, tied by the noose of the Law, constrained by his gravity and held back by Arjuna, I wreak no havoc! But if the King Dharma unleashes me, I shall crush the evil band of Dhṛtarāṣṭra with the swordlike flats of my hands, as a lion flattens small game!" And at once Bhīṣma and Droṇa and Vidura spoke: "Bear with it! With you anything is possible!"

Karṇa said:

> **63.1** There are three who own no property,
> A student, a slave, a dependent woman:
> The wife of a slave, you are *his* now, my dear;
> A masterless slave wench, you are now slave wealth!
>
> Come in and serve us with your attentions:
> That is the chore you have left in this house.
> Dhṛtarāṣṭra's men, and not the Pārthas,
> Are now your masters, child of a king!

Now quickly choose you another husband
Who will not gamble your freedom away:
For license with masters is never censured:
That is the slave's rule, remember it!

Won have been Nakula, Bhīmasena,
Yudhiṣṭhira, Sahadeva, Arjuna!
Become a slave, come inside, Yājñasenī!
The ones who are won are no longer your men.

5 What use are now to the Pārtha himself,
His gallantry and his manliness?
In the midst of the hall he has gambled away
The daughter of Drupada, king of Pāñcāla!

Vaiśaṃpāyana said:

Hearing this, Bhīma bore it no longer;
A man tormented, he panted hard;
But avowed to the king and trapped by the Law,
Burning him down with wrath-shot eye,

Bhīma said:

I do not anger at a *sūta*'s son,
For the Law of serfdom is surely upon us:
But could our enemies now have held me,
If you had not thrown for her, my liege?

Vaiśaṃpāyana said:

10–15 When he had heard the words of Rādheya, Prince Duryodhana said to Yudhiṣṭhira, who was sitting silent and mindless, "Bhīma and Arjuna and the twins follow your orders, king. Answer the question, whether you think she has been won!" This he said to the Kaunteya, and crazed by his ascendancy, he took his cloth and looked invitingly at Pāñcālī. Then, smiling up at Rādheya, and taunting Bhīma, he exposed to Draupadī who was watching him his left thigh, soft like a banana tree and auspiciously marked – an elephant trunk and a thunderbolt in one. The Wolf-Belly saw it and, widening his bloodshot eyes, spoke up in the midst of the kings, willing the assembly to listen: "May the Wolf-Belly never share the world of his fathers, if I fail to break that thigh with my club in a great battle!" And as he raged, flames of fire burst forth from all the orifices of his body, as from the hollows of a tree that is on fire.

Vidura said:

Kings! Watch for the ultimate danger from Bhīma!
Kings! Watch it as if it were Varuṇa's noose!
For surely the hostile fate has emerged
That the Gods set of old for the Bhāratas.

This has been an overplay, Dhārtarāṣṭras,
Who fight over a woman in this hall!
Your security now seems much imperiled,
For evil counsels the Kurus now spell.

Kurus, quickly decide on the Law of the case.
If it's wrongly perceived the assembly will suffer.
If this gamester here had staked her before,
He'd have been undefeated and still been her master.

Like a stake that is won in a dream is the stake,
If the stake is put up by one who does not own it!
You have listened to Gāndhārī's son,
Now Kurus, don't run from the Law of the case!

Duryodhana said:

20 I stay with the word of Bhīmasena
And Arjuna's word and the word of the twins:
If they say Yudhiṣṭhira wasn't their master,
Then Yājñasenī, you won't be a slave!

Arjuna said:

The king was our master when first he played us,
Great-spirited Dharma, the son of Kuntī:
But whose master is he who has lost himself?
That you should decide, ye Kurus assembled!

Vaiśaṃpāyana said:

And there in the house of the King Dhṛtarāṣṭra
At the *agnihotra* a jackal barked,
The donkeys, they brayed in response, O king,
And so on all sides the grisly birds.

And Vidura, sage of all portents, listened
To the horrible sound, so did Saubala;
And Bhīṣma and Droṇa and wise Gautama
Made loud declarations of "Peace!" and "Peace!"

Thereupon Gāndhārī and Vidura the wise,
Who both had observed that ghastly omen,
At once unhappily told the king;
Whereupon the king gave voice to his word:

25 "You're lost, Duryodhana, shallow-brain,
Who in this hall of the bulls of the Kurus
Berated a woman most uncouthly,
And her a Draupadī, married by Law!"

Having spoken the wise Dhṛtarāṣṭra withdrew,
For he wished for the weal of his allies-in-law;
Kṛṣṇā Pāñcālī he pacified,
And thinking with insight, informed of the facts,

Dhṛtarāṣṭra said:
Choose a boon from me, Pāñcālī, whatever you wish; for you are to me the most distinguished of my daughters-in-law, bent as you are on the Law!

Draupadī said:
30 If you give me a boon, bull of the Bharatas, I choose this: the illustrious Yudhiṣṭhira, observer of every Law, shall be no slave! Do not let these little boys, who do not know my determined son, say of Prativindhya when he happens to come in, "Here comes the son of a slave!" He has been a *king*'s son, as no man has been anywhere. Spoiled as he is, he shall die, Bhārata, when he finds out that he has been a slave's son!

Dhṛtarāṣṭra said:
I give you a second boon, good woman, ask me! My heart has convinced me that you do not deserve only a single boon.

Draupadī said:
With their chariots and bows I choose Bhīmasena and Dhanaṃjaya, Nakula and Sahadeva, as my second boon!

Dhṛtarāṣṭra said:
Choose a third boon from us; two boons do not honor you enough. For of all of my daughters-in-law you are the best, for you walk in the Law.

Draupadī said:
35 Greed kills Law, Sir, I cannot make another wish. I am not worthy to take a third boon from you, best of kings. As they say, the commoner has one boon, the baron and his lady two, but three are the king's, great king, and a hundred the brahmin's. They were laid low, my husbands, but they have been saved: and they will find the good things, king, with their own good acts!

Karṇa said:
64.1 Of all the women of mankind, famous for their beauty, of whom we have heard, no one have we heard accomplished such a deed! While the Pārthas and the Dhārtarāṣṭras are raging beyond measure, Kṛṣṇā Draupadī has become the salvation of the Pāṇḍavas! When they were sinking, boatless and drowning, in the plumbless ocean, the Pāñcālī became the Pāṇḍavas' boat, to set them ashore!

Vaiśaṃpāyana said:
5 Hearing this amidst the Kurus, that a woman had become the refuge of the sons of Pāṇḍu, resentful Bhīmasena said glumly, "Devala has declared that there are three stars in man – offspring, deeds, and knowledge; for creatures live on through them. When the body has become impure, void of life, emptied, and cast off by the kinsmen, it is these three that survive of a man. Our light has been darkened, for our wife has been defiled, Dhanaṃjaya: how can offspring be born from one defiled?"

Arjuna said:
Bhāratas never babble of the insults, spoken or unspoken, from a lower man. The best people always remember only the good acts, not the hostilities they have been shown, acknowledging them because they have confidence in themselves.

Bhīma said:
10 I shall here and now kill all the enemies that have assembled! Or you go outside, Bhārata, lord among the kings, and cut them to their roots! What is the use for us to argue here, why suffer, Bhārata? I am going to kill them here and now, and you sway this world!

Vaiśaṃpāyana said:
When Bhīmasena had spoken, surrounded by his younger brothers like a lion amidst deer, he kept glancing at his club. While the Pārtha of unsullied deeds sought to appease and cool him off, the powerful strong-armed Bhīma began to sweat with his inner heat. From the ears and the other orifices of the raging man fire issued forth, smoking and sparking. His face became fierce to behold, with its folds of knitted brows, as the face of Yama himself when the end of the

Eon has come. Yudhiṣṭhira restrained the strong-armed Bhīma with his arm, O Bhārata. "Don't!" he said. "Stay quiet!" And when he had restrained the strong-armed man, whose eyes were bloodshot with rage, Yudhiṣṭhira went up to his father Dhṛtarāṣṭra and folded his hands.

Yudhiṣṭhira said:

65.1 King, what should we do? Command us, you are our master. For we always wish to obey your behest, Bhārata.

Dhṛtarāṣṭra said:

Ajātaśatru, good luck to you! Go ye in peace and comfort. I give you my leave: rule your own kingdom with your own treasures. But keep in mind this admonition that I, an old man, utter; I have thought it through with my mind, as it is proper and beneficent above all.

5 Yudhiṣṭhira, my wise son, you know the subtle course of the Laws, you are courteous and you attend to your elders. Where there is wisdom there is serenity: become serene, Bhārata. An ax does not sink in if it is not on wood, but on wood it cuts. The best among men do not remember hostilities; they see the virtues, not the faults, and they do not stoop to enmity. It is the lowliest that hurl insults in a quarrel, Yudhiṣṭhira; the middling ones return the insults, but the best and the steady ones never babble about hostile insults, spoken or unspoken. The good only remember the good that was done, not the hostile deeds, acknowledging it because they have confidence in themselves.

10 You have behaved nobly in this meeting of good people, therefore, my son, do not brood in your heart on Duryodhana's offensiveness. Look at your mother Gāndhārī, and at me, your old blind father before you, who longs for your virtues. It was from affection that I allowed this dicing game, as I wished to see my friends and find out the strengths and weaknesses of my sons. King, the Kurus whose ruler you are and whose councillor is the sagacious Vidura, expert in all the fields of knowledge, are they to be pitied? In you there is Law, in Arjuna prowess, in Bhīmasena might, in the twins, foremost among men, there is faith and obedience to their elders.

15 Ajātaśatru, good luck to you! Return to the Khāṇḍava Tract. May you have brotherly bonds with your brethren, and may your mind abide by the Law!

Vaiśaṃpāyana said:

At his words Yudhiṣṭhira the King Dharma, first of the Bharatas, having fulfilled the full covenant of the nobles, departed with his brothers. Riding their cloudlike chariots they started with Kṛṣṇā, and in cheerful spirits, for their good city Indraprastha.

The Drilling Woods

Janamejaya said:

295.1 After the Pāṇḍavas suffered dire distress when Kṛṣṇā had been abducted, and had gained her back, what did they do?

Vaiśaṃpāyana said:

5 After they suffered dire distress when Kṛṣṇā had been abducted, King Acyuta and his brothers left Kāmyaka. Yudhiṣṭhira once more went to lovely Dvaitavana by Mārkaṇḍeya's fetching hermitage where the roots and fruit were sweet. The Pāṇḍavas all kept to a diet of fruit and ate sparingly while they dwelled there with Kṛṣṇā, O Bhārata. Living in Dvaitavana, King Yudhiṣṭhira, son of Kuntī, Bhīmasena, Arjuna, and the twin sons of Mādrī, those Law-spirited enemy-burners of strict vows, found when acting boldly in a brahmin's cause great sorrow that ended in happiness.

10 While Ajātaśatru was sitting with his brothers in the forest, a brahmin came running to him and said in anguish, "My gear with my drilling woods was hanging from a tree, and it got caught in the antlers of a deer that was rubbing against it. The big deer ran away with it, king, dashing fast from the hermitage, leaping with great speed. Follow its trail quickly and attack the big deer. Bring it back, Pāṇḍavas, so my *agnihotra* is not spoiled!"

15 When Yudhiṣṭhira heard the brahmin's words, he was upset; and the Kaunteya took his bow and rushed off with his brothers. All the bowmen, bulls among men, girt themselves and hurried off in the brahmin's cause and quickly pursued the deer. Shooting eared shafts, reeds, and iron arrows, the warlike Pāṇḍavas yet did not hit the deer that they saw close by. And while they were so busying themselves, the deer disappeared. The mindful men no longer saw the deer, and they were tired and discouraged. In the depths of the forest the Pāṇḍavas sought shelter in the cool shade of a banyan tree and, their bodies sore with hunger and thirst, sat down together. While they were sitting there, Nakula said with vexation and impatience to his eldest brother, O chief of the Kurus,

> "The Law never lapses in this our house,
> Nor does laziness thwart our purposeful ends –
> Then why are we, who are peerless among
> All creatures, again in danger, O King?"

Yudhiṣṭhira said:

296.1 Misfortune has neither limit, condition, nor cause. The Law distributes it here according to both good and bad.

Bhīma said:

The reason we are in danger is that I did not kill the usher who brought Kṛṣṇā to the Hall like a servant!

Arjuna said:

The reason we are in danger is that I tolerated the harsh, bone-piercing words that the *sūta*'s son spoke!

Sahadeva said:

The reason we are in danger is that I did not kill Śakuni when he had defeated you in the dicing game, Bhārata!

Vaiśaṃpāyana said:

5 King Yudhiṣṭhira said to Nakula, "Climb a tree, Mādreya, and look in the ten directions. Look for water close by, or trees that grow near water, for your brothers are tired, friend, and thirsty."

10 Nakula agreed, quickly climbed a tree, looked in all directions, and said to his eldest brother, "I see plenty of trees that grow near water, king, and I hear the screeching of cranes there is water here, no doubt of that." Thereupon Kuntī's son Yudhiṣṭhira, steadfast in truth, said to him, "Go, friend, and quickly fetch water to drink." Nakula agreed and at his eldest brother's orders he rushed to the water, which he reached shortly. He saw pure water surrounded by cranes, but when he wanted to drink, he heard a voice from heaven: "Commit no violence, friend. This is my old property. Answer my questions, Mādreya, then you may drink and fetch." Nakula, who was very thirsty, did not heed these words and drank the cool water. And having drunk he collapsed.

15 When Nakula was long returning, Kuntī's son Yudhiṣṭhira said to his brother Sahadeva, heroic enemy-tamer, "Your brother is long, Sahadeva, your senior brother. Go fetch your brother, and bring water." Sahadeva agreed, went in the same direction, and saw his brother collapsed on the ground. Burning with grief for his brother and being sorely pressed by thirst, he ran to the water, and the voice said, "Commit no violence, friend. This is my old property. Answer my questions if you please, then you may drink and fetch." Sahadeva, who was thirsty, did not heed these words, and drank the cool water. And having drunk he collapsed.

20–25 Then Kuntī's son Yudhiṣṭhira said to Vijaya, "Your brothers have been long gone, Terrifier, plower of your enemies. Go fetch them, hail to thee! and bring water." At these words Guḍākeśa took his bows and arrows and with sword drawn the sagacious man made for the lake. Then he of the white horses saw his tiger-like brothers fallen where they had gone to fetch water. The Kaunteya, a lion among men, struck by grief when he saw them as though asleep, raised his bow and looked into the forest. The left-handed archer saw no creature at all in the vast wilderness, and wearily he rushed to the water. As he did so the voice spoke from the sky, "Why did you come near? You cannot take this water by force. If you answer my questions, Kaunteya, then you shall drink and fetch the water, Bhārata!" Thus having been halted the Pārtha said, "Stop me where I can see you, so that you, pierced by my arrows, won't speak like this again!" The Pārtha pelted that entire region with enchanted arrows, displaying his skill at sound shooting. Discharging eared shafts, and iron arrows, O bull of the Bharatas, he showered the sky with many swarms of arrows.

The Yakṣa said:

30 What does this shooting profit you, Pārtha? Answer my questions and drink. If you do not answer you shall cease to be as soon as you drink!

Vaiśaṃpāyana said:

But after shooting off his never-failing arrows, Arjuna was so pressed by thirst that without paying heed to the questions he drank, and at once he collapsed.

35 Then Kuntī's son Yudhiṣṭhira said to Bhīmasena, "Nakula, Sahadeva, and the unvanquished Terrifier have now been gone for water a long time, and they are not coming back. Fetch them, Bhārata, hail to thee! and bring back water." Bhīmasena agreed and went to the same spot where his brothers, tigers among men, had been felled. Upon seeing them, and being sorely pressed by thirst, strong-armed Bhīma thought that it was the work of Yakṣas or Rākṣasas and reflected that he certainly would have to put up a fight. "But I shall first drink the water," and so the wolf-bellied Pārtha, bull among men, thirstily ran to the water.

The Yakṣa said:

Do not commit violence, friend. This is my old property. But answer my questions, Kaunteya, and you shall drink and fetch.

Vaiśaṃpāyana said:

At these words of the Yakṣa of boundless splendor, he did not pay heed, drank, and collapsed at once.

40 Thereupon Kuntī's son the king, bull among men, began pondering, and the strong-armed man rose up with his mind on fire. He entered the vast wilderness, whence all sound of people had gone. *Ruru* deer frequented the woods, and bear and fowl, it was made beautiful by dark and luminous trees, and it was buzzing with bees and birds as the glorious man made his entrance. Walking in the forest the illustrious prince set eyes upon that lake adorned with piles of gold, as though it had been fashioned by Viśvakarman, on that lake covered with lotus beds, *negundo* lilies, and reeds, with *ketakas, karavīras*, and *pippalas.* And wearily he approached the lake and looked at it with amazement.

Vaiśaṃpāyana said:

297.1 5 There he saw his brothers, the likes of Śakra in weight, fallen like the World Guardians when they are toppled at the end of the Eon. On seeing Arjuna felled, with his bows and arrows scattered, and Bhīmasena, and the twins, all motionless and lifeless, he shed tears of grief and sighed long and hotly. In his mind he wondered, "Who has felled the heroes? There is no mark of a weapon on them, nor is there a sign of anyone else. Methinks it is some great being that has slain my brothers. I must ponder this with my full mind – or after I have drunk I shall find out. Well may it be that this is the work ordained secretly by Duryodhana, and set afoot by the Gāndhāra prince of the crooked mind as always. What hero would put his trust in that man of evil mind and unmade spirit, for whom right and wrong are the same? Or this may be the design of that evil spirit through hidden henchmen!"

10 Thus the strong-armed prince thought in various ways. It occurred to him that the water was not poisoned, as his brothers' faces were healthy of color. "Who," he thought, "but Yama who finishes in Time could best these superb men with the force of a flood one by one?" With this conclusion he waded into the water; and as he plunged in he heard from the sky –

The Yakṣa said:

A crane that lives on duckweed and fishes,
I have brought your brothers in the power of death.
You, son of a king, shall be the fifth
If you do not reply to the questions I ask!

Commit no violence, friend, this is my old property. But answer my questions, Kaunteya, then drink and fetch!

Yudhiṣṭhira said:

15 I ask you, who are you, a God, the chief of the Rudras, the Vasus, or the Maruts? This is not the doing of a Śakuni! Who in his splendor has felled unto earth the four mountains Himālaya, Pariyātra, Vindhya, and Malaya? First among the strong, a supremely great deed have you accomplished, which neither Gods, nor Gandharvas, nor Asuras, nor Rākṣasas would be able to do, a great miracle have you wrought in a great battle. I do not know the task you have, I do not fathom your intentions. Great curiosity has been aroused in me, and terror has come over me. You who have brought anguish to my heart and fever to my head, who, I ask you, are you who stand there?

The Yakṣa said:

I am a Yakṣa, hail to thee! I am no bird of the water. It is I who felled all your august brothers!

Vaiśaṃpāyana said:

20 Upon hearing the ominous, rough-spoken words that the Yakṣa had spoken, O king, he kept coming closer. And the bull of the Bharatas saw standing on a dam an odd-eyed, big-bodied Yakṣa, tall as a palm, fiery like fire and sun, unconquerable and mountainous, who was chiding him powerfully in a voice as deep as a thunderclap.

The Yakṣa said:

I stopped these brothers of yours time and again, king, when they tried to take water by force. Then I finished them off. This water is not to be drunk by anyone here who wants to live, king. Pārtha, do not commit violence! This is my old property. But answer my questions, Kaunteya, and you may drink and fetch.

Yudhiṣṭhira said:

25 I do not at all covet your old property, Yakṣa, for strict people never approve of such coveting. As a person himself gives an account of himself, I shall answer your questions according to my lights, my lord. Ask me!

The Yakṣa said:

What causes the sun to rise, and what are its companions? What makes it set, and on what is it founded?

Yudhiṣṭhira said:

Brahman makes the sun rise, and the Gods are its companions. The Law makes it set, and on truth is it founded.

The Yakṣa said:

By what does one become learned, by what does one attain to great things, by what does one have a second, king, by what does one gain insight?

Yydhiṣṭhiru said:

By learning one becomes learned, by austerities one attains to great things; one has a second in perseverance, one gains insight by attending on one's elders.

The Yakṣa said:

30 What is the divine nature of the brahmins, what is their Law, like that of the strict, what is their human nature, what is their vice as of those without strictness?

Yudhiṣṭhira said:

Veda study is their divine nature, austerity their Law, as it is of the strict; mortality is their human nature, detraction their vice, as it is of those without strictness.

The Yakṣa said:

What is the human nature of the barons, what their Law, as it is of the strict? What is their human nature, what their vice, as it is of those without strictness?

Yudhiṣṭhira said:

Weaponry is their divine nature, sacrifice their Law, as it is of the strict; fear is their human nature, desertion their vice, as it is of those without strictness.

The Yakṣa said:

Which is the one sacrificial chant, which is the one sacrificial formula? What cuts down the sacrifice, what does the sacrifice not exceed?

Yudhiṣṭhira said:

35 Breath is the sacrificial chant, mind the sacrificial formula; speech alone cuts down the sacrifice, and the sacrifice does not exceed speech.

The Yakṣa said:

What is the best of the dropping, what is the best of the falling, what is the best of the standing, what is the best of the speaking?

Yudhiṣṭhira said:

Rain is the best of the dropping, seed the best of the falling, cows the best of the standing, a son the best of the speaking.

The Yakṣa said:

Who breathes, experiences the objects of the senses, is intelligent, honored in the world, and respected by all creatures – yet is not alive?

Yudhiṣṭhira said:

He who makes no offerings to the five, to wit Gods, guests, dependents, ancestors, and himself, may breathe but is not alive.

The Yakṣa said:

40 What has more weight than the earth, what is higher than heaven, what is faster than the wind, what more numerous than men?

Yudhiṣṭhira said:

The mother has more weight than the earth, the father is higher than heaven, the mind is faster than the wind, worries are more numerous than men.

The Yakṣa said:

What does not close the eyes when asleep, what does not stir when born, what has no heart, what grows by speeding along?

Yudhiṣṭhira said:

A fish does not close the eyes when asleep, an egg does not stir when born, a rock has no heart, a river grows by speeding along.

The Yakṣa said:

What is the friend of the traveler, what the friend at home, what the friend of the sick man, what the friend of the moribund?

Yudiṣṭhira said:

45 The caravan is the friend of the traveler, the wife is the friend at home, the physician is the friend of the sick man, charity the friend of the moribund.

The Yakṣa said:

What travels alone, what once born is born again, what is the cure for snow, what is the great acre?

Yudhiṣṭhira said:

The sun travels alone, the moon is reborn, fire is the cure of snow, the earth is the great acre.

The Yakṣa said:

What in a word makes the Law, what in a word is fame, what in a word leads to heaven, what in a word is happiness?

Yudhiṣṭhira said:

Ability in a word makes the Law, giving in a word is fame, truth in a word leads to heaven, character in a word is happiness.

The Yakṣa said:

50 What is the self of a man, what is the friend made by fate, what is the support of his life, what is his highest resort?

Yudhiṣṭhira said:

A son is the self of a man, a wife is the friend made by fate, the monsoon is the support of his life, charity is his highest resort.

The Yakṣa said:

What is the greatest of riches, what is the greatest of possessions, what is the greatest of boons, what is the greatest of comforts?

Yudhiṣṭhira said:

Ability is the greatest of riches, learning the greatest of possessions, health the greatest of boons, contentment the greatest of comforts.

The Yakṣa said:

What is the highest Law in the world, what Law always bears fruit, what does not grieve when tamed, what bond never comes loose?

Yudhiṣṭhira said:

55 Uncruelty is the highest Law, the Law of the *Veda* always bears fruit, the mind does not grieve when tamed, the bond of the good never comes loose.

The Yakṣa said:

Abandoning what does one become friendly, abandoning what does one not grieve, abandoning what does one become rich, abandoning what does one become happy?

Yudhiṣṭhira said:

Abandoning pride one becomes friendly, abandoning anger one does not grieve, abandoning desire one does become rich, abandoning greed one becomes happy.

The Yakṣa said:
How is a man dead, how is a kingdom dead, how is a *śrāddha* dead, how is a sacrifice dead?

Yudhiṣṭhira said:
A poor man is dead, a kingless kingdom is dead, a *śrāddha* without a learned brahmin is dead, a sacrifice without payment is dead.

The Yakṣa said:
60 What is the right direction? What is called water? What is food, Pārtha, and what poison? Tell me the time for a *śrāddha*, then you may drink and fetch.

Yudhiṣṭhira said:
The strict are the right direction, space is water, the cow is food, a request is poison; and a brahmin is the right time for a *śrāddha* – or do you think otherwise, Yakṣa?

The Yakṣa said:
You have answered my questions correctly, enemy-burner! Now tell me, who is a man, and what man owns all riches?

Yudhiṣṭhira said:
The repute of a good deed touches heaven and earth; one is called a man as long as his repute lasts. And *he* possesses all riches to whom the pleasing and displeasing are the same, and happiness and unhappiness, past and future.

The Yakṣa said:
65 You have explained man and the baronial man of all riches. For that, one of your brothers shall live, whoever you please.

Yudhiṣṭhira said:
The dark one with the red eyes, shot up like a tall *śāla* tree, with the wide chest and the long arms, O Yakṣa, he shall live – Nakula!

The Yakṣa said:
70 You have Bhīmasena, you rely on Arjuna, then why, king, do you want their rival Nakula to live? You give up Bhīma, whose strength is the match of a myriad elephants, and want Nakula to live? People say you hold this Bhīmasena so dearly, then by what greater affection do you want his rival to live? All the Pāṇḍavas rely on the strength of Arjuna's arms, yet you abandon him and want Nakula to live?

Yudhiṣṭhira said:
Uncruelty is the highest of Laws, this I know as the final truth. And I will not be cruel, so, Yakṣa, Nakula shall live! "The king is by character always lawful." This do people know of me; and I shall not stray from my Law – Nakula shall live, Yakṣa! As Kuntī was, so was Mādrī; I allow no difference. I want the same for both my mothers – Nakula shall live, Yakṣa!

The Yakṣa said:
Uncruelty you hold superior to profit and pleasure: for that all your brothers shall live, Bharata bull!

Vaiśaṃpāyana said:
298.1 At that Yakṣa's word the Pāṇḍavas stood up, and the hunger and thirst of all of them instantly disappeared.

Yudhiṣṭhira said:
5 I ask you, who are you, a God, who stands invincibly on one leg in the lake? I do not think you are a Yakṣa. Are you one of the Vasus or Rudras, or the chief of the Maruts, or the Thunderbolt-wielder, the lord of the Thirty? For these brothers of mine can fight hundreds and thousands, and I fail to perceive the manner in which they could be brought down. I observe that their faculties have returned now that they have been peaceably awakened – you are our friend, or are you our father?

The Yakṣa said:
10 I am your begetter, son, the God Dharma, O man of mild prowess! Know, Bull of the Bharatas, that I have come out of a desire to see you. Fame, truth, self-control, purity, uprightness, modesty, steadfastness, liberality, austerities, and chastity are my bodies. Nonviolence, equanimity, tranquillity, austerity, purity, and unenviousness – know that these are the doors to me. It is fortunate that you are devoted to the five, and fortunate that you have conquered the six states; two occur early, two in the middle, and two at the end, leading to the world hereafter. I am Dharma, hail to thee! and have come here to try you. I am pleased with your want of cruelty.

Prince sans blame, I shall grant you a boon. Choose a boon, Indra of kings, for I shall grant it to you, blameless man. No mishap befalls those men who are devoted to me!

Yudhiṣṭhira said:
May the fires of the brahmin whose drilling sticks that deer carried off not be disrupted! That shall be my first boon.

Dharma said:
I took the drilling woods of the brahmin in the guise of a deer, Lord Kaunteya, in order to test you.

Vaiśaṃpāyana said:
The blessed lord promised in answer, "I shall grant it! Choose another boon, hail to thee, God-like man."

Yudhiṣṭhira said:
15 The twelve years in the forest have passed, the thirteenth is at hand. May people not recognize us wherever we dwell.

Vaiśaṃpāyana said:
20 The blessed lord promised in answer, "I grant it!" and once more gave comfort to the Kaunteya, whose prowess was his truth. "Even though you may roam this earth in your own persons, no one in the three worlds will recognize you, Bhārata! By my grace you, scions of Kuru, shall live this thirteenth year hidden and unrecognized in the city of Virāṭa. Whatever appearance anyone of you fancies, that appearance you all shall have according to your wish. Return these drilling woods to the brahmin, for I stole them in the guise of a deer in order to try you.

"Now choose a third boon, son, one incomparably great, for you have sprung from me, and Vidura partakes of a portion of me."

Yudhiṣṭhira said:
I have set eyes on your person, on you the everlasting God of Gods. I shall contentedly accept that boon, father, which you yourself will give me. May I conquer greed, and folly, and anger forever, my lord, and may my mind always be on charity, austerity, and truthfulness.

Dharma said:
25 By your very nature are you endowed with all virtues, Pāṇḍava. You are the King Dharma. Again you shall have what you ask.

Vaiśaṃpāyana said:
Having said this Dharma disappeared, the blessed lord who prospers the worlds; and the high-minded Pāṇḍavas slept peacefully together. Rested, the heroes all returned to the hermitage and gave the drilling woods to the austere brahmin.

A self-controlled man, the master of his senses,
Who recites the great story of the *Revival*
And Encounter of father and son shall live
For a hundred years with his sons and grandsons.

And people who know this good tale will never
Delight in lawlessness, nor in estranging
Old friends, nor in theft or adultery,
Nor in any ignoble way of life.

Vaiśaṃpāyana said:
299.1 5 When the Pāṇḍavas, whose prowess was their truth, had been dismissed by Dharma, and were about to embark upon a life of concealment in the thirteenth year, the sagacious men of strict vows seated themselves humbly; and the great-spirited and well-taught brothers spoke with folded hands to the ascetics who out of devotion for them had dwelled in the forest with them, in order to ask their leave to end the sojourn to which they had so avowedly held. "It is known to you entirely how we have been plundered of our kingdom and possessions in various ways by the deceitful Dhārtarāṣṭras. We now have lived in the forest, with much hardship, for twelve years, and during the remaining thirteenth year, the span of our life of concealment, shall remain hidden with equal hardship. Pray give us leave. Suyodhana of wicked soul. Karṇa and Saubala will, when they find us out, make trouble for our townsfolk and kinsmen and be committed in their efforts, for they are endlessly resentful of us. Shall it come to pass that we once more will live as kings in our royal domains in the company of brahmins?"

As he said this, the pure King Yudhiṣṭhira, the son of Dharma, felt so oppressed by sorrow and grief that he choked with tears and fainted.

10–15 All the brahmins and his brothers comforted him; and thereupon Dhaumya spoke these words of great import in reply to the king: "Sire, you are wise, controlled, true to your promises, and master of your senses, and such men do not lose their heads in any emergency. Even the great-spirited Gods in case of emergencies have often gone into hiding in various places to subdue their rivals. Indra went to the Niṣadhas, hid away in a hermitage on a mountain plateau, and accomplished the feat of subduing the power of his enemies. Viṣṇu, before he was to lie in Aditi's womb, lived for a long while in hiding, wearing a horse's head, to kill off the Daityas. You have heard how he who has the form of Brahman assumed the shape of a dwarf and hid, and with his strides took the kingdom from Bali. You have heard, son, what the brahmin seer Aurva accomplished in the worlds while lying hidden in his mother's thigh. You have heard, Law-wise prince, what Hari accomplished when he entered and hid in Śakra's thunderbolt in order to subdue Vṛtra. You have heard what the Fire did for the Gods after entering the waters and staying concealed. Likewise Vivasvat of supreme splendor lived on earth in hiding and burned down all his enemies. Viṣṇu lived in Daśaratha's house, and in disguise the God of terrible deeds killed Ten-headed Rāvaṇa in battle. Thus these great-spirited beings lived in hiding and vanquished their enemies in battle. So shall you triumph!"

20 Yudhiṣṭhira, gratefully comforted by these words of the Law-wise Dhaumya, no more wavered from the spirit of the *śāstras* and that of his own. Then the strong-armed and powerful Bhīmasena, strong of the strong, spoke to the king, raising his spirits: "Out of deference to you, great king, and in a spirit obedient to the Law, the Gāṇḍīva bowman has not burst into violence yet. I constantly keep Sahadeva and Nakula in check – these enemy-killers of terrible prowess are well capable of crushing the foes. We shall not desert whatever task you lay on us. You yourself must dispose it all, and we shall speedily vanquish the enemies!"

25 When Bhīmasena had spoken, the brahmins pronounced the most solemn benedictions, said farewell to the Bharatas, and went each to his own house. All the eminent *Veda*-wise ascetics and hermits spoke blessings according to the rules, hoping to see them again. Then the five sagacious Pāṇḍavas rose with Dhaumya; and taking Kṛṣṇā the heroes set out.

They journeyed the distance of a shout from that place for a reason, and on the morrow those tiger-like men, who stood ready to begin their life of concealment, sat down together in council; and they all knew different arts, were experts in counseling, and knew the time of peace and the time of war.

The Temptation of Karṇa

Dhṛtarāṣṭra said:

138.1 Saṃjaya, before Madhusūdana rode out amidst princes and councilors, he had Karṇa mount his chariot. What did that slayer of enemy heroes say to Rādheya inside the chariot, what blandishments did Govinda offer the *sūta*'s son? Relate to me what Kṛṣṇa, with his voice roaring like a flood or a cloud, said to Karṇa, whether gently or sharply?

Saṃjaya said:

5 Hear from me, Bhārata, what Madhusūdana of the boundless spirit had to say to Rādheya in the course of their conversing, in words that were smooth and gentle, friendly, informed with Law, truthful, and helpful, to be cherished in the heart.

Vāsudeva said:

Rādheya, you have attended to brahmins learned in the Veda, and you have questioned them about truths without demurring. You, Karṇa, know the sempiternal sayings of the Veda, and you are well-grounded in the subtleties of the scriptures regarding the Law.

10 Now, those who know the scriptures teach that the son born to a woman before her marriage is as much counted the son of her wedded husband as the son she bears in marriage. You, Karṇa, were born that way: under

Law you are the son of Pāṇḍu. Under the constraint of the books of the Law, come with me and you shall be a king. The Pārthas are your kin on your father's side, the Vṛṣṇis on your mother's side: recognize, bull among men, both these lineages of your kinsmen!

15 Come with me today, my son; the Pāṇḍavas shall have to recognize you as the Kaunteya senior to Yudhiṣṭhira. The five Pāṇḍavas shall clasp your feet as your brothers, and so shall the five sons of Draupadī, and the unvanquished son of Subhadrā. The kings and the sons of kings who have trooped together in the Pāṇḍava's cause, and all the Andhaka-Vṛṣṇis shall clasp your feet. Baronesses and daughters of kings shall bring golden, silver, and earthen vessels, herbs, all seeds, all gems and shrubs for your inauguration. And at the sixth turn you shall lie with Draupadī!

Today brahmins representing all four Vedas shall consecrate you, assisted by the very priest of the Pāṇḍavas, while you are seated on the tiger skin: so shall the five Pāṇḍava brothers, bulls among men, the Draupadeyas, the Pāñcālas, and Cedis. I myself shall consecrate you King and Lord of the Land, and Kuntī's son Yudhiṣṭhira shall be your Young King. Kuntī's law-spirited son Yudhiṣṭhira shall mount the chariot of state behind you, holding the white fan.

20 Kaunteya! Mighty Bhīmasena Kaunteya himself shall hold the grand white umbrella over you, the King consecrated! Arjuna shall drive the chariot drawn by his white horses, tinkling with hundreds of bells and covered with tiger hides. Abhimanyu, Nakula, Sahadeva, and the five Draupadeyas shall always be at your beck and call.

25 The Pāñcālas will follow your banner, and the great warrior Śikhaṇḍin, and I myself will follow you; and all the Andhaka-Vṛṣṇis, the Dāśārhas, and Daśārṇas shall be your retinue, lord of the people! Enjoy your kingship, with your Pāṇḍava brothers, amidst prayers and oblations and manifold benisons. The Draviḍas and Kuntalas shall be your vanguard with the Āndhras, Tālacaras, Cūcupas, and Veṇupas. Bards and minstrels shall today sing your praises in many a song. And the Pāṇḍavas shall proclaim the Triumph of Vasuṣeṇa.

You, Kaunteya, surrounded by the Pārthas as the moon by the stars, reign you over the realm and bestow blessing on Kuntī! Your friends shall shudder with joy, your enemies with fear. Today, let there be brotherhood between you and your Pāṇḍava brothers!

Karṇa said:

139.1–5 I have no doubt at all, Keśava, that you are speaking to me out of friendship and affection, and so as a friend have my best interests at heart, Vārṣṇeya. I understand it all: under the Law, under the constraints of the scriptures concerning the Law I am, as you hold, the son of Pāṇḍu, Kṛṣṇa. An unmarried maiden conceived me by the Sun, Janārdana, and at the behest of the Sun she abandoned me at birth. Yes, Kṛṣṇa, under Law I was born the son of Pāṇḍu. But Kuntī cast me out as though I had been stillborn! And Adhiratha, a *sūta*, no sooner did he see me than he carried me to his home, Madhusūdana, and proffered me to Rādhā, with *love*! Out of *love* for me the milk of Rādhā's breasts poured forth at once, and she accepted my piss and shit, Mādhava! How could a man like me deny her the ancestral offering? A man who knows the Law and always took care to listen to the scriptures on the Law? Adhiratha, the *sūta*, thinks of me as his son, and my *love* demands that I think of him as my father.

10 He had my birth rites performed, Mādhava, by the Rules found in Scripture, out of *love* for his son, Janārdana. He had the brahmins name me Vasuṣeṇa, and when I was old enough, he married me to wives, Keśava. I have sons and grandsons by them, Janārdana, and my heart has bonds of *love* with them, Kṛṣṇa!

15 Govinda, neither joy nor fear, nor all of earth nor piles of gold can make me a traitor to my word. For thirteen years I have enjoyed unrivaled royal power in Dhṛtarāṣṭra's lineage by relying on Duryodhana. I have offered up much and often, but always with *sūtas*. I have performed domestic and marital rites, but always with *sūtas*. Duryodhana has raised arms and prepared for war with the Pāṇḍavas, because he relies on me, Kṛṣṇa of the Vṛṣṇis. Therefore he has confidently chosen me to be the main opponent of the Left-handed Archer in a chariot duel in the war, Acyuta. Neither death nor capture, neither fear nor greed can make me break my promise to the sagacious Dhārtarāṣṭra, Janārdana. If I now refuse to enter the chariot duel with the Left-handed Archer, Hṛṣīkeśa, it will bring both me and the Pārtha disgrace in the world.

20–25 No doubt you mean well, Madhusūdana, and no doubt, either, that the Pāṇḍavas will accomplish everything, with your guidance. So you should suppress word of our taking counsel here, best of men; that would be best, I think, joy of all the Yādavas. If the law-spirited king of strict vows knows that I am Kuntī's first-born son, he will not accept the kingdom; and if I were then to obtain this large, prosperous kingdom, I would hand it over to Duryodhana, Madhusūdana, enemy-tamer! Let the law-spirited Yudhiṣṭhira be king forever, he who has Hṛṣīkeśa as his guide, Dhanaṃjaya as his warrior. His is the earth who has the great warrior Bhīmasena, Nakula, Sahadeva, the Draupadeyas, O Mādhava, and Uttamaujas, Yudhāmanyu, Satyadharman, Somaki, Caidya and Cekitāna, the unvanquished Śikhaṇḍin, the firefly-colored Kekaya brothers, the rainbow-hued Kuntibhoja, that great warrior, and Bhīmasena's uncle, and the warrior Senājit, Śankha son of Virāṭa, and you as his treasury, Janārdana. Great is this gathering of the baronage that has been achieved, Keśava. And this kingdom, blazing and renowned among all kings, has now been won.

30–40 Vārṣṇeya, the Dhārtarāṣṭra will hold a grand sacrifice of war. Of this sacrifice you shall be the Witness, Janārdana, and you shall be the Adhvaryu priest at the ritual. The Terrifier with the monkey standard stands girt as the Hotar; Gāṇḍīva will be the ladle; the bravery of men the sacrificial butter. The *aindra, pāśupata, brāhma*, and *sthūṇākarṇa* missiles will be the spells employed by the Left-handed Archer. Saubhadra, taking after his father, if not overtaking him, in prowess, will act perfectly as the Grāvastut priest. Mighty Bhīma will be the Udgātar and Prastotar, that tigerlike man who with his roars on the battlefield finishes off an army of elephants. The eternal king, law-spirited Yudhiṣṭhira, well-versed in recitations and oblations, will act as the Brahmán. The sounds of the conches, the drums, the kettledrums, and the piercing lion roars will be the Subrahmaṇyā invocation. Mādrī's two glorious sons Nakula and Sahadeva of great valor will fill the office of the Śamitar priest. The clean chariot spears with their spotted staffs will serve as the sacrificial poles at this sacrifice, Janārdana. The eared arrows, hollow reeds, iron shafts and calf-tooth piles, and the javelins will be the Soma jars, and the bows the strainers. Swords will be the potsherds, skulls the Puroḍāśa cakes, and blood will be the oblation at this sacrifice, Kṛṣṇa. The spears and bright clubs will be the kindling and enclosing sticks; the pupils of Droṇa and Kṛpa Śāradvata the Sadasyas. The arrows shot by the Gāṇḍīva bowman, the great warriors, and Droṇa and his son will be the pillows. Sātyaki shall act as Pratiprasthātar, the Dhārtarāṣṭra as the Sacrificer, his great army as the Wife. Mighty Ghaṭotkaca will be the Śamitar when this Overnight Sacrifice is spun out, strong-armed hero. Majestic Dhṛṣṭadyumna shall be the sacrificial fee when the fire rite takes place, he who was born from the fire.

45–50 The insults I heaped on the Pāṇḍavas, to please Duryodhana, those I regret. When you see me cut down by the Left-handed Archer, it will be the Re-piling of the Fire of their sacrifice. When the Pāṇḍava drinks the blood of Duḥśāsana, bellowing his roar, it will be the Soma draught. When the two Pāñcālyas fell Droṇa and Bhīṣma, that will be the Conclusion of the sacrifice, Janārdana. When the mighty Bhīmasena kills Duryodhana, then the great sacrifice of the Dhārtarāṣṭra will end. The weeping of the gathered daughters-in-law and granddaughters-in-law, whose masters, sons, and protectors have been slain, with the mourning of Gāndhārī at the sacrificial site now teeming with dogs, vultures, and ospreys, will be the Final Bath of this sacrifice, Janārdana.

May these barons, old in learning and days, O bull among barons, not die a useless death for your sake, Madhusūdana. Let the full circle of the baronage find their death by the sword on the Field of the Kurus, holiest in all three worlds, Keśava. Ordain here, lotus-eyed Vārṣṇeya, what you desire, so that the baronage in its totality may ascend to heaven.

55 As long as the mountains will stand and the rivers flow, Janārdana, so long and forevermore shall last the sound of the fame of this war. Brahmins shall in their gatherings narrate the Great War of the Bhāratas, proclaiming the glory of the barons.

Keśava, lead the Kaunteya to the battle, and keep this council of ours secret, enemy-burner.

Saṃjaya said:

140.1 Having heard Karṇa's reply, Keśava, slayer of enemy heroes, smiled; then he laughed and said, "Does the offer of a kingdom not tempt you, Karṇa? Do you not wish to rule the earth I am giving you?"

> There is not a shadow of doubt remaining
> That victory's sure of the Pāṇḍavas:
> The Pāṇḍava's banner of Triumph is out,
> The terrible king of the apes has been raised!
>
> Celestial art did Bhauvana fashion:
> It is raised like the banner of Indra himself;
> It shows many creatures that terrify,
> Celestial creatures that horrify.
>
> 5 It is never entangled in rocks or trees,
> Upward and across it stretches a league;
> The illustrious flag of Dhanaṃjaya, Karṇa,
> Is raised with a glow that resembles the fire's.

10–15 When you see the man of the white horses on the battlefield with Kṛṣṇa driving his chariot, employing the missiles of Indra, Fire, and Wind, and hear the whip-crack of Gāṇḍīva as of a thunderbolt, then there will be no more Kṛta Age, no more Tretā, no more Dvāpara. When you see Kuntī's son Yudhiṣṭhira on the battlefield, protecting his grand-army with spells and oblations, unassailable like the sun burning the host of the enemy, then there will be no more Kṛta, no more Tretā, no more Dvāpara. When you see the mighty Bhīmasena on the battlefield, dancing his war dance after drinking Duḥśāsana's blood, like a rutting elephant that has killed a challenging tusker, then there will be no more Kṛta, no more Tretā, no more Dvāpara. When you see Mādrī's warrior sons on the battlefield, routing the army of the Dhārtarāṣṭras like elephants, shattering the chariots of enemy heroes as they plunge into the clash of arms, then there will be no more Kṛta, no more Tretā, no more Dvāpara. When you see on the battlefield Droṇa. Śāṃtanava, Kṛpa, King Suyodhana, and Jayadratha Saindhava storming to the attack and halted by the Left-handed Archer, then there will be no more Kṛta, no more Tretā, no more Dvāpara.

Go hence, Karṇa, and say to Droṇa, Śaṃtanava, and Kṛpa: this is a propitious month, with fodder and fuel plentifully at hand, abounding with ripe grains and plants, with plenty of fruit and hardly any mosquitoes. There is no mud, the water is tasty, the weather is pleasant, neither too hot nor too cold. Seven days from now it will be New Moon: let then the battle be joined, for they say that that is the Day of Indra.

20 Likewise say to all the kings who have come to battle, "I shall accomplish for you all that you desire." The kings and princes who follow Duryodhana's orders will, in finding their death by the sword, attain to the highest goal.

Saṃjaya said:

141.1 5 Upon hearing Keśava's words, benevolent and propitious, Karṇa paid homage to Kṛṣṇa Madhusūdana, and said, "Why, strong-armed man, did you seek to delude me when you knew already? The total destruction that looms for the earth is caused by Śakuni, me, Duḥśāsana, and Dhṛtarāṣṭra's son King Duryodhana. There is no doubt, Kṛṣṇa, that a great battle impends between the Pāṇḍavas and Kurus, grisly and mired in blood. The kings and princes who follow Duryodhana's orders will journey to Yama's realm, burned by the fire of the weapons in the war. Many nightmarish dreams are being seen,

Madhusūdana, and dreadful portents and calamitous omens, hair-raising and manifold, which presage that victory will be Yudhiṣṭhira's and defeat Duryodhana's, Vārṣṇeya. The luminous planet Saturn is sharply threatening the constellation Rohiṇī, menacing the creatures even more. Mars, in retrograde position to Jyeṣṭhā, is aiming for Anurādhā, Madhusūdana, as though pleading for the peace of friendship.

10–15 Surely great danger is at hand for the Kurus, Kṛṣṇa, for the planet threatens Citrā in particular, Vārṣṇeya. The spot on the moon is distorted, while Rāhu is about to attack the sun. Meteors are falling from the sky with hurricanes and earthquakes. The elephants are trumpeting, the horses are shedding tears and take no pleasure in water and fodder, Mādhava. When such portents appear, they say a horrendous danger is near that will destroy the creatures, strong-armed one. Horses, elephants, and men are eating little in all the armies of the Dhārtarāṣṭra, Keśava, yet their feces are massive. The wise say that that is a sign of defeat, Madhusūdana. They say, Kṛṣṇa, that the mounts of the Pāṇḍavas are in good spirits and that the wild beasts are circumambulating their camp, a sign of victory, but all animals go the reverse way around the Dhārtarāṣṭra, Keśava, and there are also disembodied voices, a sign of his defeat. Peacocks, flower birds, wild geese, cranes, *cātakas*, and *jīvaṃjīvaka* flocks follow the Pāṇḍavas, while vultures, crows, *baḍas*, kites, ghouls, jackals, and swarms of mosquitoes follow the Kauravas.

20–25 In the Dhārtarāṣṭra's armies there is no sound of drums, but the drums of the Pāṇḍavas sound forth unstruck. The wells in the Dhārtarāṣṭra's camp gurgle like bullocks, presaging his defeat. The God rains a rain of flesh and blood. A brilliant Gandharva city hovers nearby with walls, moats, ramparts, and handsome gate towers. A black mace obfuscates the sun at dawn and dusk, predicting great danger, and a single jackal howls horrifyingly, a sign of Duryodhana's defeat. Black-necked birds hover terrifyingly, then fly into the dusk, a sign of his defeat. He hates first of all the brahmins, Madhusūdana, and then his elders and loyal retainers, a sign of his defeat. The eastern horizon is blood-red, the southern darkling like swords, and the western mud-colored like an unbaked pot, Madhusūdana. All the horizons of the Dhārtarāṣṭra are on fire, Mādhava, and with these portentous signs they foredoom great danger.

30–40 I had a dream in which I saw Yudhiṣṭhira and his brothers ascend to a thousand-pillared palace, Acyuta. All wore white turbans and white robes, and I saw that they all had beautiful stools. In my vision I saw you drape the blood-fouled earth with entrails, Kṛṣṇa Janārdana. A boundlessly august Yudhiṣṭhira mounted a pile of bones and joyously ate rice mixed with *ghee* from a gold platter. I saw Yudhiṣṭhira swallow the earth which you had served him – clearly he shall enjoy the rule of the earth. Wolf-Belly of the terrible feats had climbed a steep mountain and with his club in hand the tigerlike man seemed to survey this earth – clearly he shall destroy us all in a great battle. I know, Hṛṣīkeśa, that where there is Law there is triumph. Dhanaṃjaya carrying Gāṇḍīva had mounted a white elephant, together with you, Hṛṣīkeśa, blazing with sublime luster. All of you shall – about that I have no doubts – slaughter all the kings led by Duryodhana in battle, Kṛṣṇa. Nakula, Sahadeva, and the great warrior Sātyaki, decked with pure bracelets and necklaces, wearing white garlands and robes, tigerlike man, had mounted on men, the three stately men wearing white umbrellas and robes. In the Dhārtarāṣṭra's armies too I saw three white-turbaned men, Janārdana Keśava – know who they are: Aśvatthāman, Kṛpa, and Kṛtavarman Sātvata. All other kings wore red turbans, Mādhava. Mounted on a camel cart, O strong-armed Janārdana, Bhīṣma and Droṇa accompanied by me and the Dhārtarāṣṭra traveled to the region ruled by Agastya, Lord Janārdana: soon we shall reach the dwelling of Yama; I and the other kings and the circle of barons shall doubtless enter the fire of Gāṇḍīva.

Kṛṣṇa said:

Of a certainty, the destruction of the earth is now near, for my words do not reach your heart, Karṇa. When the destruction of all creatures is at hand, bad policy disguised as good does not stir from the heart, my friend.

Karṇa said:

45 Perhaps we shall see you again, strong-armed Kṛṣṇa, if we escape alive from the great battle, the carnage of heroes. Or surely we shall meet in heaven, Kṛṣṇa – yes, there we shall meet again next, prince sans blame.

Saṃjaya said:

Speaking thus, Karṇa clasped the Mādhava tightly; then, dismissed by Keśava, he came down from the pit of the chariot. Riding his own gold-adorned chariot, Rādheya dejectedly returned with us. Keśava rode off with Sātyaki at a fast pace, again and again urging his charioteer, "Go! Go!"

Vaiśampāyana said:

142.1–5 When Kṛṣṇa's diplomacy had failed and he had departed from the Kurus for the Pāṇḍavas, the Steward went to Pṛthā and spoke softly in sorrow, "You know, mother of living sons, that my heart always inclines to kindliness. I may shout, but Suyodhana does not take my advice. Yonder, King Yudhiṣṭhira, armed with the Cedis, Pāñcālas, and Kekayas, with Bhīma and Arjuna, Kṛṣṇa, Yuyudhāna, and the twins, and encamped at Upaplavya, still only wishes for Law out of love for his kinsmen, like a weak man although he is strong. King Dhṛtarāṣṭra here, on the other hand, while old in years does not make peace. Infected by the madness of his son, he walks the path of lawlessness. Because of the bad judgment of Jayadratha, Karṇa, Duḥśāsana, and Saubala the breach goes on. But the Law and its consequences will overtake those who lawlessly stole that most law-loving kingdom. Who would not run a fever when the Kurus steal the Law by force? When Keśava comes back without peace, the Pāṇḍavas shall arm for battle, and the bad policy of the Kurus will become the assassin of heroes. I worry and worry, and find no sleep by day or night."

10–15 Listening to his words, which were spoken by one who meant well, Kuntī, sick with grief herself, sighed aloud and reflected in her mind, "Accursed be this wealth for the sake of which there will be great carnage in the slaughter of kinsmen, for there will only be defeat in this family war. If the Pāṇḍavas, Cedis, Pāñcālas, and the Yādavas together fight the Bhāratas, what could be worse than that? I do see that there is evil in war, surely, but so is defeat in war evil. For the dispossessed it is better to die, for there is no victory in the killing of kin. Grandfather Śāṃtanava and the Teacher, master of warriors, and Karṇa increase my fears in the cause of the Dhārtarāṣṭra. Droṇa the Teacher would never willingly fight with his pupils for personal gain, and why would Grandfather not have good feelings toward the Pāṇḍavas? It is only *he* who perversely follows the folly of the evil-hearted Dhārtarāṣṭra, who always has hated the Pāṇḍavas wickedly. Karṇa is obdurate in a great cause, and always strong enough to visit disaster on the Pāṇḍavas; and that burns me now. Today I hope to soften Karṇa's heart toward the Pāṇḍavas, when I approach him and show him the truth.

20–25 "When the blessed Durvāsas was satisfied and granted me the boon of conjuring up Gods, while I lived honorably in father Kuntibhoja's house, I thought in many ways with beating heart, right there in the king's women's quarters, about the strength and weakness of spells and the power of a brahmin's word. I thought and thought, being both a woman and a child, protected by my trusted nurse and surrounded by my friends, shunning mistakes and guarding my father's good name, "How can I do something good for myself and yet not sin?" thinking of the brahmin and bowing to him. Then, on having attained the boon that enabled such a course I, out of curiosity and childishness, being just a girl, made God the Sun come to me. Why should he whom I carried as a girl, not obey my word, which is proper and good for his brothers, when he has been received back as my son?"

30 When Kuntī had taken this ultimate decision, she embarked upon her task and went to the river Bhāgīrathī. On the bank of the Ganges Pṛthā heard the sound of her compassionate and truthful son's recitations. She stood miserably behind her son, who faced east with his hands raised, and waited for the recitation to end. She, wedded wife of a Kauravya, a Princess of the Vṛṣṇis, stood in the shade of Karṇa's upper garment like a withered garland of lotuses, hurting from the heat of the sun. He prayed until the heat reached his back, being strict in his vows; then he turned around and saw Kuntī. He saluted her and waited for her to speak with folded hands, as was proper, this proud and splendid man, first of the upholders of the Law.

Karṇa said:

143.1 I, Karṇa, son of Rādhā and Adhiratha, salute you. Why has your ladyship come? Tell me what I must do for you.

Kuntī said:

5–10 You are the son of Kuntī, not of Rādhā, nor is Adhiratha your father. You have not been born in the line of *sūtas*, Karṇa. Learn what I am telling you. I gave birth to you before I was married. You are my first-born whom I carried in my womb in the palace of Kuntibhoja. You are a *Pārtha*, my son! He, the God who makes light and spreads heat, he Virocana begot you on me, Karṇa, to be the greatest of swordsmen. The child of a God, with inborn earrings and armor, you were borne by me in my father's house, covered with glory, invincible son. It is not at all right for you, son, innocently to serve the Dhārtarāṣṭras without knowing your real brothers. In the decisions of Law *that* is reckoned the fruit of the Law of men that as parents – and also as a one-eyed mother – they rest content with their son. Cut yourself off from the Dhārtarāṣṭras and enjoy Yudhiṣṭhira's fortune, the fortune once won by Arjuna and then greedily stolen by scoundrels. Let the Kurus today witness the meeting of Karṇa and Arjuna in a spirit of brotherhood. Let Karṇa and Arjuna be like Rāma and Janārdana. When the two of you are united in spirit, what could you not achieve in the world! Surrounded by your five brothers, you shall surely shine forth, Karṇa, like Brahmā surrounded by the Vedas and their Branches. Endowed with virtues, the eldest and the best among relations who are the best, your title will no longer be that of the son of a *sūta*; you shall be a heroic *Pārtha*!

Vaiśampāyana said:

144.1 Thereupon Karṇa heard a voice that issued from the sun, affectionate and not to be gainsaid, which the sun uttered like a father: "Pṛthā has spoken the truth, Karṇa, obey your mother's word. The greatest good will befall you, tiger among men, if you do as she says." And thus addressed by his mother, and by his father the Sun himself, Karṇa's mind did not falter, for he stood fast by the truth.

Karṇa said:

5 It is not that I do not believe the words you have spoken, *ksatriya* lady, or deny that for me the gateway to the Law is to carry out your behest. But the irreparable wrong you have done me by casting me out has destroyed the name and fame I could have had. Born a *kṣatriya*, I have yet not received the respect due a baron. What enemy could have done me greater harm than you have? When there was time to act you did not show me your present compassion. And now you have laid orders on me, the son to whom you denied the sacraments. You have never acted in my interest like a mother, and now, here you are, enlightening me solely in your own interest.

10–15 Who would not tremble before a Dhanaṃjaya aided by a Kṛṣṇa? Who would not call me a coward, if I now joined the Pārthas? I who never had been known as their brother now stand revealed as one, at the hour of battle. If I now go to the Pāṇḍavas, what will the baronage call me? The Dhārtarāṣṭras have let me share in all their comforts and have honored me much at all times: how could I, *I* betray them now? Now that they are embroiled in a feud with the others, they attend to me at all times and honor me as much as the Vasus honor Vāsava. How could I shatter their hopes now, if they think that with my prowess they can engage their enemies? How could I desert them now when they see in me the boat they need to cross over this impassable battle and find the farther shore of this shoreless ocean? Now the hour has struck for all the men who have lived off the Dhārtarāṣṭra, and I have to discharge my duty heedless of my life. Those evil men who, after having been well supported to their heart's content, pay no heed to what has been done for them and fecklessly undo past benefactions when the time of duty arrives, wicked despoilers of their kings and thieves of their masters' riceball, gain neither this world nor the next.

20 Yes, I shall fight your sons in the cause of Dhṛtarāṣṭra's son with all my power and strength – I will *not* lie to you. While trying to persevere in the humane conduct that becomes a decent man, I will *not* carry out your word, beneficial though it may be. Yet, your effort with me shall not lack fruit. I shall not kill your sons in the battle, though I can withstand and slay them – that is, your sons Yudhiṣṭhira, Bhīma and the twins, excepting Arjuna. Arjuna I shall fight in Yudhiṣṭhira's army. In killing Arjuna on the battlefield I shall find my reward, or reap fame if the Left-handed Archer kills me. So never shall your sons number less than five, glorious woman: either without Arjuna but with Karṇa, or with Arjuna, if I am killed.

Vaiśaṃpāyana said:

25 Having heard Karṇa's answer, Kuntī shuddered from sorrow; and embracing her son, she said to Karṇa, who was unfaltering in his fortitude, "So it must be then – the Kauravas will go to their perdition, as you have said, Karṇa. Fate is all-powerful. But promise me, enemy-plougher: the safety you have granted your four brothers, of that pledge you will acquit yourself! Good health and good luck," said Pṛthā to Karṇa. Pleased, Karṇa saluted her. Then both went their separate ways.

Vaiśaṃpāyana said:

145.1 Returning to Upaplavya from Hāstinapura, enemy-tamer Keśava reported everything to the Pāṇḍavas. After they had discussed it for a long time and consulted again and again, Śauri went to his own camp to rest. The five Pāṇḍava brothers dismissed all the kings, headed by Virāṭa. When the sun set, they worshiped the twilight. Then their thoughts went to Kṛṣṇa, and they had the Dāśārha fetched and deliberated again.

Yudhiṣṭhira said:

5 What did you tell the son of Dhṛtarāṣṭra in the assembly hall, lotus-eyed one, when you had gone to the City of the Elephant? Please repeat it to me.

Vāsudeva said:

What I told the son of Dhṛtarāṣṭra in the assembly hall, when I had gone to the City of the Elephant, was true, salutary, and beneficial. But the scoundrel did not accept it.

Yudhiṣṭhira said:

10 When that man had gone off the right path, Hṛṣīkeśa, what did grandfather, the elder of the Kurus, have to say to the truculent Duryodhana? And what did our Teacher, the strong-armed Bhāradvāja, and our junior father the Steward, the first of the upholders of Law, tell the son of Dhṛtarāṣṭra in sorrow over his sons? What, too, did all the kings who sat together in the hall have to say? Tell what happened, Janārdana. You did report what the two chief Kurus said to that fool who thinks he is clever, overcome by lust and greed. But unpleasant matters do not stick in my mind, Keśava. I want to hear what they said, Lord Govinda. Act, friend, the time is passing by; for you are our recourse, you our protector, you our guru.

Vāsudeva said:

Hear then, king, what King Suyodhana was told amidst the Kurus, O Indra among kings, in the assembly hall. Listen to me.

15 After I had made my address, Dhṛtarāṣṭra's son laughed, whereupon an outraged Bhīṣma said to him, "Duryodhana, listen to what I have to say for the good of the family; and when you have heard it, tiger among kings, do what is in the interest of your own family.

20 "My father was the world-renowned Śaṃtanu, king, and I was his only son, the best of all who have sons, my son. The thought occurred to him, 'How may I have a second son? The wise say that having one son is having none. How may the family continue to exist and spread its fame?' Knowing his desire I brought him Kālī, who was to be my mother. For the sake of my father and family I swore a difficult oath, as you well know, to be neither king nor father. And here I live confidently, keeping my promise. From her the law-spirited Vicitravīrya was born, strong-armed, illustrious scion of the House of Kuru, my younger brother.

"When father had gone to heaven, I installed Vicitravīrya in my kingdom as the king, while I myself became his retainer below him. You have often heard how I brought him suitable brides in marriage after vanquishing a whole gathering of princes. Later I became embroiled in a duel with Rāma – he was banished by his townsmen out of fear for Rāma. Being too greatly attached to his wives, he succumbed to exhaustion.

"When Indra no longer rained on the kingless kingdom, the subjects hastened to me, driven by hunger and fear.

The subjects said:

25 " 'All the subjects are dwindling! You be our king and revive us! Be blessed, drive away the plagues, increaser of Śaṃtanu's house. All your subjects are suffering from most terrible diseases and but few remain, son of the Ganges. Pray rescue us! Dispel the sicknesses, hero, and rule the subjects by the Law, lest the kingdom fall in ruins while you are alive.' "

Bhīṣma said:

30 "The wailing of the subjects failed to shake my mind, and recalling the code of the strict, I kept my promise. The townspeople, my good mother, Kālī, retainers, house priests, and learned brahmins, great king, all kept urging me in great distress, 'Be our king! The kingdom that was ruled by Pratīpa is going to perish now that it has fallen to you. For the sake of our well-being be you our king, O sage!' At their words I folded my hands, greatly distressed and unhappy, and told them again and again the promise I had made out of deference to my father, son, that I would remain a celibate and not be king for the good of the lineage. With folded hands I again and again placated my mother, king, saying, 'Mother, though born from Śaṃtanu and carrying on the lineage of Kuru, I cannot belie my oath, withal for your own sake. Do not lay the yoke on me. I am your servant and slave, son-loving mother!'

35–40 "Having thus placated my mother and the people, I solicited the great hermit Vyāsa for my brother's wives. Together with my mother, great king. I propitiated the seer and solicited him for offspring; and he bestowed his grace and begot three sons then, best of the Bharatas. Being blind and thus lacking the faculty of sight, your father could not be king, and Pāṇḍu, great-spirited and world-renowned, became king. He was the king and his sons are their father's heirs. Do not quarrel, son, give them half the kingdom. What man can rule the kingdom as long as I am alive? Do not ignore my words, for I always have your peace at heart. I do not discriminate, son, between you and them, king. This is also the opinion of your father, of Gāndhārī and of Vidura. If the elders are to be heard, do not disobey my words, lest you destroy everybody, yourself and the earth."

Vāsudeva said:

146.1–5 When Bhīṣma had spoken, eloquent Droṇa addressed Duryodhana in the midst of the kings, blessings upon thee. "Just as Pratīpa's son Śaṃtanu," he said, "rose in the cause of his lineage, son, so Devavrata Bhīṣma has stood for the interests of the family. Thereafter Pāṇḍu, lord of men, true to his word, master of his senses, became the king of the Kurus, law-spirited, of good vows, and devoted. Later he, who increased the dynasty of Kuru, gave the realm to the wise Dhṛtarāṣṭra, his elder, and to Vidura, his junior. Then, after having placed him firmly on the lion throne, king, the Kauravya went to the forest with his two wives, prince sans blame.

10 "Vidura stood below him like a humble servant, and the tigerlike man waited on him, holding up the tail-hair fan. All the subjects properly accepted Dhṛtarāṣṭra as the lord of the realm, just as they had King Pāṇḍu, my son. After entrusting the kingdom to Dhṛtarāṣṭra and Vidura, Pāṇḍu, the conqueror of enemy cities, roamed all of earth. Vidura, true to his word, was in charge of generating revenue, gifts, the supervision of the servants, and the upkeep of all. Mighty Bhīṣma, conqueror of enemy cities, was in charge of war and peace and oversaw the personal care of the king. Strong-armed King Dhṛtarāṣṭra sat on the lion throne, always attended by the great-spirited Vidura.

15 "Why do you, though born in this family, resolve to break up the family? Enjoy your comforts in unison with your brethren, lord of the people! I am not saying this out of either lack of nerve or hope of personal gain: I eat what Bhīṣma gives me, not you, best of kings. I do not want my livelihood from you, lord of the people. Where Bhīṣma goes goes Droṇa. Do what Bhīṣma says. Give the sons of Pāṇḍu half the kingdom, plougher of enemies. I have always served both you and them equally as teacher, son. The man of the white horses means as much to me as Aśvatthāman. Why use many words? Victory lies where Law lies."

20–25 When Droṇa had thus spoken, great king, true-spoken and Law-wise Vidura lifted his voice, turning to his father and looking him in the face, "Devavrata, listen to what I have to say. This dynasty of Kuru was lost and you rescued it – now you pay no heed to my complaints. Who is this defiler of his family, this Duryodhana, that you follow the judgment of this man who is possessed with greed, ignoble, ungrateful, his mind diseased with avarice, disobedient to the commandments of his father, who sees Law and Profit? The Kurus are doomed because of Duryodhana: act, great king, so that they need not perish. After you had created me and the lustrous King Dhṛtarāṣṭra as a painter creates a painting, do not destroy us now. Do not, strong-armed hero, look away at the sight of the destruction of the Kurus, like a Prajāpati who creates the creatures to destroy them. Or if your wits fail you, now that destruction impends, go to the forest with me and Dhṛtarāṣṭra, and the kingdom shall be safely ruled by the Pāṇḍavas. Have mercy, tiger among kings, we face a holocaust of Pāṇḍavas and Kurus and boundlessly august kings!"

Having spoken Vidura fell silent, with sorrow in his heart, lost in his thoughts and sighing again and again.

Thereupon King Subala's daughter herself,
Afeared of the death of the family, spoke
Irately in front of the kings to her son,
Mean-hearted, cruel Duryodhana.

"Let the kings who have entered this hall of the king,
The brahmin seers and others in council
Pay heed: before them I state the guilt
Of you and your councilors' band who are evil!

"The realm of the Kurus is ruled by succession:
That's the family Law come down to us.
You, wicked of mind and most cruel of deed,
Kill the realm of the Kurus by means that are crooked.

30 "The wise Dhṛtarāṣṭra now stands in the realm
And by him stands farsighted Vidura.
Overreaching them both, how dare you aspire
In your folly to kingship, Duryodhana?

"The King and the Steward of mighty prowess
Are subject to Bhīṣma as long as he stands;
But the son of the river, great-spirited, does not
Aspire to the realm since he knows the Law.

"This kingdom was Pāṇḍu's inalienably,
And his sons now rank, and nobody else;
This kingdom entire is the Pāṇḍavas' own,
Ancestral, bequeathed to their sons and theirs.

"What the great-souled chief of the Kurus has said,
Devavrata the sage, whose promise is true,
We must accept it all as Law undiminished,
If we are to guard the Law of our own.

"With this man of great vows' consent let the king
In like manner speak, and Vidura also,
And let it be done at their charge by our friends,
Keeping Law in the front for a long time to come.

35 "Yudhiṣṭhira, son of the Law, shall rule
This realm of the Kurus, to which he succeeded,
Exhorted by King Dhṛtarāṣṭra himself,
And placed at the head by Śaṃtanu's son!"

Vāsudeva said:

147.1 When Gāndhārī had spoken, King Dhṛarāṣṭra addressed Duryodhana in the midst of the princes, O king, "Duryodhana, listen to what I shall have to say to you, my son, and carry it out, and be blessed, if you respect your father.

5–10 "Soma Prajāpati founded the dynasty of the Kurus in the beginning, and Nahuṣa's son Yayāti was the sixth from Soma. He had five sons, all most eminent royal seers, and the eldest of them was the mighty Lord Yadu. The youngest, Pūru, who increased our dynasty, was born from Śarmiṣṭhā, the daughter of Vṛṣaparvan. Yadu, O best of the Bharatas, was the son of Devayānī, and on her side the grandson of Śukra Kāvya of immense splendor. The founder of the Yādavas, strong and esteemed for his bravery, despised the baronage, being full of pride and slow of wit. Befuddled by his pride in his strength, he did not abide by his father's command – this unvanquished prince despised his father and brothers. Yadu grew mighty on four-cornered earth and after subjugating the kings dwelled in the City of the Elephant. His father, Yayāti Nāhuṣa, in fury cursed his son, O Gāndhāri, and cast him from the kingdom. Yayāti in his rage also cursed those sons of his who had followed their brother, so proud of his strength. That best of kings thereupon installed his youngest son Pūru, who took his orders obediently, in the kingdom.

15–20 "Thus even an eldest son is not born to kingship, if he is prideful, while the youngest are born to be kings by their deference to their elders. Likewise my father's grandfather, Pratīpa, who knew all the Laws, a king famed in the three worlds: to this lion among kings, who ruled the kingdom under Law, three famous Godlike sons were born. Devāpi was the eldest, Bāhlīka came after him, and steadfast Śaṃtanu, my grandfather, son, was the third. But Devāpi of great splendor and the best of kings, law-abiding, veracious, and obedient to his father, had a skin disease. Devāpi was loved by the townfolk and country people, esteemed by the good, and dear to the hearts of young and old. Wise, true to his promises, intent on the interests of all creatures, abiding by the commands of his father and the brahmins, he was a beloved brother to Bāhlīka and the great-spirited Śaṃtanu – indeed the brotherliness of these great-spirited men was exemplary.

"In the course of time his father, best among kings, had the necessaries fetched for the Royal Consecration according to precept, and the overlord had all the auspicious formalities performed. Then the brahmins and elders, supported by town and country folk, forbade the consecration of Devāpi. When the king heard about the interdiction of the consecration, his throat was choked with tears and he grieved over his son.

25 "Thus this generous, Law-wise, true-spoken prince, beloved by the subjects, was yet flawed by his skin disease. The Gods do not approve of a king who is lacking in limbs, and with this in mind the bulls of the twice-born stopped their good king. Thereupon, with sorrowing spirit and grieving over his son, Pratīpa died; and seeing him dead Devāpi took shelter in the forest. Bāhlīka had left the realm and established himself in the family of his maternal uncle. He abandoned his father and brothers and acquired a wealthy town. With Bāhlīka's leave, world-famous Śaṃtanu upon his father's death ruled the kingdom as king, O king.

30 "Likewise I myself, the eldest, was upon much thought barred from the kingdom by the sagacious Pāṇḍu for being 'lacking in limbs,' Bhārata, and Pāṇḍu, though the younger, succeeded to the kingdom as king. Upon his demise the kingdom became his sons', enemy-tamer. If I could not inherit the realm, how can you seek it?

"Great-souled Yudhiṣṭhira is the Heir;
This realm has lawfully fallen to him.
The master is he of the Kaurava people,
For him to rule in majesty.

"He is true to his promises, never distracted,
Upright and prepared to obey his kin,
Beloved of the subjects, kind to his friends,
In control of his senses, support of the good.

"Forgiveness, forbearance, uprightness, control,
Avowedness to truth, great learning and zeal,
Compassion as well as authority –
Yudhiṣṭhira has all the virtues of kings.

"Not the son of a king and ignoble in conduct,
Avaricious, ill-intentioned to kin,

How can you, a lout, pretend to seize
This realm that others are lawfully heir to?

35 "Cast off your delusion and render them half
Of the realm and requisite mounts and retainers;
Only then, lord of men, may you and your brothers
Still have the rest of your lives to live!"

Vāsudeva said:

148.1 5 When Bhīṣma had thus spoken, and Droṇa, Vidura, Gāndhārī, and Dhṛtarāṣṭra, the fool paid no heed. Shrugging them off he rose irately, his eyes bloodshot with rage; and the kings hurried after him, laying down their lives. He ordered those kings, whose minds were warped, "March out to the field of the Kurus! Today it is Puṣya," again and again. Thereupon the kings departed with their troops, after making Bhīṣma supreme commander, exultant and urged on by Time. Eleven armies of kings had massed, and at their head shone Bhīṣma with his palm-tree standard.

10–15 Therefore, lord of your people, dispose what is meet and proper. I have reported all that befell in the assembly of the Kurus, all that was said in my presence by Bhīṣma, Droṇa, Vidura, Gāndhārī, and Dhṛtarāṣṭra, King Bhārata. First I used a conciliatory approach, hoping for a sense of brotherliness to prevail, to prevent a breach in the dynasty of Kuru, and to further the well-being of the subjects. When conciliatoriness failed, I tried alienation and recited your feats, human and divine. When Suyodhana ignored my conciliatory speech, I convened all the kings and attempted to sow discord. I displayed dreadful and terrifying miracles and superhuman exploits, Lord Bhārata. I threatened the kings, denigrated Suyodhana, and intimidated Rādheya and Saubala time and again. Again and again I pointed to the meanness of the Dhārtarāṣṭras and heaped blame on them, trying to alienate those kings over and over again with words and advice. Once more conciliatory, I mentioned gifts, in order to prevent a breach in the dynasty of Kuru and accomplish my mission, saying, "Those boys, those Pāṇḍavas, will shed their pride and submit to Dhṛtarāṣṭra, Bhīṣma, and Vidura. Let them proffer you the kingdom and themselves remain no more masters. Let it be as the king and Gāṅgeya and Vidura have stated. Let the whole realm be yours, let go of just five villages. Surely your father can afford to support them, greatest of kings!" Yet at such words the evil man did not change his mind.

Now I see no other course open but the fourth – punishment. The kings are marching to Kurukṣetra to their doom! I have told all that befell in the assembly of the Kurus: they will *not* give you the kingdom without war, Pāṇḍava. Driven to destroy, they now face death.

Chapter 5

The *Bhagavad Gītā*

The *Bhagavad Gītā* is a discourse between Arjuna and Kṛṣṇa, both central figures of the epic tale the *Mahābhārata*, the "Great History of the descendants of Bharata." This dialogue, which takes place amid the armies of the Pāṇḍava brothers and Kaurava brothers, is born from Arjuna's panic about fighting with his own blood relatives. Just as the war is about to begin, Arjuna, the third Pāṇḍava brother, drops his weapons, unable to fight, and conveys his dilemma to Kṛṣṇa, his charioteer. The immediate conversation that follows consists of arguments put forth by Kṛṣṇa to convince Arjuna to follow his *dharma* as a *kṣatriya* and, therefore, to fight. If one were to link this injunction to the larger social system within which Arjuna found himself, it becomes clear that the teaching is merely to maintain and uphold the societal structures, namely the *varṇa* system.

Subsequent conversations revolve around the prerequisites and practices for obtaining *mokṣa*, liberation, from the cycle of birth and rebirth. In these sections Arjuna learns about how to be a proper *yogi* and about *bhakti*, devotion, to Kṛṣṇa. *Bhakti*, devotion, is much more available than either the ritual expertise required in the *Vedas* or the esoteric and coded knowledge of the *Upaniṣads*. Another central theme in the *Gītā* concerns how to act, yet not accumulate any *karma*. To this end Kṛṣṇa teaches that acting *niṣkāmakarma*, without desire for the fruits of one's action, does not result in the accumulation of *karma*. Actions, moreover, are best offered to him as an act of *bhakti*.

Many concepts in the *Gītā* are perfumed with theories that parallel those propounded by the Sāmkhyā School of Indian philosophy (codified in 350–450 CE by Īśvarakṛṣṇa in his *Sāmkhyā Kārikas*). The authors of the *Gītā* brought together many of the prevailing ideas and beliefs in the text.

It is likely that the *Gītā* was inserted into the *Mahābhārata*. It may be that the *Gītā* was added to take advantage of the popularity of the *Mahābhārata* and thereby convey its theological and philosophical message to a larger group.[1] The centrality of *bhakti* in the text also indicates that the intended audience was a diverse one and was not limited to the *brāhmaṇas*.

Like the *Upaniṣads*, the *Gītā* was not intended to put forth a consistent theological system. This, of course, does not prevent Hindus and Hindu philosophers from reading the text as if it were. This led to a number of rival commentaries, each proposing to synthesize an otherwise varied text.

Chapters 1 and 2 of the *Gītā* are included here and set the stage for the conversation to follow. In them Arjuna expressed his terror and Kṛṣṇa offers several arguments from very different perspectives in order to try to convince him. The section from Chapter 5 concerns *niṣkāmakarma* while Chapter 9 concerns the other major theme, namely *bhakti*. Here Kṛṣṇa explains to Arjuna that devotion can take many forms and is available to all people, regardless of *varṇa*, class. Chapter 11, from which Oppenheimer, the father of the atomic bomb, purportedly quoted upon seeing a nuclear blast, is the moment when Kṛṣṇa reveals himself to be God to an awed and reverent Arjuna. In the subsequent chapter, Chapter 12, Kṛṣṇa instructs Arjuna about proper *bhakti* devotion again. Chapter 18, the final chapter of the *Gītā* ties together many of the themes, *yoga, bhakti*, and others outlined in the earlier chapters.

Note

1 John Brockington, "The Sanskrit Epics" in G. Flood (ed.), *A Blackwell Companion to Hinduism*. Oxford: Blackwell Publishing, 2003.

Further reading

Brockington, John, "The Sanskrit Epics" in G. Flood (ed.), *A Blackwell Companion to Hinduism*. Oxford: Blackwell Publishing, 2003.

Miller, Barbara Stoler, *The Bhagavad Gita: Krishna's Counsel in Time of War*. New York: Bantam, 1991.

Minor, Robert N., *Bhagavad-Gītā: An Exegetical Commentary*. Columbia, MO: South Asia Books, 1982.

Minor, Robert N. (ed.), *Modern Indian Interpreters of the Bhagavadgita*. Albany, NY: State University of New York Press, 1986.

Robinson, Catherine A., *Interpretations of the Bhagavad-Gītā and Images of the Hindu Tradition: The Song of the Lord*. London: Routledge, 2006.

Rosen, Steven J. (ed.), *Holy War: Violence and the Bhagavad Gita*. Hampton, VA: Deepak Heritage Books, 2002.

Zaehner, R. C., *The Bhagavad-Gītā, with a Commentary Based on the Original Sources*. Oxford: Clarendon Press, 1969.

Bhagavad Gītā

The First Teaching
Arjuna's Dejection

Dhritarashtra

Sanjaya, tell me what my sons
and the sons of Pandu did when they met,
wanting to battle on the field of Kuru,
on the field of sacred duty? 1

Sanjaya

Your son Duryodhana, the king,
seeing the Pandava forces arrayed,
approached his teacher Drona
and spoke in command. 2

"My teacher, see
the great Pandava army arrayed
by Drupada's son,
your pupil, intent on revenge. 3

Here are heroes, mighty archers
equal to Bhima and Arjuna in warfare,
Yuyudhana, Virata, and Drupada,
your sworn foe on his great chariot. 4

Here too are Dhrishtaketu, Cekitana,
and the brave king of Benares;
Purujit, Kuntibhoja,
and the manly king of the Shibis. 5

Yudhamanyu is bold,
and Uttamaujas is brave;
the sons of Subhadra and Draupadi
all command great chariots. 6

Now, honored priest, mark
the superb men on our side
as I tell you the names
of my army's leaders. 7

They are you and Bhishma,
Karna and Kripa, a victor in battles,
your own son Ashvatthama,
Vikarna, and the son of Somadatta. 8

Many other heroes also risk
their lives for my sake,
bearing varied weapons
and skilled in the ways of war. 9

Guarded by Bhishma, the strength
of our army is without limit;
but the strength of their army,
guarded by Bhima, is limited. 10

In all the movements of battle,
you and your men,
stationed according to plan,
must guard Bhishma well!" 11

Bhishma, fiery elder of the Kurus,
roared his lion's roar
and blew his conch horn,
exciting Duryodhana's delight. 12

Conches and kettledrums,
cymbals, tabors, and trumpets
were sounded at once
and the din of tumult arose. 13

Standing on their great chariot
yoked with white stallions,
Krishna and Arjuna, Pandu's son,
sounded their divine conches. 14

Krishna blew Pancajanya, won from a demon;
Arjuna blew Devadatta, a gift of the gods;
fierce wolf-bellied Bhima blew Paundra,
his great conch of the east. 15

Yudhishthira, Kunti's son, the king,
blew Anantavijaya, conch of boundless victory;
his twin brothers Nakula and Sahadeva
blew conches resonant and jewel toned. 16

The king of Benares, a superb archer,
and Shikhandin on his great chariot,
Drishtadyumna, Virata, and indomitable
Satyaki,
all blew their conches. 17

Drupada, with his five grandsons,
and Subhadra's strong-armed son,
each in his turn blew
their conches, O King. 18

The noise tore the hearts
of Dhritarashtra's sons,
and tumult echoed
through heaven and earth. 19

Arjuna, his war flag a rampant monkey,
saw Dhritarashtra's sons assembled

Excerpts from Barbara Stoler Miller (tr.), *The Bhagavad-Gītā*. New York: Bantam Books, 1986.

as weapons were ready to clash,
and he lifted his bow. 20

He told his charioteer:
"Krishna,
halt my chariot
between the armies! 21

Far enough for me to see
these men who lust for war,
ready to fight with me
in the strain of battle. 22

I see men gathered here,
eager to fight,
bent on serving the folly
of Dhritarashtra's son." 23

When Arjuna had spoken,
Krishna halted
their splendid chariot
between the armies. 24

Facing Bhishma and Drona
and all the great kings,
he said, "Arjuna, see
the Kuru men assembled here!" 25

Arjuna saw them standing there:
fathers, grandfathers, teachers,
uncles, brothers, sons,
grandsons, and friends. 26

He surveyed his elders
and companions in both armies,
all his kinsmen
assembled together. 27

Dejected, filled with strange pity,
he said this:
"Krishna, I see my kinsmen
gathered here, wanting war. 28

My limbs sink,
my mouth is parched,
my body trembles,
the hair bristles on my flesh. 29

The magic bow slips
from my hand, my skin burns,
I cannot stand still,
my mind reels. 30

I see omens of chaos,
Krishna; I see no good
in killing my kinsmen
in battle. 31

Krishna, I seek no victory,
or kingship or pleasures.
What use to us are kingship,
delights, or life itself? 32

We sought kingship, delights,
and pleasures for the sake of those
assembled to abandon their lives
and fortunes in battle. 33

They are teachers, fathers, sons,
and grandfathers, uncles, grandsons,
fathers and brothers of wives,
and other men of our family. 34

I do not want to kill them
even if I am killed, Krishna;
not for kingship of all three worlds,
much less for the earth! 35

What joy is there for us, Krishna,
in killing Dhritarashtra's sons?
Evil will haunt us if we kill them,
though their bows are drawn to kill. 36

Honor forbids us to kill
our cousins, Dhritarashtra's sons;
how can we know happiness
if we kill our own kinsmen? 37

The greed that distorts their reason
blinds them to the sin they commit
in ruining the family, blinds them
to the crime of betraying friends. 38

How can we ignore the wisdom
of turning from this evil
when we see the sin
of family destruction, Krishna? 39

When the family is ruined,
the timeless laws of family duty
perish; and when duty is lost,
chaos overwhelms the family. 40

In overwhelming chaos, Krishna,
women of the family are corrupted;
and when women are corrupted,
disorder is born in society. 41

This discord drags the violators
and the family itself to hell;
for ancestors fall when rites
of offering rice and water lapse. 42

The sins of men who violate
the family create disorder in society

that undermines the constant laws
of caste and family duty. 43

Krishna, we have heard
that a place in hell
is reserved for men
who undermine family duties. 44

I lament the great sin
we commit when our greed
for kingship and pleasures
drives us to kill our kinsmen. 45

If Dhritarashtra's armed sons
kill me in battle when I am unarmed
and offer no resistance,
it will be my reward." 46

Saying this in the time of war,
Arjuna slumped into the chariot
and laid down his bow and arrows,
his mind tormented by grief. 47

The Second Teaching

Philosophy and Spiritual Discipline

Sanjaya

Arjuna sat dejected,
filled with pity,
his sad eyes blurred by tears.
Krishna gave him counsel. 1

Lord Krishna

Why this cowardice
in time of crisis, Arjuna?
The coward is ignoble, shameful,
foreign to the ways of heaven. 2

Don't yield to impotence!
It is unnatural in you!
Banish this petty weakness from your heart.
Rise to the fight, Arjuna! 3

Arjuna

Krishna, how can I fight
against Bhishma and Drona
with arrows
when they deserve my worship? 4

It is better in this world
to beg for scraps of food
than to eat meals
smeared with the blood
of elders I killed
at the height of their power
while their goals
were still desires. 5

We don't know which weight
is worse to bear –
our conquering them
or their conquering us.
We will not want to live
if we kill
the sons of Dhritarashtra
assembled before us. 6

The flaw of pity
blights my very being;
conflicting sacred duties
confound my reason.
I ask you to tell me
decisively – Which is better?
I am your pupil.
Teach me what I seek! 7

I see nothing
that could drive away
the grief
that withers my senses;
even if I won kingdoms
of unrivaled wealth
on earth
and sovereignty over gods. 8

Sanjaya

Arjuna told this
to Krishna – then saying,
"I shall not fight,"
he fell silent. 9

Mocking him gently,
Krishna gave this counsel
as Arjuna sat dejected,
between the two armies. 10

Lord Krishna

You grieve for those beyond grief,
and you speak words of insight;
but learned men do not grieve
for the dead or the living. 11

Never have I not existed,
nor you, nor these kings;

and never in the future
shall we cease to exist. 12

Just as the embodied self
enters childhood, youth, and old age,
so does it enter another body;
this does not confound a steadfast man. 13

Contacts with matter make us feel
heat and cold, pleasure and pain.
Arjuna, you must learn to endure
fleeting things – they come and go! 14

When these cannot torment a man,
when suffering and joy are equal
for him and he has courage,
he is fit for immortality. 15

Nothing of nonbeing comes to be,
nor does being cease to exist;
the boundary between these two
is seen by men who see reality. 16

Indestructible is the presence
that pervades all this;
no one can destroy
this unchanging reality. 17

Our bodies are known to end,
but the embodied self is enduring,
indestructible, and immeasurable;
therefore, Arjuna, fight the battle! 18

He who thinks this self a killer
and he who thinks it killed,
both fail to understand;
it does not kill, nor is it killed. 19

It is not born,
it does not die;
having been,
it will never not be;
unborn, enduring,
constant, and primordial,
it is not killed
when the body is killed. 20

Arjuna, when a man knows the self
to be indestructible, enduring, unborn,
unchanging, how does he kill
or cause anyone to kill? 21

As a man discards
worn-out clothes
to put on new
and different ones,
so the embodied self
discards
its worn-out bodies
to take on other new ones. 22

Weapons do not cut it,
fire does not burn it,
waters do not wet it,
wind does not wither it. 23

It cannot be cut or burned;
it cannot be wet or withered;
it is enduring, all-pervasive,
fixed, immovable, and timeless. 24

It is called unmanifest,
inconceivable, and immutable;
since you know that to be so,
you should not grieve! 25

If you think of its birth
and death as ever-recurring,
then too, Great Warrior,
you have no cause to grieve! 26

Death is certain for anyone born,
and birth is certain for the dead;
since the cycle is inevitable,
you have no cause to grieve! 27

Creatures are unmanifest in origin,
manifest in the midst of life,
and unmanifest again in the end.
Since this is so, why do you lament? 28

Rarely someone
sees it,
rarely another
speaks it,
rarely anyone
hears it –
even hearing it,
no one really knows it. 29

The self embodied in the body
of every being is indestructible;
you have no cause to grieve
for all these creatures, Arjuna! 30

Look to your own duty;
do not tremble before it;
nothing is better for a warrior
than a battle of sacred duty. 31

The doors of heaven open
for warriors who rejoice
to have a battle like this
thrust on them by chance. 32

If you fail to wage this war
of sacred duty,
you will abandon your own duty
and fame only to gain evil. 33

People will tell
of your undying shame,
and for a man of honor
shame is worse than death. 34

The great chariot warriors will think
you deserted in fear of battle;
you will be despised
by those who held you in esteem. 35

Your enemies will slander you,
scorning your skill
in so many unspeakable ways –
could any suffering be worse? 36

If you are killed, you win heaven;
if you triumph, you enjoy the earth;
therefore, Arjuna, stand up
and resolve to fight the battle! 37

Impartial to joy and suffering,
gain and loss, victory and defeat,
arm yourself for the battle,
lest you fall into evil. 38

Understanding is defined in terms of
philosophy;
now hear it in spiritual discipline.
Armed with this understanding, Arjuna,
you will escape the bondage of action. 39

No effort in this world
is lost or wasted;
a fragment of sacred duty
saves you from great fear. 40

This understanding is unique
in its inner core of resolve;
diffuse and pointless are the ways
irresolute men understand. 41

Undiscerning men who delight
in the tenets of ritual lore
utter florid speech, proclaiming,
"There is nothing else!" 42

Driven by desire, they strive after heaven
and contrive to win powers and delights,
but their intricate ritual language
bears only the fruit of action in rebirth. 43

Obsessed with powers and delights,
their reason lost in words,
they do not find in contemplation
this understanding of inner resolve. 44

Arjuna, the realm of sacred lore
is nature – beyond its triad of qualities,
dualities, and mundane rewards,
be forever lucid, alive to your self. 45

For the discerning priest,
all of sacred lore
has no more value than a well
when water flows everywhere. 46

Be intent on action,
not on the fruits of action;
avoid attraction to the fruits
and attachment to inaction! 47

Perform actions, firm in discipline,
relinquishing attachment;
be impartial to failure and success –
this equanimity is called discipline. 48

Arjuna, action is far inferior
to the discipline of understanding;
so seek refuge in understanding – pitiful
are men drawn by fruits of action. 49

Disciplined by understanding,
one abandons both good and evil deeds;
so arm yourself for discipline –
discipline is skill in actions. 50

Wise men disciplined by understanding
relinquish the fruit born of action;
freed from these bonds of rebirth,
they reach a place beyond decay. 51

When your understanding passes beyond
the swamp of delusion,
you will be indifferent to all
that is heard in sacred lore. 52

When your understanding turns
from sacred lore to stand fixed,
immovable in contemplation,
then you will reach discipline. 53

Arjuna

Krishna, what defines a man
deep in contemplation whose insight
and thought are sure? How would he
speak?
How would he sit? How would he move? 54

Lord Krishna

When he gives up desires in his mind,
is content with the self within himself,
then he is said to be a man
whose insight is sure, Arjuna. 55

When suffering does not disturb his mind,
when his craving for pleasures has vanished,
when attraction, fear, and anger are gone,
he is called a sage whose thought is sure. 56

When he shows no preference
in fortune or misfortune
and neither exults nor hates,
his insight is sure. 57

When, like a tortoise retracting
its limbs, he withdraws his senses
completely from sensuous objects,
his insight is sure. 58

Sensuous objects fade
when the embodied self abstains from food;
the taste lingers, but it too fades
in the vision of higher truth. 59

Even when a man of wisdom
tries to control them, Arjuna,
the bewildering senses
attack his mind with violence. 60

Controlling them all,
with discipline he should focus on me;
when his senses are under control,
his insight is sure. 61

Brooding about sensuous objects
makes attachment to them grow;
from attachment desire arises,
from desire anger is born. 62

From anger comes confusion;
from confusion memory lapses;
from broken memory understanding is lost;
from loss of understanding, he is ruined. 63

But a man of inner strength
whose senses experience objects
without attraction and hatred,
in self-control, finds serenity. 64

In serenity, all his sorrows
dissolve;
his reason becomes serene,
his understanding sure. 65

Without discipline,
he has no understanding or inner power;
without inner power, he has no peace;
and without peace where is joy? 66

If his mind submits to the play
of the senses,
they drive away insight,
as wind drives a ship on water. 67

So, Great Warrior, when withdrawal
of the senses
from sense objects is complete,
discernment is firm. 68

When it is night for all creatures,
a master of restraint is awake;
when they are awake, it is night
for the sage who sees reality. 69

As the mountainous depths
of the ocean
are unmoved when waters
rush into it,
so the man unmoved
when desires enter him
attains a peace that eludes
the man of many desires. 70

When he renounces all desires
and acts without craving,
possessiveness,
or individuality, he finds peace. 71

This is the place of the infinite spirit;
achieving it, one is freed from delusion;
abiding in it even at the time of death,
one finds the pure calm of infinity. 72

The Third Teaching
Discipline of Action

[...]
Janaka and other ancient kings
attained perfection by action alone;
seeing the way to preserve
the world, you should act. 20

Whatever a leader does,
the ordinary people also do.
He sets the standard
for the world to follow. 21

In the three worlds,
there is nothing I must do,
nothing unattained to be attained,
yet I engage in action. 22

What if I did not engage
relentlessly in action?
Men retrace my path
at every turn, Arjuna. 23

These worlds would collapse
if I did not perform action;
I would create disorder in society,
living beings would be destroyed. 24

As the ignorant act with attachment
to actions, Arjuna,
so wise men should act with detachment
to preserve the world. 25

No wise man disturbs the understanding
of ignorant men attached to action;
he should inspire them,
performing all actions with discipline. 26

Actions are all effected
by the qualities of nature;
but deluded by individuality,
the self thinks, "I am the actor." 27

When he can discriminate
the actions of nature's qualities
and think, "The qualities depend
on other qualities," he is detached. 28

Those deluded by the qualities of nature
are attached to their actions;
a man who knows this should not upset
these dull men of partial knowledge. 29

Surrender all actions to me,
and fix your reason on your inner self;
without hope or possessiveness,
your fever subdued, fight the battle! 30

Men who always follow my thought,
trusting it without finding fault,
are freed
even by their actions. 31

But those who find fault
and fail to follow my thought,
know that they are lost fools,
deluded by every bit of knowledge. 32

Even a man of knowledge
behaves in accord with his own nature;
creatures all conform to nature;
what can one do to restrain them? 33

Attraction and hatred are poised
in the object of every sense experience;
a man must not fall prey
to these two brigands lurking on his path! 34

Your own duty done imperfectly
is better than another man's done well.
It is better to die in one's own duty;
another man's duty is perilous. 35

Arjuna

Krishna, what makes a person
commit evil
against his own will,
as if compelled by force? 36

Lord Krishna

It is desire and anger, arising
from nature's quality of passion;
know it here as the enemy,
voracious and very evil! 37

As fire is obscured by smoke
and a mirror by dirt,
as an embryo is veiled by its caul,
so is knowledge obscured by this. 38

Knowledge is obscured
by the wise man's eternal enemy,
which takes form as desire,
an insatiable fire, Arjuna. 39

The senses, mind, and understanding
are said to harbor desire;
with these desire obscures knowledge
and confounds the embodied self. 40

Therefore, first restrain
your senses, Arjuna,
then kill this evil
that ruins knowledge and judgment. 41

Men say that the senses are superior
to their objects, the mind superior to the senses,
understanding superior to the mind;
higher than understanding is the self. 42

Knowing the self beyond understanding,
sustain the self with the self.
Great Warrior, kill the enemy
menacing you in the form of desire! 43

The Fourth Teaching
Knowledge

Lord Krishna

I taught this undying discipline
to the shining sun, first of mortals,
who told it to Manu, the progenitor of man;
Manu told it to the solar king Ikshvaku. 1

Royal sages knew this discipline,
which the tradition handed down;
but over the course of time
it has decayed, Arjuna. 2

This is the ancient discipline
that I have taught to you today;
you are my devotee and my friend,
and this is the deepest mystery. 3

Arjuna

Your birth followed the birth
of the sun;
how can I comprehend that you taught it
in the beginning? 4

Lord Krishna

I have passed through many births
and so have you;
I know them all,
but you do not, Arjuna. 5

The Fifth Teaching
Renunciation of Action

Arjuna

Krishna, you praise renunciation
of actions and then discipline;
tell me with certainty
which is the better of these two. 1

Lord Krishna

Renunciation and discipline in action
both effect good beyond measure;
but of the two, discipline in action
surpasses renunciation of action. 2

The man of eternal renunciation
is one who neither hates nor desires;
beyond dualities,
he is easily freed from bondage. 3

Simpletons separate philosophy
and discipline, but the learned do not;
applying one correctly, a man
finds the fruit of both. 4

Men of discipline reach the same place
that philosophers attain;
he really sees who sees philosophy
and discipline to be one. 5

Renunciation is difficult to attain
without discipline;
a sage armed with discipline
soon reaches the infinite spirit. 6

Armed with discipline, he purifies
and subdues the self, masters his senses,
unites himself with the self of all creatures;
even when he acts, he is not defiled. 7

Seeing, hearing, touching, smelling,
eating, walking, sleeping, breathing,
the disciplined man who knows reality
should think, "I do nothing at all." 8

When talking, giving, taking,
opening and closing his eyes,
he keeps thinking, "It is the senses
that engage in sense objects." 9

A man who relinquishes attachment
and dedicates actions to the infinite spirit
is not stained by evil,
like a lotus leaf unstained by water. 10

Relinquishing attachment,
men of discipline perform action
with body, mind, understanding, and senses
for the purification of the self. 11

Relinquishing the fruit of action,
the disciplined man attains perfect peace;
the undisciplined man is in bondage,
attached to the fruit of his desire. 12

Renouncing all actions with the mind,
the masterful embodied self
dwells at ease in its nine-gated fortress –
it neither acts nor causes action. 13

The lord of the world
does not create agency or actions,

or a union of fruits with actions;
but his being unfolds into existence. 14

The lord does not partake
of anyone's evil or good conduct;
knowledge is obscured by ignorance,
so people are deluded. 15

When ignorance is destroyed
by knowledge of the self,
then, like the sun, knowledge
illumines ultimate reality. 16

That becomes their understanding,
their self, their basis, and their goal,
and they reach a state beyond return,
their sin dispelled by knowledge. 17

Learned men see with an equal eye
a scholarly and dignified priest,
a cow, an elephant, a dog,
and even an outcaste scavenger. 18

Men who master the worldly world
have equanimity –
they exist in the infinite spirit,
in its flawless equilibrium. 19

The Ninth Teaching
The Sublime Mystery

Lord Krishna

I will teach the deepest mystery
to you since you find no fault;
realizing it with knowledge and judgment,
you will be free from misfortune. 1

This science and mystery of kings
is the supreme purifier,
intuitive, true to duty,
joyous to perform, unchanging. 2

Without faith in sacred duty,
men fail to reach me, Arjuna;
they return to the cycle
of death and rebirth. 3

The whole universe is pervaded
by my unmanifest form;
all creatures exist in me,
but I do not exist in them. 4

Behold the power of my discipline;
these creatures are really not in me;
my self quickens creatures,
sustaining them without being in them. 5

Just as the wide-moving wind
is constantly present in space,
so all creatures exist in me;
understand it to be so! 6

As an eon ends, all creatures
fold into my nature, Arjuna;
and I create them again
as a new eon begins. 7

Gathering in my own nature,
again and again I freely create
this whole throng of creatures,
helpless in the force of my nature. 8

These actions do not bind me,
since I remain detached
in all my actions, Arjuna,
as if I stood apart from them. 9

Nature, with me as her inner eye,
bears animate and inanimate beings;
and by reason of this, Arjuna,
the universe continues to turn. 10

Deluded men despise me
in the human form I have assumed,
ignorant of my higher existence
as the great lord of creatures. 11

Reason warped, hope, action,
and knowledge wasted,
they fall prey to a seductive
fiendish, demonic nature. 12

In single-minded dedication, great souls
devote themselves to my divine nature,
knowing me as unchanging,
the origin of creatures. 13

Always glorifying me,
striving, firm in their vows,
paying me homage with devotion,
they worship me, always disciplined. 14

Sacrificing through knowledge,
others worship my universal presence
in its unity
and in its many different aspects. 15

I am the rite, the sacrifice,
the libation for the dead, the healing herb,
the sacred hymn, the clarified butter,
the fire, the oblation. 16

I am the universal father,
mother, granter of all, grandfather,
object of knowledge, purifier,
holy syllable OM, threefold sacred lore. 17

I am the way, sustainer, lord,
witness, shelter, refuge, friend,
source, dissolution, stability,
treasure, and unchanging seed. 18

I am heat that withholds
and sends down the rains;
I am immortality and death;
both being and nonbeing am I. 19

Men learned in sacred lore,
Soma drinkers, their sins absolved,
worship me with sacrifices,
seeking to win heaven.
Reaching the holy world of Indra,
king of the gods,
they savor the heavenly delights
of the gods in the celestial sphere. 20

When they have long enjoyed
the world of heaven
and their merit is exhausted,
they enter the mortal world;
following the duties
ordained in sacred lore,
desiring desires,
they obtain what is transient. 21

Men who worship me,
thinking solely of me,
always disciplined,
win the reward I secure. 22

When devoted men sacrifice
to other deities with faith,
they sacrifice to me, Arjuna,
however aberrant the rites. 23

I am the enjoyer
and the lord of all sacrifices;
they do not know me in reality,
and so they fail. 24

Votaries of the gods go to the gods,
ancestor-worshippers go to the ancestors,
those who propitiate ghosts go to them,
and my worshippers go to me. 25

The leaf or flower or fruit or water
that he offers with devotion,
I take from the man of self-restraint
in response to his devotion. 26

Whatever you do – what you take,
what you offer, what you give,
what penances you perform –
do as an offering to me, Arjuna! 27

You will be freed from the bonds of action,
from the fruit of fortune and misfortune;
armed with the discipline of renunciation,
your self liberated, you will join me. 28

I am impartial to all creatures,
and no one is hateful or dear to me;
but men devoted to me are in me,
and I am within them. 29

If he is devoted solely to me,
even a violent criminal
must be deemed a man of virtue,
for his resolve is right. 30

His spirit quickens to sacred duty,
and he finds eternal peace;
Arjuna, know that no one
devoted to me is lost. 31

If they rely on me, Arjuna,
women, commoners, men of low rank,
even men born in the womb of evil,
reach the highest way. 32

How easy it is then for holy priests
and devoted royal sages –
in this transient world of sorrow,
devote yourself to me! 33

Keep me in your mind and devotion,
sacrifice to me, bow to me,
discipline your self toward me,
and you will reach me! 34

The Eleventh Teaching

The Vision of Krishna's Totality

Arjuna

To favor me you revealed
the deepest mystery of the self,
and by your words
my delusion is dispelled. 1

I heard from you in detail
how creatures come to be and die,
Krishna, and about the self
in its immutable greatness. 2

Just as you have described
yourself, I wish to see your form
in all its majesty,
Krishna, Supreme among Men. 3

If you think I can see it,
reveal to me
your immutable self,
Krishna, Lord of Discipline. 4

Lord Krishna

Arjuna, see my forms
in hundreds and thousands;
diverse, divine,
of many colors and shapes. 5

See the sun gods, gods of light,
howling storm gods, twin gods of dawn,
and gods of wind, Arjuna,
wondrous forms not seen before. 6

Arjuna, see all the universe,
animate and inanimate,
and whatever else you wish to see;
all stands here as one in my body. 7

But you cannot see me
with your own eye;
I will give you a divine eye to see
the majesty of my discipline. 8

Sanjaya

O King, saying this, Krishna,
the great lord of discipline,
revealed to Arjuna
the true majesty of his form. 9

It was a multiform, wondrous vision,
with countless mouths and eyes
and celestial ornaments,
brandishing many divine weapons. 10

Everywhere was boundless divinity
containing all astonishing things,
wearing divine garlands and garments,
annointed with divine perfume. 11

If the light of a thousand suns
were to rise in the sky at once,
it would be like the light
of that great spirit. 12

Arjuna saw all the universe
in its many ways and parts,
standing as one in the body
of the god of gods. 13

Then filled with amazement,
his hair bristling on his flesh,
Arjuna bowed his head to the god,
joined his hands in homage, and spoke. 14

Arjuna

I see the gods
in your body, O God,
and hordes
of varied creatures:
Brahma, the cosmic creator,
on his lotus throne,
all the seers
and celestial serpents. 15

I see your boundless form
everywhere,
the countless arms,
bellies, mouths, and eyes;
Lord of All,
I see no end,
or middle or beginning
to your totality. 16

I see you blazing
through the fiery rays
of your crown, mace, and discus,
hard to behold
in the burning light
of fire and sun
that surrounds
your measureless presence. 17

You are to be known
as supreme eternity,
the deepest treasure
of all that is,
the immutable guardian
of enduring sacred duty;
I think you are
man's timeless spirit. 18

I see no beginning
or middle or end to you;
only boundless strength
in your endless arms,
the moon and sun in your eyes,
your mouths of consuming flames,
your own brilliance
scorching this universe. 19

You alone
fill the space
between heaven and earth
and all the directions;
seeing this awesome,
terrible form of yours,
Great Soul,
the three worlds
tremble. 20

Throngs of gods enter you,
some in their terror
make gestures of homage
to invoke you;
throngs of great sages
and saints
hail you and praise you
in resounding hymns. 21

Howling storm gods, sun gods,
bright gods, and gods of ritual,
gods of the universe,
twin gods of dawn, wind gods,
vapor-drinking ghosts,
throngs of celestial musicians,
demigods, demons, and saints,
all gaze at you amazed. 22

Seeing the many mouths
and eyes
of your great form,
its many arms,
thighs, feet,
bellies, and fangs,
the worlds tremble
and so do I. 23

Vishnu, seeing you brush
the clouds with flames
of countless colors,
your mouths agape,
your huge eyes blazing,
my inner self quakes
and I find no resolve
or tranquility. 24

Seeing the fangs
protruding
from your mouths
like the fires of time,
I lose my bearings
and I find no refuge;
be gracious, Lord of Gods,
Shelter of the Universe. 25

All those sons
of the blind king
Dhritarashtra
come accompanied
by troops of kings,
by the generals Bhishma,
Drona, Karna,
and by our battle leaders. 26

Rushing through
your fangs
into grim
mouths,
some are dangling
from heads
crushed
between your teeth. 27

As roiling
river waters
stream headlong
toward the sea,
so do these human
heroes enter
into your blazing
mouths. 28

As moths
in the frenzy
of destruction
fly into a blazing flame,
worlds
in the frenzy
of destruction
enter your mouths. 29

You lick at the worlds
around you,
devouring them
with flaming mouths;
and your terrible fires
scorch the entire universe,
filling it, Vishnu,
with violent rays. 30

Tell me –
who are you
in this terrible form?
Homage to you, Best of Gods!
Be gracious! I want to know you
as you are in your beginning.
I do not comprehend
the course of your ways. 31

Lord Krishna

I am time grown old,
creating world destruction,
set in motion
to annihilate the worlds;
even without you,
all these warriors
arrayed in hostile ranks
will cease to exist. 32

Therefore, arise
and win glory!
Conquer your foes
and fulfill your kingship!
They are already
killed by me.
Be just my instrument,
the archer at my side! 33

Drona, Bhishma, Jayadratha,
and Karna,
and all the other battle heroes,
are killed by me.
Kill them
without wavering;
fight, and you will conquer
your foes in battle! 34

Sanjaya

Hearing Krishna's words,
Arjuna trembled
under his crown,
and he joined his hands
in reverent homage;
terrified of his fear,
he bowed to Krishna
and stammered in reply. 35

Arjuna

Krishna, the universe
responds
with joy and rapture
to your glory,
terrified demons
flee in far directions,
and saints throng
to bow in homage. 36

Why should they not bow
in homage to you, Great Soul,
Original Creator,
more venerable than the creator Brahma?
Boundless Lord of Gods,
Shelter of All That Is,
you are eternity,
being, nonbeing, and beyond. 37

You are the original god,
the primordial spirit of man,
the deepest treasure
of all that is,
knower and what is to be known,
the supreme abode;
you pervade the universe,
Lord of Boundless Form. 38

You are the gods of wind,
death, fire, and water;
the moon; the lord of life;
and the great ancestor.
Homage to you,
a thousand times homage!
I bow in homage to you
again and yet again. 39

I bow in homage
before you and behind you;
I bow everywhere
to your omnipresence!
You have boundless strength
and limitless force;
you fulfill
all that you are. 40

Thinking you a friend,
I boldly said,
"Welcome, Krishna!
Welcome, cousin, friend!"
From negligence,
or through love,
I failed to know
your greatness. 41

If in jest
I offended you,
alone
or publicly,
at sport, rest,
sitting, or at meals,
I beg your patience,
unfathomable Krishna. 42

You are father of the world
of animate and inanimate things,
its venerable teacher,
most worthy of worship,
without equal.
Where in all three worlds
is another to match
your extraordinary power? 43

I bow to you,
I prostrate my body,
I beg you to be gracious,
Worshipful Lord –
as a father to a son,
a friend to a friend,
a lover to a beloved,
O God, bear with me. 44

I am thrilled,
and yet my mind
trembles with fear
at seeing
what has not been seen before.
Show me, God, the form I know –
be gracious, Lord of Gods,
Shelter of the World. 45

I want to see you
as before,
with your crown and mace,
and the discus in your hand.
O Thousand-Armed God,
assume the four-armed form
embodied
in your totality. 46

Lord Krishna

To grace you, Arjuna,
I revealed
through self-discipline
my higher form,
which no one but you
has ever beheld –
brilliant, total,
boundless, primal. 47

Not through sacred lore
or sacrificial ritual
or study or charity,
not by rites
or by terrible penances
can I be seen in this form
in the world of men
by anyone but you, Great Hero. 48

Do not tremble
or suffer confusion
from seeing
my horrific form;
your fear dispelled,
your mind full of love,
see my form again
as it was. 49

Sanjaya

Saying this to Arjuna,
Krishna once more
revealed
his intimate form;
resuming his gentle body,
the great spirit
let the terrified hero
regain his breath. 50

Arjuna

Seeing your gentle human form,
Krishna, I recover
my own nature,
and my reason is restored. 51

Lord Krishna

This form you have seen
is rarely revealed;
the gods are constantly craving
for a vision of this form. 52

Not through sacred lore,
penances, charity, or sacrificial rites
can I be seen in the form
that you saw me. 53

By devotion alone
can I, as I really am,
be known and seen
and entered into, Arjuna. 54

Acting only for me, intent on me,
free from attachment,
hostile to no creature, Arjuna,
a man of devotion comes to me. 55

The Twelfth Teaching
Devotion

Arjuna

Who best knows discipline:
men who worship you with devotion,
ever disciplined, or men who worship
the imperishable, unmanifest? 1

Lord Krishna

I deem most disciplined
men of enduring discipline
who worship me with true faith,
entrusting their minds to me. 2

Men reach me too who worship
what is imperishable, ineffable, unmanifest,
omnipresent, inconceivable,
immutable at the summit of existence. 3

Mastering their senses,
with equanimity toward everything,
they reach me, rejoicing
in the welfare of all creatures. 4

It is more arduous when their reason
clings to my unmanifest nature;
for men constrained by bodies,
the unmanifest way is hard to attain. 5

But men intent on me
renounce all actions to me
and worship me, meditating
with singular discipline. 6

When they entrust reason to me,
Arjuna, I soon arise
to rescue them from the ocean
of death and rebirth. 7

Focus your mind on me,
let your understanding enter me;
then you will dwell
in me without doubt. 8

If you cannot concentrate
your thought firmly on me,
then seek to reach me, Arjuna,
by discipline in practice. 9

Even if you fail in practice,
dedicate yourself to action;
performing actions for my sake,
you will achieve success. 10

If you are powerless to do
even this, rely on my discipline,
be self-controlled,
and reject all fruit of action. 11

Knowledge is better than practice,
meditation better than knowledge,
rejecting fruits of action
is better still – it brings peace. 12

One who bears hate for no creature
is friendly, compassionate, unselfish,
free of individuality, patient,
the same in suffering and joy. 13

Content always, disciplined,
self-controlled, firm in his resolve,
his mind and understanding dedicated to me,
devoted to me, he is dear to me. 14

The world does not flee from him,
nor does he flee from the world;
free of delight, rage, fear,
and disgust, he is dear to me. 15

Disinterested, pure, skilled,
indifferent, untroubled,
relinquishing all involvements,
devoted to me, he is dear to me. 16

He does not rejoice or hate,
grieve or feel desire;
relinquishing fortune and misfortune,
the man of devotion is dear to me. 17

Impartial to foe and friend,
honor and contempt,
cold and heat, joy and suffering,
he is free from attachment. 18

Neutral to blame and praise,
silent, content with his fate,
unsheltered, firm in thought,
the man of devotion is dear to me. 19

Even more dear to me are devotees
who cherish this elixir of sacred duty
as I have taught it,
intent on me in their faith. 20

The Eighteenth Teaching
The Wondrous Dialogue Concludes

Arjuna

Krishna, I want to know
the real essence
of both renunciation
and relinquishment. 1

Lord Krishna

Giving up actions based on desire,
the poets know as "renunciation";
relinquishing all fruit of action,
learned men call "relinquishment." 2

Some wise men say all action
is flawed and must be relinquished;
others say action in sacrifice, charity,
and penance must not be relinquished. 3

Arjuna, hear my decision
about relinquishment;
it is rightly declared
to be of three kinds. 4

Action in sacrifice, charity,
and penance is to be performed,
not relinquished – for wise men,
they are acts of sanctity. 5

But even these actions
should be done by relinquishing to me
attachment and the fruit of action –
this is my decisive idea. 6

Renunciation of prescribed action
is inappropriate;
relinquished in delusion,
it becomes a way of dark inertia. 7

When one passionately relinquishes
difficult action from fear
of bodily harm, he cannot win
the fruit of relinquishment. 8

But if one performs prescribed action
because it must be done,
relinquishing attachment and the fruit,
his relinquishment is a lucid act. 9

He does not disdain unskilled action
nor cling to skilled action;
in his lucidity the relinquisher
is wise and his doubts are cut away. 10

A man burdened by his body
cannot completely relinquish actions,
but a relinquisher is defined
as one who can relinquish the fruits. 11

The fruit of action haunts men
in death if they fail to relinquish
all forms, unwanted, wanted, and mixed –
but not if men renounce them. 12

Arjuna, learn from me
the five causes
for the success of all actions
as explained in philosophical analysis. 13

They are the material basis,
the agent, the different instruments,
various kinds of behavior,
and finally fate, the fifth. 14

Whatever action one initiates
through body, speech, and mind,
be it proper or perverse,
these five causes are present. 15

This being so, when a man
of poor understanding and misjudgment
sees himself as the only agent,
he cannot be said to see. 16

When one is free of individuality
and his understanding is untainted,
even if he kills these people,
he does not kill and is not bound. 17

Knowledge, its object, and its subject
are the triple stimulus of action;
instrument, act, and agent
are the constituents of action. 18

Knowledge, action, agent are threefold,
differentiated by qualities of nature;
hear how this has been explained
in the philosophical analysis of qualities. 19

Know that through lucid knowledge
one sees in all creatures
a single, unchanging existence,
undivided within its divisions. 20

Know passionate knowledge
as that which regards
various distinct existences
separately in all creatures. 21

But knowledge that clings
to a single thing as if it were the whole,
limited, lacking a sense of reality,
is known for its dark inertia. 22

Action known for its lucidity
is necessary, free of attachment,
performed without attraction or hatred
by one who seeks no fruit. 23

Action called passionate
is performed with great effort
by an individualist
who seeks to satisfy his desires. 24

Action defined by dark inertia
is undertaken in delusion,
without concern for consequences,
for death or violence, or for manhood. 25

An agent called pure
has no attachment or individualism,
is resolute and energetic,
unchanged in failure and success. 26

An agent said to be passionate
is anxious to gain the fruit of action,
greedy, essentially violent, impure,
subject to excitement and grief. 27

An agent defined by dark inertia
is undisciplined, vulgar, stubborn,
fraudulent, dishonest, lazy,
depressed, and slow to act. 28

Listen as I tell you without reserve
about understanding and resolve,
each in three aspects,
according to the qualities of nature. 29

In one who knows activity and rest,
acts of right and wrong,
bravery and fear, bondage and freedom,
understanding is lucid. 30

When one fails to discern
sacred duty from chaos,
right acts from wrong,
understanding is passionate. 31

When it thinks in perverse ways,
is covered in darkness,
imagining chaos to be sacred duty,
understanding is darkly inert. 32

When it sustains acts
of mind, breath, and senses
through discipline without wavering,
resolve is lucid. 33

When it sustains with attachment
duty, desire, and wealth,
craving their fruits,
resolve is passionate. 34

When a fool cannot escape
dreaming, fear, grief,
depression, and intoxication,
courage is darkly inert. 35

Arjuna, now hear about joy,
the three ways of finding delight
through practice
that brings an end to suffering. 36

The joy of lucidity
at first seems like poison
but is in the end like ambrosia,
from the calm of self-understanding. 37

The joy that is passionate
at first seems like ambrosia
when senses encounter sense objects,
but in the end it is like poison. 38

The joy arising from sleep,
laziness, and negligence,
self-deluding from beginning to end,
is said to be darkly inert. 39

There is no being on earth
or among the gods in heaven
free from the triad of qualities
that are born of nature. 40

The actions of priests, warriors,
commoners, and servants
are apportioned by qualities
born of their intrinsic being. 41

Tranquility, control, penance,
purity, patience and honesty,
knowledge, judgment, and piety
are intrinsic to the action of a priest. 42

Heroism, fiery energy, resolve,
skill, refusal to retreat in battle,
charity, and majesty in conduct
are intrinsic to the action of a warrior. 43

Farming, herding cattle, and commerce
are intrinsic to the action of a commoner;
action that is essentially service
is intrinsic to the servant. 44

Each one achieves success
by focusing on his own action;
hear how one finds success
by focusing on his own action. 45

By his own action a man finds success,
worshipping the source
of all creatures' activity,
the presence pervading all that is. 46

Better to do one's own duty imperfectly
than to do another man's well;
doing action intrinsic to his being,
a man avoids guilt. 47

Arjuna, a man should not relinquish
action he is born to, even if it is flawed;
all undertakings are marred by a flaw,
as fire is obscured by smoke. 48

His understanding everywhere detached,
the self mastered, longing gone,
one finds through renunciation
the supreme success beyond action. 49

Understand in summary from me
how when he achieves success
one attains the infinite spirit,
the highest state of knowledge. 50

Armed with his purified understanding,
subduing the self with resolve,
relinquishing sensuous objects,
avoiding attraction and hatred; 51

Observing solitude, barely eating,
restraining speech, body, and mind;
practicing discipline in meditation,
cultivating dispassion; 52

Freeing himself from individuality, force,
pride, desire, anger, acquisitiveness;
unpossessive, tranquil,
he is at one with the infinite spirit. 53

Being at one with the infinite spirit,
serene in himself, he does not grieve or crave;
impartial toward all creatures,
he achieves supreme devotion to me. 54

Through devotion he discerns me,
just who and how vast I really am;
and knowing me in reality,
he enters into my presence. 55

Always performing all actions,
taking refuge in me,
he attains through my grace
the eternal place beyond change. 56

Through reason, renounce all works
in me, focus on me;
relying on the discipline of understanding,
always keep me in your thought. 57

If I am in your thought, by my grace
you will transcend all dangers;
but if you are deafened
by individuality, you will be lost. 58

Your resolve is futile
if a sense of individuality
makes you think, "I shall not fight" –
nature will compel you to. 59

You are bound by your own action,
intrinsic to your being, Arjuna;
even against your will you must do
what delusion now makes you refuse. 60

Arjuna, the lord resides
in the heart of all creatures,
making them reel magically,
as if a machine moved them. 61

With your whole being, Arjuna,
take refuge in him alone –
from his grace you will attain
the eternal place that is peace. 62

This knowledge I have taught
is more arcane than any mystery –
consider it completely,
then act as you choose. 63

Listen to my profound words,
the deepest mystery of all,
for you are precious to me
and I tell you for your good. 64

Keep your mind on me,
be my devotee, sacrificing, bow to me –
you will come to me, I promise,
for you are dear to me. 65

Relinquishing all sacred duties to me,
make me your only refuge;
do not grieve,
for I shall free you from all evils. 66

You must not speak of this
to one who is without penance and devotion,
or who does not wish to hear,
or who finds fault with me. 67

When he shares this deepest mystery
with others devoted to me,
giving me his total devotion,
a man will come to me without doubt. 68

No mortal can perform
service for me that I value more,
and no other man on earth
will be more dear to me than he is. 69

I judge the man who studies
our dialogue on sacred duty
to offer me sacrifice
through sacrifice in knowledge. 70

If he listens in faith,
finding no fault, a man is free
and will attain the cherished worlds
of those who act in virtue. 71

Arjuna, have you listened
with your full powers of reason?
Has the delusion of ignorance
now been destroyed? 72

Arjuna

Krishna, my delusion is destroyed,
and by your grace I have regained memory;
I stand here, my doubt dispelled,
ready to act on your words. 73

Sanjaya

As I heard this wondrous dialogue
between Krishna and Arjuna,
the man of great soul,
the hair bristled on my flesh. 74

By grace of the epic poet Vyasa, I heard
the mystery of supreme discipline
recounted by Krishna himself,
the lord of discipline incarnate. 75

O King, when I keep remembering
this wondrous and holy dialogue
between Krishna and Arjuna,
I rejoice again and again. 76

In my memory I recall again
and again Krishna's wondrous form –
great is my amazement, King;
I rejoice again and again. 77

Where Krishna is lord of discipline
and Arjuna is the archer,
there do fortune, victory, abundance,
and morality exist, so I think. 78

Chapter 6

The *Rāmāyaṇa* of Vālmīki

The most well-known story in South Asia is arguably the *Rāmāyaṇa* of Vālmīki. An epic tale of epic proportions (it is 20,000 verses), it has been told and retold innumerable times and has spread to Cambodia and Bali as well as to other parts of South East Asia.[1] Though it has changed in each of its *avatāras*, incarnations, the basic plot revolving around the complexities of upholding *dharma* that was solidified by the first century CE, has remained somewhat the same in each retelling. The tale thus concerns the adventures of Prince Rāma, who is an *avatāra* of Viṣṇu, the archetypal *kṣatriya*, and an exemplary follower of *dharma*, and the trials and tribulations he undergoes in order to rescue his wife Sītā who was kidnapped by the *rākṣasa* king Rāvaṇa. Despite the complexities of *dharma*, the plot is *prima facie* uncomplicated: Prince Rāma, who is the son of King Daśaratha of Ayodhyā, marries Sītā, daughter of King Janaka of Videha. After returning to Ayodhyā with his wife, Rāma is told that his father will abdicate so Rāma prepares to be consecrated as the new king. Kaikeyī, Daśaratha's second wife, forces Rāma to leave Ayodhyā and to live exiled in the Daṇḍaka forest for 14 years. She does so by reason of a favor that Daśaratha owes to her. Rāma accompanied by Sītā, and his devoted and loyal brother Lakṣmaṇa, travel into the Daṇḍaka forest to begin their odyssey. Their idyllic yet arduous life, however, is interrupted when Rāvaṇa, the *rākṣasa* king of Ír-Laṅkā, kidnaps Sītā who he wants to keep as his wife. Rāma and Lakṣmaṇa chase after her and, en route, meet the monkey king Sugrīva and his general, Hanumān who assist them to locate Sītā in Laṅkā. Hanumān serves Rāma faithfully and becomes his most ardent devotee.[2] After building a bridge from India to Laṅkā with the help of the monkey army, righteous Rāma kills wicked Rāvaṇa and Sītā is rescued. Though one would think that the reunited couple would live happily ever after, trouble arises when the citizens of Ayodhyā doubt that Sītā has been faithful to her husband Rāma while under Rāvaṇa's lustful and leering gaze. To this end, Rāma demands that Sītā dutifully undergo the *agnipaīikṣa*, trial by fire, whereby she is to enter a fire and survive the flames unscathed to prove that she is a *satī*, virtuous wife, her purity and virtue.[3] Despite this, she is nonetheless banished to the *āśrama*, hermitage, of Vālmiki where she gives birth to twins. When Rāma discovers her and his sons and asks her to return, Sītā beseeches the Earth, who is her mother ("Sītā" means furrow), which splits open and swallows her.

The central theme of the *Rāmāyaṇa* is *dharma* and it pervades nearly every story and embedded story in the epic. First, Daśaratha must follow his *dharma* by keeping his word to Kaikeyī. Next, Rāma must follow his *dharma* by obeying the words of his father, counter-intuitive as they may seem. Sītā must also follow *pativrata*, wifely duty, and her *dharma* as an *atī*, virtuous women, by following her exiled husband into the forest. Finally, when it seems as if *dharma* has triumphed over *adharma*, when Rāvaṇa is killed, Sītā is obliged to prove that she too has followed her *dharma* as a wife, so that Rāma may fulfill his *dharma* as king of Ayodhyā.[4]

The story, as already mentioned, has captured the imagination of South Asia and parts of South East Asia. Angkor Wat, built by the Khmer king Suryavarman II between 1113 and 1150 CE in Siem Reap, Cambodia, contains, for example, enormous bas-relief carvings from the Cambodian version of the *Rāmāyaṇa*. And, in recent times, between 1987 and 1988, a 78-episode TV serial of the *Rāmāyaṇa* directed by Ramanand Sagar, aired. The serial was so popular that much of India came to a standstill when it was shown. The segments where *dharma* was most controversial, such as Sītā's *agnipalikṣa*, became a flashpoint for public debates. The *Rāmāyaṇa* is also performed as a play in many villages in India and South East Asia and the text is ritually chanted on auspicious occasions such as the Rāmanavami, Rāma's birthday.[5]

The centrality of Rāma and the *Rāmāyaṇa* has serious consequences when, on December 6, 1992, the Babri Masjid, a mosque believed by some Hindus to have been built on the site where there once existed the Rām Janmabhūmi Temple, was destroyed by zealous Rāma devotees. This temple, as the name indicates, was believed to have been built in the same place where Rāma was born. Though the historical accuracy of these claims is still under dispute, the catastrophic conflagration points towards the centrality of the *Rāmāyaṇa*.[6]

The first few passages included here are from the *Bālakāṇḍa*, *Childhood Volume*, of Vālmīki's text. The first *sarga*, chapter, of the *Bālakāṇḍa* is a brief summary of the basic plot of the *Rāmāyaṇa*. *Sarga* 65 is the story of how Rāma travels to Videha to win Sītā as his wife. King Janaka, her father, stipulates that eligible suitors must pass a feat of strength, to break Śiva's bow, in order to be married to Sītā. Rāma breaks the bow, weds Sītā, and returns triumphantly to Ayodhyā.

The next selection is from the *Araṇyakāṇḍa*, *Forest*, volume. *Sarga* 16 is crucial to the plot and involves Śūrpaṇakhā, Rāvaṇa's sister. She spies on Rāma and Lakṣmaṇa in the Daṇḍaka forest and becomes infatuated with Rāma. After imploring him to abandon Sītā and then threatening Sītā when Rāma refuses, she is mutilated by Lakṣmaṇa.[7] In *sargas* 30 and 31, Śūrpaṇakha retreats to Laṅkā, narrates her misfortune to her brother, seeking assistance to avenge her mutilation. Consequently, in *sarga* 32 Rāvaṇa himself becomes infatuated with Sītā merely from his sister's description. He then plots, in *sargas* 33, 34, and 35 with the demon Mārīca to capture Sītā by means of a ruse, despite Marīcā's advice not to.

In *sargas* 40–48, the clever trick is enacted when Marīcā takes the form of a deer and entices Sītā, who asks Rāma to chase after the deer. Lakṣmaṇa is left to protect Sītā but, at Sītā's behest he is forced to leave her, in spite of his better judgment. She is subsequently kidnapped by Rāvaṇa and taken to Laṅkā. These *sargas* include debates between Sītā and Lakṣmaṇa and between Rāvaṇa and Sītā.

Notes

1 See Paula Richman, *Many Rāmāyaṇas: The Diversity of a Narrative Tradition in South Asia*. Berkeley: University of California Press, 1991.

2 See Philip Lutgentdorf, *Hanuman's Tale: The Messages of a Divine Monkey*. Oxford: Oxford University Press, 2007.

3 See Linda Hess, "Rejecting Sita: Indian Reponses to the Ideal Man's Cruel Treatment of His Ideal Wife." *Journal of the American Academy of Religion*. 67(1), 1999: 1–32.

4 See Robert Goldman, "*Eṣa Dharmaḥ Sanātanaḥ*: Shifting Moral Values and the Indian Epics" in P. Bilimoria and J. N. Mohanty (eds.), *Relativism, Suffering and Beyond: Essays in Memory of Bimal K. Matilal*. Delhi: Oxford University Press, 1997.

5 See Joyce Burkhalter Flueckiger and Laurie J. Sears (eds.), *Boundaries of the Text: Epic Performances in South and Southeast Asia*. Ann Arbor, MI: Center for South and Southeast Asian Studies, University of Michigan, 1991 and Mandakranta Bose (ed.), *The Rāmāyaṇa Revisited*. Oxford: Oxford University Press, 2004.

6 See P. V. Narasimha Rao, *Ayodhya: 6 December 1992*. Delhi: Penguin Books, 2006. See S. Gopal (ed.), *Anatomy of a Confrontation: The Babri Masjid-Ram Janmbhumi Issue*. Delhi: Penguin Books, 1991.

7 See Kathleen Erndl, "The Mutilation of Śūrpaṇakhā" in Paula Richman, *Many Rāmāyaṇas: The Diversity of a Narrative Tradition in South Asia*. Berkeley, CA: University of California Press, 1991.

Further reading

Bose, Mandakranta (ed.), *The Rāmāyaṇa Revisited*. Oxford: Oxford University Press, 2004.

Brockington, John, *The Sanskrit Epics*. Leiden and Boston: Brill, 1998.

Brockington, John, "The Sanskrit Epics" in G. Flood (ed.), *A Blackwell Companion to Hinduism*. Oxford: Blackwell Publishing, 2003.

Erndl, Kathleen, "The Mutilation of Śūrpaṇakhā" in Paula Richman, *Many Rāmāyaṇas: The Diversity of a Narrative Tradition in South Asia*. Berkeley, CA: University of California Press, 1991.

Goldman, Robert, "*Eṣa Dharmaḥ Sanātanaḥ*: Shifting Moral Values and the Indian Epics" in P. Bilimoria and J. N. Mohanty (eds.), *Relativism, Suffering and Beyond: Essays in Memory of Bimal K. Matilal*. Delhi: Oxford University Press, 1997.

Gopal, S. (ed.), *Anatomy of a Confrontation: The Babri Masjid-Ram Janmbhumi Issue*. Delhi: Penguin Books, 1991.

Hess, Linda, "Rejecting Sita: Indian Reponses to the Ideal Man's Cruel Treatment of His Ideal Wife." *Journal of the American Academy of Religion*. 67(1), 1999: 1–32.

Lutgentdorf, Philip, *Hanuman's Tale: The Messages of a Divine Monkey*. Oxford: Oxford University Press, 2007.

Rao, P. V. Narasimha, *Ayodhya: 6 December 1992*. Delhi: Penguin Books, 2006.

Richman, Paula, *Many Rāmāyaṇas: The Diversity of a Narrative Tradition in South Asia*. Berkeley, CA: University of California Press, 1991.

The *Rāmāyaṇa*

Bālakāṇḍa

Sarga 1

1. Vālmīki, the ascetic, questioned the eloquent Nārada, bull among sages, always devoted to asceticism and study of the sacred texts.

2. "Is there a man in the world today who is truly virtuous? Who is there who is mighty and yet knows both what is right and how to act upon it? Who always speaks the truth and holds firmly to his vows?

3. "Who exemplifies proper conduct and is benevolent to all creatures? Who is learned, capable, and a pleasure to behold?

4. "Who is self-controlled, having subdued his anger? Who is both judicious and free from envy? Who, when his fury is aroused in battle, is feared even by the gods?

5. "This is what I want to hear, for my desire to know is very strong. Great seer, you must know of such a man."

6. When Nārada, who was familiar with all the three worlds, heard Vālmīki's words, he was delighted. "Listen;" he replied and spoke these words:

7. "The many virtues you have named are hard to find. Let me think a moment, sage, before I speak. Hear now of a man who has them all.

8. "His name is Rāma and he was born in the House of Ikṣvāku. All men know of him, for he is self-controlled, mighty, radiant, steadfast, and masterful.

9. "He is wise and grounded in proper conduct. Eloquent and majestic, he annihilates his enemies. His shoulders are broad and his arms mighty. His neck is like a conch shell and his jaws are powerful.

10. "His chest is vast, and a subduer of his enemies, he wields a huge bow. His collarbone is set deep in muscle, his arms reach down to his knees, and his head is finely made. His brow is noble and his gait full of grace.

11. "His proportions are perfect and his limbs well-formed and symmetrical. Dark is his complexion and he is valorous. His chest is fully fleshed; he has large eyes. He is splendid and marked with all auspicious signs.

12. "He knows the ways of righteousness and is always true to his word. The welfare of his subjects is his constant concern. He is renowned, learned, pure, disciplined, and contemplative.

13. "He is the protector of all living things and the guardian of righteousness. Versed in the essence of the *vedas* and their subsidiary sciences, he is equally expert in the science of arms.

14. "He is versed in the essence of every science, learned in traditional lore, and highly intelligent. All the people love him, for he is good, cheerful, and clever.

15. "He is the constant resort of good men, as is the ocean of rivers. For he is noble and equable in all circumstances and always a pleasure to behold.

16. "The delight of his mother Kausalyā, he is gifted with every virtue. For he is as deep as the ocean and as unyielding as the Himalayas.

17. "He is as mighty as Viṣṇu, but as pleasant to behold as the moon. In his wrath he resembles the fire at the end of time, yet he rivals the earth in forbearance.

18–19. "In charity he is the equal of Kubera, giver of wealth, and in truthfulness like a second Dharma, the god of righteousness. Moved by affection for him, Daśaratha, lord of the earth, wished to appoint this Rāma, his beloved eldest son, as prince regent. For he was truly valorous, possessed all these virtues, and was gifted with other excellent virtues.

Excerpts from Robert Goldman (tr.), *The Rāmāyaṇa of Vālmīki*, Vol. 1. Princeton, NJ: Princeton University Press, 1984; and from Sheldon Pollock (tr.), *The Rāmāyaṇa of Vālmīki*, Vol. 3. Princeton, NJ: Princeton University Press, 1990.

20. "Seeing the preparations for the consecration, the king's wife, Queen Kaikeyī, who had long before been granted a boon, now asked for it. She demanded that Rāma be exiled and that Bharata be consecrated in his place.

21. "Because he was a man true to his word, King Daśaratha was caught in the trap of his own righteousness and had to exile his dear son Rāma.

22. "Keeping the promise, the hero entered the forest, because of the command implicit in a father's word and in order to please Kaikeyī.

23. "Out of love for him, his beloved and obedient brother Lakṣmaṇa, the delight of Sumitrā, followed him as he set forth.

24. "And his wife Sītā, the best of women, possessed of every grace, followed Rāma as Rohiṇī does the hare-marked moon.

25. "He was followed far on his way by his father, Daśaratha, and the people of the city. But at the town of Śṛṅgavera on the banks of the Ganges he dismissed his charioteer.

26. "Wandering from wood to wood, they crossed great rivers until, on the instructions of Bharadvāja, they came to Mount Citrakūṭa.

27. "There the three of them built a pleasant dwelling. Delighting in the forest and resembling celestial *gandharvas*, they lived there happily.

28. "When Rāma had gone to Mount Citrakūṭa, King Daśaratha was stricken with grief for his son and loudly lamenting him, went to heaven.

29. "When he was dead, the brahmans, led by Vasiṣṭha, urged Bharata to become king, but that mighty man did not desire kingship. Instead the hero went to the forest to beg for grace at Rāma's feet.

30. "But Bharata's elder brother only gave his sandals as a token of his sovereignty and repeatedly urged Bharata to return.

31. "Unable to accomplish his desire, Bharata touched Rāma's feet and ruled the kingdom from the village of Nandigrāma in expectation of Rāma's return.

32. "But Rāma, seeing that the people of the city had come there, entered the Daṇḍaka forest with single-minded resolution.

33. "He killed the *rākṣasa* Virādha and met Śarabhaṅga, Sutīkṣṇa, Agastya, and Agastya's brother.

34. "On the advice of Agastya, and with the greatest pleasure, he accepted Indra's bow as well as a sword and two quivers, whose arrows were inexhaustible.

35. "While Rāma was living in the forest with the woodland creatures, all the seers came to see him about killing the *asuras* and *rākṣasas*.

36. "While dwelling there, he disfigured the *rākṣasa* woman Śūrpaṇakhā, who lived in Janasthāna and could take any form at will.

37–38. "Then Rāma slew in battle all the *rākṣasas* who had been sent against him on the strength of Śūrpaṇakhā's report – Khara, Triśiras, and the *rākṣasa* Dūṣaṇa, as well as all of their followers. Fourteen thousand *rākṣasas* were slain.

39. "But Rāvaṇa, hearing of the slaughter of his kinsmen, went mad with rage and chose a *rākṣasa* named Mārīca to assist him.

40. "Mārīca tried to dissuade Rāvaṇa many times, saying, 'Rāvaṇa, you would do well not to meddle with this mighty man.'

41. "But Rāvaṇa, who was driven by his fate, paid no heed to Mārīca's words and went with him to Rāma's ashram.

42. "With the help of that master of illusion, he lured both sons of the king far away. Then, having slain the vulture Jaṭāyus, he carried off Rāma's wife.

43. "Finding the vulture dying and hearing that Maithilī had been abducted, Rāghava was consumed with grief. Beside himself with grief, he lamented loudly.

44–45. "In sorrow, he cremated the vulture Jaṭāyus. Then, searching the forest for Sītā, he met a *rākṣasa* named Kabandha, deformed and dreadful to behold. The great-armed man killed and cremated him so that he went to heaven.

46. "But Kabandha had first told him, 'Rāghava, you must go to the hermit woman Śabarī, for she is cunning in all ways of righteousness and lives accordingly.' And so the powerful destroyer of his foes came to Śabarī.

47. "Rāma, the son of Daśaratha, was duly honored by Śabarī. Then, on the shores of Lake Pampā, he met the monkey Hanumān.

48. "Acting on Hanumān's advice, mighty Rāma met Sugrīva and told him all that had happened.

49. "Sensing that he had found a friend, the sorrowful king of the monkeys told Rāma the whole story of his feud. And the monkey told him also of Vālin's might.

50. "Rāma vowed to kill Vālin, but Sugrīva remained doubtful of Rāghava's strength.

51. "So to reassure him, Rāghava kicked the great corpse of Dundubhi ten whole leagues with his big toe.

52. "Furthermore, with a single mighty arrow he pierced seven *sāla* trees, a hill, and even the underworld Rasātala, thus inspiring confidence.

53. "The great monkey was confident, and, his mind at ease, he went with Rāma to the cave Kiṣkindhā.

54. "Then the foremost of monkeys, Sugrīva, yellow as gold, gave a great roar. At that roar, the lord of the monkeys, Vālin, came forth.

55. "Rāghava then killed Vālin in battle at the request of Sugrīva and made Sugrīva king in his place.

56. "Eager to find Janaka's daughter, that bull among monkeys assembled all the monkeys and sent them out in all directions.

57. "On the advice of the vulture Sampāti, mighty Hanumān leaped over the salt sea, a hundred leagues in breadth.

58. "Reaching the city of Laṅkā, which was ruled by Rāvaṇa, he saw Sītā brooding in a grove of *aśoka* trees.

59. "He gave her a token of recognition and told her all that had happened. Then, when he had comforted Vaidehī, he smashed the gate.

60. "He killed five generals of the army and seven ministers' sons as well. Then, after crushing the hero Akṣa, he was captured.

61. "Knowing that he could free himself from their magic weapon by means of a boon he had received from Grandfather Brahmā, the hero suffered the *rākṣasas* to bind him as they would.

62. "The great monkey then burned the city of Laṅkā, sparing Sītā Maithilī, and returned to tell the good news to Rāma.

63. "Approaching great Rāma, the immeasurable monkey walked reverently around him and told him just what had happened, saying, 'I have seen Sītā.'

64. "Rāma went with Sugrīva to the seashore, where he made the ocean tremble with arrows blazing like the sun.

65. "The ocean, lord of rivers, revealed himself, and, following the ocean's advice, Rāma had Nala build a bridge.

66. "By this means he went to the city of Laṅkā, and having killed Rāvaṇa in battle, he consecrated Vibhīṣaṇa as lord of the *rākṣasas* in Laṅkā.

67. "The three worlds, including all that moves and is fixed, and the hosts of gods and seers were delighted by that mighty feat of great Rāma.

68. "All the gods were thoroughly delighted and worshiped Rāma. Having accomplished what he had to do, he was freed from anxiety and rejoiced.

69. "He received boons from the gods and revived the fallen monkeys. Then, mounting the flying chariot Puṣpaka, he went to Nandigrāma.

70. "In Nandigrāma the blameless man and his brothers put off the knotted hair of ascetics. Thus did Rāma regain Sītā and recover his kingdom.

71. "His people are pleased and joyful, contented, well-fed, and righteous. They are also free from physical and mental afflictions and the danger of famine.

72. "Nowhere in his realm do men experience the death of a son. Women are never widowed and remain always faithful to their husbands.

73. "Just as in the Golden Age, there is no danger whatever of fire or wind, and no creatures are lost in floods.

74. "He performs hundreds of Horse Sacrifices involving vast quantities of gold. And, in

accordance with custom, he donates tens and hundreds of millions of cows to the learned.

75. "Rāghava is establishing hundreds of royal lines and has set the four social orders each to its own work in the world.

76. "When he has ruled the kingdom for 11,000 years, Rāma will go to the world of Brahmā.

77. "Whoever reads this history of Rāma, which is purifying, destructive of sin, holy, and the equal of the *vedas*, is freed from all sins.

78. "A man who reads this *Rāmāyaṇa* story, which leads to long life, will after death rejoice in heaven together with his sons, grandsons, and attendants.

79. "A brahman who reads it becomes eloquent, a kshatriya becomes a lord of the earth, a *vaiśya* acquires profit from his goods, and even a lowly *śūdra* achieves greatness."

The end of the first *sarga* of the *Bālakāṇḍa* of the *Śrī Rāmāyaṇa*.

[...]

Sarga 65

1. In the clear dawn, Janaka, the lord of men, performed his ritual duties and summoned great Viśvāmitra and the two Rāghavas.

2. The righteous man paid homage to him and the two Rāghavas with rites set down in the traditional texts and then spoke:

3. "Welcome to you, holy one. What can I do for you, sinless man? Command me, sir, for I am yours to command."

4. Addressed in this fashion by great Janaka, the righteous sage, skilled in speech, said these words to that hero:

5. "These two kshatriyas are the world-renowned sons of Daśaratha. They wish to see that best of bows you have in your possession.

6. "Please show it to them, and when they have once attained their desire by seeing the bow, the princes will return home as they please."

7. Addressed in this fashion, Janaka replied to the great sage, "You must first learn the purpose for which the bow is here.

8. "Holy man, there was once a king named Devarāta, sixth in descent from Nimi. Great Śiva left it as a trust in his hands.

9. "Long ago, at the time of the destruction of Dakṣa's sacrifice, the mighty Rudra bent this bow, and in his anger, spoke contemptuously to the gods:

10. " 'Since you failed to set aside a portion for me who desire a portion, o gods, I shall cut off your precious heads with this bow.'

11. "In despair, bull among sages, the gods all propitiated him, Bhava, the lord of gods, so that at length he was pleased with them.

12. "Filled with pleasure, he gave the bow to all the great gods.

13. "Lord, it was that very jewel of a bow belonging to the great god of gods that was given as a trust to our forebear.

14. "Now one time, as I was plowing a field, a girl sprang up behind my plow. I found her as I was clearing the field, and she is thus known by the name Sītā, furrow.

15. "Sprung from the earth, she has been raised as my daughter, and since she was not born from the womb, my daughter has been set apart as one for whom the only bride-price is great strength.

16. "Many kings have come, bull among sages, and asked for the hand of this girl who sprang from the earth and has been raised as my daughter.

17. "But, holy man, although all the rulers of the earth are asking for this girl, I have not given my daughter in marriage, reflecting that she is one whose bride-price is great strength.

18. "So all the kings assembled, bull among sages, and came to Mithilā eager to test their strength.

19. "Since they wished to test their strength, I offered them the bow. But they could not even grasp it, much less lift it.

20. "Now you must know, great sage, that when I saw these mighty kings had little strength, I rejected them all.

21. "But when the strength of the kings had been called into question, bull among sages, they all laid siege to Mithilā in great anger.

22. "Feeling themselves slighted, bull among sages, they were filled with great fury and harassed the city of Mithilā.

23. "By the time a full year had passed, all my resources were exhausted, best of sages, and I was truly miserable.

24. "Therefore, I propitiated all the hosts of gods with austerities, and since they were pleased with me, the gods gave me an army complete with the four divisions.

25. "Then those wicked kings, whose strength had been called into question, were broken. They fled with their ministers in all directions, stripped of their strength while being slaughtered.

26. "This, then, is the incomparably splendid bow, tiger among sages, firm in your vows. I shall show it to Rāma and Lakṣmaṇa.

27. "And if, sage, Rāma, son of Daśaratha, can string this bow, I will give him my daughter, who was not born from the womb."

The end of the sixty-fifth *sarga* of the *Bālakāṇḍa* of the *Śrī Rāmāyaṇa*.

Sarga 66

1. When the great sage Viśvāmitra had listened to King Janaka's words, he said to him, "Show Rāma the bow."

2. So King Janaka gave the order to his ministers, "Bring the celestial bow and see that it is perfumed and adorned with garlands."

3. Commanded by Janaka, the ministers entered the city and, placing the bow before them, came forth on the king's orders.

4. Five thousand tall.and brawny men were hard-put to drag its eight-wheeled chest.

5. But when they brought the iron chest that held the bow, his counsellors addressed the godlike King Janaka:

6. "Your majesty, best of kings, lord of Mithilā, here is the great bow, worshiped by all the kings. If you wish it, it shall be seen."

7. Hearing their words, the king cupped his hands in reverence and spoke to great Viśvāmitra, Rāma, and Lakṣmaṇa:

8. "Here is the great bow, brahman, that the Janakas worship and the mighty kings were unable to string.

9–10. "All the hosts of gods, *asuras, rākṣasas*, and the foremost among the *gandharvas* and *yakṣas, kinnaras*, and great serpents are incapable of bending this bow, stringing it, fitting an arrow to it, drawing its string, or even lifting it. What chance is there then for men?

11. "Yes, bull among sages, it is the greatest of bows that has been brought. Illustrious sage, please show it to the two princes."

12. When righteous Viśvāmitra heard what Janaka said, he turned to Rāghava and said, "Rāma, my son, behold the bow."

13. Following the great seer's instructions, Rāma opened the chest in which the bow lay and regarding it closely, he spoke:

14. "Now, brahman, I shall touch this great bow with my hand. I shall attempt to lift and even string it."

15. "Very well," replied both king and sage. So following the sage's instructions, he easily grasped the bow in the middle.

16. Then, as though it were mere play to him, the righteous prince, the delight of the Raghus, strung the bow as thousands watched.

17. The mighty man affixed the bowstring and fitting an arrow to it, drew it back. But, in so doing, the best of men broke the bow in the middle.

18. There was a tremendous noise loud as a thunderclap, and a mighty trembling shook the earth, as if a mountain had been torn asunder.

19. Of all those men, only the great sage, the king, and the two Rāghavas remained standing; the rest fell, stunned by the noise.

20. When the people had come to their senses, the eloquent king, free from his anxiety, cupped his hands in reverence and addressed the bull among sages:

21. "Holy man, I have witnessed the might of Daśaratha's son Rāma. It is marvelous and inconceivable. I had no notion of it.

22. "With Rāma, Daśaratha's son, for her husband, my daughter Sītā will bring glory to the House of the Janakas.

23. "And so, Kauśika, my vow that great strength should be her only bride-price has been proven true. For my daughter Sītā, as dear to me as life itself, shall be given in marriage to Rāma.

24. "Bless you, Kauśika brahman, with your permission, my counsellors shall set out at once for Ayodhyā in swift chariots.

25. "With courteous words they shall bring the king to my city. And they shall tell him all about the betrothal of my daughter, whose only bride-price was strength.

26. "They shall also tell the king that the Kākutsthas are under the sage's protection. The king will be delighted. Now, let them go swiftly and bring him here."

27. "So be it," Kauśika replied. The righteous king then spoke to his counsellors, and when they had received their orders, he dispatched them to Ayodhyā.

The end of the sixty-sixth *sarga* of the *Bālakāṇḍa* of the *Śrī Rāmāyaṇa*.

Sarga 67

1. Instructed by Janaka, his messengers spent three nights on the road and then entered the city of Ayodhyā, their horses exhausted.

2. In accordance with the orders of their king, the messengers entered the royal dwelling and saw the aged king, godlike Daśaratha.

3. Cupping their hands in reverence, restrained yet free from anxiety, they all spoke sweet words to the king:

4–5. "Great king, King Janaka of Mithilā, delight of his people, and his brahmans repeatedly inquire in sweet and affectionate words after the continuing well-being of you, your preceptors, priests, and attendants.

6. "And having thus made inquiry about your continuing well-being, Vaideha, the lord of Mithilā, with Kauśika's permission, addresses these words to you:

7. " 'You know my longstanding vow that my daughter's only bride-price shall be strength. You know, too, that the kings, lacking strength, have been made angry and hostile.

8. " 'Now your majesty, this very same daughter of mine has been won by your heroic son who chanced to come here following Viśvāmitra.

9. " 'For, your majesty, great king, the great Rāma has broken my celestial bow in the middle, before a vast assembly of the people.

10. " 'Therefore, I must give Sītā, whose only bride-price was strength, to this great man. Please permit this, for I wish to make good my vow.

11. " 'Come quickly, great king, with your preceptors, setting your family priest before you. Please come and see the two Rāghavas.

12. " 'Please make my happiness complete, lord of kings, for you too shall obtain happiness on account of your two sons.' "

13. Such was the sweet speech of the lord of Videha, sanctioned by both Viśvāmitra and Śatānanda.

14. When the king heard the messengers' words, he was utterly delighted. Addressing Vasiṣṭha, Vāmadeva, and his other counsellors, he spoke:

15. "The increaser of Kausalyā's joy is staying in Videha with his brother Lakṣmaṇa, under the protection of the son of Kuśika.

16. "Great Janaka has witnessed Kākutstha's might, and he wishes to give Rāghava his daughter.

17. "If this news pleases you, then let us quickly go to great Janaka's city. Let there be no delay."

18. His counsellors and all the great seers replied, "Excellent." At this the king was greatly delighted and said to them, "The journey will begin tomorrow."

19. All the virtuous counsellors of Janaka, lord of men, were delighted. They spent the night there and were shown the greatest honor.

The end of the sixty-seventh *sarga* of the *Bālakāṇḍa* of the *Śrī Rāmāyaṇa*.

[. . .]

Araṇyakāṇḍa

[...]

Sarga 16

1. After their bath Rāma, Sītā, and Lakṣmaṇa left the bank of the Godāvarī for their ashram.

2. Returning to the ashram, Rāghava and Lakṣmaṇa performed the morning rites and then returned to the leaf hut.

3. Great-armed Rāma sat with Sītā before the leaf hut, shining like the moon beside the sparkling star Citrā, and began to converse with his brother Lakṣmaṇa about one thing and another.

4. As Rāma was sitting there engrossed in conversation, a certain *rākṣasa* woman chanced to come that way.

5. She was the sister of Rāvaṇa, the ten-necked *rākṣasa*, and her name was Śūrpaṇakhā. Coming upon Rāma, she stared at him as if he were one of the thirty gods.

6–7. Rāma had long arms, the chest of a lion, eyes like lotus petals. Though delicate, he was very strong and bore all the signs of royalty. He was swarthy as the blue lotus, radiant as the love-god Kandarpa, the very image of Indra – and when the *rākṣasa* woman saw him, she grew wild with desire.

8–10. Rāma was handsome, the *rākṣasa* woman was ugly, he was shapely and slim of waist, she misshapen and potbellied; his eyes were large, hers were beady, his hair was jet black, and hers the color of copper; he always said just the right thing and in a sweet voice, her words were sinister and her voice struck terror; he was young, attractive, and well mannered, she ill mannered, repellent, an old hag. And yet, the god of love, who comes to life in our bodies, had taken possession of her, and so she addressed Rāma:

11. "Your hair is matted in the manner of ascetics, yet you have a wife with you and bear bow and arrows. How is it you have come into this region, the haunt of *rākṣasas*?"

12. Questioned in this fashion by the *rākṣasa* woman Śūrpaṇakhā, the slayer of enemies in his open manner proceeded to tell her everything.

13. "There was a king named Daśaratha, courageous as one of the thirty gods. I am his eldest son, named Rāma, known to people far and wide.

14. "This is Lakṣmaṇa, my devoted younger brother, and this my wife, the princess of Videha, known as Sītā.

15. "I was compelled to come to live in the forest by command of my mother and my father, the lord of men, and I wanted to do what is right, for doing right has always been my chief concern.

16. "But I should like to know about you. Tell me, who are you? To whom do you belong? For what purpose have you come here? Tell me truthfully."

17. Hearing his words and consumed with passion, the *rākṣasa* woman replied, "Listen, then, Rāma, I shall tell you, and my words will be truthful.

18. "My name is Śūrpaṇakhā. I am a *rākṣasa* woman, who can take on any form at will, and I roam this wilderness all alone, striking terror into every living thing.

19. "The *rākṣasa* named Rāvaṇa, the lord of all *rākṣasas*, is my brother, so too the powerful Kumbhakarṇa, who lies ever fast asleep.

20. "So is Vibhīṣaṇa, but he is righteous and does not behave like a *rākṣasa*. My other brothers are Khara and Dūṣaṇa, famed for their might in battle.

21. "But I am prepared to defy them all, Rāma, for I have never seen anyone like you. I approach you as I would a husband, with true love, best of men. Be my husband forevermore; what do you want with Sītā?

22. "She is ugly and misshapen and unworthy of you. I alone am suited to you; look upon me as your wife.

23. "I will devour this misshapen slut, this hideous human female with her pinched waist, along with this brother of yours.

24. "And then, my beloved, you shall roam Daṇḍaka with me, viewing all the different mountain peaks and forests."

25. Thus addressed by the wild-eyed creature, Kākutstha burst out laughing but then went on to reply with customary eloquence.

The end of the sixteenth *sarga* of the *Araṇyakāṇḍa* of the *Śrī Rāmāyaṇa*.

Sarga 17

1. As Śūrpaṇakhā stood there bound tight in the bonds of desire, Rāma smiled and, humoring her, replied in jest:

2. "I am already married, my lady, and I love my wife. And for women such as you, to have a rival wife is a source of bitter sorrow.

3. "But my younger brother here is of good character, handsome, powerful, majestic, and still unmarried. His name is Lakṣmaṇa.

4. "He had never had a woman before and is in need of a wife. He is young and handsome and will make a good husband, one suited to such beauty as yours.

5. "Accept my brother as your husband, large-eyed, shapely lady. With no rival wife the two of you will be inseparable as sunlight and Mount Meru."

6. When the *rākṣasa* woman, wild with desire, heard Rāma address her in this way, she promptly forsook him and said to Lakṣmaṇa:

7. "I shall make you a lovely wife, one befitting your beauty. And together we shall roam so pleasantly all through Daṇḍaka."

8. Lakṣmaṇa smiled at the words of the *rākṣasa* woman Śūrpaṇakhā and with customary eloquence made this fitting reply:

9. "Why would you want to be my wife, lotuslike beauty? I am completely subject to the will of my noble brother; I am a slave, and she who is my wife must be a slave as well.

10. "Become instead the junior wife of my noble brother, large-eyed lady of unblemished beauty. He is prosperous, and with him your fortunes, too, will prosper and you will be happy.

11. "Soon enough he will turn away from this misshapen slut, this hideous old wife with her pinched waist, and give his love to you alone.

12. "What man with any sense would reject this singular beauty of yours, my fair and shapely lady, and bestow his affections on a human female?"

13. So Lakṣmaṇa spoke, and the potbellied, hideous creature, unused to teasing, thought he was in earnest.

14. Then as Rāma, the invincible slayer of enemies, sat with Sītā before the leaf hut, the *rākṣasa* woman addressed him once more, wild with desire.

15. "It is on account of this misshapen slut, this hideous old wife with her pinched waist, that you care so little for me.

16. "I am going to devour this human female at once, before your very eyes; then, free of any rival, I shall live happily with you."

17. And with this, she flew into a rage, and with eyes flashing like firebrands she shot toward the fawn-eyed princess, like a giant meteor toward the star Rohiṇī.

18. But as she was about to fall upon Sītā, like the very noose of Death, mighty Rāma angrily restrained her and said to Lakṣmaṇa:

19. "Never tease savage, ignoble creatures, Saumitri. Look at Vaidehī, dear brother; she is frightened half to death.

20. "Now, tiger among men, mutilate this misshapen slut, this potbellied, lustful *rākṣasa* woman."

21. So Rāma spoke, and powerful Lakṣmaṇa, in full view of his brother, drew his sword and in a rage cut off the creature's ears and nose.

22. The dreadful Śūrpaṇakhā, her ears and nose hacked off, gave out an earsplitting roar as she fled back into the forest the way she hàd come.

23. Mutilated, spattered with blood, and all the more dreadful now, the *rākṣasa* woman roared incessantly, like a storm cloud when the rains come.

24. Gushing blood all over, a terror to behold, she disappeared into the deep forest, howling, her arms outstretched.

25. She made her way then to her brother, the awesome Khara, who was in Janasthāna together with a troop of *rākṣasas*. Mutilated,

she fell before him to the ground, like a bolt of lightning from the sky.

26. Spattered with blood, wild with fear and confusion, Khara's sister told him the whole story – how Rāma had come into the forest with his wife and Lakṣmaṇa, and how she herself had been mutilated.

The end of the seventeenth *sarga* of the *Araṇyakāṇḍa* of the *Śrī Rāmāyaṇa*.
[...]

Sarga 30

1–2. Now, when Śūrpaṇakhā saw how Rāma all alone had killed the fourteen thousand awesome *rākṣasas* in battle, and Dūṣaṇa, Triśiras, and Khara as well, once more like a storm cloud she let out a deafening roar.

3. When she saw the feat accomplished by Rāma, impossible for anyone else to do, she set out in wild panic for Laṅkā, where Rāvaṇa held sway.

4. She found Rāvaṇa in his splendid palace, radiant in his power, his advisers sitting beside him like the Maruts next to Vāsava.

5. He was seated upon a golden throne radiant as the sun, and he looked like a fire on a golden altar blazing with rich oblations.

6. A hero invincible in combat with gods, *gandharvas*, spirits, or great seers, he looked like Death himself with jaws agape.

7. He carried lightning-bolt wounds received in clashes with gods and *asuras*. His chest was seamed with scars where Airāvata's pointed tusks had gored him.

8. He had twenty arms and ten necks. His regalia was a wonder to behold. A broad-chested, mighty king, he was marked with all the marks of royalty.

9. He sparkled with earrings of burnished gold and the glossy beryl he wore. His arms were handsome, his teeth bright white, his mouth huge, and he was as tall as a mountain.

10. In combat with gods his body had been wounded in hundreds of places, by blows from Viṣṇu's discus and all the other weapons of the gods.

11. He could effortlessly perturb the imperturbable seas, level mountaintops, and vanquish the gods.

12. A breaker of laws he would violate the wives of other men, and use any unearthly weapon to obstruct the sacrifice.

13. It was he who had gone to the city of Bhogavatī, defeated Vāsuki and Takṣaka, and abducted Takṣaka's wife.

14. It was he who had gone to Mount Kailāsa and conquered the man-borne Kubera, stealing his aerial chariot, Puṣpaka, that flies where one desires.

15. It was he who in a mighty rage would destroy the gardens of the gods, the heavenly forest Caitraratha with its lotus pond, and Nandana forest.

16. It was he who, tall as a mountain peak, would extend his arms and prevent the glorious powers, the sun and moon, from rising.

17. It was he who long ago in the great forest had practiced austerities for ten thousand years and unflinchingly cut off his own heads as offering to the Self-existent Brahmā.

18. It was he who had no longer to fear death in combat with any beings – gods, *dānavas, gandharvas, piśācas*, great birds, or serpents – any beings but men.

19. It was he who in overweening pride of power would pollute the holy *soma* at the seats of the oblation, when in the course of their rites the brahmans consecrated it with vedic hymns.

20. He would disrupt sacrifices at their climax, then murder the brahmans. He was savage and wicked, cruel and ruthless, delighting in the misfortune of others. He was Rāvaṇa, "he who makes all creatures wail," the terror of all the worlds.

21. The *rākṣasa* woman beheld this savage and powerful brother of hers, clad in heavenly garments and jewels, adorned with heavenly garlands, the illustrious lord of *rākṣasas*, delight of the House of the Paulastyas.

22. Śūrpaṇakhā, who once lived free from fear, now wild with fear and confusion, told him the dreadful story of how the great prince

had mutilated her. As she displayed herself, his eyes grew wide and blazed.

The end of the thirtieth *sarga* of the *Araṇyakāṇḍa* of the *Śrī Rāmāyaṇa*.

Sarga 31

1. As Rāvaṇa, who made the worlds wail, sat among his ministers, Śūrpaṇakhā in her rage and desolation addressed him with harsh words:

2. "Drunk as you are on sensual pleasures, so licentious and unbridled, you overlook the one thing you must not, the presence of terrible danger.

3. "When a lord of the earth is lustful, addicted to vulgar pleasures, a slave to his passions, his subjects see him as no better than a cremation fire.

4. "If a king fails to attend to affairs himself and in timely fashion, those affairs come to grief, so too his kingdom and the king himself.

5. "The ruler of men who is not his own master, grants no audience, or makes no use of spies is shunned by men as elephants shun a muddy riverbank.

6. "If rulers of men are not their own masters and fail to protect their realm, their grandeur disappears, like mountains sunk beneath the sea.

7. "How can you stay king when, though staunchly opposed by gods, *gandharvas*, and *dānavas*, you do not even bother to use spies?

8. "Rulers of men who do not master espionage, diplomacy, or their treasuries, your highness, are no more than common men.

9. "Kings are called farsighted precisely because, through their spies, they can see anything, however far away.

10. "Surrounded by worthless advisers, you have made no use of spies, I am sure, and thus are unaware that your people, and Janasthāna, have been destroyed.

11. "Fourteen thousand awesome *rākṣasas* killed by a single man – Rāma – and with them Khara and Dūṣaṇa.

12. "Tireless Rāma attacked Janasthāna, and he has made Daṇḍaka safe and won security for the seers.

13. "But, consumed with lust, negligent, and no longer your own master, Rāvaṇa, you are unaware of the danger present in your realm.

14. "In times of trouble no one runs to aid a king who has been cruel and ungenerous, negligent, haughty, and treacherous.

15. "When a ruler of men is arrogant and aloof, conceited and quick to anger, in times of trouble even his own people will slay him.

16. "A king who ignores his affairs, blind to dangers, is quickly toppled from his kingship – and the wretch is then not worth a straw.

17. "Dry logs have some use, even clods of dirt or dust, but not a ruler of the earth fallen from power.

18. "For no matter how able, a king deposed is as useless as a wornout garment or crushed garland.

19. "But a king who is alert, well informed, and self-controlled, knowing what must be done and acting in keeping with righteousness, enjoys a long reign.

20. "The king who, though his eyes be closed in sleep, watches with the eye of diplomacy, who shows his grace no less than anger, is honored by his people.

21. "But you are a fool, Rāvaṇa, and devoid of such virtues, and so lack spies to tell you of the massacre of the *rākṣasas*.

22. "A king who misjudges his enemy, is addicted to sensual pleasures, fails to recognize the proper time and place for things, gives no thought to weighing the pros and cons of an issue – such a king soon ruins his kingdom and himself."

23. Rāvaṇa paid heed as she recited his failings in this fashion, and for some time afterward the lord of nightstalkers, with all his wealth and pride and power, sat lost in thought.

The end of the thirty-first *sarga* of the *Araṇyakāṇḍa* of the *Śrī Rāmāyaṇa*.

Sarga 32

1. When the raging Śūrpaṇakhā had finished her harsh speech, Rāvaṇa, too, was filled with rage and from where he sat among his ministers he began to question her:

2. "Who is this Rāma? What does he look like? How powerful is he, how bold? And for what reason has he entered the impassable Daṇḍaka wilderness?

3. "What weapon could Rāma possibly have used to kill the *rākṣasas* in combat, to kill Khara, Dūṣaṇa, and Triśiras?"

4. Questioned in this fashion by the lord of the *rākṣasas*, the *rākṣasa* woman, blind with rage, proceeded to tell all she knew of Rāma.

5. "Rāma is the son of Daśaratha. He has long arms and large eyes and resembles Kandarpa, god of love, though clad in barkcloth and black hides.

6. "He has a bow like Śakra's, banded with gold, and drawing it to its fullest he shoots flaming iron shafts that, like snakes, carry deadly poison.

7. "I could not even see powerful Rāma take up his terrible arrows in combat, draw his bow, or shoot.

8. "But I could see the army cut down by the shower of arrows, like a tall stand of grain cut down by Indra with a shower of hailstones.

9–10. "Fighting on foot, all alone, with those sharp arrows he killed fourteen thousand awesome *rākṣasas* in a split second, and a second later killed Khara and Dūṣaṇa as well. He has made Daṇḍaka safe and won security for the seers.

11. "I alone just barely escaped from the great and celebrated Rāma: Although he treated me with contempt, he shrank from killing a woman.

12. "He has a mighty brother, of equal prowess and virtue, who is loyal and devoted to him, the brave Lakṣmaṇa.

13. "Implacable and invincible, sure of victory with his boldness, power, and intelligence, he is always there, Rāma's right arm, a veritable second self.

14. "Rāma has a lawful wife named Sītā, princess of Videha. And what a glorious woman she is, with her large eyes, slender waist, and full hips.

15. "No goddess, no *gandharva* woman, no *yakṣa* or *kinnara* woman, no mortal woman so beautiful have I ever seen before on the face of this earth.

16. "He who claims Sītā as wife and receives her delighted embraces has more reason to live than anyone else in all the worlds, the breaker of fortresses, Indra himself, included.

17. "She is a woman of good character, with a form beyond all praise, a beauty unequaled on earth. She would make a perfect wife for you, and you a perfect husband for her.

18. "How broad her hips, how full and high her breasts, how lovely her face. Why, I all but brought her back to be your wife.

19. "The moment you saw Vaidehī's full-moon face, you would find yourself at the mercy of the arrows of Manmatha, god of love.

20. "If you have any interest in taking her to wife, put your best foot forward at once to win her.

21. "At the same time, lord of *rākṣasas*, do one last act of kindness for the *rākṣasas*, and slay that cruel Rāma, who is living a hermit's life.

22. "When you have killed him and Lakṣmaṇa, the great chariot-fighter, with your sharp arrows, you will then enjoy the widowed Sītā to your heart's content.

23. "If what I am saying meets with your approval, Rāvaṇa, lord of *rākṣasas*, do as I say without a moment's hesitation.

24. "Now that you have heard how the nightstalkers of Janasthāna were killed by the unerring arrows of Rāma, and how Khara and Dūṣaṇa were killed, you must act at once."

The end of the thirty-second *sarga* of the *Araṇyakāṇḍa* of the *Śrī Rāmāyaṇa*.

Sarga 33

1. When Rāvaṇa had heard Śūrpaṇakhā's horrifying tale, he dismissed his advisers and turned his thoughts to the question at hand.

2–3. After pondering the question, examining it carefully, and weighing the pros and cons, the strengths and weaknesses, he decided exactly what to do, and firmly resolved made his way to the lovely carriage house.

4. The overlord of *rākṣasas* went secretly to the carriage house and urgently told his driver to make ready the chariot.

5. At this, the charioteer stepped lively and at once made ready the chariot, a splendid one prized by his master.

6–7. It was a golden, jewel-encrusted chariot that flew where one desires. Harnessed to it were asses decked out with trappings of gold, their faces like those of *piśācas*. The majestic overlord of *rākṣasas*, younger brother of Kubera, bestower of riches, ascended the chariot; with the rumble of a storm cloud he set out for the ocean, lord of streams and rivers.

8. Ten-faced Rāvaṇa carried with him a white yak-tail fan and white parasol, and he sparkled with jewelry of burnished gold and the glossy beryl he wore.

9. Dressed in regalia a wonder to behold, with his ten heads he resembled the ten-peaked king of mountains; he had twenty arms, this enemy of the thirty gods, this slayer of lordly sages.

10. Aboard his chariot that flew where one desires, the overlord of *rākṣasas* appeared like a thundercloud in the sky ringed with lightning and a flight of cranes.

11. Powerful Rāvaṇa gazed down upon the rocky coast, dotted with thousands of different fruit-bearing and flowering trees;

12. Lotus ponds with cool clear water, and sprawling ashrams with sacrificial altars;

13. Plantain trees and *āḍhikas* growing densely, and coconut palms lending their beauty, along with *sālas, tālas, tamālas*, and other flowering trees.

14–15. Supreme seers given to rigorous fasting graced it; great serpents and birds, *gandharvas* and *kinnaras* by the thousand; perfected beings who had mastered desire, celestial bards, *ājas, vaikhānasas, māṣas, vālakhilyas*, and *marīcipas.*

16. There were *apsarases* by the thousands, all expert in the sports of lovemaking. Their jewelry and garlands were heavenly, heavenly too their beauty.

17. It was a place the majestic wives of the gods would visit and touch with majesty, where hosts of *dānavas* wandered, and gods, who drink the nectar of immortality.

18. It was full of geese, *krauñca* birds, and cormorants, and the call of cranes set it ringing. There were lovely carpets of cat's-eye beryl, made smooth and glossy by the ocean's force.

19–20. Hastening onward, the younger brother of Kubera, bestower of riches, saw on all sides spacious white chariots that could fly where one desires. They belonged to those who had conquered higher worlds by their acts of asceticism; all were decked with heavenly garlands and gave forth the sound of pipes and singing. There were *gandharvas* and *apsarases* to be seen as well.

21–25ab. He saw pleasant forests of sandalwood, thousands of trees with gratifying redolence and roots juicy with resin; forests and orchards of fine aloe, noble *takkolas* and fragrant fruit-trees, *tamāla* flowers and pepper-plant shrubs; heaps of pearls drying on the shore, carpets of conch shells, mounds of coral, mountains of gold and silver everywhere; enchanting cascades and pools of clear water.

25cd–26ab. His gaze fell on cities crowded with elephants, horses, and chariots, filled with grain and riches, adorned with women like perfect jewels.

26cd–27ab. Such was the shore of the ocean, king of rivers, everywhere level and smooth, with breezes gently caressing. It was as if the very summit of heaven had come into view.

27cd–28ab. And there he saw a banyan tree where seers were gathered. Massive as a storm cloud, its branches extended a hundred leagues in every direction.

28cd–ef. To one of these branches, once upon a time, mighty Garuḍa had come, carrying a huge tortoise and elephant on which to feed.

29. But the leafy branch suddenly gave way under the weight of mighty Suparṇa, greatest of birds.

30. Upon it supreme seers had gathered together: *vaikhānasas, māṣas, vālakhilyas, marīcipas, ajas*, and *dhūmras*.

31–32. In compassion for them, righteous Garuḍa rushed up and caught the branch – a hundred leagues long – in a single claw, both elephant and tortoise clinging to it still. After devouring their flesh, the greatest of birds used the branch to lay waste the realm of the Niṣādas. He had freed the great sages and felt delight beyond compare.

33. And this delight made him twice as bold and resolute: He resolved to go in quest of the nectar of immortality.

34. Shattering the iron latticework and breaking into the supernal treasure house, he stole the nectar from its hiding place in the palace of great Indra.

35. This was the banyan called Subhadra that Rāvaṇa, younger brother of Kubera, bestower of riches, now beheld. Hosts of great seers still frequented it, and the claw marks left by Suparṇa were still to be seen.

36. Reaching the further shore of the ocean, lord of rivers, he saw an ashram in a secluded, holy, and lovely stretch of forest.

37. And there he saw the *rākṣasa* Mārīca, who wore black hides, matted hair, and bark-cloth, and practiced rigorous fasting.

38. Rāvaṇa met with him according to custom, and thereafter, clever speaker that he was, addressed these words to the *rākṣasa*.

The end of the thirty-third *sarga* of the *Araṇyakāṇḍa* of the *Śrī Rāmāyaṇa*.

Sarga 34

1. "Mārīca, my friend, hear what I have to tell you. I am troubled, and my sole refuge from these troubles is you.

2–3. "You know Janasthāna, where once lived my brother Khara, great-armed Dūṣaṇa, my sister Śūrpaṇakhā, the mighty *rākṣasa* Triśiras, an eater of raw flesh, and many another heroic night-stalker who was tried and tested.

4–5. "On my orders the *rākṣasas* had made their dwelling there, oppressing the sages who followed the ways of righteousness in the great wilderness – fourteen thousand awesome *rākṣasas*, heroes tried and tested, who bowed to the will of Khara.

6. "But recently these *rākṣasas* of Janasthāna, powerful and ever vigilant, met in combat with Rāma.

7. "Rāma, in a fury, but without one harsh word, set his bow and arrows to work on the field of battle.

8. "And with his keen arrows this mere man, fighting on foot, killed fourteen thousand ferocious *rākṣasas*.

9. "He killed Khara and cut down Dūṣaṇa in combat, he killed Triśiras as well and has made Daṇḍaka safe.

10. "This Rāma who destroyed the army is a short-lived mortal, scum of the kshatriya, a man whose father cast him out in anger, him and his wife.

11. "A man of no character, a cruel, vicious, greedy, intemperate fool, he has forsaken righteousness and in his unrighteousness takes pleasure in others' misery.

12. "It was him who, without provocation, in an act of brute force mutilated my sister in the wilderness, cutting off her ears and nose.

13. "He has a wife named Sītā, a woman like the daughter of the gods. I mean to abduct her by force from Janasthāna, and you must help me.

14. "For with you at my side to help me, powerful Mārīca, you and my brothers, I would think nothing of facing all the gods united in battle.

15. "So you have to help me, *rākṣasa*, as I know you can, for you have no equal in might, in battle, and in pride.

16. "This is the reason I come to you, nightstalker. Now listen, and I shall tell you what you can do to help me.

17. "Turn yourself into a golden deer dappled with silver spots and go grazing near Rāma's ashram within view of Sītā.

18. "When Sītā sees you transformed as this deer, she will surely tell her husband and Lakṣmaṇa to capture you.

19. "Then, with the two of them gone and the place deserted, nothing can stop me from carrying Sītā off, as Rāhu the Eclipse makes off with the moonlight.

20. "Afterward, with Rāma in agony over the theft of his wife, I know I can easily slay him and so gain my innermost heart's desire."

21. But the moment great Mārīca heard talk of Rāma, his mouth went dry and he was seized with utter terror.

22. Acquainted as he was with Rāma's prowess in great battles, he grew terrified, and his heart sank in despair. Cupping his hands in reverence, he made a forthright reply for both Rāvaṇa's good and his own.

The end of the thirty-fourth *sarga* of the *Araṇyakāṇḍa* of the *Śrī Rāmāyaṇa*.

Sarga 35

1. After listening to the words of the lord of *rākṣasas*, the wise Mārīca, a clever speaker himself, replied:

2. "How easy to find those who say what you want to hear, your majesty; how difficult to find one who gives – or heeds – unpleasant but sound advice.

3. "Clearly you know nothing of Rāma, since you are too careless to make use of spies – not how great his might, how distinguished his virtues, how much like great Indra or Varuṇa he is.

4. "I fear no *rākṣasa* on earth will be safe from harm, my friend; I fear that Rāma in his rage will empty the world of them.

5. "I fear the daughter of Janaka was born to take your life. I fear some awful doom will strike because of Sītā.

6. "I fear the city of Laṅkā, ruled by a lord like you – dissolute and a slave to his passions – will perish, and with it you and all the *rākṣasas*.

7. "A king like you, of poor judgment and poor character, a slave to his passions, takes bad advice and ends up destroying his kingdom, his people, and himself.

8–9. "Rāma, the delight of Kausalyā, was not disowned by his father. It is absolutely false to say he knows no bounds, is greedy, of bad character, or the 'scum of the kshatriyas.' He is not lacking in virtue or righteousness, nor is he vicious; on the contrary, he is devoted to the welfare of all creatures.

10. "When the righteous prince saw how Kaikeyī tricked his father, he accepted forest exile to preserve the truth of his father's word.

11. "To please Kaikeyī and his father, Daśaratha, he gave up the luxuries of kingship and entered Daṇḍaka forest.

12. "Rāma is not cruel, my friend, or stupid or intemperate. You must not say such things; they are groundless lies.

13. "Rāma is righteousness incarnate, a just man who strives for truth. He is king of all this world, like Vāsava of all the gods.

14. "His might it is that protects Vaidehī; how then can you dream of taking her by force? Easier to take the sunlight from the sun.

15. "In battle, this Rāma suddenly ignites, an all-consuming fire, whose bow and sword are kindling, whose arrows licking tongues: Do not walk right into it.

16–17. "Armed with his bow and arrows, this hero implacably destroys the armies of his foes. When the mouth of his bow gapes wide and blazes and the fiery tongues of his arrows dart out, Rāma becomes Death himself. Do not get too near him, my friend, lest you lose every pleasure, your kingship, and the life you hold so dear.

18. "Janaka's daughter belongs to one of immeasurable might. You will not carry her off in the forest, not when she can rely on Rāma's bow.

19. "He loves fair-waisted Sītā more than life itself, and she has always been a faithful wife. He is a blazing fire, and she the flame that leaps from it.

20. "What can you possibly gain, overlord of *rākṣasas*, by this futile adventure? For the moment you face him in battle your life is

finished – your life, your every pleasure, your hard-won kingship.

21. "Consult with all those advisers of yours who are righteous, Vibhīṣaṇa first and foremost, and only then decide.

22. "Weigh the pros and cons, the strengths and weaknesses, and honestly compare your power and Rāghava's; then decide where your true interests lie and do what is best.

23. "As for me, I am sure it is not best for you to meet the prince of Kosala in battle. Listen to me a moment longer, overlord of nightstalkers, and I shall tell you what is best and prudent."

The end of the thirty-fifth *sarga* of the *Araṇyakāṇḍa* of the *Śrī Rāmāyaṇa*.

Sarga 36

1. "Once upon a time I, too, wandered this earth in pride of power, tall as a mountain and possessing the strength of a thousand elephants.

2. "Looking like a blue-black cloud, wearing a crest jewel and earrings of burnished gold and armed with an iron cudgel, I would roam Daṇḍaka wilderness, feeding on the flesh of seers and striking fear into all the world.

3. "But then the great sage, righteous Viśvāmitra, who was terrified of me, came in person to Daśaratha and addressed the lord of men as follows:

4. " 'Let Rāma come and vigilantly protect me at the time of the lunar sacrifice, lord of men, for I am terribly afraid of Mārīca.'

5. "So the great and illustrious sage Viśvāmitra spoke, and righteous King Daśaratha replied to him:

6. " 'Rāghava is a mere twelve years old and unpracticed in arms. I, on the other hand, am prepared to go with all the army at my command and slay your enemy, best of sages, just as you desire.'

7. "Thus the king spoke, and the sage once again addressed him: 'No one on earth but Rāma has the power it takes to defeat that *rākṣasa*.

8. " 'A mere boy he may be, but he is mighty and capable of subduing him. I will take Rāma and go. My blessings on you, slayer of foes.'

9. "Thus the sage Viśvāmitra spoke, and taking the prince he returned in high spirits to his own ashram.

10. "When the sage was consecrated for sacrifice in Daṇḍaka wilderness, Rāma took up his position nearby, brandishing his shining bow.

11. "He was just a beardless youth, standing bow in hand, clad only in a loincloth – yet majestic and swarthy, with lovely eyes, a top-knot, and a garland of gold.

12. "Rāma shed the radiance of his might over Daṇḍaka wilderness, looking like the newly risen crescent moon.

13. "It was then I came, resembling a storm cloud, wearing earrings of burnished gold. Powerful in my possession of a boon, I arrogantly approached the ashram.

14. "He saw me as I entered, and instantly I raised my weapon, but all he did on seeing me was calmly string his bow.

15. "In my folly I was contemptuous of Rāghava – 'He is just a boy,' I thought – and so I charged headlong at Viśvāmitra's altar.

16. "Then he shot a dart, sharp and murderous, and its impact hurled me into the ocean, a hundred leagues away.

17. "The force of Rāma's arrow carried me far away and dropped me insensible in the bottomless waters of the ocean. When much later I regained consciousness, my friend, I made my way back to the city of Laṅkā.

18. "Thus did I escape on that occasion, but my companions were cut down by this 'mere boy, unpracticed in arms,' the tireless Rāma.

19. "So if, despite my warning, you quarrel with Rāma, it will not be long before terrible misfortune befalls you and you perish.

20. "And upon the *rākṣasas* – all of whose care it is to master the sports of lovemaking and hold crowded fairs and festivals – you shall bring down misery and disaster.

21. "On account of Maithilī you shall see Laṅkā laid to waste, with its array of mansions

and palaces, and all the precious objects that adorn it.

22. "For though they may commit no evil themselves the innocent perish through the evils of their allies, like fish in a pool of snakes.

23. "You shall see the *rākṣasas*, who anoint their bodies with heavenly sandalwood cream and adorn themselves, with heavenly jewelry – you shall see them lying dead upon the ground through no one's fault but your own.

24. "And you shall see the surviving night-stalkers fleeing in the ten directions with their wives – if their wives have not been carried off – and seeking refuge in vain.

25. "Yes, you shall surely see Laṅkā enmeshed in a net of arrows, engulfed in fiery flames, its dwellings burnt to cinders.

[. . .]

Sarga 40

1. So Mārīca spoke, but for all his harsh talk he stood in dread of the lord of nightstalkers. Wretchedly, then, he said to Rāvaṇa, "Well, let us go.

2. "The instant Rāma sets eyes on me again, raises his sword, his bow and arrow, or some other weapon to slay me, my life is at an end.

3. "But what can I do in the face of such perversity as yours? So here, I am coming, my friend. I wish you well, nightstalker."

4. The *rākṣasa* was delighted by his words, and embracing him warmly, he said:

5. "There are the brave words I had hoped to hear from you. You were some other night-stalker a moment ago; now you are Mārīca.

6. "Here stands my flying chariot, studded with jewels and harnessed with asses, their faces like those of *piśācas*. Come aboard with me at once."

7. Rāvaṇa and Mārīca then boarded the palatial chariot and at once left the circle of ashrams behind.

8–9. And so, viewing the towns far below, the expanses of forest, the mountains, streams, kingdoms, and cities, they arrived in due course in Daṇḍaka wilderness. And then Mārīca and Rāvaṇa, overlord of *rākṣasas*, beheld the ashram of Rāghava.

10. Alighting from the gilded chariot, Rāvaṇa took Mārīca by the hand and said:

11. "What you see here, surrounded by plantain trees, is the site of Rāma's ashram. Quickly now, my friend, do what we came here to do."

12. Hearing Rāvaṇa's words, the *rākṣasa* Mārīca turned himself into a deer and began to graze near the entrance to Rāma's ashram.

13–16. The deer's horns were tipped with rare gems, his face mottled dark and light, one part like pink lotuses and the other like blue. His ears were like sapphires or blue lotuses, his neck gently elongated, his belly gleaming sapphire. His flanks were like the pale, velvety *madhūka* flower, the rest golden lotus shoots, and his hooves glowed cat's-eye beryl. He was slim and slender of leg, and brilliantly crowned with a tail tinged with every color of the rainbow. He was studded with all sorts of precious stones that lent him a glossy and captivating hue. In an instant the *rākṣasa* had changed himself into this magnificent deer.

17–18. It was a lovely and captivating form, sparkling with all its precious metals, that the *rākṣasa* assumed to entice Vaidehī. And shedding a brilliant radiance over the forest and Rāma's ashram, he duly went grazing in the meadows all around.

19. Dappled with hundreds of silver spots, a lovely sight to see, he grazed among the trees, breaking off and nibbling the tender shoots.

20. Back and forth he went to the plantain grove and among the *karṇikāra* trees, at a slow pace, trying to catch Sītā's eye.

21. What a brilliant spectacle the great deer made, with his back the hue of blue lilies, as he leisurely grazed in the vicinity of Rāma's ashram.

22. Going back and forth, appearing suddenly here and suddenly there, the splendid deer went grazing.

23. One moment he would frisk about, then lie upon the ground; he would approach the ashram's entrance and then withdraw amid a herd of deer.

24. And once more he would return with the other deer following behind, hoping Sītā would notice him, this *rākṣasa* become a deer.

25–26ab. He gamboled about, meandering in graceful circles. Other forest animals stared at him, came close and sniffed, and then all scampered off in every direction.

26cd–27ab. For he was still a *rākṣasa*, of course, who liked nothing more than killing animals. But to hide his true nature he did not eat these forest animals, though they were close enough to touch.

27cd–28ab. At this very moment, lovely eyed Vaidehī, busily picking flowers, came out beyond the trees.

28cd–29ab. The fair-faced woman with flashing eyes wandered about picking flowers, *karṇikāra, aśoka*, and mango flowers.

29cd–ef. The beautiful lady, not meant for life in the wilderness, caught sight of the jewel-studded deer, his limbs sparkling with gems and pearls.

30. She with her sparkling teeth and ruby lips stood there, eyes blossoming with wonder, staring longingly at the deer and his hide of silvery metal.

31. And the magical deer saw. Rāma's beloved, too, and stopped to graze there, illuminating, it seemed, all the forest.

32. And when Sītā, daughter of Janaka, saw that jewel-studded deer, the likes of which no one had ever seen before, she stood lost in sheer wonder.

The end of the fortieth *sarga* of the *Araṇyakāṇḍa* of the *Śrī Rāmāyaṇa*.

Sarga 41

1–2 The flawless beauty with full hips and a complexion of polished gold was picking flowers when she spotted the deer with his beautiful flanks of gold and silver hue. In delight she cried out to her husband and to Lakṣmaṇa, who stood armed and ready.

3. Rāma and Lakṣmaṇa, those tigers among men, glanced up in Vaidehī's direction at her call, and saw the deer.

4. Seeing him Lakṣmaṇa at once became suspicious and said to Rāma, "I am sure that deer is none other than the *rākṣasa* Mārīca.

5. "When kings who delight in the hunt enter the forest, Rāma, this evil creature, who can take on any form at will, assumes this or that disguise and kills them.

6. "He knows magic, tiger among men, and this is the magic form of a deer he has taken on, as dazzling to the eye as a mirage.

7. "For nowhere in all the world, Rāghava, master of the world, does there exist such a deer, sparkling with gems. I am certain this is magic."

8. But even as Kākutstha was speaking thus, bright-smiling Sītā interrupted – the deception had taken her reason away – and said in great delight:

9. "Dear husband, what an exquisite deer! He has stolen my heart away. Please catch him for me, my great-armed husband. He shall be our plaything.

10–11. "Here at our ashram many beautiful animals come wandering in droves: yaks and antelope, apes, herds of spotted gazelle, monkeys, and *kinnaras*. Lovely and powerful animals are always grazing here, my great-armed husband.

12. "But never before have we seen an animal such as this, your majesty, none so brilliant, tame, and radiant as this magnificent deer.

13. "His body sparkles with different colors and is speckled with chips of precious stones; he illuminates the entire forest, shining like the hare-marked moon.

14. "What coloring, what beauty, what sweet sounds he makes. He has utterly stolen my heart away, this amazing, sparkling deer.

15. "If you can catch him alive the deer will be a thing to marvel at, a source of wonder.

16. "And when our sojourn in the forest has ended and we are back in the kingdom once again, this deer will adorn the women's quarters.

17. "The heavenly form of this deer will be a source of wonder for Bharata, my brother-in-law, and for my mothers-in-law as well, my lord.

18. "But if you cannot catch the splendid deer alive, tiger among men, then his hide would be a source of great pleasure to me.

19. "Were the creature to be killed, I should like his golden skin to be stretched over a cushion of straw, to make a seat.

20. "You might think it willful, heartless, or unladylike of me, but I am so filled with wonder at the beauty of this creature.

21. "Even the mind of Rāghava is lost in wonder at the sight of him; with his golden hide and horns of precious gems, he shows all the brilliance of the morning sun, all the luster of the starry heavens."

22. When Rāghava heard these words of Sītā's and looked at the amazing deer, he addressed his brother Lakṣmaṇa in delight:

23. "Just see how Vaidehī longs to have this deer, Lakṣmaṇa. Because of his surpassing beauty he shall die today.

24. "Not in the renowned forest of Nandana, nor in famous Caitraratha, let alone on earth, Saumitri, is any such deer to be found.

25. "The lovely patterns on the deer's pelt, both with the nap and against it, are brilliantly flecked with chips of gold.

26. "Look how when he yawns his gleaming, flamelike tongue darts from his mouth like lightning from a cloud.

27. "His face gleams with sapphire and crystal, his belly glows with conch shell and pearl. Indeed, this indescribable deer could beguile the heart of anyone.

28. "Anyone would be lost in wonder to see this heavenly form fashioned of every precious stone, glittering like gold.

29. "Both for meat and sport, Lakṣmaṇa, kings armed with bows go hunting and kill animals in the deep forest.

30. "In the deep forests they gather riches with determination, precious metals of all sorts, veined with gems and gold.

31. "But here is all the wealth a man could ask for, Lakṣmaṇa, riches enough to swell his coffers, just as Śukra's coffers come to be swelled with all the wealth men dream of.

32. "Those who know the theory behind material success and those who achieve it, Lakṣmaṇa, say a man in want of something should go and get it without hesitation.

33. "Yes, fair-waisted Vaidehī shall seat herself next to me upon the precious golden hide of this rare deer.

34. "There is no hide, I should think – antelope's or gazelle's, goat's or ewe's – that could be so soft to the touch.

35. "This majestic deer and the heavenly deer that roams the sky are both of them heavenly – that deer of the stars and this deer of the earth.

36. "Then again, if it turns out to be 'the magic of that *rākṣasa*,' as you tell me, Lakṣmaṇa, then it is my duty to slay him.

37. "For the savage, impious Mārīca used to roam the forests injuring the bulls among sages.

38. "He has killed many a king and expert bowman out hunting, and so this deer, if it be he, must be slain.

39. "Once upon a time Vātāpi lived in this place. He had utter contempt for ascetic brahmans and would kill them from within their stomachs, as her foal will kill a she-mule when it comes to be born.

40. "But finally one day he met up with the greatest sage in the world, the mighty Agastya. As usual he had himself served up to him as food.

41. "At the conclusion of the feast the holy one perceived that Vātāpi was about to assume his true form again. Smiling slyly he said to him:

42. " 'It was reckless of you, Vātāpi, to show such mighty contempt to the best twice-born in this mortal world. And for that you are now to be digested.'

43. "Just as happened with Vātāpi, Lakṣmaṇa, no *rākṣasa* can hope to live that treats with scorn someone like me, who is constant in righteousness and self-controlled.

44ab. "Now that he has fallen into my hands I will slay him, just as Agastya slew Vātāpi.

44cd–45ab. "But you must remain here to protect Maithilī, armed and on your guard, delight of the Raghus. For our first responsibility is to her.

45cd–46ab. "I intend to go at once, Saumitri, and bring back the deer dead or alive.

46cd–47ab. "Just see how Vaidehī longs for the hide of this deer, Lakṣmaṇa. And because of his splendid hide the deer shall die today.

47cd–48. "Stay in the ashram with Sītā, Lakṣmaṇa, and be on your guard. I intend to kill the dappled deer with my first shot, and afterward skin him and come straight back.

49. "With the aid of wise Jaṭāyus, the capable and all-powerful bird, take care of Maithilī. Be on your guard every moment, Lakṣmaṇa, and suspicious of everything."

The end of the forty-first *sarga* of the *Araṇyakāṇḍa* of the *Śrī Rāmāyaṇa*.

Sarga 42

1. After instructing his brother the mighty prince, delight of the Raghus, strapped on his gold-hilted sword.

2. He then strapped on a pair of quivers and took up his proper ornament – the bow with triple curve – and set off at a rapid pace.

3. The deer spied the lord of kings rushing toward him and he led him on, now timorously hiding, now showing himself again.

4. With sword strapped on and taking up his bow, Rāma ran toward the deer, imagining he saw his form shimmering before him.

5–6. At one moment he would spot him running through the deep forest, temptingly near, and would take his bow in hand, only to look once more and find the deer beyond the range of his arrow. In one stretch of forest he came into sight leaping through the air in frightful panic, and then he passed into another stretch and out of sight.

7. Like the disk of the autumn moon veiled in tatters of cloud, he was seen one instant and gone the next.

8. Now appearing, now disappearing, he drew Rāghava far away, and helplessly deluded by him Kākutstha flew into a rage.

9. Then the deer halted in exhaustion and withdrew to a shady spot in the meadow, not far away, where Rāma spotted him surrounded by other animals of the forest.

10. Seeing the deer mighty Rāma was determined to kill him. The powerful prince nocked his sturdy bow and drew it back with power.

11. Aiming at the deer he shot a gleaming, flaming arrow fashioned by Brahmā that glared like a snake as it darted forth.

12. The supreme arrow penetrated the illusory deer form and like a bolt of lightning pierced the heart, Mārīca's heart.

13. The deer leaped high as a palm tree and with a ghastly shriek fell to the ground, tormented by the arrow, his life ebbing away. And as Mārīca lay there dying, the shape he had assumed began to disappear.

14. Knowing the time had come, in Rāghava's own voice he cried out, "Oh Sītā! Oh Lakṣmaṇa!"

15. Pierced to the quick by an arrow unlike any other, Mārīca once more took on the form of a massive *rākṣasa*, giving up the deer form and his life.

16. Struck by the arrow, he became a *rākṣasa* once more, with huge fangs, a necklace of gold, sparkling earrings, and every other ornament to adorn him.

17. Seeing that dreadful sight, the *rākṣasa* fallen on the ground, Rāma thought suddenly of Sītā and recalled what Lakṣmaṇa had said.

18. "With his dying breath this *rākṣasa* cried out at the top of his voice, 'Oh Sītā! Oh Lakṣmaṇa!' How will Sītā react to hearing this?

19. "And great-armed Lakṣmaṇa, what will be his state of mind?" As these thoughts came to righteous Rāma, the hair on his body bristled with dread.

20. Then Rāma's consternation gave way to a feeling of fear that shot through him with sharp pangs: The deer he had slain was in fact a *rākṣasa*, the voice it had used was his own.

21. He killed another dappled deer and taking the meat hurriedly retraced his steps to Janasthāna.

The end of the forty-second *sarga* of the *Araṇyakāṇḍa* of the *Śrī Rāmāyaṇa*.

Sarga 43

1. Now, when Sītā heard that cry of distress, in her husband's own voice, coming from the forest, she said to Lakṣmaṇa, "Go and find out what has happened to Rāghava.

2. "My heart – my very life – is jarred from its place by the sound of his crying in deep distress that I heard so clearly.

3–4. "You must rescue your brother, who cries out in the forest. Run to your brother at once, for he needs help! The *rākṣasas* have him in their power, like a bull fallen among lions." So she spoke, but Lakṣmaṇa, heeding his brother's command, did not go.

5–6. Then the daughter of Janaka angrily said to him, "You wear the guise of a friend to your brother, Saumitri, but act like his foe, refusing to aid him in his extremity. You hope Rāma perishes, Lakṣmaṇa, isn't that so? And it is all because of me.

7. "I think you would be happy should some disaster befall your brother. You have no real affection for him, so you stand there calmly with the splendid prince gone from sight.

8. "For with him in danger and me here, how could I prevent what you came here with the sole intention of doing?"

9. So Sītā, princess of Videha, spoke, overwhelmed with tears and grief, and Lakṣmaṇa replied to her as she stood there frightened as a doe.

10–11. "My lady, there is no one, god or man, *gandharva*, great bird, or *rākṣasa*, *piśāca*, *kinnara*, beast, or dreaded *dānava* – no one, fair lady, who could match Rāma, the peer of Vāsava, in battle.

12. "Rāma cannot be killed in battle. You must not talk this way, for I dare not leave you in the forest with Rāghava gone.

13. "His power cannot be withstood, not by any powers however vast, not by all three worlds up in arms, or the deathless gods themselves, their lord included.

14. "Let your heart rest easy, do not be alarmed. Your husband will soon return, after killing that splendid deer.

15. "That was clearly not his voice, or any belonging to a god. It was the magic of that *rākṣasa*, unreal as a mirage.

16. "You were entrusted to my safekeeping, shapely Vaidehī, by the great Rāma. I dare not leave you here alone.

17. "Then too, dear lady, because of the slaughter at Janasthāna, where Khara perished, we have earned the hostility of the night-stalkers.

18. "*Rākṣasas* delight in causing trouble, Vaidehī, they make all kinds of noises in the deep forest. You need not worry."

19. Though what he said was true, Sītā was enraged by Lakṣmaṇa's words. Her eyes blazed bright red as she made this harsh reply:

20. "Ignoble, cruel man, disgrace to your House! How pitiful this attempt of yours. I feel certain you are pleased with all this, and that is why you can talk the way you do.

21. "It is nothing new, Lakṣmaṇa, for rivals to be so evil, cruel rivals like you always plotting in secret.

22. "You treacherously followed Rāma to the forest, the two of you alone: You are either in the employ of Bharata or secretly plotting to get me.

23. "I am married to Rāma, a husband dark as a lotus, with eyes like lotus petals. How could I ever give my love to some ordinary man?

24. "I would not hesitate to take my life before your very eyes, Saumitri, for I could not live upon this earth one moment without Rāma."

25. Such were the words Sītā spoke to Lakṣmaṇa, so harsh they made his hair bristle with horror. But he controlled himself, and with hands cupped in reverence he addressed her:

26. "I dare not answer, Maithilī, for you are a deity in my eyes. And yet inappropriate words from a woman come as nothing new.

27. "This is the nature of women the whole world over: Women care nothing for righteousness, they are flighty, sharp-tongued, and divisive.

28. "May all the inhabitants of the forest give ear and bear me witness how my words of reason met so harsh a reply from you.

29. "Curse you and be damned, that you could so suspect me, when I am only following the orders of my guru. How like a woman to be so perverse!

30. "I am going to Kākutstha. I wish you well, fair woman. May the spirits of the forest, each and every one, protect you, large-eyed lady.

31. "How ominous the portents that manifest themselves to me! I pray I find you here when I return with Rāma."

32. Now, when Lakṣmaṇa addressed her in this fashion, Janaka's daughter began to weep. Overwhelmed with tears she hotly replied:

33. "Parted from Rāma I will drown myself in the Godāvarī, Lakṣmaṇa, I will hang myself or hurl my body upon some rocky place.

34. "Or I will drink deadly poison or throw myself into a blazing fire. I would never touch any man but Rāghava, not even with my foot!"

35. Such were the insults Sītā hurled at Lakṣmaṇa in her sorrow, and sorrowfully she wept and struck her belly with her fists.

36. At the sight of large-eyed Sītā so deeply anguished and weeping, Saumitri was beside himself and tried to comfort her, but she would say nothing more to her husband's brother.

37. Then, cupping his hands in reverence and bowing slightly, Lakṣmaṇa, the self-respecting prince, said goodbye to Sītā. And as he set forth to find Rāma, he turned around again and again and looked back at Maithilī.

The end of the forty-third *sarga* of the *Araṇyakāṇḍa* of the *Śrī Rāmāyaṇa*.

Sarga 44

1. Rāghava's younger brother, angered by her harsh words and sorely longing for Rāma, set forth without further delay.

2. This was the opening ten-necked Rāvaṇa had been waiting for, and he took advantage of it at once. Assuming the guise of a wandering mendicant, he turned his steps toward Vaidehī.

3. Clad in a soft saffron robe, with topknot, parasol, and sandals, and goodly staff and water pitcher hanging at his left shoulder – disguised like this, as a mendicant – he approached Vaidehī.

4. Both brothers had left her, and in his pride of power he advanced upon her, like total darkness advancing upon the twilight, when both sun and moon have left.

5. He gazed at the glorious young princess as ominously as a planet might gaze upon the star Rohiṇī when the hare-marked moon is absent.

6. At the appearance of the dreaded, evil creature, the trees that grew in Janasthāna stopped rustling and the wind died down.

7. At the sight of him peering around with his blood-red eyes, the swift current of the Godāvarī river began to slacken in fear.

8. Ten-necked Rāvaṇa had waited for an opening, and Rāma had given him one. In the guise of a beggar he drew near to Vaidehī.

9. As Vaidehī sat grieving for her husband, the unholy Rāvaṇa in the guise of a holy man edged closer to her, like the sluggish planet, Saturn, closing in on Citrā, the sparkling star.

10–11. Like a deep well concealed by grass, the evil one in the guise of a holy man stood watching Vaidehī, illustrious wife of Rāma – the beautiful woman with lovely teeth and lips, and a face like the full moon – as she sat in the leaf hut tormented with grief and tears.

12. The blackhearted stalker of the night stole ever closer to Vaidehī, the woman dressed in garments of yellow silk, and with eyes like lotus petals.

13. With arrows of Manmatha, god of love, lodged deep within his heart, and the sounds of the *vedas* on his lips, the overlord of *rākṣasas* appeared before the deserted hut and courteously spoke.

14. Rāvaṇa began singing her praises, that loveliest of women in the three worlds, a radiant beauty, like the goddess Śrī herself without the lotus.

15. "Who are you, golden woman dressed in garments of yellow silk, wearing a lovely lotus garland, and like a lotus pond yourself?

16. "Are you the goddess Modesty or Fame? Are you Śrī or lovely Lakṣmī or perhaps an *apsaras*, lovely lady? Could you be Prosperity, shapely woman, or easygoing Pleasure?

17. "Your teeth are bright white, tapered, and even; your eyes are large and clear, rosy at the corner, black in the center.

18–19. "Your hips are full and broad, your thighs smooth as an elephant's trunk. And these, your delightful breasts, how round they are, so firm and gently heaving; how full and lovely, smooth as two palm fruits, with their nipples standing stiff and the rarest gems to adorn them.

20. "Graceful lady with your lovely smile, lovely teeth, and lovely eyes, you have swept my heart away like a river in flood that sweeps away its banks.

21. "Your waist I could compass with my fingers; how fine is your hair, how firm your breasts. No goddess, no *gandharva* woman, no *yakṣa* or *kinnara* woman, no mortal woman so beautiful have I ever seen before on the face of this earth.

22. "Your beauty, unrivaled in all the worlds, your delicacy and youth, and the fact of your living here in the woods stir the deepest feelings in me.

23. "I urge you to go home, this is no place for you to be living. For this is the lair of dreaded *rākṣasas*, who can change their form at will.

24. "In the most delightful palaces, in luxuriant, fragrant city gardens is where you should be strolling.

25. "To my mind you deserve the finest garlands and beverages and raiment, and the finest husband, lovely black-eyed lady.

26. "Could you be one of the Rudras or Maruts, sweet-smiling, shapely woman, or one of the Vasus, perhaps? You look like a goddess to me.

27. "But *gandharvas* do not pass this way, nor do gods or *kinnaras*, for this is the lair of *rākṣasas*. How is it you have come here?

28. "There are monkeys here, lions, panthers, and tigers, apes, hyenas, and flesh-eating birds. How is it you do not fear them?

29. "And the dreaded elephants that go running wild, maddened by rut – how is it you do not fear them, lovely lady, all alone in the deep wilderness?

30. "Who are you, to whom do you belong, where do you come from, my precious, and why are you wandering all alone through Daṇḍaka, the haunt of dreaded *rākṣasas*?"

31. Such was the praise evil Rāvaṇa lavished on Vaidehī. But seeing he had come in the garb of a brahman, Maithilī honored him with all the acts of hospitality due a guest.

32. First she brought forward a cushion and offered water for his feet, and then she called him when food was ready, for he looked kindly enough.

33. When Maithilī observed that he had come in the garb of a twice-born – a brahman with a begging bowl and saffron robe; when she saw these accoutrements, it was impossible to refuse him, and so she extended him an invitation befitting a brahman.

34. "Here is a cushion, brahman, please be seated and accept this water for your feet. Here I have made ready for you the best fare the forest has to offer. You may partake of it freely."

35. So Maithilī extended him a cordial invitation, and as Rāvaṇa gazed at her, the wife of the lord of men, he confirmed his resolve to take her by force, and with that, consigned himself to death.

36. Her husband in his honest garb had gone to hunt the magic deer, and she waited for him and Lakṣmaṇa, scanning the horizon. But she saw neither Rāma nor Lakṣmaṇa – only the deep, green forest.

The end of the forty-fourth *sarga* of the *Araṇyakāṇḍa* of the *Śrī Rāmāyaṇa*.

Sarga 45

1. When Rāvaṇa came in the guise of a mendicant to carry off Vaidehī, he had first put some

questions to her. Of her own accord she now began to tell her story.

2. For Sītā had thought a moment: "He is a brahman and my guest. If I do not reply he will curse me." She then spoke these words:

3. "I am the daughter of Janaka, the great king of Mithilā. My name is Sītā, may it please the best of twice-born, and I am the wife of Rāma.

4. "For twelve years I lived in the house of Rāghava, enjoying such pleasures as mortals enjoy. I had all I could desire.

5. "Then, in the thirteenth year, the king in concert with his kingly counselors approved the royal consecration of my husband.

6. "But just as the preparations for Rāghava's consecration were under way, a mother-in-law of mine named Kaikeyī asked her husband for a boon.

7. "You see, Kaikeyī had already married my father-in-law for a consideration. So she had two things she now could ask of her husband, the best of kings and a man who always kept his word: One was the consecration of Bharata, the other, my husband's banishment.

8. " 'From this day forth I will not eat, or drink, or sleep, I will put an end to my life if Rāma is consecrated.'

9. "Such were Kaikeyī's words, and though my father-in-law, who had always shown her respect, begged her with offers of commensurate riches, she would not do what he begged of her.

10ab–874. "Rāma, my mighty husband, was then twenty-five years old, and I had just passed my eighteenth birthday.

10cd–ef. "His name is renowned throughout the world, his eyes are large, his arms strong. He is virtuous, honest, truthful, and devoted to the welfare of all people.

11. "When Rāma came into his father's presence for the consecration to begin, it was Kaikeyī who addressed my husband, in a rush of words:

12. " 'Listen to me, Rāghava, and hear what your father has decreed. The kingship is to be given to Bharata uncontested.

13. " 'As for you, you are to live in the forest for nine years and five. Go into banishment, Kākutstha, and save your father from falsehood.'

14. "Without a trace of fear my husband Rāma answered Kaikeyī, 'So be it,' and in firm compliance with his vow did just as she had told him.

15. "For Rāma has taken a solemn vow, brahman, one never to be broken: always to give and not receive, to tell the truth and not lie.

16. "Rāma has a constant companion, his half brother Lakṣmaṇa, a tiger among men and mighty slayer of enemies in battle.

17. "This brother Lakṣmaṇa, who keeps to the ways of righteousness, firm in his vows, followed bow in hand when Rāma went into banishment with me.

18. "And so the three of us were driven from the kingdom for the sake of Kaikeyī. Thus it is under compulsion, best of twice-born, that we now wander the dense forest.

19. "Rest a moment; or you can even pass the night here if you like. My husband will soon return bringing an abundance of food from the forest.

20. "But can you just tell me your name, your clan, and family? How is it that you, a brahman, wander all alone in Daṇḍaka wilderness?"

21. So Sītā, wife of Rāma, spoke, and powerful Rāvaṇa, overlord of *rākṣasas*, made a reply that froze her blood:

22. "I am he who terrifies the worlds, with all their gods, *asuras*, and great serpents. I am Rāvaṇa, Sītā, supreme lord of the hosts of *rākṣasas*.

23. "Now that I have set eyes on you, flawless, golden lady dressed in silk, I shall no longer take any pleasure in my own wives.

24. "From one place and another I have carried off many splendid women. May it please you to become chief queen over every one of them.

25. "In the middle of the ocean lies my vast city Lañkā, perched upon a mountain peak and ringed by the sea.

26. "There, my radiant Sītā, you shall stroll with me through the forests, never longing for this life you are leading in the wilderness.

27. "Five thousand slave women all adorned with ornaments shall wait upon you hand and foot, Sītā, if you become my wife."

28. So Rāvaṇa spoke, but Janaka's daughter, that faultless beauty, angrily and with utter contempt for the *rākṣasa* replied:

29. "I am faithful to Rāma, my husband, the equal of great Indra, unshakable as a great mountain, imperturbable as the great sea.

30. "I am faithful to Rāma, the great-armed, great-chested prince, who moves with the boldness of a lion, a lionlike man, a lion among men.

31. "I am faithful to Rāma, the king's most cherished son, a great-armed, mighty prince of wide renown and strict self-control, whose face is like the full moon.

32. "As for you, you are a jackal in the presence of a lioness, to come here seeking me, whom you can never have. You could no more touch me than touch the radiance of the sun.

33. "You must be seeing many a golden tree of death, ill-fated Rāvaṇa, if you seek to gain the beloved wife of Rāghava.

34. "You are seeking to pluck the fang from the mouth of a poisonous snake, the tooth from the mouth of a hungry lion in pursuit, the foe to all beasts.

35. "You are seeking to carry off Mandara, greatest of mountains, in your hand, to drink the *kālakūṭa* poison and take no harm of it.

36. "You are rubbing your eye with a needle, licking a razor with your tongue, if you seek to violate the beloved wife of Rāghava.

37. "You are seeking to cross the ocean with a boulder tied around your neck, to take into your hands the very sun and moon, if you seek to assault the beloved wife of Rāghava.

38. "You have seen a blazing fire and seek to carry it away in a cloth, if you seek to carry off the virtuous wife of Rāma.

39. "You are seeking to walk atop a row of iron-headed spears, if you seek to violate the proper wife of Rāma.

40. "As different as a lion and a jackal in the forest, the ocean and a ditch, rare wine and gruel, so different are Dāśarathi and you.

41. "As different as gold and lead, sandalwood paste and slime, a bull elephant and a cat in the forest, so different are Dāśarathi and you.

42. "As different as Garuḍa, the son of Vinatā, and a crow, a peacock and a gull, a vulture and a crane in the forest, so different are Dāśarathi and you.

43. "As long as Rāma walks the earth, mighty as thousand-eyed Indra, armed with his bow and arrow, you may take me but could never enjoy me, no more than a fly the diamond chip it swallows."

44. Such were the words the good woman addressed to the evil nightstalker, but a shudder passed through her body, and she began to quiver like a slender plantain tree tossed by the wind.

45. And when Rāvaṇa, mighty as Death himself, observed how Sītā was trembling, he thought to frighten her still further by telling of his House, his power, the name he had won for himself, and the deeds he had done.

The end of the forty-fifth *sarga* of the *Araṇyakāṇḍa* of the *Śrī Rāmāyaṇa*.

Sarga 46

1. Even as Sītā was speaking in this manner, Rāvaṇa flew into a passion, and knitting his brow into a frown he harshly replied:

2. "I am half brother to Vaiśravaṇa, lovely lady. My name is Rāvaṇa, if you please, the mighty ten-necked one.

3. "In fear of me the gods, *gandharvas*, *piśācas*, great birds, and serpents flee in terror, as all things born are put to flight by fear of Death.

4. "In connection with some issue between us Vaiśravaṇa, my half brother, and I came into conflict. In a rage I attacked and defeated him in battle.

5. "Tormented by fear of me he left his own prosperous realm and now dwells on Kailāsa,

highest of mountains, with only men to convey him.

6. "For the aerial chariot that flies where one desires, the lovely Puṣpaka, once belonged to him. But I took it by force of arms, my beauty, and now ride upon it through the sky.

7. "At the mere sight of my face, Maithilī, once my anger has been provoked, the gods with Indra at their head flee in terror.

8. "In my presence the wind blows cautiously, and the sun's hot rays turn cold in fear.

9. "The leaves on the trees stop rustling, and the rivers slacken their current wherever I am, wherever I go.

10. "On the further shore of the ocean lies my lovely city, Laṅkā, grand as Indra's Amarāvatī, thronged with dreaded *rākṣasas*.

11. "It is a lovely, dazzling city ringed by a white rampart, with gateways made of gold and towers of cat's-eye beryl.

12. "It is crowded with elephants, horses, and chariots, the sound of pipes resounds there, and its gardens are beautiful, filled with trees bearing any fruit one wants.

13. "Living there with me, proud princess Sītā, you shall forget what it was like to have been a mortal woman.

14. "Enjoying not only the pleasures mortals enjoy, lovely lady, but divine pleasures, too, you shall soon forget that short-lived mortal, Rāma.

15. "So meager is his power that King Daśaratha, in order to enthrone a favored son, was able to drive him into the forest, first-born though he was.

16. "What use is this witless Rāma to you, large-eyed woman, a miserable ascetic who lets himself be deposed from the kingship?

17. "The lord of all *rākṣasas* has come here in person, of his own accord. Do not reject him, whom the arrows of Manmatha, god of love, have so badly wounded.

18. "For if you do reject me, timid lady, you shall live to regret it, just like Urvaśī after she spurned Purūravas."

19. So he spoke, but Vaidehī was overcome with rage – her eyes grew red, and though all alone in that deserted spot, she made this harsh reply to the lord of *rākṣasas*:

20. "How can you want to commit such an outrage, you who claim Vaiśravaṇa as brother, a god to whom all beings pay homage?

21. "The *rākṣasas* shall inevitably perish, Rāvaṇa, all who have you for their king, a cruel, imprudent, intemperate king.

22. "A man might abduct Indra's wife, Śacī herself, and still hope to save his life, but he who carries me off, the wife of Rāma, has no life left to save.

23. "One might steal the incomparable Śacī from the hand that wields the thunderbolt and long remain alive. But violate a woman like me, *rākṣasa*, and even drinking the nectar of immortality will be no escape for you."

The end of the forty-sixth *sarga* of the *Araṇyakāṇḍa* of the *Śrī Rāmāyaṇa*.

Sarga 47

1. Hearing Sītā's words the awesome ten-necked Rāvaṇa struck his hands together and made ready to assume his massive form.

2. Again he addressed Maithilī, and far more severely than before: "It seems you did not hear, madwoman, when I spoke of my strength and valor.

3. "I can lift the earth in my arms while standing in the sky; I can drink up the ocean, I can slay Death in battle.

4. "I can shatter the earth with my sharp arrows, madwoman, or bring the sun to a halt. I can take on any form at will. You see before you a husband ready to grant your every wish."

5. And as Rāvaṇa spoke thus in his wild rage, his yellow-rimmed eyes turned fiery red.

6. Then suddenly Rāvaṇa, younger brother to Vaiśravaṇa, abandoned the kindly form of beggar and assumed his true shape, one such as Doom itself must have.

7. With eyes flaming bright red, with earrings of burnished gold, with bow and arrows, he became once more the majestic ten-faced stalker of the night.

8. He had thrown off the guise of mendicant and assumed his own form again, the colossal shape of Rāvaṇa, overlord of *rākṣasas.*

9–10. With eyes flaming bright red in his rage, lowering like a bank of storm clouds, clad in a red garment Rāvaṇa stood before Maithilī, staring at her, perfect jewel of a woman, with her jet-black hair, her sunlike radiance, and the fine clothes and ornaments that she wore. And he said:

11. "If you seek a husband whose fame has spread throughout the three worlds, shapely woman, be mine. I am a lord worthy of you.

12. "Love me forever. I shall be a lover to win your praise, and never, my beauty, will I do anything to displease you. Give up this love for a mortal being, and bestow your love on me.

13. "What possible virtues could make you love this short-lived Rāma, a failure, stripped of kingship? You think you are so smart, but what a fool you really are!

14. "He is a simpleton, who at the bidding of a woman abandoned his kingdom and loved ones to come and live in this forest, the haunt of wild beasts."

15. And so speaking to Sītā, princess of Mithilā, who deserved the same kindness she always showed others, Rāvaṇa seized her as the planet Budha might seize the star Rohiṇī in the sky.

16. With his left hand he seized lotus-eyed Sītā by her hair and with his right hand by her thighs.

17. With his long arms and sharp fangs he resembled a mountain peak; seeing him advancing like Death himself, the spirits of the forest fled overpowered by fear.

18. Then with a dreadful rumble Rāvaṇa's great chariot came into view, that unearthly chariot fashioned by magic, with wheels of gold, and harnessed with asses.

19. With loud, harsh threats he then clutched Vaidehī to his breast and boarded the chariot.

20. Caught in Rāvaṇa's grip and wild with despair, the glorious Sītā screamed at the top of her voice, crying, "Rāma!" But Rāma was far away in the forest.

21. Filled with desire for one who was filled with loathing for him, Rāvaṇa flew up holding her writhing like a serpent queen.

22. As the lord of *rākṣasas* carried her off through the sky, she screamed shrilly like a woman gone mad, in agony, or delirious:

23. "Oh great-armed Lakṣmaṇa, you have always sought favor with your guru. Don't you know that I am being carried off by a *rākṣasa*, who can change his form at will?

24. "And you, Rāghava, you renounced all life's pleasures, everything of value, for the sake of righteousness. Don't you see me being carried off in defiance of all that is right?

25. "And surely, slayer of enemies, you are the one to discipline wrongdoers. Why then don't you punish so evil a creature as Rāvaṇa?

26. "But no, the result of wrongdoing is not seen right away. Time is a factor in this, as in the ripening of grain.

27. "And as for you, Doom must have robbed you of your senses to do what you have done. Disaster shall befall you at the hands of Rāma, a terrible disaster that will end your life.

28. "Ah, now Kaikeyī and all her family must be satisfied. Rāma's lawful wife has been taken from him, that glorious prince whom nothing but righteousness could satisfy.

29. "Janasthāna, I call on you and you *karṇikāra* trees in full blossom: Tell Rāma at once that Rāvaṇa is carrying off Sītā.

30. "I greet you, Mount Prasravaṇa, with your flower garlands and massive peaks: Quickly tell Rāma that Rāvaṇa is carrying off Sītā.

31. "I greet you, Godāvarī river, alive with the call of geese and cranes: Tell Rāma at once that Rāvaṇa is carrying off Sītā.

32. "And you spirits that inhabit the different trees of this forest, I salute you all: Tell my husband that I have been carried off.

33–34. "All creatures that live in this place, I appeal to you for help, all you flocks of birds and herds of beasts: Tell my husband that the woman he loves more than life itself is being carried off, that Sītā has been carried away, helpless, by Rāvaṇa.

35. "Once the powerful, great-armed prince discovers where I am – albeit in the

other world – he shall come in all his valor and bring me home, were it Vaivasvata himself, god of death, who had carried me off.

36. "Jaṭāyus, tell Rāma and Lakṣmaṇa just how I was carried off, tell the whole story, from beginning to end!"

The end of the forty-seventh *sarga* of the *Araṇyakāṇḍa* of the *Śrī Rāmāyaṇa*.

Sarga 48

1. From deep in sleep Jaṭāyus heard her cry. He glanced up and all at once saw them, Rāvaṇa and Vaidehī.

2. The great, majestic bird, tall as a mountaintop, his beak sharp as a razor, then called out these wise words from his tree:

3. "Ten-necked Rāvaṇa, I am Jaṭāyus, the powerful king of vultures who keeps to the ancient ways of righteousness and puts his trust in truth.

4. "Rāma, son of Daśaratha, is king of all the world, the equal of great Indra and Varuṇa, and dedicated to the welfare of all creatures in the world.

5. "The shapely woman you now seek to carry off belongs to him, the master of the world. Her name is Sītā, and she is his glorious, lawful wife.

6. "How could any king who keeps to the ways of righteousness defile the wife of another man, and a king's wife at that, who is inviolable above all? It is a despicable thing, powerful Rāvaṇa, to defile the wife of another. Put the thought out of your mind.

7. "A wise man should not do what others would censure. One must look upon the wives of other men as no less inviolable than one's own.

8. "It is according to how kings behave, delight of the Paulastyas, that the learned decide questions of profit, pleasure, or righteousness not settled in the sacred texts.

9. "For a king is righteousness, pleasure, and the ultimate repository of wealth; the king is the root from which all conduct springs, be it good or evil.

10. "You are evil and reckless by nature, foremost of *rākṣasas*. How could you possibly have secured your lofty position of power? It is as though a sinner had acquired a celestial chariot.

11. "Indeed, one can never change one's true nature. The noble do not linger long in the dwelling of the wicked.

12. "Mighty Rāma is a righteous prince and has never wronged you in your city or realm. Why is it you are wronging him now?

13–14. "If Khara, coming to Janasthāna on Śūrpaṇakhā's account, overstepped all bounds and so was slain by tireless Rāma, tell me now in all honesty, what crime is Rāma guilty of that you should go and carry off this woman, the wife of the master of the world?

15. "Release Vaidehī at once or he shall consume you with his terrible eye, as fiery as the lightning bolt of Indra that consumed the demon Vṛtra.

16. "A poisonous snake is caught in the hem of your cloak and you do not know it; the noose of Doom is wound around your neck and you do not see it.

17. "A man should only bear a load, my friend, that does not bring him to his knees; he should only eat the food he can safely digest.

18. "Who would attempt a deed that can bring him no righteous merit, no worldly fame or glory, nothing but physical pain?

19. "It was sixty thousand years ago I was born, Rāvaṇa, and all that time I have justly reigned in the kingship of my fathers and forefathers.

20. "I am old and you are young; you are mounted, clad in armor, and bear a bow and arrows. Still, you shall not take Vaidehī and go your way unscathed.

Chapter 7

The *Purāṇas*, Stories of the Ancient Past

The *Purāṇas*, Stories of the Ancient Past, are, like the *Mahābhārata* and the *Rāmāyaṇa*, texts whose origins are oral. First recited by *sūtas*, bards, to *kṣatriyas*, there are 18 *mahā-purāṇas*, major *Purāṇas*, and 18 *upapurāṇas*, minor *Purāṇas*. Though these numbers may seem fixed, there are many more texts than these that are considered to belong to this genre of texts.[1] To complicate matters further, *Purāṇas* are not an exclusively Hindu genre because there are Jain *Purāṇas* as well as vernacular *Purāṇas* that have been translated into Sanskrit or have remained in the vernacular.[2]

As their name conveys, the *Purāṇas* are largely stories of events that have taken place in the past. These include creation myths and accounts of the destruction of the universe, stories about royal genealogies, and stories about, and biographies of, gods and goddesses. These stories were composed in ways that made them entertaining and accessible. Unlike the *Vedas* and *Upaniṣads* that were only for virtuosos and other elites, the *Purāṇas* had non-experts as their intended audience. The *Purāṇic* stories were also popular accounts for the consumption of the masses. That some were in the vernacular coincides with this intention. In recent times many stories from the *Purāṇas* have become even more accessible thanks to Anant Pai, the developer and publisher of the legendary *Amar Chitra Katha* comic books.[3]

The goal of the *Purāṇas* was primarily to inspire *bhakti*, devotion. The *Purāṇas* were part of larger changes in the history of Hinduism where theism replaced more abstract forms of worship, where *bhakti*, devotion, to personalized gods and goddesses was held as highest. These stories, then, made the gods and goddesses welcoming and approachable in the minds of their listeners.

The *Purāṇas* served sectarian purposes as well and there are *Purāṇas* dedicated solely to the edification of particular gods or goddesses. The *Viṣṇu Purāṇa*, for example, centered upon stories about Viṣṇu, while the *Śiva Purāṇa*, nor surprisingly, centered upon Śiva. Even within the Vaiṣṇava sects there were *Purāṇas* devoted to particular *avatāras*, such as the *Bhāgavata Purāṇa*, which is a biography of Kṛṣṇa. In each of these *Purāṇic* cosmologies one god (or goddess) was treated as supreme. A theological perspective, though not a systematic one, surrounding the given deity was developed within each text. Seeking consistency across *Purāṇic* worlds is thus futile since they were never to be taken altogether to present a coherent worldview.

The first grouping contains myths about the origin and destruction of the universe. "The Origins and Nature of Time," taken from *Mārkaṇḍeya Purāṇa* (42.61–73), is a description of the four *yugas*, ages. "The Four Ages" continues with this theme and is from the *Kūrma Purāṇa* (1.27.16–57). "The Kali Age" and the "The Dissolution of the World in Vṣṇu" are about the last *yuga* and subsequent destruction and are both from the *Viṣṇu Purāṇa* (4.24.70–97 and 6.3.14–41 respectively).

The next three sets are taken from several sects, including the Vaiśṇava, Śaiva, and Devi sects. The first cluster is Viṣṇu-oriented and includes myths about him and his *avatāras*. "The Twelve *Avatāras* of Viṣṇu" (*Matsya Purāṇa* 47.32–52) and "The Twenty-two *Avatāras* of Viṣṇu" (*Garuḍa Purāṇa* 1.12–35) are lists and short descriptions of his various *avatāras*. The latter includes the Jina and the Buddha as *avatāras* of Viṣṇu. This points towards the Hindu practice to include non-Hindu traditions within its fold.[4] "The Churning of the Ocean" is a well-known creation myth that appears in the *Viṣṇu Purāṇa* (1.9.2–116). This myth spread throughout South and South East Asia as is evident in the enormous bas-relief stone carving of this myth in the Agkor Wat temple in Siem Reap, Cambodia. "Viṣṇu and Śrī" is a brief account of the relationship between the god and goddess and masculinity and femininity and is found in the *Viṣṇu Purāṇa* (1.8.17–35). Other than Durga and Kālī, all goddesses in Hinduism are held to be consorts of gods and this account points towards these correlations.

Among the *avatāras* of Viṣṇu, Kṛṣṇa is one of the most popular. This next section includes several myths, all taken from the *Viṣṇu Purāṇa* that revolve around the life of the mischieveous *bāla*, baby, Kṛṣṇa. Stories of infant Kṛṣṇa are easily comprehensible and lend themselves towards creating *bhakti* in their listeners. I have included here "The Conception of Kṛṣṇa" (5.1.5–33) and "The Birth of Kṛṣṇa" (5.3.1–29) and the provocative tale of "Pūtanā, the Child Killer" (5.5.1–23) whose attempt to suckle and thus to murder Kṛṣṇa with her deadly breast milk fails. The last myth is "Mt. Govardhana" and is a story of Kṛṣṇa protecting his worshippers from the wrath of Indra, a god central to the *Vedas*. It points towards some significant changes in orientation from a sacrifice-oriented-Vedic world to a Viṣṇu-centered *bhakti* one (5.11.1–25).

Another set of sectarian *Purāṇas* focus upon Śiva. "The Test of Pārvatī's *Tapas*," taken from *Śiva Satarudra Purāṇa* (33.1–63), is a tale about his greatest *bhakta*, devotee, namely Pārvatī, who later became his wife. In it Pārvātī practices severe austerities and is awarded with his love. "Dakṣa's Insult" (*Śiva Vāyavīya Purāṇa* 1.18.4–59) is the story of Satī, Śiva's first wife (later reborn as Pārvatī), who, after her father insults Śiva, immolates herself and becomes the first *satī*, virtuous wife. "Gaṇeśa" (from Śiva *Rudra Purāṇa* 13.15–39) is the story of the birth of the ever-popular elephant-headed deity who is worshiped as the mischievous god of obstructions and beginnings. Since Śiva is believed to be the god of oppositions, within him is found both male and female principles. These beliefs are presented in "The Origin of Women" (*Śiva Satarudra Purāṇa* 3.1–31) and "Hari-Hara" (*Vāmana Purāṇa* 36.1–9, 19–31).[5]

The last collection of myths concerns the goddess. "The Death of Mahiṣa, the Buffalo Demon" (*Mārkeṇḍeya Devīmāhātmya Purāṇa* 80.21–44) is the story of the goddess Durgā while "The Birth of Kālī and the Final Battle" is another presentation of the ferocity and war-like nature of the goddess (*Mārkeṇḍeya Devīmāhātmya Purāṇa* 84.1–25, 89.29–37). As already mentioned, unlike other goddesses in the Hindu tradition, neither Durgā nor Kālī are consorts of gods.

Notes

1 Ludo Rocher, for example, lists 82 *Purāṇas*. See Ludo Rocher, *The Puranas*. Wiesbaden: Otto Harrasowitz, 1986.

2 Fred Matchett, "The Purāṇas" in G. Flood (ed.), *A Blackwell Companion to Hinduism*. Oxford: Blackwell Publishing, 2003, p. 129.

3 See Frances Prichett, "The World of *Amar Chitra Katha*" in L. Babb and S. Wadley (eds.), *Media and the Transformation of Religion in South Asia*. Philadelphia: University of Pennsylvania Press, 1995.

4 For more on this practice, deemed "Inklusivismus" by Paul Hacker, see his "Religiöse Toleranz und Intoleranz im Hinduismus" in L. Schmithausen (ed.), *Kleine Schriften*. Wiesbaden: Steiner, 1978.

5 For analyses of myths about Śiva, see Wendy Doniger O'Flaherty's *Śiva: The Erotic Ascetic*. Oxford: Oxford University Press, 1973.

Further reading

Doniger, Wendy (ed.), *Purāṇa Perennis: Reciprocity and Transformation in Hindu and Jaina Texts*. New York: State University of New York Press, 1993.

Hacker, Paul, "Religiöse Toleranz und Intoleranz im Hinduismus" in L. Schmithausen (ed.), *Kleine Schriften*. Wiesbaden: Steiner, 1978.

Matchett, Fred, "The Purāṇas" in G. Flood (ed.), *A Blackwell Companion to Hinduism*. Oxford: Blackwell Publishing, 2003.

O'Flaherty, Wendy Doniger, *Śiva: The Erotic Ascetic*. Oxford: Oxford University Press, 1973.

Prichett, Frances, "The World of *Amar Chitra Katha*" in L. Babb and S. Wadley (eds.), *Media and the Transformation of Religion in South Asia*. Philadelphia: University of Pennsylvania Press, 1995.

Rocher, Ludo, *The Puranas*. Wiesbaden: Otto Harrasowitz, 1986.

The *Purāṇas*

Origins

The Origin and Nature of Time

When this whole world goes to dissolution in Prakṛti, then it is said by the learned to be reabsorbed into its original nature. When the unmanifest abides in its own self, when the created world is annihilated, Prakṛti and Puruṣa exist with the same nature. Then the two qualities, *tamas* and *sattva*, rest in balance, interwoven, with nothing lacking and nothing to spare. Like sesamum oil in seeds, like ghee in milk, so does *rajas* reside in *tamas* and *sattva*.

A day of the supreme lord is as long as a life-span from the birth of Brahmā, namely two *parārdhas*. Of equal length is the night of the world's dissolution. This supreme one, whose work is unequalled, whose nature is inconceivable, the cause of everything, first beginning of creation, wakes up at the start of the day. As soon as the lord of creation has penetrated Prakṛti and Puruṣa he agitates them by intense Yoga. Just as a spring-breeze invades the mind of a young woman to excite her, so does he in yogic form enter into Prakṛti and Puruṣa. When Pradhāna is aroused, the god called Brahmā who is lying in the egg arises, as I have already told you. So the lord of Prakṛti is first the agitator; then he is what is to be agitated by means of expansion and contraction, even while he rests in the state of Pradhāna. This womb of the world, born possessing *rajas* but without qualities, proceeds to create as Brahmā. Then he, in the form of Brahmā, having an excess of *sattva*, pours forth humankind; having become Viṣṇu, he protects them with Dharma. And when, in the shape of Rudra, abounding in *tamas*, he has destroyed the whole creation, the three worlds, he – of three qualities and without qualities, both – lies down to sleep. As he is first the purveyor of the field of existence, then the protector and the destroyer, he gets this name: the one composed of Brahmā, Viṣṇu and Hara. As Brahmā he pours forth the worlds; as Rudra he destroys; and he is also in between as Viṣṇu: these are the three conditions of the self-existent. *Rajas* is Brahmā; *tamas* is Rudra; Viṣṇu, lord of creation, is *sattva*. These are the three gods (and these are the three qualities). All three are paired, each joined to his quality. Not for an instant's separation do they abandon each other. Thus Brahmā, four-faced god of gods, is first in the world. Having assumed the quality of *rajas* he exists as creator. Brahmā, the golden embryo, origin of the gods, without beginning so to speak, resting in the calyx of the world lotus, was born in the beginning. His life-span is one hundred years according to the Brahmā count. Hear me relate its length. A *kāṣṭhā* is said to equal fifteen *nimeṣas*; thirty *kāṣṭhās*, one *kalā*; and thirty *kalās*, one *muhūrta*. A day and a night are known by men to be thirty *muhūrtas*; an *ahorātra*, a day and a night; and a month is said to consist of two fortnights, with thirty days and nights. A half-year (*ayana*) is made up of six such months; a year is two *ayanas*: southern and northern. This year is a day and night of the gods; its day is the *ayana* called northern. The four Ages known as Kṛta, Tretā, Dvāpara and Kali comprise 12,000 divine years. Hear from me their distribution.

Kṛta is said to last 4,000 years, the morning twilight, 400 and the evening twilight the same. There are reckoned 3,000 divine years in the Tretā, 300 in its morning twilight and the same allotted to the evening twilight. 2,000 years are counted in the Dvāpara with 200 years in each twilight. And in the Kali there are 1,000 divine years, O best of the twice-born; its morning and evening twilights are said to be 100 years each. These 12,000 year counts of the Ages are made by

---

Excerpts from Cornelia Dimmitt and J. A. B. van Buitenen (eds.), *Classical Hindu Mythology: A Reader in the Sanskrit Purāṇas*. Philadelphia: Temple University Press, 1978.

the sages. This period multiplied by 1,000 is called a day and night of Brahmā. In a day of Brahmā there should be 14 Manus. 1,000 periods of four Ages are allotted to these Manus, according to their distribution. The gods, the seven seers together with Indra, Manu and the kings who are his sons are poured forth together with Manu and annihilated as in the past. Seventy-one Manvantaras plus some additional years are distributed over 1,000 periods of four Ages. Hear me tell the length of the Manvantara in human years: one Manvantara numbers 367,020,000 years in all. Hear me recount the aforementioned Manvantara by divine years: one such Manvantara is 852,000 years. Fourteen of these are said to constitute a day of Brahmā. The occasional dissolution is said by the wise to come at the end of it. Bhūrloka, Bhuvarloka, Svarloka and their inhabitants then proceed to destruction while Maharloka survives. Consumed by heat, its residents retreat to Janaloka. And when the three worlds are one great ocean, Brahmā sleeps in the night. That night is the same length as his day; at the end of the night the world is poured forth again. And so passes one Brahmā year; his life lasts one hundred years. One hundred of his years is called *para*; fifty years is termed *parārdha* (half a *para*). One half of his life has passed, O best of the twice-born, at the end of which is the final great Eon known as Pādma. The present one, O twice-born, is the first Eon of the second half of Brahmā's life, called Vārāha.

The Four Ages

The first Age is called Kṛta by the wise, the next Tretā. The third is said to be Dvāpara, O Pārtha, and Kali the fourth. The highest virtue is said to be meditation in the Kṛta, knowledge in the Tretā, sacrifice, they say, in the Dvāpara and gift-giving in the Kali. Brahmā is god in the Kṛta Age, lord Sun in the Tretā, in the Dvāpara the divine Viṣṇu and great lord Rudra in the Kali. Brahmā, Viṣṇu and the Sun are all worshipped in the Kali. Lord Rudra, who carries the Pināka, is honored in all four Ages. Eternal Dharma is four-footed in the Kṛta Age, three-footed in the Tretā Yuga, and stands two-footed in the Dvāpara. In Tiṣya, missing three feet, it barely survives. In the Kṛta, birth occurs through sexual intercourse. All creatures are continually content, with their livelihood spontaneously arising out of their pleasure in doing it. In this Kṛta Age there is no distinction between the best and the worst of them, O city-conqueror; their life, happiness and beauty are equal. They are free from sorrow, full of goodness, much given to solitude; devoted to meditation, intent upon *tapas*, their final end is Mahādeva. They act without self-interest; their minds are always joyful; they have no permanent home; they live in the mountains or by the oceans.

In the course of time the spontaneous arising of pleasure came to an end in the Tretā. When the natural propensity for pleasure was lost, another perfection came into being. When the subtleness of waters [their spontaneous welling forth] had ceased, then rain in the shape of clouds poured forth from thunderheads. As soon as earth's surface was covered by the fallen rain there appeared trees called homes. All food came from these trees; indeed, at the beginning of the Tretā Age all creatures subsisted entirely on them. Then, after a long period of degeneration, their disposition became unexpectedly passionate and greedy. Because of their decadence, in the course of time all these trees known as homes disappeared. After they had vanished, those who were born from intercourse became confused. They set their hearts on success, but yet paid attention to truthfulness. The trees they called homes then reappeared and brought forth clothing, fruit and ornaments. In their holes was potent honey not collected by bees, with sweet smell, color and taste. In fact, at the start of the Tretā Age all beings lived on this honey and were happy, well-fed and free from trouble. Then, after a time, they once again turned to greed, forcibly seizing these trees whose honey was not gathered by bees. And once more, because of their misdeeds, through their fault, the wishing-trees abounding in honey everywhere disappeared. Suffering acutely through intense rain and oppressed by the opposites of cold and heat, they made shelters. After the wishing-trees with their copious honey were lost, those who were hiding from the opposing elements pondered how to make a living. So success came again to them in the Tretā Age: another type of rain, conducive to their livelihood, fell in accordance with their desire. Then a continual succession of supernal rains flowed down the valleys, bore the waters downward, and thus became rivers. The drops of water which once again covered the earth's surface then became herbs through the commingling of earth and water. Fourteen kinds of trees – both flowering and fruit-bearing – took root, some appropriate to barren soil, some to untilled land, some to unsowed soil, and some to village and forest. Then greed and passion arose again everywhere, inevitably, due to the predestined purpose of the Tretā Age. And people seized the rivers, fields, mountains, clumps of trees and herbs, overcoming them by their strength. Because of their perversity, the herbs reentered earth. Pṛthu milked the earth by command of the Fathers. Then all the people, insensate with anger, due to the influence of the times, captured each other's land, wives and wealth by their own power. Knowing this, the unborn lord Brahmā emitted the kṣatriyas for the purpose of setting limits and for the benefit of the brahmins. In the Tretā the lord instituted the rules of class and stage in life and also the performance of sacrifice without injury to cattle.

In the Dvāpara, however, differences of opinion continually occurred among men, as did passion, greed and war, and a lack of firm resolve regarding truth. In the Tretā the four-footed Veda was laid down as a unit whereas in the Dvāpara and the others it was divided into four parts by Vyāsa. They were re-divided by the sons of the seer who commited errors in judgment by way of distinctive divisions of *mantra* and *brāhmaṇa*; the errors were due to changes in accents and phonemes. Because of certain differences of opinion here and there, the collections of Ṛg, Yajus and Sāma Vedas were compiled by the seers of *śruti* according to their various characteristics; also the Brāhmaṇa, the Kalpasūtras, the recitations and mantras; Itihāsa and Purāṇa, and the Dharmaśāstras, O one of strong vow. Disgust with existence arose among mankind along with death, calamity and disease through suffering born in speech, mind and body. From disgust there arose among human beings reflections on liberation from suffering, and from such reflection arose indifference to worldly desires, and from indifference the perception of fault. In the Dvāpara, then, wisdom arose from the observation of error. This behavior, along with *rajas* and *tamas*, is remembered of the Dvāpara. In the first age, the Kṛta, there was virtue; it continued throughout the Tretā, became confused in the Dvāpara, and is lost altogether in the Kali.

In Tiṣya, men confounded by *tamas* continually perpetrate trickery, envy and the murder of ascetics. In the Kali there is fatal disease, continuous hunger and fear, awful dread of drought and revolution in the lands. Evil creatures born in the Tiṣya – wicked, unprincipled, weak in wit and strong in anger – speak lies. Fear arises among people because of brahmin errors in behavior: crimes, lack of knowledge, evil conduct and ill-gotten gains. In the Kali the twice-born are ignorant of the Vedas. Nor do they perform sacrifice; others of inferior intellect do the sacrifice, and they recite the Vedas incorrectly. In this Kali age there will occur the association of śūdras with brahmins through *mantras*, marriages and the practice of sleeping and sitting together. Kings who are mostly śūdras will have brahmins killed; abortion and hero-murder will prevail in this age, O king!

The Kali Age

All kings occupying the earth in the Kali Age will be wanting in tranquillity, strong in anger, taking pleasure at all times in lying and dishonesty, inflicting death on women, children and cows, prone to take the paltry possessions of others, with character that is mostly *tamas*, rising to power and soon falling. They will be short-lived, ambitious, of little virtue and greedy. People will follow the customs of others and be adulterated with them; peculiar, undisciplined barbarians will be vigorously supported by the rulers. Because they go on living with perversion, they will be ruined. The destruction of the world will occur because of the departure from virtue and profit, little by little, day by day. Money alone will confer nobility. Power will be the sole definition of virtue. Pleasure will be the only reason for marriage. Lust will be the only reason for womanhood. Falsehood will win out in disputes. Being dry of water will be the only definition of land. The sacred thread alone will distinguish brahmins. Praiseworthiness will be measured by accumulated wealth. Wearing the *linga* will be sufficient cause for religious retreat. Impropriety will be considered good conduct, and only feebleness will be the reason for unemployment. Boldness and arrogance will become equivalent to scholarship. Only those without wealth will show honesty. Just a bath will amount to purification, and charity will be the only virtue. Abduction will be marriage. Simply to be well-dressed will signify propriety. And any water hard to reach will be deemed a pilgrimage site. The pretense of greatness will be the proof of it, and powerful men with many severe faults will rule over all the classes on earth. Oppressed by their excessively greedy rulers, people will hide in valleys between mountains where they will gather honey, vegetables, roots, fruits, birds, flowers and so forth. Suffering from cold, wind, heat and rain, they will put on clothes made of tree-bark and leaves. And no one will live as long as twenty-three years. Thus in the Kali Age humankind will be utterly destroyed.

The Dissolution of the World in Viṣṇu

At the end of a thousand periods of four Ages, when the earth's surface is for the most part wasted, there arises a dreadful drought that lasts for a hundred years. Then all these earthly beings whose strength has declined perish completely through oppression. And so the imperishable lord Viṣṇu, who abides in himself, adopts the form of Rudra, and exerts himself to act in order to destroy all creatures. Permeating the seven rays of the sun, the lord Viṣṇu then drinks up all the waters, O excellent sage. When he has consumed all the waters that had gone to the world of creatures, he dries up the earth's surface. Oceans, rivers and flowing mountain streams as well as whatever water lies in the Pātālas – all this he leads to dissolution. Then due to his power, those same seven rays become seven suns, invigorated by the absorption of water. These seven blazing suns ignite all three worlds, above and below, along with the surface of the Netherworld, O twice-born. The three worlds, O twice-born one, consumed by these fiery suns, complete with mountains, rivers and the expanse of the ocean, become arid. Then the whole triple world whose water and trees are burned away, and this earth as well, become as bare as a turtle's back. Likewise, when the monstrous fire has burned up these Pātālas, it rises to the earth and utterly devours its surface. And a frightful tornado of flame rolls through the entire Bhuvarloka and Svarloka. The three worlds then blaze like a frying-pan; all things moving and unmoving are consumed by the surrounding flames. The inhabitants of these two worlds, overcome by heat, their duties done, retreat to Maharloka, O great seer. Still seared by the heat they flee again; seeking safety in a different place, they hurry thence to Janaloka. So when Janārdana in Rudra's form has consumed all creation, he produces clouds from the breath of his mouth that look like a herd of elephants, emitting lightning, roaring loudly. Thus do dreadful clouds arise in the sky. Some are dark like the blossom of the blue lotus; some look like the white water-lily; some are the color of smoke; and others are yellow. Some resemble a donkey's hue; others are like red lacquer; some have the appearance of a cat's-eye gem; and some are like sapphire. Still others are white as a conch shell or jasmine, or similar to collyrium; some are like fireflies, while others resemble peacocks. Huge clouds arise resembling red or yellow arsenic, and others look like a blue-jay's wing. Some of these clouds are like fine towns, and some like mountains; others resemble houses, and still others, mounds of earth. These dense, elephantine clouds fill up the surface of the sky, roaring loudly. Pouring down rain they completely extinguish this dreadful fire which has overtaken the three worlds. And when the fire is thoroughly quenched, the clouds raining day and night overwhelm the entire world with water, O excellent seer. When they have completely inundated the atmosphere with copious streams of water, then, O twice-born, they flood Bhuvarloka on high. When everything movable and immovable in the world has perished in the watery darkness, these vast clouds pour down rain for another one hundred years. So is it at the end of every Eon, O excellent seer, by the majesty of the eternal Vāsudeva, the supreme lord.

When the waters come to rest, having reached the realm of the seven seers, then this single ocean completely covers the three worlds. Wind blown out of Viṣṇu's mouth makes the clouds disappear in a hundred years. When the eternal lord, fashioner of all creatures, inconceivable, the condition of creation, the beginning of everything who has no beginning himself, has entirely consumed the wind, then, reposing on Śeṣa in the single ocean, the lord, first creator, rests in the form of Brahmā, praised by Sanaka and others, the seers who went to Janaloka, and also meditated upon by those who went to Brahmaloka seeking freedom. Resting in meditative sleep, in the divine form of his own illusive power, Viṣṇu, destroyer of Madhu, concentrates on the form of himself called Vāsudeva. This is the dissolution called occasional, O Maitreya; the occasion is that Hari rests in the form of Brahmā. When the soul of all awakens, then the world stirs; when the imperishable one has gone to his bed of illusion, it falls completely asleep. A day of Brahmā, born from the lotus, lasts a thousand periods of four Ages; a night, when the world is destroyed and made into a vast ocean, is of the same length. At the end of the night, Viṣṇu, unborn, having awakened, takes the form of Brahmā in order to create, as it has already been told to you.

The Twelve Avatāras *of Viṣṇu*

When the end of an Age rolls around and time has lost its strength, then lord Viṣṇu abandons his divine form to be born among men. When the gods and demons go to war, then Hari is born.

Long ago when the Daitya Hiraṇyakáśipu ruled the triple world, and later when the three worlds were governed by Bali, there was real friendship between the gods and demons, who equally abided by the orders of these two rulers. But then the world became disordered, overrun with demons, and grievous and ferocious death-dealing war began between the demons and the gods who sought Bali's destruction.

When Bhṛgu cast his curse on both the gods and demons, Viṣṇu was born among men for the maintenance of Dharma.... There were in all twelve ferocious battles fought between the gods and demons over the shares of the sacrifice, from the battle of the Boar to the battle of Ṣaṇḍa and Marka. Hear now their designations.

First was the Man-Lion, second was the Dwarf, third was the Boar and fourth was the Churning of the Nectar. Fifth there was the battle of Tāraka, and the sixth was called Āḍīvaka, the Heron and the Crane. The seventh was over Tripura, the eighth dealt with Andhaka and the ninth was the killing of Vṛtra. Tenth came the battle of the Creator, eleventh, the Halāhala poison, and twelfth, the dreadful Kolāhala.

The demon Hiraṇyakaśipu was felled by the Man-Lion and Bali was captured by the Dwarf who traversed the triple world so long ago. Hiraṇyākṣa was slain in a duel when he fought with the celestials, and the Boar parted the ocean with his tusks. Prahlāda was defeated in battle by Indra at the churning of the ocean, and Virocana, Prahlāda's son, who was always trying to kill Indra, was slain in the Tāraka war when Indra attacked him with great courage. This Tāraka could never tolerate anything about the gods.

In the Andhaka battle, all the Dānavas in the triple world were slain by Tryambaka, and the demons and Piśācas were also destroyed. When the gods, humans and the Fathers were utterly annihilated, the awful Vṛtra was murdered in the Hālāhala battle, along with the demons. Vṛtra was checked by the mighty Indra who, accompanied by Viṣṇu and Vipracitta (who knew Yoga), and concealed by Māyā, penetrated the emblem on his flag during the Dhvaja battle, then killed him along with his younger brothers.

The bull and both Ṣaṇḍa and Marka were killed in the Kolāhala war at the concluding ceremony of the sacrifice after being surrounded by the gods, who were victorious over all the assembled Daityas and Dānavas. These are the twelve wars that took place between the gods and demons, wreaking havoc on gods and demons alike, for the benefit of creation.

The Twenty-Two Avatāras *of Viṣṇu*

Nārāyaṇa is the only god, overlord of the gods, supreme soul and unequalled Brahman, "source of this world and everything in it." For the protection of his creation, the unborn, undying Vāsudeva made various *avatāras*, such as the tortoise Kumāra and other forms.

The god Hari, first undertaking the tortoise creation, performed the difficult *brahmacarya* vow without interruption, O brahmin. Second, for the prosperity of the world, the lord of sacrifices took the form of a boar to raise up the earth, which had sunk to the netherworld Rasātala. Third, he poured forth the sages; becoming a divine seer himself, he produced the Sātvata doctrine, by virtue of which actions become free of their consequences. Fourth, worshiped by the gods and the demons, Hari performed *tapas*, having become Naranārāyaṇa for the protection of Dharma.

Fifth, as the lord of the Siddhas named Kapila, he proclaimed Sāṃkhya to the gods; this definitive account of the true principles of existence had been lost in the course of time. Sixth, as Atri, born of Anasūyā, he taught the school of Logic to Ālarka, Prahlāda and others. Then seventh, he was born in the Svāyambhuva Manvantara as the Sacrifice, son of Ruci and Ākūti, sacrificing with his truthful counselors, the hosts of the gods. Eighth, born of Nābhi and Merudevī, he was Urukrama, who showed the way to women that is honored in all stages of life. Solicited by the sages, ninth, he adopted the form of Pṛthu who milked from the earth the great herbs that strengthened the brahmins and other creatures.

Tenth, he took the form of a fish during the flood in the Cākṣusa Manvantara, rescuing Manu Vaivasvata from the waters with a boat which was earth. Eleventh, the lord in the form of a tortoise carried Mt. Mandara on his back to help the gods and demons who were churning the ocean. Twelfth, he took the form of Dhanvantari and, thirteenth, he nourished the gods by adopting the body of the woman Mohinī, who deluded the demons. Becoming Narasiṃha in the fourteenth *avatāra* he ripped apart the mighty Daitya chief as a plaiter of straw mats shreds his reeds. Fifteenth, as a little dwarf, he went to Bali's sacrifice and asked for three steps, planning to take the three worlds in return. In the sixteenth descent, angry at seeing kings hostile to brahmins, he rid the earth of kṣatriyas twenty-one times.

Then, in the seventeenth, he was born to Satyavatī and Parāśara; seeing the ignorance of mankind, he made branches on the tree which is the Veda. Having next become a man-god, out of desire to do a task for the gods, he subdued the ocean and did other chores as well. In the nineteenth and twentieth *avatāras*, he was born twice among the Vṛṣṇis as Rāma and Kṛṣṇa and in these forms he removed the burden from earth. Next, at the close of time's twilight, he will become the son of a Jina among the non-Āryans, named Buddha, in order to delude the foes of the gods. In the future, in the eighth twilight, when the kings have largely disappeared from earth, he will be born the son of Viṣṇuyaśas, as the lord of creation called Kalkin.

Innumerable are the *avatāras* of Hari, who contains the ocean of being, O twice-born ones! Those who know the Veda, the Manus and all the others are said to be portions of this same Viṣṇu. From them the various creatures are born; they are to be honored by means of vows and other observances.

The Churning of the Ocean

When the sage Durvāsas, a portion of Śankara, was journeying around this earth, he saw a heavenly garland in the hand of a Vidyādharī. The perfume of its *santānaka* flowers filled the whole woods where the forest-dwellers revelled, O brahmin. When he saw that beautiful wreath, this brahmin who was fulfilling a demented vow asked the full-hipped Vidhyādhara woman for it. At his demand, the slender-limbed, large-eyed Vidhyādharī gave him the garland, prostrating herself respectfully before him. Accepting the ornament he put it on his own head; looking like a madman, O Maitreya, the brahmin roamed the earth.

This lunatic saw Śaci's lord approaching, sitting on Airāvata – Indra, who is first lord of the three worlds – accompanied by the great gods. Lifting from his own head that garland full of frenzied bees, like a crazy man he threw it at the king of the immortals. Indra caught it and put it on Airāvata's head where that wreath shone like the river Ganges on the peak of Kailāsa.

Attracted by the fragrance, the elephant, his eyes clouded with rut, smelled it with his trunk, and threw it on the ground. At this the excellent seer Durvāsas grew angry. Furious, O Maitreya, he said to the king of the gods, "Drunk with power, your soul is corrupted, O Vāsava! You are too arrogant! You have rejected this garland I have given you which is the abode of Śrī! You have not prostrated yourself and exclaimed 'How lucky am I!' Nor have you put it on your head, your cheeks blooming with delight! Because you have not honored this wreath I gave you, fool, your prosperity in the three worlds will come to naught! Thinking that I am like all the other brahmins, Śakra, you have insulted me with your arrogant manner. Because you have thrown the garland I gave you on the ground, you will no longer enjoy good fortune in any of the three worlds. You are treating me haughtily and with contempt, king of the gods, me whose anger when it arises terrifies all creatures moving and unmoving!"

Mahendra, speedily alighting from the elephant's back, went to pacify the blameless sage Durvāsas. When Indra had prostrated himself before him and placated him, the excellent seer Durvāsas spoke to the Thousand-Eyed god: "I am not a man with a compassionate heart; nor is forgiveness part of my nature as it is for other seers, O Śakra. Know me to be Durvāsas! You have been filled with self-importance by Gautama and others to no purpose. Know that I am Durvāsas, whose sum and substance is implacability. You have been rendered haughty by Vasiṣtha and others whose core is compassion, who sing your praises on high. Because of this you now treat me, too, with contempt. Who in the three worlds remains unafraid after seeing my glowering face with knitted brow and my blazing knot of hair? Enough said, god of the Hundred Sacrifices, I will not forgive you, however much you try to appease me!" Speaking, the brahmin left, and the king of the gods mounted Airāvata once again, O brahmin, and went to Amarāvatī.

From then on the three worlds, and Śakra too, were bereft of good fortune and desolate with withered plants and herbs. No sacrifices were made, no ascetics practiced *tapas*, and people neglected gift-giving and other laws. The worlds were utterly dispirited; people became covetous even of trifles, O excellent twice-born one, their senses afflicted by greed and other weaknesses. . . .

When the three worlds were steeped in misfortune in this way and were without mettle, the Daityas and Dānavas, overcome by greed, turned their power against the gods. The Daityas made war on the luckless, powerless gods. Defeated by the Daityas, Indra and the rest of the thirty gods, led by Fire, fled for refuge to the eminent Grandfather. When the gods told him what had happened, Brahmā said to them: "You should seek shelter with the demon-destroyer, the lord of both higher and lower creation, Viṣṇu, the causeless cause of creation, the lord, the master of Prajāpatis, the eternal, unvanquished god. Go to Viṣṇu, cause of the unborn Prakṛti and Puruṣa, who dispels the suffering of those who bow to him. He will bestow on you supreme good." When he had thus admonished all the gods, Brahmā, Grandfather of the worlds, went with them to the farther shore of the ocean of milk. Having accompanied the thirty gods, the Grandfather extolled the supreme lord Hari with sweet speech. . . .

So praised, the blessed supreme lord appeared before their eyes, bearing conch and discus, O Maitreya. When the gods saw this unprecedented form, carrying conch, discus and mace, radiating a rich aura of splendor, all of them, led by the Grandfather, bowed low, their eyes staring in shock. They praised the lotus-eyed one: "Praise, praise be to you who are without distinctions! You are Brahmā, you are the Pināka-bearer, you are Indra, Agni, Wind, Varuṇa, Sun, Yama. You are the Vasus, Maruts, Sādhyas, the hosts of Viśvedevas. You are this host of deities who stands before you here. You are he who pours forth the world, pervader of all. You are the sacrifice, you are the cry of "*Vaṣaṭ!*" You are the syllable *OṂ*, you are Prajāpati. You are the knowledge and what is to be known, the soul of the universe. The whole world consists of you. In distress we have come to you for refuge, O Viṣṇu, since we have been defeated by the Daityas. Have mercy on us, O gracious All-Soul! Nourish us with your strength! So long as one does not turn to you for refuge, destroyer of all evil, there is suffering and longing, confusion and unhappiness. O tranquil soul, bestow your favor on us who have come to you for help! Nourish the strength of us all, O protector."

When he had been praised in this manner by the prostrate immortals, the lord Hari with serene aspect, the creator of the universe, said this: "Yes, gods, I will strengthen your power. I shall tell you what you must do. Take all the herbs to the ocean of milk along with the Daityas; then you, together with the Daityas and Dānavas, must throw them all into that ocean in order to make the nectar. Then, using Mt. Mandara as a stirring stick and Vāsuki as a twirling rope, churn the ocean for the nectar while I stand by to help. To enlist the help of the Daityas, tell them diplomatically that they will enjoy the same fruit as you. And then you, the immortals, will become strong from drinking the nectar that arises from the churning of the ocean. I shall arrange it so that the enemies of the thirty gods will not get any nectar, but only the suffering gods themselves."

So directed by the god of gods, all the gods joined with the demons in a compact to produce the nectar. After gathering various herbs, the gods, Daityas and Dānavas threw them into the water of the ocean of milk whose glow was as clear as the sky in autumn. Taking Mt. Mandara as the staff and Vāsuki as the rope, O Maitreya, they began to churn vigorously for the nectar. All the gods gathered with Kṛṣṇa at Vāsuki's tail while all the Daityas were stationed at his head. Then all the demons of limitless energy lost their power because of the violent blast of fiery heat that came from the hissing mouth of the snake. But the gods were invigorated by the rainclouds blown towards his tail by the wind coming from that hissing mouth.

In the middle of the milky ocean lord Hari himself appeared in the form of a tortoise to support the rotating mountain while it was churned, O great seer. Keśava appeared in one form in the midst of the gods, bearing mace and discus; in another form he pulled the snake-king with the Daityas; and in a third gigantic form, unseen by gods and demons alike, he strode up the mountain, O Maitreya. Hari then infused the serpent-king with strength, and in his original form invigorated the gods with power.

Out of the middle of this ocean of milk that was being churned by gods and demons, there first arose Surabhi, source of the oblation, honored by the deities. Both gods and Dānavas were delighted, great seer, their minds excited, their eyes unblinking. Even as the heavenly Siddhas were thinking "What is this?" the goddess Vāruṇī appeared, her eyes rolling with intoxication. Next from the whirling milk ocean came the Pārijāta tree, perfuming the world with its fragrance and delighting the wives of the gods. And then, Maitreya, a most marvellous throng of Apsarases, endowed with the virtues of beauty and nobility, sprang up from the milky ocean. Next appeared the cool-rayed moon which Maheśvara took as his own, as the snakes took the poison which arose from the ocean of milk. Finally the god Dhanvantari himself came up, clad in white, carrying a water-jar full of the nectar, whereupon all the mindful Daityas and Dānavas became joyful, Maitreya, along with the seers.

After this, the goddess Śrī of vibrant beauty arose from this milk, standing in a blossoming lotus with a lotus in her hand. With joy the great seers assembled there praised her with the Śrīsūkta; and the Gandharvas, led by Viśvāvasu, sang before her while the throngs of Apsarases, led by Ghṛtācī, danced. The Ganges and other rivers approached her with their waters for bathing. The elephants of the four quarters holding up golden vessels of pure water bathed the goddess, the great mistress of all the worlds. The ocean in bodily form gave her a wreath of unfading lotuses, while Viśvakarman wrought ornaments for her body. Wearing celestial garlands and garments, bathed and adorned with decorations, with all the gods looking on, she went to Hari's chest. While resting on Hari's chest, Lakṣmī made the gods know instant supreme bliss just by looking at the two of them, O Maitreya.

But the Daityas led by Vipracitti, forsaken by Lakṣmī, were dismayed. So they stole the jar full of potent nectar that was in Dhanvantari's hand. Whereupon Viṣṇu fooled them with an illusion. Assuming the body of a woman, the lord took the cup from the Dānavas and gave it to the gods. At this, the heavenly host, Śakra and the other gods, drank the nectar. With weapons and swords raised on high, the Daityas attacked the thirty gods. Defeated by the powerful deities who had consumed the nectar, the demons then fled in all directions and entered the netherworld.

After this the gods rejoiced, prostrating themselves before the one who bears conch, discus and mace, and Indra ruled in his heaven once again. The sun, serenely shining, went on his way, and the heavenly bodies followed their paths, excellent seer. The blessed god Fire blazed brightly on high and all creatures put their minds on Dharma. Good Fortune inhabited the three worlds, excellent brahmin, and Indra, chief of the thirty gods, became resplendent once more. Regaining the third heaven, Śakra went to his lion's throne from which he ruled the gods, giving praise to the lotus-bearing goddess.

Viṣṇu and Śrī

The eternal Śrī, loyal to Viṣṇu, is the mother of the world. Just as Viṣṇu pervades the universe, O excellent brahmin, so does she. Viṣṇu is meaning; Śrī is speech. She is conduct; Hari is behavior. Viṣṇu is knowledge; she is insight. He is Dharma; she is virtuous action.

Viṣṇu is the creator; Śrī is creation. She is the earth and Hari earth's upholder. The eternal Lakṣmī is contentment, O Maitreya; the blessed lord is satisfaction. Śrī is wish, the lord desire. He is the sacrifice, she the fee. The goddesss is the offering of butter, Janārdana the sacrificial cake. At the sacrifice, Lakṣmī is the women's hut, Madhusūdana the sacrificial site. Lakṣmī is the altar, Hari the sacrificial pole. Śrī is the firewood, the lord the sacred grass. The lord has the nature of the Sāma Veda; the lotus-born Śrī is the *udgītha*. Lakṣmī is the *svāhā* cry; Jagannātha Vāsudeva is the oblation-eating fire.

Śauri the lord is Śankara, and Lakṣmī is Gaurī, excellent brahmin. Keśava is the sun, Maitreya, and the lotus-dwelling goddess is its light. Viṣṇu is the host of the Fathers, Padmā the *svadhā* offering of constant nourishment. Śrī is the sky; Viṣṇu, the Self of everything, is wide-open space. Śrī's husband is the moon; its beauty is the constant Śrī. Lakṣmī is fortitude, enacted in the world, Hari the all-pervading wind. Govinda is the ocean, O brahmin; Śrī is the shore, great seer.

Lakṣmī bears the form of Indrāṇī, while Madhusūdana is Indra, her spouse, among the gods. The discus-bearing Viṣṇu is Yama personified; the lotus-dwelling Lakṣmī is his wife. Śrī is prosperity; the god who possesses Śrī is the lord of wealth himself. Illustrious Lakṣmī is Gaurī; Keśava is Varuṇa himself. Śrī is the host of gods, chief brahmin, and Hari is lord of the host.

He who bears a mace in his right hand is reliability, O excellent twice-born one; Lakṣmī is power. Lakṣmī is the instant, the lord the wink of an eye. He is the hour; she is the second. Lakṣmī is light; he is the lamp. Hari is everything and lord of everything as well. Śrī, mother of the world, is a forest creeper while Viṣṇu is a tree. Śrī is the starry night; the god who carries mace and discus is the day. Viṣṇu, granter of wishes, is the bridegroom; the lotus-dwelling goddess is the bride.

Appearing in the form of a male river is the lord, while Śrī takes form as a female river. The lotus-eyed god is a banner; the lotus-dweller is a flag. Lakṣmī is desire, O Maitreya, and Jagannātha Nārāyaṇa is greed. Together Lakṣmī and Govinda are passion and love.

What more is there to tell? In summary, let it be said that among gods, beasts and human beings, Hari is all that is known as male, and Śrī all that is known as female. There is nothing more beyond these two!

Kṛṣṇa

The Conception of Kṛṣṇa

Once upon a time, great seer, Vasudeva married Devaka's daughter, the august Devakī, who was like a goddess. At the wedding of Vasudeva and Devakī, Kaṃsa, joy of the Bhojas, drove their coach as charioteer. Respectfully addressing Kaṃsa, a voice in the atmosphere, deep-sounding and rumbling like the clouds, spoke aloud, "Fool! You will be robbed of your life by the eighth embryo of that woman you are carrying in your chariot along with her spouse!" Giving ear to this, the mighty Kaṃsa unsheathed his sword and threatened Devakī, whereupon Vasudeva spoke up, "Don't kill Devakī, O blameless lord! I will deliver over to you each embryo that arises in her womb!"

"So be it!" replied Kaṃsa to Vasudeva, excellent twice-born one, and he ceased his attempt to kill Devakī out of respect for her husband's word.

Meanwhile Earth, oppressed by a heavy burden, went to the assembly for the inhabitants of the triple heaven on Mt. Meru. Prostrating herself before Brahmā and all the gods, she related everything, speaking piteously of her distress:

"Agni is the *guru* of gold, Sūrya the *guru* of cows; my *guru* and that of all the worlds is Nārāyaṇa. He is the lord of the Prajāpatis, of Brahmā, the first-born even of the elder gods. He is Time, consisting of minutes, seconds and instants, his body unmanifest. All of you together, excellent deities, comprise but a portion of him. The Ādityas, Maruts, Sādhyas, Rudras, Vasus, Aśvins and Fire, the Fathers who are creators of the world, headed by Atri – all these are the body of the immeasurable great-souled Viṣṇu. Yakṣas, Rākṣasas, Daityas, Piśācas, Uragas and Dānavas, Gandharvas and Apsarases comprise the body of the great-souled Viṣṇu. Space glittering with planets, the Pleiades and the stars, fire, water, wind and I myself as well as the sense objects – all these consist in Viṣṇu. Moreover, these manifold forms of his proceed by night and day in the reciprocal relationship of master and servant, like the waves on the ocean.

"At present the Daityas, led by Kālanemi, have overthrown the world of mortals and oppress all creatures night and day. That great demon Kālanemi, who was once slain by the powerful lord Viṣṇu, has now been born as Kaṃsa, Ugrasena's son! And other mighty evil-souled heroic Asuras have been born in the houses of kings – the impetuous and violent demons Ariṣṭa (Disaster), Dhenuka (Little Cow), Keśin (Flame-Hair), Pralamba (Long-Nose), Naraka (Hell) and the terrible demon Sunda, and Bāṇa, son of Bali – so numerous I cannot count them all. Many such demons with divine shapes and hordes of strong, powerful, arrogant Daitya chiefs roam on top of me. O immortal gods, I tell you that I cannot hold out any longer, so depressed am I by the weight of these demons. O lordly ones, remove my burden lest, so distressed, I plunge into the netherworld!"

Having heard Earth's speech and urged on by the thirty immortals, Brahmā spoke in order to alleviate Earth's burden, "Everything Earth says is true, heaven-dwellers. You and I and Bhava all consist in Nārāyaṇa. . . . Come, let us go to the fine shore of the ocean of milk and worship Hari there; he should hear all about this. When the all-soul who is embodied in the world descends on earth with a portion of himself for the world's benefit, he supports Dharma in every way." So speaking, the Grandfather went to Hari together with the gods, where with attentive mind they hymned him whose banner bears Garuḍa. . . .

"This earth, lord, whose mountains are pressed down by great demons who have arisen on her, comes to you, who are the refuge of the worlds, to lift her burden, O god whose substance is boundless. We stand before you here – Indra, foe of Vṛtra, the wondrous Nāsatyas and Daśra, the Rudras and Vasus with the Sun, headed by Wind and Fire. Tell us, guardian of the gods, what are we all to do? By following your command, we will always remain pure."

Praised in this manner, the supreme lord god pulled two hairs from his head, great seer, one white, one black. And he said to the gods, "These two hairs of mine will descend to earth and remove the painful burden from the world. All the gods should also descend to earth, along with their portions, in order to do battle with these wild demons that have appeared. Then all the Daityas on earth will most certainly go to perdition, crushed by my glance. One of my hairs, O gods, will become the eighth embryo in the womb of the divine Devakī, Vasudeva's wife. Descending on earth in this form, it will destroy Kālanemi who has been reborn as Kaṃsa." So saying, Hari vanished. Prostrating themselves before the invisible Hari, great seer, the gods went to the top of Mt. Meru and descended to the surface of the earth.

When Kaṃsa heard the god's plan from Nārada, who said, "Devakī's eighth embryo will be Kṛṣṇa, upholder of the earth!" he held both Devakī and Vasudeva captive in their house. As he had previously promised, Vasudeva turned each child over to Kaṃsa, O brahmins. They say that these six sons became the children of Hiraṇyakaśipu, after Sleep, sent by Viṣṇu, had bestowed the embryos on Devakī, one by one. It is this *yogic* sleep of Viṣṇu, the illusion of which is vast, that deludes all creation with ignorance.

Lord Hari said to her, "Sleep, at my order, go and take the six embryos which are resting on the bottom of the underworld and put them one at a time into Devakī's womb. When these six have been destroyed by Kaṃsa, the seventh in her womb will be an infinitesimal portion of myself called Śesa. In Gokula there lives another wife of Vasudeva, Rohiṇī. During her confinement, which will be at the same time as Devakī's, you are to put Devakī's embryo into her womb. People will say that Devakī's seventh conception has ended in miscarriage, aborted by her fear of the Bhoja king. Because it has been extracted in this way the embryo will be called Saṃkarṣaṇa throughout the world; he will be a hero resembling the peak of the White Mountain.

"Then I myself will take shape in the holy womb of Devakī, while you go without delay into Yaśodā's womb. And in the month of Nabhas, during the rainy season, at night, I will be born as Kṛṣṇa, the eighth embryo, and you will be the ninth. Vasudeva, his mind prompted by my power, will lead me to Yaśodā's bed and you, blameless one, to that of Devakī.

"Now when Kaṃsa discovers you, O goddess, he will dash you against a rocky mountain peak. But you will attain a dwelling place in the sky, where Śakra of a thousand eyes will honor you out of respect for me. His head bowed reverently, he will accept you as his sister. After killing Śumbha, Niśumbha and thousands of other demons, you will adorn the earth with countless shrines. You are prosperity, humility, patience, beauty, fortitude, modesty, wealth, dawn, heaven and earth – and whatever else there is, you are. Those who will praise you with heads bowed in the morning and afternoon, calling you Āryā, Durgā, Ambikā, womb of the Veda, Bhadrā, and Bhadrakālī, the goddess who gives rest and happiness – to those who worship you I will give whatever they desire, by my graciousness. Honored with offerings of wine, meat and other enjoyable things, you will be liberally beneficent toward the desires of all people. By my grace, good mistress, humankind will know no danger. Go, goddess, and do as I have said."

Thus addressed by the god of gods, the midwife of creation then deposited the six embryos in Devakī, as told, and exchanged the seventh. When she put the seventh into Rohiṇī, Hari entered Devakī to benefit the three worlds. On the day that Yoganidrā began to grow in Yaśodā's womb exactly as Parameṣṭhin had directed, all the planets circled in the sky. When Viṣṇu's portion went to earth, O brahmin, all the seasons sparkled. No one could look upon Devakī because of her great brilliance; when they beheld her flaming radiance, their minds trembled. Unseen by men and women, day and night the hosts of gods praised Devakī as she bore Viṣṇu in her body.

The Birth of Kṛṣṇa

Thus eulogized by the gods, Devakī bore in her womb the god with the lotus eyes, savior of the world. On the day of his birth, the great-souled Acyuta, awakening the lotus which is the world, appeared in the dawn which is Devakī to bring joy to the whole world like the light of the moon. Virtuous people were satisfied, fierce winds grew calm, and rivers ran clear when Janārdana was born. The oceans made sweet music with their waves while the lords of the Gandharvas sang and bevies of Apsarases danced. Gods in the heaven rained showers of flowers upon earth and smokeless fires blazed up afresh when Janārdana was born. Rainclouds rumbled softly, pouring down showers of blossoms, O brahmin, midway through the night when Janārdana, support of all, was born.

When his father, Anakadundubhi, saw his son born with four arms, pure as the petal of a blue lotus blossom, and with the *śrīvatsa* whorl on his chest, he celebrated him with song. Praising him with gracious words, the great-minded father, who still feared Kaṃsa, said to his son, excellent twice-born ones:

"You have been born, overlord of the gods! O god, abandon, by your grace, this divine form with conch, discus and mace! When Kaṃsa learns, O god, that you have descended this very day into my house, he will kill me outright! Be gracious, lord, you whose form is infinite, complete, embodied in the universe, who bears the worlds within your body even while in the womb. O god of gods, you who bear the form of an infant made visible by illusion, abandon this four-armed form, O universal soul, lest Kaṃsa born of Diti know of your descent!"

"Long ago," said Viṣṇu to Devakī, "out of desire for a son you worshiped me. That propitiation, goddess, has now born fruit for you in that I am born from your own womb!" So speaking, the lord fell silent, excellent seer, and Vasudeva went outside.

As Anakadundubhi carried out his son in the dead of night, the guards were gripped by Sleep, as were the guardians of Mathurā's gate. As they went in the night under cover of the clouds that were raining torrents of water, the serpent Śeṣa followed Anakadundubhi and sheltered him with his hoods. Carrying Viṣṇu, Vasudeva crossed the deep river Yamunā with its hundreds of whirlpools, but it only reached up to his knees.

On the bank of the river he saw the cowherd elders, Nanda and the others, who had come to bring taxes to Kaṃsa. At that time O Maitreya, Yaśodā, too, was fooled by Sleep whom she bore as her daughter, while the people were also deluded. Vasudeva, of infinite splendor, put down the boy, picked up the girl from Yaśodā's bed and quickly left. When she awoke and saw that she had borne a son who was as dark as a blue lotus petal, Yaśodā was ecstatic with joy.

Vasudeva carried the girl to his own house, put her into Devakī's bed and lay down there as before. Hearing the crying of a child, the guards rose up and told Kaṃsa of Devakī's delivery, O brahmin. Going at once to her side, Kaṃsa seized the little girl. Devakī tried to prevent him with strangled cries of "Let go! Let go" but he dashed the baby onto a rock. When she was thrown down, she rose into the sky where she assumed a vast body with eight weapon-bearing arms. Then she laughed aloud, enraged, and said to Kaṃsa, "Why did you hurl me on the ground, O Kaṃsa? The one who will destroy you is now born! He who himself consists of all the gods has been the cause of your death once before; ponder this and look to your own welfare at once!"

So speaking, the goddess left, with her heavenly garlands and ornaments. Before the eyes of the Bhoja king she sped through the sky, lauded by the Siddhas.

Pūtanā, the Child-Killer

Vasudeva went to Nanda's wagon where Nanda, overjoyed, exclaimed, "A son has just been born to me!" Vasudeva spoke to him courteously, "Good fortune! Even though you are old, you have had a son! You have paid the king's annual tax, which was the reason you came here. Now there is no further cause for you to remain here with your goods. Why stay now that you have done your duty? Nanda, you should return at once to your own home Gokula. I too have a little son who has been born of Rohiṇī. Please take him with you and protect him as your own." At these words, having paid their taxes, the cowherds led by Nanda put their belongings into their wagons and departed in great numbers.

One night while they were living in Gokula, the child-killer Pūtanā picked up the sleeping Kṛṣṇa and gave him her breast. Every child to whom Pūtanā gives suck at night has his body destroyed. But Kṛṣṇa grabbed her nipple, squeezed it tightly with both hands and furiously sucked out the milk, together with her life. Screeching loudly, the cords of her muscles cut asunder, the ghastly Pūtanā fell dying to the ground.

The inhabitants of Vraja woke up, startled by her screams, and saw Kṛṣṇa on Pūtanā's lap as she lay dead on the ground. Yaśodā too appeared, trembling with fear. Grabbing up Kṛṣṇa, excellent brahmin, she waved a cow's tail over him to ward off evil. And the cowherd Nanda put cow dung on Kṛṣṇa's head to protect him, saying:

"May Hari protect you, he who is the source of all creatures, from whose navel has sprung the lotus which is the origin of the world. May Keśava protect you, the god who raised up earth on the tip of his tusk when he took the form of a boar. May Janārdana protect you on all sides, the lord in the form of Narasiṃha who split asunder his enemy's chest with his claws. May Vāmana always protect you, he who bestrode the three worlds in a wink with weapons flashing. May Govinda guard your head, Keśava your throat, Viṣṇu your genitals and belly, and Janārdana your shins and feet. May the imperishable Nārāyaṇa, whose sovereignty is flawless, watch over your face, arms, forearms, your mind and all your senses. May those ghosts, goblins and demons who oppose you go to perdition when they are struck by the sound of the conch of Viṣṇu, who holds in his hand the bow, discus and mace. May Vaikuṇṭha protect you in the principal quarters, Madhusūdana in the intermediate directions, Hṛṣīkeśa in the sky, and Mahīdhara on earth!"

Wishing him godspeed the cowherd Nanda laid the boy to rest on his little cot under the wagon. And when the cowherds saw the monstrous cadaver of the dead Pūtanā, they were shocked and terrified.

Mt. Govardhana

When the cowherds had been persuaded by Kṛṣṇa to make their offerings to the mountain instead of to Indra, Śakra became filled with fury, O Maitreya. He summoned a troop of rainclouds named Saṃvartaka and addressed them, "*Bhoḥ! Bhoḥ*, you clouds, hear what I have to say, and act immediately on my orders! The evil-minded cowherd Nanda, together with the other cowherds, proud of the power of Kṛṣṇa's protection, had disrupted my sacrifice! Harry with rain and wind, according to my command, those cows which are their ultimate livelihood and the cause of their support. Riding on my mountainous elephant I shall assist you in the storm."

At his command, the thunderclouds loosed a horrendous storm in order to destroy the cows, O brahmin. Then in a flash the earth, horizons and sky became one under the mighty downpour of water. A huge flood poured from the clouds as they shook from the blows of whip-like lightning, and the circle of the horizon was filled with thunder. The world was darkened by the incessant raining of the clouds, as if it were nothing but water, above, below and across.

The trembling cows, buffeted by the fierce wind and rain, with shrunken withers, necks and thighs, began to die. Some stood there sheltering their calves under their chests, great seer, while others lost their calves to the flood waters. And the sad-faced calves, their necks shaken by the wind, cried out in feeble voices, "Help! Help!" as if they were sick.

When Hari saw all Gokula, cows, men and women together, so miserable, O Maitreya, he began to ponder, "This has been done by Indra, who is angry because of the loss of his offerings. I must now rescue the entire cowpen! I shall root up this mountain with its broad expanse of rock, and firmly hold it aloft over Gokula like a wide umbrella."

Having made up his mind, Kṛṣṇa lifted Mt. Govardhana with one hand and playfully held it aloft! Then Śauri, holding the uprooted mountain, said to the cowherds with a smile, "Now quickly hide under here where I have stopped the rain. You may stay here contentedly, as in a windless spot, without fear of the mountain falling down."

At Kṛṣṇa's words the cowherds, who were being pelted by the rain, entered under the mountain with their herds, and so did the cowherd women with their belongings piled on carts. And so Kṛṣṇa held that mountain steadily aloft to the delight of the inhabitants of Vraja, their eyes thrilled with wonder. As Kṛṣṇa supported that mountain, his deed was celebrated by the delighted cowherd men and women with eyes wide with joy.

For seven nights huge clouds sent by Indra poured rain on Nanda's Gokula, O brahmin, in order to annihilate the cowherds. But since they were protected by the mighty mountain held on high, that slayer of Bala, his promise proven false, dispersed the clouds. After the sky was free of clouds and Indra's promise had been shown to be empty, the happy people of Gokula came out and returned to their own homes. And Kṛṣṇa then returned Mt. Govardhana to its own place as the inhabitants of Vraja looked on with wonder in their faces.

The Test of Pārvatī's Tapas

Hear with pleasure, O Sanatkumāra, the story of the most purifying *avatāra* of the great-souled lord Śiva called Jaṭila. Long ago Satī, Dakṣa's daughter, abandoned her body at her father's feast after he insulted her and she was reborn as Śivā, daughter of Menā and the snowy mountain Himavat. Desiring Śankara for her husband, she went to the deep forest with two companions and practiced pure *tapas*; Śiva, skilled in various sports, sent the Seven Seers to the site of Pārvatī's *tapas* to examine her asceticism in person. Arriving there, these sages performed their inspection scrupulously, but even with their utmost efforts they were unable to distract her. They returned to Śiva, bowed, and told him what had happened. Thus having accomplished their task, they returned respectfully to Svarloka.

After the seers had gone home, lord Śankara, the begetter, decided to investigate Śivā's behavior himself. The mighty lord, who had himself become a serene ascetic through the appeasement of desire took the form of a *brahmacārin*, this our most wondrous lord. In the body of an ancient brahmin, glowing with his own luster, the luminous one who carried a staff and umbrella was happy at heart. Thus bearing the body of a matted-haired ascetic, Śambhu Śankara who is kind to his devotees went at once with great joy to the forest of the mountain daughter.

There he saw the goddess standing at a fire altar surrounded by her companions, pure like an auspicious digit of the moon. When Śambhu, who is loyal to his devotees, saw the goddess, he approached her eagerly in a friendly manner. When she saw him coming, this marvelous and splendid brahmin, his body covered with fine hair, his aspect serene, with a staff and animal skin, in the person of an aged *brahmacārin* with matted hair carrying a water jar, she worshiped him most graciously with all the offerings of *pūjā*. After joyfully honoring the *brahmacārin*, the goddess Pārvatī inquired respectfully about his health, "Who are you who have come here in the form of a *brahmacārin*? Where have you come from to brighten this forest? Speak, O choicest of those who know the Veda!"

Thus questioned by Pārvatī, the twice-born *brahmacārin* graciously replied at once in order to test Śivā's intentions, "Be assured that I am a twice-born *brahmacārin*. I am an ascetic, going where I please, a benefactor who gives help to others."

As he said this, Śankara the *brahmacārin* who is kind to his devotees stood at her side concealing his true nature. "What can I say, great goddess? There is nothing more to be said. A great perversion is going on here, I see, conduct that will bring disaster. For in your early youth when you should be enjoying fine pleasures and the attentions of others, you are doing *tapas* to no purpose at all! Who are you? Whose daughter are you? Why are you practicing *tapas* in this lonely forest, *tapas* that is hard to master even for self-controlled seers?"

At these words, the supreme goddess began to laugh and replied politely to the excellent *brahmacārin*, "Hear my whole story, O wise brahmin *brahmacārin*. I was born in the land of Bharata, in the house of Himavat. Before that I was born in the House of Dakṣa as the maiden Satī, beloved of Śankara. When my father insulted me about my husband, I abandoned by body through Yoga. In this birth, O twice-born one, I won Śiva again by my great merit, but after reducing Manmatha to ashes, he abandoned me and went away. When Śankara left my father's house to do *tapas*, I was ashamed. So I came here for *tapas* myself, following the word of my *guru*. With mind, speech and action I have chosen Śankara as my lord.

"All this is the truth I speak and not a lie. Yet I realize my purpose is most difficult to obtain. How am I to succeed? In any case, it is because of my heart's desire that I am now practicing *tapas*. Disregarding all the other gods who are headed by Indra, leaving aside even Viṣṇu and Brahmā, I want in truth to win for my husband only the one who holds the Pināka!"

When he heard these determined words of Pārvatī, O seer, the matted-haired Rudra said this with a smile, "What an idea you have in your head, goddess, daughter of Himācala! Abandoning the gods for Rudra, you practice *tapas*! I am well acquainted with this Rudra, so listen to what I say. He has a bull on his banner. He is not a normal man. His hair is unkempt. He is always alone by himself. Above all, he is indifferent to the world. Therefore do not yoke your mind to this Rudra! Your lovely form, goddess, is wholly opposite to that of Hara. What you propose offends me; but you are free to do as you choose."

After saying this, Rudra in his *brahmacārin* form continued to ridicule himself in various ways before her in order to test her. When she heard the brahmin's untoward words, the goddess Pārvatī, greatly provoked, answered him who was reviling Śiva, "This much I am sure of, that there is someone here who deserves to be killed, even though he appears at the moment to be inviolable. You must be some imposter who has come here in the guise of a *brahmacārin* in order to insult Śiva! Now I am angry with you, fool! You cannot possibly know Śiva, for your face is turned away from him. It infuriates me that I have honored you! On earth, one who insults Śiva has all the merit he has accumulated since birth reduced to ashes. And one who so much as touches a despiser of Śiva must perform expiation. Fie on you, dirty thief! Vile man, I know this Śiva whom you have described. He is the supreme lord! He adopts various forms through illusion so that you cannot know him definitively. Yet Rudra, granter of my wishes, beloved of the virtuous, is utterly without alteration!"

After Śivā, the goddess, had said this, she recited the truth about Śiva, describing Rudra as the unmanifest Brahman who is without characteristics. After listening to the goddess' words, the twice-born *brahmacārin* started once again to speak, but the mountain-born Śivā, turning her face away from any further abuse of Śiva, her mind's fancy fixed on him, spoke quickly to her companion:

"Stop this horrid brahmin from speaking out as he wishes, friend, or he will once again insult Śiva! The sin of one who reviles Śiva is not his alone, but those who listen to the insult also share in the guilt. Anyone, without exception, who reviles Śiva is to be killed by his servants. A brahmin who does so is to be shunned; one should leave his company at once. This wicked man is again going to speak ill of Śiva, but because he is a brahmin, he is not to be killed. He is, however, to be ignored and avoided at all costs. Let us leave this place at once and go somewhere else immediately so we will not have to converse further with this idiot!"

After Umā had said this, seer, and just as she was lifting one foot to go, Śiva appeared before her and caught hold of her garment. Assuming his divine form as it appears to those who meditate on him, Śiva made himself visible to Śivā and spoke to her while her face was still turned away from him.

"If you leave me, where will you go? O Śivā, I will not leave you alone. I have tested you, blameless woman, and find you firmly devoted to me. I came to you in the form of a *brahmacārin* and said to you many things, all out of desire for your own welfare. I am profoundly pleased with your special devotion. Tell me what your heart desires! There is nothing you do not deserve! Because of your *tapas*, I shall be your servant from this moment on. Due to your loveliness, each instant without you lasts an Age. Cast off your modesty! Become my wife forevermore! Come, beloved. I shall go to my mountain at once, together with you."

Śivā became overjoyed at hearing these words of the lord of the gods and abandoned immediately all the hardships of *tapas*. Trembling at the sight of Śiva's celestial form, Śivā kept her face modestly turned down and replied respectfully to the lord, "If you are pleased with me and if you have compassion for me, then be my husband, O lord of the gods."

Thus addressed by Śivā, Śiva took her hand according to custom and went to Mt. Kailāsa with her. Having won her husband, the mountain-born girl performed the divine offices for the gods.

Dakṣa's Insult

Hear as I relate how Dakṣa offended all the immortals with his wickedness and deliberate negligence. Once long ago all the gods, demons, Siddhas and supreme sages went to Mt. Himavat to see the lord. Both the god and goddess sat on their celestial thrones and gave audience to these gods and other beings, O excellent brahmins. Dakṣa too went there with the immortals at the same time to see his son-in-law Hara and Satī, who was his own daughter. The god and goddess were so exalted that, upon his arrival, no special privilege was accorded to Dakṣa over the other gods.

Ignorant of the divine nature of his host and hostess, and erroneously thinking Satī to be just his daughter and no more, Dakṣa became hostile. He was impelled by fate as well as by this enmity. At a later time, when Dakṣa was consecrated for a sacrifice in his own domain, he refused to invite Bhava, whom he regarded as an enemy, and he began to despise his own daughter as well. He entertained all his other sons-in-law in turn and paid his respects to them a hundred-fold, but not to Śiva.

When Rudrāṇī heard from Nārada's mouth that they were all assembled at her father's house, she informed Rudra and went there herself. The great goddess ascended her celestial chariot, which was ready nearby. Open on all sides and easy to mount, it was endowed with auspicious marks and was beautiful beyond measure. Resembling refined gold, it was covered with glittering gems, the top canopy made of pearls and wreathed with garlands. It was encircled by hundreds of jeweled posts with steps fashioned of diamond and gateposts of coral. Blanketed with flowers it bore a large, sparkling gem-encrusted throne, a window of diamond-studded lattice-work and a flawless mosaic of precious stones. The forepart of the chariot was decorated with a cloud-white standard bearing the sign of a mighty bull and adorned with a jeweled staff. Its great portal was guarded by invincible Gaṇeśvaras with colorful staffs in their hands, their bodies protected by mail inlaid with precious gems. The chariot abounded with women skilled in drum, rhythm, song, flute and lute, who were smartly dressed and clever in speech. The great goddess mounted this heavenly chariot along with her beloved companions.

Two of Rudra's lovely handmaidens took up a pair of beautiful yaktail fans with diamond-studded handles and wafted them back and forth. Between the two chowrie plumes the face of the goddess appeared like a lotus in the middle of two fighting geese. Over her crown-jewel, her servant Sumālinī, full of love, held a moon-like parasol strewn with pearls. That shimmering parasol shone above the face of the goddess like the orb of the moon over a jar of nectar. The smiling Śubhāvatī sat in front of Satī and delighted her by playing dice with her. And Suyaśā waited on the goddess after putting the lovely jeweled sandals of her mistress between her own breasts. One woman with limbs as gorgeous as gold held up a shining mirror, another a palm-leaf fan and still another a betel-box. One comely woman held in her hand a fine pet parrot, another carried beautiful fragrant flowers, while another lotus-eyed woman bore a jewel box. And again, one carried finely strained oil and the best collyrium, while others in similar positions did their own appointed tasks. Surrounding their mistress, the women attended her on all sides. The great goddess shone forth in their midst like a digit of the autumn moon in the center of a circle of stars.

Immediately following the sounding of conches, the great kettledrum was beaten announcing departure. Melodious instruments sang aloud without being played, accompanied by the beat of clapping hands and the sound of hundreds of drums. At the same time 800,000 Gaṇeśas marched in front, their splendor equalling Maheśa's. In their midst astride a bull, like a *guru* on an elephant, proceeded the illustrious lord of the *gaṇas*, worshiped by the moon and by Nandin the bull. Divine drums resounded in the heavens and beautiful clouds rumbled in the sky while all the seers danced and the Yogins and Siddhas rejoiced.

Rainclouds massed on all sides poured forth a shower of flowers on the canopy as the great goddess, accompanied everywhere by the hosts of other gods, entered her father's house as though in a flash. When Dakṣa saw her, infuriated because of his own loss of face, he ignored her, and paid scant attention even to her younger sisters. Then the moon-faced goddess Ambikā spoke strong words in a cool and collected manner to her father who was sitting in the *sadas*.

"Dear father, you are not worshiping properly according to the rules the god who commands all beings from Brahmā to the Piśācas! As if this weren't enough, you have made a pitiful, disgraceful *pūjā* to me, your eldest daughter. How could you?" Thus addressed, Dakṣa, truculent from rancor, said to her, "My other daughters are finer, more distinguished and more worthy of honor than you! Moreover I gladly hold in high esteem their husbands who are in all virtues superior to your spouse, the three-eyed one! That dark *tamasic* Śarva is arrogant in his soul, yet you revere him. Bhava offends me. For this I repudiate you!"

At this, the goddess furiously replied to her father Dakṣa, "Let all those who sit in the sacrificial *sadas* give ear to the mistress of the universe! Dakṣa, you have insulted my husband before me for no good reason, the great lord of the world in whom no faults exist. *Śruti* says that those who steal knowledge, those who betray a teacher, those who defile the lord of the Vedas are all great sinners who should be punished. Because of this, as your fate you will immediately suffer cruel and severe punishment befitting your egregious sin. Because you have failed to worship Tryambaka, the god of gods, be assured that your wicked family is ruined!"

After saying this to her father, the offended Satī, her wrath spent, abandoned her body and went to Mt. Himavat. That excellent mountain had been practicing severe *tapas* for a long time and now attained the fruit of his merit. To grant a favor to the lord of the mountain, the goddess made him her own father by Yogic illusion. After Satī, afflicted with distress, had reproached Dakṣa and left him, the *mantras* too disappeared, and so the sacrifice was prevented from taking place.

When he heard of the goddess' departure, the destroyer of Tripura became enraged at Dakṣa and the seers and cursed them. "O Dakṣa," he said, "you despise Satī because of me while you honor all your other daughters and their husbands. Because of this, all your daughters will originate together at the sacrifice of Brahmā in the Vaivasvata Manvantara without benefit of a womb. In the Cākṣusa Manvantara, you will be a human king, the grandson of Pracīṇabarhis and son of Pracetas. At that time, too, I shall obstruct you again and again, hard-souled one, even in actions that conform to Duty, Success and Love."

Thus addressed by Rudra of infinite splendor, the miserable Dakṣa abandoned the body that had been born from Svāyambhuva and fell to the ground.

Gaṇeśa

Once upon a time while Pārvatī was taking a bath, the always auspicious Śiva threatened Nandin, who was guarding her door, and went into the house. When that lovely woman, the mother of the world, saw Śankara arrive so unexpectedly, she stood up, embarrassed. After this happened, the auspicious Pārvatī, supreme Māyā, the supernal goddess, became eager to follow the good advice given earlier by a friend, thinking to herself, "I should have a servant of my very own! He should be favorable to me, a man of accomplishment who will obey my command and no other, one who will not stray even a hair's breadth from my side!"

Thinking these thoughts, the goddess fashioned from the dirt of her body a young man who possessed all these good characteristics. He was handsome, flawless of limb, sturdy, well-adorned, and most valorous and strong. She gave to him various garments, abundant ornaments and an incomparable blessing. "You are my very own son!" she said, "I have no one else here who is mine alone."

At her words, the youth bowed and said to Śivā, "What task have you found for me? I shall do as you tell me." Thus addressed, Śivā answered her son, "Dear son, hear my words. From now on you shall be my doorkeeper. You are my very own child; I have no one whatsoever here but you who belongs to me. Let no one into my house without my permission, my son, no matter who, no matter where. Use force if necessary, dear son. I mean this truly!" And so speaking, she gave him a hard stick, O seer. Gazing at his handsome body, she was thrilled with delight.

Then she kissed his face lovingly, embraced him with affection and stationed him, staff in hand, at her door as chief of her *gaṇas*. And the beloved son of the goddess, the great heroic *gaṇa*, stood at the door of her house, holding the staff in his hand, out of desire to please Pārvatī. After she had put her son Gaṇeśa, lord of the *gaṇas*, in front of her door, Śivā herself stayed inside to bathe with her companions.

At that moment Śiva, skilled in various sports, arrived eagerly at the door, O lion among seers. Not knowing he was lord Śiva, Gaṇeśa said, "You may not enter here, O god, without permission of my mother who is inside bathing. Where do you think you're going? Get out at once!" Saying this, Gaṇeśa brandished his staff to stop Śiva.

Looking at him, Śiva said, "You silly fool, who are you to keep me out? Don't you recognize me, stupid? I am none other than Śiva himself!" But Gaṇeśa struck the great lord of many sports with his stick. This infuriated Śiva who said once again to his son, "You are an imbecile not to know me! I am Śiva, the husband of Pārvatī, daughter of the mountain! I shall go into my own house, idiot. Why are you standing in my way?"

After the god had spoken Gaṇeśa grew angry with Maheśa, who was going into the house, O brahmin, so he hit him again with his staff. At this Śiva became enraged. Mustering his own *gaṇas*, he asked them, "Who is this person? What is he up to? What is going on here, *gaṇas*, while you just stand there and watch?"...

The *gaṇas*, filled with fury, went to the guardian of the door at Śiva's behest and questioned the son of the mountain daughter. "Who are you? Where have you come from? What are you going to do? Get out now if you want to live! Now listen to us. We are Śiva's best *gaṇas* and doorkeepers. We have come to stop you, by order of lord Śankara. We can see that you are a *gaṇa* too, so we will spare your life, but otherwise you would be killed! For your own sake, stay far away from us. Why risk death by staying here?"

Even after this speech, Pārvatī's son Gaṇeśa showed no fear. Rebuking Śankara's *gaṇas*, he refused to budge from the doorway. When they had heard all he had to say, the *gaṇas* of Śiva who had gone there returned to the lord and told him what had happened....

After hearing their words, Śiva said, "Listen, all you *gaṇas*. It is not right to go to battle over this, for you are my very own *gaṇas* and that other *gaṇa* belongs to my wife Gaurī. On the other hand, if I back down, O *gaṇas*, people might say, 'Śambhu is always cowed by his wife!' It is a weighty matter to know the right thing to do. That *gaṇa* by himself is only a mere child. What power can he have? Moreover, *gaṇas*, in the world you are experts in battle, and you belong to me. Why should you avoid a fight and thereby become useless to me? How can a woman be so obstinate, especially to her husband? It is she who is responsible for this! Now the mountain daughter will reap the fruit of her act! Listen carefully to what I say, all my heroes: wage all-out war! Let it come out as it will!" After making this speech, O brahmin, Śankara who is skilled in various sports stopped talking, excellent seer, according to the way of the world.

Thus addressed by their lord, the *gaṇas* made a supreme resolve to do his bidding. United, they went to Śivā's house. When Gaṇeśa saw the eminent *gaṇas* approach, armed for battle, he said to them, "Come if you will, all you lords of the *gaṇas* following Śiva's command! I am only one boy who obeys the order of Śivā. Nevertheless, the goddess Pārvatī shall witness the strength of her son, while Śiva shall see the power of his own *gaṇas*! The fight that is about to take place between a child and mighty men is a contest between Bhavānī and Śiva. You are skilled in warfare, since you have fought before; I am a boy who has never been to battle. Nevertheless, I shall put you to shame in this conflict between the mountain-born woman and Śiva! For my part, I have nothing against you, but I shall humble you before Pārvatī and Śiva! Now that you know this, O *gaṇa* lords, let the battle be joined! Look to your master and I shall look to my mother. Let the outcome be as it will be, for no one in the three worlds can stop it now!"

Thus challenged, the *gaṇas* grabbed up all kinds of weapons and assaulted him, their arms bristling with sticks. They ground their teeth, cried "*Hūṃ!*" over and over again and attacked him shouting, "Look at him! There he is!" Nandin approached first, seized Gaṇeśa's foot and tugged at it while Bhṛgin grabbed the other foot. As they pulled at his feet, the *gaṇa* beat back their hands which clung to his sandals.

Then Gaṇapati, the heroic son of the goddess, seized a huge iron-stubbed club and stood at the door, bashing them all with it. Some had their hands severed, the backs of others were shattered, while still others had their heads and skulls cut off. The knees of some were smashed, the shoulders of others. All those who faced Gaṇeśa were hit in the chest. Some fell to the ground, while others fled in all directions. Some had their feet cut off while others retreated towards Śarva. There was not a one among them who faced up to Gaṇeśa in battle. Like deer who see a lion, they fled in all the ten directions. When all the *gaṇas* by the thousands had run away, Gaṇeśa returned to stand at the beautiful door. That destroyer of them all was a terrifying sight, looking like Time at the end of the Eon. . . .

After waging war with his army for a long time, O seer, even Śiva grew dismayed at the sight of his formidable foe. He stood in the middle of his troops thinking, "Gaṇeśa can only be killed by a trick! For surely there is no other way." Then all the gods and Maheśa's *gaṇas* were delighted to see both Śiva, embodied with qualities, and Viṣṇu come to the battle. Greeting each other with affection, they all celebrated. And Gaṇeśa, the heroic son of *śakti*, with his staff, following the way of heroes, was the first to worship Viṣṇu who brings happiness to all.

Then Viṣṇu said to Śiva, "You shall kill your enemy, O lord, but not without trickery, for he is hard to reach and full of *tamas*. I shall create a delusion." He conferred with Śaṃbhu, and after receiving Śiva's command, Viṣṇu began to prepare his trick. . . .

The heroic son of Śivā, endowed with great strength, saw the great lord Śaṃbhu arrive, trident in hand, eager for the kill. Recalling his mother's lotus feet, and emboldened by the *śakti* of Śivā, the mighty hero Gaṇeśa struck him in the hand with his spear. When Śiva whose protection is good saw the trident fall from his hand, he took up the Pināka bow, but the lord of the *gaṇas* made that too fall to the ground with a blow of his iron-studded staff. Since five of his hands had been clubbed, Śiva took up the trident with five others. "Aho!" he cried in the way of the world, "a great calamity has befallen me! Surely nothing worse than this can happen to the *gaṇas*!"

Meanwhile, the heroic Gaṇeśa, full of the power bestowed by *śakti*, attacked all the gods and *gaṇas* with his cudgel. Set upon by his club, they dispersed into the ten directions. None remained in combat with that wondrous fighter. When Viṣṇu saw that *gaṇa*, he exclaimed, "This is a lucky one! He is most powerful, most manly, a great hero fond of battle! I have seen many deities, Daityas, Dānavas,

Yakṣas, Gandharvas and Rākṣasas, but there is none to equal this guardian in brilliance, beauty, valor and other fine qualities in any of the three worlds!"

As he was speaking in this manner, the *gaṇa* lord, son of *śakti*, brandished his club and hurled it at Viṣṇu. Recollecting the lotus-like feet of Śiva, Hari took up his discus and swiftly shattered that iron-studded club. The *gaṇa* then hurled a chip of the club at Hari, but the bird Garuḍa caught it and rendered it powerless. Thus did the time pass as the two mighty heroes, Viṣṇu and Gaṇeśa, fought with each other.

Once again, the choicest hero, the mighty son of *śakti*, recalling Śivā, took up his matchless staff and struck Viṣṇu with it. Unable to withstand the blow, Viṣṇu fell to the ground. But he sprang up at once and battled again with that son of Śivā. Seizing his opportunity at last, the trident-wielding Śiva took his stand in the north and cut off the head of Gaṇeśa with his trident. When Gaṇeśa lost his head, both the army of the *gaṇas* and the army of the gods stood stock still, rooted to the earth.

After Gaṇeśa was killed, the *gaṇas* held a great festival to the sound of hand drums and kettle drums. Śiva was sorry that he had cut off Gaṇeśa's head, O lord of seers, but the mountain-born goddess Pārvatī was furious: "What will I do? Where will I go? Alas, alas, misery engulfs me. How will I ever lose this grief and sorrow that now are mine? All the gods and *gaṇas* have killed my son. I shall wreak utter havoc! I shall bring about the dissolution of the world!"

Grieving in this manner, the great goddess of the universe, enraged, fashioned in an instant hundreds of thousands of *śaktis*, or powers. Once created, they bowed to the mother of the world, blazed forth and said, "O Mother, tell us what to do!" At their words, O lord of seers, Mahāmāyā, Śaṃbhu's *śakti*, she who is Prakṛti, full of fury, answered them all. "O *śaktis*, O goddesses, you are to annihilate the world without a moment's pause. O my companions, devour with a vengeance the gods, sages, Yakṣas, Rākṣasas, my very own followers and all the rest as well!"

At her command, all the *śaktis*, consumed with rage, prepared to destroy all the gods and other creatures. They went forth to spread devastation, as fire licks up grass. The leaders of the *gaṇas* – Viṣṇu, Brahmā, Śankara and Indra, Kubera, king of the Yakṣas, Skanda and Sūrya – all these they sought to obliterate without ceasing. No matter where one looked, there were the *śaktis*! There were multitudes of them – Karālī (Gape-Mouth), Kubjakā (Hunch-Back), Khaṃjā (Cripple), Lambaśīrsā (Droop-Head) – and they all snatched up the gods in their hands and hurled them into their open mouths.

Witnessing this devastation, Hara, Brahmā, Hari, Indra and all the rest of the gods, *gaṇas* and seers said to themselves, "What is this goddess doing, this untimely annihilation of the world?" Thus they were uncertain and lost hope for their own lives. Gathering together, they conferred with each other, saying, "We must consider what to do!" Thus deliberating, they talked rapidly among themselves. "Only when the mountain goddess is satisfied will peace return to the world, and not otherwise, not even with a myriad efforts! Even Śiva, skilled in all sports, the deluder of the world, is filled with sorrow like the rest of us!"

A million gods were annihilated while Śivā was enraged; none could prevail. There was no one whatsoever to withstand the mountain-born goddess, O seer, whether her own devotee or that of another, whether god or Dānava, *gaṇa* or guardian of the quarters, whether Yakṣa, Kinnara or seer, not even Viṣṇu, Brahmā or lord Śankara himself! When they beheld her dazzling splendor flashing in all directions, all the gods were terrified and retreated to some distance away.

Meanwhile Nārada of divine sight arrived – you, O seer – to benefit the gods and *gaṇas*. After bowing to Brahmá, Viṣṇu, Śankara and myself, he met with them and spoke, reflecting on what was to be done. All the gods conferred with the great-souled Nārada, saying in unison, "How can our suffering be ended?" To this he replied, "As long as the mountain-born goddess is without compassion, you will be miserable. Make no mistake about this!"

And then the seers headed by Nārada went to Śivā and all propitiated her in order to appease her fury. Over and over again they bowed, singing hymns by the numbers. Placating her with devotion, they said to her, at the command of the gods and *gaṇas*:

"O Mother of the world, praise be to you! To you, Śivā! Glory be to you, Caṇḍikā, to Kalyāṇī, praise! O Mother, you are the primordial *śakti*, creatress of everything. You are the power that protects, the power that destroys! O goddess, be content! Be serene! Glory be to you, O goddess! The triple world is destitute because of your rage!"

Thus hymned by the seers led by Nārada, the supreme goddess continued to look furious and spoke not a word to them. So all the seers bowed again to her lotus feet and spoke diplomatically once more to Śivā with devotion, their hands folded in reverence:

"Forgive us, O goddess! Devastation is upon us! Your master stands before you, Ambikā, look at him! We are the gods Viṣṇu, Brahmā and the others, O goddess. We are your very own creatures who stand before you with our hands folded in worship. Forgive our fault, supreme goddess! All of us are utterly miserable. O Śivā, grant us peace!"

So speaking, all the seers, wretched and confused, stood together in front of Caṇḍikā with their hands folded in obeisance. When she heard what they said, Caṇḍikā grew pleased. And she answered those seers with a mind filled with compassion: "If you can revive my son, I shall stop my devastation. If you honor him and make him overseer of everything, then there will be peace in the world. In no other way will you be happy again."

Thus addressed, all the seers led by Nārada went to tell the gods what had happened. After they heard the story, all the miserable gods led by Śakra bowed, folded their hands, and related it all to Śankara. At their words, Śiva said, "Do whatever is necessary to benefit the worlds. Go the north and cut off the head of whomever you first encounter. After doing this, join that head to Gaṇeśa's body."

All this was done by the gods according to Śiva's order. They brought the body, washed it by the rules and worshiped it. Then turning their faces to the north, they went out. The first thing they met was an elephant with a single tusk. Taking its head, all the deities fastened it firmly to the body of Gaṇeśa. Worshiping Śiva, Viṣṇu and Brahmā, they bowed and said, "We have done as you told us. Now you must finish the task." And the gods and attendants beamed with happiness at these words, having obeyed the command of Śiva.

Again Brahmā, Viṣṇu and the gods bowed to their master, the lord who is without characteristics, god Śiva himself, and said, "Since all of us were born from your *tejas*, or energy, now let your *tejas* enter this body by means of the recitation of Vedic *mantras*!" And calling Śiva to mind, they all sprinkled blessed holy water on the corpse while reciting *mantras*. At the mere touch of the drops of water, Gaṇeśa regained both consciousness and life. The boy arose, by Śiva's wish, as though from sleep. He was handsome, noble and resplendent, with a pleasing shape, a jolly manner and a ruddy elephant head.

Everyone rejoiced, their sorrows banished, O lord of seers, at the sight of Śivā's son restored to life. Filled with happiness, they showed him to the goddess. When she saw her son alive, she too was overcome with joy.

The Origin of Women

Hear, friend of great wisdom, about the matchless form of Śiva called Ardhanarīnara, half woman, half man, who grants wishes and fulfills the desire of the creator. When all the creatures poured forth by Brahmā failed to reproduce, he grew disturbed in his mind and suffered greatly on account of this misfortune. Then Brahmā heard an unearthly voice speak out, "Make a creation born from coupling!" and he decided to do so. But since no race of women had yet arisen from the lord, the lotus-born god was not able to produce a copulative creation.

When it occurred to him that such creatures could not be born without the power of Śaṃbhu, Brahmā began to practice great *tapas* while concentrating, with love in his heart, on the supreme lord conjoined with Śiva, the supreme *śakti*. Soon Śiva grew pleased with Svāyambhuva, the self-existent, who was yoked in intense *tapas*, so he assumed the wish-granting form of the lord whose consciousness is complete, and came before Brahmā as half woman, half man.

When he saw the god Śankara united with delightful *śakti*, Brahmā bowed formally and praised him with folded hands. Then the lord Mahādeva, creator of the universe, spoke most graciously to Svāyambhuva with a voice like rumbling clouds, "My dear Grandfather, blessed son, truly I know the whole of your heart's desire. You are now doing *tapas* so that your creatures will multiply. I am pleased with your *tapas* and I shall grant your wish!" And as he spoke these sweet words – they were both noble and naturally gentle – Śiva separated the goddess Śivā from a part of his body.

When he saw this supreme *śakti* detached from Śiva, the creator prostrated himself before her, his soul humbled, and asked, "In the beginning I was emitted first by your master, the god of gods, O Śivā, after which all creatures were charged with their duties by the great-souled Śaṃbhu. Out of my mind I fashioned the gods and all the other creatures, O Śivā, but they do not reproduce themselves. I must create them over and over again. I want to make all my creatures multiply by producing henceforth a creation that proceeds from copulation. But the immortal race of women has not yet emerged from you, and I have no power to produce them myself. Indeed, all the *śaktis* originate from you. Therefore I am asking you for the supreme *śakti*, which is the mistress of the universe!

"Glory be to you, O Śivā, mother, beloved of Śiva! Give me the power to pour forth the race of women! O mother, know that the world with its moving and unmoving beings is hallowed by having its source in you. And I ask from you another favor, O goddess of boons. Have compassion on me and grant my desire! Praise be to you, mother of the world! For the increase of moving and unmoving beings, with the lord as your spouse, O omnipresent woman, become the daughter of my son Dakṣa, O mother of welfare!"

Thus implored by Brahmā, the goddess, supreme mistress, gave that power to Brahmā, the creator, saying, "Let it be so." Whereupon Śivā, the goddess who is Śiva's *śakti*, consisting of the world, emitted from between her eyebrows a single *śakti* whose brilliance equaled her own. When Hara, best of the gods, the great lord who is a flood of compassion, player of games, saw that *śakti*, he addressed the mother of welfare with a smile, "O goddess who has been propitiated by the *tapas* of Brahmā Parameṣṭhin, be gracious! Out of your great affection, grant his entire desire!"

The goddess accepted the command of the supreme lord with a nod of her head and became Dakṣa's daughter, as Brahmā had requested. Having lent her incomparable power to Brahmā, O seer, Śivā entered lord Śaṃbhu's body and lord Śaṃbhu disappeared.

From that time onward, the female sex has been established in this world. Brahmā gained bliss and creation by copulation was born. Now you have heard the story of that great supreme form of Śiva, half woman, half man, dear one, who brings abundant wellbeing to the virtuous. Whoever recites or hears this holy story enjoys complete happiness and attains the ultimate goal.

Hari-Hara

The gods went to the dwelling place of Viṣṇu, enemy of Mura, made obeisance to the god and asked him why the world was so disturbed. When he heard their words, the blessed lord said, "Let us go to the abode of Hara. He is very wise; he will know why the world is shaking, with its moving and unmoving beings." Thus addressed by Vāsudeva, the gods, led by Indra, set out for

Mt. Mandara with Janārdana in front. Enveloped in darkest ignorance, they thought the mountain was empty, for they saw there neither god nor goddess, nor even Nandin the bull.

When the glorious Viṣṇu perceived that the eyes of the gods were clouded, he began to speak, "Don't you see the great lord who stands before you?" And they replied, "No, we do not see the lord of the gods, the husband of the mountain-born goddess! And we do not know what has deprived us of our sight!"

Then he who consists of the world said to them, "You yourselves have offended the god! Intent on your own self-interest, you have most wickedly destroyed the embryo of Śiva's wife Mṛḍāṇī. Because of this, knowledge and discrimination have been taken away by the god who bears a trident. It is for this reason that you do not see him even though he is standing right in front of you!

"Therefore, for the purification of your bodies and in order to see the god, most diligently expiate yourselves by the *taptakṛcchra* vow and take a ritual bath at the place of the lord, using 150 jars of milk, O gods." . . . And so the gods performed the *taptakṛcchra* vow by reciting the Śatarudrīya hymn and subsisting successively on hot water, hot milk, hot *ghī* and air for three days each.

After they had observed this vow, the gods were released from evil. Their stains removed, they addressed Vāsudeva, lord of the gods, "O Jagannātha, tell us where to find Śaṃbhu! Keśava, we are going to bathe him with ablutions of milk and other substances, according to the rules." At this, lord Viṣṇu told the gods, "Śankara resides in my body. Don't you see him here? This is the established Yoga!"

"No, we don't see in you the slayer of Tripura!" they replied. "Tell us the truth, O lord of gods, where is Maheśa?" Then the immortal-souled Hari, enemy of Mura, exhibited to them the divine *linga* of the lord Hara which was lying on the lotus of his heart. Whereupon the gods one by one bathed that endless, eternal, firm, immortal *linga* with milk and other offerings. They smeared it with yellow ointment and with fragrant sandal paste and then zealously worshiped the god with *bilva* leaves and lotus flowers. Perfuming the air with aloes, they devotedly proffered the best herbs. Reciting his 1,008 names, they bowed before the lord, pondering in their hearts how the two gods, Hari and Īśvara, could have entered into union since they had sprung from *sattva* and *tamas*, respectively.

The immortal lord knew what they were thinking, and so he assumed a universal form that bore all the auspicious marks and possessed every kind of weapon. The gods saw him at last with his three eyes, wearing earrings made of snakes and lotuses, sporting a topknot of matted hair, with a banner bearing bird and bull, along with Mādhava, whose chest bore a serpent necklace, and whose loins were draped with a yellow garment and an antelope skin; he was holding a discus and a sword in his hands, carrying a plough and a bow, and possessed the Pināka, the trident and the Ajagava weapon, with knotted hair, a skull-topped staff, a skull and a bell, and was making the skies echo with the call of his conch, O great seer.

When the gods, led by the one who sits on a lotus, saw Hari-Śankara, they bowed before him and cried aloud, "Praise be to you, immortal all-pervader!" And they considered the two to be wholly one.

The Goddess

The Death of Mahiṣa, the Buffalo Demon

When his army was being destroyed in this manner, the demon Mahiṣa himself, in the form of a buffalo, terrorized the troops of the goddess. Some of them he beat with his snout, others he trampled with his hooves, still others he lashed with his tail, while some were ripped to shreds by his horns. Some were thrown to the ground by his bellowing and the speed of his charge while others were felled by the gusts of his panting breath. After felling her troops, the demon rushed to attack the lion that was with the great goddess. At this Ambikā became enraged. The mighty; virile buffalo, whose hooves pounded the earth, also grew furious, smashing the lofty mountains with his horns and bellowing aloud. Trampled by his violent sallies, the earth was shattered, and the ocean, lashed by his hairy tail, overflowed on all sides. Shaken by his slashing horns, the troops were utterly dispersed. Mountains tumbled by the hundreds from the sky, struck down by the wind of his snorting breath.

When she saw this great demon attacking, swelling with rage, Caṇḍikā then became furious enough to destroy him. She threw her noose and lassoed the great Asura. Thus trapped in that mighty battle, he abandoned his buffalo shape and became a lion. At the moment Ambikā cut off its head, a man appeared; sword in hand. As soon as Ambikā cut down that man along with his sword and shield, the demon became a huge elephant. With a roar he dragged the goddess's lion along with his trunk, but while he was pulling the lion, she cut off his trunk with her sword. Then the great demon resumed his wondrous buffalo shape, causing all three worlds with their moving and unmoving creatures to tremble.

Provoked by this, Caṇḍikā, mother of the world, guzzled her supreme liquor, laughing and red-eyed. And the Asura, puffed up with pride in his own strength and bravery, bellowed aloud and tossed mountains at Caṇḍikā with his horns. Pulverizing those mountains that were hurled at her with arrows sent aloft, the goddess, excited by anger, her mouth red with liquor, cried out to him and his invincible troop, "Roar and bellow, but only as long as I drink the mead, you fool! In a moment the gods will be howling at you when you die by my hand!" So speaking, the goddess flew up and trod on his throat with her foot, piercing him with her spear. Crushed by her foot, overcome by the power of that goddess, the demon came half-way out of his own mouth. Still battling in this way, he was felled by the goddess who cut off his head with her mighty sword. So that demon Mahiṣa, his army and his allies, who had so distressed the three worlds, were all annihilated by the goddess.

At Mahiṣa's death, all the gods and demons, mankind and all creatures living in the three worlds cried "Victory!" And when the entire army of the lamenting Daityas was annihilated, the whole host of the gods went into exultant rapture. The gods and the great celestial seers praised that goddess, while Gandharva lords sang aloud and hosts of Apsarases danced.

The Birth of Kālī and the Final Battle

As they had been commanded, the Daityas, led by Caṇḍa and Muṇḍa, formed a four-fold army and sallied forth, their weapons raised aloft. They saw the goddess, smiling slightly, positioned on her lion atop the great golden peak of a mighty mountain. When they saw her, they made zealous efforts to seize her, while other demons from the battle approached her with bows and swords drawn. Then Ambikā became violently angry with her enemies, her face growing black as ink with rage. Suddenly there issued forth from between her eyebrows Kālī, with protruding fangs, carrying a sword and a noose, with a mottled, skull-topped staff, adorned with a necklace of human skulls, covered with a tiger-skin, gruesome with shriveled flesh. Her mouth gaping wide, her lolling tongue terrifying, her eyes red and sunken, she filled the whole of space with her howling. Attacking and killing the mighty demons, she devoured the armed force of the enemies of the gods. Seizing with one hand the elephants with their back-riders, drivers, warriors and bells, she hurled them into her maw. In the same way she chewed up warriors with their horses, chariots and charioteers, grinding them up most horribly with her teeth. One she grabbed by the hair of the head, another by the nape of the neck, another she trod underfoot while another she crushed against her chest. The mighty striking and throwing weapons loosed by those demons she caught in her mouth and pulverised in fury. She ravaged the entire army of powerful evil-souled Asuras; some she devoured while others she trampled; some were slain by the sword, others bashed by her skull-topped club, while other demons went to perdition crushed by the sharp points of her teeth.

Seeing the sudden demise of the whole Daitya army, Caṇḍa rushed to attack that most horrendous goddess Kālī. The great demon covered the terrible-eyed goddess with a shower of arrows while Muṇḍa hurled discuses by the thousands. Caught in her mouth, those weapons shone like myriad orbs of the sun entering the belly of the clouds. Then howling horribly, Kālī laughed aloud malevolently, her maw gaping wide, her fangs glittering, awful to behold. Astride her huge lion, the goddess rushed against Caṇḍa; grabbing his head by the hair, she decapitated him with her sword. When he saw Caṇḍa dead, Muṇḍa attacked, but she threw him too to the ground, stabbing him with her sword in rage. Seeing both Caṇḍa and the mighty Muṇḍa felled, the remains of the army fled in all directions, overcome with fear.

Grabbing the heads of the two demons, Kālī approached Caṇḍikā and shrieked, cackling with fierce, demoniac laughter, "I offer you Caṇḍa and Muṇḍa as the grand victims in the sacrifice of battle. Now you yourself will kill Śumbha and Niśumbha!" Witnessing this presentation of the two great Asuras, the eminent Caṇḍikā spoke graciously to Kālī, "Since you have captured Caṇḍa and Muṇḍa and have brought them to me, O goddess, you will be known as Cāmuṇḍā!" . . .

So speaking, the honorable goddess Caṇḍikā of fierce mettle vanished on the spot before the eyes of the gods. And all the gods, their enemies felled, performed their tasks without harassment and enjoyed their shares of the sacrifices. When Śumbha, enemy of the gods, world-destroyer, of mighty power and valor, had been slain in battle and the most valiant Niśumbha had been crushed, the rest of the Daityas went to the netherworld.

In such a way, then, does the divine goddess, although eternal, take birth again and again to protect creation. This world is deluded by her; it is begotten by her; it is she who gives knowledge when prayed to and prosperity when pleased. By Mahākālī is this entire egg of Brahmā pervaded, lord of men. At the awful time of dissolution she takes on the form of Mahāmārī, the great destructress of the world. She is also its unborn source; eternal, she sustains creatures in time. As Lakṣmī, or Good Fortune, she bestows wealth on men's homes in times of prosperity. In times of disaster she appears as Misfortune for their annihilation. When the goddess is praised and worshiped with flowers, incense, perfume and other gifts, she gives wealth, sons, a mind set upon Dharma, and happiness to all mankind.

Chapter 8

The *Bhāgavata Purāṇa*

The *Bhāgavata Purāṇa* is one of the many *Purāṇas*, Stories of the Ancient Past. Like other *Purāṇas* it was orally transmitted and composed. The *Bhāgavata*, as it is known to its readers, is devoted largely to Kṛṣṇa, one of the *avatāras*, incarnations, of the god Viṣṇu. Kṛṣṇa, who appears as an adult in the *Mahābhārata*, is depicted in the *Bhāgavata* amidst *līlā*, play, as a baby, a child, and as an amorous young adult cavorting with *gopīs*, cowgirls. The stories are intended to inspire *bhakti* for listeners. These purportedly biographical accounts of Kṛṣṇa thus play an essential role in the devotional life of worshipers of Kṛṣṇa.[1]

Imagery of Kṛṣṇa most often is taken from snippets of well-known stories from the *Bhāgavata*. These images and the stories which they portray inspire *bhakti*, devotion, in Kṛṣṇa. The stories are to have taken place in Vṛndāvana, now known as Vraj. Many devotees of Kṛṣṇa travel to Vraj (Braj) on a pilgrimage, and visit the sites that are associated with each story.[2]

Twelve *skandhas*, cantos, in length, the *Bhāgavata* was central to several traditions of Hinduism, including the Mādhva tradition of Vedānta and, in the west, the International Society for Krishna Consciousness which has its roots in the Bengali tradition of Caitanya. Its significance is evident given that many of these traditions expanded the canon to include the *Bhāgavata* and even to write *bhāṣyas*, commentaries, on it. These traditions largely ignored the amorous side of Kṛṣṇa in favor of the *dharmic*, dutiful, whose presence was to protect the world and maintain the stability of society.

Several of the stories included here are popular ones. The first story, *The Banishment of Kāliya* (10.16) is a well-liked story about young Kṛṣṇa's battle with Kāliya the sea snake. This story portrays Kṛṣṇa as a protector of the world who defeats those who conflict with *dharma*. 10.24, *Kṛṣṇa Diverts Indra's Sacrifice*, and *Kṛṣṇa Lifts Mount Govardhana* relate the story of how Kṛṣṇa makes his devotees turn their attention away from Indra, who was a god from the *Vedas*. The implication, is that *Vedic* practices are being supplanted by *bhakti* ones. Kṛṣṇa lifts Mount Govardhana to protect his devotees from Indra's wrath.

Chapters 10.29, 30, and 31 concern Kṛṣṇa as a dallying lover who tempts the *gopīs* to abandon their duties to chase after the flirtatious god. He is intimate with each *gopī* and, when he leaves them, each longs to be united with him again. Such stories are intended to convey the image of the ideal *bhakta*, devotee, who is willing to renounce all in search of god. These themes of love are also to be found in Bengali *bhakti* poetry, written much later, but still directed towards Kṛṣṇa.[3] 10.80 and 10.81, *The Story of Śrīdāma* and *The Episode of the Flat Rice*, relate a tale of a poor but devoted friend of Kṛṣṇa who is awarded for his *bhakti* devotion. The last excerpt, 11.31, *Kṛṣṇa Returns to his own Abode*, relates how Kṛṣṇa leaves earth and references *līlā*, divine play, and the importance of *bhakti*.

Notes

1 Edwin Bryant (tr.), *Krishna: The Beautiful Legend of God*. New York: Penguin, 2003.
2 David Haberman, *Journey Through the Twelve Forests: An Encounter with Krishna*. New York: Oxford University Press, 1994.
3 Edward Dimock, *In Praise of Krishna*. Chicago: University of Chicago Press, 1967.

Further reading

Bryant, Edwin (tr.), *Krishna: The Beautiful Legend of God*. New York: Penguin, 2003.
Dimock, Edward, *In Praise of Krishna*. Chicago: University of Chicago Press, 1967.
Haberman, David, *Journey Through the Twelve Forests: An Encounter with Krishna*, New York: Oxford University Press, 1994.
Hardy, Friedhelm, *Viraha-bhakti: The Early History of Krsna Devotion in South India*. Delhi: Oxford University Press, 2001.
Hawley, John Stratton, *Krishna, the Butter Thief.* Princeton, NJ: Princeton University Press, 1983.
Hiltebeitel, Alf, *The Ritual of Battle: Krishna in the Mahābhārata*. Albany, NY: State University of New York Press, 1990.
Singer, Milton (ed.), *Krishna: Myths, Rites, and Attitudes*. Chicago: University of Chicago Press, 1966.

The Bhāgavata Purāṇa

Chapter 16

The Banishment of Kāliya

1. *Śrī* Śuka said:

'After seeing the Yamunā polluted by the black snake, Kṛṣṇa, the Almighty Lord, desired to purify it, and so banished that serpent.'

2. The king said:

'How did *Bhagavān* subdue the serpent in the depths of the waters? How had the snake come to reside there for so many ages? Please relate how this took place, O *brāhmaṇa*.

3. Who could be satiated from tasting the nectar of the exalted pastimes of the all-pervasive Gopāla [Kṛṣṇa], O *brāhmaṇa*? He acts according to his own pleasure.'

4. *Śrī* Śuka said:

'In the Yamunā river there was a pool which was boiling from the fire of Kāliya's poison. Birds flying overhead plummeted into it.

5. All moving and non-moving living entities in the vicinity of the shore died when touched by the spray borne by the wind from the poison-laden waves of the pool.

6. Seeing the contaminated river and the potency of that highly toxic poison, Kṛṣṇa, whose incarnation was to subdue the wicked, climbed a very high *kadamba* tree. With his belt well-fastened, he slapped his arms and jumped into the poisonous water.

7. The serpent was greatly provoked by the force of the supreme being's plunge. He exhaled poison into masses of matter, which overflowed in waves on all sides of the serpent's pool. Lethal from the toxicity of the poison, these waves flooded for a distance of over one hundred bows. But what is this for Kṛṣṇa, who has unlimited power?

8. Kāliya, whose eyes were his ears, heard the commotion of the water churned by the mighty arms of Kṛṣṇa, who was sporting in the pond, as powerful as a mighty elephant, O king. Observing such a lack of respect for his abode, Kāliya came forth, unable to tolerate it.

9. Kṛṣṇa was playing without fear of anyone. Dressed in yellow, and bearing the mark of *śrīvatsa*, he was delicately youthful, gorgeous to behold and luminous as a cloud. His beautiful face was smiling, and his feet resembled the inside of a lotus. Kāliya furiously bit Kṛṣṇa's tender parts and wrapped his coils around him.

10. Seeing Kṛṣṇa apparently motionless and enveloped by the coils of the serpent, his dear friends the *gopas* collapsed in great distress, their minds overcome by fear, sorrow and pain. They had dedicated their desires, their wives, their wealth, their relatives and their own selves to Kṛṣṇa.

11. The cows, bulls and female calves were greatly distressed. With their eyes fixed on Kṛṣṇa, they were bellowing fearfully and stood as if weeping.

12. Then three kinds of extremely terrifying and ominous portents – on the earth, in the sky, and on people – arose in Vraj. They forewarned of imminent danger.

13. Learning that Kṛṣṇa had gone to graze the cows without Balarāma, the *gopas*, led by Nanda, were struck with fear on seeing these portents.

14. Because of the inauspicious signs, and unaware of who Kṛṣṇa really was, the *gopas* thought Kṛṣṇa had met his death. Their minds were absorbed in Kṛṣṇa and they had surrendered their life to him, and so they were struck by fear, distress and pain.

15. All the cowherd folk, from children to elders and women, O king, feeling miserable, left Gokula anxious for a sight of Kṛṣṇa.

16. Seeing them despairing in this way, Lord Balarāma, the descendant of Madhu, laughed, knowing the power of his younger brother. But he said nothing.

Excerpts from Edwin Bryant (tr.), *Krishna: The Beautiful Legend of God.* Harmondsworth: Penguin Books, 2003.

17. Searching for their beloved Kṛṣṇa along the path by means of his footprints, which were marked with the signs of God, the cowherd folk went to the banks of the Yamunā.

18. Seeing the footsteps of the Lord of their community here and there mixed in with the other footprints of the cows on the path, O king, they rushed along. These footprints bore the marks of the flag, the thunderbolt, the goad, the barley and the lotus.

19. Seeing Kṛṣṇa motionless in the body of water in the distance and enveloped in the coils of the serpent in the lake, and seeing the cows and cowherd men in distress everywhere, the cowherd folk were struck with utter despair and cried out in anguish.

20. The *gopīs*' minds were attached to the unlimited Lord. Remembering his affectionate smiles, glances and words, they were overcome with utter grief as their beloved was being seized by the serpent. They perceived the three worlds as void without their dear one.

21. They prevented Kṛṣṇa's mother from following her child [into the lake], although they were as distressed as she. Pouring out their sorrow, and telling stories about the darling of Vraj, each one remained still as a corpse, their eyes fixed on the face of Kṛṣṇa.

22. Lord Balarāma was aware of the potency of Kṛṣṇa. Seeing Nanda and the others, for whom Kṛṣṇa was their very life, about to enter the lake, he restrained them.

23. Kṛṣṇa remained for some time, assuming the behavior of a human being in this manner. Then, seeing that his own Gokula community, including women and children, which had no shelter other than in him, was in great distress, he realized that it was on his account and rose up from the bonds of the serpent.

24. The serpent, his coils tormented by the extended body of Kṛṣṇa, released him. Enraged, the serpent raised his hoods and drew himself erect as he looked at the Lord. His face had unmoving eyes like burning charcoal and he was breathing through his nostrils as from pots of poison.

25. Kṛṣṇa circled around him, toying with him. Like Garuḍa [Suparṇaka], the king of birds, Kṛṣṇa manoeuvred around waiting for his opportunity. The serpent had eyes fiery with dreadful poison and repeatedly licked the two corners of his mouth with his forked tongue.

26. Bending the raised neck of the serpent, whose strength had been depleted by this circling around, Kṛṣṇa, the original being, climbed on to its massive hoods. Then, the original teacher of all art forms danced, his lotus feet made red by contact with the heaps of jewels on the serpent's head.

27. Then his followers – the celestial *gandharvas, siddhas*, sages, *cāraṇas*, and young wives of the gods – seeing that Kṛṣṇa had begun to dance, immediately approached in delight with eulogies, offerings, flowers, songs, musical instruments and various types of drums such as *mṛdaṅgas, paṇavas* and *ānakas*.

28. Kṛṣṇa, chastiser of the wicked, crushed whichever head of that hundred-and-one-headed snake would not bend with blows of his feet, O king. The snake's span of life was running out and he was whirling around. He vomited blood profusely from his nose and mouth and was overcome by utter desperation.

29. The serpent was breathing fiercely from anger and was discharging poison from his eyes. Whichever head he raised up, Kṛṣṇa forced him to bow low, striking it with his feet as he danced. As he was being worshipped with flowers, that most ancient being forced the snake to submit in the lake.

30. The serpent, his body broken, and his 1,000 hoods battered by that extraordinary dancing, was spewing blood from his mouths, O king. He remembered that most ancient being, Nārāyaṇa, the teacher of all moving and non-moving entities, and surrendered to him in his mind.

31. The wives of the snake, whose hood umbrellas had been smashed by heel blows, saw that he had been crushed by the extreme weight of Kṛṣṇa, who bears the universe in his abdomen. They approached the original being

in distress, with the locks of their hair, ornaments and clothing loosened.

32. Deeply agitated in mind and with their children placed in front of them, they prostrated their bodies on the ground, and offered obeisance to Kṛṣṇa, the Lord of creatures. These righteous ladies folded their hands in supplication and approached the giver of shelter for shelter, desiring the liberation of their wicked husband.

33. The serpent's wives said: "Punishment is certainly fitting for this offender. Your incarnation is for the subjugation of the wicked. You view sons and even enemies with impartiality. In fact, you mete out punishment after considering its benefits.

34. In fact, what has happened to us is your Lordship's blessing. Your punishment of the unrighteous is undoubtedly that which destroys their sin. Even your anger is considered really to be a blessing for this embodied soul who has found himself in the form of this snake.

35. He has renounced his pride and paid his respects – what austere practice did he previously perform so that your Lordship, who is the life of everything, is satisfied? Or was it his righteous and compassionate behaviour towards all living entities?

36. We do not know what were the grounds of his qualification for contacting the dust from your feet, O Lord. The goddess of fortune, a lady, undertook ascetic practices out of a desire for those feet – she gave up pleasures, and maintained her vow for a long time.

37. Those who have attained the dust of your feet do not desire the highest heaven, nor sovereignty over the earth, nor the highest situation [of Brahmā], nor lordship over the lower worlds, nor the mystic powers of *yoga*, nor freedom from rebirth.

38. This lord of serpents, although *tāmasic* in birth after birth and controlled by anger, has obtained that which is difficult for others to obtain, O master. Abounding wealth appears before the eyes of the embodied soul, wandering in the cycle of *saṃsāra*, who desires to obtain this.

39. Reverence to you, *Bhagavān*. You are the great soul, the supreme being, the abode of the world, the world, transcendence, and the supreme soul.

40. Reverence to you, *brahman*. You are the storehouse of knowledge and wisdom, unlimited in powers, without qualities, changeless and original.

41. You are time, the hub of time, the witness of the phases of time, the universe, its observer and maker, and the cause of the universe.

42. You are the soul in the heart, the mind, the vital airs, the senses and the subtle elements. The ability to see you in person is hidden by [people's] pride and the three *guṇas*.

43. You are unlimited, subtle, pre-eminent, wise, the fulfilment of different doctrines, the potency of the speaker and that which is spoken.

44. You are the root of all epistemology, the author and source of scripture. Reverence again and again to you who are the Veda and who are activity and inactivity.

45. Reverence to you Kṛṣṇa, son of Vasudeva. Reverence to Rāma, Pradyumna, Aniruddha, Lord of the Sātvatas.

46. Reverence to you who are the light of the *guṇas*, who cover yourself with the *guṇas*, who can be inferred from the activity of the *guṇas*, who are the witness of the *guṇas* and who are self-knowing.

47. Your pastimes are unfathomable, and you are the conclusion of everything that has been expounded. You are a sage accustomed to silence – let there be obeisance unto you, O Hṛṣīkeśa [Kṛṣṇa].

48. Reverence to you. You know the workings of that which is superior and that which is inferior. You are the overseer of everything, you are transcendent as well as immanent, and you are the witness as well as the cause of this world.

49. Although you are neutral, it is actually you, O omnipresent one, who have brought about the birth, maintenance and destruction of this world by means of the *guṇas*. You are the upholder of the power of time. Through your glance, you awaken the latent

dispositions of each of the *guṇas*, within everything that exists. Your pastimes are infallible.

50. The bodies of whatever exists in the three worlds are from you. They are born of those beings who are peaceful [*sāttvic*], agitated [*rājasic*] as well as ignorant [*tāmasic*]. The peaceful ones are the ones who are dear to you. As the Lord, you now wish to protect the righteous out of a desire to preserve *dharma*.

51. The master should tolerate a solitary transgression performed by his own subject. You have a peaceful nature, so please forgive this fool who is ignorant of you.

52. Be merciful, O *Bhagavān*. This serpent is giving up his life. Our husband is our life – please return him to us. We are women, and should be pitied by those who are righteous.

53. We are your servants: tell us what we should do. One is undoubtedly freed from all kinds of fear by complying with your command with faith." '

54. *Śrī* Śuka said:

'When he was extolled in this way by the wives of the serpent, *Bhagavān* released the broken-headed snake, who was unconscious from the blows of his feet.

55. The wretched Kāliya slowly regained his vital airs and senses. Breathing again with difficulty, he spoke to Hari with his hands joined in submission.

56. Kāliya said: "We are miscreants, full of wrath and *tāmasic* from birth. One renounces one's personal nature with difficulty, O Lord, because it clings to falsehood.

57. This universe is an emanation of the *guṇas*, and has been generated by you, O creator. It contains a variety of natures, potencies, powers, wombs, latent dispositions and forms.

58. And in this universe, O *Bhagavān*, we serpents are extremely wrathful as a species. How can we, who are deluded, shake off your *māyā* by ourselves? It is so hard to cast off.

59. Your Lordship is the means to do this. You are the all-knowing Lord of the universe. Bestow either compassion or chastisement on us as you see fit." '

60. *Śrī* Śuka said:

'After listening to this, *Bhagavān*, who took human form for a purpose, spoke these words: "You should not remain here, serpent. Go to the ocean with your relatives and wives. Do not delay. Let the cows and people enjoy the river.

61. Any mortal being who remembers my command to you, and recites it at the two junctures of day and night, will never experience fear of you.

62. Whoever fasts and bathes here, the place of my pastime, or satisfies the gods with water, or worships while remembering me, is freed from all sins.

63. You left the island of Ramaṇaka out of fear of the eagle, Garuḍa, and took shelter of this lake. He will not eat you. You have been marked by my feet." '

64. The sage said:

'When he had been let free by Kṛṣṇa *Bhagavān*, whose activities are marvellous, the snake, along with his wives, worshipped Kṛṣṇa with joy and with respect.

65–66. He worshipped and pleased the Lord of the universe, whose banner is Garuḍa, with celestial clothes, garlands, jewels, outstanding ornaments, divine scents, ointments and a magnificent garland of blue lotuses. When he was granted leave to go, he circumambulated Kṛṣṇa and saluted him in good spirits.

67. Then he left for an island in the ocean with his wives, friends and sons. From that time on, the nectarean water of the Yamunā became free from poison through the mercy of *Bhagavān*, who had assumed a human form for sport.'

[. . .]

Chapter 24

Kṛṣṇa Diverts Indra's Sacrifice

1. *Śrī* Śuka said:

'As he was residing there in Vraj with Balarāma, *Bhagavān* Kṛṣṇa saw the *gopas* making preparations for Indra's sacrifice.

2. *Bhagavān* Kṛṣṇa is the seer of everything as well as the soul of everything; despite knowing all about it, he bowed down reverentially and inquired of the elders headed by Nanda:

3. "Tell me, father, what is this bustle that has arisen? Why is this sacrifice being performed, from what incentive and by whom?

4–5. Explain this to me, father – I am curious to hear about it and my desire is great. Surely, the deeds of *sādhus* are not secret. They see the *ātmā* within everything in this world. They do not distinguish between what is their own and what is another's, and they have no friends, enemies or neutral relationships. It is said that a neutral party is to be avoided like an enemy, but a friend is like one's own self.

6. These people perform actions [the purpose of which] they either understand or do not understand. Success in action will be granted to the one who has knowledge, but not for the one who is ignorant.

7. This being so, is this act of *yoga* something that has received careful deliberation, or is it popular practice? This should be clearly explained to me, for I am asking."

8. *Śrī* Nanda said: "*Bhagavān* Indra is the rain. The clouds are the manifestations of his being. They release water, the nourishing life-force of living things.

9. He is the lord and master of the clouds, my son; other people also worship him, just as we do, by sacrifices of the products of his flow of water.

10. They subsist with the remnants in order to accomplish the threefold goals of life. The rain-god produces fruit for people engaged in human undertakings.

11. The person who neglects this duty handed down by tradition, out of lust, animosity, fear or greed, definitely does not achieve auspicious results." '

12. *Śrī* Śuka said:

'After hearing the words of Nanda and the other residents of Vraj, Keśava spoke to his father, provoking the indignation of Indra.

13. *Śrī Bhagavān* said: "The living entity is born because of *karma* and perishes because of *karma*. Happiness, distress, fear and security all arrive because of *karma* alone.

14. Even if there is some kind of a controller who awards the fruit of the *karma* of other people, he can only interact with a person engaged in action. He is certainly not the master of one who does not engage in action.

15. What can Indra do to living beings who are following their own *karma*? He is incapable of doing anything other than what has been determined as a result of people's own nature.

16. People are actually controlled by their own nature and they act according to their own nature. This whole universe with gods, demons and humankind exists in its own nature.

17. It is as a result of *karma* that the living being accepts and then gives up higher and lower bodies. It is *karma* alone that is the enemy, friend or impartial observer, the *guru* and the lord.

18. One's deity is actually that through which one is able to subsist easily. Therefore, grounded in one's own nature and performing one's duty, one should worship *karma*.

19. If one entity is the means of subsistence, while another entity is dependent on something else, then one cannot find security in the latter, just as an unfaithful woman will not find security in a paramour.

20. A *brāhmaṇa* should subsist by means of the Veda, the *kṣatriya* by the protection of the earth, the *vaiśya* by business, and the *śūdra* by service to the twice-born.

21. There are four types of business: agriculture, trade and cow-protection, as well as money-lending, which is said to be the fourth. From these, we have always taken subsistence from the cows.

22. The causes of maintenance, production and destruction are *sattva, rajas* and *tamas. Rajas* produces the entire universe, which is given shape by mutual interaction.

23. The clouds are propelled by *raja*, and they shower water everywhere. Living beings prosper as a result of clouds alone. What can the mighty Indra do?

24. Cities are not for us, father, nor are inhabited countries, villages and homesteads. We are forest-dwellers, living in forests and hills.

25. Therefore, let us begin a sacrifice for Mount Govardhana, the *brāhmaṇas* and the cows. Let this sacrifice be accomplished with these very utensils that are for Indra's sacrifice!

26. People should prepare various types of cooked food, starting with soup and ending with a pudding made from rice, as well as *saṃyāva, āpūpa* and *śuṣkalī* cakes. And all the milk-products should be collected.

27–28. The sacrificial fires should receive oblations from the *brāhmaṇas* who recite the Veda. All of you should give many kinds of food and donations of cows to the *brāhmaṇas*, as well as to others also, up to the *cāṇḍālas* [outcastes], and dogs, as is appropriate. And, after grass has been given to the cows, offerings should be made to the mountain.

29. Then, when you are nicely adorned, adequately smeared [with sandalwood paste], handsomely dressed and well fed, walk round the cows, the *brāhmaṇas*, the fire and the hill in a clockwise direction.

30. This is my opinion, father, which can be followed if it is approved. Such a sacrifice will be pleasing to the cows, the *brāhmaṇas* and the mountains, and to me as well."'

31. *Śrī* Śuka said:

'Hearing those words spoken by *Bhagavān* Kṛṣṇa, who, in the form of time, desired to destroy the pride of Indra, Nanda and the others accepted his words as appropriate.

32–33. They prepared everything just as Madhusūdana [Kṛṣṇa] had said. Auspicious blessings were chanted, and offerings presented with full respect to the twice-born and to the hill with those same utensils, as well as grass to the cows. Then, they circumambulated the hill, with their riches – their cattle – in front.

34. The beautifully adorned *gopīs* mounted the carts, which were yoked to the oxen. They were singing of the exploits of Kṛṣṇa in harmony with the uttering of blessings of the twice-born.

35. Then Kṛṣṇa transformed himself into another body to gain the confidence of the *gopas*. Saying: "I am the mountain!" the huge form ate the lavish offering.

36. Together with the people of Vraj, Kṛṣṇa prostrated himself before that form – which was really himself – saying: "*Aho!* Look – this mountain is assuming a form! It has bestowed its favour upon us.

37. Assuming any form at will, it kills the human residents of the forest who disregard it. We should prostrate ourselves before it for the protection of our cows and ourselves."

38. After performing the sacrifice to the twice-born, the cows and the hill, as directed by Vāsudeva in this fashion, the *gopas* went to Vraj along with Kṛṣṇa.'

Chapter 25

Kṛṣṇa Lifts Mount Govardhana

1. *Śī* Śuka said:

'At this, O king, Indra understood that his own worship had been abandoned, and became enraged with the *gopas*, led by Nanda, who had accepted Kṛṣṇa as their Lord.

2. Considering himself Lord, Indra summoned the host of clouds called Samvartaka which bring about the annihilation of the universe. Furious, he spoke the following words:

3. "Just see how intoxicated the forest-dwelling *gopas* are because of the wealth [of the forest]. They have taken refuge with Kṛṣṇa, a mortal, and now they neglect the gods.

4. Abandoning meditative knowledge, they desire to cross over the ocean of material existence through ritualistic so-called sacrifices which are like unstable boats.

5. By taking refuge with Kṛṣṇa, a boastful, childish, stubborn, ignorant mortal who thinks himself to be a great scholar, the *gopas* have made an enemy of me.

6. Destroy the arrogance of these people caused by the conceit of riches. They are steeped in wealth and their egos have been inflated by Kṛṣṇa. Bring destruction to their livestock.

7. As for me, I will mount my elephant Airāvata, and follow you to Vraj accompanied by the immensely powerful host of Maruts, with the intention of destroying the cattle station of Nanda." '

8. *Śrī* Śuka said:

'Ordered on this way by Indra, the clouds, unleashed from their moorings, deluged rain on Nanda's Gokula.

9. Flashing forth with lightning and roaring with claps of thunder, they showered down hail, urged on by the fierce hosts of Maruts.

10. The clouds released incessant torrents of rain as thick as pillars, and the earth became inundated with floods. Low ground could not be distinguished from high ground.

11. The livestock, shivering because of the high wind and rain, and the *gopas* and *gopīs*, afflicted by cold, approached Kṛṣṇa for protection.

12. Covering their heads and shielding their children with their bodies, shivering and tormented by the rain, they approached the soles of the feet of the Lord:

13. "Kṛṣṇa, most virtuous Kṛṣṇa, master – you are compassionate towards your devotees. Please protect Gokula, which accepts you as Lord, from the wrath of this divinity."

14. Seeing them pounded unconscious by the excessive wind and hail, Lord Hari reflected on what Indra had done in his fury:

15. "Indra unleashes rain full of hail and mighty winds out of season in order to destroy us because we neglected his offering.

16. Consequently, I will employ suitable countermeasures through my mystic power. I will destroy the ignorance and pride born of opulence of those who, out of stupidity, think of themselves as lords of the world.

17. The bewilderment caused by thinking of oneself as lord is inappropriate for the demigods, who are endowed with a godly nature. If I break the pride of the impure for their peace of mind it is an appropriate thing to do.

18. Therefore, I make this pledge: I shall protect the cowherd community by my own mystic power. They accept me as their Lord, their shelter is in me and they are my family."

19. Saying this, Viṣṇu lifted up the mountain of Govardhana with one hand and held it effortlessly, as a child holds a mushroom.

20. Then the Lord spoke to the cowherds: "Mother, father and residents of Vraj, enter the cavity under the mountain with your herds of cows whenever you wish.

21. Do not be afraid that the mountain might fall from my hand during this time. Enough of your fear of the rain and wind! I have arranged shelter from them for you."

22. At this, reassured by Kṛṣṇa, they entered the cavity with their wealth, their herds and dependants as far as there was room for them.

23. Giving up concern for hunger and thirst, and any expectation of comfort, Kṛṣṇa held up the mountain for seven days. Watched by the residents of Vraj, he did not move from the spot.

24. Subdued and helpless, and with his plan thwarted, Indra reined in his clouds. He was awed by Kṛṣṇa's mystic power.

25. When he saw that the sky was cloudless, the fierce rain and wind had ceased, and that the sun had arisen, Govardhanadhara [Kṛṣṇa], he who lifted Mount Govardhana, spoke to the *gopas*:

26. "Don't be afraid, O *gopas*, and come out with your wives, possessions and children. The wind and rain have ceased, and the rivers are for the most part without [flood] water."

27. At this, the *gopas*, women, children and elders each took their own cows and their utensils, which had been loaded on to carts, and came out slowly.

28. While all watched, *Bhagavān*, the Lord, effortlessly put back the hill where it had been.

29. The people of Vraj were filled with the force of love, and came to embrace him, or whatever was appropriate. And with joy the *gopīs* offered auspicious blessings, and with love worshipped him with offerings of yogurt and unhusked barley, and other such items.

30. Overcome with love, Yaśodā, Rohiṇī, Nanda and Balarāma, best of the strong, embraced Kṛṣṇa and offered blessings.

31. The hosts of gods, the *siddhas, sādhyas, gandharvas* and *cāraṇas* in the heavens,

satisfied, praised Kṛṣṇa and let fall showers of flowers, O Parīkṣit, descendant of Pṛthu.

32. Directed by the gods, they played conches and kettledrums in heaven, while the leaders of the *gandharvas*, headed by Tumburu, sang.

33. Then, O king, Hari, together with Balarāma, went to his own cow-pen surrounded by the friendly cowherders. The *gopīs* happily went on their way singing about such deeds as this. Their hearts were touched.'

[...]

Chapter 29

The Description of the Rāsa *Pastime*

1. *Śrī* Śuka, the son of Bādarāyaṇa, said:

'Even *Bhagavān*, God himself, beholding those nights, with autumnal jasmine [*mallikā*] flowers blossoming, called upon his divine power of *yogamāyā*, and turned his thoughts towards enjoying love.

2. At that time, the moon, king of the constellations, arose in the east, covering the face of the heavens with its copper-coloured soothing rays. It wiped away the cares of the onlookers, like a lover who has been absent for a long time wipes away the cares of his beloved.

3. Seeing that full disc, heralder of the white night-lilies, reddened with fresh vermilion powder, its splendour like the face of Lakṣmī, the goddess of fortune, and seeing the forest coloured by its silky rays, Kṛṣṇa played [his flute] softly, capturing the hearts of the beautiful-eyed women.

4. The music aroused Kāma. When they heard it, the women of Vraj, enchanted by Kṛṣṇa, came to their lover, their earrings swinging in their haste, and unknown to one another.

5. Some, who were milking cows, abandoned the milking and approached eagerly. Others had put milk on the fire, but then came without even removing [the milk or] the cakes [from the oven].

6–7. Others interrupted serving food, feeding their babies milk, and attending to their husbands. Still others were eating, but left their food. Others were putting on make-up, washing, or applying mascara to their eyes. They all went to be near Kṛṣṇa, their clothes and ornaments in disarray.

8. Their hearts had been stolen by Govinda, so they did not turn back when husbands, fathers, brothers and relatives tried to prevent them. They were in a state of rapture.

9. Some *gopīs*, not being able to find a way to leave, remained at home and thought of Kṛṣṇa with eyes closed, completely absorbed in meditation.

10–11. [The *karma*] from their impious deeds was destroyed by the intense and intolerable pain of separation from their lover, and their auspicious deeds were diminished by the complete fulfilment resulting from the intimate contact with Acyuta that they obtained through meditation. Their bondage was destroyed, and they immediately left their bodies made of the *guṇas*. Uniting with the supreme soul, they considered him their lover.'

12. *Śrī* Parīkṣit said:

'O sage, they related to Kṛṣṇa as their supreme lover, not as *brahman*, the absolute truth. So how did the flow of the *guṇas*, in which their minds were absorbed, cease for the *gopīs*?'

13. *Śrī* Śuka said:

'This was explained to you previously: in the same way as the king of the Cedis, Śiśupāla, attained perfection despite hating Hṛṣīkeśa. What then of those dear to Adhokṣaja [Kṛṣṇa]?

14. God appears for the supreme good of humanity, O king. He is immeasurable and eternal. As the controller of the *guṇas*, he is beyond the *guṇas*.

15. Those who always dedicate their desire, anger, fear, affection, sense of identity and friendship to Hari enter for certain into his state of being.

16. You should not show such surprise at Lord Kṛṣṇa. He is unborn and the master of all masters of *yoga*. From him the whole universe attains liberation.

17. The Lord saw that the women of Vraj had arrived in his presence. Being the best of

speakers, he addressed them, captivating them with the charm of his words:

18. "Welcome – you are most fortunate. What can I do to please you? Is everything well in Vraj? Tell me the purpose of your coming.

19. This fearsome dark night is frequented by ferocious creatures. Go back to Vraj, O slender-waisted ones; this place is not fit for women.

20. Your mothers, fathers, sons, brothers and husbands are worried because they cannot find you. Do not cause your relatives concern.

21–22. You have seen the forest, adorned with flowers, coloured by the rays of the full moon, and made beautiful by the blossoms of the trees quivering playfully in the breeze of the Yamunā river. Therefore hurry now to the cow-pen and serve your husbands – you are chaste ladies. The babies and calves are crying; suckle them and milk them.

23. Or perhaps your hearts are captivated, and you have come out of love for me. This is commendable of you – living beings delight in me.

24. The highest *dharma* [duty] of a woman is to serve her husband faithfully, to ensure the well-being of her relatives, and to nourish her children.

25. A husband who is not a sinner, even though he be of bad character, ill-fated, old, dull-headed, sick or poor, should not be abandoned by women who desire to attain heaven.

26. Without exception, the adultery of a woman of good birth does not lead to heaven. It is scandalous, fear-laden, worthless, fraught with difficulty and abhorrent.

27. Love for me comes from hearing about me, seeing me, meditating on me and reciting my glories – not in this way, by physical proximity. Therefore, return to your homes."

28. Hearing Govinda speak these unwelcome words, the dejected *gopīs* had their aspirations dashed and were inconsolable in their distress.

29. They stood silently, their red *bimba*-fruit-coloured lips faded by their sighs, and the vermilion powder on their breasts smeared by the mascara carried by their tears. Casting down their faces out of sorrow and scratching the ground with their feet, they were weighed down by extreme unhappiness.

30. Wiping their eyes, and having checked their tears somewhat, the *gopīs* spoke to Kṛṣṇa, their beloved, with voices faltering with agitation. They were utterly devoted, and had sacrificed all desires for his sake, but he had replied to them as if he were anything but their beloved:

31. "You should not speak to us in such a heartless fashion, O Lord. Renouncing all enjoyments of the senses, we are devoted to the soles of your feet. Reciprocate, you obstinate one, just as the Lord, the original being, reciprocates with those who desire liberation. Do not reject us.

32. You, the knower of *dharma*, have declared that the occupational *dharma* of women consists of attending to friends, husbands and children. Then let this be our *dharma* when it comes to you, the source of this advice, O Lord – after all, you are the soul within all relatives. Indeed, you are the most dear of all embodied beings.

33. You are the eternal beloved, O soul of all, and so the learned place their affection in you. What is the use of husbands and children who simply cause problems? Therefore, O supreme Lord, be pleased with us. Do not dash our hopes. They have been sustained by you for such a long time, O lotus-eyed one.

34. Our hearts, which were absorbed in our households, have been stolen away with ease by you, as have our hands from domestic chores. Our feet cannot move one step from the soles of your lotus feet. How can we go to Vraj? And, besides, what would we do there?

35. O beloved, pour the nectar of your lips on the fire dwelling in our hearts which has been kindled by your musical harmonies, your glances and your smiles. If you do not, we will traverse the path to your feet through meditation, our bodies consumed by the fire born of separation.

36. Lotus-eyed Kṛṣṇa, you are dear to the forest-dwelling hermits. Somewhere or other, for a moment, we providentially touched the

soles of your feet, which belong to the goddess of fortune. Alas, from that moment, instantly enamoured of you, we became incapable of remaining in the presence of any other man.

37. The goddess of fortune aspires to the dust of those lotus feet which is worshipped by your servants, even though she has obtained a place on your chest along with Tulasī. Other gods, even, strive to attract her personal glance. In the same way, we solicit the dust of your feet.

38. It is you who banish distress – therefore be compassionate to us. In the desire to worship you, we have given up our homes and arrived at the soles of your feet. Allow us, whose hearts are burning with intense desire born from your beautiful smiles and glances, to be your servants, O ornament of men.

39. We have gazed on your face covered with curls, with its smiles and glances, and on your honeyed lips placed between your cheeks made beautiful with earrings. And we have beheld your two strong arms, which bestow fearlessness, and your chest, which is the exclusive delight of the goddess of fortune. After this, we have become your servants.

40. Dear Kṛṣṇa, what women in the three worlds would not stray from the behaviour proper to Āryans, when thrown into turmoil by the melodies of your flute, which vibrates harmoniously? And what woman would not stray after seeing this, your form, which brings good fortune to the three worlds and causes the hair of cows, birds, trees and deer to stand on end with bliss?

41. It is clear that you have accepted birth to remove the tribulations and fears of Vraj just as the Lord, the primeval person, protects the denizens of heaven. Therefore, since you are the friend of the afflicted, place your lotus hands on the burning breasts and heads of your servants." '

42. *Śrī* Śuka said:

'The master of the masters of *yoga*, hearing their despairing words, laughed and engaged in amorous pleasures from compassion, even though his satisfaction is self-contained.

43. Kṛṣṇa, the infallible one, whose conduct is upright, shone forth with the assembled *gopīs*, who were dazzling with jasmine teeth and broad smiles. As the *gopīs'* faces blossomed from the glances of their beloved, Kṛṣṇa appeared like the moon surrounded by stars.

44. Praised in song, and singing loudly himself, the Lord of hundreds of women, wearing a garland of *vaijayantī* flowers, frolicked in the forest, making it beautiful.

45–46. Accompanied by the *gopīs*, Kṛṣṇa approached the bank of the river. Its cool sand was swept by a wind bearing the scent of *kumuda* flowers and refreshing from its contact with the waves. Arousing Kāma in the young women of Vraj with jokes, smiles and glances, playfully scratching their breasts, girdles, thighs, hair and hands with his nails, and embracing them with outstretched arms, he gave them pleasure.

47. Such attention from Kṛṣṇa *Bhagavān*, the supreme soul, made the *gopīs* proud. Indeed, they thought themselves to be the best of women on earth.

48. Keśava saw their pride, which was born from the exhilaration of their good fortune, and vanished from the spot out of kindness, in order to moderate [their pride].'

Chapter 30

Searching for Kṛṣṇa in the Rāsa *Pastime*

1. *Śrī* Śuka said:

'When *Bhagavān* suddenly vanished, the women of Vraj were filled with remorse at his disappearance. They were like female elephants who had lost sight of the leader of the herd.

2. Intoxicated by the pleasing gestures, playfulness and words, as well as by the quivering glances, smiles of love and movements of Kṛṣṇa, the husband of Ramā, the goddess of fortune, their minds were overwhelmed. They acted out each of those behaviours, their hearts [dedicated] to him.

3. Those beloved women were so bewildered by Kṛṣṇa's pastimes that their bodies imitated their darling in the way they moved, smiled, glanced, spoke, and so forth. With their hearts [dedicated] to him, the women declared: "I am he!"

4. Singing loudly in unison only about him, they searched from grove to grove, like mad women. They asked the trees about the supreme being who, like space, is inside and outside living creatures:

5. "O *aśvattha* tree! O *plakṣa* tree! O *nyagrodha* tree! Have you seen the son of Nanda at all? He has stolen our minds with his glances and smiles of love, and has gone.

6. O *kurabaka, aśoka, nāga, punnāga* and *campaka* trees! Has the younger brother of Balarāma [passed] by here? His smile steals away the pride of haughty women.

7. O auspicious *tulasī* plant, you who are dear to Govinda! Have you seen your most beloved, Acyuta, wearing you [as a garland covered] with swarms of bees?

8. O *mālatī* plant! O *mallikā* plant! O *jātī* plant! O *yūthikā* plant! Has Mādhava [Kṛṣṇa] passed by, awakening your love with the touch of his hand? Have you seen him?

9. O *cūta* [mango], *priyāla, panasa* [breadfruit], *asana, kovidāra, jambū* [rose-apple], *arka, bilva* [wood-apple], *bakula, āmra* [mango], *kadamba* and *nipa* trees, and those others which grow on the shore of the Yamunā river and which exist to benefit others! Point us to the path [taken] by Kṛṣṇa. We have lost our hearts.

10. O earth, you are beautiful in that the hairs of your body [the trees] stand up from the bliss of the touch of the feet of Keśava [Kṛṣṇa]. What ascetic practice have you performed? Is the cause of this these very feet [of Kṛṣṇa]? Or is it because of the step of Urukrama? Or rather from the embrace of the body of Varāha?

11. O wife of the deer, has Acyuta passed by here with his beloved, his limbs giving pleasure to your eyes? O friend, the scent from the jasmine garland of the Lord of our group is wafting here – a garland coloured with breast saffron contracted from the body of his lover.

12. O trees, did the younger brother of Balarāma wander here? Was he followed by swarms of bees, blinded with intoxication, on his *tulasī* [garland]? With his arm placed on the shoulder of his beloved, he [must have been] holding a lotus flower. And did he acknowledge with glances of love your bowing down?

13. Ask these creeping plants! Just see, although they are embracing the arms of the forest tree, they surely must have been touched by his fingernails, for they are bristling with ecstasy."

14. The *gopīs*, [uttering] these crazed words, became perplexed in their search for Kṛṣṇa. With their hearts [dedicated] to him, each of them imitated the *līlā* of *Bhagavān*.

15. One, who was acting as if she were Kṛṣṇa, suckled the breast of someone else, who was playing the part of Pūtanā. Another became an infant, began crying, and then kicked another one, who was acting as a cart, with her foot.

16. After changing into a demon, one *gopī* kidnapped another, who was imagining herself to be the child Kṛṣṇa. Yet another crawled around, dragging her two feet, accompanied by the sounds from her jewellery.

17. Two *gopīs* enacted the roles of Kṛṣṇa and Balarāma, and others behaved as *gopas*. Yet another struck a *gopī* who had become Vatsa, the calf demon, while someone else there struck the *gopī* who was playing the role of Baka, the crane demon.

18. One called the cows who were far away, as Kṛṣṇa would have done. Others praised one *gopī* who was sporting and playing the flute in imitation of him: "Bravo!"

19. Another, wandering about, placed her arm on someone else, and said: "There can be no doubt that I am Kṛṣṇa. Look at how gracefully I move." Her mind was intent on him:

20. "Do not fear the wind and the rain. I have arranged protection." Saying this, one *gopī*, exerting herself, lifted up her garment with one hand.

21. Another *gopī* mounted and stepped on the head of another with her foot, O king, and said: "Go, wicked snake! There is no doubt that I have undertaken birth as the chastiser of the wicked."

22. Someone there said: "Hey *gopas*, look at the terrible forest fire! Close your eyes, I will with ease arrange for your protection!"

23. One slender-waisted *gopī* was tied to a mortar with a flower garland by another one. The former, her beautiful eyes afraid, covered her face and adopted a posture of fear.

24. Inquiring thus after Kṛṣṇa from the creeping plants and trees of Vṛndāvana, the *gopīs* noticed the footprints of the supreme soul in a certain part of the forest:

25. "These footprints are certainly those of the great soul, the son of Nanda," they said. "They are recognizable from such marks as the flag, the lotus flower, the thunderbolt, the goad and the barley."

26. Following Kṛṣṇa's tracks further, footprint by footprint, the women noticed that they were clearly interspersed with the footprints of a young woman. They discussed this together in distress:

27. "Whose footprints are these? She is going with the son of Nanda, his forearm placed on her shoulder, like a female elephant with a male elephant.

28. She has worshipped *Bhagavān* Hari, the Lord. Consequently, Govinda was pleased, and so has abandoned us and led that *gopī* to a secluded place.

29. Just see, O friends, how fortunate are these particles of dust from the lotus feet of Govinda. Brahmā, Śiva and the goddess of fortune, Ramā [Śrī], place them on their heads to remove their sins.

30. The footprints of that woman are causing us great distress because she alone of the *gopīs* is enjoying the lips of Acyuta in a secluded place.

31. Now, right here, her footprints are no longer visible: the lover has lifted up his beloved, whose feet with their delicate soles are bruised by the blades of grass.

31a. Look, *gopīs*, at these deeper footprints of lusty Kṛṣṇa weighed down by carrying the young woman. And here the beloved has been put down by that great soul in order to [gather] flowers.

32. Look, here the lover plucked flowers for the beloved: these two footprints are incomplete because he stood on tip-toe.

33. Here, lusty Kṛṣṇa decorated that lusty woman's hair. Surely he sat here while making his lover a crown with those [flowers]." '

34. [*Śrī* Śuka said]:

'Kṛṣṇa took pleasure with that *gopī*, although he is complete, content within himself and delights in his own self. He was displaying the wretchedness of lusty men and women because of their depravity.

35–36. The dispirited *gopīs* wandered about pointing [things] out in this way. The *gopī*, whom Kṛṣṇa had taken to the forest after abandoning the other women, then thought that she was the best of all women: "Kṛṣṇa, my beloved, has abandoned the [other] *gopīs* who were impelled by Kāma and dedicated himself to me."

37. Then, after going to a spot in the wood, the proud woman spoke to Keśava [Kṛṣṇa]: "I am unable to walk any further. Take me wherever your mind [desires]."

38. At this request, Kṛṣṇa told his beloved that she should climb on his shoulder, but then he disappeared. The young woman was filled with remorse:

39. "O Lord, lover, dearest! Where are you? Where are you, mighty-armed one? Reveal your presence to me, friend – I am your miserable servant!" '

40. *Śrī* Śuka said:

'The *gopīs*, searching for the path of *Bhagavān*, saw a distressed girl not far away who was disorientated by the separation from her beloved.

41. Hearing her story of how she had first received respect from Mādhava [Kṛṣṇa], and then humiliation because of her bad faith, they were astounded.

42. After this, they went as far into the forest as the moon gave light. Then, seeing that darkness had descended there, the women returned.

43. Their minds absorbed in Kṛṣṇa, the *gopīs*' conversations focused on him, their activities centred on him, and they dedicated their hearts to him. Simply by singing about his qualities, they forgot their own homes.

44. Meditating on Kṛṣṇa, they reached the bank of the Kālindī [Yamunā] river again. Gathering together they sang about Kṛṣṇa, longing for his arrival.'

Chapter 31

The Gopīs' *Song in the* Rāsa *Pastime*

1. 'The *gopīs* said: "Vraj has become pre-eminent because of your birth; indeed, Indirā [Lakṣmī] resides there permanently. O loved one, show yourself! Your devotees, whose lives are sustained in you, are searching for you everywhere.

2. You are taking our life, O Lord of autumn; your glance excels in beauty the heart of a beautiful lotus perfectly born in autumn from a pool of water. We are your maidservants [and do not ask for] any payment. Isn't this killing us, O bestower of favours?

3. O bull among men, we have been continuously protected by you from destruction from the poisonous water, from the wicked demon, from the winds and rains, from fire and lightning, from the bull Ariṣṭa, from the son of Maya [Vyomāsura], and from fear from all sides.

4. You are not, in fact, the son of a *gopī*. You are the witness of the inner self of all embodied beings. Being petitioned by Brahmā, you become manifest in the family of the Sātvatas, O friend, for the protection of the universe.

5. Place your lotus hand on the head of those who have approached you out of fear of the material world, O foremost of the Vṛṣṇi clan. Your hand, which holds the hand of Śrī [Lakṣmī], bestows fearlessness and fulfils desires, O lover.

6. You are the hero of women, and you take away the pain of the people of Vraj! The pride of your devotees is annihilated by your smile! Accept your maidservants, friend! Show us your beautiful lotus face!

7. Place your lotus feet upon our breasts. Your feet have been placed on the hoods of the serpent [Kāliya] and follow the animals to the pasture. They are the abode of the goddess of fortune, Śrī, and they remove the sins of submissive embodied beings. Excise Kāma, who dwells within our hearts.

8. O hero, these women obedient to your will are stunned by your sweet voice, your charming words which please the mind and the intelligence, and your lotus eyes. Reinvigorate us with the intoxicating liquid of your lips.

9. Those who repeat the sweetness of your words in this world are munificent. These words are praised by poets, spread abroad, and are auspicious to hear. They are life-giving for those who are suffering. They remove sins and bring good fortune.

10. Your bursts of laughter, pleasing looks of love, and pastimes are auspicious to contemplate. Those meetings in secret places touch our hearts, you cheater, and perturb us thoroughly.

11. When you go from Vraj grazing the animals, O Lord, your feet, beautiful as lotuses, are troubled by blades of grass and corn stubble, and so we feel distress. You are our beloved.

12. You possess a lotus face, surrounded by blue locks of hair which you constantly display covered with thick dust at the end of the day. You arouse Kāma in the heart, O hero.

13. O lover, place your most beneficent lotus feet on our breasts. They fulfil the desires of the humble and should be meditated upon in trouble, O destroyer of anxiety. They are worshipped by the lotus-born Brahmā, and are the ornament of the earth.

14. Bestow upon us the nectar of your lips, O hero, which have been thoroughly kissed by the flute as it plays music. It destroys sorrow, increases the pleasures of love, and causes men to forget other passions.

15. When you, Lord, go to the forest during the day, a moment becomes a *yuga* for those who do not see you. He who created eyelashes

is dull-witted, from the perspective of those beholding your beautiful face, with its curled locks of hair.

16. Acyuta, you are the knower of [people's] movements. Bewildered by your song, we have thoroughly neglected our husbands, sons, family, brothers and kinsfolk, and come before you. Who would abandon women in the night, you rogue?

17. We have become unsettled from contemplating your broad chest, the abode of Śrī, the goddess of fortune, as well as your looks of love, your smiling face and the meetings in secret places which aroused Kāma. We long for you intensely all the time.

18. Your incarnation is for the good of the universe, and dispels the distress of the people of Vraj. Deliver a little of that [medicine] which removes the ailment from the hearts of your devotees to us. Our hearts yearn for you.

19. We gently place your tender lotus feet on our rough breasts with trepidation. You wander in the forest on them and our minds are disturbed: what if they have been hurt by small stones? Your Lordship is our life."'

[. . .]

Chapter 80

The Story of Śrīdāmā

1. The king said:

'O *Bhagavān* [Śuka]. I desire to hear of some other of the great-souled Mukunda's heroic deeds; his heroic deeds are infinite, O master.

2. What judicious person, disillusioned by sensual pursuits and who has repeatedly heard the stories of Uttamaśloka [Kṛṣṇa], O *brāhmaṇa*, could desist [from hearing them]?

3. It is by speech that one praises his qualities, it is hands that perform his deeds, mind that contemplates him dwelling in all that is moving and non-moving, and the ear that listens to his holy stories.

4. It is the head that bows down to his two types of manifestation, the eye that perceives him, and the limbs that always worship the water from the feet of the devotees of Viṣṇu.

5. Sūta said:

'Questioned by Viṣṇurāta [Parīkṣit], *Bhagavān* Bādarāyaṇi [Śukadeva] – whose heart was immersed in *Bhagavān* Vāsudeva – spoke.'

6. *Śrī* Śuka said:

'There was a noble *brāhmaṇa* friend of Kṛṣṇa, a peaceful soul, and knower of *brahman*. He was detached from the objects of the senses, and his senses were disciplined.

7. He was a householder who subsisted on whatever came his way fortuitously. His wife, emaciated by hunger, was in a similar ragged state.

8. The chaste wife, her face drawn, approached her poor husband. Despondent and shaking, she said to him:

9. "*Brāhmaṇa* – you actually are the friend of *Bhagavān* Kṛṣṇa, who is the best of the Satvata clan and the husband of Śrī, the goddess of fortune herself. He is the giver of shelter and is devoted to *brāhmaṇas*.

10. You are very fortunate. Approach him, for he is the ultimate resort for the saintly. He will give you much wealth since you are a desperate householder.

11. Kṛṣṇa, the Lord of the Andhaka, Vṛṣṇi and Bhoja clans, is now in Dvārakā. He is the *guru* of the world, and gives even his own self to one who remembers his lotus feet – what is it, then, for him to give wealth and worldly desires, which are not very favoured, to his devotee?"

12–13. The *brāhmaṇa* was entreated profusely and repeatedly by his wife. Thinking, "The sight of Uttamaśloka is actually the highest blessing," he made a decision to go: "If there is any gift in the house, give it to me, auspicious lady," he said.

14. She begged four handfuls of flat rice from the *brāhmaṇas*, tied them up in a piece of cloth and gave them to her husband to be used as a gift.

15. The distinguished *brāhmaṇa* took them and set off for Dvārakā, thinking: "Is it possible that I will catch a sight of Kṛṣṇa?"

16. Accompanied by *brāhmaṇas*, he passed three outside walls and three contingents of

guards between the unassailable houses of the Andhaka and Vṛṣṇi clans, who followed the laws of Acyuta.

17. There were 16,000 houses for Hari's queens. The *brāhmaṇa* entered one of them, which was magnificent – it was as if he had entered the bliss of *brahman*.

18. Acyuta was seated on a couch with his beloved, but saw the *brāhmaṇa* from a distance. He immediately rose up, went towards the *brāhmaṇa* and embraced him joyfully with two arms.

19. The delighted lotus-eyed Kṛṣṇa was ecstatic from the bodily contact with his dear friend, the *brāhmaṇa* sage, and shed tears from his eyes.

20–21. Then he seated the *brāhmaṇa* on his own couch, and offered his friend gifts. After this, *Bhagavān*, the purifier of the world, washed the *brāhmaṇa*'s feet, and placed the washing water on his head, O king. He then smeared him with heavenly scents, and with sandalwood, aloe and vermilion.

22. With joy he honoured his friend with fragrant incense and rows of lamps, and presented him with betel nut and a cow. Then he welcomed him.

23. The goddess herself attended that weak, dirty, tattered and emaciated *brāhmaṇa*, by fanning him with a whisk.

24. When the people in the inner quarters saw how the ascetic had been worshipped with great love by Kṛṣṇa of spotless fame, they were astonished:

25–26. "What pious deed did this ascetic mendicant perform? He is without wealth, and shunned as the lowest in this world, yet this person is honoured by Kṛṣṇa, the *guru* of the three worlds, and the shelter of the goddess of fortune. Kṛṣṇa left Śrī sitting on the couch and embraced the *brāhmaṇa*, as if he were his elder brother."

27. Kṛṣṇa and the *brāhmaṇa* grasped each other's hands, and talked about pleasing past events that had happened when they were both in *gurukula* school at the house of their *guru*.

28. *Śrī Bhagavān* said: "O *brāhmaṇa*, you are a knower of *dharma*; did you take a wife in marriage when you returned home from the *guru*'s school after he had received the student remuneration from you, or not?

29. I know that your mind is usually focused on your household affairs without craving, and hence you are not gratified by wealth, O learned one.

30. Some people renounce the material world and perform their activities for the welfare of the world – just as I do – with their minds unaffected by lust.

31. Do you remember, O *brāhmaṇa*, our residence in the house of the *guru*? It is there that a twice-born understands that which is to be understood, and experiences that which is beyond *tamas*.

32. The first personification of the *guru* is as the one from whom there is birth in this world. Then, there is the *guru* of the sacred duties of the twice-born, and then there is the *guru* who is the giver of knowledge. I myself am as the latter, dear *brāhmaṇa*.

33. Those among the followers of the *varṇāśrama* social system who are wise to their own interests cross over the ocean of *saṃsāra* by [following] my words. I am the *guru*.

34. I am not as satisfied by worship, birth, austere practices and tranquillity of mind as I am by obedience to the *guru*.

35. Do you remember, O *brāhmaṇa*, what happened when we were living with the *guru*? Once, we were sent by the *guru*'s wives to fetch kindling wood.

36. We entered an enormous forest at the wrong time of year, O *brāhmaṇa*. There was fierce wind and rain, and harsh thunder.

37. The sun had set at that point, and the quarters were enveloped in darkness. High ground and low ground were covered with water, and nothing could be recognized.

38. Wind and water pounded us continually and relentlessly, and we could not discern the directions in the flood of water. Grasping each other's hands in the forest, we wandered about in distress.

39. When the sun arose, our *guru*, Sāndīpani, who knew all this and was conducting a search, saw us, his distressed disciples. He said:

40. '*Aho!* Hey boys! You have been put to great distress for our sake. Dedicated to me as you are, you have neglected even your own selves, which are so dear to embodied beings.

41. The offering of oneself and all one's possessions with a pure mind to the *guru* is the type of offering the true disciple should make to the guru.

42. I am satisfied with you, O best of the twice-born. May your desires be fulfilled, and may your recitations of Vedic hymns be invocations that remain potent both in this world and in the next.'

43. We [experienced] many such things when we were living in the *guru*'s house. It is by the grace of the *guru* alone that a person succeeds in attaining peace."

44. The *brāhmaṇa* said: "Your desires are fulfilled, O God of gods and *guru* of the universe. What could remain unaccomplished for us when our residence with the *guru* was in your company?

45. Your body is *brahman*, composed of the Vedas, and the fount of all benefit, O all-pervading one – your residing in the house of the *guru* is the ultimate play-acting." '

Chapter 81

The Episode of the Flat Rice

1. *Śrī* Śuka said:

'Hari was chatting in this way with the best of the *brāhmaṇas*. Knowing the minds of all creatures, he addressed the *brāhmaṇa* with a smile.

2. *Bhagavān* Kṛṣṇa, who is the goal of the saintly, and devoted to *brāhmaṇas*, was looking at the dear *brāhmaṇa* with an expression of love. Kṛṣṇa was laughing.

3. *Śrī Bhagavān* said: "What gift did you bring for me from home, O *brāhmaṇa*? Something brought with love by my devotees, even if insignificant, becomes great, while something brought by a non-devotee is not able to give me satisfaction, even if it is great.

4. I accept whatever is presented with love by a devout soul who offers me a leaf, flower, fruit or water with devotion."

5. Although he was questioned in this way, the *brāhmaṇa* did not present Kṛṣṇa, the husband of Śrī, the goddess of fortune, with the handful of flat rice, O king. He held his face down and became embarrassed.

6. Kṛṣṇa directly sees the *ātmā* of all creatures and knew the reason for the *brāhmaṇa*'s coming. He thought: "This *brāhmaṇa* was never desirous of wealth previously.

7. On the contrary, my friend has come to me as a favour to his chaste wife. I will bestow wealth on him that is hard even for the gods to come by."

8. With these thoughts, Kṛṣṇa himself grabbed the flat rice that had been tied up in the strip of cloth from the twice-born *brāhmaṇa*, and said: "What is this?

9. What you have brought for me is delightful, dear friend. These grains of flat rice will satisfy me, and thus the universe!"

10. Saying this, Kṛṣṇa immediately devoured a handful, and then took a second one to devour. At this, Śrī, who is devoted to him, grasped the hand of the highest God, and said:

11. "This much is enough to grant a person an abundance of all types of prosperity both in this world and the next, O soul of the universe; it is sufficient for your satisfaction."

12. The *brāhmaṇa* ate, drank and resided happily in Acyuta's palace that night; he thought he was in heaven.

13. When the next day arrived, he was respectfully saluted by Kṛṣṇa, the cause of the universe, whose happiness comes from himself, and set out for his own residence. He made the journey blissfully.

14. He went home without having obtained wealth from Kṛṣṇa – since, being embarrassed, he did not solicit it himself – but he was ecstatic from seeing that great being.

15. The *brāhmaṇa* said: "*Aho!* I have seen the devotion to *brāhmaṇas* of the Lord who is dedicated to *brāhmaṇas*. I, the poorest of the poor, have been embraced by him who carries Lakṣmī, the goddess of fortune, on his chest.

16. Who am I but a poor sinner? And who is Kṛṣṇa but the abode of Śrī, the goddess of

fortune? Nonetheless I, who can be called a *brāhmaṇa* in name only, was embraced in his arms.

17. I was made to spend the night on the bed enjoyed by his beloved as if I were his brother. When I was tired, I was fanned by his queen, who held a fly-whisk in her hand.

18. I was worshipped like a god by the God of gods and God of *brāhmaṇas* with the highest service – the massaging of feet.

19. Worship of his feet is the root of all perfections, of wealth both in this world and in the lower worlds, and of [the attainment] of the celestial regions and liberation.

20. Thinking, 'This poor person might not remember me if he obtains wealth, but will revel in it excessively,' the merciful [Lord] did not even give me some token wealth."

21. Thinking this inwardly, the *brāhmaṇa* arrived in the vicinity of his home. The area was covered on all sides by palaces that resembled the sun, fire and the moon.

22. It was covered with various parks and groves brimming with flocks of cooing birds and there were lakes of *ambuja* lotuses, blue *utpala* lotuses, red *kumuda* lotuses and white *kahlāra* lotuses in full bloom.

23. It was populated by handsomely adorned men, and by women with doe-like eyes. "What is this? Whose place is it? How has it become like this?" he thought.

24. While the most fortunate *brāhmaṇa* was thinking like this, the men and women, who were as brilliant as gods, welcomed him with much music and song.

25. When his wife heard that her husband had arrived, she became very excited with joy. She quickly came out of the house, like the beautiful goddess Śrī coming out from her dwelling.

26. The husband saw his chaste wife, who had tears in her eyes from the pain of love. With her eyes closed, she silently offered respect to him and embraced him in her mind.

27. The *brāhmaṇa* saw his wife, who looked like a glittering goddess travelling in a celestial vehicle. She was radiant in the midst of maidservants wearing golden neck ornaments. He was astonished.

28. Delighted, he entered his own palace in her company. It was endowed with 100 jewelled columns, just like the residence of the great Indra.

29. It had ivory beds resembling the foam of milk, couches with golden appendages, and fly-whisks and fans with golden handles.

30. The chairs were golden, with soft cushions, and there were glittering canopies hanging with strings of pearls.

31. The women were adorned with gems, and gem lamps shone in walls of pure crystal containing huge emeralds.

32. The *brāhmaṇa* saw the extravagance of unlimited wealth there and deliberated calmly about his unexpected abundance:

33. "Since I have always been poor and unfortunate, the cause of my prosperity could certainly not have happened other than by the glance of that greatly powerful and eminent member of the Yadu dynasty, Kṛṣṇa.

34. No doubt, Kṛṣṇa, the enjoyer of abundance, without saying anything, personally notices and bestows abundance on a person present before him who only intends to solicit. My friend Kṛṣṇa, the best of the descendants of Daśārha, is like a rain cloud.

35. Whatever is given by himself, he makes out to be insignificant, and whatever is done by his friend, even if of no consequence, he makes out to be great. I brought a handful of flat rice, and that great Soul accepted it with love.

36. May my service, friendship, camaraderie and affection for Kṛṣṇa continue birth after birth, and may I feel devotion for his followers, who are attached to him, that noble-minded fount of qualities.

37. *Bhagavān* does not personally arrange conspicuous wealth, power or sovereignty for his devotee, whose intelligence is limited. Being wise, the unborn one foresees the downfall of the wealthy brought about by pride."

38. When he had understood this, the *brāhmaṇa*, who was absolutely devoted to Janārdana and not over-lustful, enjoyed

relations with his wife while renouncing the objects of enjoyment.

39. *Brāhmaṇas* are the masters for Lord Hari, the God of gods and Lord of sacrifice. There is no deity higher than them.

40. Thus, the *brāhmaṇa, Bhagavān*'s friend, saw how the unconquered one becomes conquered by his own servants in this way. The bondage of his *ātmā* was released through the power of his meditation on Kṛṣṇa. He then attained Kṛṣṇa's abode, the goal of the saintly.

41. A person who has heard about the devotion to *brāhmaṇas* by the Lord of *brāhmaṇas* attains love for *Bhagavān*, and is released from the bondage of *karma*.'

[. . .]

Chapter 31

Kṛṣṇa Returns to his own Abode

1. *Śrī* Śuka said:

'Then, Brahmā, Śiva, along with his consort, the gods, led by the great Indra, the sages and the progenitors of the universe came there. So did the forefathers, *siddhas, gandharvas, vidyādharas*, mighty serpents, *cāraṇas, yakṣas, rākṣasas, kinnaras, apsaras* and the twice-born *brāhmaṇas*.

3. Singing and reciting the birth and deeds of Śauri [Kṛṣṇa], they were highly excited and eager to witness the departure of *Bhagavān*, God [to his transcendent abode].

4. Crowding the sky with rows of celestial vehicles, and filled with great devotion, they showered down streams of flowers.

5. When *Bhagavān* Kṛṣṇa saw grandfather Brahmā and [the gods] who were manifestations of his own power, he closed his eyes and fixed his mind on himself.

6. Without burning his body – which is pleasing to the whole world and the object of meditation and trance – with the fire of *yogic* concentration, Kṛṣṇa entered his own abode.

7. Kettledrums resounded in the heavens, and flowers fell from the sky, and Truth, Dharma, Resolution, Fame and Opulence followed him.

8. The gods and everyone, headed by Brahmā, were dumb-founded, but they were not able to see Kṛṣṇa entering his abode, since his path is unknown.

9. As mortals cannot trace the path of a moving lightning flash which has left a ring of clouds, so the path of Kṛṣṇa could not be traced by the gods.

10. Brahmā, Rudra and others who had witnessed Hari's *yogic* method were full of amazement and returned to their respective planets, glorifying him.

11. O king, you should consider the activities of birth and of departure of the supreme among human beings to be the role-playing of *māyā*, just like that of an actor. After creating this world from himself, he enters it, sports in it and, in the end, withdraws from it and remains retired in his own glory.

12. Kṛṣṇa, the giver of protection, brought the *guru*'s son from the abode of Yama, Lord of death, in his mortal body; he saved you when you were burned by the ultimate weapon; he defeated Lord Śiva, who is death even for death himself; and he brought the hunter Jarā to the celestial world – how could he be incapable of protecting his own self?

13. Although he is the sole cause of the origin, maintenance and disappearance of everything, and the wielder of all *śakti* powers, he did not desire to leave his form behind in this world – since what is the use of this world? – but demonstrated the path of those who are situated in the self.

14. One who rises early in the morning, and glorifies Kṛṣṇa's supreme departure in a devotional frame of mind, also attains to that highest destination.

15. Dāruka went to Dvārakā and fell at the feet of Vasudeva and Ugrasena, soaking their feet with his tears because of the separation from Kṛṣṇa.

16. He told of the total destruction of the Vṛṣṇi clan, O king. When they heard this, the people felt faint at heart, and swooned with grief.

17. Overwhelmed at the loss of Kṛṣṇa, his relatives rushed to that place, beat their faces and fell down unconscious.

18. Devakī, Rohiṇī and Vasudeva were overcome with grief at not finding their two sons, Kṛṣṇa and Balarāma, and fainted.

19. Overwhelmed by separation from *Bhagavān* Kṛṣṇa, they relinquished their lives on the spot. The women embraced their husbands and climbed upon the funeral pyre, Parīkṣit, my dear son.

20. The wives of Balarāma, too, embraced his body and entered the flames. The wives of Vasudeva embraced his body, as did Hari's daughters-in-law [the bodies of their husbands] such as Pradyumna and others, as they entered the fire. Kṛṣṇa's wives Rukmiṇī and the others, for whom Kṛṣṇa is their life and soul, did the same.

21. Arjuna was stricken by the loss of his dear friend Kṛṣṇa, but consoled himself by the words of truth spoken by Kṛṣṇa.

22. Arjuna made arrangements, according to custom and seniority, for the funerary rites of his deceased relatives whose family lineages had been destroyed.

23. The ocean immediately submerged Dvārakā when it was abandoned by Hari, O great king, leaving only the residence of the beautiful *Bhagavān* Kṛṣṇa.

24. *Bhagavān* Madhusūdana is eternally present there. It is the most auspicious of auspicious places, and removes all impurities simply by remembrance of it.

25. Dhanañjaya took the survivors of those who had been slaughtered – the women, children and elders – and settled them in Indraprastha. Then he consecrated Vajra, the son of Aniruddha, on the throne there.

26. When your grandfathers [the Pāṇḍavas] heard about the destruction of their friends, O king, they made you the preserver of the dynasty, and then they all set out on the great journey.

27. Any mortal who recites these birth and deeds of Viṣṇu, the Lords of lords, with faith, is freed from all sins.

28. In conclusion, anyone who recites the delightful deeds of the incarnations of Hari, *Bhagavān*, and the most auspicious stories of his childhood, as are described here and in other sources, achieves the highest devotion for Kṛṣṇa, who is the goal of swan-like devotees.'

This ends the translation of the beautiful story of Kṛṣṇa.

Chapter 9

Mānavadharmaśāstra, The Law Code of Manu

Mānavadharmaśātra, The Law Code of Manu, is among the most well-known and most notorious texts in India. It is classified as a *dharmaśāstra*, treatise on *dharma*,[1] along with the *Yājñavalkya, Nāradam* and *Parāśara dharmaśāstras*. Among these, *Manu* is the oldest and most famous. Composed between 200 BC and 200 CE, the authors of *Manu* sought to consolidate, codify, and unify the prevailing laws. Though the text is named after "Manu" this does not mean that Manu composed it. It is more than likely that several authors composed the text and that appending the name "Manu," who was purportedly the first man in the universe, to their work gave it legitimacy.

Manu was one of the first texts to become part of the European world. Translated in 1794 by William Jones, the text was translated into several languages, including French and German. Nietzsche, the German philosopher, mentioned the text several times in his corpus. The British, moreover, looked towards it as a pre-eminent example of Hindu law and they thus integrated it into their rule of India. Its infamy largely derives from the simple fact that it was composed by *brāhmaṇas*, members of the priestly class, and that its laws maintained the status quo and class inequalities. Ambedkar, the spokesman of the so-called "Untouchables," was public in 1935 about his disgust for the text. Encouraged by his hatred for the text, copies were burned by untouchable men a short while later.[2]

Manu is centered upon issues of *śuddha*, purity and *aśuddha*, impurity.[3] It offers a detailed account of how to act in almost every imaginable situation and simultaneously maintain one's purity. There are rules about when and how to eat, to bathe, to have intercourse, to get married, what sort of woman would be an ideal wife, what sort would not, funerary practices, and so on. These rules about how to behave in the world were differentiated according to *varṇa*, class, *āśrama*,[4] stage of life, and gender. In addition to these, one also finds punishments for crimes that ought to be administered by *kṣatriya* rulers. Not surprisingly, the degree of the punishment was often indexed to the *varṇa, āśrama*, and gender of the criminal. As Doniger characterizes it, "all aspects of *dharma* are 'context-sensitive'."[5] That is, the *dharma* of a person is indexed to *varṇa, āsrama*, gender, and sometimes even the particular circumstance.

The question arises as to whether or not the texts were prescriptive or descriptive. That is, did they put forth ideals towards which society ought to aspire or were they detailed characterizations of what was actually transpiring? In all likelihood, people were aware of the ideals but may not have followed them.[6] Even today, Hindus are aware of *Manu* (though they may not know much of the content) though they refer to it as an unattainable or superannuated ideal.

The selections here exemplify the breadth and depth of *Mānavadharmaśāstra*. The selections from Chapter 1 set the tone for the rest of the text as they address the foundations of the socio-religious world envisioned. Sections 1.51–1.86, "*Excursus*: Cosmic Cycles," "Transmission of the Law," and "*Excursus*: Time and Cosmology," are descriptions of the divine origins of the text as well as characterization of the four *yugas*, ages.[7] "*Excursus*: Occupations of Social Classes, 1.87–91, is a presentation of the *varṇa* system. Section 1.92–101 is a detailed discussion of the "Excellence of the Brahmin." The section ends with passages about the utility of studying the *Law Code* itself (1.102–1.11).

Chapter 2 is the first presentation of *dharma* and the selections here begin with an analysis of the necessity for law, its sources, suggestions about how to read the law, and who has competence to do so (2.1–16). Before turning to the *saṃskāras*, consecratory rites, there is a brief section on the land in which this law applies (2.17–25). Verses 2.26–249 all concern the consecratory and initiatory practices of *dvija*, twice born,[8] men. These include childhood rites, initiation into *brahmacārya*, Vedic studentship (2.36–64), and the prescribed behavior for these students. In 2.66–68 one finds an identity made between a woman's marriage and the male initiation rites. The remainder of this section (2.69–249) consists of rules pertaining to the life of a student.

Chapter 3 concerns the next step that a student is to take, namely to get married. Verses 3.4–19 are explanations of how to choose a wife. Verses 3.20–44 are about the marriage ceremony and taxonomy of the types of marriages. Intercourse is enjoined in 3.45–47 while the verses that follow concern purchasing a wife (3.51–54), honoring women (3.55–59) and how to maintain marital harmony (3.60–66). The remainder of this section (3.67–141) consists of rules pertaining to the life of a *gṛhasthā*, a householder. 3.122–141 in this section is a description of the *piṇḍa* ceremony, an annual ceremony in which deceased ancestors are ritually honored and fed *piṇḍas*, balls of rice.

The selections from Chapter 4 are a continuation of the rules and regulations of the *gṛhasthā* including proper livelihoods, and daily practice and observances. Verses 4.40–44 are rules about the prescribed relationship that one should have with one's wife. Prohibitions relating to violence (4.162–169), food (4.205–225), and meat (4.27–57) are addressed here. As already mentioned, the maintenance of one's *śuddhatva* purity, was an essential component of the *dharmaśāstras*. To this end, verses 5.58–116 are methods for re-purifying oneself. The final section here is laws relating to women and their duties towards their husbands (5.147–168). Another well-known passage (5.147–149) concerning the dependence of a woman on her father, husband, and children can be found here.

Chapter 6 consists of rules pertaining to the life of the *vanaprastha*, forest hermit, who is in the third stage of the *āśrama* system (6.1–32) and the *saṁnyāsin*, the renunciant ascetic who is in the fourth and final stage (6.33–86). The selection from Chapter 6 ends with a discussion of the superiority of the householder and indirectly, the importance of maintaining the status quo (6.87–90).

Chapter 7 consists of laws for and divine origins of the king (7.1–25). Chapter 8 includes lists of crimes and punishments to be administered by the king. Verses 8.352–384 address sexual crimes against women. The last portion of this chapter is verses enjoining the king to maintain the *varṇa* system and includes a description of the prescribed occupations of each *varṇa* (7.410–420).

The selections from Chapter 9 include laws concerning the husband and wife and other laws and punishment to be instituted by the king. Verse 9.2 is another infamous verse about the need to control, protect, and guard a woman. In contrast, 9.26–30 concerns the importance of the wife. Verses 9.229–234 are lists of *doṣas*, faults, and types of punishments while 9.35–9.49 are lists of *doṣas* that cause one to lose one's caste and class. In addition there are two short sections at the end of the chapter that are the rules of *Vaiśyas* (9.326–333) and for *Śūdras* (9.334–335).

Chapter 10 is the rules for *apāddharma*, time of calamity. These are places where the rules can be bent and altered. The size and importance of this chapter suggests that, although there are strict laws, this does not mean that they were strictly enforced or that they were immutable. There are certain circumstances, catalogued here, in which the rules can change. The first few sections of this chapter (10.1–10.73) are focused upon the issues that result when people reproduce across class and caste lines, the so-called "mixed classes." Even occupations may change in such times as is evidenced in verses 10.74–129.

Chapter 11 is include here in its entirety and it concerns *prāyaścittas*, penances to restore purity when one transgresses. There are more lists of activities that cause loss of caste including killing a *brāhmaṇa* (11.73–90), drinking liquor (11.91–98), and having sex with an elder's wife (11.104–108). Verses 11.181–182 are rules about associating with outcastes. Other sections of the chapter include rules about excommunication (11.183–186) and gaining readmission (11.187–190).

Notes

1 The word *dharma* has an enormous semantic range but in this context it can easily be translated as "law" or "duty."

2 Patrick Olivelle (tr.), *The Law Code of Manu*. Oxford: Oxford University Press, 2004, p. xvii.

3 T. N. Madan, "Concerning the Categories *Śubha* and *Śuddha* in Hindu Culture: *An Exploratory Essay*" in J. Carman and F. A. Marglin (eds.), *Purity and Auspiciousness in Indian Society.* Leiden: E. J. Brill, 1985.

4 There are four *āśramas.* These are *brahmacārya*, celibate student, *gṛhasthā*, householder, *vanaprasthā*, forest dweller, and *saṃnyāsi*, ascetic renunciant. See Patrick Olivelle, *The Āśrama System.* Oxford: Oxford University Press, 1993.

5 Wendy Doniger, *The Laws of Manu.* London: Penguin Books, 1991, p. xlvi.

6 Doniger, *The Laws of Manu*, pp. lvii–lxi.

7 These *yugas* are also described in the *Purāṇas.*

8 The term *dvija* is in reference to the *upanayana*, initiation ceremony, that was available only to *brāhmaṇas, kṣatriyas, and vaiśyas.* See 2.36 and 2.37 of this section.

Further reading

Doniger, Wendy, *The Laws of Manu*. London: Penguin Books, 1991.
Flood, Gavin, *An Introduction to Hinduism*. Cambridge: Cambridge University Press, 1999.
Madan, T. N., "Concerning the Categories *Śubha* and *Śuddha* in Hindu Culture: *An Exploratory Essay*" in J. Carman and F. A. Marglin (eds.), *Purity and Auspiciousness in Indian Society*. Leiden: E. J. Brill, 1985.
Olivelle, Patrick (tr.), *The Āśrama System*. Oxford: Oxford University Press, 1993.
Olivelle, Patrick, *The Law Code of Manu*. Oxford: Oxford University Press, 2004.
Rocher, Ludo, "The *Dharmaśāstras*" in G. Flood (ed.), *A Blackwell Companion to Hinduism*. Oxford: Blackwell Publishing, 2003.

Manu

Chapter One

Creation

[. . .]

Excursus: Cosmic Cycles

[51] 'After bringing forth in this manner this whole world and me, that One of inconceivable prowess once again disappeared into his own body, striking down time with time. [52] When that god is awake, then this creation is astir; but when he is asleep in deep repose, then the whole world lies dormant. [53] When he is soundly asleep, embodied beings, whose nature is to act, withdraw from their respective activities, and their minds become languid. [54] When they dissolve together into that One of immense body, then he, whose body contains all beings, sleeps tranquil and at ease. [55] Plunging himself into darkness, he lingers there for a long time together with his sense organs and ceases to perform his own activities. Then he emerges from that bodily frame. [56] When, after becoming a minute particle, he enters, conjoined, the seminal form of mobile and immobile beings, then he discharges the bodily frame.

[57] 'In this manner, by waking and sleeping, that Imperishable One incessantly brings to life and tears down this whole world, both the mobile and the immobile.

Transmission of the Law

[58] 'After composing this treatise, he himself in the beginning imparted it according to rule to me alone; and I, in turn, to Marīci and the other sages. [59] Bhṛgu here will relate that treatise to you completely, for this sage has learnt the whole treatise in its entirety from me.'

[60] When Manu had spoken to him in this manner, the great sage Bhṛgu was delighted. He then said to all those seers: 'Listen!'

Excursus: Time and Cosmology

[61–2] There are six further Manus in the lineage of this Manu, the son of the Self-existent One: Svārociṣa, Auttami, Tāmasa, Raivata, Cākṣuṣa of great energy, and the son of Vivasvat. Possessing great nobility and might, they each have brought forth their own progeny.

[63] These seven Manus of immense energy, with the son of the Self-existent One at their head, gave rise to and secured this whole world, the mobile and the immobile, each in his own Epoch.

[64] Eighteen Nimeṣas ('winks') make a Kāṣṭha ('second'), thirty Kāṣṭhas a Kalā ('minute'), thirty Kalās a Muhūrta ('hour'), and thirty Muhūrtas a day-and-night. [65] The sun divides the day and the night, both the human and the divine. The night is meant for creatures to sleep, and the day to engage in activities.

[66] For ancestors, a month constitutes a day and a night, divided into the two fortnights. The dark fortnight is the day for engaging in activities, and the bright fortnight is the night for sleeping. [67] For gods, a year is a day and a night and their division is this: the day is the northward passage of the sun, and the night is its southward passage.

[68] Listen now to a concise account of the duration of a day-and-night of Brahmā and of each Age in proper sequence. [69] The Kṛta Age is said to last 4,000 years. It is preceded by a twilight lasting 400 years and followed by a twilight of the same length. [70] For each of the three subsequent Ages, as also for the twilights that precede and follow them, the first number of the thousands and the hundreds is progressively diminished by one. [71] These four Ages, computed at the very beginning as lasting 12,000 years, are said to constitute a single Age of the gods. [72] The sum total of 1,000 divine Ages should be regarded as a single day of Brahmā, and his night as having the very same duration. [73] Those who know this propitious day of Brahmā lasting 1,000 Ages, as also his

Excerpts from Patrick Olivelle (tr.), *The Law Code of Manu*. Oxford: Oxford University Press, 2004.

night with the same duration – they are people who truly know day and night.

[74] At the end of that day-and-night, he awakens from his sleep; and when he has woken up, he brings forth the mind, which is both existent and non-existent. [75] The mind, driven by the desire to create, transmutes the creation. From the mind is born ether, whose distinctive quality is said to be sound. [76] From ether, as it is being transmuted, is born wind – powerful, pure, and bearing all odours – whose distinctive quality is thought to be touch. [77] From the wind, as it is being transmuted, is produced light – shining, brilliant, and dispelling darkness – whose distinctive quality, tradition says, is visible appearance. [78] From light, as it is being transmuted, comes water, with taste as its distinctive quality; and from water, earth, with smell as its distinctive quality. That is how this creation was at the beginning.

[79] The divine Age mentioned previously as lasting 12,000 years – that multiplied 71 times is here referred to as an 'Epoch of a Manu'. [80] The countless Epochs of Manu, as also creation and dissolution – the Supreme Lord does this again and again as a kind of sport.

[81] In the Kṛta Age, the Law is whole, possessing all four feet; and so is truth. People never acquire any property through unlawful means. [82] By acquiring such property, however, the Law is stripped of one foot in each of the subsequent Ages; through theft, falsehood, and fraud, the Law disappears a foot at a time.

[83] In the Kṛta Age, people are free from sickness, succeed in all their pursuits, and have a life span of 400 years. In the Tretā and each of the subsequent Ages, however, their life span is shortened by a quarter. [84] The life span of mortals given in the Veda, the benefits of rites, and the power of embodied beings – they all come to fruition in the world in conformity with each Age.

[85] There is one set of Laws for men in the Kṛta Age, another in the Tretā, still another in the Dvāpara, and a different set in the Kali, in keeping with the progressive shortening taking place in each Age. [86] Ascetic toil, they say, is supreme in the Kṛta Age; knowledge in Tretā; sacrifice in Dvāpara; and gift-giving alone in Kali.

Excursus: Occupations of Social Classes

[87] For the protection of this whole creation, that One of dazzling brilliance assigned separate activities for those born from the mouth, arms, thighs, and feet. [88] To Brahmins, he assigned reciting and teaching the Veda, offering and officiating at sacrifices, and receiving and giving gifts. [89] To the Kṣatriya, he allotted protecting the subjects, giving gifts, offering sacrifices, reciting the Veda, and avoiding attachment to sensory objects; [90] and to the Vaiśya, looking after animals, giving gifts, offering sacrifices, reciting the Veda, trade, moneylending, and agriculture. [91] A single activity did the Lord allot to the Śudra, however: the ungrudging service of those very social classes (10.74–80).

Excursus: Excellence of the Brahmin

[92] A man is said to be purer above the navel. Therefore, the Self-existent One has declared, the mouth is his purest part. [93] Because he arose from the loftiest part of the body, because he is the eldest, and because he retains the Veda, the Brahmin is by Law the lord of this whole creation. [94] For, in the beginning, the Self-existent One heated himself with ascetic toil and brought him forth from his own mouth to convey divine oblations and ancestral offerings and to protect this whole world. [95] What creature can surpass him through whose mouth the denizens of the triple heaven always eat their oblations, and the forefathers their offerings.

[96] Among creatures, living beings are the best; among living beings, those who subsist by intelligence; among those who subsist by intelligence, human beings; and among human beings, Brahmins – so the tradition declares. [97] Among Brahmins, the learned are the best; among the learned, those who have made the resolve; among those who have made the resolve, the doers; and among doers, the Vedic savants.

[98] A Brahmin's birth alone represents the everlasting physical frame of the Law; for,

born on account of the Law, he is fit for becoming Brahman. [99] For when a Brahmin is born, a pre-eminent birth takes place on earth – a ruler of all creatures to guard the storehouse of Laws. [100] This whole world – whatever there is on earth – is the property of the Brahmin. Because of his eminence and high birth, the Brahmin has a clear right to this whole world. [101] The Brahmin eats only what belongs to him, wears what belongs to him, and gives what belongs to him; it is by the kindness of the Brahmin that other people eat.

Excursus: Treatise of Manu

[102] To determine which activities are proper to him and which to the remaining classes in their proper order, Manu, the wise son of the Self-existent, composed this treatise. [103] It should be studied diligently and taught to his pupils properly by a learned Brahmin, and by no one else.

[104] When a Brahmin who keeps to his vows studies this treatise, he is never sullied by faults arising from mental, oral, or physical activities; [105] he purifies those alongside whom he eats (3.183–6), as also seven generations of his lineage before him and seven after him; he alone, moreover, has a right to this entire earth.

[106] This treatise is the best good-luck incantation; it expands the intellect; it procures everlasting fame; and it is the ultimate bliss. [107] In this, the Law has been set forth in full – the good and the bad qualities of actions and the timeless norms of proper conduct – for all four social classes.

[108] Proper conduct is the highest Law, as well as what is declared in the Veda and given in traditional texts. Applying himself always to this treatise, therefore, let a twice-born man remain constantly self-possessed. [109] When a Brahmin has fallen away from proper conduct, he does not reap the fruit of the Veda; but when he holds fast to proper conduct, tradition says, he enjoys its full reward. [110] Seeing thus that the Law proceeds from proper conduct, the sages understood proper conduct to be the ultimate root of all ascetic toil. [. . .]

Chapter Two
The Law

[1] Learn the Law always adhered to by people who are erudite, virtuous, and free from love and hate, the Law assented to by the heart.

Excursus: Desire

[2] To be motivated by desire is not commended, but it is impossible here to be free from desire; for it is desire that prompts vedic study and the performance of vedic rites. [3] Intention is the root of desire; intention is the wellspring of sacrifices; and intention triggers every religious observance and every rule of restraint – so the tradition declares. [4] Nowhere in this world do we see any activity done by a man free from desire; for whatever at all that a man may do, it is the work of someone who desired it. [5] By engaging in them properly, a man attains the world of the immortals and, in this world, obtains all his desires just as he intended.

Sources of Law

[6] The root of the Law is the entire Veda; the tradition and practice of those who know the Veda; the conduct of good people; and what is pleasing to oneself. [7] Whatever Law Manu has proclaimed with respect to anyone, all that has been taught in the Veda, for it contains all knowledge. [8] After subjecting all this to close scrutiny with the eye of knowledge, a learned man should apply himself to the Law proper to him on the authority of the scriptures; [9] for by following the Law proclaimed in scripture and tradition, a man achieves fame in this world and unsurpassed happiness after death.

[10] 'Scripture' should be recognized as 'Veda', and 'tradition' as 'Law Treatise'. These two should never be called into question in any matter, for it is from them that the Law has shined forth. [11] If a twice-born disparages these two by relying on the science of logic, he ought to be ostracized by good people as an infidel and a denigrator of the Veda.

Knowledge of the Law

[12] Veda, tradition, the conduct of good people, and what is pleasing to oneself – these, they say, are the four visible marks of the Law. [13] The knowledge of the Law is prescribed for people who are unattached to wealth or pleasures; and for people who seek to know the Law, scripture is the highest authority.

Contradictions in Law

[14] When there are two contradictory scriptural provisions on some issue, however, tradition takes them both to be the Law with respect to it; for wise men have correctly pronounced them both to be the Law. [15] After sunrise, before sunrise, and at daybreak – the sacrifice takes place at any of these times; so states a vedic scripture.

Competence to Study the Law

[16] A man for whom it is prescribed that the rites beginning with the impregnation ceremony and ending with the funeral are to be performed with the recitation of vedic formulas – no one but he is to be recognized as entitled to study this treatise.

The Sacred Land

[17] The land created by the gods and lying between the divine rivers Sarasvatī and Dṛṣadvatī is called 'Brahmāvarta' – the region of Brahman. [18] The conduct handed down from generation to generation among the social classes and the intermediate classes of that land is called the 'conduct of good people'.

[19] Kurukṣetra and the lands of the Matsyas, Pañcālas, and Śūrasenakas constitute the 'land of Brahmin seers', which borders on the Brahmāvarta. [20] All the people on earth should learn their respective practices from a Brahmin born in that land.

[21] The land between the Himalaya and Vindhya ranges, to the east of Vinaśana and west of Prayāga, is known as the 'Middle Region'.

[22] The land between the same mountain ranges extending from the eastern to the western sea is what the wise call 'Āryāvarta' – the region of the Āryas.

[23] The natural range of the black buck is to be recognized as the land fit for sacrifice; beyond that is the land of foreigners.

[24] Twice-born people should diligently settle in these lands; but a Śūdra, when he is starved for livelihood, may live in any region at all.

> [25] I have described to you above succinctly the source of the Law, as also the origin of this whole world. Learn now the Laws of the social classes.

Consecratory Rites

[26] The consecration of the body, beginning with the ceremony of impregnation, should be performed for twice-born men by means of the sacred vedic rites, a consecration that cleanses a man both here and in the hereafter. [27] The fire offerings for the benefit of the foetus, the birth rite, the first cutting of hair, and the tying of the Muñja-grass cord – by these rites the taint of semen and womb is wiped from twice-born men. [28] Vedic recitation, religious observances, fire offerings, study of the triple Veda, ritual offerings, sons, the five great sacrifices, and sacrifices – by these a man's body is made 'brāhmic'.

Childhood Rites

[29] The rule is that the birth rite of a male child must be performed before his umbilical cord is cut; he is fed gold, honey, and ghee to the accompaniment of vedic formulas.

[30] One should see to it that the child's naming ceremony is performed on the tenth or the twelfth day after birth, on a day or at a time that is auspicious, or under a favourable constellation. [31] For a Brahmin, the name should connote auspiciousness; for a Kṣatriya, strength; for a Vaiśya, wealth; and for a Śūdra, disdain. [32] For a Brahmin, the name should connote happiness; for a Kṣatriya, protection; for a Vaiśya, prosperity; and for a Śūdra, service. [33] For girls, the name should be easy to pronounce and without fierce connotations, have a clear meaning,

be charming and auspicious, end in a long final syllable, and contain a word for blessing.

[34] In the fourth month, one should perform the ceremony of taking the child out of the house; and in the sixth month, the feeding with rice, as also any other auspicious ceremony cherished in the family.

[35] The first cutting of hair, according to the Law, should be performed for all twice-born children in the first or the third year, in accordance with the dictates of scripture.

Vedic Initiation

Time for Initiation [36] For a Brahmin, the vedic initiation should be carried out in the eighth year from conception; for a Kṣatriya, in the eleventh year from conception; and for a Vaiśya, in the twelfth year from conception. [37] For a Brahmin desiring eminence in vedic knowledge, it should be carried out in the fifth year; for a Kṣatriya aspiring to power, in the sixth year; and for a Vaiśya aspiring to a spirit of enterprise, in the seventh year.

Failure to be Initiated [38] For a Brahmin, the time for Sāvitrī does not lapse until the sixteenth year; for a Kṣatriya, until the twenty-second; and for a Vaiśya, until the twenty-fourth. [39] If, after those times, any of these three has not undergone consecration at the proper time, he becomes a Vrātya (10.20–23), fallen from Sāvitrī (2.38 n.) and spurned by Āryas. [40] Even in a time of adversity, a Brahmin should never establish vedic or matrimonial links with such people, unless they have been cleansed according to rule.

Insignia: I [41] Students should wear the skin of a black antelope, a Ruru deer, or a male goat, and clothes of hemp, flax, or wool, according to the direct order of classes.

[42] For a Brahmin, the girdle should be made with a triple cord of Muñja grass, smooth and soft; for a Kṣatriya, with a bowstring of Mūrvā hemp; and for a Vaiśya, with a string of hemp. [43] When Muñja grass is unavailable, they should be made with Kuśa grass, the Aśmantaka plant, or Balvaja grass. One should wrap the girdle around the waist three times and make one, three, or five knots.

[44] For a Brahmin, the sacrificial cord is made with a triple strand of cotton thread twisted upward; for a Kṣatriya, with strands of hemp; and for a Vaiśya, with woollen strands.

[45] A Brahmin, according to the Law, is entitled to a wood-apple or Palāśa staff; a Kṣatriya, to a banyan or Khadira staff; and a Vaiśya, to a Pīlu or Udumbara staff. [46] In terms of length, a Brahmin's staff should reach the hair; a Kṣatriya's the forehead; and a Vaiśya's the nose. [47] Every staff should be straight, without blemishes, pleasing to the eye, not liable to alarm people, with the bark intact, and undamaged by fire.

Food [48] Taking his chosen staff, he should worship the sun, walk around the fire clockwise, and go on his begging round according to rule. [49] An initiated Brahmin should beg placing the word 'Madam' at the beginning; a Kṣatriya, in the middle; and a Vaiśya, at the end. [50] The very first time, he should beg from his mother, his sister, or his own mother's sister, or from some other woman who would not snub him.

[51] After collecting as much almsfood as he needs without guile, he should present it to his teacher, purify himself by sipping some water, and eat it facing the east. [52] Facing the east while eating procures long life; facing the south procures fame; facing the west procures prosperity; and facing the north procures truth. [53] A twice-born should always eat food after sipping some water and with a collected mind; after eating also he should sip water in the proper manner and rub water on the orifices.

[54] He must always revere his food and eat it without disdain. When he sees the food, he should rejoice, look pleased, and receive it joyfully in every way. [55] For when food is revered, it always bestows strength and vigour; but when it is eaten without being revered, it destroys them both.

[56] He must not give his leftovers to anyone, eat between meals, engage in overeating, or go anywhere while he is sullied with remnants. [57] Eating too much harms his health, reduces his life expectancy, impedes heaven, hinders

merit, and is despised by people; therefore, he should avoid it.

Sipping [58] A Brahmin should sip water at all times with the part of the palm linked to Brahmā, Prajāpati, or gods, but never with the part linked to ancestors. [59] They call the flat surface at the base of the thumb the part linked to Brahmā; the base of the fingers, the part linked to Prajāpati; the finger tips, the part linked to gods; and the area beneath these two, the part linked to ancestors.

[60] He should first sip water three times, then wipe his mouth twice, and finally rub water on his orifices, body, and head (2.53 n.). [61] A man who knows the Law and desires to become pure should always do the sipping in a secluded place, using water that is not warm or frothy, employing the appropriate part of the palm, and facing east or north. [62] A Brahmin is purified by water reaching the heart; a Kṣatriya, by water reaching the throat; a Vaiśya, by water taken into the mouth; and a Śūdra, by water wetting the lips.

Insignia: II [63] When the right hand is raised, a twice-born man is called '*upavītin*' – wearing the cord in the sacrificial mode; when the left hand is raised, he is called '*prācīnāvītin*' – wearing the cord toward the east; and when it is worn around the neck, he is called '*nivītin*' – wearing the cord down.

[64] When the girdle, antelope skin, staff, sacrificial cord, or water pot is damaged, he should throw it in water and take a new one with the appropriate ritual formula.

Shaving Ceremony

[65] The rule is that for a Brahmin the shaving ceremony is to be performed in the sixteenth year; for a Kṣatriya, in the twenty-second; and for a Vaiśya, in the twenty-fourth (2.38 n.).

Consecratory Rites for Women

[66] For females, on the other hand, this entire series should be performed at the proper time and in the proper sequence, but without reciting any vedic formula, for the purpose of consecrating their bodies.

[67] For females, tradition tells us, the marriage ceremony equals the rite of vedic consecration; serving the husband equals living with the teacher; and care of the house equals the tending of the sacred fires.

> [68] I have explained above the initiatory rite of twice-born men, a rite that signals a new birth and is sanctifying. Learn now the activities connected with it.

The Student

Instruction

[69] After initiating a pupil, the teacher should at the outset train him in purification, proper conduct, fire rituals, and twilight worship.

[70] When the pupil is ready for vedic recitation, he should sip water in the prescribed manner, dress in light clothing, bring his organs under control, face the north, and join his palms in '*brahmāñjali*' – then should he be taught. [71] At the beginning and at the end of a vedic lesson, he should always clasp his teacher's feet and recite the Veda with joined palms – tradition calls this '*brahmāñjali*', the vedic joining of palms. [72] He should clasp his teacher's feet by crossing his hands, touching the teacher's right foot with his right hand and the teacher's left with his left.

[73] When he is ready for vedic recitation, he should say to the teacher, 'Teach, Sir (*bho*)!', without being lazy at any time; and when commanded 'Stop!', he should cease. [74] At the beginning and at the end of vedic recitation, the student should always recite the syllable OṂ. If it is not recited at the beginning, the Veda slips away; if it is not recited at the end, the Veda wastes away. [75] When he is seated on sacred grass with the tips toward the east, cleansed by the purificatory blades of grass, and purified by controlling his breath three times – then he becomes competent to recite OṂ.

The Syllable OṂ [76] The phonemes 'a', 'u', and 'm' – Prajāpati extracted these from the three Vedas, as also '*bhū*', earth; '*bhuvaḥ*', mid-space; and '*svar*', heaven. [77] Also from the three Vedas, Prajāpati, the Supreme Lord, squeezed out foot by foot the Sāvitrī verse: 'That. . . .'

[78] By softly reciting this syllable and this verse preceded by the Calls during the two twilights, a Brahmin who knows the Veda wins the merit of reciting the Veda itself. [79] By reciting these three one thousand times outside the village, a Brahmin is freed from even a grievous sin within a month, like a snake from its slough. [80] Someone who is a Brahmin, a Kṣatriya, or a Vaiśya by birth invites the censure of good people by cutting himself off from this verse and from the timely performance of his rite.

[81] The three inexhaustible Great Calls preceded by OṂ and the three-footed Sāvitrī verse should be recognized as the mouth of the Veda. [82] When a man recites this verse tirelessly for three years, becoming wind and assuming an ethereal form, he reaches the highest Brahman. [83] The highest Brahman is the monosyllable OṂ; the highest ascetic toil is the control of breath; nothing is higher than the Sāvitrī; and truth is better than ascetic silence. [84] Offering ghee while seated, offering oblations while standing – all such vedic rites perish. The syllable (*akṣara*) OṂ should be recognized as imperishable (*akṣara*); it is Brahman, it is Prajāpati.

Soft Recitation [85] The sacrifice consisting of soft recitation is ten times better than the sacrifice consisting of prescribed rites – a hundred times, if the recitation is done inaudibly; and a thousand times, if it is done mentally. [86] The four types of cooked oblations along with the sacrifices consisting of prescribed rites – all these are not worth a sixteenth part of the sacrifice consisting of soft recitation. [87] Only by soft recitation does a Brahmin achieve success; on this there is no doubt. Whether he does anything else or not, a Maitra, they say, is the true Brahmin.

Excursus: Control of the Organs

[88] As his organs meander amidst the alluring sense objects, a learned man should strive hard to control them, like a charioteer his horses.

[89] I will explain precisely and in their proper order the eleven organs described by wise men of old: [90] ear, skin, eyes, tongue, and the fifth, nostrils; anus, sexual organ, hands, feet, and speech, listed by tradition as the tenth. [91] Of these, the five in order beginning with the ear are called the organs of perception; and the five beginning with the anus, the organs of action. [92] Know that the eleventh is the mind, which, by virtue of its own distinctive quality, belongs to both groups. So, by mastering it, one masters both those quintets.

[93] By attachment to the organs, a man undoubtedly becomes corrupted; but by bringing them under control, he achieves success. [94] Desire is never quenched by enjoying desires; like a fire fed with ghee, it only waxes stronger. [95] Between a man who obtains all these and a man who gives them all up – giving up all desires is far better than obtaining them all. [96] Corrupted as these organs are by sensory objects, one cannot bring them under control as effectively by abstinence as by constant insight. [97] Vedas, gifts, sacrifices, constraints, and ascetic toils – none of these is ever successful for a man with a corrupt heart.

[98] When a man feels neither elation nor revulsion at hearing, touching, seeing, eating, or smelling anything, he should be recognized as a man who has mastered his organs. [99] Of all these organs, however, if a single one slips away, through that his wisdom slips away, like water through the foot of a skin. [100] By bringing the full range of his organs under control and by restraining his mind, a man will achieve all his goals without having to shrivel up his body through yoga.

Twilight Worship

[101] At the morning twilight, he should stand reciting softly the Sāvitrī verse until the sun comes into view; at the evening twilight, however, he should always remain seated until Ursa Major becomes clearly visible. [102] When he stands reciting softly at the morning twilight, he banishes any sin committed during the night; and when he sits at the evening

twilight, he removes any taint contracted during the day. [103] A man who neither stands at the morning twilight nor sits at the evening twilight should be excluded like a Śūdra from all rites of the twice-born.

Vedic Recitation

[104] Intent on carrying out the ritual of daily recitation, he should go into the wilderness and, controlled and composed, recite at least the Sāvitrī verse near a place of water.

[105] Rules regarding the suspension of vedic recitation have no bearing on Vedic Supplements, on daily vedic recitation, and on ritual formulas used in fire offerings. [106] The daily vedic recitation is not subject to suspension, for tradition calls it a sacrificial session consisting of vedic recitation; it is a meritorious rite at which the vedic recitation takes the place of the burnt oblation and the factors causing a suspension act as the oblatory exclamation Vaṣaṭ.

[107] When someone, after purifying and controlling himself, performs his vedic recitation for a year according to rule, that recitation will rain milk, curd, ghee, and honey on him every single day.

Persons Competent to Receive Vedic Instruction

[108] Kindling the sacred fire, begging almsfood, sleeping on the floor, and doing what is beneficial to his teacher – a twice-born who has undergone vedic initiation should do these until he has performed the rite of returning home.

[109] The son of his teacher, a person who offers obedient service, a person who has given him knowledge, a virtuous person, an honest person, someone close to him, a capable man, someone who gives him money, a good man, and one who is his own – these ten may be taught the Veda in accordance with the Law. [110] He must never impart instruction to anyone who has not requested it or who has requested it in an improper way; for in this world, a wise man, though learned, should conduct himself like an idiot. [111] A man who imparts in violation of the Law and a man who requests in violation of the Law – of these two, the one or the other will incur death or enmity.

[112] Do not sow knowledge where there is no merit or money, or at least proportionate service; you don't sow good seed on brackish soil. [113] Even in a time of dreadful adversity, a vedic savant should rather die with his knowledge; let him not sow it on barren soil.

[114] Vedic knowledge came up to the Brahmin and said, 'I am your treasure. Guard me! Do not hand me over to a malcontent. I shall thus become supremely strong. [115] A man you know to be honest, restrained, and chaste – only to such a Brahmin should you disclose me, as to a vigilant guardian of your treasure.'

[116] If, however, a man learns the Veda without permission by listening to someone who is reciting it, he is guilty of stealing the Veda and will go to hell.

Salutation

[117] He should greet first the person from whom he received knowledge – whether it is the knowledge of worldly matters, of the Veda, or of the inner self. [118] A well-disciplined Brahmin, although he knows just the Sāvitrī verse, is far better than an undisciplined one who eats all types of food and deals in all types of merchandise, though he may know all three Vedas.

[119] He should not sit on a bed or seat occupied by a superior, and he should rise from the bed or seat he is occupying before he greets such a person; [120] for when an older person comes near, the life-breaths of a younger person rise up, and as he rises up and greets him, he retrieves them. [121] When someone is conscientious about greeting and always renders assistance to the elderly, he obtains an increase in these four: life span, wisdom, fame, and power.

[122] When a Brahmin is greeting an older person, he must state his name after the greeting, saying, 'I am so-and-so'. [123] When

greeting people who are ignorant of the greeting containing the proper name, as also any woman, a wise man should simply say 'I'. [124] When he uses the greeting containing his own name, he should say '*bho*' at the end; the meaning of '*bho*' contains the essential meanings of all proper names – that is the tradition handed down by the seers. [125] In greeting a Brahmin, he should say, 'May you live long, gentle Sir!'; and at the end of the name, he should pronounce 'a' and prolate the previous syllable. [126] A learned man should not greet a Brahmin who does not know how to return a greeting; he is no better than a Śūdra.

[127] When he meets a Brahmin, he should ask him whether he is doing well (*kuśala*); a Kṣatriya, whether he is all right (*anāmaya*); a Vaiśya, whether his property is secure (*kṣema*); and a Śūdra, whether he is in good health (*ārogya*). [128] A person consecrated for sacrifice should not be addressed by name even if he is younger; a man conversant with the Law should address such a person using the words '*bho*' or 'Sir' (*bhavat*). [129] He should address a woman who is another man's wife and who is not a blood relative of his using the words 'Madam', 'Dear Lady', or 'Sister'. [130] He should rise up and say, 'I am so-and-so' to his maternal and paternal uncles, fathers-in-law, officiating priests, and elders who are younger than he. [131] He should honour a maternal aunt, a wife of a maternal uncle, a mother-in-law, and a paternal aunt as he would his teacher's wife; they are equal to his teacher's wife.

[132] The feet of his brother's wife of the same social class, he should clasp every day; but the feet of the wives of his paternal and maternal relatives, only after returning from a journey. [133] Towards a sister of his father and mother and towards his own older sister, he should behave as towards his own mother; but the mother is more venerable than they.

Precedence

[134] Among fellow citizens, people with an age difference of ten years are regarded as friends; among fellow artisans, people with an age difference of five years; among vedic scholars, people with an age difference of three years; and among blood relatives, only people with a slight age difference.

[135] A 10-year-old Brahmin and a 100-year-old king, one should know, stand with respect to each other as a father to a son; but of the two, the Brahmin is the father. [136] Wealth, kin, age, ritual life, and the fifth, knowledge – these are the grounds for respect; and each subsequent one carries greater weight than each preceding. [137] Among persons of the three classes, one who possesses more of and to a higher degree these five grounds is more deserving of respect; and so is a Śūdra who is in his nineties.

[138] One should give way to people in vehicles or in their nineties, the sick, people carrying loads, women, bath-graduates, kings, and bridegrooms. [139] When such people encounter each other, however, a bath-graduate and a king are to receive greater honour; but when a king and a bath-graduate encounter each other, the king pays honour to the bath-graduate.

Teacher

[140] The twice-born man who initiates a pupil and teaches him the Veda together with the ritual books and the secret texts is called 'Teacher'. [141] A man who teaches a section of the Veda or else the Vedic Supplements (2.105 n.) for a living is called 'Tutor'. [142] The Brahmin who performs the rites beginning with the ceremony of impregnation according to rule and nourishes with food is called 'Elder'. [143] The person who, after he has been chosen by someone, sets up the sacred fires and performs the cooked oblations and sacrifices such as the Agniṣṭoma offering on his behalf is called here his 'Officiating Priest'.

[144] He should consider the man who fills both his ears faithfully with the Veda as his father and mother and never show hostility towards him. [145] The teacher is ten times greater than the tutor; the father is a hundred times greater than the teacher; but the mother is a thousand times greater than the father.

[146] Between the man who gave life and the man who gave the Veda, the man who gave the Veda is the more venerable father; for a Brahmin's birth in the Veda is everlasting, both here and in the hereafter. [147] When, through lust for each other, his father and mother engender him and he is conceived in the womb, he should consider that as his mere coming into existence. [148] But the birth that a teacher who has fathomed the Veda brings about according to rule by means of the Sāvitrī verse – that is his true birth, that is not subject to old age and death.

[149] A man who assists someone with vedic knowledge, be it a little or a lot, is also acknowledged here as his elder in recognition of that assistance with vedic knowledge.

[150] Even a younger Brahmin who brings about the vedic birth of an older individual and trains him in the Law proper to him becomes his father according to the Law. [151] The child sage, son of Aṅgiras, gave vedic instruction to his fathers; and having excelled them in knowledge, he called them 'Little Children'. [152] They became infuriated and raised the issue with the gods. The gods convened and told them: 'The child addressed you properly. [153] An ignorant man, surely, is the child, and the man who imparts the Veda is the father; for they address an ignorant man as "Child" and a man who imparts the Veda as "Father".'

[154] The seers have established this Law: 'In our eyes, only a vedic savant is an eminent man'; eminence does not come from age, grey hairs, wealth, or kin. [155] For Brahmins, seniority depends on knowledge, for Kṣatriyas on valour, and for Vaiśyas on grain and wealth; for Śūdras alone it depends on age. [156] A man does not become a 'senior' simply because his hair has turned grey. Gods call a man with vedic learning a 'senior', even though he may be young.

[157] Like an elephant made of wood, like a deer made of leather, is a Brahmin without vedic learning; these three only bear the name. [158] As fruitless as a eunuch with women, as fruitless as a cow with a cow, and as fruitless as a gift given to an ignorant man, is a Brahmin ignorant of the Veda.

[159] A man who wishes to promote the Law should instruct creatures about what is best without hurting them, employing pleasant and gentle words. [160] Only a man whose mind and speech have been purified and are always well-guarded acquires the entire fruit of reaching the end of the Veda. [161] Though deeply hurt, let him never use cutting words, show hostility to others in thought or deed, or use aberrant language that would alarm people.

[162] Let a Brahmin always shrink from praise, as he would from poison; let him ever yearn for scorn, as he would for ambrosia – [163] for, a man who is scorned sleeps at ease, wakes up at ease, goes about in this world at ease; but the man who scorned him perishes.

Vedic Study

[164] A twice-born whose body has been consecrated following this orderly sequence should gradually amass the riches of ascetic toil consisting of vedic study while he resides with his teacher. [165] A twice-born should study the entire Veda together with the secret texts (2.140 n.), as he carries out the various observances and special ascetic practices enjoined by vedic injunctions. [166] A Brahmin planning on undergoing ascetic toil should simply recite the Veda constantly; for vedic recitation is recognized here as the highest ascetic toil for a Brahmin. [167] When a twice-born, even while wearing a garland, performs his vedic recitation every day according to his ability, he is surely practising the fiercest ascetic toil down to the very tips of his nails. [168] When a Brahmin expends great effort in other matters without studying the Veda, while still alive he is quickly reduced to the status of a Śūdra, together with his children.

[169] According to a scriptural injunction, the first birth of a Brahmin is from his mother; the second takes place at the tying of the Muñja-grass girdle (2.27 n.), and the third at the consecration for a sacrifice. [170] Of these, the one signalled by the tying of the Muñja-grass girdle is his birth from the Veda. At this birth, the Sāvitrī verse is said to be his mother,

and the teacher his father. [171] The teacher is called the father because he imparts the Veda, for a man does not become competent to perform any rite until the tying of the Muñja-grass girdle. [172] Such a man should not pronounce any vedic text, except when he offers a funerary oblation, for he is equal to a Śūdra until he is born from the Veda.

Observances

[173] After he has undergone vedic initiation, he is to be instructed in the observances and then taught the Veda in the proper order and according to rule. [174] The very same skin, cord, girdle, staff, and garment prescribed for him after his initiation are prescribed for him also during the observances.

[175] Bringing all his organs under control, a vedic student living with his teacher should observe these restrictions in order to increase his ascetic toil. [176] Every day, after purifying himself by bathing, he should offer quenching libations to gods, seers, and ancestors; worship the gods; and put firewood into the sacred fire. [177] He should avoid honey, meat, perfumes, garlands, savoury foods, women, all foods that have turned sour, causing injury to living beings, [178] rubbing oil on the body, putting collyrium on the eyes, using footwear or an umbrella, lust, hatred, greed, dancing, singing, playing musical instruments, [179] gambling, gossiping, slander, lies, looking at and touching women, and hurting others.

[180] He should always sleep alone and never ejaculate his semen; for when he voluntarily ejaculates his semen, he breaks his vow. [181] When a Brahmin student ejaculates his semen involuntarily in sleep, he should bathe, worship the sun, and softly recite three times the verse: 'May the virile strength return again to me. . . .'

Begging and Daily Duties [182] He should fetch a pot of water, flowers, cow dung, loose soil, and Kuśa grass – as much as required – and beg for food every day.

[183] Having made himself pure, a vedic student should gather alms-food every day from the houses of persons who do not neglect the Veda or sacrifices and who have distinguished themselves in the activities proper to them. [184] He should not beg from his teacher's family or from the families of his paternal or maternal relatives. When houses of other people are unavailable, however, he may beg from these, avoiding those listed earlier when those listed later are available. [185] When the kinds of person mentioned above are not available, he may beg from the entire village after purifying himself and curbing his speech; but he should avoid heinous sinners.

[186] Having fetched firewood from afar, he should stack it above ground; and using that firewood, he should make offerings in the fire diligently morning and evening.

[187] If he fails to beg food or to put firewood into the sacred fire for seven nights without being sick, he should perform the penitential observance prescribed for a student who has broken his vow of chastity (11.119–24).

[188] Subsisting on almsfood every day, a votary should never eat a meal given by one person; tradition says that for a votary subsisting on almsfood is equal to a fast. [189] When he is invited, however, he may freely eat at an offering to the gods while keeping to his vow, and at an offering to ancestors, conducting himself like a seer; doing so does not violate his vow. [190] Wise men sanction this activity only for Brahmins; this kind of activity is not commended at all for Kṣatriyas and Vaiśyas.

Conduct towards the Teacher

[191] When he is ordered by the teacher – or even when he is not – he should apply himself every day to vedic recitation and to activities beneficial to his teacher.

[192] Bringing his body, speech, organs of perception, and mind under control, he should stand with joined palms looking at his teacher's face. [193] He must always keep his right arm uncovered, comport himself properly, cover himself well, and, when he is told 'Be seated', sit down facing the teacher.

[194] In his teacher's presence, his food, clothes, and apparel should always be of a lesser quality than his teacher's. He should wake up before his teacher and go to bed after him.

[195] He must never answer or converse with his teacher while lying down, seated, eating, standing, or facing away; [196] he should do so standing up if the teacher is seated, approaching him if he is standing, going up to meet him if he is walking towards him, running after him if he is running, [197] going around to face him if he is turned away from him, coming close to him if he is far away, and bending down if he is lying down or standing at a lower level. [198] In his teacher's presence, he should always occupy a lower couch or seat; and, within his teacher's sight, he must not sit as he pleases.

[199] Even out of sight, he must not refer to his teacher by just his name or mimic his walk, speech, or mannerisms. [200] Wherever his teacher is slandered or reviled, he should either cover his ears or go somewhere else. [201] By slandering his teacher, he becomes an ass; by reviling him, a dog; by living off him, a worm; and by being jealous of him, an insect.

[202] When he is far away or angry, he must not pay his respects to his teacher; nor should he do so in the presence of a woman. When he is riding in a vehicle or seated on a chair, he should greet his teacher only after getting down. [203] He must not sit down with his teacher in such a way that the wind blows from the teacher towards him or from him towards the teacher; nor should he talk about anything out of his teacher's hearing. [204] He may sit by his teacher on a cart drawn by an ox, horse, or camel; on a terrace or a spread of grass; or on a mat, rock, bench, or boat.

Teacher's Teacher and Other Instructors [205] In the presence of his teacher's teacher, he should behave towards him as towards his own teacher; and he must not greet his own elders unless he is permitted by his teacher.

[206] He should always behave in the very same manner towards his vedic instructors and his own blood relatives, as also towards those who keep him from what is unrighteous and who teach him what is beneficial.

Members of Teacher's Family [207] Towards distinguished persons, as well as towards the teacher's Ārya sons and the teacher's own relatives, he should always behave just as he does towards his teacher.

[208] A teacher's son who teaches him – whether that son is younger than or of the same age as himself, or even if he is only a student of the ritual – is entitled to the same respect as his teacher. [209] He must not massage the limbs of his teacher's son, assist him at his bath, eat his leftovers, or wash his feet.

[210] The teacher's wives of equal class should receive the same honour as the teacher, but wives of unequal class should be honoured by rising up and greeting them. [211] He must not apply oil on his teacher's wife, assist her at her bath, massage her limbs, or do her hair. [212] Anyone who is over 20 and able to distinguish between the attractive and the unattractive should not greet here a young wife of his teacher by clasping her feet. [213] It is the very nature of women here to corrupt men. On that account, prudent men are never off guard in the presence of alluring young women. [214] For an alluring young woman is capable of leading astray not only the ignorant but even learned men under the sway of anger and lust. [215] He must not sit alone with his mother, sister, or daughter; the array of sensory organs is powerful and overpowers even a learned man. [216] A young man may freely pay his respects to the young wives of his teacher, however, by prostrating himself on the ground according to rule and saying: 'I am so-and-so.' [217] Recalling the Law followed by good people, he should clasp the feet of his teacher's wives upon his return from a journey and greet them every day.

[218] As a man discovers water by digging with a spade, so a student, offering obedient service, discovers the knowledge contained in his teacher.

Rules of Conduct

[219] A student may shave his head or keep his hair matted; or else he may keep just his topknot matted.

He should never let the sun rise or set while he is asleep in a village. [220] If the sun should rise or set while he is asleep, whether deliberately or inadvertently, he should fast for one day while engaging in soft recitation. [221] If, after he had been asleep at sunrise or sunset, he does not perform the penance, he becomes saddled with a great sin. [222] After purifying himself by sipping water and becoming self-possessed, he should worship both twilights every day, softly reciting the prescribed formula in a clean spot and according to rule (2.103).

[223] If he sees a woman or a low-born man doing something conducive to welfare, he should do all of that diligently, or anything else that he is fond of. [224] Some say that Law and Wealth are conducive to welfare; others, Pleasure and Wealth; and still others, Law alone or Wealth alone. But the settled rule is this: the entire triple set is conducive to welfare.

Mother, Father, Teacher [225] Teacher, father, mother, and older brother – these should never be treated with contempt especially by a Brahmin, even though he may be deeply hurt. [226] The teacher is the embodiment of Brahman; the father is the embodiment of Prajāpati; the mother is the embodiment of Earth; and one's brother is the embodiment of oneself. [227] The tribulations that a mother and a father undergo when humans are born cannot be repaid even in hundreds of years.

[228] He should do what is pleasing to these two every day, and always what is pleasing to his teacher. When these three are gratified, he obtains the fullness of ascetic toil. [229] Obedient service to these three is said to be the highest form of ascetic toil. Without their consent, he should not follow any other rule of conduct. [230] For they alone are the three worlds; they alone are the three orders of life; they alone are the three Vedas; and they alone are called the three sacred fires. [231] The householder's fire is clearly the father; the southern fire, tradition says, is the mother; and the offertorial fire is the teacher – this is the most excellent triad of sacred fires.

[232] A householder who does not neglect these three will win the three worlds; and, shining with his own body, he will rejoice in heaven like a god. [233] He obtains this world by devotion to his mother, and the middle world by devotion to his father; but he obtains the world of Brahman only by obedient service to his teacher. [234] When someone has attended to these three, he has attended to all his duties; should someone not attend to them, all his rites bear him no fruit. [235] So long as these three are alive, he should not follow another rule of conduct; taking delight in what is pleasing and beneficial to them, he should always render them obedient service. [236] Whenever he undertakes any mental, verbal, or physical activity for the sake of the next world without inconveniencing them, he should inform them of it.

[237] When these three are gratified, a man has done all he has to do. This is the highest Law itself in person; all else is called subsidiary Law.

Non-Brahmin Teachers [238] A man with faith should accept fine learning even from a low-caste man; the highest Law even from a man of the lowest caste; and a splendid woman even from a bad family. [239] One should take ambrosia even from poison; words of wisdom even from a child; a good example even from an enemy; and gold even from filth. [240] Women, gems, learning, Law, purification, and words of wisdom, as well as crafts of various kinds, may be accepted from anyone.

[241] In a time of adversity, the rules allow a man to study the Veda under a person who is not a Brahmin; and, as long as he is studying, he should walk after that teacher and serve him obediently. [242] If he desires to attain the highest state, a pupil should not live all his life with a teacher who is not a Brahmin or who is a Brahmin but not a vedic scholar.

Life-long Student: I

[243] If he wishes to live with his teacher's family all his life, however, he should diligently serve the teacher until he is freed from his body. [244] When a Brahmin obediently serves his teacher until his body comes to an end, he goes immediately to the eternal abode of Brahman.

Conclusion of Study

[245] Knowing the Law, he must not give any present to his teacher beforehand; but when, with his teacher's permission, he is ready to take his final bath, he should present the teacher with a gift according to his ability – [246] land, gold, a cow, or a horse; or at least an umbrella or footwear; or grain, vegetables, or clothes – and thus gladden his teacher.

Life-long Student: II

[247] If his teacher happens to die, he should maintain the same conduct towards his teacher's son possessing the right qualities – or towards his teacher's wife, or towards a person belonging to his teacher's ancestry (5.60 n.) – as he did towards his teacher. [248] If none of these is available, he should end his life by serving the sacred fire faithfully, standing during the day and seated at night (6.22 n.). [249] When a Brahmin lives the life of a vedic student in this manner without breaking his vow, he will go to the highest station and will not be reborn on earth again.

Chapter Three

Marriage

Conclusion of Study

[1] He should carry out the observance relating to the three Vedas at his teacher's house, an observance lasting thirty-six years, or one-half or one-quarter of that time, or else until he has learnt them.

[2] After he has learnt in the proper order the three Vedas or two of them, or at least one, without violating his chastity, he should undertake the householder's order of life. [3] When he has returned in accordance with the Law proper to him and received his vedic inheritance from his father, he should be honoured at the outset with the gift of a cow, as he sits on a couch wearing a garland.

Selection of a Bride

[4] After he has taken the concluding bath with his teacher's permission and performed the rite of returning home according to rule, the twice-born should marry a wife belonging to the same class and possessing the right bodily characteristics.

[5] A girl who belongs to an ancestry (5.60 n.) different from his mother's and to a lineage different from his father's, and who is unrelated to him by marriage, is recommended for marriage by a twice-born man.

[6] He should avoid these ten families when contracting a marriage alliance, even though they may be prominent and rich in cattle, goats, sheep, money, and grain: [7] families negligent about rites, deficient in male issue, without vedic learning, and with hairy bodies, as well as families prone to haemorrhoids, tuberculosis, dyspepsia, epilepsy, leukoderma, or leprosy.

[8] He must not marry a girl who has red hair or an extra limb; who is sickly; who is without or with too much bodily hair; who is a blabbermouth or jaundiced-looking; [9] who is named after a constellation, a tree, a river, a very low caste, a mountain, a bird, a snake, or a servant; or who has a frightening name. [10] He should marry a woman who is not deficient in any limb; who has a pleasant name; who walks like a goose or an elephant; and who has fine body and head hair, small teeth, and delicate limbs.

[11] A wise man must not marry a girl who has no brother or whose father is unknown, for fear that the Law of 'female-son' may be in force.

[12] At the first marriage, a woman of equal class is recommended for twice-born men; but for those who proceed further through lust, these are, in order, the preferable women. [13] A Śūdra may take only a Śūdra woman as wife; a Vaiśya, the latter and a woman of his own class; a Kṣatriya, the latter two and a woman of his own class; and a Brahmin, the latter three and a woman of his own class.

Prohibition of a Śūdra Wife [14] Not a single story mentions a Brahmin or a Kṣatriya taking a Śūdra wife even when they were going through a time of adversity. [15] When twice-born men foolishly marry low-caste wives, they quickly reduce even their families and children to the rank of Śūdras.

[16] According to Atri and the son of Utathya, a man falls from his caste by marrying a Śūdra woman; according to Śaunaka, by fathering a son through her; and according to Bhṛgu, by producing all his offspring through her. [17] By taking a Śūdra woman to bed, a Brahmin will descend along the downward course; and by begetting a son through her, he falls from the very rank of a Brahmin. [18] When such a woman plays the leading role in his divine, ancestral, and hospitality rites, gods and ancestors do not partake of them, and he will not go to heaven. [19] No expiation is prescribed for a man who drinks the saliva from the lips of a Śūdra woman, who is tainted by her breath, and who begets himself in her.

Types of Marriage

[20] Listen now in brief to these eight types of marriage for all four classes, some beneficial both here and in the hereafter, and some not. [21] They are the Brāhma, the Divine, the Seer's, the Prājāpatya, the Demonic, the Gāndharva, the Fiendish, and the Ghoulish, which is the eighth and the worst. [22] Which of these is lawful for which class, their respective merits and defects, the merits and demerits of each with respect to procreation – I will explain all this to you.

[23] The first six in the order enumerated should be considered lawful for Brahmins; the last four for Kṣatriyas; the same four, with the exception of the Fiendish, for Vaiśyas and Śūdras. [24] The first four, sages say, are recommended for Brahmins; the Fiendish alone for Kṣatriyas; and the Demonic for Vaiśyas and Śūdras. [25] The tradition recorded here, however, considers three of the last five as lawful and two as unlawful; one should never engage in the Demonic or the Ghoulish. [26] The two marriages proclaimed earlier, the Gāndharva and the Fiendish, whether undertaken separately or conjointly, are viewed by tradition as lawful for Kṣatriyas.

[27] When a man dresses a girl up, honours her, invites on his own a man of learning and virtue, and gives her to him, it is said to be the 'Brāhma' Law. [28] When a man, while a sacrifice is being carried out properly, adorns his daughter and gives her to the officiating priest as he is performing the rite, it is called the 'Divine' Law. [29] When a man accepts a bull and a cow, or two pairs of them, from the bridegroom in accordance with the Law and gives a girl to him according to rule, it is called the 'Seer's' Law. [30] When a man honours the girl and gives her after exhorting them with the words: 'May you jointly fulfil the Law,' tradition calls it the 'Prājāpatya' procedure. [31] When a girl is given after the payment of money to the girl's relatives and to the girl herself according to the man's ability and out of his own free will, it is called the 'Demonic' Law. [32] When the girl and the groom have sex with each other voluntarily, that is the 'Gāndharva' marriage based on sexual union and originating from love. [33] When someone violently abducts a girl from her house as she is shrieking and weeping by causing death, mayhem, and destruction, it is called the 'Fiendish' procedure. [34] When someone secretly rapes a woman who is asleep, drunk, or mentally deranged, it is the eighth known as 'Ghoulish', the most evil of marriages.

[35] Giving a girl away by simply pouring water is recommended for Brahmins, while among the other classes it may be done through mutual love.

Sons from Different Types of Marriage [36] Brahmins, listen now as I describe accurately all that Manu has said regarding the merits of each of these marriages.

[37] A son who is born to a woman married according to the 'Brāhma' rite and who does good deeds rescues from evil ten generations of forefathers before him and ten generations after him, with himself as the twenty-first; [38] a son born to a woman married according to the

'Divine' rite rescues seven generations before him and seven after him; a son born to a woman married according to the 'Seer's' rite, three before and three after; and a son born to a woman married according to 'Prājāpatya' marriage, six before and six after.

[39] From all four types of marriage beginning, in order, with 'Brāhma' are born sons who are eminent in vedic knowledge and respected by cultured people. [40] Endowed with beauty, spirit, and virtue, possessing wealth and fame, furnished with every delight, and righteous to the highest degree, they will live a hundred years. [41] But in the others – the remaining wicked types of marriage – are born sons whose speech is cruel and false and who hate the Veda and the Law.

[42] From irreproachable marriages are born children beyond reproach; from reproachable marriages are born children inviting people's reproach. Therefore, a man should avoid reproachable marriages.

Marriage Rite [43] The consecratory rite of taking the hand in marriage is prescribed only for brides of equal class. The following should be recognized as the procedure for the rite of marriage when brides are of unequal class. [44] When marrying an upper-class man, a Kṣatriya bride should take hold of an arrow, a Vaiśya bride a goad, and a Śūdra bride the hem of his garment.

Sexual Union

[45] Finding his gratification always in his wife, he should have sex with her during her season. Devoted solely to her, he may go to her also when he wants sexual pleasure, except on the days of the moon's change.

[46] The natural season of women, according to tradition, consists of sixteen nights, together with the other four days proscribed by good people. [47] Of these nights, the first four as well as the eleventh and the thirteenth are disapproved; the remaining ten nights are recommended.

[48] Sons are born when he has sex on even nights, and girls on odd nights. Desiring a son, therefore, he should have sex with his wife on even nights during her season. [49] When the man's semen is dominant, it turns out to be a boy; when the woman's is dominant, a girl; and when both are equal, a hermaphrodite or a twin boy and girl. When both are weak or scanty, no conception takes place.

[50] Regardless of the order of life in which a man lives, if he avoids women during the forbidden nights and during the other eight nights, he becomes a true celibate.

Purchasing a Wife

[51] A learned father must never accept even the slightest bride-price for his daughter; for by greedily accepting a bride-price, a man becomes a trafficker in his offspring. [52] When relatives foolishly live off a woman's wealth – slave women, vehicles, or clothes – those evil men will descend along the downward course.

[53] At a 'Seer's' marriage, some say, the bull and cow constitute the bride-price. That is totally false. Whether the amount is great or small, it is still a sale. [54] When women's relatives do not take the bride-price for themselves, it does not constitute a sale. It is an act of respect to women, a simple token of benevolence.

Honouring Women

[55] If they desire an abundance of good fortune, fathers, brothers, husbands, and brothers-in-law should revere their women and provide them with adornments.

[56] Where women are revered, there the gods rejoice; but where they are not, no rite bears any fruit. [57] Where female relatives grieve, that family soon comes to ruin; but where they do not grieve, it always prospers. [58] When female relatives, not receiving due reverence, curse any house, it comes to total ruin, as if struck down by witchcraft.

[59] If men want to become prosperous, therefore, they should always honour the women on joyful occasions and festive days with gifts of adornments, clothes, and food.

Marital Harmony

[60] Good fortune smiles incessantly on a family where the husband always finds delight in his wife, and the wife in her husband.

[61] For, if the wife does not sparkle, she does not arouse her husband. And if the husband is not aroused, there will be no offspring. [62] When the wife sparkles, so does the entire household; but when she ceases to sparkle, so does the entire household.

Degradation of Families

[63] By contracting aberrant marriages, by neglecting rites, and by failing to study the Veda, respectable families quickly come to ruin; as also by disregarding Brahmins. [64] By practising crafts, by engaging in trade, by having children only from a Śūdra wife, by dealing in cattle, horses, and vehicles, by engaging in agriculture, by entering a king's service, [65] by officiating at sacrifices of people at whose sacrifices one is forbidden to officiate, and by denying the efficacy of rites, respectable families fall into disrepute; as also those families bereft of vedic knowledge.

[66] When they are rich in vedic knowledge, however, even poor families attain the status of 'respectable family' and achieve great fame.

The Householder

[67] A householder should perform the domestic rites in his nuptial fire according to rule, as also the five great sacrifices and the daily cooking.

Great Sacrifices

[68] A householder has five slaughter-houses: fireplace, grindstone, broom, mortar and pestle, and water pot. By his use of them, he is fettered. [69] To expiate successively for each of these, the great seers devised the five great sacrifices to be carried out daily by householders.

[70] The sacrifice to the Veda is teaching; the sacrifice to ancestors is the quenching libation; the sacrifice to gods is the burnt offering; the sacrifice to beings is the Bali offering; and the sacrifice to humans is the honouring of guests. [71] If a man never fails to offer these five great sacrifices to the best of his ability, he remains unsullied by the taints of his slaughter-houses in spite of living permanently at home. [72] Gods, guests, dependants, ancestors, and oneself – when someone does not make offerings to these five, he has breath but no life at all.

[73] The five sacrifices are called Ahuta, Huta, Prahuta, Brāhmya-Huta, and Prāśita. [74] The Ahuta – 'not offered in the fire' – is soft recitation. The Huta – 'offered in the fire' – is a burnt offering. The Prahuta – 'offered by scattering' – is the Bali offering to beings. The Brāhmya-Huta – 'offered in Brahmins' – is the worship of Brahmins. The Prāśita – 'consumed' – is the quenching libation to ancestors.

[75] He should apply himself here daily to his vedic recitation and to making offerings to gods; for by applying himself to making offerings to gods, he upholds this world, both the mobile and the immobile. [76] An oblation duly consigned to the fire reaches the sun; from the sun comes rain; from rain, food; and from food, offspring.

[77] As all living beings exist dependent on air, so people in other orders of life exist dependent on the householder. [78] Because it is householders who sustain people in all three orders of life every day by giving them knowledge and food, the householder represents the most senior order of life. [79] This is the order that must be shouldered assiduously by anyone who desires undecaying heaven and absolute happiness, an order that cannot be shouldered by people with feeble faculties.

[80] Seers, ancestors, gods, beings, and guests seek favours from the householder, which a wise man should grant them. [81] He should duly honour the seers by private vedic recitation, gods with burnt oblations, ancestors with an ancestral offering, humans with food, and beings with a Bali offering.

Ancestral Offerings [82] He should make an ancestral offering every day with food or water, or even with milk, roots, and fruits, gladdening his ancestors thereby. [83] He should feed at least a single Brahmin for the benefit of his ancestors as part of the five great sacrifices; at this, he should never feed even a single Brahmin in connection with the offering to the All-gods.

Divine Offerings [84] From the oblation to All-gods that has been cooked, a Brahmin should offer portions in the domestic fire to the following deities every day and according to rule: [85] first to Fire and to Soma; then to both of them together; to the All-gods; to Dhanvantari; [86] to Kuhū – the goddess of the new moon; to Anumati – the goddess of the full moon; to Prajāpati; to heaven and earth together; and finally to Sviṣṭakṛt – Fire who makes the offering flawless.

Bali Offerings [87] In this manner, having offered the burnt oblation properly, he should make the Bali offerings to Indra, Death, Lord of the waters (Varuṇa), and Moon, together with their attendants, making the offerings clockwise in the direction of each quarter. [88] He should make an offering by the door, saying: 'To the Maruts!'; by the water pot, saying: 'To the waters!'; and by the mortar and pestle, saying 'To trees!' [89] He should make a Bali offering to Śrī – the goddess of prosperity – by the head of the bed; to Bhadrakālī – the auspicious black goddess – by the foot of the bed; and to Brahman and the Lord of the house in the middle of the house.

[90] He should throw into the air a Bali offering to All-gods, as well as to beings that roam during the day and to those that roam at night. [91] In the back house, he should make a Bali offering to Sarvānnabhūti – the power of all food. The remainder of the Bali oblation he should offer towards the south for the ancestors. [92] He should also gently place on the ground offerings for dogs, outcastes, dog-cookers, persons with evil diseases, crows, and worms.

[93] When a Brahmin honours all beings in this manner every day, he takes on a body of effulgence and goes by the direct route to the supreme abode.

Honouring Guests [94] After completing in this manner the Bali offering, he should feed a guest before anyone else and give almsfood to a mendicant student of the Veda according to rule. [95] By giving almsfood, a twice-born householder obtains as much merit as he does by giving a cow to a poor man according to rule.

[96] He should garnish some almsfood or a pot of water and present it in accordance with the rules to a Brahmin who knows the true meaning of the Veda. [97] Divine and ancestral oblations of ignorant men come to naught when the donors offer them foolishly to Brahmins who are the equivalent of ashes. [98] Oblations offered in the fires that are the mouths of Brahmins, fires set ablaze by knowledge and ascetic toil, rescue a man from danger and from grievous sin.

[99] When a guest arrives, he should offer him a seat and water and give him food as well according to rule, after garnishing it according to his ability. [100] When a Brahmin resides without being treated with respect, he takes away all the good works of even a man who lives by gleaning ears of grain (4.5 n.) or who makes daily offerings in the five sacred fires (3.185 n.). [101] Some straw, a place on the floor, water, and fourth, a pleasant word of welcome – at least these are never wanting in the houses of good people.

[102] Tradition defines a guest as a Brahmin who spends just one night. He is called 'guest' because his stay is brief. [103] A Brahmin living in the same village or on a social visit cannot be considered a guest even when he comes to a house which has a wife or even sacred fires. [104] When foolish householders become attached to other people's cooking, the result is that after death they are born as the cattle of those who gave them food.

[105] A householder must never turn away a guest led there by the sun in the evening; and whether he arrives at the proper time or not, he should not let him remain in his house without food. [106] Nor should he eat anything that he does not serve his guest. Honouring a guest leads to wealth, fame, long life, and heaven.

[107] Guests of the highest status should receive the highest treatment with respect to

seating, room, bed, accompanying them as they leave, and paying honour to them; those of equal status should receive equal treatment; and those of inferior status should receive inferior treatment. [108] If another guest arrives after he has completed the offering to All-gods, however, he should provide him also with food according to his ability; but he need not make a fresh Bali offering.

[109] A Brahmin must not advertise his family and lineage for the sake of a meal; for the wise call a man who flaunts these for a meal 'an eater of vomit'.

[110] A Kṣatriya is not called a 'guest' in the house of a Brahmin; nor is a Vaiśya, a Śūdra, a friend, a relative, or an elder. [111] If, however, a Kṣatriya comes to his house fulfilling the conditions of a guest, he may freely feed him also after the Brahmins have finished their meal. [112] Even when a Vaiśya or a Śūdra arrives at his house fulfilling the conditions of a guest, he should show kindness and feed him along with his servants. [113] Even when others, such as his friends, visit his house out of mutual affection, he should make as special a preparation of food as he can and feed them along with his wife. [114] Newly married women, young girls, the sick, and pregnant women – these he may feed without hesitation right after the guests.

[115] When a fool eats before he gives food to these persons, as he eats he is unaware that he is being eaten by dogs and vultures. [116] Once the Brahmins, the dependants, and the servants have finished their meal, only then should the husband and wife eat what is left over. [117] After he has honoured the gods, seers, humans, ancestors, and the guardian deities of the house, the householder should eat what remains. [118] A man who cooks only for his own sake eats nothing but sin; for the food prescribed for good men is this – eating the leftovers of a sacrifice.

[119] He should honour a king, an officiating priest, a bath-graduate, an elder, a friend, a father-in-law, and a maternal uncle with a honey-mixture when they visit him after the lapse of one year. [120] The rule is that a king and a vedic scholar should be honoured with a honey-mixture when a sacrifice is about to take place, but never outside the context of a sacrifice.

[121] When the evening meal is cooked, the wife should make a Bali offering without reciting vedic formulas. This is called 'offering to All-gods', and it is prescribed both in the evening and in the morning.

Ancestral Offerings

[122] After he has offered the sacrifice to ancestors, a Brahmin who possesses a sacred fire should perform the monthly ancestral rite called the 'supplementary offering of rice balls' on the new-moon day. [123] The wise call the monthly offering to ancestors the 'supplementary offering', and it should be performed diligently using the recommended kinds of meat.

[124] Who are the Brahmins to be fed at this rite and who are to be avoided? How many? And with what kinds of food? – I will explain all that completely.

Number of Invitees [125] Even if he is rich, he should feed two at an offering to gods, three at an offering to ancestors, or one at either offering; he should not indulge in feeding a large number. [126] A large number is detrimental to five things: offering proper hospitality, doing things at the right place and the right time, carrying out purifications, and finding Brahmins of quality. Therefore, he must not try to get a large number.

Quality of Invitees [127] This rite for the deceased performed at the new moon is well known by the name 'ancestral offering'. When a man is devoted to it, the same non-vedic rite for the deceased benefits him always.

[128] Donors should present a divine or ancestral offering only to a vedic scholar; what is given to such an eminently worthy Brahmin yields abundant fruit. [129] He should feed even a single learned man at each rite to gods or ancestors rather than a lot of men ignorant

of the Veda; he reaps thereby copious fruit. [130] He should search far and wide for a Brahmin who has mastered the Veda; such a man is the proper recipient of divine and ancestral offerings, and tradition calls him a 'guest'. [131] For when one man who knows the Veda is gratified there, in terms of the Law he is worth all the men ignorant of the Veda who may eat there, be they in their millions. [132] Divine and ancestral offerings should be given to a man renowned for his knowledge, for hands smeared with blood cannot be cleansed with more blood. [133] A man will have to eat as many red-hot spikes, spears, and iron balls as the rice balls that someone ignorant of the Veda eats at his divine or ancestral offerings.

[134] Some Brahmins apply themselves to knowledge, some to ascetic toil, others to both ascetic toil and vedic recitation, and still others to ritual activities. [135] He should diligently present divine offerings only to those who apply themselves to knowledge, but he may present ancestral offerings to any of the four according to rule. [136] Between a man whose father is not a vedic savant but whose son has mastered the Veda and a man whose father has mastered the Veda but whose son is not a vedic savant, [137] the man whose father is a vedic savant should be considered as superior. The other deserves honour for the sake of venerating the Veda.

[138] A friend must not be fed at an ancestral offering; he is to be courted with presents. A twice-born who is deemed neither friend nor foe is the one who should be fed at an ancestral offering. [139] When a friend takes centre stage at his divine or ancestral offerings, he reaps no fruit from them after death. [140] When a man foolishly strikes up friendships by means of an ancestral offering, that lowest of twice-born, using ancestral offerings to make friends, will fall from heaven. [141] Such a sacrificial gift is ghoulish and twice-born people call it 'feeding-one-another'. It remains in this very world, like a blind cow in a single stall.

[. . .]

Chapter Four

The Bath-Graduate

[1] After spending the first quarter of his life at his teacher's, a twice-born man should marry a wife and spend the second quarter of his life at home.

Right Livelihood

[2] Except during a time of adversity, a Brahmin ought to sustain himself by following a livelihood that causes little or no harm to creatures. [3] He should gather wealth just sufficient for his subsistence through irreproachable activities that are specific to him, without fatiguing his body.

[4] Let him sustain himself by means of 'true' and 'immortal', or by means of 'mortal' and 'fatal', or even by means of 'truth-cum-falsehood'; but under no circumstances by means of the 'dog's life'. [5] Gleaning and picking should be considered the 'true'; what is received unasked is the 'immortal'; almsfood that is begged is the 'mortal'; and agriculture, tradition says, is the 'fatal'. [6] Trade is the 'truth-cum-falsehood', and he may sustain himself even by that. Service is called the 'dog's life'; therefore, he should avoid it altogether.

[7] Let him be a man who stores grain sufficient to fill a granary, a man who stores grain sufficient to fill a jar, a man who has sufficient grain to last three days, or a man who keeps nothing for the next day. [8] Among all these four types of twice-born householders, each should be recognized as superior to the ones preceding it and better at winning the heavenly world, according to the Law. [9] One of these may engage in the six activities; another may live by three; yet another by two; and a fourth may subsist through the sacrificial session of the Veda. [10] A man who lives by gleaning and picking should be totally dedicated to the daily fire sacrifice and always offer only the sacrifices at the new- and full-moon days and at the solstices. [11] He must never follow a worldly occupation for the sake of livelihood,

but subsist by means of a pure, upright, and honest livelihood proper to a Brahmin.

[12] One who seeks happiness should become supremely content and self-controlled, for happiness is rooted in contentment and its opposite is the root of unhappiness.

Observances

[13] Subsisting by one of these means of livelihood, a twice-born who is a bath-graduate should follow these observances, which procure heaven, long life, and fame.

[14] He should perform diligently the daily rituals specific to him prescribed in the Veda; for, by performing them according to his ability, he attains the highest state. [15] He must never seek to obtain wealth (*artha*) with excessive passion, through forbidden activities, when he already has sufficient wealth, or from just anyone even in a time of adversity; [16] nor shall he be passionately attached to any of the sensory objects (*artha*) out of lust, but using his mind he should stamp out any excessive attachment to them. [17] He should forsake all pursuits (*artha*) that interfere with his vedic recitation, eking out a living some way or other, for that recitation constitutes the fulfilment of all his obligations. [18] He should comport himself here in such a way that his attire, speech, and mind are in harmony with his age, occupation, wealth (*artha*), learning, and family background.

Study

[19] Every day, he should explore the treatises – those that aid in the quick development of one's mind, those that facilitate the acquisition of wealth, and those that promote well-being – as well as ancillary texts of the Veda; [20] for, the more a man studies treatises, the more he comes to understand and the more brightly shines his understanding.

Ritual Duties

[21] He must never fail to offer every day and according to his ability the sacrifices to seers, gods, beings, humans, and ancestors.

[22] Some individuals who are experts in the sacrificial science and free from striving offer these great sacrifices incessantly in just their organs. [23] Others offer breath in speech and speech in breath every day, recognizing that the sacrifice reaches its inexhaustible consummation in speech and breath. [24] Still other Brahmins offer these sacrifices daily through knowledge alone, recognizing by the eye of knowledge that the execution of those sacrifices is rooted in knowledge.

[25] A twice-born man, moreover, should always offer the fire sacrifice at the beginning and end of each day and night; the new-moon and the full-moon sacrifice at the end of each fortnight; [26] the new-harvest sacrifice at the end of each harvest; the seasonal sacrifices at the end of each season; an animal sacrifice at the end of each half-year; and Soma sacrifices at the end of each year. [27] A twice-born who has established the sacred fires, if he wants to live a long life, must never eat a new crop without offering the new-harvest sacrifice, or meat without offering an animal sacrifice; [28] for his sacred fires crave for the new crop and meat and, if they have not been honoured with an offering of the new crop and an animal oblation, yearn to eat his very lifebreaths.

Reception of Guests

[29] No guest should stay at his house without being honoured with a seat, food, and a bed, or with water, roots, and fruits, according to his ability. [30] He must never honour the following even with a word of welcome: ascetics of heretical sects; individuals engaging in improper activities, observing the 'cat vow', or following the way of herons; hypocrites; and sophists. [31] At rites for gods and ancestors, he should honour individuals who have bathed after completing the Vedas, vedic learning, or vedic vows, who are vedic scholars, or who are householders, but avoid individuals different from these. [32] As far as he is able, a householder should give to those who do not cook and share with all beings without causing hardship to himself.

Rules of Conduct: I

[33] If a bath-graduate is tormented by hunger, he may request money from the king, from a client at whose sacrifices he officiates, or from a resident pupil, but from no one else – that is the settled rule. [34] If he has the capacity, a Brahmin bath-graduate should never torment himself with hunger or, if he has the means, wear dirty or worn-out clothes.

[35] He shall keep his nails clipped, his hair and beard trimmed, and himself restrained; wear white clothes; remain pure; and apply himself every day to his vedic recitation and to activities conducive to his own welfare. [36] He shall carry a bamboo staff, a waterpot filled with water, and a broom of sacred grass, and wear a sacrificial cord and a pair of bright gold earrings.

[37] He must never look at the sun as it rises or sets, when it is eclipsed or reflected in water, or when it is in the middle of the sky. [38] He must not step over a rope to which a calf is tied, run in the rain, or look at his reflection in water – that is the fixed rule. [39] A mound of earth, a cow, a god, a Brahmin, ghee, honey, and a crossroads – he should circumambulate these clockwise, as also notable trees.

Relationship with Women

[40] Though aroused, he must never have sex with his wife after the onset of her menstrual period, or even lie on the same bed with her; [41] for when a man has sex with a woman besmirched with menstrual blood, his wisdom, energy, strength, sight, and life-force waste away. [42] When he avoids a woman besmirched with menstrual blood, his wisdom, energy, strength, sight, and life-force will wax stronger.

[43] He must never eat with his wife or look at her while she is eating, sneezing, yawning, or seated at ease; [44] nor should the Brahmin, if he wants energy, look at her while she is applying collyrium to her eyes or oil on her body, or when she is undressed or giving birth.

Voiding Urine and Excrement

[45] He must never eat food wearing just a single garment; bathe naked; or urinate on a road, on ashes, in a cow pen, [46] on ploughed land, into water, onto a mound or a hill, in a dilapidated temple, onto an anthill, [47] into occupied animal holes, while walking or standing, by a river bank, or at the top of a hill. [48] He must never void urine or excrement facing the wind, a fire, a Brahmin, the sun, water, or cows.

[49] Restraining his voice, remaining steadfastly attentive, covering his body, and wrapping his head, he should ease himself after strewing the ground with sticks, clods, leaves, or grass. [50] During the day, he should void urine and excrement facing the north, at night facing the south, and at the two twilights in the same way as during the day. [51] Under a shadow or in a place that is pitch-dark, a Brahmin may do so during the day or at night facing any direction he pleases, as also when he fears for his life.

[52] When someone urinates towards a fire, the sun, the moon, water, a twice-born man, a cow, or the wind, his wisdom perishes.

Rules of Conduct: II

[53] He must never blow on a fire with his mouth; look at a woman when she is naked; throw anything filthy into a fire; warm his feet over it; [54] place it under his bed; step over it; place it by his feet; hurt living creatures; [55] eat, travel, or sleep during the time of twilight; scribble on the ground; take off his own garland; [56] deposit urine, excrement, sputum, blood, poison, or anything smeared with filth in water; [57] sleep alone in an abandoned house; awaken a sleeping superior; speak with a menstruating woman; or go to a sacrifice uninvited.

[58] Within an enclosure for the sacred fire, in a cow pen, in the presence of Brahmins, during his vedic recitation, and while eating, he shall keep his right arm uncovered (2.193 n.). [59] He must never prevent a cow from suckling her calf or report it to anyone. When he sees a rainbow in the sky, he should wisely refrain from pointing it out to anyone.

[60] He must never reside in a village full of unrighteous people or where diseases run rampant; go on a journey alone; stay long on a mountain; [61] or live in a kingdom ruled by a Śūdra, teeming with unrighteous people, overrun by people belonging to heretical ascetic sects, or swamped by lowest-born people.

[62] He must never eat anything from which the oil has been extracted; eat beyond capacity; eat very early in the morning or very late in the evening; eat again in the evening after taking his meal in the morning; [63] undertake useless activities; drink water from his cupped hands; eat food placed on his lap; be in any way inquisitive; [64] dance; sing; play a musical instrument; clap; whistle; make noises when sexually excited; [65] wash his feet in a brass vessel at any time; eat from a broken plate or from one that looks repulsive to him; [66] or use footwear, a garment, a sacrificial cord, an ornament, a garland, or a waterpot previously used by others.

[. . .]

Avoiding Violence

[162] He must never cause harm to his teacher, instructor, father, mother, elder, Brahmins, cows, and all who are given to austerities. [163] He should eschew infidelity, denigrating the Vedas, disparaging the gods, hatred, arrogance, pride, anger, and harshness.

[164] He must not raise a stick against another person or bring it down on anyone in anger, except a son or a pupil; these he may beat in order to discipline them (8.299). [165] If a twice-born merely threatens a Brahmin with murderous intent, he will meander in the Tāmisra hell for one hundred years. [166] If he strikes him deliberately in anger with even a blade of grass, he will be reborn in evil wombs for twenty-one births. [167] If a man foolishly draws blood from the body of a Brahmin who is not attacking him, he will experience intense suffering after death. [168] A man who draws blood will be eaten by others in the next world for as many years as the number of dust particles from the earth that the spilled blood lumps together.

[169] A wise man, therefore, must never threaten a twice-born person, strike him even with a blade of grass, or draw blood from his body.

[. . .]

Unfit Food

[205] A Brahmin must never partake of food at a sacrifice offered by someone who is not a vedic scholar or who officiates as a priest for a large number of people, or at one offered by a woman or an effeminate man (3.150 n.). [206] When such persons offer an oblation, it is unpropitious for virtuous people and disagreeable to gods; therefore, he should avoid it.

[207] He must also never eat the following: food given by someone who is drunk, angry, or sick; food contaminated with hair or insects or touched deliberately with the foot; [208] food looked at by a murderer of a Brahmin, touched by a menstruating woman, pecked by a bird, or touched by a dog; [209] food smelled by a cow; in a special way, food given after a public announcement; food given by a group or by a prostitute; food that is despised by learned men; [210] food given by a thief, a musician, a carpenter, a usurer, a man consecrated for a sacrifice, a miser, a prisoner, a shackled man, [211] a heinous sinner (2.185 n.), a eunuch, a promiscuous woman, or a hypocrite; food that has turned sour or is stale; food of a Śūdra; leftovers (2.56 n.); [212] food given by a physician, a hunter, a cruel man, someone who eats left-overs, or an Ugra; food of a woman impure by reason of childbirth; food served at a meal where someone sips water during the meal; food given during the ten days of impurity resulting from a birth; [213] food given without respect; meat procured capriciously (5.27); food given by a woman without a husband; food of an enemy, the chief of a town, or an outcaste; food someone has sneezed upon; [214] food given by a slanderer, a liar, a trafficker in rituals, an actor, a tailor, an ingrate, [215] a blacksmith, a Niṣāda, a theatrical performer, a goldsmith, a basket-weaver, an arms merchant, [216] those who raise dogs, liquor merchants, a washerman, a dyer, a heartless man, someone who lets his wife's

paramour live in his house [217] or who condones a paramour, or someone who is bossed by his wife in every way; food of persons during the first ten days after a death in their family; food offered to a newly deceased person, and unappetizing food.

[218] The food of a king robs his energy; the food of a Śūdra, his eminence in vedic knowledge; the food of a goldsmith, his life-force; and the food of a leather-worker, his fame. [219] The food of an artisan destroys his offspring, and the food of a dyer, his strength. The food of a group or of a prostitute cuts him off from the worlds. [220] The food of a physician is pus; the food of a promiscuous woman is semen; the food of a usurer is excrement; and the food of an arms merchant is filth. [221] The food of those others who have been listed in order as people whose food is unfit to be eaten – the wise declare that to be skin, bones, and hair.

[222] If someone eats the food of any one of them unintentionally, he should fast for three days; if he eats intentionally – as also when he consumes semen, urine, or excrement – he should perform an arduous penance (11.212).

[223] A learned twice-born must never eat cooked food given by a Śūdra who lacks a spirit of generosity (3.202 n.). If he is without sustenance, he may accept from such a man only raw provisions sufficient for a single day.

[224] The gods once evaluated the food of a miserly vedic scholar and that of a generous usurer and pronounced the two to be equal. [225] Prajāpati came up to them and said, 'Don't make equal what is unequal. The food of the generous man is cleansed by the spirit of generosity, whereas the other food is defiled by the lack of generosity.'

[. . .]

Chapter Five

Food Eating Meat

[27] He may eat meat when it is sacrificially consecrated, at the behest of Brahmins, when he is ritually commissioned according to rule, and when his life is at risk.

[28] Prajāpati created this whole world as food for lifebreath; all beings, the mobile and the immobile, are nourishment for lifebreath. [29] The immobile are food for the mobile; the fangless for the fanged; the handless for the handed; and the timid for the brave. [30] The eater is not defiled by eating living beings suitable for eating, even if he eats them day after day; for the creator himself fashioned both the eaters and the living beings suitable for eating.

[31] 'The sacrifice is the reason for eating meat' – this, the tradition says, is the rule of gods. Doing it for any other purpose is called the rule of fiends. [32] When a man eats meat – whether it was purchased, procured by himself, or offered by someone else – after making an offering to gods and ancestors, he does not become defiled. [33] Except in a time of adversity, a twice-born man who knows the rules must never eat meat in contravention of the rules; if he eats meat in contravention of the rules, after death he will be eaten forcibly by those very animals. [34] In the afterlife, the sin of someone who hunts animals for profit is not as great as that of a man who eats meat procured capriciously. [35] If a man refuses to eat meat after he has been ritually commissioned according to rule (5.27 n.), after death he will become an animal for twenty-one lifetimes. [36] A Brahmin must never eat animals that have not been consecrated with ritual formulas. Abiding by the eternal rule, however, he must eat those that have been consecrated with ritual formulas.

[37] If he gets the urge, let him make an animal out of butter or flour; but he must never entertain the desire to kill an animal for a futile reason. [38] When a man kills an animal for a futile reason, after death he will be subject in birth after birth to being slain as many times as the number of hairs on that animal.

[39] The Self-existent One himself created domestic animals for sacrifice, and the sacrifice is for the prosperity of this whole world. Within the sacrifice, therefore, killing is not killing. [40] When plants, domestic animals, trees, beasts, and birds die for the sake of a sacrifice,

they will in turn earn superior births. [41] The honey-mixture (3.119 n.), a sacrifice, an offering to gods or ancestors – at no other occasion than these, Manu has declared, may animals be killed. [42] When a twice-born man who knows the true meaning of the Veda kills animals for these purposes, he leads himself and those animals to the highest state. [43] Whether he lives at home, at his teacher's, or in the wilderness, a twice-born man who is self-possessed must never, even in a time of adversity, carry out a killing that is not sanctioned by the Veda. [44] When a killing is sanctioned by the Veda and well-established in this mobile and immobile creation, it should be regarded definitely as a non-killing; for it is from the Veda that the Law has shined forth.

[45] If someone, craving his own pleasure, harms harmless creatures, he will not find happiness anywhere while he is still alive or after death. [46] When someone has no desire to tie up, kill, or cause pain to living creatures and seeks the welfare of all beings, he obtains endless bliss. [47] Whatever a man contemplates, whatever a man undertakes, whatever a man takes a liking to – all that he obtains without effort, when he does no harm to any creature.

[48] One can never obtain meat without causing injury to living beings, and killing living beings is an impediment to heaven; he should, therefore, abstain from meat. [49] Reflecting on how meat is obtained and on how embodied creatures are tied up and killed, he should quit eating any kind of meat. [50] When a man refrains from eating meat like a goblin, except when the rules prescribe it, he is loved by the world and is not tormented by diseases.

[51] The man who authorizes, the man who butchers, the man who slaughters, the man who buys or sells, the man who cooks, the man who serves, and the man who eats – these are all killers. [52] There is no greater sinner than a man who, outside of an offering to gods or ancestors, wants to make his own flesh thrive at the expense of someone else's.

[53] A man who abstains from meat and a man who offers the horse sacrifice every year for a hundred years – the reward for their meritorious acts is the same. [54] Even by living on pure fruits and roots and by eating the food of sages, a man fails to obtain as great a reward as he would by abstaining completely from meat.

[55] 'Me he (*māṃ sa*) will eat in the next world, whose meat (*māṃsa*) I eat in this world' – this, the wise declare, is what gave the name to and discloses the true nature of 'meat' (*māṃsa*).

[56] There is no fault in eating meat, in drinking liquor, or in having sex; that is the natural activity of creatures. Abstaining from such activity, however, brings great rewards.

> [57] I will now explain the purification after a death, as well as the purification of things, precisely and in their proper order for all four classes.

Bodily Purification

Death or Birth of a Person Belonging to the Same Ancestry

[58] Someone who has teethed, someone younger, or someone who has had his first cutting of hair (2.35) – when any of these dies, all his relatives become impure; the same is prescribed after the birth of a child. [59] A ten-day period of impurity following a death is prescribed for those who belong to the same ancestry; alternatively, that period may last until the collection of bones, or for three days, or for a single day.

[60] The relationship based on common ancestry stops with the seventh generation; the relationship based on offering libations, on the other hand, stops only when someone's birth and name are no longer remembered.

[61] The same holds true at a birth. The birth-impurity, however, affects only the mother and the father. The mother alone is subject to the period of birth-impurity; the father becomes pure by bathing. [Number 62 is omitted] [63] On the contrary, it is after spilling his seed that a man is purified by simply bathing; the impurity resulting from a seminal relationship adheres to him for three days.

[64] Those who touch the corpse are purified in ten days, but those who offer libations in three. [65] A pupil who performs the funerary rites of his deceased teacher, on the other hand, is on a par with those who carry a corpse and is purified in ten days.

[66] After a miscarriage, a woman is purified after the same number of days as the months of her pregnancy. A menstruating woman becomes wholesome by taking a bath after her menstrual flow has ceased.

[67] When males die before the first cutting of their hair (2.35), tradition tells us, the impurity lasts a single night; but when they die after the cutting of their hair, purity is considered to be restored after three nights. [68] When a child under two dies, its relatives should decorate its corpse and lay it down in a clean spot outside the village; the ceremony of collecting its bones is omitted. [69] Neither the consecration with fire nor the offering of water is done for such a child; after leaving it behind in the wilderness like a piece of wood, one should keep the observances for just three days. [70] Relatives should not offer libations of water for a child under three; they may do so optionally if it has teethed or if its naming ceremony has been performed.

[71] When someone who had been a fellow student dies, tradition prescribes the observances for one day. In the event of a birth, the purity of those related through offering libations (5.60 n.) is considered to be restored after three days. [72] The relations of unmarried women are purified in three days, but her siblings are purified exactly according to the prescribed rule.

[73] For three days they are to eat food without artificial salt, bathe by immersion, abstain from eating meat, and sleep separately on the floor.

Death in a Distant Region [74] The above set of rules concerning impurity after death is prescribed only when a death has occurred close by; when it has happened far away, kinsmen and relatives should know that the procedure is as follows.

[75] When someone living in a far-away place dies and one hears of it within ten days of his death, one becomes impure only for the remainder of that ten-day period. [76] If one hears of it after the lapse of ten days, one becomes impure for three days; but if it is after a year, one is purified simply by bathing. [77] When a man hears about the death of a paternal relative or the birth of a son after the lapse of ten days, he becomes pure by immersing himself in water with his clothes on. [78] When a child or someone belonging to a different ancestry dies in a far-away place, one is purified instantly by immersing oneself in water with one's clothes on.

Overlapping Periods of Impurity [79] If during one ten-day period of impurity another death or birth occurs, a Brahmin remains impure only until the end of the initial ten-day period.

Death of Significant Others [80] At the death of one's teacher, they prescribe a three-day period of impurity; and at the death of the teacher's son or wife, the settled rule is a day and a night. [81] One becomes impure for three days at the death of a vedic scholar living near by, and for two days plus the intervening night at the death of one's maternal uncle, pupil, officiating priest, or maternal relative. [82] At the death of a king, anyone residing within his realm remains impure that day from dawn to dusk or that night from dusk to dawn (4.106 n.). At the death of someone who is not a vedic scholar, a vedic savant, or an elder, one remains impure for a full day.

Periods of Impurity for Different Classes [83] A Brahmin is purified in ten days, a Kṣatriya in twelve, a Vaiśya in fifteen, and a Śūdra in a month. [84] One should not prolong the days of impurity or postpone one's fire rituals; while performing that rite, even a uterine brother (5.72 n.) becomes immune to impurity.

Impurity from Touch [85] When someone touches a Divākīrti, a menstruating woman, an outcaste, a woman who has given birth, or a corpse – as also a person who has touched any of these – he is purified by bathing. [86] At the sight of an impure person, he should make himself ritually pure by sipping water and then softly recite the Solar formulas according to his capacity, and the Pāvamānī verses to the best of his ability. [87] After touching a human bone, a Brahmin is purified by bathing if the bone was greasy, but simply by sipping water, touching a cow, or gazing at the sun, if the bone was dry.

Libations for the Dead [88] A votary shall not offer a libation until he has completed his vow; but once he has completed his vow and offered the libation, he is purified in just three days. [89] Libations are omitted in the case of people born through capricious caste mingling; those living in ascetic orders; suicides; [90] and women who have joined heretical sects, roam about at will, harm their foetus or husband, or drink liquor. [91] By carrying his own deceased teacher, tutor (2.141), father, mother, or elder, a votary (5.88 n.) does not break his vow.

Funeral Path [92] A dead Śūdra should be carried out through the southern gate of the city, and a twice-born person through the western, the northern, or the eastern gate, as appropriate.

Instant Purification of Kings [93] The taint of impurity does not affect kings, votaries, and those engaged in a sacrificial session; for they are seated on the seat of Indra and are ever one with *brahman*. [94] Instant purification is prescribed for a king on the seat of majesty – the reason for this is that he is seated for the protection of his subjects – [95] as also for people killed in a riot or battle, by lightning or the king, or in defence of cows or Brahmins, and for anyone the king wants.

[96] Soma, Fire, Sun, Wind, Indra, the Lords of wealth and water, and Yama – the king is the embodiment of these eight guardians of the world (see 7.4). [97] The lords of the world abide within the king, and no period of impurity is prescribed for him; for it is the lords of the world who both bring about and erase purity and impurity in mortal beings.

[98] When a man is killed in battle with upraised weapons according to the Kṣatriya law, the settled rule is that for him both sacrifice and purification are accomplished instantly.

[99] After completing the required rite, a Brahmin is purified by touching water, a Kṣatriya his conveyance or weapon, a Vaiśya his goad or reins, and a Śūdra his staff.

> [100] I have explained to you above, O Brahmins, the purification in the case of people belonging to the same ancestry (5.60 n.). Listen now to the purification after death in the case of all those belonging to different ancestries.

Death of a Person Belonging to a Different Ancestry

[101] If a Brahmin carries the corpse of a twice-born person unrelated to him by ancestry as if he were a relative, or if he carries a close (2.109 n.) relative of his mother, he is purified in three days. [102] If he eats their food, on the other hand, his purification takes ten full days; but if he neither eats their food nor stays at their house, it takes just one day. [103] If someone willingly follows a corpse, whether it is that of a paternal relative or of someone else, he is purified after he has bathed with his clothes on, touched the fire, and eaten some ghee.

[104] When one's own people are present, one should never let a Śūdra carry a Brahmin's corpse, for a sacrificial offering defiled by a Śūdra's touch does not lead a person to heaven.

Means of Purification

[105] Knowledge, austerity, fire, food, earth, mind, water, smearing with cow dung, wind, rites, sun, time – these are the agents of purification for embodied beings.

[106] Purifying oneself with respect to wealth, tradition tells us, is the highest of all purifications; for the truly pure man is the one who is pure with respect to wealth, not the one who becomes pure by using earth and water.

[107] Learned men are purified by forbearance; those who do forbidden things, by giving gifts; those who commit secret sins, by soft recitation; and pre-eminent experts in the Veda, by ascetic toil. [108] What needs cleaning is cleansed by using earth and water, a river by its current, a woman defiled in thought

by her menstrual flow, and Brahmins by renunciation. [109] The body is cleansed with water, the mind by truth, the elemental self by learning and austerity, and the intellect by knowledge.

> [110] I have explained to you above the determination with regard to bodily purification. Listen now to the determination with regard to the purification of different kinds of articles.

Purification of Articles

[111] The wise have determined that metal objects, jewels, and anything lapidary are cleaned with ash, water, and earth. [112] When they are unstained, gold vessels are cleaned with water alone, as also the aquatic, the lapidary, or any silver article that is unembellished. [113] Gold and silver issued from the union of fire and water; they are best cleaned, therefore, using their very sources. [114] The cleaning of copper, iron, brass, pewter, tin, and lead is done using as appropriate alkali, acid, and water.

[115] All liquids, tradition tells us, are cleaned by straining; solids, by sprinkling water; and wooden articles, by planing.

[116] During a sacrificial rite, sacrificial vessels are rubbed with the hand; the Camasa-cups and Graha-ladles, on the other hand, are cleaned by washing; [117] the Caru-pots, Sruk-spoons, and Sruva-spoons are cleaned with warm water, as are Sphya-swords, Śūrpa-winnows, Śakaṭa-carts, pestles, and mortars [. . .]

Law With Respect to Women

Lack of Independence

[147] Even in her own home, a female – whether she is a child, a young woman, or an old lady – should never carry out any task independently. [148] As a child, she must remain under her father's control; as a young woman, under her husband's; and when her husband is dead, under her sons'. She must never seek to live independently. [149] She must never want to separate herself from her father, husband, or sons; for by separating herself from them, a woman brings disgrace on both families.

[150] She should be always cheerful, clever at housework, careful in keeping the utensils clean, and frugal in her expenditure.

Duties towards Husband

[151] The man to whom her father or, with her father's consent, her brother gives her away – she should obey him when he is alive and not be unfaithful to him when he is dead. [152] The invocation of blessings and the sacrifice to Prajāpati are performed during marriage to procure her good fortune; the act of giving away is the reason for his lordship over her. [153] In season and out of season, in this world and in the next, the husband who performed the marriage consecration with ritual formulas always gives happiness to his woman.

[154] Though he may be bereft of virtue, given to lust, and totally devoid of good qualities, a good woman should always worship her husband like a god. [155] For women, there is no independent sacrifice, vow, or fast; a woman will be exalted in heaven by the mere fact that she has obediently served her husband. [156] A good woman, desiring to go to the same world as her husband, should never do anything displeasing to the man who took her hand, whether he is alive or dead.

[157]After her husband is dead, she may voluntarily emaciate her body by eating pure flowers, roots, and fruits; but she must never mention even the name of another man. [158] Aspiring to that unsurpassed Law of women devoted to a single husband, she should remain patient, controlled, and celibate until her death. [159] Untold thousands of Brahmins who have remained celibate from their youth have gone to heaven without producing offspring to continue their family line. [160] Just like these celibates, a good woman, though she be sonless, will go to heaven when she steadfastly adheres to the celibate life after her husband's death. [161] When a woman is unfaithful to her husband because of her strong desire for children, she is disgraced in this world and

excluded from the husband's world. [162] No recognition is given here to offspring fathered by another man or begotten on another's wife; nor is it taught anywhere that a good woman should take a second husband.

[163] When a woman abandons her own husband of lower rank and unites with a man of higher rank, she only brings disgrace upon herself in the world and is called 'a woman who has had a man before'. [164] By being unfaithful to her husband, a woman becomes disgraced in the world, takes birth in a jackal's womb, and is afflicted with evil diseases (3.159 n.).

[165] A woman who controls her mind, speech, and body and is never unfaithful to her husband attains the worlds of her husband, and virtuous people call her a 'good woman'. [166] By following this conduct, a woman who controls her mind, speech, and body obtains the highest fame in this world and the world of her husband in the next.

Funeral

[167] When a wife who has conducted herself in this manner and who belongs to the same class as her husband dies before him, a twice-born man who knows the Law should cremate her with his sacred fire and sacrificial implements. [168] After he has given his sacred fires to his predeceased wife at her funeral, he should marry a wife again and establish anew his sacred fires.

Chapter Six

Forest Hermit

[1] After living this way in the householder's order according to rule, a twice-born bath-graduate should duly live in the forest, controlling himself and mastering his organs.

Time and Procedure

[2] When a householder sees his skin wrinkled, his hair turned grey, and his children's children, he should take to the wilderness. [3] Giving up village food and all his belongings, he should go to the forest, entrusting his wife to his sons or accompanied by her.

[4] Taking with him his sacrificial fires and the implements required for his domestic fire rituals, he should depart from the village to the wilderness and live there with his organs controlled.

Mode of Life

[5] Using various kinds of ritually clean sage's food, or vegetables, roots, and fruits, he should continue to offer the same great sacrifices (3.68–70) according to rule. [6] He should wear a garment of skin or tree bark; bathe in the morning and evening; always wear matted hair; and keep his beard, body hair, and nails uncut.

Great Sacrifices [7] He should give Bali offerings and almsfood to the best of his ability with whatever food he eats and honour those who visit his hermitage with water, roots, fruits, and almsfood. [8] He should be always diligent in his vedic recitation; remain controlled, friendly, and collected; be always a giver and never a receiver of gifts; be compassionate towards all creatures; [9] offer the daily fire sacrifice in his three sacred fires according to rule, without neglecting the new-moon and full-moon sacrifices at their proper time; [10] and offer the constellation-sacrifice, the sacrifice of first fruits (4.26), the seasonal sacrifices, the Turāyaṇa sacrifice and the Dākṣāyaṇa sacrifice, in their proper sequence. [11] With ritually clean sage's foods that grow in spring and autumn and that he has gathered himself, he should offer separately the sacrificial cakes and oblations of milk-rice according to rule.

Food [12] After he has offered that most ritually clean oblation of forest produce to the gods, he may avail himself of what remains, as also of salt that he has manufactured himself.

[13] He may eat vegetables growing on land or in water; flowers, roots, and fruits coming from ritually clean trees; and oils extracted from fruits. [14] He must avoid honey, meat, the Bhauma plant, mushrooms, the Bhūstṛṇa plant, the Śigruka horseradish, and the Śleṣmātaka fruit.

[15] In the month of Āśvayuja (September–October), he must throw away the sage's food that he had previously collected, as also vegetables, roots, fruits, and old garments.

[16] He must never eat anything grown on ploughed land, even if it has been thrown away by someone; or flowers and fruits grown in a village, even if he is in dire straits.

[17] He may eat food that has been cooked with fire or ripened by time; he may use a grindstone or use his teeth as a mortar; [18] he may clean up immediately after eating or maintain a supply of food sufficient for a month, six months, or a year.

[19] Having gathered food to the best of his ability, he may eat it at night, during the day, at every fourth mealtime, or at every eighth mealtime; [20] or he may maintain himself during the bright and dark halves of the month according to the lunar rule (11.217), or eat boiled barley-gruel once at the end of each half-month; [21] or he may subsist permanently on just flowers, roots, and fruits that have ripened by time and wilted on their own – abiding by the Vaikhānasa doctrine.

Austerities [22] He should roll on the ground or stand on tiptoes all day; spend the day standing and the night seated, bathing at dawn, midday, and dusk; [23] surround himself with the five fires in the summer; live in the open air during the rainy season; and wear wet clothes in the winter – gradually intensifying his ascetic toil. [24] Bathing at dawn, noon, and dusk, he should offer quenching libations to ancestors and gods, and engaging in ever harsher ascetic toil, he should inflict punishment on his body.

Homeless Ascetic [25] After depositing his sacred fires in his body according to rule, he should become a sage without house or fire, subsisting on roots and fruits, [26] making no effort to obtain pleasurable things, remaining celibate, sleeping on the ground, showing no attachment to any place of shelter, and making his home at the foot of a tree.

[27] He should beg for almsfood just sufficient to sustain life only from Brahmin ascetics and from other twice-born householders living in the forest. [28] Or, while continuing to live in the forest, he may collect almsfood from a village and eat eight mouthfuls, receiving the almsfood in a leaf-cone, in a potsherd, or in the hand.

Conclusion

[29] To attain the full perfection of his self, a Brahmin living in the forest must pursue these and other observances, as also the various Upaniṣadic scriptures, [30] and, to enhance his knowledge and ascetic toil and to purify his body, also those pursued by seers, Brahmins, and householders.

[31] Or he may set out in a north-easterly direction and, subsisting on water and air, walk straight on steadfastly until his body drops dead. [32] When a Brahmin has discarded his body through any one of these means employed by the great seers, freed from sorrow and fear, he will be exalted in the world of Brahman.

Wandering Ascetic

[33] After spending the third quarter of his life this way in the forest, he should cast off his attachments and wander about as an ascetic during the fourth. [34] When a man goes forth as an ascetic after he has moved from order to order, offered sacrifices, subdued his senses, and become worn out by giving alms and oblations, he will prosper after death.

Qualification

[35] Only after he has paid his three debts, should a man set his mind on renunciation; if he devotes himself to renunciation without paying them, he will proceed downward. [36] Only after he has studied the Vedas according to rule, fathered sons in keeping with the Law, and offered sacrifices according to his ability, should a man set his mind on renunciation; [37] if a twice-born seeks renunciation without studying the Vedas, without fathering sons, and without offering sacrifices, he will proceed downward (6.35 n.).

Initiation

[38] Only after he has offered a sacrifice to Prajāpati at which all his possessions are given as the sacrificial gift and after he has deposited the sacred fires within himself (6.25 n.), should a Brahmin go forth from his home as an ascetic.

[39] Worlds of resplendent energy await a vedic savant who goes forth from his home as an ascetic after bestowing freedom from fear on all creatures. [40] Because that twice-born has not been the cause of even the slightest fear to creatures, he has nothing to fear from anyone after he is freed from his body.

[41] After departing from home with a cloth for straining water, the sage should wander about, ignoring the sensual delights presented to him.

Mode of Life

[42] To achieve success, he must always wander alone, without any companions; recognizing that success comes to the solitary man, he will forsake no one and no one will forsake him. [43] He should live without fire or house, enter a village to obtain food, be dispassionate, keep no store, and remain a silent sage and mentally composed. [44] A bowl, the foot of a tree, a ragged piece of cloth, a solitary life, and equanimity towards all – these are the marks of a renouncer.

[45] He should long neither for death nor for life, but simply await his appointed time, as a servant his wages. [46] He should place his foot on a spot purified by his sight, drink water purified by a cloth, speak words purified by truth, and follow conduct purified by the mind.

[47] He must bear harsh words with patience; never treat anyone with contempt; never start a feud with anyone merely for the sake of this body; [48] never show ire towards anyone who is irate with him; bless those who curse him; and never utter an untrue word scattered across the seven gates.

[49] Taking delight in what pertains to the self, he should remain seated without longings or sensual attachments. With himself as his only companion, he should walk about here, seeking felicity.

Begging and Food

[50] He must never try to obtain almsfood by interpreting portents or omens, by his knowledge of astrology or palmistry, by giving counsel, or by engaging in debates.

[51] He should never visit a house crowded with ascetics, Brahmins, birds, dogs, or other beggars; [52] and always go about with his head and beard shaved, with his nails clipped, carrying a bowl, a staff, and a water-pot, and without causing harm to any creature.

[53] His bowls must be non-metallic and undamaged; and tradition says that they are to be cleaned with just water, like Camasa-cups at a sacrifice (5.116). [54] A gourd, a wooden bowl, a clay bowl, and a wicker bowl – Manu, the son of the Self-existent One, has proclaimed these as the bowls of ascetics.

[55] He may go on his begging round only once a day. He must not be overly attached to getting a lot; for when an ascetic is overly attached to almsfood, he becomes attached also to sensual objects. [56] An ascetic should go on his daily begging round only when the smoke has cleared, the pestles are at rest, the embers are extinguished, the people have finished their meal, and the dishes have been put away.

[57] When he receives nothing, he must not become dejected; when he receives something, it must not make him elated. He should gather food just sufficient to sustain his life and become free from attachment to his belongings. [58] He should hold anything received with a show of reverence in total disdain; even an ascetic who has freed himself is shackled by what is received with a show of reverence. [59] By eating little and by spending the day standing and the night seated (6.22 n.) in solitude, he should pull his organs back as they are being drawn away by sensory objects. [60] By restraining his organs, by stamping out love and hatred, and by ceasing to harm any creature, he becomes fit for immortality.

Yogic Meditation

[61] He should reflect on the diverse paths humans take as a result of their evil deeds; on how they fall into hell; on the tortures they endure in the abode of Yama; [62] on how they are separated from the ones they love and united with the ones they hate; on how they are overcome by old age and tormented by diseases; [63] on how the inner self departs from this body, takes birth again in a womb, and migrates through tens of billions of wombs; [64] and on how embodied beings become linked with pain as a result of pursuing what is against the Law and with imperishable happiness as a result of pursuing the Law as one's goal.

[65] By yogic meditation, he should also reflect on the subtle nature of the highest self and on its appearance in the highest and the lowest of bodies (6.73).

Conduct [66] Though decked in finery, he should pursue the Law in whichever order he may live, treating all creatures alike; an emblem does not accomplish the Law. [67] Although the fruit of the Kataka tree makes water clear, yet the water does not become clear by mere mention of its name.

[68] To protect living creatures, he should walk always – whether at night or during the day – only after inspecting the ground even at the cost of bodily discomfort. [69] To purify himself of killing living creatures unintentionally during the day or at night, an ascetic should bathe and control his breath six times.

Breath Control [70] Controlling the breath even three times according to rule while reciting the Calls and the syllable OṂ is to be considered the highest type of ascetic toil for a Brahmin. [71] As the impurities of metallic ores are burnt away when they are blasted in a furnace, so the faults of the organs are burnt away by suppressing the breath.

Meditation [72] He should burn away his faults by suppressing his breath, his taints by concentration, his attachments by the withdrawal of senses, and his base qualities by meditation. [73] Through the practice of meditation, he should discern the course of this inner self through the highest and the lowest of creatures (6.65), a difficult course to grasp for persons with uncultivated minds.

[74] When a man possesses right understanding, he is not fettered by actions; but when he lacks understanding, he enters the transmigratory cycle. [75] By ceasing to harm living creatures, by withdrawing the organs from their attachments, by performing vedic rites, and by practising fierce austerities, individuals do attain that state here on earth.

Meditation on the Body [76] Constructed with beams of bones, fastened with tendons, plastered with flesh and blood, covered with skin, foul-smelling, filled with urine and excrement, [77] infested with old age and sorrow, the abode of sickness, full of pain, covered with dust, and impermanent – he must abandon this dwelling place of ghosts. [78] When a tree falls from a river bank, the bird leaves the tree; when he abandons this body in like manner, he escapes the alligator's painful grasp.

Final Goal [79] Consigning his good deeds to people he likes and his evil deeds to people he dislikes, he attains the eternal Brahman through the practice of meditation. [80] When by the passion of his spirit he frees himself from attachment to every object of passion, then he wins eternal happiness both here and in the hereafter. [81] When he gives up all attachments gradually in this manner, freed from all the pairs of opposites, he comes to rest in Brahman alone.

[82] Everything prescribed here is contingent on meditation; for no one ignorant of the highest self can reap the fruits of his rites. [83] He should practise the soft recitation of vedic texts relating to sacrifice, gods, and self, as also those named 'Vedānta' – [84] this is the refuge of the ignorant, as indeed of the learned; this is the refuge of those who seek heaven, as of those who yearn for the infinite.

[85] If a twice-born lives as a wandering ascetic following the above sequence of practices, he will cast off his sins in this world and attain the highest Brahman.

[86] I have explained to you above the Law pertaining to self-controlled ascetics. Listen

now to the ritual discipline of vedic retirees (1.114 n.).

Vedic Retiree

Superiority of the Householder

[87] Student, householder, forest hermit, and ascetic: these four distinct orders have their origin in the householder. [88] All of these, when they are undertaken in their proper sequence as spelled out in the sacred texts, lead a Brahmin who acts in the prescribed manner to the highest state. [89] Among all of them, however, according to the dictates of vedic scripture, the householder is said to be the best, for he supports the other three. [90] As all rivers and rivulets ultimately end up in the ocean, so people of all the orders ultimately end up in the householder.
[. . .]

Chapter Seven

The Law for the King

[1] I will explain the Laws pertaining to kings – how a king should conduct himself, how he came into being, and how he can attain the highest success.

Origin of the King

[2] A Kṣatriya who has received the vedic consecration according to rule has the obligation to protect this whole world in accordance with the norms; [3] for when people here were without a king and fleeing in all directions out of fear, to protect this whole world the Lord created the king [4] by extracting eternal particles from Indra, Wind, Yama, Sun, Fire, Varuṇa, Moon, and the Lord of wealth.

[5] Because the king was fashioned out of particles from these chiefs of the gods, he overpowers all beings by reason of his energy. [6] Like the sun, indeed, he burns eyes and minds; no one on earth can bear to gaze upon him. [7] He is Fire, he is Wind, he is the Sun, he is the Moon, he is the King of the Law [Yama], he is Kubera, he is Varuṇa, and he is the Great Indra – by reason of his power.

[8] A king, though a mere child, must never be treated with disrespect, thinking he is just a human being; for it is a great deity who stands here in human form. [9] When approached recklessly, a fire burns only that single man, but the fire that is the king burns his family, together with all his livestock and wealth.

[10] After examining truthfully the task to be accomplished, his own strength, the time, and the place, he assumes in turn every aspect in order to fully implement the Law; [11] he, in whose benevolence lies Padmā, the goddess of prosperity, in whose valour lies victory, and in whose anger lies death – for he is made from the energies of them all.

[12] The man who in his folly hates him perishes without doubt; for the king makes up his mind to destroy him quickly. [13] When the king issues a Law favourable to those he favours or unfavourable to those out of favour, therefore, no one should transgress that Law.

Punishment [14] For the king's sake, the Lord formerly created Punishment, his son – the Law and protector of all beings – made from the energy of Brahman. [15] It is the fear of him that makes all beings, both the mobile and the immobile, accede to being used and not deviate from the Law proper to them.

[16] The king should administer appropriate Punishment on men who behave improperly, after examining truthfully the place and the time, as well as their strength and learning. [17] Punishment is the king; he is the male; he is the leader; he is the ruler; and, tradition tells us, he stands as the surety for the Law with respect to the four orders of life. [18] Punishment disciplines all the subjects, Punishment alone protects them, and Punishment watches over them as they sleep – Punishment is the Law, the wise declare. [19] When he is wielded properly after careful examination, he gives delight to all the subjects; but when he is administered without careful examination, he wreaks total havoc.

[20] If the king fails to administer Punishment tirelessly on those who ought to be punished,

the stronger would grill the weak like fish on a spit; [21] crows would devour the sacrificial cakes; dogs would lap up the sacrificial offerings; no one would have any right of ownership; and everything would turn topsy-turvy. [22] The whole world is subdued through Punishment, for an honest man is hard to find; clearly, it is the fear of Punishment that makes the whole creation accede to being used (7.15 n.). [23] Gods, demons, Gandharvas, fiends, birds, and snakes – even these accede to being used only when coerced by Punishment. [24] All the social classes would become corrupted, all boundaries would be breached, and all the people would revolt, as a result of blunders committed with respect to Punishment. [25] Wherever Punishment, dark-hued and red-eyed, prowls about as the slayer of evil-doers, there the subjects do not go astray – so long as its administrator ascertains correctly.

[. . .]

Grounds for Litigation: XIV Violence

[344] If a king desires to obtain the seat of Indra and inexhaustible and imperishable fame, he should never ignore even for a moment a man who perpetrates violence. [345] A man who perpetrates violence should be considered far more evil than someone who is offensive in speech, who steals, or who assaults with a rod. [346] A king who condones a man who engages in violence is quickly brought to ruin and becomes the object of hatred.

[347] The king must never release violent men who strike terror in all creatures eyeing either friendship or a large monetary gain.

Permissible Violence [348] Twice-born men may take up arms when the Law is thwarted or when the vicissitudes of time bring calamity upon twice-born classes. [349] When a man kills in accordance with the Law to protect his life, in a conflict over sacrificial fees, or in defence of women or Brahmins, he remains untainted.

[350] When an assailant attacks with the intent to kill – whether he is an elder, a child, an old person, or a learned Brahmin – one may surely kill him without hesitation. [351] In killing an assailant, the killer incurs no fault; whether it is done openly or in secret, wrath there recoils on wrath.

Grounds for Litigation: XV Sexual Crimes against Women

Sexual Crimes against Married Women [352] When men violate the wives of others, the king should disfigure their bodies with punishments that inspire terror and then execute them; [353] for such violations give rise to the mixing of social classes among the people, creating deviation from the Law that tears out the very root and leads to the destruction of everything.

[354] When a man carries on a conversation secretly with another man's wife, he is subject to the lowest fine if he has been previously accused of similar offences. [355] If someone who has not been previously accused engages in such conversation for a good reason, however, no guilt attaches to him, for he has committed no transgression.

[356] If a man converses with the wife of another at a sacred ford, in a wild tract, in a forest, or at the confluence of rivers, he is guilty of adultery. [357] Doing favours, dallying, touching the ornaments or clothes, and sitting together on a bed – all this, tradition tells us, constitutes adultery. [358] When a man touches a woman at an inappropriate place or permits her to touch him – all such acts done with mutual consent, tradition tells us, constitute adultery.

[359] In the case of adultery, everyone other than a Brahmin merits the death penalty; women of all four classes are to be guarded always with the utmost care.

[360] Mendicants, bards, men consecrated for sacrifice, and artisans may converse with women, unless they have been explicitly banned. [361] A man should never converse with women when he has been forbidden to do so; when someone speaks after being forbidden, he ought to be fined 1 Suvarṇa.

[362] The above rule does not apply to wives of travelling performers or to wives who earn a

living on their own, for such men get their women to attach themselves to men and, concealing themselves, get them to have sexual liaisons. [363] When someone engages in secret conversations with such women, as also with female slaves serving a single master and with female wandering ascetics, he shall be compelled to pay a small fine.

Male Sexual Assault [364] A man who defiles a virgin against her will merits immediate execution. When a man of equal status defiles a willing virgin, however, he is not subject to execution. [365] No fine should be imposed on a virgin who falls in love with a man superior to herself; but if she makes love to a man inferior to herself, she should be put under restraint and confined to her house. [366] When a man of inferior status makes love to a superior woman, however, he merits execution; if he makes love to a woman of equal status, he should pay a bride-price if her father so desires.

[367] If a man arrogantly violates a virgin by force, two of his fingers should be cut off immediately, and he should also be fined 600. [368] A man of equal status who defiles a willing girl shall not be subject to the cutting of his fingers, but he should be compelled to pay a fine of 200 to deter repetition.

Female Sexual Assault [369] If a virgin violates another virgin, she should be fined 200, pay three times the bride-price, and receive ten lashes. [370] When a woman violates a virgin, however, her head ought to be shaved immediately – alternatively, two of her fingers should be cut off – and she should be paraded on a donkey.

Adultery [371] When a woman, arrogant because of the eminence of her relatives and her own feminine qualities, becomes unfaithful to her husband, the king should have her devoured by dogs in a public square frequented by many. [372] He should have the male offender burnt upon a heated iron bed; they should stack logs and burn up that villain there.

[373] When a convict is accused again within a year, the fine is doubled; likewise when a man has sex with a Vrātya or a Caṇḍāla woman. [374] When a Śūdra has sex with a guarded or unguarded woman of a twice-born class – he loses a limb and all his possessions, if she was unguarded. If she was guarded, a Śūdra loses everything; [375] a Vaiśya is imprisoned for a year and all his property is confiscated; and a Kṣatriya is fined 1,000 and his head is shaved using urine. [376] If a Vaiśya or a Kṣatriya has sex with an unguarded Brahmin woman, the Vaiśya is fined 500 and the Kṣatriya 1,000. [377] If any of these two has sex with a guarded Brahmin woman, he should be punished in the same way as a Śūdra or he should be burnt with a straw-fire. [378] A Brahmin who has forcible sex with a guarded Brahmin woman should be fined 1,000; for sex with a willing partner, he should be fined 500.

[379] Shaving the head is prescribed as the death penalty for Brahmins; but the other social classes are actually subject to the death penalty. [380] The king should never put a Brahmin to death, even if he has committed every sort of crime; he should banish such a Brahmin from his kingdom along with all his property, without causing him hurt. [381] There is no greater violation of the Law on earth than killing a Brahmin; therefore, a king should not even think of killing a Brahmin.

[382] If a Vaiśya has sex with a guarded Kṣatriya woman or a Kṣatriya with a guarded Vaiśya woman, both ought to receive the same punishment as a man who has sex with an unguarded Brahmin woman. [383] When a Brahmin has sex with those two types of guarded women, however, he should be compelled to pay a fine of 1,000; likewise, when a Kṣatriya or a Vaiśya has sex with a Śūdra woman, the fine is 1,000. [384] For sex with an unguarded Kṣatriya woman, a Vaiśya is fined 500, but a Kṣatriya has his head shaved using urine or is levied the same fine. [385] When a Brahmin has sex with an unguarded Kṣatriya or Vaiśya woman or with a Śūdra woman, he shall be fined 500, but 1,000 for sex with a lowest-born woman.

[*Excursus*]

Miscellanea [386] The king in whose capital there is no thief, no adulterer, no person who uses offensive speech, no person who uses violence, and no person who commits physical assault, will attain the world of Indra. [387] The suppression of these five within his territory secures for the king paramountcy among his peers and fame among his people.

[388] If the patron of a sacrifice gets rid of an officiating priest or an officiating priest the patron when both are capable of performing the rite and are untainted by any fault, each is fined 100.

[389] A mother, father, wife, or son ought never to be abandoned. Anyone who abandons these when they have not fallen from their caste shall be fined 600 by the king.

[390] When twice-born men living in hermitages are arguing with each other about any duty, the king should never pronounce on the Law, if he cares for his own welfare. [391] Accompanied by Brahmins, the king should first pay them due reverence, pacify them initially with soothing words, and then teach them the Law specific to them.

[392] When a Brahmin fails to feed his two worthy neighbours – the one living in front of his house and the one behind – at a festival attended by twenty Brahmins, he ought to be fined 1 Māṣaka. [393] When a vedic scholar fails to feed another virtuous vedic scholar at auspicious rites, he should be compelled to give twice that amount of food and a gold Māṣaka.

[394] A blind man, an idiot, a cripple, a man over 70, and someone who takes care of vedic scholars – no one should compel these to pay any tax.

[395] The king should always honour vedic scholars, the sick and the afflicted, children, the aged, the poor, men from illustrious families, and Āryas.

[396] A washerman shall wash clothes thoroughly and gently on a smooth cotton-wood board. He must not use some clothes to carry the other clothes or let others wear those clothes.

[397] A weaver receiving thread weighing 10 Palas must return cloth weighing 1 Pala more; if he does otherwise, he should be compelled to pay a fine of 12.

[. . .]

Occupations of Social Classes [410] The king should make Vaiśyas pursue trade, moneylending, agriculture, and cattle herding, and make Śūdras engage in the service of twice-born people.

[411] A Brahmin should support a Kṣatriya or a Vaiśya who is starved for a livelihood out of compassion and employ them in activities proper to them. [412] If a Brahmin makes twice-born men who have undergone vedic initiation do slave labour against their will through greed and to show off his power, the king should fine him 600. [413] He may, however, make a Śūdra, whether he is bought or not, do slave labour; for the Śūdra was created by the Self-existent One solely to do slave labour for the Brahmin.

[414] Even when he is released by his master, a Śūdra is not freed from his slave status; for that is innate in him and who can remove it from him? [415] There are seven kinds of slaves: a man captured in war, a man who makes himself a slave to receive food, a slave born in the house, a purchased slave, a gifted slave, a hereditary slave, and a man enslaved for punishment.

[416] Wife, son, and slave – all these three, tradition tells us, are without property. Whatever they may earn becomes the property of the man to whom they belong.

[417] A Brahmin may confidently seize property from a Śūdra, because there is nothing that he owns; for he is a man whose property may be taken by his master.

[418] The king should strenuously make Vaiśyas and Śūdras perform the activities specific to them; for when they deviate from their specific activities, they throw this world into confusion.

[419] Every day the king should pay attention to his administrative centres, conveyances, daily income and expenditure, mines, and treasury. [420] When the king thus brings to a satisfactory conclusion all these legal matters, he gets rid of all sins and attains the highest state.

Chapter Nine

Grounds for Litigation: XVI Law Concerning Husband and Wife

[1] For a husband and wife who stay on the path pointed out by the Law, I shall declare the eternal Laws for both when they are together and when they are apart.

Guarding the Wife [2] Day and night men should keep their women from acting independently; for, attached as they are to sensual pleasures, men should keep them under their control. [3] Her father guards her in her childhood, her husband guards her in her youth, and her sons guard her in her old age; a woman is not qualified to act independently (5.147–9).

[4] A father is reprehensible, if he does not give her away at the proper time; a husband, if he does not have sex with her at the right time; and a son, if he fails to guard his mother when her husband is dead. [5] Women in particular should be guarded against even the slightest evil inclination, for when they are left unguarded, they bring grief to both families (5.149 n.). [6] Seeing that this is clearly the highest Law of all social classes, even weak husbands strive to guard their wives; [7] for by carefully guarding his wife, a man guards his offspring, his character, his family, himself, and the Law specific to him.

[8] The husband enters the wife, becomes a foetus, and is born in this world. This, indeed, is what gives the name to and discloses the true nature of 'wife' (*jāyā*) – that he is born (*jāyate*) again in her. [9] For, a wife bears a son resembling the man she loves; to ensure the purity of his offspring, therefore, he should carefully guard his wife.

[10] No man is able to thoroughly guard women by force; but by using the following strategies, he will be able to guard them thoroughly. [11] He should employ her in the collection and the disbursement of his wealth, in cleaning, in meritorious activity, in cooking food, and in looking after household goods. [12] When they are kept confined within the house by trusted men, they are not truly guarded; only when they guard themselves by themselves are they truly well guarded.

[13] Drinking, associating with bad people, living away from the husband, travel, sleep, and staying in the houses of others – these are the six things that corrupt women. [14] They pay no attention to beauty, they pay no heed to age; whether he is handsome or ugly, they make love to him with the single thought, 'He's a man!' [15] Lechery, fickleness of mind, and hard-heartedness are innate in them; even when they are carefully guarded in this world, therefore, they become hostile towards their husbands. [16] Recognizing thus the nature produced in them at creation by Prajāpati, a man should make the utmost effort at guarding them. [17] Bed, seat, ornaments, lust, hatred, behaviour unworthy of an Ārya, malice, and bad conduct – Manu assigned these to women.

[18] No rite is performed for women with the recitation of ritual formulas – that is well-established Law. 'Without strength or ritual formula, women are the untruth' – that is the fixed rule. [19] There are, likewise, numerous scriptural passages recited in the sacred books. Listen to a sample of these intended to expose the true character of women. [20] Here is an illustration of it: 'May my father keep from me the seed that my mother, roaming about unfaithful to her husband, craved!' [21] When a woman contemplates anything harmful to her husband in her mind, this is said to be a thorough expiation of that infidelity.

Elevation of Wife to Husband's Status [22] When a wife unites with her husband according to rule, she takes on the qualities he has, like a river uniting with the ocean. [23] Akṣamālā, a woman of the lowest birth when she united with Vasiṣṭha – as also Śārṅgī with Mandapāla – became worthy of great respect. [24] These and other women of low birth attained high status in this world by reason of the eminent qualities of their respective husbands.

[25] I have described above the splendid conduct of a husband and wife commonly practised in the world. Next, listen to the Laws that pertain to progeny, Laws that bring happiness here and in the hereafter.

Importance of Wife [26] On account of offspring, a wife is the bearer of many blessings, worthy of honour, and the light within a home; indeed, in a home no distinction at all exists between a wife (*strī*) and Śrī, the Goddess of Fortune. [27] She begets children; and when they are born, she brings them up – day in, day out, the wife, evidently, is the linchpin of domestic affairs. [28] Offspring, rites prescribed by Law, obedient service, the highest sensuous delights, and procuring heaven for oneself and one's forefathers – all this depends on the wife.

[29] A woman who controls her mind, speech, and body and is never unfaithful to her husband attains the worlds of her husband, and virtuous people call her a 'good woman' (= 5.165). [30] By being unfaithful to her husband, on the other hand, a woman becomes disgraced in the world, takes birth in a jackal's womb, and is afflicted with evil diseases (= 5.164).

[. . .]

Excursus: Types of Punishment

[229] When a Kṣatriya, a Vaiśya, or a Śūdra is unable to pay a fine, he should acquit himself of the debt through work; a Brahmin, on the other hand, should pay it off in instalments.

[230] The king should punish women, children, the insane, the elderly, the poor, those without guardians, and the sick with a lash, a cane, a rope, and the like.

[231] When those appointed to adjudicate lawsuits, inflamed by the heat of money, undermine cases brought by litigants, the king should confiscate all their property. [232] He should put to death those who forge royal edicts, corrupt the constituents of the realm, or kill women, children or Brahmins, as also those who give aid to his enemies.

[233] Whenever something has been adjudicated and a judgement issued, he should recognize it as executed according to the Law and not bring it back again. [234] If an official or a judge settles a case wrongly, the king himself should settle it and fine him 1,000.

Grievous Sins Causing Loss of Caste [235] A murderer of a Brahmin, a man who drinks liquor, a thief, and a man who has sex with an elder's wife – all these men should be considered individually as guilty of a grievous sin causing loss of caste (11.55 n.).

[236] If any of these four fails to perform the penance, the king should determine for them a punishment, both corporal and pecuniary, that accords with the Law. [237] For sex with an elder's wife, the man should be branded with the mark of a vagina; for drinking liquor, with the sign of a tavern; for stealing, with the figure of a dog's foot; and for killing a Brahmin, with the figure of a headless man. [238] These wretched men – with whom one is not permitted to eat, to participate at a sacrifice, to recite the Veda, or to contract marriages – shall roam the earth, excluded from all activities relating to the Law. [239] Branded with marks, they shall be forsaken by their paternal and maternal relations; they should be shown no compassion and paid no reverence – that is Manu's decree.

[240] If they do perform the prescribed penance, on the other hand, the king should not brand the higher classes on the forehead, but make them pay the highest fine. [241] For these offences, the middle fine should be imposed on a Brahmin, or he should be exiled from the realm along with his property and belongings. [242] When others commit these sins, however, they deserve to have all their property confiscated, if they did them thoughtlessly, or to be executed, if they did them wilfully.

[243] A good king must never take the property of someone guilty of a grievous sin causing loss of caste; if he takes it out of greed, he becomes tainted with the same sin.

[244] He should offer that fine to Varuṇa by casting it into water, or present it to a Brahmin endowed with learning and virtue. [245] Varuṇa is the lord of punishment, for he holds the rod of punishment over kings; and a Brahmin who has mastered the Veda is the lord of the entire world. [246] When a king refrains from taking the fines of evil-doers, in that land are born in due course men with long lives; [247] the farmers' crops ripen, each as it was sown; children do not die; and no deformed child is born.

[248] If a man of a lower class deliberately torments Brahmins, the king should kill him using graphic modes of execution (9.279 n.) that strike terror into men. [249] A king incurs as great a sin by releasing someone who ought to be executed as by executing someone who ought not to be executed; but he gains merit by its proper exercise.

[...]

Rules of Action for Vaiśyas and Śūdras

Rules for Vaiśyas

[326] After undergoing initiatory consecration and getting married, a Vaiśya should devote himself constantly to trade and to looking after farm animals; [327] for, after creating them, Prajāpati handed over to the Vaiśya the farm animals, and to the Brahmin and the king, all creatures.

[328] 'I don't want to look after farm animals' – a Vaiśya should never entertain such a wish, and when there is a willing Vaiśya, under no circumstances shall anyone else look after them. [329] He shall acquaint himself with the relative values of gems, pearls, coral, metals, threads, perfumes, and condiments. [330] He should be knowledgeable about sowing seeds, the good and bad qualities of farmland, all the various ways of weighing and measuring, [331] the desirable and undesirable properties of goods, the good and bad aspects of regions, the probable profit and loss of merchandise, and how best to raise farm animals. [332] He should be well-informed about the wages to be paid to servants, the different languages of people, the manner of storing goods, and the procedures of buying and selling.

[333] He should make the utmost effort at making his assets grow in accordance with the Law and diligently distribute food to all creatures.

Rules for Śūdras

[334] For the Śūdra, on the other hand, the highest Law leading to bliss is simply to render obedient service to distinguished Brahmin householders who are learned in the Veda. [335] When he keeps himself pure, obediently serves the highest class, is soft-spoken and humble, and always takes refuge in Brahmins, he obtains a higher birth.

Conclusion of the Law Outside Times of Adversity

[336] I have described above the splendid rules of action for the social classes outside times of adversity. Listen now to the rules for them in the proper order for times of adversity.

Chapter Ten

Rules for Times of Adversity

Mixed Classes

The Four Classes [1] Devoted to their respective activities, the three twice-born classes should study the Veda; but it is the Brahmin who should teach them, not the other two – that is the firm principle. [2] The Brahmin must know the means of livelihood of all according to rule, and he should both teach them to the others and follow them himself.

[3] Because of his distinctive qualities, the eminence of his origin, his observance of restrictive practices, and the distinctive nature of his consecration, the Brahmin is the lord of all the classes.

[4] Three classes – Brahmin, Kṣatriya, and Vaiśya – are twice-born; the fourth, Śūdra, has a single birth. There is no fifth.

[5] In all the classes, children born in the direct order of class to wives who are of equal class and married as virgins should be recognized as belonging to the same class by birth. [6] Sons fathered by twice-born men on wives of the class immediately below theirs are considered only 'similar', disdained as they are due to their mother's defect.

[7] That is the eternal rule with respect to those born from women of the class immediately below. The following should be recognized as the righteous rule with respect to those born from women two or three classes below.

Mixed Classes: First Discourse [8] From a Brahmin man by a Vaiśya girl is born a son called Ambaṣṭha; and by a Śūdra girl, a Niṣāda, also called Pāraśava. [9] From a Kṣatriya man by a Śūdra girl is born a son called Ugra, who is cruel in his behaviour and in his dealings, a being with the physical characteristics of both a Kṣatriya and a Śūdra.

[10] A Brahmin's children by the three lower classes, a Kṣatriya's by the two lower classes, and a Vaiśya's by the one lower class – tradition calls these six 'low-born' (10.46 n.).

[11] From a Kṣatriya man by a Brahmin girl is born a Sūta by caste; sons of a Vaiśya by Kṣatriya and Brahmin women are a Māgadha and a Vaideha, respectively; [12] and from a Śūdra by Vaiśya, Kṣatriya, and Brahmin women are born respectively an Āyogava, a Kṣattṛ, and a Cāṇḍāla, the worst of all men – so originates the intermixture of classes.

[13] As when there is a difference of two classes in a birth, tradition calls them Ambaṣṭha and Ugra if the difference is in the direct order; in like manner they are Kṣatṛ and Vaideha, if it is in the inverse order. [14] The sons of twice-born men by women of the class immediately below theirs that have been enumerated in their proper order – they are given the name 'Promixate', because of their mother's defect.

Mixed Classes: Second Discourse [15] From a Brahmin man by an Ugra girl is born a son called Āvṛta; by an Ambaṣṭha girl, an Ābhīra; and by an Āyogava girl, a Dhigvaṇa.

[16] From a Śūdra man are born in the inverse order three 'low-borns': Āyogava, Kṣattṛ, and Cāṇḍāla, the worst of all men. [17] Three further 'low-borns' (10.46 n.) are born in the inverse order: from a Vaiśya man, a Māgadha and a Vaideha; and from a Kṣatriya man, a Sūta.

[18] From a Niṣāda man by a Śūdra woman is born a Pulkasa by caste; a son born from a Śūdra man by a Niṣāda woman, tradition tells us, is a Kukkuṭa. [19] A child born from a Kṣattṛ man by an Ugra woman is said to be a Śvapāka; and from a Vaidehaka man by an Ambaṣṭha woman, a Veṇa.

[20] When children fathered by twice-born men on women of equal class do not keep the observances and have fallen from the Sāvitrī (2.38 n.), they should be called by the name Vrātya (2.39). [21] From a Vrātya of the Brahmin class are born the evil-natured Bhṛjjakaṇṭaka, the Āvantya, the Vāṭadhāna, the Puṣpadha, and the Śaikha. [22] From a Vrātya of the Kṣatriya class are born the Jhalla, the Malla, the Licchivi, the Naṭa, the Karaṇa, the Khasa, and the Draviḍa. [23] From a Vrātya of the Vaiśya class are born the Sudhanvan, the Ācārya, the Kāruṣa, the Vijanman, the Maitra, and the Sātvata.

Mixed Classes: Third Discourse [24] By adultery among the classes, by marrying forbidden women, and by abandoning the activities proper to them, originate the intermixture of classes. [25] I will enumerate completely those who are of mixed origin, born in the direct and in the inverse order and mutually connected.

[26] Sūta, Vaidehaka, Cāṇḍāla, the worst of men, Māgadha, Kṣatṛ, and Āyogava – [27] these six beget children similar in class to themselves by women of their own class, by women of their mother's caste, and by women of higher castes. [28] As from two of the three classes is born a child that is one's own self – being born from a woman of his own class because of the contiguity – so the same process applies to excluded men. [29] These same men beget on each other's wives large numbers of excluded children even more vile than they and despicable. [30] Just as a Śūdra man begets an excluded child from a Brahmin woman, so also an excluded man begets from women of the four classes a child subject to even greater exclusion.

[31] Having sex in the inverse order, excluded men beget children subject to even greater exclusion, the low-born beget low-born children, generating as many as fifteen classes. [32] On an Āyogava woman – a Dasyu man begets a Sairandra, who, although not a slave, gains his livelihood as a slave, is skilled at adorning and personal attendance, and lives by trapping animals; [33] a Vaideha man begets a Maitreyaka, who has a sweet voice, eulogizes men constantly, and rings the bell at dawn; [34] and a Niṣāda man begets a Mārgava, that is, a Dāśa, who lives by working on ships and whom people living in Āryāvarta (2.22) call a Kaivarta. [35] By Āyogava women, who are non-Āryas, wear the clothes of the dead, and eat despicable food, are born severally these three low-borns.

[36] From a Niṣāda man is born a Kārāvara, who works on leather; from a Vaidehaka, an Andhra and a Meda, both of whom dwell outside the village. [37] On a Vaideha woman – a Cāṇḍāla man begets a Pāṇḍusopāka, who deals in bamboo; and a Niṣāda man begets an Āhiṇḍika. [38] On a Pulkasa woman, a Cāṇḍāla man begets a Sopāka, a wicked man who gains his living as an executioner and is despised by good people. [39] A son born to a Niṣāda woman by a Cāṇḍāla man is an Antyāvasāyin, who operates in cemeteries and is despised even by excluded people.

[40] These castes arising from intermixture and described above according to their fathers and mothers – whether they conceal their caste or are open about it – should be recognized by their respective activities (10.57).

[41] The six types of son born to women belonging to one's own or the class immediately below have characteristics of a twice-born; but tradition regards all the 'delinquent-born' (10.46 n.) as having the same characteristics as Śūdras. [42] By the power of austerity and semen, in each succeeding generation they attain here among men a higher or a lower status by birth.

[43] By neglecting rites and by failing to visit Brahmins, however, these men of Ksatriya birth have gradually reached in the world the level of Śūdras – [44] Puṇḍrakas, Coḍas, Draviḍas, Kāmbojas, Yavanas, Śakas, Pāradas, Pahlavas, Cīnas, Kirātas, and Daradas. [45] All the castes in the world that are outside those born from the mouth, arms, thighs, and feet – whether they speak foreign or Ārya languages – tradition calls Dasyus.

Occupations, Residence, and Dress [46] The 'low-born' among the twice-born, as well as those that tradition calls 'delinquent-born', should live by occupations despised by the twice-born – [47] to Sūtas, management of horses and chariots; to Ambaṣṭhas, medicine; to Vaidehakas, taking care of women; to Māgadhas, trade; [48] to Niṣādas, fishing; to Āyogavas, carpentry; to Medas, Andras, Cuñcus, and Madgus, hunting wild animals; [49] to Kṣattṛs, Ugras, and Pulkasas, trapping and killing animals living in burrows; to Dhigvaṇas, working in leather; and to Veṇas, playing drums.

[50] These should live by memorial trees and in cemeteries, hills, and groves, well-recognizable and living by the occupations specific to them.

Cāṇḍālas and Śvapacas [51] Cāṇḍālas and Śvapacas, however, must live outside the village and they should be made Apapātras. Their property consists of dogs and donkeys, [52] their garments are the clothes of the dead; they eat in broken vessels; their ornaments are of iron; and they constantly roam about.

[53] A man who follows the Law should never seek any dealings with them. All their transactions shall be among themselves, and they must marry their own kind. [54] They depend on others for their food, and it should be given in a broken vessel. They must not go about in villages and towns at night; [55] they may go around during the day to perform some task at the command of the king, wearing distinguishing marks. They should carry away the corpses of those without relatives – that is the settled rule. [56] They should always execute those condemned to death in the manner prescribed by authoritative texts and at the command of the king; and they may take the clothes, beds, and ornaments of those condemned to death.

Further Discourse on Mixed Classes [57] An unknown man without the proper complexion, born from a squalid womb, a non-Ārya with some measure of Ārya features – one should detect such a man by his activities (10.40). [58] Un-Ārya conduct, harshness, cruelty, and the neglect of rites reveal in this world a man who is born from a squalid womb. [59] He will possess the character of either his father or his mother, or of both; a man born from an evil womb is never able to conceal his nature. [60] If he is the result of a mixed union, even a man born in a prominent family will undoubtedly partake of his parents' character to a greater or a lesser extent.

[61] Wherever these 'delinquent-born' (10.46 n.) individuals, who corrupt the social classes, are born, that realm quickly comes to ruin together with its inhabitants.

Advance to Higher Classes [62] For excluded individuals, giving up their life without artifice for the sake of a Brahmin or a cow, or in the defence of women or children is the means for achieving success.

[63] Abstention from injuring, truthfulness, refraining from anger, purification, and mastering the organs – this, Manu has declared, is the gist of the Law for the four classes.

[64] If an offspring of a Brahmin man from a Śūdra woman were to bear children from a superior partner, within seven generations the inferior attains the superior caste; [65] a Śūdra thus attains the rank of a Brahmin, and so does a Brahmin the rank of a Śūdra – one should understand that this rule holds good also for offspring born from a Kṣatriya or a Vaiśya man.

[66] If it be asked: who is superior? A child born accidentally to a Brahmin man by a non-Ārya woman or a child of a non-Ārya man by a Brahmin woman? [67] This is the resolution: a child born to an Ārya man by a non-Ārya woman becomes an Ārya by reason of his attributes, while a child born to a non-Ārya man by an Ārya woman is a non-Ārya. [68] Neither of these should be permitted to receive vedic initiation – that is the settled Law; the former because of the inferiority of his birth and the latter because he was born in the inverse order of class. [69] As a good seed sprouting in a good field grows vigorously, so a child born to an Ārya man by an Ārya woman is worthy of receiving all the consecratory rites.

[70] Some wise men extol the seed, others the field, and yet others both the seed and the field. In this regard, the settled rule is as follows. [71] A seed planted in a bad field dies midstream; a field without seed also is just bare land. [72] By the power of the seed, children born from animals became seers, receiving honour and acclaim; therefore, they extol the seed (9.32–56).

[73] The creator evaluated a non-Ārya who acts like an Ārya and an Ārya who acts like a non-Ārya and declared: 'They are neither equal nor unequal.'

Occupations of the Four Classes

[74] Brahmins who are established in that whose source is the Veda and are devoted to the activities specific to them should duly live by the six occupations in their proper order: [75] teaching and studying, offering sacrifices and officiating at sacrifices, and giving and accepting gifts are the six occupations of a highest-born person.

[76] Of these six activities, however, three provide him with a livelihood: officiating at sacrifices, teaching, and accepting gifts from a completely pure person.

[77] From the Brahmin, three Laws are suspended with respect to the Kṣatriya: teaching and officiating at sacrifices, and the third, accepting gifts; [78] the same are suspended also with respect to the Vaiśya – that is the settled rule; for Manu, the Prajāpati, has not prescribed these Laws with respect to these two.

[79] Use of arms and weapons has been prescribed as the livelihood for the Kṣatriya; and trade, animal husbandry, and agriculture for the Vaiśya. Their Law, however, is giving gifts, studying, and offering sacrifices. [80] Among the activities specific to each, the most admirable are: studying the Veda for the Brahmin,

protecting the people for a Kṣatriya, and trade alone for the Vaiśya.

Occupations in Times of Adversity

Brahmins [81] When a Brahmin is unable to earn a living by means of the activities specific to him given above, he may live by means of the Kṣatriya Law, for the latter is the one right below him. [82] If it be asked: what happens if he is unable to earn a living by either of these two means? Taking up agriculture or cattle-herding, he should earn a living by the occupation of a Vaiśya.

[83] A Brahmin, or even a Kṣatriya, who earns a living by the Vaiśya occupation, should try his best to avoid agriculture, which involves injury to living beings and dependence on others. [84] People think that agriculture is something wholesome. Yet it is an occupation condemned by good people; the plough with an iron tip lacerates the ground as well as creatures living in it.

[85] When someone, deprived of livelihood, is forced to abandon this strict adherence to the Law, he may sell goods traded by Vaiśyas to increase his wealth, with the following exceptions. [86] He should avoid condiments of every kind; cooked food; sesame seeds; stones; salt; farm animals; human beings; [87] every type of dyed cloth; cloth made of hemp, flax, or wool even if they are undyed; fruits; roots; medicines; [88] water; weapons; poison; meat; Soma; all types of perfume; milk; honey; curd; ghee; oil; beeswax; molasses; Kuśa grass; [89] all wild animals; fanged animals; birds; liquor; indigo; lac; and all one-hoofed animals.

[90] An individual engaged in agriculture may freely sell pure sesame seeds that he has cultivated himself, provided they are to be used for purposes relating to the Law and have not been stored for long. [91] If someone uses sesame seeds for purposes other than eating, anointing the body, and giving as a gift, he will become a worm and plunge into the excrement of dogs together with his ancestors.

[92] By selling meat, lac, or salt, a Brahmin falls immediately from his caste; by selling milk, he becomes a Śūdra in three days; [93] but by selling here the other commodities deliberately, a Brahmin is reduced in seven days to the rank of a Vaiśya.

[94] Condiments may be bartered for condiments – but never salt for condiments – cooked food for uncooked food, and sesame seeds for an equal amount of grain.

Kṣatriyas [95] A Kṣatriya who has fallen on hard times may earn his living by all the above means; but under no circumstances should he even think of living by a superior occupation. [96] If a man of inferior birth out of greed lives by activities specific to his superiors, the king shall confiscate all his property and promptly send him into exile. [97] Far better to carry out one's own Law imperfectly than that of someone else perfectly; for a man who lives according to someone else's Law falls immediately from his caste.

Vaiśyas [98] When a Vaiśya is unable to sustain himself through the Law proper to him, he may live by the occupation of even a Śūdra, refraining, however, from forbidden acts; and he should discontinue it when he is able.

Śūdras [99] When a Śūdra is unable to enter into the service of twice-born men and is faced with the loss of his sons and wife, he may earn a living by the activities of artisans – [100] that is, the activities of artisans and various kinds of crafts the practice of which best serves the twice-born.

Further Occupations for Brahmins [101] A Brahmin firmly committed to his way of life and unwilling to follow the Vaiśya occupations may pursue the following Law when he is languishing through lack of a livelihood. [102] A Brahmin who has fallen on hard times may accept gifts from anybody; that something pure can be sullied is impossible according to the Law. [103] By teaching, officiating at the sacrifices of, and accepting gifts from, despicable individuals, Brahmins do not incur any sin, for they are like fire and water.

[104] When someone facing death eats food given by anyone at all, he remains unsullied by sin, as the sky by mud. [105] Ajīgarta, tormented by hunger, went up to his son to kill him;

and he was not tainted with sin, as he was seeking to allay his hunger. [106] Vāmadeva, a man with a clear vision of what accords with and what is against the Law, finding himself in dire straits and trying to save his life, wanted to eat dog's meat, and yet remained unsullied. [107] Bharadvāja, a man of great austerities, when he and his sons were tormented by hunger in a desolate forest, accepted many cows from the carpenter Bṛbu. [108] Viśvāmitra, a man with a clear vision of what accords with and what is against the Law, when he was tormented by hunger, came to eat the rump of a dog, taking it from the hand of a Cāṇḍāla.

[109] Accepting gifts, officiating at sacrifices, and teaching – among these, accepting gifts is the worst and the most reprehensible for a Brahmin with respect to the hereafter. [110] Officiating at sacrifices and teaching always pertain to those who have undergone consecratory rites, whereas accepting pertains even to a lowest-born Śūdra. [111] A sin committed by teaching or officiating at a sacrifice is removed by soft recitation and oblations, but a sin incurred by accepting a gift is removed only by discarding it and performing ascetic toil. [112] A Brahmin without a livelihood may even glean or pick single grains (4.5 n.) from anywhere; gleaning is superior to accepting gifts, and picking single grains is superior to even that.

[113] When Brahmin bath-graduates are in dire straits and want wares or money, they should petition the king; if he refuses to give, they ought to abandon him.

[114] Unploughed land is less tainted than ploughed land; and among a cow, a goat, a sheep, gold, grain, and cooked food, each preceding one is less tainted than each subsequent.

Acquisition of Property [115] Seven means of acquiring wealth are in accordance with the Law: inheritance, finding, purchase, conquest, investment, work, and acceptance of gifts from good people. [116] The ten means of livelihood are: learning, craft, employment, service, cattle-herding, trade, agriculture, fortitude, begging, and lending on interest.

[117] A Brahmin or a Kṣatriya must never lend money on interest; to pursue activities dictated by the Law, however, he may lend to an evil man at a small interest.

[118] Even if a Kṣatriya collects 25 per cent as his share during a time of adversity, he is freed from that taint by protecting his subject to the best of his ability. [119] The Law specific to him is conquest, and he must not turn back in the face of danger; when he protects Vaiśyas with his weapons, he may collect a levy in accordance with the Law: [120] from Vaiśyas, a one-sixth share of the grain crop and a duty of one-twentieth on other commodities, with a minimum of 1 Kārṣāpaṇa; and from Śūdras, artisans, and craftsmen, the contribution of their services.

Livelihood of Śūdras [121] If a Śūdra desires to earn a living, he may serve a Kṣatriya, or he may seek to earn a living by serving even a wealthy Vaiśya. [122] He should serve Brahmins for the sake of heaven or for the sake of both, for when he has the name 'Brahmin' attached to him, he has done all there is to do. [123] The service of a Brahmin alone is declared to be the pre-eminent activity of a Śūdra, for whatever other work he may do brings him no reward.

[124] They must allocate a suitable livelihood for him from their own family resources, taking into account his ability and skill, and the number of his dependants. [125] They should give him leftover food, old clothes, grain that has been cast aside, and the old household items.

[126] A Śūdra is not affected by any sin causing loss of caste, nor is he entitled to any consecratory rite. He has no qualification with regard to the Law, but he is not prohibited from following the Law. [127] Those who know the Law and yearn to follow it, however, incur no sin and receive praise when they imitate the practices of good men, without reciting any ritual formulas; [128] for a Śūdra obtains this world and the next without enduring disdain to the extent that he imitates the practices of good men without giving way to envy.

[129] Even a capable Śūdra must not accumulate wealth; for when a Śūdra becomes wealthy, he harasses Brahmins.

Conclusion of the Laws of the Four Classes

[130] I have described above the Laws for the four classes during times of adversity; when they are properly followed, people attain the highest state.
[131] I have described above the entire set of rules pertaining to the Law of the four classes. Next, I will explain the splendid rules pertaining to penance.

Chapter Eleven

Penances

Excursus: Occasions for Giving and Begging

[1] A man seeking to extend his line; a man preparing to perform a sacrifice; a traveller; a man who has performed the sacrifice at which all his possessions are given away; a man who begs for the sake of his teacher, father, or mother; a student of the Veda; and a sick man – [2] these nine should be known as 'bath-graduates', Brahmins who are beggars pursuant to the Law. Gifts must be given to these destitutes in proportion to their eminence in vedic learning.

[3] To these Brahmins food should be given along with the sacrificial fees; to others, it is said, cooked food should be given outside the sacrificial arena. [4] The king should bestow all sorts of precious gifts on Brahmins learned in the Veda according to their merits, as well as fees for the purpose of sacrifices.

[5] When a married man marries another wife after begging for the expenses, his reward is only sensual pleasure; the resultant offspring belongs to the man who defrayed the expenses.

[7] A man who has sufficient resources to maintain his dependants for three years, or someone who has more than that, is entitled to drink Soma. [8] If a twice-born man who possesses fewer resources than that drinks Soma, he will not reap its reward, even though he may never have drunk Soma before. [9] When a man of means gives to outsiders while his own people live in misery, that is counterfeit Law, dripping with honey but poisonous to taste. [10] If a man does anything for his welfare after death to the detriment of his dependants, it will make him unhappy both when he is alive and after he is dead.

[11] While a righteous king is ruling, if a man offering a sacrifice finds that his sacrifice is interrupted for want of a single item, he may, especially if he is a Brahmin, [12] take that article from the house of a Vaiśya who has a large herd of animals but has failed to perform rites or to drink Soma, in order to complete the sacrifice. [13] He may freely take two or three items from the house of a Śūdra; for a Śūdra has nothing to do with sacrifices. [14] He may also take it without a second thought even from the house of a man who has a hundred cows but has not established his sacred fires or from that of a man who has a thousand cows but has not offered a sacrifice. [15] He may also take it from a man who is always a taker and never a giver, if he refuses to give it; thus his fame will spread and his merits will increase.

[16] Likewise, when a man has not eaten during six mealtimes (6.19 n.), at the seventh mealtime he may take from someone who performs no rites, keeping to the rule of leaving no provisions for the next day, [17] and taking it from his threshing floor, field, or house, or from any place where he can find something. If the man questions him, however, he should confess it to him.

[18] A Kṣatriya must never take anything belonging to a Brahmin; if he has no sustenance, however, he may take what belongs to a Dasyu or a man who neglects his rites. [19] When a man takes money from evil persons and gives them to the virtuous, he makes himself a raft and carries them both to the other side. [20] The wise call the wealth of those devoted to sacrifice the property of gods; the possessions of those who do not offer sacrifice, on the contrary, is called the property of demons.

[21] A righteous king should never punish such a man, for it is because of the Kṣatriya's foolishness that the Brahmin is languishing with hunger. [22] After finding out who his

dependants are and enquiring into his learning and virtue, the king should provide him with provisions for a righteous livelihood from his own house. [23] After providing him with a livelihood, he should protect him in every way, for by protecting him the king receives from him one-sixth of his merits.

[24] A man who knows the Law should never beg money from a Śūdra to perform a sacrifice; for when the patron of a sacrifice begs in this way, after death he is reborn a Cāṇḍāla. [25] If a Brahmin begs money for a sacrifice and does not devote all of it to that purpose, he will become a Bhāsa vulture or a crow for one hundred years.

[26] If a man seizes what belongs to a god or a Brahmin out of greed, in the next world that evil man will live on the leftovers of vultures.

Excursus: Miscellaneous Topics

Times of Adversity [27] If he is unable to perform the prescribed animal and Soma sacrifices, he should offer as an expiation the Vaiśvānara oblation at the turn of the year.

[28] When during a normal time a twice-born follows the Law according to the mode for a time of adversity, he will not receive its reward after death – that is indisputable. [29] All the gods, the Sādhyas, and the great Brahmin sages, afraid of death during times of adversity, created a substitute for the rule. [30] When someone, though able to follow the principal mode, yet lives according to the secondary mode, that fool will obtain no reward for it after death.

Power of Brahmins [31] A Brahmin who knows the Law shall not inform the king about any matter; solely with his own power should he chastise men who do him harm. [32] Between the king's power and his own, his own power is far more potent. A twice-born, therefore, should punish enemies solely with his own power, [33] and make use of vedic texts of Atharva-Āṅgīrasa – that is indisputable. Clearly, speech is the Brahmin's weapon; with that a twice-born should strike down his enemies.

[34] A Kṣatriya overcomes his adversities by the power of his arms; a Vaiśya and a Śūdra, by means of wealth; and a Brahmin, through soft recitation and sacrifices. [35] A Brahmin is called the creator, the chastiser, the teacher, and the benefactor; one should never say anything unpleasant to him or use harsh words against him.

Sacrifices [36] A girl, a young woman, an uneducated man, or a fool should never act as the officiant at the daily fire sacrifice, nor should a man who is in great anguish or who has not undergone initiatory consecration; [37] for, when these perform the offering, both they and the person to whom the fire sacrifice belongs fall into hell. Therefore, only a man who has mastered the Veda and is an expert in the vedic rituals should be an officiant.

[38] When a Brahmin fails to give a horse dedicated to Prajāpati as a sacrificial fee at the rite for establishing the sacred fires in spite of having the resources to do so, he is reduced to the level of one who has not established his sacred fires. [39] A man who has mastered his organs and has a spirit of generosity may perform other meritorious acts; but under no circumstances should he offer sacrifices here with inadequate sacrificial fees. [40] Organs, honour, heaven, life span, fame, offspring and livestock – a sacrifice with inadequate sacrificial fees destroys all these; a man with inadequate resources, therefore, should not offer a sacrifice (11.7–8).

[41] If a Brahmin who has established his sacred fires abandons his fires deliberately, he should perform the lunar penance (11.217) for one month; for it is equal to killing a hero.

[42] Those who perform their daily fire sacrifice by obtaining money from a Śūdra are considered reprehensible among vedic savants, for they are the officiating priests of Śūdras. [43] Stepping with his foot on the heads of these ignorant men who serve the fires of Śūdras, the giver crosses over difficulties.

Justification of Penance

[44] When a man fails to carry out prescribed acts, performs disapproved acts, and is attached to the sensory objects, he is subject to a penance.

[45] The wise acknowledge a penance for a sin committed unintentionally; some, on the basis of vedic evidence, admit it even for a deliberately committed sin. [46] A sin committed unintentionally is cleansed by vedic recitation, whereas a sin committed deliberately through folly is cleansed with various types of penance. [47] When a twice-born, either by fate or by what he did in a previous life, finds himself in a condition requiring the performance of a penance, he should not associate with good people before performing that penance.

[48] Some evil men become disfigured because of the bad deeds committed in this world, and some because of deeds done in a previous life. [49] A man who steals gold gets rotten nails; a man who drinks liquor, black teeth; the murderer of a Brahmin, consumption; a man who has sex with his elder's wife, skin disease; [50] a slanderer, a smelly nose; an informant, a smelly mouth; a man who steals grain, the loss of a limb; a man who adulterates grain, an excess limb; [51] a man who steals food, dyspepsia; a man who steals speech, smelly breath; a man who steals clothes, leukoderma; and a man who steals horses, lame legs. [53] In this way, as a result of the remnants of their past deeds, are born individuals despised by good people: the mentally retarded, the mute, the blind, and the deaf, as well as those who are deformed.

[54] Therefore, one should always do penances to purify oneself; for individuals whose sins have not been expiated are born with detestable characteristics.

Categories of Sin

Grievous Sins Causing Loss of Caste [55] Killing a Brahmin, drinking liquor, stealing, and having sex with an elder's wife – they call these 'grievous sins causing loss of caste'; and so is establishing any links with such individuals (11.181–2).

[56] A lie concerning one's superiority, a slander that reaches the king's ear, and false accusations against an elder are equal to killing a Brahmin. [57] Abandoning the Veda, reviling the Veda, giving false testimony, killing a friend, eating unfit food or forbidden food – these six are equal to drinking liquor. [58] Stealing deposits, men, horses, silver, land, diamonds, or gems, tradition tells us, is equal to stealing gold. [59] Sexual intercourse with uterine sisters, unmarried girls, lowest-born women, and the wives of a friend or son, they say, is equal to sex with an elder's wife.

Secondary Sins Causing Loss of Caste [60] Killing a cow; officiating at the sacrifice of an individual at whose sacrifice one is forbidden to officiate; adultery; selling oneself; forsaking one's teacher, mother, father, vedic recitation, sacred fire, or son; [61] an elder brother permitting a younger brother to marry before him; a younger brother marrying before his older brother; giving a girl in marriage to or officiating at a sacrifice of either of these; [62] deflowering a virgin; usury; breaking the vow; selling a reservoir, park, wife, or son; [63] remaining as a Vrātya (2.39); abandoning a relative; giving instruction as a paid teacher; receiving instruction from a paid teacher; selling proscribed commodities; [64] supervising any kind of mine; constructing large equipment; injuring plants; living off one's wife; sorcery; root-witchcraft; [65] cutting down live trees for firewood; undertaking activities solely for one's own sake; eating reprehensible food; [66] remaining without establishing the sacred fires; acting like a woman; non-payment of debts; studying fallacious treatises; living a corrupt life; engaging in vices; [67] stealing grain, base metals, and livestock; sex with women who drink; killing a woman, a Śūdra, a Vaiśya, or a Kṣatriya; and being an infidel – these are secondary sins causing loss of caste.

Further Categories of Sin [68] Making a Brahmin cry, smelling liquor or substances that should not be smelt, cheating, and sexual intercourse with a man – tradition calls these sins that cause exclusion from caste.

[69] Killing donkeys, horses, camels, deer, elephants, goats, sheep, fish, snakes, or buffaloes – these should be known as sins that cause a man to be of a mixed caste (10.8 f.).

[70] Accepting wealth from despicable men, trade, serving a Śūdra, and telling lies – these should be recognized as sins that make a man unworthy of receiving gifts.

[71] Killing worms, insects, or birds; eating anything that has come into contact with liquor; stealing fruits, firewood, or flowers; and lack of steadfastness – these make a man impure.

[72] Listen now attentively to the specific observances by which all these sins individually enumerated above may be removed.

Penances for Grievous Sins Causing Loss of Caste

Killing a Brahmin [73] A man who has killed a Brahmin should construct a hut and live in the forest for twelve years, eating alms-food and making the head of a corpse his banner, in order to purify himself.

[74] Or, if he so wishes, he may make himself a target for armed men who are cognizant of his state. Or, he may throw himself headlong three times into a blazing fire. [75] Or, he may offer a horse sacrifice, a Svarjit sacrifice, a Gosava sacrifice, an Abhijt sacrifice, a Viśvajit sacrifice, a Trivṛt sacrifice, or an Agniṣṭut sacrifice. [76] Or, to rid himself of the Brahmin's murder, he may walk one hundred leagues reciting one of the Vedas, eating little, and keeping his organs under control. [77] Or, he may present to a Brahmin learned in the Vedas all his possessions, or wealth sufficient to maintain a person, or else a house with furniture. [78] Or, he may walk upstream along the Sarasvatī, subsisting on sacrificial food. Or, he may recite three times softly one Collection of the Veda, while limiting his food. [79] Or, after getting his hair shaved, he may live in the outskirts of the village, in a cowshed, in a hermitage, or at the foot of a tree, taking pleasure in doing what is beneficial to cows and Brahmins. [80] Or, he may duly give up his life for the sake of a Brahmin or a cow; one who protects a cow or Brahmin is freed from the murder of a Brahmin. [81] Or, he becomes freed from it by fighting at least three times in defence of a Brahmin, by recovering all the property of a Brahmin, or by losing his life for the sake of a Brahmin.

[82] Thus always remaining steadfast in his vow, collected in mind, and chaste, he rids himself of the Brahmin's murder at the end of the twelfth year.

[83] Or, he is freed from his sin by proclaiming it in a gathering of the gods of earth and the gods of men and participating at the bath concluding a horse sacrifice. [84] The Brahmin is said to be the root of the Law, and the Kṣatriya its crest; therefore, by broadcasting a sin at a gathering of theirs, he becomes purified. [85] By his very origin, a Brahmin is a deity even for the gods and the authoritative source of knowledge for the world; the Veda clearly is the reason for this. [86] When even three of them who know the Veda declare an expiation for sins, it is sufficient for their purification; for the speech of the learned is a means of purification.

[87] By resorting to any one of the above procedures with a collected mind, a Brahmin will rid himself of the sin of killing a Brahmin by means of his self-control.

[88] One must perform the same observance for killing a foetus whose sex cannot be identified, a Kṣatriya or a Vaiśya who is engaged in a sacrifice, or a woman soon after her menstrual period; [89] for bearing false testimony; for assailing an elder; for stealing a deposit; and for killing a woman or a friend.

[90] This purification is enjoined for killing a Brahmin unintentionally; for killing a Brahmin deliberately, there is no prescribed expiation.

Drinking Liquor [91] If a twice-born man in his folly drinks liquor, he should drink boiling-hot liquor; when his body is scalded by it, he will be released from that sin. [92] Or, he may drink boiling-hot cow's urine, water, milk, ghee, or watery cow dung until he dies. [93] Or, he may eat only broken grain or oil-cake once a day during the night for a full year, wearing a garment of hair, keeping his hair matted, and carrying a banner, in order to remove the guilt of drinking liquor.

[94] Liquor is clearly the filth of various grains; sin is also called filth. Therefore, Brahmins, Kṣatriyas, and Vaiśyas must not drink liquor. [95] It should be understood that there are three kinds of liquor: one made from molasses, another from ground grain, and a third from honey. Just as drinking one of them is forbidden to Brahmins, so are all. [96] Intoxicants, meat, liquor, and spirits are the food of demons and fiends; they must not be consumed by a Brahmin, who eats the oblations to the gods. [97] When a Brahmin is intoxicated, he may tumble into filth, blabber vedic texts, or do other improper things. [98] If the *brahman* resident in a man's body is drenched with liquor even once, his Brahmin nature departs from him and he sinks to the level of a Śūdra.

[99] I have described above the various expiations for drinking liquor. Next, I will explain the expiation for stealing gold.

Stealing Gold [100] A Brahmin who has stolen gold should go up to the king, proclaim his deed, and say: 'Lord, punish me!' [101] Taking the pestle, the king himself should strike him once. A thief is purified by being put to death or, if he is a Brahmin, solely by ascetic toil.

[102] If a twice-born wants to rid himself of the sin of stealing gold by means of ascetic toil, however, he should carry out the observance prescribed for killing a Brahmin, living in the wilderness and dressed in tree bark (6.6).

[103] A twice-born should eliminate the sin resulting from stealing by means of the above observances. The sin of having sexual intercourse with an elder's wife, on the other hand, he should remove by means of the following observances.

Sex with an Elder's Wife [104] A man who had sex with an elder's wife should proclaim his crime and lie down on a heated iron bed, or embrace a red-hot metal cylinder; he is purified by death. [105] Or, he may cut off his penis and testicles by himself, hold them in his cupped hands, and walk straight towards the south-west until he falls down dead. [106] Or, he may perform the Prājāpatya penance (11.212) for one year with a collected mind, carrying a bed-post, dressed in tree bark (6.6), wearing a long beard, and living in a desolate forest. [107] Or, he may perform the lunar penance (11.217) for three months, keeping his organs under control and subsisting on sacrificial food or barley gruel, so as to remove the sin of sexual intercourse with an elder's wife.

[108] Men guilty of a grievous sin causing loss of caste should eliminate their sin by means of the above observances, but men guilty of a secondary sin causing loss of caste should do so by means of the various observances given below.

Penances for Secondary Sins Causing Loss of Caste

Killing a Cow [109] A man guilty of a secondary sin causing loss of caste by killing a cow should drink barley gruel for a month and live in a cow pen with his hair shaved and wrapped in the skin of that cow. [110] During two months, he should eat a small amount of food without artificial salt at every fourth mealtime (6.19 n.), bathing with cow's urine, and keeping his organs under control. [111] During the day, he should follow those cows, remain standing, and inhale their dust; at night, after attending to them and paying them homage, he should remain seated on his haunches. [112] When they stand, he should stand behind them; when they walk, he should also walk behind them; when they sit down, he should likewise sit down, self-controlled and free from rancour. [113] When a cow is sick, is threatened by dangers from thieves, tigers, and the like, has fallen down, or has got stuck in mud, he should free her with all his strength. [114] When it is hot, raining, or cold, or when the wind is blowing strong, he must never find shelter for himself without first providing it for the cow to the best of his ability. [115] When a cow is eating from his own or another's house, field, or threshing floor, or when the calf is drinking milk, he must not inform anybody of it.

[116] When a man who has killed a cow follows cows in this manner, in three months he rids himself of the sin resulting from killing a cow. [117] After he has duly completed this observance, furthermore, he should give ten cows along with a bull or, if that is impossible, all his possessions to those who know the Veda.

Other Secondary Sins [118] The very same observance should be performed by twice-born men who commit any secondary sin causing loss of caste, with the exception of a vedic student who has broken his vow of chastity, in order to purify themselves; alternatively, they may perform the lunar penance (11.217).

Student Breaking the Vow of Chastity [119] A vedic student who has broken his vow of chastity should offer at night a one-eyed donkey to Nirṛti at a crossroads, employing the ritual procedure of a cooked oblation.

[120] After offering the oblations in the fire according to rule, he should finally offer oblations of ghee to Wind, Indra, Teacher, and Fire, reciting the verse: 'May the Maruts. . . .' [121] Vedic savants who know the Law declare that when a twice-born votary ejaculates his semen intentionally he breaks his vow. [122] When a votary breaks his vow of chastity, the vedic energy within him enters these four: Wind, Indra, Teacher, and Fire. [123] When he has committed this sin, he should wear the skin of a donkey and beg food from seven houses, proclaiming his deed. [124] Subsisting on the almsfood obtained from them once a day and bathing three times a day, he is purified in a year.

Penances for the Remaining Categories of Sin

[125] Someone who has committed any of the acts that cause exclusion from caste (11.68) should perform a Sāntapana penance (11.213) if he did it deliberately, and a Prājāpatya penance (11.212) if he did it inadvertently.

[126] For committing acts that cause a person to be of a mixed caste or that make a person unworthy of receiving gifts (11.69–70), the purification is to perform the lunar penance (11.217) for one month, and for those that make a person impure (11.71), the purification is to drink hot barley gruel for three days.

Excursus: Penances for Injury to Living Beings

Homicide [127] One-quarter the penance for the murder of a Brahmin is prescribed by tradition for the murder of a Kṣatriya; one-eighth for the murder of a virtuous Vaiśya; and one-sixteenth for the murder of a Śūdra.

[128] If a Brahmin kills a Kṣatriya unintentionally, however, he should give one thousand cows and a bull to purify himself. [129] Or, he may perform during three years the observance prescribed for killing a Brahmin, keeping himself controlled, wearing matted hair, living far away from the village, and making his home at the foot of a tree. [130] A Brahmin who kills a virtuous Vaiśya should perform the same observance for one year, or give one hundred cows along with a bull. [131] One who kills a Śūdra should perform the same vow completely for six months, or give ten white cows along with a bull to a Brahmin.

Killing Animals [132] For killing a cat, a mongoose, a blue jay, a frog, a dog, a monitor lizard, an owl, or a crow, a man should perform the observance for killing a Śūdra. [133] Alternatively, he may drink milk for three days, or walk a distance of one league (11.76 n.), or bathe in a river, or recite softly the hymn addressed to the waters (8.106 n.).

[134] For killing a snake, a Brahmin should give an iron spade; for killing a castrate, a load of straw and a Māṣa of lead; [135] for killing a boar, a pot of ghee; for killing a partridge, a Droṇa of sesame seeds; for killing a parrot, a 2-year-old calf; and for killing a Krauñca crane, a 3-year-old calf. [136] For killing a ruddy goose, a Balāka flamingo, a Baka heron, a peacock, a monkey, a Śyena hawk, or a Bhāsa vulture, he should give a cow to a Brahmin. [137] For killing a horse, he should give a garment;

for killing an elephant, five black bulls; for killing a goat or a sheep, a draught ox; and for killing a donkey, a 1-year-old calf. [138] For killing wild animals, he should give a milk cow if they are carnivorous, and a heifer if they are non-carnivorous; for killing a camel, one Kṛṣṇala. [139] For killing a licentious woman belong to any of the four classes, he should give a leather bag, a bow, a goat, and a sheep, respectively. [140] If a twice-born is unable to expiate the killing of snakes and the rest by giving gifts, to remove the sin he may perform one arduous penance (11.212) for each.

[141] For killing one thousand creatures with bones or a cart-full of boneless creatures, he should perform the observance for killing a Śūdra. [142] For killing creatures with bones, he should give a little something to a Brahmin; when he kills boneless creatures, he is purified by controlling his breath.

Injuring Vegetation [143] For cutting down fruit trees a person should recite softly one hundred Ṛc verses; so also for cutting down shrubs, vines, creepers, or flowering plants.

[144] For killing any kind of creature growing in food stuffs, condiments, fruits, or flowers, the purification is to consume ghee.

[145] For needlessly tearing out cultivated plants or ones that grow spontaneously in the forest, he should follow a cow for one day, subsisting on milk (11.109–15).

[146] Through these observances a man should remove all sins he has committed deliberately or inadvertently by causing injury. Listen now to the observances relating to eating food that ought not to be eaten.

Excursus: Penances for Eating Forbidden Food

[147] When someone drinks Vāruṇī liquor inadvertently, he is purified only by undergoing vedic initiation. If he drinks it intentionally, no penance is prescribed; its penance ends in death – that is the settled rule. [148] If someone drinks water that has stood in a vessel for keeping liquor or an intoxicant (11.96 n.), he should drink milk boiled with Śaṅkhapuṣpī plant for five days. [149] If he touches, gives, or receives according to rule an intoxicant, or drinks water left over by a Śūdra, he should drink water boiled with Kuśa grass for three days. [150] If a Brahmin who has drunk Soma, however, smells the odour coming from a man who has drunk liquor, he is purified by controlling his breath three times while submerged in water and then consuming ghee. [151] Persons of all three twice-born classes ought to undergo re-initiation if they inadvertently consume urine or excrement, or anything that has come into contact with liquor.

[152] Shaving, girdle, staff, begging, and the vows are dispensed with in the rite of re-initiation of twice-born men.

[153] If someone eats the food of individuals whose food is not to be eaten or the leftovers of a woman or a Śūdra, or consumes forbidden meat, he should drink barley gruel for seven days. [154] When a twice-born drinks anything turned sour or pungent decoctions, even though they may be pure, he remains ritually impure until it has been excreted.

[155] If a twice-born consumes the urine or excrement of a village pig, a donkey, a camel, a jackal, a monkey, or a crow, he should perform the lunar penance (11.217). [156] He should perform the same observance after eating dried meat, the Bhauma plant, mushrooms (6.14 n.), the meat of an unknown animal (5.17), or meat from a slaughter-house.

[157] The hot-arduous penance (11.215) is the purification for eating the meat of carnivorous animals, pigs, camels, cocks, humans, crows, or donkeys.

[158] If a twice-born student who has not performed the rite of return eats food given at a monthly ancestral rite, he should fast for three days and remain in water for one day. [159] If someone observing the student vow eats honey or meat in any way, he should perform the standard arduous penance (11.212 n.) and complete the remainder of his vow.

[160] If someone eats anything that has become impure from the mouth of a cat, crow, rat, dog,

or mongoose, or that has been contaminated by hair or insects, he should drink a decoction of the Brahmasuvarcalā plant.

[161] A person who desires to remain pure should never eat unfit food (5.5 n.); he should vomit any such thing that he has eaten inadvertently or purify himself quickly with the various methods of purification.

> [162] I have described above the various rules pertaining to the observances for eating food that ought not to be eaten. Listen now to the rules pertaining to the observances that remove the sin of theft.

Excursus: Penances for Theft

[163] A Brahmin who deliberately steals grain, cooked food, or money from the house of someone belonging to his own caste is purified by performing the arduous penance (11.212) for one year. [164] For stealing men, women, a field, a house, or water from a well or a tank, tradition prescribes the lunar penance (11.217) as purification.

[165] If he steals articles of little value from the house of someone else, to purify himself he should return the stolen goods and perform the Sāntapana penance (11.213). [166] For stealing food or delicacies, as also a vehicle, a bed, a seat, flowers, roots, or fruits, the purification consists of consuming the five products of the cow. [167] For stealing grass, wood, trees, dried food, molasses, clothes, skins, or meat, he should abstain from food for three days. [168] For stealing gems, pearls, coral, copper, silver, iron, brass, or stone, he should subsist on broken grains for twelve days. [169] For stealing cotton, silk, wool, a single-hoofed or double-hoofed animal, a bird, perfume, medicinal herbs, or a rope, he should subsist on milk for three days.

> [170] Through these observances, a twice-born should remove a sin incurred by stealing. The sin incurred by having sex with a woman with whom sex is forbidden, on the other hand, he should remove by means of the following observances.

Excursus: Penances for Sexual Offences

[171] If a man has sexual intercourse with his uterine sisters, the wives of a friend or son, unmarried girls, or lowest-born women, he should perform the observance prescribed for sex with an elder's wife (see 11.58).

[172] If he has sex with his sister – the daughter of his father's or mother's sister – or the daughter of his mother's uterine brother, he should perform the lunar penance (11.217). [173] A wise man must not take these three to be his wife. Marriage with them is forbidden because they are blood relatives, and anyone marrying them proceeds downward (6.35 n.).

[174] If someone ejaculates his semen in nonhuman females, in a man, in a menstruating woman, in any place other than the vagina, or on water, he should perform the Sāntapana penance (11.213). [175] If a twice-born has sexual intercourse with a man or a woman in an oxcart, on water, or during the day, he should bathe with his clothes on.

[176] If a Brahmin has sex with Cāṇḍāla or lowest-born women, or eats food or accepts presents given by them, he falls from his caste if he does it inadvertently and becomes equal to them if he does it intentionally.

[177] The husband should keep an adulterous wife confined in a single room and make her perform the observance prescribed for a man who has sex with another man's wife. [178] If she commits adultery again when solicited by a man of the same caste, tradition prescribes an arduous penance (11.212) and a lunar penance (11.217) as the means of her purification.

[179] The sin that a twice-born commits in a single night by having sex with a Śūdra woman he removes in three years by living on almsfood and performing soft recitations every day.

> [180] I have described above the expiation for all four kinds of sinner. Listen now to the following expiations for those who associate with outcastes.

Association with Outcastes

[181] When someone associates with an outcaste by officiating at sacrifices, by teaching, and by contracting marriages – but not by occupying the same vehicle or seat or by eating together – in one year he himself becomes an outcaste.

[182] When a man forges links (2.40 n.) with any one of these outcastes, he should perform the same observance prescribed for that man in order to purify himself of his linkage with him.

Excommunication [183] In the evening of an inauspicious day and in the presence of his blood relations, officiating priests, and teachers, the rite of offering water to the outcaste should be performed by the relatives belonging to his ancestry (5.60 n.) together with his relatives by marriage. [184] A slave woman should overturn a pot filled with water with her foot, as for a dead man; and they, along with his relatives by marriage, shall observe a period of impurity for a day and a night. [185] They should suspend conversing or sitting together with him, giving him his inheritance, and even ordinary interaction with him. [186] The rights of primogeniture are also suspended in his case, along with the pre-emptive property owed to the eldest; the pre-emptive share of the eldest should go to a younger brother of his with the highest qualities.

Re-admission [187] After he has performed the penance, however, they should bathe in a sacred body of water and, along with him, throw into it a brand-new pot filled with water. [188] After he has thrown that pot in the water and entered his own house, he should participate in all the activities of the relatives just as he had done before.

[189] These same rules should be adhered to also in the case of women who become outcastes; but they should be provided with clothes, food, and drink, and permitted to live near the house.

[190] No one should transact any business with uncleansed sinners; and under no circumstances should anyone abhor those who have been cleansed.

Excursus: Miscellanea on Sin and Penance

[191] One must not live together with people who have killed children, women, or those who come to them for protection, or with people who are ingrates, even if they have been purified in accordance with the Law.

[192] When any twice-born men have not been taught the Sāvitrī verse according to rule (2.38 n.), one should make them undergo three arduous penances and have them initiated according to rule. [193] One should prescribe the same when twice-born men who have followed wrong occupations or neglected the Veda seek to perform a penance.

[194] When Brahmins have acquired wealth through a reprehensible activity, they are purified by giving away that wealth and by engaging in soft recitation and ascetic toil. [195] A man is freed from the sin of accepting gifts from a bad individual by softly reciting the Sāvitrī verse three thousand times with a collected mind and by subsisting on milk for a month while remaining in a cow pen. [196] When that man, emaciated by the fast, returns from the cow pen and remains bowing down, they should ask him: 'Friend, do you seek equality?' [197] Saying 'Truly' to the Brahmins, he should scatter some grass for the cows. At that place made holy by the cows, they should perform his re-admission.

[198] If someone officiates at a sacrifice of Vrātyas (2.39), performs the funeral of outsiders, or carries out a rite of sorcery or an Ahīna sacrifice, he is purified by doing an arduous penance (11.212) three times.

[199] When a twice-born has forsaken someone who has come to him for protection or has misused the Veda, he removes that sin by subsisting on barley for one year.

[200] When a man has been bitten by a dog, a jackal, a donkey, a carnivorous animal of the village, a man, a horse, a camel, or a pig, he is purified by controlling his breath.

[201] Eating at every sixth mealtime (6.19 n.) for one month, reciting a Vedic Collection, offering daily a Śākalā oblation – these are

the means of purification for individuals alongside whom it is unfit to eat.

[202] When a Brahmin deliberately gets onto a camel-cart or a donkey-cart, he is purified by bathing naked and controlling his breath. [203] If someone in distress discharges his bodily waste either without water or in water, he is purified by bathing with his clothes on outside the village and then touching a cow.

[204] For neglecting the daily rites prescribed by the Veda and for breaking the vow of a bath-graduate, the penance is fasting. [205] When someone says 'Hum' to a Brahmin or addresses a superior as 'you', he should bathe, fast the rest of the day, and placate that person by paying him obeisance. [206] If he strikes such a man with even a blade of grass, throttles his neck with a cloth, or defeats him in an argument, he should placate him by prostrating himself on the ground. [207] By wanting to hurt a Brahmin, a man goes to hell – if he threatens him, for one hundred years; if he strikes him, for one thousand years. [208] As many particles of dust as the blood of a twice-born lumps together, for so many thousands of years will the man who spilled it live in hell (4.168). [209] For threatening, he should perform an arduous penance (11.212); for striking, a very arduous penance (11.214); and for spilling a Brahmin's blood, both an arduous and a very arduous penance.

[210] For the removal of sins for which no expiation has been specified, one should fix a penance after taking into consideration both the type of sin and the strength of the sinner.

> [211] I will describe to you the means whereby a human being may remove sins, means employed by gods, seers, and ancestors.

Types of Generic Penance [212] A twice-born practising the *Prājāpatya* penance should eat in the morning for three days and in the evening for three days, eat what is received unasked for three days, and abstain from food during the final three days.

[213] Subsisting on cow's urine, cow dung, milk, curd, ghee, and water boiled with Kuśa grass, and fasting during one day – tradition calls this the Sāntapana penance.

[214] A twice-born practising the Atikṛcchra (very arduous) penance should eat as before (11.212) one mouthful a day during the three three-day periods and fast during the final three days.

[215] A Brahmin practising the Taptakṛcchra (hot-arduous) penance should drink hot water, hot milk, hot ghee, and hot air during each three-day period and bathe once with a collected mind.

[216] When a man, controlled and vigilant, abstains from food for twelve days, it is called the Parāka penance, which removes all sins.

[217] He should decrease his food by one rice-ball a day during the dark fortnight and increase it likewise during the bright fortnight, bathing three times a day – tradition calls this Cāndrāyaṇa (the lunar penance). [218] This same procedure in its entirety should be followed when a man, with his mind controlled, performs the lunar observance with its middle shaped like a barley corn, beginning it on the first day of the bright fortnight.

[219] A man practising the lunar penance of ascetics should eat each day at noon eight rice-balls from the sacrificial oblation, controlling himself. [220] A Brahmin should eat four rice-balls in the morning with a collected mind and four after sunset – tradition calls this the lunar penance of children.

[221] If a man eats thrice eighty rice-balls from the sacrificial oblation in any manner whatsoever during one month with a collected mind, he obtains residence in the same world as the Moon.

[222] This observance was practised by the Rudras, the Ādityas, the Vasus, and the Maruts, along with the great seers, to free themselves from all evil.

Observances by the Penitent [223] He should offer a burnt oblation every day by himself, reciting the Great Calls; and he should practise abstention from injuring, truthfulness, abstention from anger, and honesty. [224] He should enter water with his clothes three times during the day and three times during the night, and under no circumstance may he speak with women, Śūdras, or outcastes. [225] He must remain standing during the day and seated at night or, if he is unable, lie down on the ground (6.22 n.). He must remain chaste and devoted to his vow, paying homage to teachers, gods, and Brahmins. [226] He should recite softly the Sāvitrī verse and the purificatory texts every day to the best of his ability, remaining diligent in this way with respect to all observances carried out for the purpose of a penance.

[227] By these observances should twice-born persons cleanse themselves of public sins; they may cleanse themselves of secret sins, however, through ritual formulas and burnt offerings.

Four Means of Expiation [228] A sinner is freed from his sin by declaring it publicly, by being contrite, by performing ascetic toil, and by reciting the Veda; during a time of adversity, also by giving gifts.

[229] To the extent a man on his own publicly acknowledges an infraction of the Law he has committed, to that extent is he freed from that infraction, like a snake from his slough.

[230] The more his mind abhors that evil deed, the more his body is freed from that infraction; [231] for when a man is contrite about a sin he has committed, he is freed from that sin. 'I will never do so again' – by this forswearing he is purified. [232] Having thus contemplated in his mind the consequences his actions have on his afterlife, he should always pursue wholesome activities with his thoughts, speech, and body. [233] If a man commits a reprehensible act, whether it is inadvertent or deliberate, he must not commit it a second time if he wants to be freed from it.

[234] If someone's mind is not at ease with respect to a particular act he has committed, he should practise ascetic toil for it until his mind is assuaged. [235] All happiness here, whether divine or human, has ascetic toil as its root, as its middle, and as its end – so have wise men who saw the Veda declared. [236] Knowledge is the ascetic toil for a Brahmin; protection, for a Kṣatriya; trade, for a Vaiśya; and service, for a Śūdra. [237] Solely by ascetic toil do well-disciplined seers, subsisting on fruits, roots, and air, observe the three worlds together with their mobile and immobile creatures. [238] Solely by ascetic toil do medicines, antidotes, spells, and the various divine conditions become effective; for ascetic toil is the means by which they become effective. [239] What is difficult to cross, what is difficult to obtain, what is difficult to enter, what is difficult to do – all that is accomplished by ascetic toil, for it is difficult to prevail over ascetic toil. [240] Persons guilty of a grievous sin causing loss of caste, as also others who have committed misdeeds, are freed from their sins simply by ascetic toil vigorously carried out. [241] Insects, snakes, moths, animals, birds, and immobile creatures attain heaven by the power of ascetic toil. [242] Whatever sin people commit through their mind, word, or body – with ascetic toil as their only wealth, they quickly burn off all that simply by ascetic toil. [243] The denizens of heaven accept the offerings of a Brahmin purified solely by ascetic toil, and they fulfil his desires. [244] Prajāpati, the Lord, created this Treatise solely by ascetic toil; the seers, likewise, obtained the Vedas by ascetic toil. [245] Thus did the gods proclaim this grandeur of ascetic toil, as they observed the sacred origin of this whole world from ascetic toil.

[246] Reciting the Veda daily to the best of one's ability, performing the great sacrifices, and forbearance quickly destroy sins, even those rising from grievous acts causing loss of caste. [247] As a fire by its energy burns up in an instant a piece of kindling placed in it, so a man who knows the Veda burns up all sins by the fire of his knowledge.

Further Means of Expiation [249] Controlling the breath sixteen times while reciting the syllable OṂ along with the Calls, when it is performed every day, purifies even the murderer of a learned Brahmin (4.208 n.) within one month.

[250] Even a man who has drunk liquor is purified by reciting softly Kutsa's hymn, 'Burning away our evil . . . ', the triple verse of Vasiṣṭha, 'To welcome the Dawn . . . ', the Māhitra hymn, and the Śuddhavatī verses.

[251] A man who has stolen gold, on the other hand, becomes instantly stainless by reciting softly the Asyavāmīya hymn and the Śiva-saṃkalpa formulas.

[252] A man who has had sex with an elder's wife is freed from his sin by reciting softly the hymns Haviṣpāntīya, 'No anxiety, no danger . . . ', and 'This, yes, this is my inclination . . . ', and the Puruṣa hymn.

[253] A man who wants to remove grave or slight sins should recite softly during one year the verse 'We placate . . . ,' and the verse 'Whatever offence . . . ' [254] If a man has accepted a forbidden gift or has eaten reprehensible food, he is purified in three days by reciting softly the Taratsamandī hymn. [255] A man who has committed many sins is purified by reciting the Somāraudra hymn and the three verses 'Aryaman . . . ' while bathing in a river. [256] A sinner should recite softly the seven verses 'Indra . . . ' for half a year; but if someone commits a reprehensible act in the water, he should subsist for a month on almsfood. [257] A twice-born removes even a grave sin by offering oblations of ghee during one year while reciting the Śākalahomīya formulas or by reciting softly the verse 'Adoration . . . '.

[258] A man guilty of a grievous sin causing loss of caste should follow cows with a collected mind; he becomes purified by subsisting on almsfood and reciting the Pāvamāṇī verses for one year (11.109–17). [259] Or, if a man, being ritually pure, recites three times a Vedic Collection in the wilderness and cleanses himself by means of three Parāka penances, he is freed from all the sins causing loss of caste. [260] If a man, self-controlled, fasts for three days while bathing three times a day and reciting the Aghamarṣaṇa hymn three times, he is freed from all the sins causing loss of caste. [261] As the horse sacrifice, the king of sacrifices, removes all sins, so the Aghamarṣaṇa hymn removes all sins.

[262] Even if he has slaughtered these three worlds and even if he has eaten food of anyone at all, no sin taints a Brahmin who retains the Ṛg-veda in his memory. [263] If a man recites three times with a collected mind the Collection of the Ṛg-veda, the Yajur-veda, or the Sāma-veda, along with the secret texts (2.140 n.), he is freed from all sins. [264] As a clod dissolves quickly when it falls into a large lake, so all sins become submerged in the triple Veda. [265] The Ṛg verses, the primary Yajus formulas, and the diverse Sāman chants – these should be known as the triple Veda. A man who knows it is one who knows the Veda. [266] The primary tri-syllabic Veda, upon which the triple Veda is based, is another secret triple Veda. A man who knows it is one who knows the Veda.

Part II

Contemporary Texts and Issues

Chapter 10

Papers Relating to East India Affairs, viz. Hindoo Widows, and Voluntary Immolations

The *(Parliamentary) Papers* are a detailed catalogue of the *satīs*, widow self-immolations, which were performed in India between 1797 and 1830. Published in London by the House of Commons, they exemplify the predicament faced by the British as they tried to permit and regulate an act that they thought was fundamentally wrong, yet found intriguing and exotic. This was indeed a challenge given that the British government sought to:

> consult with religious opinions, customs, and prejudices of the natives, in all cases in which has been practicable, consistently with the principles of morality, reason and humanity.[1]

These papers thus integrated accounts of particular cases, list and tables of the *satīs*, as well as documented debates about the legitimacy and authenticity of the *sati*. The catalogue included headings for the name, age, and *varṇa-jāti* of the *satī*, as well as the date of her immolation, number of children, her dead husband's name, and the place where the *satī* took place.

The accounts published in these *Papers* were the source of debate and discussion both in Britain and in India. It served to rally together those with political, economic, and missionary interests.[2] Such debates were part of the media coverage and helped to characterize India as "backward and barbaric."[3] Concurrently Rāja Rammohan Ray, the public intellectual of the Bengali Renaissance, published his own dialogues about the practice. The complexities facing the British as well as Indian thinkers who were exposed to Enlightenment ideals are present in these writings and accounts.

The first set of passages included here are descriptions of two *satīs*, one that took place in 1797 and another in 1805. The second set is a series of "Judicial Consultations" that concern the rules and regulations for permissible *satīs* which largely concerned ascertaining if the *satī*-to-be was cognizant of her choice, a willing participant, and was not drugged or coerced in any way. The third set is a series of questions posed to several *paṇḍits* about the authenticity and legitimacy of *satī* in Hinduism. Their answers involve citations from the Shaster (i.e. *śāstras*). These are most similar to Ray's "Translation of a Conference between an Advocate for, and an Opponent of, the Practice of Burning Widows Alive."

Notes

1 *Papers Relating to East India Affairs, viz. Hindoo Widows, and Voluntary Immolations.* London: House of Commons, 1821–1830, p. 24.
2 Andrea Major, *Pious Flames: European Encounters with Sati.* Oxford: Oxford University Press, 2006, p. 123.
3 Major, *Pious Flames*, p. 126.

Further reading

Courtright, Paul, "*Satī*, Sacrifice, and Marriage: The Modernity of Tradition" in L. Harlan and P. Courtright (eds.), *From the Margins of Hindu Marriage: Essays on Gender, Religion, and Culture.* New York: Oxford University Press, 1995.

Hawley, John Stratton (ed.), *Sati, The Blessing and the Curse: The Burning of Wives in India.* New York: Oxford University Press, 1994.

Major, Andrea, *Pious Flames: European Encounters with Sati.* Oxford: Oxford University Press, 2006.

Mani, Lata, *Contentious Traditions: The Debate on Sati in Colonial India.* Berkeley, CA: University of California Press, 1998.

Weinberg-Thomas, Catherine, *Widow Burning in India* (tr. by J. Mehlman and D. G. White). Oxford: Oxford University Press, 2000.

Hindoo Widows, &c.

Extract BENGAL Judicial Consultations, the 19th May 1797.

N° 1. – (Criminal.) – Acting Magistrate of Midnapore, to the Honourable Sir John Shore, bart. Governor General in Council, Fort William.

Honourable Sir, – On receiving information this morning from the cutwal, that a child, by name Kumly, intended sacrificing herself with her husband, I thought it my duty to endeavour to prevent its taking place. She is scarcely nine years of age, and I am convinced can give no good reason whatever for so doing. Her aunt, who accompanied her, used her endeavours to dissuade her from such an act, but the superstition of the higher order of Hindoos has filled her head with such notions of its propriety, that I fear the business may yet sooner or later be accomplished. I may have erred in interfering with their religion, of which they say this is a part, but as the information was brought to me, I thought it my duty as magistrate to prevent it, as also from motives of humanity, and hope my conduct will meet with your approbation.

I have, &c. (signed)
James Battray, act[g] mag[ts].
Zillah Midnapore, 17th May 1797.

Ordered, That the acting magistrate be informed, that the Governor General in Council desires he will use every means of persuasion in his power, to induce Kumly to relinquish her intention of sacrificing herself; and that he will also endeavour to persuade her family to exert their influence in discouraging her from the execution of such an intention.

Extract BENGAL Judicial Consultations, 7th February 1805.

N° 6. – (Criminal.) – Acting Magistrate of the zillah of Bohar, to George Dowdeswell, esq. Secretary to Government; Judicial Department.

Sir, – A CIRCUMSTANCE has occurred at this place, which I think it my duty to represent to you, for the information of his excellency the most noble the Governor General in Council.

Yesterday morning the police darogah of Gya reported to me, that a man of the cast of bunnya had died on the night of the 2d instant, and that his relations were preparing to burn the corpse; that they also intended to burn the wife of the deceased (a girl of twelve years of age) upon the same pile. The darogah likewise stated to me that some friends of the girl had applied privately to him to prevent her burning herself; adding, as the father and friends of the deceased were persuading her to it, they could not interfere publicly, without incurring censure and disgrace from the rest of their tribe.

Upon receiving this report, I directed the darogah to proceed to the spot where the pile had been erected, (and where the corpse of the deceased, and the girl had been previously conveyed), to ascertain if it was voluntary on the part of the girl, and at the same time to endeavour to dissuade her from being guilty of such a rash act.

On the darogah's arrival at the place, he found the girl surrounded by an immense concourse of people, and the friends of the deceased preparing to set fire to the pile, upon which they had already placed the corpse, and were persuading the girl to ascend it also. She appeared to be in a perfect state of

Excerpts from House of Commons, *Papers Relating to East India Affairs, viz. Hindoo Widows and Voluntary Immolations*. London: House of Commons, 1821.

stupefaction or intoxication, and as it did not appear to be the wish of her friends that she should burn herself, I deemed it incumbent on me to exercise my authority, as magistrate, to prevent it; and I am since given to understand that the girl and her friends are extremely grateful for my interposition.

As I am not aware of the existence of any order or regulation to prevent such a barbarous proceeding, and as the prejudices of the natives may be affected by an interference on the part of the magistrate, I beg that you will represent the case to his excellency the most noble the Governor General in Council, for such orders as his lordship may be pleased to pass for the guidance of the magistrate in future.

I have, &c. (signed) *J. R. Elphinstone*,
acting magistrate.
Zillah Behar, 4th January 1805.

The secretary was directed to write the following letter to the register of the nizamut adawlut, on the 5th instant.

N° 7. – To S. T. Goad, esq. Register of the Nizamut Adawlut.

Sir, – I am directed by his excellency the most noble the Governor General in Council, to desire that you will lay before the court of nizamut adawlut the enclosed copy of a letter, from the acting magistrate of Behar, respecting a woman whom he had prevented from burning herself with the body of her deceased husband.

2. The nizamut adawlut is aware that it is one of the fundamental maxims of the British government to consult the religious opinions, customs, and prejudices of the natives, in all cases in which it has been practicable, consistently with the principles of morality, reason and humanity. On adverting however to the circumstances stated by the acting magistrate of Behar, respecting the case of the woman mentioned in his letter, particularly to the extreme youth of the party, and her reported state of intoxication or stupefaction, when the ceremony of burning the body of her late husband took place, the Governor General in Council considers it to be an indispensable duty to ascertain whether this unnatural and inhuman custom can be abolished altogether; or if that desirable object should appear to be impracticable, consistently with the principles above noticed, to adopt such measures as shall in future prevent, as far as possible, any undue influence over the minds of women in the situation above described; and more particularly the abuse noticed by the acting magistrate of Behar, of suspending their reasoning faculties by means of intoxication.

3. The nizamut adawlut is accordingly requested to ascertain, in the first instance, by means of a reference to the pundits, how far the practice above noticed is founded in the religious opinions of the Hindoos. Should that practice be not grounded in any precept of their law, the Governor General in Council would hope that the custom, which at present prevails among the Hindoo women, of burning themselves with the bodies of their deceased husbands, might gradually, if not immediately, be altogether abolished. If however the entire abolition of the practice in question, should appear to the nizamut adawlut to be impracticable in itself, or to be inexpedient, as offending any established religious opinion of the Hindoos, the Governor General in Council requests that the court will take into its consideration, the best means of preventing the abuses above noticed; so that, at all events, means may be adopted to prevent the illegal and unwarrantable practice of administering intoxicating medicines to women in the situation above described, and to rescue from destruction such females, as, from immaturity of years, or other circumstances, cannot be considered capable of judging for themselves, in a case of so serious and awful a nature, as that to which these remarks refer.

Council Chamber, 5th Feb. 1805.
I have, &c. (signed) *G. Dowdeswell*,
secretary to government,
Judicial Department.

Extract BENGAL Judicial Consultations, 5th December 1812.

N° 6. – (Criminal.) – Acting Register of the Nizamut Adawlut to George Dowdeswell, esq. Secretary to Government in the Judicial Department.

Para. 1. – Sir, – I AM directed by the court of nizamut adawlut to acknowledge the receipt of your letter dated 5th February last.

2. For the purpose of obtaining the information required by his excellency the most noble the Governor General in Council, the nizamut adawlut proposed a question to the pundits of the court; and subsequently made a further reference to them; the answers to which, together with translations, are submitted for the information of his excellency the Governor General in Council.

3. It appears to the court, from the opinions delivered by the law officers, that the practice of widows burning themselves with the bodies of their deceased husbands, is founded on the religious notions of the Hindoos, and is expressly stated, with approbation, in their law. The practice, as there recognized, is voluntary on the part of the widow, and grounded on a prejudice respecting the consequent benefit to herself and her husband in another world. It is however prohibited by the Hindoo law in certain circumstances, though encouraged in others; and the administering of intoxicating drugs to women about to burn themselves is pronounced by the pundits of the court to be illegal, and contrary to usage. It does not appear that a woman having declared an intention of burning herself, but receding from it at any time before the commencement of the prescribed ceremonies, would forfeit her rank in life, or suffer any degradation in point of cast; but it may be concluded from the answer of the law officers, that if she recede after the ceremonies are begun she would be an outcast until a severe penance has been undergone by her.

4. The court are fully sensible how much it is to be wished that this practice, horrid and revolting even as a voluntary one, should be prohibited and entirely abolished. Various incitements, especially that of promised happiness in another world, presented to an afflicted mind at the instant of the greatest sorrow, must too often induce a woman hastily to declare her intention of burning herself, and the fear of contempt and degradation may make her persist in the design through the very short interval which follows until its accomplishment. It cannot be doubted that persuasion is, at least sometimes, employed (though the contrary is said to be more frequent) to induce a widow to declare the design of burning herself, or to persist in it after making that declaration; and the instance reported by the acting magistrate of zillah Behar, is a sufficient ground for supposing that most unwarrantable means are sometimes used to give the appearance of a voluntary act to that which the woman neither intended nor consented to.

5. The court being aware that some usages which were formerly prevalent, and which were authorized, or even enjoined by the Hindoo law, have either gradually fallen into disuse, or been actually prohibited by Hindoo princes, thought it expedient to make inquiries, with the view of ascertaining whether this custom, though sanctioned by Hindoo law, might not be immediately abolished, without greatly offending the religious prejudices of the people. From these inquiries, conducted with caution, lest any alarm should be excited, the court have reason to believe that the prejudices in favour of this custom, are at present so strongly impressed on the minds of the inhabitants, in most parts of these provinces, that all casts of Hindoos would be extremely tenacious of its continuance. In others, (particularly in Tirhoot) more rational opinions are prevalent; and this inhuman custom has there almost entirely ceased; while, in some districts, the usage may be considered as nearly confined to particular casts (the khetree and kayuth especially), being either

discountenanced, or little practised, in the other tribes.

6. Under this information, the court apprehend that it would be impracticable at the present time, consistently with the principle invariably observed by the British government, of manifesting every possible indulgence to the religious opinions and prejudices of the natives, to abolish the custom in question; whilst such a measure would, in all probability, excite a considerable degree of alarm and dissatisfaction in the minds of the Hindoo inhabitants of these provinces. The court are accordingly of opinion, that the immediate adoption of a measure of the above nature would be highly inexpedient. It appears, however, to the court, that hopes may be reasonably entertained that this very desirable object may be gradually effected, and at no distant period of time.

7. With this view, and for the purpose of preventing any illegal, unwarrantable, and criminal practices, such as occurred in the instance reported by the acting magistrate of zillah Behar, the nizamut adawlut propose, should it be approved by his excellency the Governor General in Council, to issue instructions to the magistrates of the several cities and zillahs to the following purport: –

"That the magistrates shall direct the police officers under their authority, to use their utmost care to obtain the earliest information whenever it is intended to burn a woman with the body of her husband.

"That the police officers be directed to take immediate measures on receipt of such information, either by repairing in person to the place where the woman may be, or by deputing one of the police officers under them, to ascertain the circumstances, and particularly the age of the woman, and whether her intention of burning herself be entirely voluntary.

"In the event of the declaration having been forced from her, or of its being retracted by her, or of her being desirous of retracting it, or of her being found to be in a state of intoxication or stupefaction, as also in the case of her youth, or her being in a state of pregnancy, which would render the intended act illegal, it will be the duty of the police officer to take the necessary measures to prevent her being burned with her husband's body; apprising the relations, or other persons concerned, that they will be dealt with as criminals if they take further steps towards the effecting of their criminal and illegal design.

"Should no circumstances occur to require his immediate interference, he shall nevertheless continue his vigilance: and in the event of any compulsion being subsequently used, or drugs administered, producing intoxication or stupefaction, it will be his duty by all means in his power, immediately to stop so criminal a proceeding, and prevent its accomplishment.

"The officers in charge of the police will include in their monthly report to the magistrate, every instance which may occur within their respective jurisdictions, of a woman burning herself; and will separately report their proceedings, in every instance in which they may interfere for the prevention of it, immediately after the case shall have occurred.

"The magistates should give particular attention to enforce a strict observance of these instructions by the police officers under their authority."

8. The nizamut adawlut are of opinion, that in addition to these instructions to the magistrates, it might be useful for the end proposed, to publish a notification, under the authority of government, strictly prohibiting the practice of administering drugs productive of intoxication or stupefaction, and the use of any other illegal or unwarrantable means to procure the burning of a woman with the body of her husband; and declaring, that persons charged with offences of the above nature, will be liable to be committed for trial before the court of circuit; and, on conviction, to such punishment as the law directs.

9. The court hope, that by the adoption of the measures now proposed by them, the abuses which may have been hitherto sometimes practised, will be prevented for the future; and, that after information has been

obtained of the extent to which the practice is found to prevail, and of the districts in which it has fallen into disuse, or in which it is discountenanced by the principal and most respectable classes of Hindoo inhabitants, it may be immediately abolished in particular districts, and be checked and ultimately prohibited in the other parts of these provinces.

Fort William, 5th June 1805.

I am, &c. (signed)

Wm B. Bayley, acting register.

N° 7. – Question to the Pundits of the Nizamut Adawlut.

As it sometimes happens among persons professing the Hindoo religion, that upon the death of a man his widow becomes a suttee, *i. e.* burns herself with the body of her deceased husband, you are therefore asked, whether a woman is enjoined by the Shaster voluntarily to burn herself with the body of her husband, or is prohibited; and what are the conditions prescribed by the Shaster on such occasions? You are desired to give an answer in the course of fifteen days.

4th March 1805.

Answer. – Having duly considered the question proposed by the court, I now answer it to the best of my knowledge: – Every woman of the four casts (brahmin, khetry, bues and soodur) is permitted to burn herself with the body of her husband, provided she has not infant children, nor is pregnant, nor in a state of uncleanness, nor under the age of puberty; in any of which cases she is not allowed to burn herself with her husband's body.

But a woman who has infant children, and can procure another person to undertake the charge of bringing them up, is permitted to burn.

It is contrary to law, as well as to the usage of the country, to cause any woman to burn herself against her wish, by administering drugs to stupify or intoxicate her.

When women burn themselves, they pronounce the sunkulp, and perform other prescribed ceremonies previously to burning.

This rests upon the authority of Anjira, Vijasa and Vrihaspati, mooni.

"There are three millions and a half of hairs upon the human body, and every woman who burns herself with the body of her husband, will reside with him in heaven during a like number of years.

"In the same manner, as a snake-catcher drags a snake from his hole, so does a woman, who burns herself, draw her husband out of hell; and she afterwards resides with him in heaven."

The exceptions above cited, respecting women in a state of pregnancy, uncleanness, and adolescence, were communicated by Oorub and others to the mother of Sugur Raja.

No woman having infant children, or being in a state of pregnancy or uncleanness, or under the age of puberty, is permitted to burn with her husband; with the following exception, namely, that if a woman having infant children can provide for their support, through the means of another person, she is permitted to burn.

(signed) *Ghunesham Surmono.*

Additional question. – In the event of a woman declaring her intention to burn with the body of her husband, and afterwards receding from such declaration, what would be the consequence, and what treatment would she experience from her relations? – If any woman declares her intention of burning, but afterwards recedes from her declaration, without having pronounced the sunkulp and performed other ceremonies, she is not enjoined by the Shaster to undergo any *puraschit* or penance; neither is there any thing contained in the law, prohibiting her relations from associating with her.

But if a woman, after pronouncing the sunkulp, and performing other ceremonies, has not courage to proceed to the funeral pile, she may recover her purity by undergoing a severe penance; and her relations may then associate with her.

The authority for this is the following passage: –

"A woman who is prevented by worldly attachments, from ascending the funeral pile, must perform a severe penance before she can purify herself from such an offence."

(signed) *J. Walker*, head assistant.

[...]

(A.) – N° 6. – Questions proposed to Shoobee Rai Shastry, Pundit of the Sudder Dewanny Adawlut, with his Replies; 2d June 1817.

Question 1. – If a Hindoo widow be prevented from burning herself with the body of her husband, by pregnancy or other legal disability, can she perform the rite of anoomarana at any subsequent period, when the cause of disability may be removed? Let the authorities be stated.

Reply. – In answer to the question regarding a woman who is prevented by pregnancy, or other legal cause of disability, from burning herself with the body of her husband, it is declared, that such women alone are competent to perform the rite of anoomarana, as are devoted to their lords, and absent from them at the time of their death; or such women as are in the first or second day of menstruation, the disqualifying cause being here removed in a short interval.

Women, under other circumstances, are not permitted to perform the rite of anoomarana.

The authorities for the above opinion are as follow: – "Her husband having been burnt on the preceding day, whatever woman through delusion follows him on the succeeding day, she by her suicide neither conveys herself nor her husband to paradise." From the above quoted text of Purana, it would appear that the corpse of the husband being burnt on one day, it is incompetent to the widow to burn herself on another; but the text has been defined to extend to such women only, as do not fall under the description of women devoted to their lords. The requisites for such a character have been described in the Anoomarana Livek, "She may truly be called devoted to her lord, who rejoices when he is pleased; and who grieves when he is pained; and who accompanies him in death."

The following is an extract from the Anoomarana Livek: – "Let them burn the corpse of him who dies in the first or second day of his wife's menstruation; then let the widow devoted to her lord, having waited until the fourth day for the sake of being purified, holding his sandals, enter the fire." The same rule applies also to one whose husband dies in a foreign country, as appears from an extract of the Agneepoorana, "Her husband having died in another country, let the virtuous widow take his two sandals and enter the fire, she does not thereby commit the crime of suicide."

So also the Anoomarana Livek, "Let that virtuous woman enter the fire, placing them (the sandals) on her breast."

Question 2. – If a widow, not being a biha, who is absent from her husband at the time of his death, (and is consequently permitted to perform the anoomarana with some relic belonging to him), does not avail herself of this permission immediately on becoming acquainted with the death of her husband, is she at liberty to do so at a future period? State the authorities.

Reply. – That woman who, being absent from her husband at the time of his death, does not perform the rite of anoomarana immediately on becoming acquainted with that event, cannot be considered a patribrata or devoted to her lord. She is consequently not at liberty to burn herself at any subsequent period.

The authorities cited in the reply to the first question, are applicable to the support of this opinion.

Question 3. – If a woman be with her husband at the time of his decease, and without being prevented by any legal impediment, should omit to perform the act of sahamarana, can she at any subsequent period perform the rite of anoomarana? State the authorities.

Reply. – A woman who being present at the time of her husband's death, and unrestrained by a legal impediment, omits the act of sahamarana, cannot be considered a patribrata or devoted to her lord, she is consequently not at liberty to burn herself at any subsequent period.

The authorities cited in the reply to the first question, are applicable also to the support of this opinion.

(A true translation.)

(signed) *W. H. Macnaghten*,
acting deputy register.

(B.) – Question proposed to Sree Chundra Turkalunkar, Pundit to the Provincial Court of Appeal for the division of Dacca; 15 August 1815.

Is it allowable, according to the Shasters, for a woman of the jogee tribe to become a suttee; and, on the death of her husband, to bury herself alive along with his corpse; or is it not allowable?

Let a reply, in conformity with the Shasters, be furnished to the above question.

Reply to the above:

There is no authority for a woman of the jogee tribe to become a suttee, (*i. e.* to die with her husband) and to bury herself alive along with the corpse of her deceased husband. This is an act which is founded merely on practice. There exists no authority which recognizes the propriety of any other mode of sahamarana (or dying along with the husband) than that of ascending the flaming funeral pile. The practice of burying their dead, is observable among a certain class of sunyassees; on this account, the people of the jogee tribe, who conceive themselves to be descendants of those sunyassees, also bury their dead; and the wives of such jogees, observing this custom when they are anxious to accompany their deceased husbands, bury themselves in the same grave with their corpses; but they are not justified by the Shasters in doing so. Nay, it is even ordained in the Soodhee Chintamanee, that a certain description of sunyassees should be burnt after death; and therefore the wife of a jogee, consuming herself by fire, does not act repugnantly to the Shasters when she wishes to follow her deceased husband. But no authority is any where to be found which justifies a woman putting an end to her life, by burying herself alive along with her deceased husband.

(signed) *Sree Rajah Chundra Turkalunkar.*

They who from the tribe of jogees are born of a licentious sunyassee, cohabiting with a female of the brahmin tribe, during the period of her menstruation; among these, some adopt red clothing, wear shell-earrings, and travel about as jogees; others take to the trade of weaving, and lead the life of a householder. These are called jogee and nauth indiscriminately. Some of these remain in mourning for ten days, others for a month. A brahmin will not assist at their religious ceremonies. Their poohits or officiating priests are selected from persons of their own tribe.

The Shoodhee Futwa specially recognizes burning, as the only legitimate way in which a woman can accompany her deceased husband.

"When her husband dies there is no other alternative left for a virtuous woman than precipitating herself into the fire. She who ascends the funeral pile along with her deceased husband, being equal in virtue to Aroondhutee, shall meet with reverence in paradise."

In the above sentence, by using the words "she who ascends," the author must have had in contemplation those who declined to do so.

Vishnoo ordains, that, "at the death of her husband, the woman must either lead the life of a brahmacharee, or burn at the same funeral pile with him."

"I accompany my husband by mounting the fiery funeral pile." This is a common expression; Gundharee Madree, and others, perished in this manner.

The Mitateshura declares, that as long as a woman, at the death of her husband, shall omit to consume herself by fire, as long shall she continue in the form of a woman." The Mitateshura farther says, that a woman who is devoted to her lord will enter the fiery furnace; and that this is a duty common to all women who are neither pregnant, or have infant children, even to chundals.

From the above quoted passages of the Mitateshura, it would appear that this was an act fit for all women to perform, even chundals; but no other mode of accompanying a deceased husband, except that of burning, is any where authorized.

(A true translation.)

(signed) *W. Hay Macnaghten.*
(Copy.) (signed) *W. H. M.*
act^g dep^y register.

(C.) – Translation of the Answer delivered by the Hindoo Law Officers of the Court to the Question referred to them on the 29th of July 1813, respecting the practice of Hindoo Women burying themselves with the bodies of their deceased Husbands.

On the demise of persons at present designated as of the cast of jogees (these, by some means or other, being the descendants of either the valuidaca or the paramahansa orders of dyan jogees, devoted to abstract contemplation) although such persons do not practise religious contemplation; yet under the Shasters, in conformity with the custom of their family, the burial of these is enjoined, from the circumstance of burning having been forbidden, and interment directed in the cases of the ancestors Vahudaca and Paramahunsa, from whom they derive their origin. Hence the rule of burying these person's wives (who may be desirous of becoming "suttees") with the bodies of their deceased husbands, is proper. In support of the above may be adduced the following authorities: –

The text of a muni cited in the Smrite Arthasara, Parasara Madhaviya, Nernuya Sindhee, and other books: "For the solitary person devoted to abstract contemplation neither burning or mourning, nor the oblation of water, is to be performed."

Also the text of a muni cited in the same books. In the cases of the four following sunyasis, "let them burn the kutichka; bury the vahudaca; let the hansa be cast in the water; let them bury the parahunsa."

Lastly, the text of the muni, "Whatever institutes of country, cast or family, have originally been established, are to be preserved, otherwise the ruin of the subject is incurred."

(A true translation.)

(signed) *J. C. C. Sutherland,*
acting d^y register.

(D.) – Questions to the Pundits of the Sudder Dewanny Adawlut; 8th May 1817.

In the accompanying bewasta, given by Rajah Chunda Turkalunkar, pundit of the provincial court for the division of Dacca, it is stated that there is no authority in the Shaster for a woman of the jogee cast becoming a suttee, by being buried alive with the body of her husband; and on reference to the bewasta, upon this subject, which was delivered by the pundits of this court, in September 1813, it does not appear to contain any specific authorities for the practice in question. You are therefore desired to give another bewasta within a week from this date, stating explicitly whether there are any, and what authorities in the Shaster, which expressly sanction the interment of the widow of a jogee, or the burial of a Hindoo widow of any other tribe, with the body of her deceased husband, with the view of her becoming a suttee.

Opinion of the Pundits of the Sudder Dewanny Adawlut in the Jogee Case; 23d May 1817.

The Hindoo law officer of the Dacca provincial court, in a bewasta delivered by him, has stated that women of the jogee tribe are not authorized by the Shaster to commit the act of sahamarana, by burying themselves alive with the bodies of their deceased husbands. In a bewasta delivered by the pundit of the sudder dewanny adawlut, holding a contrary opinion, they are said not to have specifically stated the authorities, according to the Shaster, which justify the practice in question. They were therefore required to furnish in the space of one week a bewasta, stating whether or not there were any authorities according to the Shaster, which expressly justify women of the jogee tribe, or of any other class of Hindoos, in committing the act of sahamarana, by burying themselves alive with the bodies of their deceased husbands. They were further required to mention those authorities, if they exist.

Having examined the paper drawn up by the chief judge of this court, we proceed to furnish a reply to the best of our ability.

The Shasters do not enjoin any particular form to women of the jogee tribe, in committing the act of sahamarana; but that act is declared to be the special duty of such women as are devoted to their lords; and that devotion is exemplified by a widow's making choice of death after the decease of her husband. From time immemorial the last offices of both males and females of this tribe have been performed by burial; and for the accomplishment of the act of sahamarana the same rite has ever been resorted to. This practice has never met with any opposition. The tribe now known by the name of jogees, although not absorbed in devotion, are traditionally descended from that class of abstract mendicants termed Buhooduk and Purumhunsee. They were forbidden to burn, and enjoined to bury their dead. The injunction of burial is the only one which, according to the Shaster, can be legally applied to their descendants. The application of the same injunction would seem to be proper to widows who are desirous of performing the act of sahagumun. It is requisite that the act of sahagumun should be practised conformably to the manner in which the funeral rites of each tribe are practised. If this principle be denied, the funeral rites which have been in immemorial usage among the people of the jogee tribe must lose their validity.

The proofs of the above opinion are as follow: –

"She whose sympathy feels the pains and joys of her husband, who mourns and pines in his absence, and dies when he dies, is a good and loyal wife."

The following text of various moonshees contained in the Purawna Madheween, Nernuya Sindhoo, and other tracts: –

"Cremation, mourning and oblations of water, are not to be performed for him who has divested himself of every worldly desire, and is entirely absorbed in divine contemplation."

The following text contained in the Smriti Arthu Sara, Purawna Madheween, Nirnuya Sindhoo, and other tracts: –

"Let the corpse of a kooteechuk mendicant be burnt; that of a hunsa be cast into water; and that of a buhoodeh and purumhunsee be buried."

The following authentic text: – "The long established usages peculiar to a country, tribe, or family are to be respected; otherwise the people will be distressed."

(A true translation.)

(signed) *W. H. Macnaghten*,
acting d[y] register.

(E.) – Questions to the Pundits of the Sudder Dewanny Adawlut; 8th May 1817.

It appears from the report of the police darogah of Hemutabad, in the district of Dinagepore, that Basoodah, pullae, died on the 23rd Chyth, and was buried; that on the 25th of the same month, his widow Busturee, pullae, expressed a desire to burn with the body of her husband; and after giving notice to the police darogah, who took an agreement from the brother of the deceased for the maintenance of her children (a boy aged one year and a girl four years of age), on the 27th Chyth she took up the corpse of her husband from the earth and caused herself to be burnt with it on a funeral pile.

You are desired to state whether this practice is sanctioned by the Shaster? and if so, to mention any authorities for it.

Opinion of the Pundits of the Sudder Dewanny Adawlut on the Dinagepore Case; 23rd May 1817.

It appears from the report of the police darogah of Himmutabad, transmitted to the zillah court of Dinagepore, that a person named Bussoo Deo, pullee, died the 23rd of

Cheyt, and was buried on that day; that on the 25th of the same month, his widow Bushee, pullee, formed the resolution of dying along with him; that she communicated her intention to the darogah, who took a security bond from the brother of her late husband, who therein engaged to take upon himself the care of her two children; the one a boy aged one year, and the other a girl aged four years; and that afterwards, on the 27th of the same month, the corpse having been dug up and placed on a funeral pile, which was lighted, the widow cast herself into the flames and was consumed along with that corpse.

It is required to know whether the Shasters authorize such a practice or not. In the case of its being legal, according to the Shasters, let the authorities be stated.

Having inspected the paper drawn up by the chief judge of this court, we proceed to furnish a reply to the best of our ability.

The sahamarana, committed in the manner and at the time above specified, is a lawful act according to the Shasters; the proofs of which assertion are as follow: –

"Let such wives as are devoted to their lords, virtuous and pure, commit themselves to the fire with their husband's corpse."

A Pawranna Mantra. – "Let the person who performs the obsequies of the deceased husband perform those also of the widow who accompanies him, by ascending the same funeral pile." Buwishya Purawna.

(A true translation.)

(signed) *W. H. Macnaghten*, act[g] dep[y] reg.

(F.) – Questions to the Pundits of the Court of Sudder Dewanny Adawlut; 21st March 1817.

1. In a case of sahamarana, or a widow's burning herself with the corpse of her deceased husband, are any and what rules prescribed by the Shaster for the manner in which the rite is to be performed; particularly as to the widow's ascending the funeral pile previously to its being lighted, or subsequently casting herself into the flame? And are the same rules applicable to persons of every cast? or if not, what are the distinctions prescribed for different casts? Give a full answer to this question, with authorities from the Shaster current in Bengal and the Western Provinces respectively.

2. Is it authorized by the Shaster to bind or restrain in any manner a woman who has ascended the funeral pile of her husband, by tying her down with cords or placing bamboos over her, or using any other means to prevent her escape from the pile? If there be any authorities for such measures state them at length.

3. Are any and what persons expressly authorized by the Shaster to assist a widow in burning herself with the body of her deceased husband, in a case of sahamarana? or on a separate pile in a case of annoomaruna? If so, state the authorities; or, if not, what aid is indispensably requisite to enable a woman to become a suttee, whether by ignition or by interment.

4. State at the same time whether any persons are expressly authorized by the Shaster to assist lepers, and others afflicted with incurable diseases, in putting themselves to death, as declared in a former bewasta (recorded the 7th August 1810), to be sanctioned in the Brahma Purawna, with respect to the suicide of the deceased persons themselves.

(Copy.)

(signed) *M. H. Turnbull*, register.

(G.) – Translation of certain Questions proposed to the Hindoo Law Officers of the Sudder Dewanny Adawlut, regarding the burning of Widows, &c. and their Replies in conformity with the authorities current in Bengal and Benares.

Question 1. – In a case of sahamarana, or a widow's burning herself with the corpse of her deceased husband, are any and what rules prescribed by the Shasters for the manner in which the rite is to be performed; particularly as to the widow's ascending the funeral pile, previously to its being lighted, or subsequently casting herself into the flames? And are the same rules applicable to persons of every cast: or if not, what are the distinctions prescribed for different casts? Give a full answer to this question with authorities from the Shasters current in Bengal and the Western Provinces respectively.

Answer. – There are certain rules, prescribed both by the practice and Shasters of Bengal, to be attended to in a case of sahamarana. Whatever rules exist relative to ascending the funeral pile previously or subsequently to its being lighted, extend equally to all classes. There are no distinct rules for the different classes. In certain villages of Burdwan, a district in Bengal, the following ceremonies are observed: – When women are desirous of dying with their husbands, in the mode termed sahamarana, they signified their intention of so doing, either previously or subsequently to the death of their husbands, by placing five couries under a mangoe tree, and (having walked three times round the tree, and having broken off a branch) by sitting down at the feet of their dying or deceased lords, at the same time continuing to hold the branch in their hands.

The following rules are universally observed in Bengal: – The woman about to perform the act of sahamarana, previously to ascendingthe funeral pile, must clothe herself in new apparel, and rub lac on her feet; she must also apply cotton dyed with lac to her hands, tying it on with red thread; on her forehead she must apply minium plentifully. She must separate her hair in front, and place two combs between the partitions. After having placed couries rubbed over with turmeric, and fried wheat, in a sieve, let her ascend the funeral pile, and scatter them on all sides.

The following ceremonies are prescribed by the Shasters current in Bengal: – Ablution, achumurrun or sipping water from the palm of the hand, the repetition of the sunkulph (or declaration); the invocation of the guardians of the eight regions of the world, the sun, moon, air, ether, earth and water, soul, day, night and twilight; the ceremony of walking three times round the funeral pile; the expression by a brahmin of the texts extracted from the Rig Vida and Poorawnas; the utterance of the salutation; and lastly, the ascending the funeral pile.

The authority which enjoins the above ceremonies is the Anlyeshlee Puthulee, "Fire being applied by the sons to the funeral pile of their father, let the woman who wishes to accompany her deceased husband, having bathed, sipped water from the palm of her hand, and turning towards the east, pronounce the sunkulph or declaration. Then having made the following invocation, 'I call on you, ye guardians of the eight regions of the world, sun, moon, &c. &c.' Having walked three times round the funeral pile, having made use of the prescribed salutation, let her ascend the funeral pile; the brahmins having first repeated this text, 'Om, let these women, not to be widowed, devoted to their lords, virtuous and beautifully adorned, enter the fire with the bodies of their deceased husbands.'" The authority of the Shoodhee Futwa also confirms the above, "The fire being applied by the sons, according to the girhya, or peculiar ritual of the deceased's family, having first bathed, the widow dressed in two clean garments, holding some cusa grass in her hand, sips water from the palm of her hand, bearing fruit, flowers, tila water, and three blades of cusa grass in her hand, the brahmin utters the mystic words 'Om Tatsut;' she then bows to Narayana with the usual salutation, and utters the sunkulph (or declaration.) She then invokes the guardians of the eight regions of the earth, the sun, moon, &c. to bear witness that she follows her husband's corpse on the funeral pile. She then walks three times round the funeral pile, and makes the customary salutation; and the brahmins having recited the text of the Rig Vida and Poorawnas, she ascends the flaming funeral pile."

The following rules are to be universally observed throughout Benares by women who are anxious to depart with their deceased husbands. On the demise of her husband, a woman must abstain from lamentation. Should she lament, she must refrain from the act of sahamarana. The following practical rules are observed by some dravida women. Having ascertained that her husband is dead, or on the point of death, the widow anoints herself with oil, bathes, clothes herself in red or yellow garments, applies an additional quantity of turmeric, &c. to her forehead, rubs her arms with sandal, applies collyrium to her eyes, eats curds and rice, and if this latter be not procurable sweetmeats and curds, chews betel nut, adorns her hair with red garlands, places a red necklace round her neck, ties a cloth filled with turmeric, sooparee and betel nut on her navel; at the time of quitting the house she looks with circumspection into the chambers of all her relations for the sake of prosperity; she scatters grains of rice over the house, and ultimately leaves it, carrying a cocoa nut in her hand. She then proceeds to the place of sacrifice, accompanied by various sorts of music, having previously worshipped the peculiar deities of the city or village. Such are the ceremonies generally observed.

The Rules prescribed by the Vedas are as follow: –

The widows of ahitagnees, or such as preserve the sacrificial fires, are enjoined to proceed to the burning place in close conjunction with the corpse and the three fires. The widows of anahitagnees are merely enjoined to remain on the road in close company with the corpses of their husbands. In the place where the corpse is deposited, the formula attendant on the ceremony must be expressed in the dual number; and the widow must be made to sit down at the same time. All the ceremonies that occur on the road are to be observed in the same manner. Having arrived at the place of burning, the widow must be laid on the funeral pile at the side of her deceased husband. If she be then destitute of the wish to perform the act of sahagumun, she must be lifted off. The widow being desirous of burning with the corpse of her deceased husband (provided he was an ahitagnee) is to be laid on the pile with its face upwards, and the sacrificial vessels having been applied to his members, the widow is to be laid upon him with her face downwards. At the time of applying the fire, the pile is to be lighted for both at once; and the formula on this occasion is to be recited in the dual number. The texts, propitiatory of Yama, are also to be recited in the same manner by him who officiates at the sacrifice, standing near the funeral pile. In the case of a widow of an anahitagnee, the sacrificial vessels termed smarta being applied, the widow is to be laid beside the corpse. The remaining ceremonies are similar in both cases.

The authorities for the above opinion are the text of the Tricanda Munduree, "In crossing a river, in passing over a boundary, and in the interval between two boundaries, the fires should always accompany their owners." This passage is declared in the commentary to affect both husband and wife, as the ownership of the sacrificial fires extends to them both. The text of Apustumba, "Dying together, the pitrimedha is to be performed for them both at once; and the texts must be recited in the dual number."

The Nernuya Sindhoo quotes the text of Apustumba, which declares, that as the term Pitrimedha comprehends all ceremonies, including the act of cremation, all those ceremonies are to be performed for both at once. The same rule applies to a case of sahagamana, as to the case of both parties dying at the same moment. This appears from the text of Kupurdee, "Whenever a woman follows her deceased husband by ascending the flaming pile, the act of cremation will be simultaneous. The asthee kya, or ceremony of collecting the ashes, will be performed separately." The text of Apustumba ordains, that "the widow shall be placed on the right side of her deceased husband." If having arrived at the place of burning, she determine to burn, the ceremonies of depositing the widow, &c. must again be gone through. If she afterwards express a wish to rise, she must be lifted off; the two texts commencing with the word Oodursheree, having been previously recited. The commentary of Kupurdee on the above passage is as follows: – "In this interval, the officiating priest shall deposit;" that is to say, shall cause to be laid down the widow by the right side of her deceased husband, having recited the text commencing with the words "this woman." If the widow wishes to get off afterwards, the brother of the deceased husband, or some other brahmin, repeating the text commencing with the words Oodurshwee naree, shall lift her up. But if she subsequently refuses to rise, the fire is to be applied to both at once. The text of Apustumba, "An ahitagnee must be consumed with his three fires and sacrificial vessels." The text of Ashwalagama, "The widow of a man of the military tribe must be placed on the north side of him, together with his weapons; if she wishes to rise, the younger brother, or some other representative of her husband, or his pupil, or an old servant of the family, shall lift her up, pronouncing the text commencing with the words Oodurshwee naree." The following is the commentary of Purawna on the above passages: – "The body of the deceased being brought to the north of the fire, the head is to be turned to the south; the widow is to be made to sit to the northward of the corpse, and she, (thus lying to the north of the deceased, being devoid of courage), the younger brother of the husband, the disciple or old servant, shall salute and take hold of by the hand, repeating the texts Oodurshwee." The Nirnuya Sindhoo, "The younger brother of the deceased husband, or his disciple, shall raise up the terrified widow, laying to the northward of the deceased; the texts Oodurshwee, &c. having been repeated." In some villages situated in Benares, the following practices obtain among the widows of merchants and other traders: – The husband being laid on the funeral pile, she ascends it, placing the head of the corpse on her lap, when the fire is communicated.

Some observe the following practice: – The deceased husband being laid on the funeral pile, and the widow being about to ascend it, she takes in the palm of her hands a lamp inserted in a vessel filled with ghee; and the skirt of her garments having taken fire from the flame of that lamp, she immediately ascends the pile. The lamp so used is termed the Mainkeen Deepa. The ceremonies practically observed, differ as to the various tribes and districts.

The rules to be observed in Benares, in conformity to the Purawnas current there, are as follow: –

The sunkulph, or declaration, is to be made, in which the time and place is to be noticed, being decked with minium and collyrium, &c. The widow is to bestow presents on the by-standers; then, having approached the fire, she adorns her wrist with five jewels, and applies a pearl ornament to her nose; she then invokes the fire, sacrifices to fire, Vishnu, Yumu, the earth, water, the wind, ether, Kalapa, Brahma, Roadree, by offering an oblation of clarified butter; she then walks three times round the fire, worships her household utensils; then, holding flowers in her hand, she invokes the fire and enters it. The authorities enjoining these practices are as follow: – The Nurnuya Sindhoo, adverting to the time and place, "Let the widow first make the sunkulph or declaration, intimating her desire that she may be equal to Arundhatt; and then distribute presents, accompanying that act with the text, 'May Luchesmee and Narrayuna, the depositories of constancy and truth, being pleased with these offerings, grant me undeviating constancy. I, anxious to obtain the favour of Luchesmee and Narrayuna, and desirous of constancy, present these offerings.' Let her then, having approached the fire, fold up five jewels in the skirt of her garment, anointing herself with collyrium, and apply a pearl ornament to her nose; then let her invoke the fire with this text, 'O fire! ever to be mentioned with the term Suechu, all pervading and universal, conduct me to my husband by the path of constancy.' Let her, having offered an oblation of clarified butter, make a salutation to fire, as the lord of energy; to Vishnu, the lord of truth; to Yumu, the lord of justice; to Prethira, as presiding over the world; to the waters, as presiding over tastes; to the wind, as the lord of strength; to ether, as presiding over all; to Yumu, as presiding over justice; to the waters, as universal witnesses; to Brahma, as the lord of the Vedas; and to Roadree, as the lord of smushanus, or receptacles of the dead. Then let her, having thrice circumambulated the fire, worshipped her household utensils, and taken flowers into her hand, invoke the fire thus: 'O fire! thou secretly pervadest all beings; thou, O deity! knowest what mortals are ignorant of. Being afflicted with the dread of widowhood, I follow my lord; conduct me to my husband by the path of constancy.' Having uttered this text let her deliberately enter the fire."

Another extract from the Nernuyu Sindhoo.

Question 2. – Is it authorized by the Shasters to bind, or restrain in any manner, a woman who has ascended the funeral pile of her husband, by tying her down with cords, or placing bamboos over her, or using any other means to prevent her escape from the pile? If there be any authorities for such measures state them at length.

Answer. – No authority permits any restraint to be used. An expiation is ordained for the widow who has slipped off the pile, both in the Shoodhee Futwa and Nunuyu Sindhoo. The same is to be met with in the text of Apustumba, Keepurdie and Ashwulagunu. In the text of Narayumu, its commentary, and in the Nunuya Sindoo, mention is there also made of taking a woman off the funeral pile in the event of her being terrified, and of the persons by whom this is to be done.

The authority for the above opinion is the text of Apustumba, quoted in the Shoodhu Futwa and Nunuyu Sindhoo: "Whatever woman may have left the funeral pile, or slipped from it, through want of firmness, that woman will be purified from sin by undergoing the penance of praja putya."

The other authorities, in confirmation of the illegality of restraint, have been cited in the answer to the first question, treating of the manner in which the widow should be laid on the pile.

Question 3. – Are any, and what persons expressly authorized by the Shaster to assist a widow in burning herself with the body of her deceased husband, in a case of sahamarana? or on a separate pile, in a case of anoomarana? If so, state the authorities; or if not, what aid is indispensably requisite to enable a woman to become a suttee, whether by ignition or by interment.

Answer. – The sons or next heirs of a widow are expressly enjoined to assist her in the acts of sahamarana or anoomarana. This opinion is in conformity with the authorities current in Bengal and Benares. The text of the Vishnu Poorawna, cited in the Shoodhee Futwa and Nunuyu Sindhoo, is confirmatory of the above: "The son, grandson, great grandson, brother's offspring, or descendant of Sapinda, are competent to the performance of obsequies, O prince." The text of Yajnia Vulkia, cited in the same authorities, "He who performs the obsequies of her deceased husband shall perform also those of her, who ascending the same funeral pile, accompanies him."

Question 4. – State, at the same time, whether any persons are expressly authorized by the Shasters to assist lepers, and others afflicted with incurable diseases, in putting themselves to death, as declared in a former bewasta (recorded 7th of August 1810) to be sanctioned in the Brahma Poorawna, with respect to the suicide of the deceased persons themselves?

Answer. – The sons or nearest heirs are enjoined to assist at such suicides, as appears from the text of the Chandog Purisheshta, quoted in the Shoodhu Futwa: "Then let the sons or others, having collected a large heap of sticks, place them in the shape of a funeral pile, in an even and clean piece of ground."

(A true translation.)

(signed) *W. H. Macnaghten*,
acting deputy reg'.

Chapter 11

Rāja Rammohan Ray (1772–1833)

Rāja Rammohan Ray was an extraordinary intellectual who was one of the first modern social activists in India. A prolific author and daring thinker, his writings and ideas largely centered upon social reform. While his work and writing ranged from issues in Vedānta to Hindu theism, Ray is most known for his successful effort to convince the British to abolish the practice of *satī*, widow self-immolation. Ray, often regaled as the "Maker of Modern India" and the "Father of the Bengali Renaissance, thus had an enormous impact on the intellectual world of early nineteenth century India with consequences that reverberate in twenty-first century India.[1]

Ray lived between the scholarly *śāstraic* world of his ancestors and the material and political world of early nineteenth century Bengal. Trained in both Arabic and Persian, Ray moved up in the business and intellectual hierarchy of the British scene in Calcutta, eventually to work for 3 years for the East India Company beginning in 1757. He learned English and joined with the other Indian and British intellectuals of Calcutta in the process. At the same time Ray was vocal about inequalities that he perceived in the larger Indian world – inequalities brought on both by the British colonizers, and by the history of discrimination in Hinduism. He was well known even in the United Kingdom. When he visited there in 1833, though, his stay was cut short by his death in Bristol in 1833.

Ray's vision of Hinduism was influenced heavily by Deism and other European ideas. He corresponded with Bentham, the Utilitarian philosopher of the nineteenth century who suggested that Ray become the first Indian representative in the House of Commons.[2] He was even befriended by the Unitarians who hoped that he was at the forefront of a trend to Christianize India. These outside influences, combined with his training in traditional Indian philosophy and texts, made Ray a formidable adversary for both his British and Indian interlocutors. In 1828 Ray founded the Brāhmo Samāj. A Hindu reform movement that still exists today, the Brāhmo Samāj attempted to incorporate the changes envisioned by Ray.

The first essay, "Religious Instructions Founded on Sacred Authorities," shows the influence of Śaṃkaraācārya's Advaita Vedānta, Deism, and Unitarianism on Ray's thought. The themes of Hindu tolerance in this essay have counterparts in Vivekānānda's neo-Vedānta and has been embraced by some as a foundation of Hinduism.

The second essay, "Translation of a Conference between an Advocate for, and an Opponent of, the Practice of Burning Widows Alive," is an argument that there is no *vidhi*, injunction, in the *śāstras*, sacred texts, for *satī*. In it, Ray fights vehemently for the rights of women and for the prohibition of *satī*. Soon after, the practice was banned in Bengal. Ray's writings in this area parallel the *Papers Relating to East India Affairs, viz. Hindoo Widows, and Voluntary Immolations* published by the House of Commons.

Notes

1 See Gavin Flood, *An Introduction to Hinduism*. Cambridge: Cambridge University Press, 1999; Wilhelm Halbfass, *India and Europe: An Essay in Understanding*. Albany, NY: SUNY Press, 1988; and Bruce Robertson, *Raja Rammohan Ray*. Delhi: Oxford University Press, 1995.
2 Bruce Robertson (ed.), *The Essential Writings of Raja Rammohan Ray*. Delhi: Oxford University Press, 1999, p. xxxviii.

Further reading

Courtright, Paul, "*Satī*, Sacrifice, and Marriage: The Modernity of Tradition" in L. Harlan and P. Courtright (eds.), *From the Margins of Hindu Marriage: Essays on Gender, Religion, and Culture*. New York: Oxford University Press, 1995.

Flood, Gavin, *An Introduction to Hinduism*. Cambridge: Cambridge University Press, 1999.

Halbfass, Wilhelm, *India and Europe: An Essay in Understanding*. Albany, NY: SUNY Press, 1988.

Hawley, John Stratton (ed.), *Sati, The Blessing and the Curse: The Burning of Wives in India*. New York: Oxford University Press, 1994.

Major, Andrea, *Pious Flames: European Encounters with Sati*. Oxford: Oxford University Press, 2006.

Mani, Lata, *Contentious Traditions: The Debate on Sati in Colonial India*. Berkeley, CA: University of California Press, 1998.

Robertson, Bruce (ed.), *Raja Rammohan Ray*. Delhi: Oxford University Press, 1995.

Robertson, Bruce, *The Essential Writings of Raja Rammohan Ray*. Delhi: Oxford University Press, 1999.

Weinberg-Thomas, Catherine, *Widow Burning in India* (tr. by J. Mehlman and D. G. White). Oxford: Oxford University Press, 2000.

Religious Instructions Founded on Sacred Authorities

The following Treatise, in the form of questions and answers, contains a brief account of the worship enjoined in the sacred writings, as due to that Being who is pure as well as eternal, and to whose existence Nature gives testimony; that the faithful may easily understand and become successful in the practice of this worship. The proof of each doctrine may be found, according to the figures, in the end of the work.

As this subject is almost always expounded, in the sacred writings, by means of questions and answers, that it may be more easily comprehended, a similar plan is adopted in this place also.

1. *Question*. – What is meant by worship?
   Answer. – Worship implies the act of one with a view to please another; but when applied to the Supreme Being, it signifies a contemplation of his attributes.
2. *Q*. – To whom is worship due?
   A. – To the Author and Governor of the universe, which is incomprehensibly formed, and filled with an endless variety of men and things; in which, as shown by the zodiac, in a manner far more wonderful than the machinery of a watch, the sun, the moon, the planets, and the stars perform their rapid courses; and which is fraught with animate and inanimate matter of various kinds, locomotive and immoveable, of which there is not one particle but has its functions to perform.
3. *Q*. – What is He?
   A. – We have already mentioned that he is to be worshipped, who is the Author and Governor of the universe; yet, neither the sacred writings nor logical argument, can define his nature.
4. *Q*. – Are there no means of defining him?
   A. – It is repeatedly declared in the sacred writings, that he cannot be defined either by the intellect or by language. This appears from inference also; for, though the universe is visible, still no one can ascertain its form or extent. How then can we define the Being, whom we designate as its Author and Governor?
5. *Q*. – Is any one, on sufficient grounds, opposed to this worship?
   A. – To this worship no one can be opposed on sufficient grounds; for, as we all worship the Supreme Being, adoring him as the Author and Governor of the universe, it is impossible for any one to object to such worship; because each person considers the object whom he worships as the Author and Governor of the universe; therefore, in accordance with his own faith, he must acknowledge that this worship is his own. In the same manner, they, who consider Time or Nature, or any other Object, as the Governor of the universe, even they cannot be opposed to this worship, as bearing in mind the Author and Governor of the universe. And in China, in Tartary, in Europe, and in all other countries, where so many sects exist, all believe the object whom they adore to be the Author and Governor of the universe; consequently, they also must acknowledge, according to their own faith, that this our worship is their own.
6. *Q*. – In some places in the sacred writings it is written that the Supreme Being is imperceptible and unexpressible; and in others, that he is capable of being known. How can this be reconciled?

Excerpts from Bruce C. Robertson (ed.), *The Essential Writings of Raja Rammohan Ray.* Delhi: Oxford University Press, 1999. First Published in 1829.

A. – Where it is written that he is imperceptible and undefinable, it is meant, that his likeness cannot be conceived; and where it is said that he is capable of being known, his mere existence is referred to, that is, that there is a God, as the indescribable creation and government of this universe clearly demonstrate: in the same manner, as by the action of a body, we ascertain the existence of a spirit therein called the sentient soul, but the form or likeness of that spirit which pervades every limb and guides the body, we know not.

7. *Q.* – Are you hostile to any other worship?
A. – Certainly not; for, he who worships, be it whomsoever or whatsoever it may, considers that object as the Supreme Being, or as an object containing him; consequently, what cause have we to be hostile to him?

8. *Q.* – If you worship the Supreme Being, and other persons offer their adoration to the same Divine Being, but in a different form; what then is the difference between them and you?
A. – We differ in two ways; first, they worship under various forms and in particular places, believing the object of their worship to be the Supreme Being; but we declare that He, who is the Author of the universe, is to be worshipped; besides this, we can determine no particular form or place. Secondly, we see that they, who worship under any one particular form, are opposed to those who worship under another; but it is impossible for worshippers of any denomination to be opposed to us; as we have shown in the answer to the 5th question.

9. *Q.* – In what manner is this worship to be performed?
A. – By bearing in mind that the Author and Governor of this visible universe is the Supreme Being, and comparing this idea with the sacred writings and with reason. In this worship it is indispensibly necessary to use exertions to subdue the senses, and to read such passages as direct attention to the Supreme Spirit. Exertion to subdue the senses, signifies an endeavour to direct the will and the senses, and the conduct in such a manner as not only to prevent our own or others ill, but to secure our own and others good; in fact, what is considered injurious to ourselves, should be avoided towards others. It is obvious that as we are so constituted, that without the help of sound we can conceive no idea; therefore, by means of the texts treating of the Supreme Being, we should contemplate him. The benefits which we continually receive from fire, from air, and from the sun, likewise from the various productions of the earth, such as the different kinds of grain, drugs, fruits, and vegetables, all are dependent on him: and by considering and reasoning on the terms expressive of such ideas, the meaning itself is firmly fixed in the mind. It is repeatedly said in the sacred writings, that theological knowledge is dependent upon truth; consequently, the attainment of truth will enable us to worship the Supreme Being, who is Truth itself.

10. *Q.* – According to this worship, what rule must we establish with regard to the regulation of our food, conduct, and other worldly matters?
A. – It is proper to regulate our food and conduct agreeably to the sacred writings; therefore, he who follows no prescribed form among all those that are promulgated, but regulates his food and conduct according to his own will, is called self-willed; and to act according to our own wish, is opposed both by the Scriptures and by reason. In the Scriptures it is frequently forbidden. Let us examine it by reason. Suppose each person should, in non-conformity

with prescribed form, regulate his conduct according to his own desires, a speedy end must ensue to established societies; for to the self-willed, food, whether fit to be eaten or not, conduct proper or improper, desires lawful or unlawful, all are the same; he is guided by no rule: to him an action, performed according to the will, is faultless: but the will of all is not alike; consequently, in the fulfilment of our desires, where numerous opinions are mutually opposed, a quarrel is the most likely consequence; and the probable result of repeated quarrels, is the destruction of human beings. In fact, however, it is highly improper to spend our whole time in judging of the propriety and impropriety of certain foods, without reflecting on science or Divine truth; for be food of whatever kind it may, in a very short space of time it undergoes a change into what is considered exceedingly impure, and this impure matter is, in various places, productive of different kinds of grain; therefore, it is certainly far more preferable to adorn the mind than to think of purifying the belly.

11. *Q.* – In the performance of this worship, is any particular place, quarter, or time, necessary?
    A. – A suitable place is certainly preferable, but it is not absolutely necessary; that is to say, in whatever place, towards whatever quarter, or at whatever time, the mind is best at rest, – that place, that quarter, and that time, is the most proper for the performance of this worship.
12. *Q.* – To whom is this worship fit to be taught?
    A. – It may be taught to all, but effect being produced in each person according to his state of mental preparation, it will be proportionably successful.

12. Translation of a Conference between an Advocate for, and an Opponent of, the Practice of Burning Widows Alive

Advertisement

The little tract, of which the following is a literal translation, originally written in Bungla, has been for several weeks past in extensive circulation in those parts of the country where the practice of Widows burning themselves on the pile of their Husbands is most prevalent. An idea that the arguments it contains might tend to alter the notions that some European Gentleman entertain on this subject, has induced the Writer to lay it before the British Public also in its present dress.

Nov. 30, 1818.

Conference between an Advocate for, and an Opponent of, the Practice of Burning Widows Alive

Advocate. – I am surprised that you endeavour to oppose the practice of Concremation and Postcremation of Widows, as long observed in this country.

Opponent. – Those who have no reliance on the Shastru, and those who take delight in the self-destruction of women, may well wonder that we should oppose that suicide which is forbidden by all the Shastrus, and by every race of men.

Advocate. – You have made an improper assertion, in alleging that Concremation and Postcremation are forbidden by the Shastrus. Hear what Unggira and other saints have said on this subject:

'That woman who, on the death of her husband, ascends the burning pile with him, is exalted to heaven, as equal to Uroondhooti.

'She who follows her husband to another world, shall dwell in a region of joy for so many years as there are hairs in the human body, or thirty-five millions.

'As a serpent-catcher forcibly draws a snake from his hole, thus raising her husband by her power, she enjoys delight along with him.

'The woman who follows her husband expiates the sins of three races; her father's line, her mother's line, and the family of him to whom she was given a virgin.

'There possessing her husband as her chiefest good, herself the best of women, enjoying the highest delights, she partakes of bliss with her husband as long as fourteen Indrus reign.

'Even though the man had slain a Brahmun, or returned evil for good, or killed an intimate friend, the woman expiates those crimes.

'There is no other way known for a virtuous woman except ascending the pile of her husband. It should be understood that there is no other duty whatever after the death of her husband.'

Hear also what Vyas has written in the parable of the pigeon:

'A pigeon devoted to her husband, after his death entered the flames, and ascending to heaven, she there found her husband.'

And hear Hareet's words:

'As long as a woman shall not burn herself after her husband's death, she shall be subject to transmigration in a female form.'

Hear too what Vishnoo the saint says:

'After the death of her husband a wife must live as an ascetic, or ascend his pile.'

Now hear the words of the *Bruhmu Pooran* on the subject of Postcremation:

'If her lord die in another country, let the faithful wife place his sandals on her breast, and pure enter the fire.'

The faithful widow is declared no suicide by this text of the *Rig Ved*: 'When three days of impurity are gone she obtains obsequies.' Gotum says:

'To a Brahmunee after the death of her husband, Postcremation is not permitted. But to women of the other classes it is esteemed a chief duty.'

'Living let her benefit her husband; dying she commits suicide.'

'The woman of the Brahmun tribe that follows her dead husband cannot, on account of her self-destruction, convey either herself or her husband to heaven.'

Concremation and Postcremation being thus established by the words of many sacred lawgivers, how can you say they are forbidden by the Shastrus, and desire to prevent their practice?

Opponent. – All those passages you have quoted are indeed sacred law; and it is clear from those authorities, that if women perform Concremation or Postcremation, they will enjoy heaven for a considerable time. But attend to what Munoo and others say respecting the duty of widows: 'Let her emaciate her body, by living voluntarily on pure flowers, roots, and fruits, but let her not, when her lord is deceased, even pronounce the name of another man.'

'Let her continue till death forgiving all injuries, performing harsh duties, avoiding every sensual pleasure, and cheerfully practising the incomparable rules of virtue which have been followed by such women as were devoted to one only husband.'

Here Munoo directs, that after the death of her husband, the widow should pass her whole life as an ascetic. Therefore, the laws given by Unggira and the others whom you have quoted, being contrary to the law of Munoo, cannot be accepted; because the *Ved* declares, 'whatever Munoo has said is wholesome;' and Virhusputi, 'whatever law is contrary to the law of Munoo is not commendable.' The Ved especially declares, 'by living in the practice of regular and occasional duties the mind may be purified. Thereafter by hearing, reflecting, and constantly meditating on the Supreme Being, absorption in Bruhmu may be attained. Therefore from a desire during life of future fruition, life ought not to be destroyed.' Munoo, Yagnyuvulkyu, and others, have then, in their respective codes of laws, prescribed to widows the duties of ascetics only. By this passage of the *Ved*, therefore, and the authority of Munoo and others, the words you have quoted from Unggira and the rest are set aside; for by the express declaration of the former, widows after the death of their husbands may, by living as ascetics, obtain absorption.

Advocate. – What you have said respecting the laws of Unggira and others, that recommended the practice of Concremation and Postcremation, we do not admit: because, though a practice has not been recommended by Munoo, yet, if directed by other lawgivers, it should not on that account be considered as contrary to the law of Munoo. For instance, Munoo directs the performance of Sundhya, but says nothing of calling aloud on the name of Huri; yet Vyas prescribes calling on the name of Huri. The words of Vyas do not contradict those of Munoo. The same should be understood in the present instance. Munoo has commended widows to live as ascetics; Vishnoo and other saints direct that they should either live as ascetics or follow their husbands. Therefore the law of Munoo may be considered to be applicable as an alternative.

Opponent. – The analogy you have drawn betwixt the practice of Sundhya and invoking Huri, and that of Concremation and Postcremation, does not hold. For, in the course of the day the performance of Sundhya, at the prescribed time, does not prevent one from invoking Huri at another period; and, on the other hand, the invocation of Huri need not interfere with the performance of Sundhya. In this case, the direction of one practice is not inconsistent with that of the other. But in the case of living as an ascetic or undergoing Concremation, the performance of the one is incompatible with the observance of the other. Spending one's whole life as an ascetic after the death of a husband, is incompatible with immediate Concremation as directed by Unggira and others; and, vice versa, Concremation, as directed by Unggira and others, is inconsistent with living as an ascetic, in order to attain absorption. Therefore those two authorities are obviously contradictory of each other. More especially as Unggira, by declaring that 'there is no other way known for a virtuous woman except ascending the pile of her husband,' has made Concremation an indispensable duty. And Hareet also, in his code, by denouncing evil consequences, in his declaration, that 'as long as a woman shall not burn herself after the death of her husband, she shall be subject to transmigration in a female form,' has made this duty absolute. Therefore all those passages are in every respect contradictory to the law of Munoo and others.

Advocate. – When Unggira says that there is no other way for a widow except Concremation, and when Hareet says that the omission of it is a fault, we reconcile their words with those of Munoo, by considering them as used merely for the purpose of exalting the merit of Concremation, but not as prescribing this as an indispensable duty. All these expressions, moreover, convey a promise of reward for Concremation, and thence it appears that Concremation is only optional.

Opponent. – If, in order to reconcile them with the text of Munoo, you set down the words of Unggira and Hareet, that make the duty incumbent, as meant only to convey an exaggerated praise of Concremation, why do you not also reconcile the rest of the words of Unggira, Hareet, and others, with those in which Munoo prescribes to the widow the practice of living as an ascetic as her absolute duty? And why do you not keep aloof from witnessing the destruction of females, instead of tempting them with the inducement of future fruition? Moreover, in the text already quoted, self-destruction with the view of reward is expressly prohibited.

Advocate. – What you have quoted from Munoo and Yagnyavulkyu and the text of the *Ved* is admitted. But how can you set aside the following text of the *Rig Ved* on the subject of Concremation? 'O fire! let these women, with bodies anointed with clarified butter, eyes coloured with collyrium, and void of tears, enter thee, the parent of water, that they may not be separated from their husbands, but may be, in unison with excellent husbands, themselves sinless and jewels amongst women.'

Opponent. – This text of the *Ved*, and the former passages from Hareet and the rest whom you have quoted, all praise the practice of Concremation as leading to fruition, and are addressed to those who are occupied by sensual desires; and you cannot but admit that to follow these practices is only optional. In repeating the Sunkulpyu of Concremation, the desire of future fruition is declared as the object. The text therefore of the *Ved* which we have quoted, offering no gratifications, supersedes, in every respect, that which you have adduced, as well as all the words of Unggira and the rest. In proof we quote the text of the *Kuthopunishut*: 'Faith in God which leads to absorption is one thing; and rites which have future fruition for their object, another. Each of these, producing different consequences, holds out to man inducements to follow it. The man, who of these two chooses faith, is blessed; and he, who for the sake of reward practises rites, is dashed away from the enjoyment of eternal beatitude.' Also the *Moonduk Opunishut*: 'Rites, of which there are eighteen members, are all perishable: he who considers them as the source of blessing shall undergo repeated transmigrations; and all those fools who, immersed in the foolish practice of rites, consider themselves to be wise and learned, are repeatedly subjected to birth, disease, death, and other pains. When one blind man is guided by another, both subject themselves on their way to all kinds of distress.'

It is asserted in the *Bhugvut Geeta*, the essence of all the Smritis, Poorans, and Itihases, that, 'all those ignorant persons who attach themselves to the words of the *Veds* that convey promises of fruition, consider those falsely alluring passages as leading to real happiness; and say, that besides them there is no other reality. Agitated in their minds by these desires, they believe the abodes of the celestial gods to be the chief object; and they devote themselves to those texts which treat of ceremonies and their fruits, and entice by promises of enjoyment. Such people can have no real confidence in the Supreme Being.' Thus also do the *Moonduk Opunishut* and the *Geeta* state that, 'the science by which a knowledge of God is attained is superior to all other knowledge.' Therefore it is clear, from those passages of the *Ved* and of the *Geeta*, that the words of the *Ved* which promise fruition, are set aside by the texts of a contrary import. Moreover, the ancient saints and holy teachers, and their commentators, and yourselves, as well as we and all others, agree that Munoo is better acquainted than any other lawgiver with the spirit of the *Veds*. And he, understanding the meaning of those different texts, admitting the inferiority of that which promised fruition, and following that which conveyed no promise of gratification, has directed widows to spend their lives as ascetics. He has also defined in his 12th chapter, what acts are observed merely for the sake of gratifications, and what are not. 'Whatever act is performed for the sake of gratifications in this world or the next is called Pruburttuk, and those which are performed according to the knowledge respecting God, are called Niburttuk. All those who perform acts to procure gratifications, may enjoy heaven like the gods; and he who performs acts free from desires, procures release from the five elements of this body; that is, obtains absorption.'

Advocate. – What you have said is indeed consistent with the *Veds*, with Munoo, and with the *Bhuguvut Geeta*. But from this I fear, that the passages of the *Veds* and other Shastrus, that prescribe Concremation and Postcremation as the means of attaining heavenly enjoyments, must be considered as only meant to deceive.

Opponent. – There is no deception. The object of those passages is declared. As men have various dispositions, those whose minds are enveloped in desire, passion, and cupidity, have no inclination for the disinterested worship of the Supreme Being. If they had no Shastrus of rewards, they would at once throw aside all Shastrus, and would follow their several inclinations, like elephants unguided by the hook. In order to restrain such persons from being led only by their inclinations, the Shastru prescribes various ceremonies; as Shuenjag, for one desirous of the destruction of the enemy; Pootreshti for one desiring a son; and Justishtom for one desiring gratifications in heaven, &c.; but again reprobates such as are actuated by those desires, and at the same moment expresses contempt for such gratifications. Had the Shastru not repeatedly reprobated both those actuated by desire and the fruits desired by them, all those texts might be considered as deceitful. In proof of what I have advanced I cite the following text of the *Opunishut*: 'Knowledge and rites together offer themselves to every man. The wise man considers which of these two is the better and which the worse. By reflection, he becomes convinced of the superiority of the former, despises rites, and takes refuge in knowledge. And the unlearned, for the sake of bodily gratification, has recourse to the performance of rites.' The *Bhuguvut Geeta*: 'The Veds that treat of rites are for the sake of those who are possessed of desire; therefore, O Urjoon! do thou abstain from desires.'

Hear also the text of the *Ved* reprobating the fruits of rites: 'As in this world the fruits obtained from cultivation and labour perish, so in the next world fruits derived from rites are perishable.' Also the *Bhuguvut Geeta*: 'All those who observe the rites prescribed by the three Veds, and through those ceremonies worship me and seek for heaven, having become sinless from eating the remains of offerings, ascending to heaven, and enjoying the pleasures of the gods, after the completion of their rewards, again return to earth. Therefore, the observers of rites for the sake of rewards, repeatedly ascend to heaven, and return to the world, and cannot obtain absorption.'

Advocate. – Though what you have advanced from the *Ved* and sacred codes against the practice of Concremation and Postcremation, is not to be set aside, yet we have had the practice prescribed by Hareet and others handed down to us.

Opponent. – Such an argument is highly inconsistent with justice. It is every way improper to persuade to self-destruction, by citing passages of inadmissible authority. In the second place, it is evident from your own authorities, and the Sunkulpu recited in conformity with them, that the widow should voluntarily quit life, ascending the flaming pile of her husband. But, on the contrary, you first bind down the widow along with the corpse of her husband, and then heap over her such a quantity of wood that she cannot rise. At the time too of setting fire to the pile, you press her down with large bamboos. In what passage of Hareet or the rest do you find authority for thus binding the woman according to your practice? This then is, in fact, deliberate female murder.

Advocate. – Though Hareet and the rest do not indeed authorize this practice of binding, &c., yet were a woman after having recited the Sunkulpu not to perform Concremation, it would be sinful, and considered disgraceful by others. It is on this account that we have adopted the custom.

Opponent. – Respecting the sinfulness of such an act, that is mere talk: for in the same codes it is laid down, that the performance of a penance will obliterate the sin of quitting the pile. Or in case of inability to undergo the regular penance, absolution may be obtained by bestowing the value of a cow, or three kahuns of kowries. Therefore the sin is no cause of alarm. The disgrace in the opinion of others is also nothing: for good men regard not the blame or reproach of persons who can reprobate those who abstain from the sinful murder of women. And do you not consider how great is the sin to kill a woman; therein forsaking the fear of God, the fear of conscience, and the fear of the Shastrus, merely from a dread of the reproach of those who delight in female murder?

Advocate. – Though tying down in this manner be not authorized by the Shastrus, yet we practise it as being a custom that has been observed throughout Hindoosthan.

Opponent. – It never was the case that the practice of fastening down widows on the pile was prevalent throughout Hindoosthan: for it is but of late years that this mode has been followed, and that only in Bengal, which is but a small part of Hindoosthan. No one besides who has the fear of God and man before him, will assert that male or female murder, theft, &c., from having been long practised, cease to be vices. If, according to your argument, custom ought to set aside the precepts of the Shastrus, the inhabitants of the forests and mountains who have been in the habits of plunder, must be considered as guiltless of sin, and it would be improper to endeavour to restrain their habits. The Shastrus, and the reasonings connected with them, enable us to discriminate right and wrong. In those Shastrus such female murder is altogether forbidden. And reason also declares, that to bind down a woman for her destruction, holding out to her the inducement of heavenly rewards, is a most sinful act.

Advocate. – This practice may be sinful or any thing else, but we will not refrain from observing it. Should it cease, people would generally apprehend that if women did not perform Concremation on the death of their husbands, they might go astray; but if they burn themselves this fear is done away. Their family and relations are freed from apprehension. And if the husband could be assured during his life that his wife would follow him on the pile, his mind would be at ease from apprehensions of her misconduct.

Opponent. – What can be done, if, merely to avoid the possible danger of disgrace, you are unmercifully resolved to commit the sin of female murder. But is there not also a danger of a woman's going astray during the life-time of her husband, particularly when he resides for a long time in a distant country? What remedy then have you got against this cause of alarm?

Advocate. – There is a great difference betwixt the case of the husband's being alive, and of his death; for while a husband is alive, whether he resides near her or at a distance, a wife is under his control; she must stand in awe of him. But after his death that authority ceases, and she of course is divested of fear.

Opponent. – The Shastrus which command that a wife should live under the control of her husband during his life, direct that on his death she shall live under the authority of her husband's family, or else under that of her parental relations; and the Shastrus have authorized the ruler of the country to maintain the observance of this law. Therefore, the possibility of a woman's going astray cannot be more guarded against during the husband's life than it is after his death. For you daily see, that even while the husband is alive, he gives up his authority, and the wife separates from him. Control alone cannot restrain from evil thoughts, words, and actions; but the suggestions of wisdom and the fear of God may cause both man and woman to abstain from sin. Both the Shastrus and experience show this.

Advocate. – You have repeatedly asserted, that from want of feeling we promote female destruction. This is incorrect, for it is declared in our *Ved* and codes of law, that mercy is the root of virtue, and from our practice of hospitality, &c. our compassionate dispositions are well known.

Opponent. – That in other cases you shew charitable dispositions is acknowledged. But by witnessing from your youth the voluntary burning of women amongst your elder relatives, your neighbours, and the inhabitants of the surrounding villages, and by observing the indifference manifested at the time when the women are writhing under the torture of the flames, habits of insensibility are produced. For the same reason, when men or women are suffering the pains of death, you feel for them no sense of compassion. Like the worshippers of the female deities, who, witnessing from their infancy the slaughter of kids and buffaloes, feel no compassion for them in the time of their suffering death; while followers of Vishnoo are touched with strong feelings of pity.

Advocate. – What you have said I shall carefully consider.

Opponent. – It is to me a source of great satisfaction, that you are now ready to take this matter into your consideration. By forsaking prejudice and reflecting on the Shastru, what is really conformable to its precepts may be perceived, and the evils and disgrace brought on this country by the crime of female murder will cease.

Chapter 12

Dr B. R. Ambedkar (1891–1956)

Dr Bhimarao Ramji Ambedkar had perhaps the largest impact on political and civil life in India in the twentieth century. Born as a *Mahar*, Ambedkar was regarded as an "Untouchable,"[1] and felt the severity of the restrictions and inequalities imposed on his community by Hinduism. In spite of this history of discrimination (or because of this), Ambedkar rose up to become one of the central figures in the development of India as a constitutional democracy. Regaled as the leader of the "Untouchables," Ambedkar eventually became chairman of the constitutional committee charged to write the Indian Constitution in August 1947 and to reform the inequalities of the social world of India.[2]

Ambedkar was the most highly educated politician to serve in the Indian government at the time of Independence. He received a BA in English and Persian from Elphinstone College in Bombay in 1912. After serving as a Lieutenant in the armed forces, Ambedkar received a scholarship (1913) from the Mahārāja of Baroda to continue his academic study at Columbia University. There he was able to study with John Dewey, the educational reformer who was one of the founders of American Pragmatism, and with other influential scholars. After receiving his MA and PhD from Columbia in political science, Dr Ambedkar, traveled to England where he enrolled in Grey's Inn to become at barrister and became a student at the London School of Economics where he received an MSc in 1921. Before leaving Columbia, though, he published his first paper, "Caste in India: Their Mechanism, Genesis and Development" which was the prelude of his work to come. With this education background, Ambedkar was well equipped to dismantle the *varṇa* system in India.

In the 1950s, Ambedkar turned towards Buddhism and completely rejected the oppression of his Hindu past. He traveled to Sri Laṅkā to observe Buddhism there. After he returned to India, he publicly converted in October 1956 and himself converted more than 500,000 of his followers.[3] A few months later, in December, though, he passed away. Ambedkar's offered his own version of Buddhism that included 22 vows, several of which were vows to reject Hindu beliefs and ideology. Tying together Buddhism and Marxism, Dr Ambedkar argued that Buddhism was a universal religion that was especially suited for the oppressed and downtrodden.[4]

In addition to organizing political groups to fight for the rights of the so-called Depressed and Scheduled Classes (the "Untouchables," the Dalits), starting newspapers such as the *Janata* in 1930, and helping to design laws to achieve a much-needed social balance, Ambedkar served in 1947 as the chairman of the drafting committee of the Indian constitution. Ambedkar thus wrote a great deal to advance the cause of the Scheduled Castes, some of his writings became centers of controversy in India. He wrote, for example, a number of articles including "What the Congress and Gandhi Have Done to the Untouchables," that confronted the effect that his contemporary, Mahātma Gandhi, was having on the plight of the "Untouchables." Ambedkar also wrote several treatises on Buddhism and published *The Buddha and His Dharma* just before he died in 1956.

There are three articles included here: "Untouchability,"[5] "Caste and Class,"[6] and "Annihilation of Caste." The first two articles outline the issues that confronted Ambedkar. "Annihilation of Caste" was from a talk given in 1936 and provoked a considerable response because in it he suggests that the *śāstras* should be rejected.

Notes

1 I am using this term interchangeably with "Dalits" and "Scheduled Castes." Ambedkar himself used this terminology in his writing and identified himself as such. In so doing my intention is merely to inform the reader, not to maintain, these categories.

2 I am reliant on Valerian Rodrigues' excellent introduction in his *The Essential Writings of B. R. Ambedkar.* Delhi: Oxford University Press, 2002.

3 Peter Harvey, *An Introduction to Buddhism.* Cambridge: Cambridge University Press, 1990, p. 299.

4 See essays in Surendra Jondhale and Johannes Beltz (eds.), *Reconstructing the World: B. R. Ambedkar and Buddhism in India.* Oxford: Oxford University Press, 2004.

5 The title was given by Rodrigues from whose book these selections derive. Rodrigues took it from an excerpt from the speeches Ambedkar gave at the Constituent Assembly found in *Dr. Babasaheb Ambedkar: Writings and Speeches*, vol. 2, Bombay: Government of Maharashtra, Department of Education, 1994, pp. 491–4. This one was from "Ambedkar's Note to the Indian Franchise Committee (Lothian Committee), of which Ambedkar was a member, in 1932. Rodrigues, *Essential Writings*, p. 56.

6 Rodrigues has also titled this piece which was an excerpt from Ambedkar's never-completed *Can I Be a Hindu?* written in the 1950s. Rodriques, *Essential Writings*, p. 56.

Further reading

Ambedkar, B. R., *States and Minorities: What Are Their Rights and How to Secure Them in the Constitution of Free India.* Hyderabad [India]: Baba Saheb Dr. Ambedkar Memorial Society, 1970.

Ambedkar, B. R., *Dr. Babasaheb Ambedkar: Writings and Speeches*, vol. 2. Bombay: Government of Maharashtra, Department of Education, 1994.

Bayly, Susan, *Caste, Society and Politics in India from the Eighteenth Century to the Modern Age.* Cambridge: Cambridge University Press, 1999.

Gore, M. S., *The Social Context of an Ideology: Ambedkar's Political and Social Thought.* New Delhi: Sage Publications, 1993.

Harvey, Peter, *An Introduction to Buddhism*. Cambridge: Cambridge University Press, 1990.
Jaffrelot, Christophe, *Dr. Ambedkar and Untouchability: Fighting the Indian Caste System*. New York: Columbia University Press, 2005.
Jondhale, Surendra and Johannes Beltz (eds.), *Reconstructing the World: B. R. Ambedkar and Buddhism in India*. Oxford: Oxford University Press, 2004.
Omvedt, Gail, *Dalits and the Democratic Revolution: Dr. Ambedkar and the Dalit Movement in Colonial India*. New Delhi: Sage Publications, 1994.
Rodrigues, Valerian, *The Essential Writings of B. R. Ambedkar*. Delhi: Oxford University Press, 2002.

The Essential Writings of B. R. Ambedkar

Untouchability

I have agreed to confine the term depressed classes to untouchables only. In fact, I have myself sought to exclude from the untouchables all those in whom there cannot be the same consciousness of kind as is shared by those who suffer from the social discrimination that is inherent in the system of untouchability and who are therefore likely to exploit the untouchables for their own purposes. I have also raised no objection to the utilization of tests 7 and 8 referred to in the Committee's report for the ascertainment of the untouchable classes. But as I find that different persons seek to apply them in different ways, or put different constructions on them I feel it necessary to explain my point of view in regard to this matter.

In the first place it is urged in some quarters that whatever tests are applied for ascertaining the untouchable classes they must be applied uniformly all over India. In this connection, I desire to point out that in a matter of this sort it would hardly be appropriate to apply the same test or tests all over India. India is not a single homogeneous country. It is a continent. The various Provinces are marked by extreme diversity of conditions and there is no tie of race or language. Owing to absence of communication each Province has evolved along its own lines with its own peculiar manners and modes of social life. In such circumstances, the degree of uniformity with which most of the tests of untouchability are found to apply all over India is indeed remarkable. For instance, bar against temple entry exists everywhere in India. Even the tests of well-water and pollution by touch apply in every Province, although not with the same rigidity everywhere. But to insist on absolute uniformity in a system like that of untouchability which after all is a matter of social behaviour and which must therefore vary with the circumstances of each Province and also of each individual is simply to trifle with the problem. The Statutory Commission was quite alive to this possible line of argument and after careful consideration rejected it by recognizing the principle of diversity in the application of tests of untouchability. On page 67 of Vol. II which contains its recommendations it observed,

> It will plainly be necessary, after the main principles of the new system of representation have been settled, to entrust to some specially appointed body (like the former Franchise Committee) the task of drawing up fresh electoral rules to carry these principles into effect, and one of the tasks of such a body will be to frame for each province a definition of 'depressed classes' (which may well vary, sometimes even between parts of the same province), and to determine their numbers as so defined.

Another point which I wish to emphasize is the futility of insisting upon the application of uniform tests of untouchability all over India. It is a fundamental mistake to suppose that differences in tests of untouchability indicate differences in the conditions of the untouchables. On a correct analysis of the mental attitude they indicate, it will be found that whether the test is causing pollution by touch or refusal to use common well, the notion underlying both is one and the same. Both are outward registers of the same inward feeling of defilement, odium, aversion and contempt. Why will not a Hindu touch an untouchable? Why will not a Hindu allow an untouchable to enter the temple or use the village well? Why will not a Hindu admit an untouchable in the inn? The answer to each one of these questions is the same. It is that the untouchable

Excerpts from Valerian Rodrigues, *The Essential Writings of B. R. Ambedkar*. Delhi: Oxford University Press, 2002.

is an unclean person not fit for social intercourse. Again, why will not a Brahmin priest officiate at religious ceremonies performed by an untouchable? Why will not a barber serve an untouchable? In these cases also the answer is the same. It is that it is below dignity to do so. If our aim is to demarcate the class of people who suffer from social odium then it matters very little which test we apply. For as I have pointed out each of these tests is indicative of the same social attitude on the part of the touchables towards the untouchables.

In the second place the view is put forth that in applying the test of 'causing pollution by touch' for ascertaining the untouchable classes effect must be given to it in its literal sense – and not in its notional sense. In the literal sense untouchables are only those persons whose touch not only causes pollution and is therefore avoided, or if not avoided is washed off by purification. In the notional sense an untouchable is a person who is deemed to belong to a class which is commonly held to cause pollution by touch, although contact with such a person may for local circumstances not be avoided or may not necessitate ceremonial purification. According to those who seek to apply the test in its literal sense the conclusion would be the so-called untouchables should cease to be reckoned as untouchables wherever conditions have so changed that people do not avoid the touch of an untouchable, or do not trouble to purify themselves of the pollution caused by their touch. I cannot accept this view which, in my opinion, is based on a misconception. An individual may not be treated as an untouchable in the literal sense of the term on account of various circumstances. None the less outside the scope of such compelling circumstances he does continue to be regarded as an impure person by reason of his belonging to the untouchable class. This distinction is well brought out by the Census Superintendent of Bihar and Orissa in his Census Report of 1921 from which the following is an extract. Speaking of the relaxation of caste rules he says:

> Such incidents however which we have only noticed amongst the upper and more educated castes that are aspiring to the upper ranks, are to be regarded not as sign portending the collapse of the caste system, but of its adjustment to modern conditions. The same may be said with regard to modifications of the rules about personal contact or the touching of what is eaten or drunk. ... In places like Jamshedpur where work is done under modern conditions men of all castes and races work side by side in the mill without any misgivings regarding the caste of their neighbours. But, because the facts of everyday life make it impossible to follow the same practical rules as were followed a hundred years ago, it is not to be supposed that the distinctions of pure and impure, touchable and untouchable are no longer observed. A high caste Hindu will not allow an 'untouchable' to sit on the same seat, to smoke the same hookah or to touch his person, his seat, his food or the water that he drinks.

If this is a correct statement of the facts of life then the difference between untouchability in its literal and notional sense is a distinction which makes no difference to the ultimate situation; for as the extract shows untouchability in its notional sense persists even where untouchability in its literal sense has ceased to obtain. This is why I insist that the test of untouchability must be applied in its notional sense.

In the third place the idea is broadcast that untouchability is rapidly vanishing. I wish to utter a word of caution against the acceptance of this view, and to point out the necessity of distinguishing facts from propaganda. In my opinion what is important to be borne in mind in drawing inference from instances showing the occasional comingling of Brahmins and non-Brahmins, touchables and untouchables is that the system of caste and the system of untouchability form really the steel frame of Hindu society. This division cannot easily be wiped out for the simple reason that it is not based upon rational, economic or racial grounds. On the other hand, the chances are that untouchability will endure far longer into the future than the optimist reformer is likely to admit on account of the fact that it is based on religious dogma. What makes it so difficult, to break the system of untouchability is the religious sanction which it has behind it. At any rate the ordinary Hindu looks upon it as part of his religion and there is no doubt that in adopting towards untouchables what is deemed to be an inhuman way of behaviour he does so more from the sense of observing his religion than from any motive of deliberate cruelty. Based on religion the ordinary Hindu only relaxes the rules of untouchability where he cannot observe them. He never abandons them. For abandonment of untouchability to him involves a total abandonment of the basic religious tenets of Hinduism as understood by him and the mass of Hindus. Based on religion, untouchability will persist as all religious notions have done. Indian history records the attempts of many a Mahatma to uproot untouchability from the Indian soil. They include such great men as Buddha, Ramanuja and the Vaishnava saints of modern times. It would be hazardous to assume that a system which has withstood all this onslaught will collapse. The Hindu looks upon the observance of untouchability as an act of religious merit, and non-observance of it as sin. My view therefore is that so long as this notion prevails untouchability will prevail.

Caste and Class

An old agnostic is said to have summed up his philosophy in the following words:

> The only thing I know is that I know nothing; and I am not quite sure that I know that ...'

Sir Denzil Ibbetston undertaking to write about caste in Punjab said that the words of this agnostic about his philosophy expressed very exactly his own feelings regarding caste. It is no doubt true that owing to local circumstances there does appear a certain diversity about caste matters and that it is very difficult to make any statement regarding any one of the castes. Absolutely true as it may be, as regards one locality which will not be contradicted with equal truth as regards the same caste in some other area.

Although this may be true yet it cannot be difficult to separate the essential and fundamental features of caste from its non-essential and superficial features. An easy way to ascertain this is to ask what are the matters for which a person is liable to be excluded from caste. Mr. Bhattacharya has stated the following as causes for expulsion from caste. (1) Embracing Christianity or Islam (2) Going to Europe or America (3) Marrying a widow (4) Publicly throwing the sacred thread (5) Publicly eating beef, pork or fowl (6) Publicly eating *kachcha* food prepared by a Mahomedan, Christian or low-caste Hindu (7) Officiating at the house of a very low-caste Shudra (8) By a female going away from home for immoral purposes (9) By a widow becoming pregnant.

This list is not exhaustive and omits the three most important causes which entail expulsion from caste. They are (10) Inter-marrying outside caste (11) Interdining with persons of another caste and (12) Change of occupation. The second defect in the statement of Mr. Bhattacharya is that it does not make any distinction between essentials and non-essentials.

Of course, when a person is expelled from his caste the penalty is uniform. His friends, relatives and fellowmen refuse to partake of his hospitality. He is not invited to entertainments in their houses. He cannot obtain brides or bridegrooms for his children. Even his married daughters cannot visit him without running the risk of being excluded from his caste. His priest, his barber and washerman refuse to serve him. His fellow castemen severe their connection with him so completely that they refuse to assist him even at the funeral of a member of his household. In some cases the man excluded from caste is debarred access to public temples and to the cremation or burial ground.

These reasons for expulsion from caste indirectly show the rules and regulations of the caste. But all regulations are not fundamental. There are many which are unessential. Caste can exist even without them. The essential and unessential can be distinguished by asking another question. When can a Hindu who has lost caste regain his caste? The Hindus have a system of *prayaschitas* which are penances and which a man who has been expelled from caste must perform before he can be admitted to caste fellowship. With regard to these prayaschitas or penances certain points must be remembered. In this first place, there are caste offences for which there is no prayaschita. In the second place, the prayaschitas vary according to the offence. In some cases the prayaschitas involve a very small penalty. In other cases the penalty involved is a very severe one.

The existence of a prayaschita and the absence of it have a significance which must by clearly understood. The absence of prayaschita does not mean that anyone may commit the offence with impunity. On the contrary it means that the offence is of an immeasurable magnitude and the offender once expelled is beyond reclamation. There is no re-entry for him in the caste from which he is expelled. The existence of a prayaschita means that the offence is compoundable. The offender can take the prescribed prayaschita and obtain admission in the caste from which he is expelled.

There are two offences for which there is no penance. These are (1) change from the Hindu religion to another religion (2) Marriage with a person of another caste or another religion. It is obvious if a man loses caste for these offences he loses it permanently.

Of the other offences the prayaschitas prescribed are of the severest kind, are two – (1) interdining with a person of another caste or a non-Hindu and (2) Taking to an occupation which is not the occupation of the caste. In the case of the other offences the penalty is a light one, almost nominal.

The surest clue to find out what are the fundamental rules of caste and what caste consists in is furnished by the rules regarding prayaschitas. Those for the infringement of which there is no prayaschita constitute the very soul of caste and those for the infringement of which the prayaschita is of the severest kind make up the body of caste. It may therefore be said without any hesitation that there are four fundamental rules of caste. A caste may be defined as a social group having (a) belief in the Hindu religion and bound by certain regulations as to (b) marriage (c) food and (d) occupation. To this one more characteristic may be added, namely a social group having a common name by which it is recognized.

In the matter of marriage the regulation lays down that the caste must be endogamous. There can be no intermarriage between members of different castes. This is the first and the most fundamental idea on which the whole fabric of the caste is built up. In the matter of food the rule is that a person cannot take food from and dine with any person who does not belong to his caste. This means that only those who can intermarry can also interdine. Those who cannot intermarry cannot interdine. In other words, caste is an endogamous unit and also a communal unit. In the matter of occupation the regulation is that a person must follow the occupation which is the traditional occupation of his caste and if the caste has no occupation then he should follow the occupation of his father. In the matter of status of a person it is fixed and is hereditary. It is fixed because a person's status is determined by the status of the caste to which he belongs. It is hereditary because a Hindu is stamped with the caste to which his parents belonged, a Hindu cannot change his status because he cannot change his caste. A Hindu is born in a caste and he dies a member of the caste in which he is born. A Hindu may lose his status if he loses caste. But he cannot acquire a new or a better or different status.

What is the significance of a common name for a caste? The significance of this will be clear if we ask two questions which are very relevant and a correct answer to each is necessary for a complete idea of this institution of caste. Social groups are either organized or unorganized. When the membership of the group and the process of joining and leaving the groups, are the subject of definite social regulations and involve certain duties and privileges in relation to other members of the group, then the group is an organized group. A group is a voluntary group in which members enter with a full knowledge of what they are doing and the aims which the association is designed to fulfil. On the other hand, there are groups of which an individual person becomes a member without any act of volition, and becomes subject to social regulation and traditions over which he has no control of any kind.

Now it is hardly necessary to say that caste is a highly organized social grouping. It is not a loose or a floating body. Similarly, it is not necessary to say that caste is an involuntary grouping. A Hindu is born in a caste and he dies as a member of that caste. There is no Hindu without caste, cannot escape caste and being bounded by caste from birth to death he becomes subject to social regulations and traditions of the caste over which he has no control.

The significance of a separate name for a caste lies in this – namely, it makes caste an organized and an involuntary grouping. A separate and a distinctive name for a caste makes caste akin to a corporation with a perpetual existence and a seal of separate entity. The significance of separate names for separate castes has not been sufficiently realized by writers on caste. In doing that they have lost sight of a most distinctive feature of caste. Social groups there are and they are bound to be in every society. Many social groups in many countries can be equated to various castes in India and may be regarded as their equivalent. Potters, washermen, intellectuals as social groups are everywhere. But in other countries they have remained as unorganized and voluntary groups while in India they have become castes because in other countries the social groups were not given a name while in India they did. It is the name which the caste bears which gives it fixity and continuity and individuality. It is the name which defines who are its members and in most cases a person born in a caste carries the name of the caste as a part of his surname. Again it is the name which makes it easy for the caste to enforce its rules and regulations. It makes it easy in two ways. In the first place, the name of the caste forming a surname of the individual prevents the offender in passing off as a person belonging to another caste and thus escape the jurisdiction of the caste. Secondly, it helps to identify the offending individual and the caste to whose jurisdiction he is subject so that he is easily handed up and punished for any breach of the caste rules.

This is what caste means. Now as to the caste system. This involves the study of the mutual relations between different castes. Looked at as a collection of castes, the caste system presents several features which at once strike the observer. In the first place there is no interconnection between the various castes which form a system. Each caste is separate and distinct. It is independent and sovereign in the disposal of its internal affairs and the enforcement of caste regulations. The castes touch but they do not interpenetrate. The second feature relates to the order in which one caste stands in relation to the other castes in the system. That order is vertical and not horizontal.

Such is the caste and such is the caste system. The question is, is this enough to know the Hindu social organization? For a static conception of the Hindu social organization an idea of the caste and the caste system is enough. One need not trouble to remember more than the facts that the Hindus are divided into castes and that the castes form a system in which all hang on a thread which runs through the system in such a way that while encircling and separating one caste from another it holds them all as though it was a string of tennis balls hanging one above the other. But this will not be enough to understand caste as a dynamic phenomenon. To follow the workings of caste in action it is necessary to note one other feature of caste besides the caste system, namely the class-caste system.

The relationship between the ideas of caste and class has been a matter of lively controversy. Some say that caste is analogous to class and that there is no difference between the two. Others hold that the idea of castes is fundamentally opposed to that of class. This is an aspect of the subject of caste about which more will be said hereafter. For the present it is necessary to emphasize one feature of the caste system which has not been referred to hereinbefore. It is this. Although caste is different from and opposed to the notion of class yet the caste-system – as distinguished from caste – recognizes a class system which is somewhat different from the graded status referred to above. Just as the Hindus are divided into so many castes, castes are divided into different classes of castes. The Hindu is caste conscious. He is also class conscious. Whether he is caste conscious or class conscious depends upon the caste with which he comes in conflict. If the caste with which he comes in conflict is a caste within the class to which he belongs he is caste conscious. If the caste is outside the class to which he belongs he is class conscious. Anyone who needs any evidence on this point may study the Non-Brahmin Movement in the Madras and the Bombay Presidency. Such a study will leave no doubt that to a Hindu caste periphery is as real as class periphery and caste consciousness is as real as class consciousness.

Caste, it is said, is an evolution of the *Varna* system. I will show later on that this is nonsense. Caste is a perversion of *Varna*. At any rate it is an evolution in the opposite direction. But while caste has completely perverted the Varna system it has borrowed the class system from the Varna system. Indeed the class-caste system follows closely the class cleavages of the Varna system.

Looking at the caste system from this point of view one comes across several lines of class cleavage which run through this pyramid of castes dividing the pyramid into blocks of castes. The first line of cleavage follows the line of division noticeable in the ancient *Chaturvarna* system. The old system of Chaturvarna made a distinction between the first three *Varnas*, the *Brahmins*, *Kshatriyas*, *Vaishyas* and the fourth *Varna*, namely, the *Shudra*. The three former were classed as the regenerate classes. The *Shudra* was held as the unregenerate class. This distinction was based upon the fact that the former were entitled to wear the sacred thread and study the Vedas. The *Shudra* was entitled to neither and that is why he was regarded as the unregenerate class. The line of cleavage is still in existence and forms the basis of the present day class division separating the castes which have grown out of the vast class of *Shudras* from those which have grown out of the three classes of *Brahmins*, the *Kshatriyas* and *Vaishyas*. This line of class cleavage is the one which is expressed by the terms High Castes and Low Castes and which are short forms for the High Class Castes and Low Class Castes.

Next, after this line of cleavage, there runs through the pyramid a second line of class cleavage. It runs just below the Low Class Castes. It sets above all the castes born out of the four *Varnas* i. e., the high castes as well as the low castes above the remaining castes which I will merely describe as the 'rest'. This line of class cleavage is again a real one and follows the well-defined distinction which was a fundamental principle of the Chaturvarna system. The Chaturvarna system as is pointed out made a distinction between the four Varnas putting the three Varnas above the fourth. But it also made an equally clear distinction between those within the Chaturvarna and those outside the Chaturvarna. It had a terminology to express this distinction. Those within the Chaturvarna – high or low, Brahmin or Shudra were called *Savarna* i. e. those with the stamp of the Varna. Those outside the Chaturvarna were called *Avarna* i. e., those without the stamp of Varna. All the castes which have evolved out of the four Varnas are called Savarna Hindus – which is rendered in English by the term Caste Hindus – the 'rest' are the *Avarnas* who in present parlance are spoken of by Europeans as Non-caste Hindus i. e., those who are outside the four original castes or Varnas.

Much that is written about the caste system has reference mostly to the caste system among the Savarna Hindus. Very little is known about the Avarna Hindus. Who are these Avarna Hindus, what is their position in Hindu Society, how are they related to the Savarna Hindus are questions to which no attention has so far been paid. I am sure that without considering these questions no one can get a true picture of the social structure the Hindus have built. To leave out the class cleavage between the Savarna Hindus and the Avarna Hindus is to relate a Grimm's Fairy Tale which leaves out the witches, the goblins and the ogres.

Annihilation of Caste

I

It is a pity that caste even today has its defenders. The defences are many. It is defended on the ground that the caste system is but another name for division of labour and if division of labour is a necessary feature of every civilized society then it is argued that there is nothing wrong in the caste system. Now the first thing to be urged against this view is that caste system is not merely division of labour. *It is also a division of labourers.* Civilized society undoubtedly needs division of labour. But in no civilized society is division of labour accompanied by this unnatural division of labourers into water-tight compartments. The caste system is not merely a division of labourers which is quite different from division of labour – it is an hierarchy in which the division of labourers are graded one above the other. In no other country is the division of labour accompanied by this gradation of labourers. There is also a third point of criticism against this view of the caste system. This division of labour is not spontaneous, it is not based on natural aptitudes. Social and individual efficiency requires us to develop the capacity of an individual to the point of competency to choose and to make his own career. This principle is violated in the caste system in so far as it involves an attempt to appoint tasks to individuals in advance, selected not on the basis of trained original capacities, but on that of the social status of the parents. Looked at from another point of view this stratification of occupations which is the result of the caste system is positively pernicious. Industry is never static. It undergoes rapid and abrupt changes. With such changes an individual must be free to change his occupation. Without such freedom to adjust himself to changing circumstances it would be impossible for him to gain his livelihood. Now the caste system will not allow Hindus to take to occupations where they are wanted if they do not belong to them by heredity. If a Hindu is seen to starve rather than take to new occupations not assigned to his caste, the reason is to be found in the caste system. By not permitting readjustment of occupations, caste becomes a direct cause of much of the unemployment we see in the country. As a form of division of labour the caste system suffers from another serious defect. The division of labour brought about by the caste system is not a division based on choice. Individual sentiment, individual preference has no place in it. It is based on the dogma of predestination. Considerations of social efficiency would compel us to recognize that the greatest evil in the industrial system is not so much poverty and the suffering that it involves as the fact that so many persons have callings which make no appeal to those who are engaged in them. Such callings constantly provoke one to aversion, ill-will and the desire to evade. There are many occupations in India which on account of the fact that they are regarded as degraded by the Hindus provoke those who are engaged in them to aversion. There is a constant desire to evade and escape from such occupations which arises solely because of the blighting effect which they produce upon those who follow them owing to the slight and stigma cast upon them by the Hindu religion. What efficiency can there be in a system under which neither men's hearts nor their minds are in their work? As an economic organization caste is therefore a harmful institution, inasmuch as, it involves the subordination of man's natural powers and inclinations to the exigencies of social rules.

II

Some have dug a biological trench in defence of the caste system. It is said that the object of caste was to preserve purity of race and purity of blood. Now ethnologists are of opinion that men of pure race exist nowhere and that there has been mixture of all races in all parts of the world. Especially is this the case with the people of India. Mr D. R. Bhandarkar in his paper on *Foreign Elements in the Hindu Population* has stated that:

> There is hardly a class, or Caste in India which has not a foreign strain in it. There is an admixture of alien blood not only among the warrior classes – the Rajputs and the Marathas – but also among the Brahmins who are under the happy delusion that they are free from all foreign elements.

The caste system cannot be said to have grown as a means of preventing the admixture of races or as a means of maintaining purity of blood. As a matter of fact caste system came into being long after the different races of India had commingled in blood and culture. To hold that distinctions of castes are really distinctions of race and to treat different castes as though they were so many different races is a gross perversion of facts. What racial affinity is there between the Brahmin of the Punjab and the Brahmin of Madras? What racial affinity is there between the untouchable of Bengal and the untouchable of Madras? What racial difference is there between the Brahmin of the Punjab and the Chamar of the Punjab? What racial difference is there between the Brahmin of Madras and the Pariah of Madras? The Brahmin of the Punjab is racially of the same stock as the Chamar of the Punjab and the Brahmin of Madras is of the same race as the Pariah of Madras. The caste system does not demarcate racial division. The caste system is a social division of people of the same race. Assuming it, however, to be a case of racial divisions one may ask: What harm could there be if a mixture of races and of blood was permitted to take place in India by intermarriages between different castes? Men are no doubt divided from animals by so deep a distinction that science recognizes men and animals as two distinct species. But even scientists who believe in purity of races do not assert that the different races constitute different species of men. They are only varieties of one and the same species. As such they can interbreed and produce an offspring which is capable of breeding and which is not sterile. An immense lot of nonsense is talked about heredity and eugenics in defence of the caste system. Few would object to the caste system if it was in accord with the basic principle of eugenics because few can object to the improvement of the race by judicious mating. But one fails to understand how the caste system secures judicious mating. Caste system is a negative thing. It merely prohibits persons belonging to different castes from intermarrying. It is not a positive method of selecting which two among a given caste should marry. If caste is eugenic in origin then the origin of sub-castes must also be eugenic. But can anyone seriously maintain that the origin of sub-caste is eugenic? I think it would be absurd to contend for such a proposition and for a very obvious reason. If caste means race then differences of sub-castes cannot mean differences of race because sub-castes become *ex hypothesia* sub-divisions of one and the same race. Consequently the bar against intermarrying and interdining between sub-castes cannot be for the purpose of maintaining purity of race or of blood. If sub-castes cannot be eugenic in origin there cannot be any substance in the contention that caste is eugenic in origin. Again if castes is eugenic in origin one can understand the bar against intermarriage. But what is the purpose of the interdict placed on interdining between castes and sub-castes alike? Interdining cannot infect blood and therefore cannot be the cause either of the improvement or of deterioration of the race. This shows that caste had no scientific origin and that those who are attempting to give it an eugenic basis are trying to support by science what is grossly unscientific. Even today eugenics cannot become a practical possibility unless we have definite knowledge regarding the laws of heredity. Professor Bateson in his *Mendel's Principles of Heredity* says,

> There is nothing in the descent of the higher mental qualities to suggest that they follow any single system of transmission. It is likely that both they and the more marked developments of physical powers result rather from the coincidence of numerous factors than from the possession of any one genetic element.

To argue that the caste system was eugenic in its conception is to attribute to the forefathers of present-day Hindus a knowledge of heredity which even the modern scientists do not possess. A tree should be judged by the fruits it yields. If caste is eugenic what sort of a race of men it should have produced? Physically speaking the Hindus are a C3 people. They are a race of Pygmies and dwarfs stunted in stature and wanting in stamina. It is a nation nine-tenths of which is declared to be unfit for military service. This shows that the caste system does not embody the eugenics of modern scientists. It is a social system which embodies the arrogance and selfishness of a perverse section of the Hindus who were superior enough in social status to set it in fashion and who had authority to force it on their inferiors.

III

Caste does not result in economic efficiency. Caste cannot and has not improved the race. Caste has however done one thing. It has completely disorganized and demoralized the Hindus.

The first and foremost thing that must be recognized is that Hindu society is a myth. The name Hindu is itself a foreign name. It was given by the Mohammedans to the natives for the purpose of distinguishing themselves. It does not occur in any Sanskrit work prior to the Mohammedan invasion. They did not feel the necessity of a common name because they had no conception of their having constituted a community. Hindu society as such does not exist. It is only a collection of castes. Each caste is conscious of its existence. Its survival is the be all and end all of its existence. Castes do not even form a federation. A caste has no feeling that it is affiliated to other castes except when there is a Hindu-Muslim riot. On all other occasions each caste endeavours to segregate itself and to distinguish itself from other castes. Each caste not only dines among itself and marries among itself but each caste prescribes its own distinctive dress. What other explanation can there be of the innumerable styles of dress worn by the men and women of India which so amuse the tourists? Indeed the ideal Hindu must be like a rat living in his own hole refusing to have any contact with others. There is an utter lack among the Hindus of what the sociologists call 'consciousness of kind'. There is no Hindu consciousness of kind. In every Hindu the consciousness that exists is the consciousness of his caste. That is the reason why the

Hindus cannot be said to form a society or a nation. There are however many Indians whose patriotism does not permit them to admit that Indians are not a nation, that they are only an amorphous mass of people. They have insisted that underlying the apparent diversity there is a fundamental unity which marks the life of the Hindus in as much as there is a similarity of habits and customs, beliefs and thoughts which obtain all over the continent of India. Similarity in habits and customs, beliefs and thoughts there is. But one cannot accept the conclusion that therefore, the Hindus constitute a society. To do so is to misunderstand the essentials which go to make up a society. Men do not become a society by living in physical proximity any more than a man ceases to be a member of his society by living so many miles away from other men. Secondly, similarity in habits and customs, beliefs and thoughts is not enough to constitute men into society. Things may be passed physically from one to another like bricks. In the same way habits and customs, beliefs and thoughts of one group may be taken over by another group and there may thus appear a similarity between the two. Culture spreads by diffusion and that is why one finds similarity between various primitive tribes in the matter of their habits and customs, beliefs and thoughts, although they do not live in proximity. But no one could say that because there was this similarity the primitive tribes constituted one society. This is because similarly in certain things is not enough to constitute a society. Men constitute a society because they have things which they possess in common. To have similar things is totally different from possessing things in common. And the only way by which men can come to possess things in common with one another is by being in communication with one another. This is merely another way of saying that society continues to exist by communication indeed in communication. To make it concrete, it is not enough if men act in a way which agrees with the acts of others. Parallel activity, even if similar, is not sufficient to bind men into a society. This is proved by the fact that the festivals observed by the different castes amongst the Hindus are the same. Yet these parallel performances of similar festivals by the different castes have not bound them into one integral whole. For that purpose what is necessary is for a man to share and participate in a common activity so that the same emotions are aroused in him that animate the others. Making the individual a sharer or partner in the associated activity so that he feels its success as his success, its failure as his failure is the real thing that binds men and makes a society of them. The caste system prevents common activity and by preventing common activity it has prevented the Hindus from becoming a society with a unified life and a consciousness of its own being.

IV

The Hindus often complain of the isolation and exclusiveness of a gang or a clique and blame them for anti-social spirit. But they conveniently forget that this anti-social spirit is the worst feature of their own caste system. One caste enjoys singing a hymn of hate against another caste as much as the Germans did in singing their hymn of hate against the English during the last war. The literature of the Hindus is full of caste genealogies in which an attempt is made to give a noble origin to one caste and an ignoble origin to other castes. The *Sahyadrikhand* is a notorious instance of this class of literature. This anti-social spirit is not confined to caste alone. It has gone deeper and has poisoned the mutual relations of the sub-castes as well. In my province the Golak Brahmins, Deorukha Brahmins, Karada Brahmins, Palshe Brahmins and Chitpavan Brahmins, all claim to be subdivisions of the Brahmin caste. But the anti-social spirit that prevails between them is quite as marked and quite as virulent as the anti-social spirit that prevails between them and other non-Brahmin castes. There is nothing strange in this. An anti-social spirit is found wherever one group has 'interests of its own' which shut it out from full interaction with other groups, so that its prevailing purpose is protection of what it has got. This anti-social spirit, this spirit of protecting its own interests is as much a marked feature of the different castes in their isolation from one another as it is of nations in their isolation. The Brahmin's primary concern is to protect 'his interest' against those of the non-Brahmins and the Non-Brahmin's primary concern is to protect their interests against those of the Brahmins. The Hindus, therefore, are not merely an assortment of castes but they are so many warring groups each living for itself and for its selfish ideal. There is another feature of caste which is deplorable. The ancestors of the present-day English fought on one side or the other in the wars of the Roses and the Cromwellian War. But the descendents of those who fought on the one side do not bear any animosity – any grudge against the descendants of those who fought on the other side. The feud is forgotten. But the present-day non-Brahmins cannot forgive the present-day Brahmins for the insult their ancestors gave to Shivaji. The present-day Kayasthas will not forgive the present-day Brahmins for the infamy cast upon their forefathers by the forefathers of the latter. To what is this difference due? Obviously to the caste system. The existence of caste and caste consciousness has served to keep the memory of past feuds between castes green and has prevented solidarity.

V

The recent discussion about the excluded and partially included areas has served to draw attention to the position of what are called the aboriginal tribes in India. They number about 13 millions if not more. Apart from the questions whether their exclusion from the new Constitution is proper or improper, the fact still remains that these aborigines have remained in their primitive uncivilized state in a land which boasts of a civilization thousands of years old. Not only are they not civilized but some of them follow pursuits which have led to their being classified as criminals. Thirteen million people living in the midst of civilization are still in a savage state and are leading the life of hereditary criminals! But the Hindus have never felt ashamed of it. This is a phenomenon which in my view is quite unparallelled. What is the cause of this shameful state of affairs? Why has no attempt been made to civilize these aborigines and to lead them to take to a more honourable way of making a living? The Hindus will probably seek to account for this savage state of the aborigines by attributing to them congenital stupidity. They will probably not admit that the aborigines have remained savages because they had made no effort to civilize them, to give them medical aid, to reform them, to make them good citizens. But supposing a Hindu wished to do what the Christian missionary is doing for these aborigines, could he have done it? I submit not. Civilizing the aborigines means adopting them as your own, living in their midst, and cultivating fellow-feeling, in short loving them. How is it possible for a Hindu to do this? His whole life is one anxious effort to preserve his caste. Caste is his precious possession which he must save at any cost. He cannot consent to lose it by establishing contact with the aborigines, the remnants of the hateful Anaryas of the *Vedic* days. Not that a Hindu could not be taught the sense of duty to fallen humanity, but the trouble is that no amount of sense of duty can enable him to overcome his duty to preserve his caste. Caste is, therefore, the real explanation as to why the Hindu has let the savage remain a savage in the midst of his civilization without blushing or without feeling any sense of remorse or repentance. The Hindu has not realized that these aborigines are a source of potential danger. If these savages remain savages they may not do any harm to the Hindu. But if they are reclaimed by non-Hindus and converted to their faiths they will swell the ranks of the enemies of the Hindus. If this happens the Hindu will have to thank himself and his caste system.

VI

Not only has the Hindu made no effort for the humanitarian cause of civilizing the savages but the higher-caste Hindu have deliberately prevented the lower castes who are within the pale of Hinduism from rising to the cultural level of the higher castes. I will give two instances, one of the Sonars and the other of the Pathare Prabhus. Both are communities quite well-known in Maharashtra. Like the rest of the communities desiring to raise their status these two communities were at one time endeavouring to adopt some of the ways and habits of the Brahmins. The Sonars were styling themselves Daivadnya Brahmins and were wearing their 'dhotis' with folds on and using the word *namaskar* for salutation. Both, the folded way of wearing the 'dhoti' and the *namaskar* were special to the Brahmins. The Brahmins did not like this imitation and this attempt by Sonars to pass off as Brahmins. Under the authority of the Peshwas the Brahmins successfully put down this attempt on the part of the Sonars to adopt the ways of the Brahmins. They even got the President of the Councils of the East India Company's settlement in Bombay to issue a prohibitory order against the Sonars residing in Bombay. At one time the Pathare Prabhus had widow-remarriage as a custom of their caste. This custom of widow-remarriage was later on looked upon as a mark of social inferiority by some members of the caste especially because it was contrary to the custom prevalent among the Brahmins. With the object of raising the status of their community some Pathare Prabhus sought to stop this practice of widow-remarriage that was prevalent in their caste. The community was divided into two camps, one for and the other against the innovation. The Peshwas took the side of those in favour of widow-remarriage and thus virtually prohibited the Pathare Prabhus from following the ways of the Brahmins. The Hindus criticize the Mohammedans for having spread their religion by the use of the sword. They also ridicule Christianity on the score of the inquisition. But really speaking who is better and more worthy of our respect – the Mohammedans and Christians who attempted to thrust down the throats of unwilling persons what they regarded as necessary for their salvation or the Hindu who would not spread the light, who would endeavour to keep others in darkness, who would not consent to share his intellectual and social inheritance with those who are ready and willing to make it a part of their own make-up? I have no hesitation in saying that if the Mohammedan has been cruel, the Hindu has been mean and meanness is worse than cruelty.

VII

Whether the Hindu religion was or was not a missionary religion has been a controversial issue. Some hold the view that it was never a missionary religion. Others hold that it was. That the Hindu religion was once a missionary religion must be admitted. It could not have spread over the face of India, if it was not a missionary religion. That today it is not a missionary religion is also a fact which must be accepted. The question therefore is not whether or not the Hindu religion was a missionary religion. The real question is why did the Hindu religion cease to be a missionary religion? My answer is this: Hindu religion ceased to be a missionary religion when the caste system grew up among the Hindus. Caste is inconsistent with conversion. Inculcation of beliefs and dogmas is not the only problem that is involved in conversion. To find a place for the convert in the social life of the community is another and a much more important problem that arises in connection with conversion. That problem is where to place the convert, in what caste? It is a problem which must baffle every Hindu wishing to make aliens converts to his religion. Unlike the club the membership of a caste is not open to all and sundry. The law of caste confines its membership to person born in the caste. Castes are autonomous and there is no authority anywhere to compel a caste to admit a newcomer to its social life. Hindu society being a collection of castes and each caste being a close corporation there is no place for a convert. Thus it is the caste which has prevented the Hindus from expanding and from absorbing other religious communities. So long as caste remains, Hindu religion cannot be made a missionary religion and *Shudhi* will be both a folly and a futility.

VIII

The reason which has made *Shudhi* impossible for Hindus is also responsible for making *Sanghatan* impossible. The idea underlying *Sanghatan* is to remove from the mind of the Hindu that timidity and cowardice which so painfully mark him off from the Mohammedan and the Sikh and which have led him to adopt the low ways of treachery and cunning for protecting himself. The question naturally arises: From where does the Sikh or the Mohammedan derive his strength which makes him brave and fearless? I am sure it is not due to relative superiority of physical strength, diet or drill. It is due to the strength arising out of the feeling that all Sikhs will come to the rescue of a Sikh when he is in danger and that all Mohammedans will rush to save a Muslim if he is attacked. The Hindu can derive no such strength. He cannot feel assured that his fellows will come to his help. Being one and fated to be alone he remains powerless, develops timidity and cowardice and in a fight surrenders or runs away. The Sikh as well as the Muslim stands fearless and gives battle because he knows that though one he will not be alone. The presence of this belief in the one helps him to hold out and the absence of it in the other makes him to give way. If you pursue this matter further and ask what is it that enables the Sikh and the Mohammedan to feel so assured and why is the Hindu filled with such despair in the matter of help and assistance you will find that the reasons for this difference lie in the difference in their associated mode of living. The associated mode of life practised by the Sikhs and the Mohammedans produces fellow-feeling. The associated mode of life of the Hindus does not. Among Sikhs and Muslims there is a social cement which makes them *Bhais*. Among Hindus there is no such cement and one Hindu does not regard another Hindu as his *Bhai*. This explains why a Sikh says and feels that one Sikh, or one Khalsa is equal to *Sava Lakh* men. This explains why one Mohammedan is equal to a crowd of Hindus. This difference is undoubtedly a difference due to caste. So long as caste remains, there will be no *Sanghatan* and so long as there is no *Sanghatan* the Hindu will remain weak and meek. The Hindus claim to be a very tolerant people. In my opinion this is a mistake. On many occasions they can be intolerant and if on some occasions they are tolerant that is because they are too weak to oppose or too indifferent to oppose. This indifference of the Hindus has become so much a part of their nature that a Hindu will quite meekly tolerate an insult as well as a wrong. You see amongst them, to use the words of Morris:

> The great reading down the little, the strong beating down the weak, cruel men fearing not, kind men daring not and wise men caring not.

With the Hindu Gods all forbearing, it is not difficult to imagine the pitiable condition of the wronged and the oppressed among the Hindus. Indifferentism is the worst kind of disease that can infect a people. Why is the Hindu so indifferent? In my opinion this indifferentism is the result of the caste system which has made *Sanghatan* and cooperation even for a good cause impossible.

IX

The assertion by the individual of his own opinions and beliefs, his own independence and interest as over against group standards, group authority and group interests is the beginning of all reform. But whether the reform will continue depends upon what scope the group affords for such individual assertion. If the group is tolerant and fair-minded in dealing with such individuals they will continue to assert and in the end succeed in converting their fellows. On the other hand if the group is intolerant and does not bother about the means it adopts to stifle such individuals they will perish and the reform will die out. Now a caste has an unquestioned right to excommunicate any man who is guilty of breaking the rules of the caste and when it is realized that excommunication involves a complete cesser of social intercourse it will be agreed that as a form of punishment there is really little to choose between excommunication and death. No wonder individual Hindus have not had the courage to assert their independence by breaking the barriers of caste. It is true that man cannot get on with his fellows. But it is also true that he cannot do without them. He would like to have the society of his fellows on his terms. If he cannot get it on his terms then he will be ready to have it on any terms even amounting to complete surrender. This is because he cannot do without society. A caste is ever ready to take advantage of the helplessness of a man and insist upon complete conformity to its code in letter and in spirit. A caste can easily organize itself into a conspiracy to make the life of a reformer a hell and if a conspiracy is a crime I do not understand why such a nefarious act as an attempt to excommunicate a person for daring to act contrary to the rules of caste should not be made an offence punishable in law. But as it is, even law gives each caste an autonomy to regulate its membership and punish dissenters with excommunication. Caste in the hands of the orthodox has been a powerful weapon for persecuting the reformers and for killing all reform.

X

The effect of caste on the ethics of the Hindus is simply deplorable. Caste has killed public spirit. Caste has destroyed the sense of public charity. Caste has made public opinion impossible. A Hindu's public is his caste. His responsibility is only to his caste. His loyalty is restricted only to his caste. Virtue has become caste-ridden and morality has become caste-bound. There is no sympathy to the deserving. There is no appreciation of the meritorious. There is no charity to the needy. Suffering as such calls for no response. There is charity but it begins with the caste and ends with the caste. There is sympathy but not for men of other caste. Would a Hindu acknowledge and follow the leadership of a great and good man? The case of a Mahatma apart, the answer must be that he will follow a leader if he is a man of his caste. A Brahmin will follow a leader only if he is a Brahmin, a Kayastha if he is a Kayastha and so on. The capacity to appreciate merits in a man apart from his caste does not exist in a Hindu. There is appreciation of virtue but only when the man is a fellow caste-man. The whole morality is as bad as tribal morality. My caste-man, right or wrong; my caste-man, good or bad. It is not a case of standing by virtue and not standing by vice. It is a case of standing or not standing by the caste. Have not Hindus committed treason against their country in the interests of their caste?

XI

I would not be surprised if some of you have grown weary listening to this tiresome tale of the sad effects which caste has produced. There is nothing new in it. I will therefore turn to the constructive side of the problem. What is your ideal society if you do not want caste is a question that is bound to be asked of you. If you ask me, my ideal would be a society based on *Liberty, Equality* and *Fraternity.* And why not? What objection can there be to fraternity? I cannot imagine any. An ideal society should be mobile, should be full of channels for conveying a change taking place in one part to other parts. In an ideal society there should be many interests consciously communicated and shared. There should be varied and free points of contact with other modes of association. In other words there must be social endosmosis. This is fraternity, which is only another name for democracy. Democracy is not merely a form of government. It is primarily a mode of associated living, of conjoint communicated experience. It is essentially an attitude of respect and reverence towards fellowmen. Any objection to liberty? Few object to liberty in the sense of a right to free movement, in the sense of a right to life and limb. There is no objection to liberty in the sense of a right to property, tools and materials as being necessary for earning a living to keep the body in due state of health. Why not allow liberty to benefit by an effective and competent use of a person's powers? The supporters of caste who would allow liberty in the sense of a right to life, limb and property, would not readily consent to liberty in this sense, inasmuch as it involves liberty to choose one's profession. But to object to this kind of liberty is to perpetuate slavery. For slavery does not merely mean a legalized form of subjection. It means a state of society in which some men are forced to accept from others the purposes which control their conduct. This condition obtains even where there is no slavery in the legal sense. It is found where, as in the caste system, some persons are compelled to carry on certain prescribed callings which are not of their choice. Any objection to equality? This has obviously been the most contentious part of the slogan of the French Revolution. The objection to equality may be sound and one may have to admit that all men are not equal. But what of that? Equality may be a fiction but nonetheless one must accept it as the governing principle. A man's power is dependent upon (1) physical heredity, (2) social inheritance or endowment in the form of parental care, education, accumulation of scientific knowledge, everything which enables him to be more efficient than the savage, and finally, (3) on his own efforts. In all these three respects men are undoubtedly unequal. But the question is, shall we treat them as unequal because they are unequal? This is a question which the opponents of equality must answer. From the standpoint of the individualist it may be just to treat men unequally so far as their efforts are unequal. It may be desirable to give as much incentive as possible to the full development of everyone's powers. But what would happen if men were treated unequally as they are, in the first two respects? It is obvious that those individuals in whose favour there is also birth, education, family name, business connections and inherited wealth would be selected in the race. But selection under such circumstances would not be a selection of the able. It would be the selection of the privileged. The reason therefore, which forces that in the third respect we should treat men unequally demands that in the first two respects we should treat men as equally as possible. On the other hand it can be urged that if it is good for the social body to get the most out of its members, it can get most out of them only by making them equal as far as possible at the very start of the race. That is one reason why we cannot escape equality. But there is another reason why we must accept equality. A statesman is concerned with vast numbers of people. He has neither the time nor the knowledge to draw fine distinctions and to treat each equitably i. e. according to need or according to capacity. However desirable or reasonable an equitable treatment of men may be, humanity is not capable of assortment and classification. The statesman, therefore, must follow some rough and ready rule and that rough and ready rule is to treat all men alike not because they are alike but because classification and assortment is impossible. The doctrine of equality is glaringly fallacious but taking all in all it is the only way a statesman can proceed in politics which is a severely practical affair and which demands a severely practical test.

XII

But there is a set of reformers who hold out a different ideal. They go by the name of the

Arya Samajists and their ideal of social organization is what is called Chaturvarnya or the division of society into four classes instead of the four thousand castes that we have in India. To make it more attractive and disarm opposition the protagonists of Chaturvarnya take great care to point out that their Chaturvarnya is based not on birth but on *guna* (worth). At the outset, I must confess that notwithstanding the worth-basis of this Chaturvarnya, it is an ideal to which I cannot reconcile myself. In the first place, if under the Chaturvarnya of the Arya Samajists an individual is to take his place in the Hindu society according to his worth I do not understand why the Arya Samajists insist upon labelling men as Brahmin, Kshatriya, Vaishya and Shudra. A learned man would be honoured without his being labelled a Brahmin. A soldier would be respected without his being designated a Kshatriya. If European society honours its soldiers and its servants without giving them permanent labels, why should Hindu society find it difficult to do so is a question, which Arya Samajists have not cared to consider. There is another objection to the continuance of these labels. All reform consists in a change in the notions, sentiment and mental attitudes of the people towards men and things. It is common experience that certain names become associated with certain notions and sentiments, which determine a person's attitude towards men and things. The names, Brahmin, Kshatriya, Vaishya and Shudra, are names which are associated with a definite and fixed notion in the mind of every Hindu. That notion is that of a hierarchy based on birth. So long as these names continue, Hindus will continue to think of the Brahmin, Kshatriya, Vaishya and Shudra as hierarchical divisions of high and low, based on birth, and act accordingly. The Hindu must be made to unlearn all this. But how can this happen if the old labels remain and continue to recall to his mind old notions. If new notions are to be inculcated in the minds of people it is necessary to give them new names. To continue the old name is to make the reform futile. To allow this Chaturvarnya, based on worth to be designated by such stinking labels of Brahmin, Kshatriya, Vaishya, Shudra, indicative of social divisions based on birth, is a snare.

XIII

To me this Chaturvarnya with its old labels is utterly repellent and my whole being rebels against it. But I do not wish to rest my objection to Chaturvarnya on mere grounds of sentiments. There are more solid grounds on which I rely for my opposition to it. A close examination of this ideal has convinced me that as a system of social organization, Chaturvarnya is impracticable, harmful and has turned out to be a miserable failure. From a practical point of view, the system of Chaturvarnya raises several difficulties which its protagonists do not seem to have taken into account. The principle underlying caste is fundamentally different from the principle underlying *Varna*. Not only are they fundamentally different but they are also fundamentally opposed. The former is based on worth. How are you going to compel people who have acquired a higher status based on birth without reference to their worth to vacate that status? How are you going to compel people to recognize the status due to a man in accordance with his worth, who is occupying a lower status based on his birth? For this you must first break up the caste system, in order to be able to establish the *Varna* system. How are you going to reduce the four thousand castes, based on birth, to the four *Varnas*, based on worth? This is the first difficulty which the protagonists of the Chaturvarnya must grapple with. There is a second difficulty which the protagonists of Chaturvarnya must grapple with, if they wish to make the establishment of Chaturvarnya a success.

Chaturvarnya presupposes that you can classify people into four definite classes. Is this possible? In this respect, the ideal of Chaturvarnya has, as you will see, a close affinity to the Platonic ideal. To Plato, men fell by nature into three classes. In some individuals, he believed mere appetites dominated. He assigned them to the labouring and trading classes. Others revealed to him that over and above appetites, they have a courageous disposition. He classed them as defenders in war and guardians of internal peace. Others showed a capacity to grasp the universal reason underlying things. He made them the law-givers of the people. The criticism to which Plato's Republic is subject, is also the criticism which must apply to the system of Chaturvarnya, in so far as it proceeds upon the possibility of an accurate classification of men into four distinct classes. The chief criticism against Plato is that his idea of lumping of individuals into a few sharply marked-off classes is a very superficial view of man and his powers. Plato had no perception of the uniqueness of every individual, of his incommensurability with others, of each individual forming a class of his own. He had no recognition of the infinite diversity of active tendencies and combination of tendencies of which an individual is capable. To him, there were types of faculties or powers in the individual constitution. All this is demonstrably wrong. Modern science has shown that lumping together of individuals into a few sharply marked-off classes is a superficial view of man not worthy of serious consideration. Consequently, the utilization of the qualities of individuals is incompatible with their stratification by classes, since the qualities of individuals are so variable. Chaturvarnya must fail for the very reason for which Plato's Republic must fail, namely that it is not possible to pigeon men into holes, according as he belongs to one class or the other. That it is impossible to accurately classify people into four definite classes is proved by the fact that the original four classes have now become four thousand castes.

There is a third difficulty in the way of the establishment of the system of Chaturvarnya. How are you going to maintain the system of Chaturvarnya, supposing it was established? One important requirement for the successful working of Chaturvarnya is the maintenance of the penal system which could maintain it by its sanction. The system of Chaturvarnya must perpetually face the problem of the transgressor. Unless there is a penalty attached to the act of transgression, men will not keep to their respective classes. The whole system will break down, being contrary to human nature. Chaturvarnya cannot subsist by its own inherent goodness. It must be enforced by law. That, without penal sanction the ideal of Chaturvarnya cannot be realized is proved by the story in the Ramayana of Rama killing Shambuka. Some people seem to blame Rama because he wantonly and without reason killed Shambuka. But to blame Rama for killing Shambuka is to misunderstand the whole situation. Ram Raj was a Raj based on Chaturvarnya. As a king, Rama was bound to maintain Chaturvarnya. It was his duty therefore to kill Shambuka, the Shudra, who had transgressed his class and wanted to be a Brahmin. This is the reason why Rama killed Shambuka. But this also shows that penal sanction is necessary for the maintenance of Chaturvarnya. Not only penal sanction is necessary, but penalty of death is necessary. That is why Rama did not inflict on Shambuka a lesser punishment. That is why Manu-Smriti prescribes such heavy sentences as cutting off the tongue or pouring of molten lead in the ears of the Shudra, who recites or hears the *Veda*. The supporters of Chaturvarnya must give an assurance that they could successfully classify men and they could induce modern society in the twentieth century to reforge the penal sanctions of Manu-Smriti.

The protagonists of Chaturvarnya do not seem to have considered what is to happen to women in their system. Are they also to be divided into four classes, Brahmin, Kshatriya, Vaishya and Shudra? Or are they to be allowed to take the status of their husbands. If the status of the woman is to be the consequence of marriage what becomes of the underlying principle of Chaturvarnya, namely, that the status of a person should be based upon the worth of that person? If they are to be classified according to their worth is their classification to be nominal or real? If it is to be nominal then it is useless and then the protagonists of Chaturvarnya must admit that their system does not apply to women. If it is real, are the protagonists of Chaturvarnya prepared to follow the logical consequences of applying it to women? They must be prepared to have women priests and women soldiers. Hindu society has grown accustomed to women teachers and women barristers. It may grow accustomed to women brewers and women butchers. But he would be a bold person, who would say that it will allow women priests and women soldiers. But that will be the logical outcome of applying Chaturvarnya to women. Given these difficulties, I think no one except a congenital idiot could hope and believe in a successful regeneration of the Chaturvarnya.

XIV

Assuming that Chaturvarnya is practicable, I contend that it is the most vicious system. That the Brahmins should cultivate knowledge, that the Kshatriya should bear arms, that the Vaishya should trade and that the Shudra should serve sounds as though it was a system of division of labour. Whether the theory was intended to state that the Shudra *need not* or that whether it was intended to lay down that he *must not*, is an interesting question. The defenders of Chaturvarnya give it the first meaning. They say, why should the *Shudra* need trouble to acquire wealth, when the three *Varnas* are there to support him? Why need the *Shudra* bother to take to education, when there is the Brahmin to whom he can go when the occasion for reading or writing arises? Why need the *Shudra* worry to arm himself because there is the Kshatriya to protect him? The theory of Chaturvarnya, understood in this sense, may be said to look upon the *Shudra* as the ward and the three *Varnas* as his guardians. Thus interpreted it is a simple, elevating and alluring theory. Assuming this to be the correct view of the underlying conception of Chaturvarnya, it seems to me that the system is neither fool-proof nor knave-proof. What is to happen, if the Brahmins, Vaishyas and Kshatriyas fail to pursue knowledge, to engage in economic enterprise and to be efficient soldiers which are their respective functions? Contrary-wise, suppose that they discharge their functions but flout their duty to the *Shudra* or to one another, what is to happen to the *Shudra* if the three classes refuse to support him on fair terms or combine to keep him down? Who is to safeguard the interests of the *Shudra* or for the matter of that of the Vaishya and Kshatriya when the person, who is trying to take advantage of his ignorance is the Brahmin? Who is to defend the liberty of the *Shudra* and for the matter of that, of the Brahmin and the Vaishya when the person who is robbing him of it is the Kshatriya? Inter-dependence of one class on another class is inevitable. Even dependence of one class upon another may sometimes become allowable. But why make one person depend upon another in the matter of his vital needs? Education everyone must have. Means of defence everyone must have. These are the paramount requirements of every man for his self-preservation. How can the fact that his neighbour is educated and armed help a man who is uneducated and disarmed. The whole theory is absurd. These are the questions, which the defenders of Chaturvarnya do not seem to be troubled about. But they are very pertinent questions. Assuming their conception of Chaturvarnya that the relationship between the different classes is that of ward and guardian is the real conception underlying Chaturvarnya, it must be admitted that it makes no provision to safeguard the interests of the ward from the misdeeds of the guardian. Whether the relationship of guardian and ward was the real underlying conception, on which Chaturvarnya was based, there is no doubt that in practice the relation was that of master and servants. The three classes, Brahmins, Kshatriyas and Vaishyas although not very happy in their mutual relationship managed to work by compromise. The Brahmin flattered the Kshatriya and both let the Vaishya live in order to be able to live upon him. But the three agreed to beat down the Shudra. He was not allowed to acquire wealth lest he should be independent of the three *Varnas*. He was prohibited from acquiring knowledge lest he should keep a steady vigil regarding his interests. He was prohibited from bearing arms lest he should have the means to rebel against their authority. That this is how the *Shudras* were treated by the Tryavarnikas is evidenced by the Laws of Manu. There is no code of laws more infamous regarding social rights than the Laws of Manu. Any instance from anywhere of social injustice must pale before it. Why have the mass of people tolerated the social evils to which they have been subjected? There have been social revolutions in other countries of the world. Why have there not been social revolutions in India is a question which has incessantly troubled me. There is only one answer, which I can give and it is that the lower classes of Hindus have been completely disabled for direct action on account of this wretched system of Chaturvarnya. They could not bear arms and without arms they could not rebel. They were all ploughmen or rather condemned to be ploughmen and they never were allowed to convert their ploughshare into swords. They had no bayonets and therefore everyone who chose could and did sit upon them. On account of the Chaturvarnya, they could receive no education. They could not think out or know the way to their salvation. They were condemned to be lowly and not knowing the way of escape and not having the means of escape, they became reconciled to eternal servitude, which they accepted as their inescapable fate. It is true that even in Europe the strong have not shrunk from exploitation, nay the spoilation of the weak. But in Europe, the strong have never contrived to make the weak helpless against exploitation so shamelessly as was the case in India among the Hindus. Social war has been raging between the strong and the weak far more violently in Europe than it has ever been in India. Yet, the weak in Europe has had in his freedom of military service his *physical weapon*, in suffering his *political weapon* and in education his *moral weapon*. These three weapons for emancipation were never withheld by the strong from the weak in Europe. All these weapons were, however, denied to the masses in India by Chaturvarnya. There cannot be a more degrading system of social organization than the Chaturvarnya. It is the system which deadens, paralyses and cripples the people from helpful activity. This is no exaggeration. History bears ample evidence. There is only one period in Indian history which is a period of freedom, greatness and glory. That is the period of the Maurya Empire. At all other times the country suffered from defeat and darkness. But the Maurya period was a period when Chaturvarnya was completely annihilated, when the Shudras, who constituted the mass of the people, came into their own and became the rulers of the country. The period of defeat and darkness is the period when Chaturvarnya flourished to the damnation of the greater part of the people of the country.

XV

Chaturvarnya is not new. It is as old as the *Vedas*. That is one of the reasons why we are asked by the Arya Samajists to consider its claims. Judging from the past as a system of social organization, it has been tried and it has failed. How many times have the Brahmins annihilated the seed of the Kshatriyas! How many times have the Kshatriyas annihilated the Brahmins! The Mahabharata and the Puranas are full of incidents of the strife between the Brahmins and the Kshatriyas. They even quarreled over such petty questions as to who should salute first, as to who should give way first, the Brahmins or the Kshatriyas, when the two met in the street. Not only was the Brahmin an eyesore to the Kshatriya and the Kshatriya an eyesore to the Brahmin, it seems that the Kshatriyas had become tyrannical and the masses, disarmed as they were under the system of Chaturvarnya, were praying Almighty God for relief from their tyranny. The Bhagwad tells us very definitely that Krishna had taken *Avtar* for one sacred purpose and that was to annihilate the Kshatriyas. With these instances of rivalry and enmity between the different *Varnas* before us, I do not understand how any one can hold out Chaturvarnya as an ideal to be aimed at or as a pattern, on which Hindu society should be remodelled.

XVI

I have dealt with those, who are without you and whose hostility to your ideal is quite open. There appear to be others who are neither without you nor with you. I was hesitating whether I should deal with their point of view. But on further consideration I have come to the conclusion that I must and that for two reasons. Firstly, their attitude to the problem of caste is not merely an attitude of neutrality, but is an attitude of armed neutrality. Secondly, they probably represent a considerable body of people. Of these, there is one set which finds nothing peculiar nor odious in the caste system of the Hindus. Such Hindus cite the case of Muslims, Sikhs and Christians and find comfort in the fact that they too have castes amongst them. In considering this question you must at the outset bear in mind that nowhere is human society one single whole. It is always plural. In the world of action, the individual is one limit and society the other. Between them lie all sorts of associative arrangements of lesser and larger scope, families, friendship, cooperative associations, business combines, political parties, bands of thieves and robbers. These small groups are usually firmly welded together and are often as exclusive as castes. They have a narrow and intensive code, which is often anti-social. This is true of every society, in Europe as well as in Asia. The question to be asked in determining whether a given society is an ideal society, is not whether there are groups in it, because groups exist in all societies. The questions to be asked in determining what is an ideal society are: How numerous and varied are the interests which are consciously shared by the groups? How full and free is the interplay with other forms of associations? Are the forces that separate groups and classes more numerous than the forces that unite? What social significance is attached to this group life? Is its exclusiveness a matter of custom and convenience or is it a matter of religion? It is in the light of these questions that one must decide whether caste among non-Hindus is the same as caste among Hindus. If we apply these considerations to castes among Mohammedans, Sikhs and Christians on the one hand and to castes among Hindus on the other, you will find that caste among Non-Hindus is fundamentally different from caste among Hindus. First, the ties, which consciously make the Hindus hold together, are non-existent, while among non-Hindus there are many that hold them together. The strength of a society depends upon the presence of points of contact, possibilities of interaction between different groups which exist in it. These are what Carlyle calls 'organic filaments' *i. e.* the elastic threads which help to bring the disintegrating elements together and to reunite them. There is no integrating force among the Hindus to counteract the disintegration caused by caste while among the non-Hindus there are plenty of these organic filaments which bind them together. Again it must be borne in mind that although there are castes among non-Hindus, as there are among Hindus, caste has not the same social significance for non-Hindus as it has for Hindus. Ask Mohammedan or a Sikh, who he is? He tells you that he is a Mohammedan or a Sikh as the case may be. He does not tell you his caste although he has one and you are satisfied with his answer. When he tells you that he is a Muslim, you do not proceed to ask him whether he is a Shiya or a Sunni; Sheikh or Saiyad; Khatik or Pinjari. When he tells you he is a Sikh, you do not ask him whether he is Jat or Roda; Mazbi or Ramdasi. But you are not satisfied, if a person tells you that he is a Hindu. You feel bound to inquire into his caste. Why? Because so essential is caste in the case of a Hindu that without knowing it you do not feel sure what sort of a being he is. That caste has not the same social significance among non-Hindus as it has among Hindus is clear if you take into consideration the consequences which follow breach of caste. There may be castes among Sikhs and Mohammedans but the Sikhs and the Mohammedans will not outcaste a Sikh or a Mohammedan if he broke his caste. Indeed, the very idea of excommunication is foreign to the Sikhs and the Mohammedans. But with the Hindus the case is entirely different. He is sure to be outcasted if he broke caste. This shows the difference in the social significance of caste of Hindus and non-Hindus. This is the second point of difference. But there is also a third and a more important one. Caste among the non-Hindus has no religious consecration; but among the Hindus most decidedly it has. Among the non-Hindus, caste is only a practice, not a sacred institution. They did not originate it. With them it is only a survival. They do not regard caste as a religious dogma. Religion compels the Hindus to treat isolation and segregation of castes as a virtue. Religion does not compel the non-Hindus to take the same attitude towards caste. If Hindus wish to break caste, their religion will come in their way. But it will not be so in the case of non-Hindus. It is, therefore, a dangerous delusion to take comfort in the mere existence of caste among non-Hindus, without caring to know what place caste occupies in their life and whether there are other 'organic filaments', which subordinate the feeling of caste to the feeling of community. The sooner the Hindus are cured of this delusion the better.

The other set denies that caste presents any problem at all for the Hindus to consider. Such Hindus seek comfort in the view that the Hindus have survived and take this as a proof of their fitness to survive. This point of view is well expressed by Professor S. Radhakrishnan in his *Hindu View of Life.* Referring to Hinduism he says,

> The civilization itself has not been a short-lived one. Its historic records date back for over four thousand years and even then it had reached a stage of civilization which has continued its unbroken, though at times slow and static, course until the present day. It has stood the stress and strain of more than four or five millenniums of spiritual thought and experience. Though peoples of different races and cultures have been pouring into India from the dawn of History, Hinduism has been able to maintain its supremacy and even the proselytizing creeds backed by political power have not been able to coerce the large majority of Hindus to their views. The Hindu culture possesses some vitality which seems to be denied to some other more forceful currents. It is no more necessary to dissect Hinduism than to open a tree to see whether the sap still runs.

The name of Professor Radhakrishnan is big enough to invest with profundity whatever he says and impress the minds of his readers. But I must not hesitate to speak out my mind. For, I fear that his statement may become the basis of a vicious argument that the fact of survival is proof of fitness to survive. It seems to me that the question is not whether a community lives or dies; the question is on what plane does it live. There are different modes of survival. But all are not equally honourable. For an individual as well as for a society, there is a gulf between merely living and living worthily. To fight in a battle and to live in glory is one mode. To beat a retreat, to surrender and to live the life of a captive is also a mode of survival. It is useless for a Hindu to take comfort in the fact that he and his people have survived. What he must consider is what is the quality of their survival. If he does that, I am sure he will cease to take pride in the mere fact of survival. A Hindu's life has been a life of continuous defeat and what appears to him to be life everlasting is not living everlastingly but is really a life which is perishing everlastingly. It is a mode of survival of which every right-minded Hindu, who is not afraid to own up the truth, will feel ashamed.

XVII

There is no doubt, in my opinion, that unless you change your social order you can achieve little by way of progress. You cannot mobilize the community either for defence or for offence. You cannot build anything on the foundations of caste. You cannot build up a nation, you cannot build up a morality. Anything that you will build on the foundations of caste will crack and will never be a whole.

The only question that remains to be considered is – *How to bring about the reform of the Hindu social order? How to abolish caste?* This is a question of supreme importance. There is a view that in the reform of caste, the first step to take, is to abolish sub-castes. This view is based upon the supposition that there is a greater similarity in manners and status between sub-castes than there is between castes. I think, this is an erroneous supposition. The Brahmins of Northern and Central India are socially of lower grade, as compared with the Brahmins of the Deccan and Southern India. The former are only cooks and water-carriers while the latter occupy a high social position. On the other hand, in Northern India, the Vaishyas and Kayasthas are intellectually and socially on par with the Brahmins of the Deccan and Southern India. Again, in the matter of food there is no similarity between the Brahmins of the Deccan and Southern India, who are vegetarians and the Brahmins of Kashmir and Bengal who are non-vegetarians. On the other hand, the Brahmins of the Deccan and Southern India have more in common so far as food is concerned with such non-Brahmins as the Gujaratis, Marwaris, Banias and Jains. There is no doubt that from the standpoint of making the transit from one caste to another easy, the fusion of the Kayasthas of Northern India and the other non-Brahmins of Southern India with the non-Brahmins of the Deccan and the Dravid country is more practicable than the fusion of the Brahmins of the South with the Brahmins of the North. But assuming that the fusion of sub-castes is possible, what guarantee is there that the abolition of sub-castes will necessarily lead to the abolition of castes? On the contrary, it may happen that the process may stop with the abolition of sub-castes. In that case, the abolition of sub-castes will only help to strengthen the castes and make them more powerful and therefore more mischievous. This remedy is therefore neither practicable nor effective and may easily prove to be a wrong remedy. Another plan of action for the abolition of caste is to begin with inter-caste dinners. This also, in my opinion, is an inadequate remedy. There are many castes which allow interdining. But it is a common experience that inter-dining has not succeeded in killing the spirit of caste and the consciousness of caste. I am convinced that the real remedy is inter-marriage. Fusion of blood can alone create the feeling of being kith and kin and unless this feeling of kinship, of being kindred, becomes paramount the separatist feeling – the feeling of being aliens – created by caste will not vanish. Among the Hindus inter-marriage must necessarily be a factor of greater force in social life than it need be in the life of the non-Hindus. Where society is already well-knit by other ties, marriage is an ordinary incident of life. But where society is cut as under, marriage as a binding force becomes a matter of urgent necessity. *The real remedy for breaking caste is inter-marriage. Nothing else will serve as the solvent of caste.* Your Jat-Pat-Todak Mandal has adopted this line of attack. It is a direct and frontal attack, and I congratulate you upon a correct diagnosis and more upon your having shown the courage to tell the Hindus what is really wrong with them. Political tyranny is nothing compared to social tyranny and a reformer, who defies society, is a much more courageous man than a politician, who defies government. You are right in holding that caste will cease to be an operative force only when inter-dining and inter-marriage have become matters of common course. You have located the source of the disease. But is your prescription the right prescription for the disease? Ask yourselves this question; Why is it that a large majority of Hindus do not inter-dine and do not inter-marry? Why is it that your cause is not popular? There can be only one answer to this question and it is that inter-dining and inter-marriage are repugnant to the beliefs and dogmas which the Hindus regard as sacred. Caste is not a physical object like a wall of bricks or a line of barbed wire which prevents the Hindus from co-mingling and which has, therefore, to be pulled down. Caste is a notion, it is a state of the mind. The destruction of caste does not therefore mean the destruction of a physical barrier. It means a *notional* change. Caste may be bad. Caste may lead to conduct so gross as to be called man's inhumanity to man. All the same, it must be recognized that the Hindus observe caste not because they are inhuman or wrong headed. They observe caste because they are deeply religious. People are not wrong in observing caste. In my view, what is wrong is their religion, which has inculcated this notion of caste. If this is correct, then obviously the enemy, you must grapple with is not the people who observe caste, but the *Shastras* which teach them this religion of caste. Criticizing and ridiculing people for not inter-dining or inter-marrying or occasionally holding inter-castes dinners and celebrating inter-caste marriages, is a futile method of achieving the desired end. The real remedy is to destroy the belief in the sanctity of the *Shastras*. How do you expect to succeed, if you allow the *Shastras* to continue to mould the beliefs and opinions of the people? Not to question the authority of the *Shastras* to permit the people to believe in their sanctity and their sanctions and to blame them and to criticize them for their acts as being irrational and inhuman is an incongruous way of carrying on social reform. Reformers working for the removal of untouchability including Mahatma Gandhi, do not seem to realize that the acts of the people are merely the results of their beliefs inculcated upon their minds by the *Shastras* and that people will not change their conduct until they cease to believe in the sanctity of the *Shastras* on which their conduct is founded. No wonder that such efforts have not produced any results. You also seem to be erring in the same way as the reformers working in the cause of removing untouchability. To agitate for and to organize inter-caste dinners and inter-caste marriages is like forced feeding brought about by artificial means. Make every man and woman free from the thraldom of the *Shastras*, cleanse their minds of the pernicious notions founded on the *Shastras*, and he or she will inter-dine and inter-marry, without your telling him or her to do so.

It is no use seeking refuse in quibbles. It is no use telling people that the *Shastras* do not say what they are believed to say, grammatically read or logically interpreted. What matters is how the *Shastras* have been understood by the people. You must take the stand that Buddha took. You must take the stand which Guru Nanak took. You must not only discard the *Shastras*, you must deny their authority, as did Buddha and Nanak. You must have courage to tell the Hindus, that what is wrong with them is their religion – the religion which has produced in them this notion of the sacredness of caste. Will you show that courage?

XVIII

What are your chances of success? Social reforms fall into different species. There is a species of reform, which does not relate to the religious notion of people but is purely secular in character. There is also a species of reform, which relates to the religious notions of people. Of such a species of reform, there are two varieties. In one, the reform accords with the principles of the religions and merely invites people, who have departed from it, to revert to them and to follow them. The second is a reform which not only touches the religious principles but is diametrically opposed to those principles and invites people to depart from and to discard their authority and to act contrary to those principles. Caste is the natural outcome of certain religious beliefs which have the sanction of the *Shastras*, which are believed to contain the command of divinely inspired sages who were endowed with a supernatural wisdom and whose commands, therefore, cannot be disobeyed without committing sin. The destruction of caste is a reform which falls under the third category. To ask people to give up caste is to ask them to go contrary to their fundamental religious notions. It is obvious that the first and second species of reform are easy. But the third is a stupendous task, well-nigh impossible. The Hindus hold to the sacredness of the social order. Caste has a divine basis. You must therefore destroy the sacredness and divinity with which caste has become invested. In the last analysis, this means you must destroy the authority of the *Shastras* and the *Vedas*.

I have emphasized this question of the ways and means of destroying caste, because I think that knowing the proper ways and means is more important than knowing the ideal. If you do not know the real ways and means, all your shots are sure to be misfires. If my analysis is correct then your task is herculean. You alone can say whether you are capable of achieving it.

Speaking for myself, I see the task to be well-nigh impossible. Perhaps you would like to know why I think so. Out of the many reasons, which have led me to take this view, I will mention some, which I regard much important. One of these reasons is the attitude of hostility, which the Brahmins have shown towards this question. The Brahmins form the vanguard of the movement for political reform and in some cases also of economic reform. But they are not to be found even as camp-followers in the army raised to break down the barricades of caste. Is there any hope of the Brahmins ever taking up a lead in the future in this matter? I say no. You may ask why? You may argue that there is no reason why Brahmins should continue to shun social reform. You may argue that the Brahmins know that the bane of Hindu society is caste and as an enlightened class could not be expected to be indifferent to its consequences. You may argue that there are secular Brahmins and priestly Brahmins and if the latter do not take up the cudgels on behalf of those who want to break caste, the former will. All this of course sounds very plausible. But in all this it is forgotten that the break up of the caste system is bound to affect adversely the Brahmin caste. Having regard to this, is it reasonable to expect that the Brahmins will ever consent to lead a movement the ultimate result of which is to destroy the power and prestige of the Brahmin caste? Is it reasonable to expect the secular Brahmins to take part in a movement directed against the priestly Brahmins? In my judgment, it is useless to make a distinction between the secular Brahmins and priestly Brahmins. Both are kith and kin. They are two arms of the same body and are bound to fight for the existence of the other. In this connection, I am reminded of some very pregnant remarks made by Professor Dicey in his *English Constitution*. Speaking of the actual limitation on the legislative supremacy of Parliament, Dicey says:

> The actual exercise of authority by any sovereign whatever, and notably by Parliament, is bounded or controlled by two limitations. Of these the one is an external, and the other is an internal limitation. The external limit to the real power of a sovereign consists in the possibility or certainty that his subjects or a large number of them will disobey or resist his laws . . . The internal limit to the exercise of sovereignty arises from the nature of the sovereign power itself. Even a despot exercises his powers in accordance with his character, which is itself

> moulded by the circumstance under which he lives, including under that head the moral feelings of the time and the society to which he belongs. The Sultan could not, if he would, change the religion of the Mohammedan world, but even if he could do so, it is in the very highest degree improbable that the head of Mohammedanism should wish to overthrow the religion of Mohammed; the internal check on the exercise of the Sultan's power is at least as strong as the external limitation. People sometimes ask the idle question, why the Pope does not introduce this or that reform? The true answer is that a revolutionist is not the kind of man who becomes a Pope and that a man who becomes a Pope has no wish to be a revolutionist.

I think, these remarks apply equally to the Brahmins of India and one can say with equal truth that if a man who becomes a Pope has no wish to become a revolutionary, a man who is born a Brahmin has much less desire to become a revolutionary. Indeed, to expect a Brahmin to be a revolutionary in matters of social reform is as idle as to expect the British Parliament, as was said by Leslie Stephen, to pass an Act requiring all blue-eyed babies to be murdered.

Some of you will say that it is a matter of small concern whether the Brahmins come forward to lead the movement against caste or whether they do not. To take this view is in my judgment to ignore the part played by the intellectual class in the community. Whether you accept the theory of the great man as the maker of history or whether you do not, this much you will have to concede that in every country the intellectual class is the most influential class, if not the governing class. The intellectual class is the class which can foresee; it is the class which can advise and give lead. In no country does the mass of the people live the life of intelligent thought and action. It is largely imitative and follows the intellectual class. There is no exaggeration in saying that the entire destiny of a country depends upon its intellectual class. If the intellectual class is honest, independent and disinterested it can be trusted to take the initiative and give a proper lead when a crisis arises. It is true that intellect by itself is no virtue. It is only a means and the use of means depends upon the ends which an intellectual person pursues. An intellectual man can be a good man but he can easily be a rogue. Similarly an intellectual class may be a band of high-souled persons, ready to help, ready to emancipate erring humanity or it may easily be a gang of crooks or a body of advocates of a narrow clique from which it draws its support. You may think it a pity that the intellectual class in India is simply another name for the Brahmin caste. You may regret that the two are one; that the existence of the intellectual class should be bound with one single caste, that this intellectual class should share the interest and the aspirations of that Brahmin caste, which has regarded itself the custodian of the interest of that caste, rather than of the interests of the country. All this may be very regrettable. But the fact remains, that the Brahmins form the intellectual class of the Hindus. It is not only an intellectual class but it is a class which is held in great reverence by the rest of the Hindus. The Hindus are taught that the Brahmins are *Bhudevas* (Gods on earth) वर्णानाम् ब्राह्मण गुरू: The Hindus are taught that Brahmins alone can be their teachers. Manu says, 'If it be asked how it should be with respect to points of the Dharma which have not been specially mentioned, the answer is that which Brahmins who are *Shishthas* propound shall doubtless have legal force' (Månavadharmabåstra 12.108):

> अनाम्नातेषु धर्मेषु कथं स्यादिति चेद्भवेत्।
> यं शिष्टा ब्राह्मणा ब्रुयुः स धर्मः स्यादशङ्कितः।

When such an intellectual class, which holds the rest of the community in its grip, is opposed to the reform of caste, the chances of success in a movement for the break-up of the caste system appear to me very, very remote.

The second reason, why I say the task is impossible, will be clear if you will bear in mind that the caste system has two aspects. In one of its aspects, it divides men into separate communities. In its second aspect, it places these communities in a graded order one above the other in social status. Each castes takes its pride and its consolation in the fact that in the scale of castes it is above some other caste. As an outward mark of this gradation, there is also a gradation of social and religious rights technically spoken of as *Ashtadhikaras* and *Sanskaras*. The higher the grade of a caste, the greater the number of these rights and the lower the grade, the lesser their number. Now this gradation, this scaling of castes, makes it impossible to organize a common front against the caste system. If a caste claims the right to inter-dine and inter-marry with another caste placed above it, it is frozen, instantly it is told by mischief-mongers, and there are many Brahmins amongst such mischief-mongers, that it will have to concede inter-dining and inter-marriage with castes below it! All are slaves of the caste system. But all the slaves are not equal in status. To excite the proletariat to bring about an economic revolution, Karl Marx told them: 'You have nothing to lose except your chains.' But the artful way in which the social and religious rights are distributed among the different castes whereby some have more and some have less, makes the slogan of Karl Marx quite useless to excite the Hindus against the caste system. Castes form a graded system of sovereignties, high and low, which are jealous of their status and which know that if a general dissolution came, some of them stand to lose more of their prestige and power than others do. You cannot, therefore, have a general mobilization of the Hindus, to use a military expression, for an attack on the caste system.

XIX

Can you appeal to reason and ask the Hindus to discard caste as being contrary to reason? That raises the question: Is a Hindu free to follow his reason? Manu has laid down three sanctions to which every Hindu must conform in the matter of his behaviour. वेदः स्मृतिः सदाचारः स्वस्य च प्रियमात्मनः Here there is no place for reason to play its part. A Hindu must follow either *Veda, Smriti* or *Sadachar*. He cannot follow anything else. In the first place how are the texts of the *Vedas* and *Smritis* to be interpreted whenever any doubt arises regarding their meaning? On this important question the view of Manu is quite definite. He says (Månavadharmabåstra 2.11):

योऽवमन्येत ते मूले हेतुशास्त्राश्रयात् द्विजः।
स साधुभिर्बहिष्कार्यो नास्तिको वेदनिन्दकः॥

According to this rule, rationalism as a canon of interpreting the *Vedas* and *Smritis*, is absolutely condemned. It is regarded to be as wicked as atheism and the punishment provided for it is excommunication. Thus, where a matter is covered by the *Vedas* or the *Smritis* a Hindu cannot resort to rational thinking. Even when there is a conflict between *Vedas* and *Smritis* on matters on which they have given a positive injunction, the solution is not left to reason. When there is a conflict between two *Shrutis*, both are to be regarded as of equal authority. Either of them may be followed. No attempt is to be made to find out which of the two accords with reason. This is made clear by Manu (Månavadharmabåstra 2.14):

श्रुतिद्वैधं तु यत्र स्याप्तत्र धर्मावुभौ स्मृतौ।

'When there is a conflict between *Shruti*, and *Smriti*, the *Shruti* must prevail.' But here too, no attempt must be made to find out which of the two accords with reason. This is laid down by Manu in the following *shloka* (Månavadharmabåstra 12.95):

या वेदबाह्याः स्मृतयो याश्च काश्च कुदृष्टः।
सर्वास्ता निष्फलाः प्रेत्य तमोनिष्ठा हि तः स्मृतः॥

Again, when there is a conflict between two *Smritis*, the Manu-Smriti must prevail, but no attempt is to be made to find out which of the two accords with reason. This is the ruling given by Brihaspati (Saµskårakåya 13):

वेदायत्वोपनिबंधृत्वत् प्रमाण्यं हि मनोः स्मृतं।
मन्वर्थविपरीता तु या स्मृतिः सा न शस्यते॥

It is, therefore, clear that in any matter on which the *Shrutis* and *Smritis* have given a positive direction, a Hindu is not free to use his reasoning faculty. The same rule is laid down in the Mahabharat (Abvamedhika Pasvan 14):

पुराणं मानवो धर्मः सांगो वेदश्चिकित्सितं।
आज्ञासिद्धानि चत्वारि न हन्तव्यानि हेतुभिः॥

He must abide by their directions. The caste and *Varna* are matters, which are dealt with by the *Vedas* and the *Smritis* and consequently, appeal to reason can have no effect on a Hindu. So far as caste and *Varna* are concerned, not only do the *Shastras* do not permit the Hindu to use his reason in the decision of the question, but they have taken care to see that no occasion is left to examine in a rational way the foundations of his belief in caste and *Varna*. It must be a source of silent amusement to many a non-Hindu to find hundreds and thousands of Hindus breaking caste on certain occasions, such as railway journeys and foreign travel and yet endeavouring to maintain caste for the rest of their lives! The explanation of this phenomenon discloses another fetter on the reasoning faculties of the Hindus. Man's life is generally habitual and unreflective. Reflective thought, in the sense of active, persistent and careful consideration of any belief or supposed form or knowledge in the light of the grounds that support it and further conclusions to which it tends, is quite rare and arises only in a situation which presents a dilemma – a crisis. Railway journeys and foreign travels are really occasions of crisis in the life of a Hindu and it is natural to expect a Hindu to ask himself why he should maintain caste at all, if he cannot maintain it at all times. But he does not. He breaks caste at one step and proceeds to observe it at the next without raising any question. The reason for this astonishing conduct is to be found in the rule of the *Shastras*, which directs him to maintain caste as far as possible and to undergo *prayaschitta* when he cannot. By this theory of *prayaschitta*, the *Shastras* by following a spirit of compromise have given caste a perpetual lease of life and have smothered reflective thought which would have otherwise led to the destruction of the notion of caste.

There have been many who have worked in the cause of the abolition of caste and untouchability. Of those, who can be mentioned, Ramanuja, Kabir and others stand out prominently. Can you appeal to the acts of these reformers and exhort the Hindus to follow them? It is true that Manu has included *Sadachar* (सदाचार) as one of the sanctions along with *Shruti* and *Smriti*. Indeed, *Sadachar* has been given a higher place than *Shastras* (Kåtyåyana Smriti 37):

यद्यद्वाचर्यते येन धर्म्यं वाऽधर्म्यमेव वा।
देशस्याचरणं नित्यं चरित्रं तद्धिकीर्तितम्॥

According to this, *Sadachar*, whether, it is धर्म्य or अधर्म्य in accordance with *Shastras* or contrary to *Shastras*, must be followed. But what is the meaning of *Sadachar*? If anyone were to suppose that *Sadachar* means right or good acts *i. e.* acts of good and righteous men he would find himself greatly mistaken. *Sadachar* does not mean good acts or acts of good men. It means ancient custom *good* or *bad*. The following verse (Månavadharmabåstra 2.18) makes this clear:

यस्मिन् देशे य आचारः पारंपर्यक्रमागतः।
वर्णानां किल सर्वेषां स सदाचार उच्यते॥

As though to warn people against the view that *Sadachar* means good acts or acts of good men and fearing that people might understand it that way and follow the acts of good men, the *Smritis* have commanded the Hindus in unmistakable terms not to follow even Gods in their good deeds, if they are contrary to *Shruti, Smriti* and *Sadachar*. This may sound to be most extraordinary, most perverse, but the fact remains that न देवचरितं चरेत् is an injunction, issued to the Hindus by their *Shastras*. Reason and morality are the two most powerful weapons in the armoury of a reformer. To deprive him of the use of these weapons is to disable him for action. How are you going to break up caste, if people are not free to consider whether it accords with reason? How are you going to break up caste if people are not free to consider whether it accords with morality? The wall built around caste is impregnable and the material, of which it is built, contains none of the combustible stuff of reason and morality. Add to this the fact that inside this wall stands the army of Brahmins, who form the intellectual class, Brahmins who are the natural leaders of the Hindus, Brahmins who are there not as mere mercenary soldiers but as an army fighting for its homeland and you will get an idea why I think that breaking-up of caste amongst the Hindus is well-nigh impossible. At any rate, it would take ages before a breach is made. But whether the doing of the deed takes time or whether it can be done quickly, you must not forget that if you wish to bring about a breach in the system then you have got to apply the dynamite to the *Vedas* and the *Shastras*, which deny any part to reason, to *Vedas* and *Shastras*, which deny any part to morality. You must destroy the religion of the *Shrutis* and the *Smritis*. Nothing else will avail. This is my considered view of the matter.

XX

Some may not understand what I mean by destruction of religion; some may find the idea revolting to them and some may find it revolutionary. Let me therefore explain my position. I do not know whether you draw a distinction between principles and rules. But I do. Not only I make a distinction but I say that this distinction is real and important. Rules are practical; they are habitual ways of doing things according to prescription. But principles are intellectual; they are useful methods of judging things. Rules seek to tell an agent just what course of action to pursue. Principles do not prescribe a specific course of action. Rules, like cooking recipes, do tell just what to do and how to do it. A principle, such as that of justice, supplies a main head by reference to which he is to consider the bearings of his desires and purposes, it guides him in his thinking by suggesting to him the important consideration which he should bear in mind. This difference between rules and principles makes the acts done in pursuit of them different in quality and in content. Doing what is said to be good by virtue of a rule and doing good in the light of a principle are two different things. The principle may be wrong but the act is conscious and responsible. The rule may be right but the act is mechanical. A religious act may not be a correct act but must at least be a responsible act. To permit of this responsibility, religion must mainly be a matter of principles only. It cannot be a matter of rules. The moment it degenerates into rules it ceases to be Religion, as it kills responsibility which is the essence of a truly religious act. What is this Hindu religion? Is it a set of principles or is it a code of rules? Now the Hindu religion, as contained in the *Vedas* and the *Smritis*, is nothing but a mass of sacrificial, social, political and sanitary rules and regulations, all mixed up. What is called religion by the Hindus is nothing but a multitude of commands and prohibitions. Religion, in the sense of spiritual principles, truly universal, applicable to all races, to all countries, to all times, is not to be found in them, and if it is, it does not form the governing part of a Hindus's life. That for a Hindu, Dharma means commands and prohibitions is clear from the way the word Dharma is used in *Vedas* and the *Smritis* and understood by the commentators. The word Dharma as used in the Vedas in most cases means religious ordinances or rites. Even Jaimini in his Purva-Mimansa defines Dharma as 'a desirable goal or result that is indicated by injunctive (*Vedic*) passage'. To put it in plain language, what the Hindus call religion is really Law or at best legalized class-ethics. Frankly, I refuse to call this code of ordinances, as religion. The first evil of such a code of ordinances, misrepresented to the people as religion, is that it tends to deprive moral life of freedom and spontaneity and to reduce it (for the conscientious at any rate) to a more or less anxious and servile conformity to externally imposed rules. Under it, there is no loyalty to ideals, there is only conformity to commands. But the worst evil of this code of ordinances is that the laws it contains must be the same yesterday, today and forever. They are iniquitous in that they are not the same for one class as for another. But this iniquity is made perpetual in that they are prescribed to be the same for all generations. The objectionable part of such a scheme is not that they are made by certain persons called Prophets or Law-givers. The objectionable part is that this code has been invested with the character of finality and fixity. Happiness notoriously varies with the conditions and circumstances of a person, as well as with the conditions and circumstances of a person, as well as with the conditions of different people and epochs. That being the case, how can humanity endure this code of eternal laws, without being cramped and without being crippled? I have, therefore, no hesitation in saying that such a religion must be destroyed and I say, there is nothing irreligious in working for the destruction of such a religion. Indeed I hold that it is your bounden duty to tear the mask, to remove the misrepresentation that is caused by misnaming this law as religion. This is an essential step for you. Once you clear the minds of the people of this misconception and enable them to realize that what they are told as religion is not religion but that it is really law, you will be in a position to urge for its amendment or abolition. So long as people look upon it as religion they will not be ready for a change, because the idea of religion is generally speaking not associated with the idea of change. But the idea of law is associated with the idea of change and when people come to know that what is called religion is really law, old and archaic, they will be ready for a change, for people know and accept that law can be changed.

XXI

While I condemn a Religion of Rules, I must not be understood to hold the opinion that there is no necessity for a religion. On the contrary, I agree with Burke when he says that 'True religion is the foundation of society, the basis on which all true Civil Government rests, and both their sanction.' Consequently, when I urge that these ancient rules of life be annulled, I am anxious that its place shall be taken by a Religion of Principles, which alone can lay claim to being a true religion. Indeed, I am so convinced of the necessity of religion that I feel I ought to tell you in outline what I regard as necessary items in this religious reform. The following in my opinion should be the cardinal items in this reform: (1) There should be one and only one standard book of Hindu religion, acceptable to all Hindus and recognized by all Hindus. This of course means that all other books of Hindu religion such as *Vedas, Shastras* and *Puranas*, which are treated as sacred and authoritative, must by law cease to be so and the preaching of any doctrine, religious or social contained in these books should be penalized. (2) It should be better if priesthood among Hindus was abolished. But as this seems to be impossible, the priesthood must at least cease to be hereditary. Every person who professes to be a Hindu must be eligible for being a priest. It should be provided by law that no Hindu shall be entitled to be a priest unless he has passed an examination prescribed by the state and holds a *sanad* from the state permitting him to practise. (3) No ceremony performed by a priest who does not hold a *sanad* shall be deemed to be valid in law and it should be made penal for a person who has no *sanad* to officiate as a priest. (4) A priest should be the servant of the state and should be subject to the disciplinary action by the state in the matter of his morals, beliefs and worship, in addition to his being subject along with other citizens to the ordinary law of the land. (5) The number of priests should be limited by law according to the requirements of the state as is done in the case of the I.C.S. To some, this may sound radical. But to my mind there is nothing revolutionary in this. Every profession in India is regulated. Engineers must show proficiency, doctors must show proficiency, lawyers must show proficiency, before they are allowed to practise their professions. During the whole of their career, they must not only obey the law of the land, civil as well as criminal, but they must also obey the special code of morals prescribed by their respective professions. The priest's is the only profession where proficiency is not required. The profession of a Hindu priest is the only profession which is not subject to any code. Mentally a priest may be an idiot, physically a priest may be suffering from a foul disease, such as syphilis or gonorrhea, morally he may be a wreck. But he is fit to officiate at solemn ceremonies, to enter the *sanctum sanctorum* of a Hindu temple and worship the Hindu God. All this becomes possible among the Hindus because for a priest it is enough to be born in a priestly caste. The whole thing is abominable and is due to the fact that the priestly class among Hindus is subject neither to law nor to morality. It recognizes no duties. It knows only of rights and privileges. It is a pest which divinity seems to have let loose on the masses for their mental and moral degradation. The priestly class must be brought under control by some such legislation as I have outlined above. It will prevent it from doing mischief and from misguiding people. It will democratize it by throwing it open to every one. It will certainly help to kill the Brahminism and will also help to kill caste, which is nothing but Brahminism incarnate. Brahminism is the poison which has spoiled Hinduism. You will succeed in saving Hinduism if you will kill Brahminism. There should be no opposition to this reform from any quarter. It should be welcomed even by the Arya Samajists, because this is merely an application of their own doctrine of *guna-karma*.

Whether you do that or you do not, you must give a new doctrinal basis to your religion – a basis that will be in consonance with Liberty, Equality and Fraternity, in short, with Democracy. I am no authority on the subject. But I am told that for such religious principles as will be in consonance with Liberty, Equality and Fraternity it may not be necessary for you to borrow from foreign sources and that you could draw for such principles on the *Upanishads*. Whether you could do so without a complete remoulding, a considerable scraping and chipping off the ore they contain, is more than I can say. This means a complete change in the fundamental notions of life. It means a complete change in the values of life. It means a complete change in outlook and in attitude towards men and things. It means conversion; but if you do not like the word, I will say, it means new life. But a new life cannot enter a body that is dead. New life can enter only in a new body. The old body must die before a new body can come into existence and a new life can enter into it. To put it simply, the old must cease to be operative before the new can begin to enliven and to pulsate. This is what I meant when I said you must discard the authority of the *Shastras* and destroy the religion of the *Shastras*.

XXII

I have kept you too long. It is time I brought this address to a close. This would have been a convenient point for me to have stopped. But this would probably be my last address to a Hindu audience on a subject vitally concerning the Hindus. I would therefore like, before I close, to place before the Hindus, if they will allow me, some questions which I regard as vital and invite them seriously to consider the same.

In the first place, the Hindus must consider whether it is sufficient to take the placid view of the anthropologist that there is nothing to be said about the beliefs, habits, morals and outlooks on life, which obtain among the different peoples of the world except that they often differ; or whether it is not necessary to make an attempt to find out what kind of morality, beliefs, habits and outlook have worked best and have enabled those who possessed them to flourish, to go strong, to people the earth and to have dominion over it. As is observed by Professor Carver,

> Morality and religion, as the organized expression of moral approval and disapproval, must be regarded as factors in the struggle for existence as truly as are weapons for offence and defence, teeth and claws, horns and hoofs, furs and feathers. The social group, community, tribe or nation, which develops an unworkable scheme of morality or within which those social acts which weaken it and make it unfit it for survival, habitually create the sentiment of approval, while those which would strengthen and enable it to be expanded habitually create the sentiment of disapproval, will eventually be eliminated. It is its habits of approval or disapproval (these are the results of religion and morality) that handicap it, as really as the possession of two wings on one side with none on the other will handicap the colony of flies. It would be as futile in the one case as in the other to argue, that one system is just as good as another.

Morality and religion, therefore, are not mere matters of likes and dislikes. You may dislike exceedingly a scheme of morality, which, if universally practised within a nation, would make that nation the strongest nation on the face of the earth. Yet in spite of your dislike such a nation will become strong. You may like exceedingly a scheme of morality and an ideal of justice, which if universally practised within a nation, would make it unable to hold its own in the struggle with other nations. Yet in spite of your admiration this nation will eventuality disappear. The Hindus must, therefore, examine their religion and their morality in terms of their survival value.

Secondly, the Hindus must consider whether they should conserve the whole of their social heritage or select what is helpful and transmit to future generations only that much and not more. Professor John Dewey, who was my teacher and to whom I owe so much, has said:

> Every society gets encumbered with what is trivial, with dead wood from the past, and with what is positively perverse.... As a society becomes more enlightened, it realizes that it is responsible *not* to conserve and transmit the whole of its existing achievements, but only such as make for a better future society.

Even Burke, in spite of the vehemence with which he opposed the principle of change embodied in the French Revolution, was compelled to admit that

> A state without the means of some change is without the means of its conservation. Without such means it might even risk the loss of that part of the constitution which it wished the most religiously to preserve.

What Burke said of a state applies equally to a society.

Thirdly, the Hindus must consider whether they must not cease to worship the past as supplying its ideals. The baneful effect of this worship of the past are best summed up by Professor Dewey when he says:

> An individual can live only in the present. The present is not just something which comes after the past; much less something produced by it. It is what life is in leaving the past behind it. The study of past products will not help us to understand the present. A knowledge of the past and its heritage is of great significance when it enters into the present, but not otherwise. And the mistake of making the records and remains of the past the main material of education is that it tends to make the past a rival of the present and the present a more or less futile imitation of the past.

The principle, which makes little of the present act of living and growing, naturally looks upon the present as empty and upon the future as remote. Such a principle is inimical to progress and is an hindrance to a strong and a steady current of life.

Fourthly, the Hindus must consider whether the time has not come for them to recognize that there is nothing fixed, nothing eternal, nothing *sanatan*; that everything is changing, that change is the law of life for individuals as well as for society. In a changing society, there must be a constant revolution of old values and the Hindus must realize that if there must be standards to measure the acts of men there must also be a readiness to revise those standards.

XXIII

I have to confess that this address has become too lengthy. Whether this fault is compensated to any extent by breadth or depth is a matter for you to judge. All I claim is to have told you candidly my views. I have little to recommend them but some study and a deep concern in your destiny. If you will allow me to say, these views are the views of a man, who has been no tool of power, no flatterer of greatness. They come from one, almost the whole of whose public exertion has been one continuous struggle for liberty for the poor and for the oppressed and whose only reward has been a continuous shower of calumny and abuse from national journals and national leaders, for no other reason except that I refuse to join with them in performing the miracle – I will not say trick – of liberating the oppressed with the gold of the tyrant and raising the poor with the cash of the rich. All this may not be enough to commend my views. I think they are not likely to alter yours. But whether they do or do not, the responsibility is entirely yours. You must make your efforts to uproot caste, if not in my way, then in your way. I am sorry, I will not be with you. I have decided to change. This is not the place for giving reasons. But even when I am gone out of your fold, I will watch your movement with active sympathy and you will have my assistance for what it may be worth. Yours is a national cause. Caste is no doubt primarily the breath of the Hindus. But the Hindus have fouled the air all over and everybody is infected, Sikh, Muslim and Christian. You, therefore, deserve the support of all those who are suffering from this infection, Sikh, Muslim and Charistian. Yours is more difficult than the other national cause, namely Swaraj. In the fight for Swaraj you fight with the whole nation on your side. In this, you have to fight against the whole nation and that too, your own. But it is more important than Swaraj. There is no use having Swaraj, if you cannot defend it. More important than the question of defending Swaraj is the question of defending the Hindus under the Swaraj. In my opinion only when the Hindu society becomes a casteless society that it can hope to have strength enough to defend itself. Without such internal strength, Swaraj of Hindus may turn out to be only a step towards slavery. Good-bye and good wishes for your success.

Chapter 13

The Hindu Marriage Act, 1955

The Hindu Marriage Act (HMA) is an anomaly, given that Indian has, in theory, attempted to become a secular democracy. The HMA is part of a larger objective that began with British attempts to codify Hindu law so that they could more easily rule the many communities that were artificially united to form India. British colonial rulers hesitated to do away with indigenous laws and, in the process, sought to codify the diverse laws that already existed. This, combined with an attempt to reform Hindu practices concerning widowhood, child marriage, and the like, led to the Sati Regulation Act of 1828, the Hindu Widows' Remarriage Act of 1856, the Age of Consent Act of 1860, the Prohibition of Female Infanticide Act of 1872, and the Anand Marriage Act of 1909, among others. When India became independent in 1947, lawmakers used the British laws to further modernize and to seek unity in diversity as a way of nation building.[1]

For these reasons, the Hindu Marriage Act of 1955 is a document that sheds light on the complexities involved in unifying an otherwise diverse set of beliefs and practices under the rubric "Hindu." Such characterizations of "Hinduism" can be related to the development of Hindu political nationalism as exemplified in Vinayak Damodar Savarkar's Hindutva ideology.

The Act in its entirety is included here. Section 2 of the Act, "The Application of Act" is noteworthy as it includes Buddhist, Jains, and Sikhs in its definition of "Hindu." Also noteworthy is its characterization of the Hindu marriage ceremony in Section 7. Such taxonomies and depictions are deeply intertwined to methodological issues concerning the origins and definitions of the term "Hindu" though in these cases, governmental, rather than religious, institutions are addressing the matter.

Note

1 Werner Menski, *Hindu Law: Beyond Tradition and Modernity.* Oxford: Oxford University Press, 2003, p. 293.

Further reading

Baird, Robert D. (ed.), *Religion and Law in Independent India.* New Delhi: Manohar, 2005.

Basu, Monmayee, *Hindu Women and Marriage Law: From Sacrament to Contract.* Oxford: Oxford University Press, 2001.

Deasai, Satyajeet, *Mulla: Principles of Hindu Law.* New Delhi: LexisNexis, 2004.

Diwan, Paras, *Modern Hindu Law.* Faridabad (Harayana): Allahabad Law Agency, 2005.

Menski, Werner, *Hindu Law: Beyond Tradition and Modernity.* Oxford: Oxford University Press, 2003.

Pennington, Brian K., *Was Hinduism Invented? Britons, Indians, and the Colonial Construction of Religion.* New York: Oxford University Press, 2005.

von Stietencron, Heinrich, "Hinduism: On the Proper Use of a Deceptive Term" in G. Sontheimer and H. Kulke (eds.), *Hinduism Reconsidered*, Delhi: Manohar, 2001, pp. 32–53.

The Hindu Marriage Act, 1955

(Act 25 of 1955) [18th May, 1955]

An Act to amend and codify the law relating to marriage among Hindus.

Preliminary

1. Short title and extent –

(1) This Act may be called the Hindu Marriage Act, 1955.
(2) It extends to the whole of India except the State of Jammu and Kashmir, and applies also to Hindus domiciled in the territories to which this Act extends who are outside the said territories.

2. Application of Act –

(1) This Act applies, –
  (a) to any person who is a Hindu by religion in any of its forms or developments, including a Virashaiva, a Lingayat or a follower of the Brahmo, Prarthana or Arya Samaj;
  (b) to any person who is a Buddhist, Jaina or Sikh by religion, and
  (c) to any other person domiciled in the territories to which this Act extends who is not a Muslim, Christian, Parsi or Jew by religion, unless it is proved that any such person would not have been governed by the Hindu law or by any custom or usage as part of that law in respect of any of the matters dealt with herein if this Act had not been passed.

Explanation – The following persons are Hindus, Buddhists, Jainas or Sikhs by religion, as the case may be, –

  (a) any child, legitimate or illegitimate, both of whose parents are Hindus, Buddhists, Jainas or Sikhs by religion;
  (b) any child, legitimate or illegitimate, one of whose parents is a Hindu, Buddhist, Jaina or Sikh by religion and who is brought up as a member of tribe, community, group or family to which such parents belongs or belonged; and
  (c) any person who is a convert or reconvert to the Hindus, Buddhist, Jaina or Sikh religion.

(2) Notwithstanding anything contained in sub-section (1), nothing contained in this Act shall apply to the members of any Scheduled Tribe within the meaning of clause (25) of Article 366 of the Constitution unless the Central Government, by notification in the Official Gazette, otherwise directs.
(3) The expression "Hindus" in any portion of this Act shall be construed as if it included a person who, though not a Hindu by religion is, nevertheless, a person whom this Act applies by virtue of the provisions contained in this section.

3. Definitions – In this Act, unless the context otherwise requires, –

  (a) the expression "custom" and "usage" signify any rule which, having been continuously and uniformally observed for a long time, has obtained the force of law among Hindus in any local area, tribe, community, group or family:
   Provided that the rule is certain and not unreasonable or opposed to public policy; and
   Provided further that in the case of a rule applicable only to a family it has not been discontinued by the family;
  (b) "District Court" means, in any area for which there is a City Civil Court, that Court, and in any other area the principal Civil Court of original jurisdiction, and includes any other civil court which may be specified by the State Government, by notification in the Official Gazette, as

having jurisdiction in respect of matters dealt with in this Act;

(c) "full blood" and "half blood" – two persons are said to be related to each other by full blood when they are descended from a common ancestor by the same wife and by half blood when they are descended from a common ancestor but by different wives;

(d) "uterine blood" – two persons are said to be related to each other by uterine blood when they are descended from a common ancestor but by different husbands.

Explanation. – In Clauses (c) and (d) "ancestor" includes the father and "ancestress" the mother;

(e) "prescribed" means prescribed by rules made under this Act;

(f) (i) "Sapinda relationship" with reference to any person extends as far as the third generation (inclusive) in the line of ascent through the mother, and the fifth (inclusive) in the line of ascent through the father, the line being traced upwards in each case from the person concerned, who is to be counted as the first generation;

(ii) two persons are said to be "sapinda" of each other if one is a lineal ascendant of the other within the limits of sapinda relationship, or if they have a common lineal ascendant who is within the limits of sapinda relationship with reference to each of them;

(g) "degrees of prohibited relationship" – two persons are said to be within the "degrees of prohibited relationship" –

(i) if one is a lineal ascendant of the other; or

(ii) if one was the wife or husband of a lineal ascendant or descendant of the other; or

(iii) if one was the wife of the brother or of the father's or mother's brother or of the grandfather's or grandmother's brother or the other; or

(iv) if the two are brother and sister, uncle and niece, aunt and nephew, or children of brother and sister or of two brothers or of two sisters.

Explanation – for the purposes of clauses (f) and (g) relationship includes –

(i) relationship by half or uterine blood as well as by full blood;

(ii) illegitimate blood relationship as well as legitimate;

(iii) relationship by adoption as well as by blood; and all terms of relationship in those clauses shall be construed accordingly.

4. Overriding effect of Act – Save as otherwise expressly provided in this Act –

(a) any text, rule or interpretation of Hindu Law or any custom or usage as part of that law in force immediately before the commencement of this Act shall cease to have effect with respect to any matter for which provision is made in this Act;

(b) any other law in force immediately before the commencement of this Act shall cease to have effect in so far as it is inconsistent with any of the provisions contained in this Act.

Hindu Marriages

5. Condition for a Hindu Marriage – A marriage may be solemnized between any two Hindus, if the following conditions are fulfilled, namely:

(i) neither party has a spouse living at the time of the marriage;

(ii) at the time of the marriage, neither party, –

(a) is incapable of giving a valid consent of it in consequence of unsoundness of mind; or
(b) though capable of giving a valid consent has been suffering from mental disorder of such a kind or to such an extent as to be unfit for marriage and the procreation of children; or
(c) has been subject to recurrent attacks of insanity or epilepsy;

(iii) the bridegroom has completed the age of twenty one years and the bride the age of eighteen years at the time of the marriage;
(iv) the parties are not within the degrees of prohibited relationship unless the custom or usage governing each of them permits of a marriage between the two;
(v) the parties are not sapindas of each other, unless the custom or usage governing each of them permits of a marriage between the two;
(vi) (Omitted)

6. Guardianship in Marriage – (Omitted by Marriage Laws (Amendment) Act, 1976.

7. Ceremonies for a Hindu marriage –

(1) A Hindu marriage may be solemnized in accordance with the customary rites and ceremonies of either party thereto.
(2) Where such rites and ceremonies include the saptapadi (that is, the taking of seven steps by the bridegroom and the bride jointly before the sacred fire), the marriage becomes complete and binding when the seventh step is taken.

8. Registration of Hindu Marriages –

(1) For the purpose of facilitating the proof of Hindu marriages, the State Government may make rules providing that the parties to any such marriage may have the particulars relating to their marriage entered in such manner and subject to such condition as may be prescribed in a Hindu Marriage Register kept for the purpose.
(2) Notwithstanding anything contained in sub-section (1), the State Government may, if it is of opinion that it is necessary or expedient so to do, provide that the entering of the particulars referred to in sub-section (1) shall be compulsory in the State or in any part thereof, whether in all cases or in such cases as may be specified and where any such direction has been issued, and person contravening any rule made in this behalf shall be punishable with fine which may extend to twenty-five rupees.
(3) All rules made under this section shall be laid before the State Legislature, as soon as may be, after they are made.
(4) The Hindu Marriage Register shall at all reasonable times be open for inspection, and shall be admissible as evidence of the statements therein contained and certified extracts therefrom shall, on application, be given by the Registrar on payment to him of the prescribed fee.
(5) Notwithstanding anything contained in this section, the validity of any Hindu marriage shall in no way be affected by the omission to make the entry.

Restitution of Conjugal rights and judicial separation

9. Restitution of conjugal rights – When either the husband or the wife has, without reasonable excuse, withdrawn from the society of the other, the aggrieved party may apply, by petition to the district court, for restitution of conjugal rights and the court, on being satisfied of the truth of the statements made in such petition and that there is no legal ground why the application should not be granted, may decree restitution of conjugal rights accordingly.

Explanation – Where a question arises whether there has been reasonable excuse for withdrawal from the society, the burden of proving reasonable excuse shall be on the person who has withdrawn from the society.

10. Judicial separation –

(1) Either party to a marriage, whether solemnized before or after the commencement of this Act, may present a petition praying for a decree for judicial separation on any of the grounds specified in sub-section (1) of Section 13, and in the case of a wife also on any of the grounds might have been presented.

(2) Where a decree for judicial separation has been passed, it shall no longer be obligatory for the petitioner to cohabit with the respondent, but the court may, on the application by petition of either party and on being satisfied of the truth of the statement made in such petition, rescind the decree if it considers it just and reasonable to do so.

Nullity of Marriage and Divorce

11. Nullity of marriage and divorce – Void marriages. – Any marriage solemnized after the commencement of this Act shall be null and void and may, on a petition presented by either party thereto, against the other party be so declared by a decree of nullity if it contravenes any one of the conditions specified in clauses (i), (iv) and (v), Section 5.

12. Voidable Marriages –

(1) Any marriage solemnized, whether before or after the commencement of this Act, shall be voidable and may be annulled by a decree of nullity on any of the following grounds, namely: –
  (a) that the marriage has not been consummated owing to the impotency of the respondent; or
  (b) that the marriage is in contravention of the condition specified in clause (ii) of Section 5; or
  (c) that the consent of the petitioner, or where the consent of the guardian in marriage of the petitioner was required under Section 5 as it stood immediately before the commencement of the Child Marriage Restraint (Amendment) Act, 1978, the consent of such guardian was obtained by force or by fraud as to the nature of the ceremony or as to any material fact or circumstance concerning the respondent; or
  (d) that the respondent was at the time of the marriage pregnant by some person other than the petitioner.

(2) Notwithstanding anything contained in sub-section (1), no petition for annulling a marriage –
  (a) on the ground specified in clause (c) of sub-section (1) shall be entertained if –
    (i) the petition is presented more than one year after the force had ceased to operate or, as the case may be, the fraud had been discovered; or
    (ii) the petitioner has, with his or her full consent, lived with the other party to the marriage as husband or wife after the force had ceased to operate or, as the case may be, the fraud had been discovered;
  (b) on the ground specified in clause (d) of sub-section (1) shall be entertained unless the court is satisfied –
    (i) that the petitioner was at the time of the marriage ignorant of the facts alleged;
    (ii) that proceedings have been instituted in the case of a marriage solemnized before the commencement of this Act within one year of such commencement and in the case of marriages solemnized after such commencement

within one year from the date of the marriage; and

(iii) that marital intercourse with the consent of the petitioner has not taken place since the discovery by the petitioner of the existence of the said ground.

13. Divorce –

(1) Any marriage solemnized, whether before or after the commencement of the Act, may, on a petition presented by either the husband or the wife, be dissolved by a decree of divorce on the ground that the other party –

(i) has, after the solemnization of the marriage had voluntary sexual intercourse with any person other than his or her spouse; or

(ia) has, after the solemnization of the marriage, treated the petitioner with cruelty; or

(ib) has deserted the petitioner for a continuous period of not less than two years immediately preceding the presentation of the petition; or

(ii) has ceased to be a Hindu by conversion to another religion; or

(iii) has been incurably of unsound mind, or has suffering continuously or intermittently from mental disorder of such a kind and to such an extent that the petitioner cannot reasonably be expected to live with the respondent.

Explanation – In this clause –

(a) the expression "mental disorder" means mental illness, arrested or incomplete development of mind, psychopathic disorder or any other disorder or disability of mind and include schizophrenia;

(b) the expression "psychopathic disorder" means a persistent disorder or disability of mind (whether or not including sub-normality of intelligence) which results in abnormally aggressive or seriously irresponsible conduct on the part of the other party and whether or not it requires or is susceptible to medical treatment; or

(iv) has been suffering from a virulent and incurable form of leprosy; or

(v) has been suffering from veneral disease in a communicable form; or

(vi) has renounced the world by entering any religious order; or

(vii) has not been heard of as being alive for a period of seven years or more by those persons who would naturally have heard of it, had that party been alive;

Explanation – In this sub-section, the expression "desertion" means the desertion of the petitioner by the other party to the marriage without reasonable cause and without the consent or against the wish of such party, and includes the willful neglect of the petitioner by the other party to the marriage, and its grammatical variations and cognate expression shall be construed accordingly.

(1-A) Either party to a marriage, whether solemnized before or after the commencement of this Act, may also present a petition for the dissolution of the marriage by a decree of divorce on the ground –

(i) that there has been no resumption of cohabitation as between the parties to the marriage for a period of one year or upwards after the passing of a decree for judicial separation in a proceeding to which they were parties; or

(ii) that there has been no restitution of conjugal rights as between the parties to the marriage for a period of one year or upward after the passing of a decree of restitution of conjugal rights in a proceeding to which they were parties.

(2) A wife may also present a petition for the dissolution of her marriage by a decree of divorce on the ground –

(i) in the case of any marriage solemnized before the commencement of this Act, that the husband had married again before the commencement or that any other wife of the husband married before such commencement was alive at the time of the solemnization of the marriage of the petitioner:

Provided that in either case the other wife is alive at the time of the presentation of the petition;

(ii) that the husband has, since the solemnization of the marriage, been guilty of rape, sodomy or bestiality; or

(iii) that in a suit under Section 18 of the Hindu Adoptions and Maintenance Act, (78 of 1956), or in a proceeding under Section 125 of the Code of Criminal Procedure, 1973, (Act 2 of 1974) or under corresponding Section 488 of the Code of Criminal Procedure, (5 of 1898), a decree or order, as the case may be, has been passed against the husband awarding maintenance to the wife notwithstanding that she was living apart and that since the passing of such decree or order, cohabitation between the parties has not been resumed for one year or upwards; or

(iv) that her marriage (whether consummated or not) was solemnized before she attained the age of fifteen years and she has repudiated the marriage after attaining that age but before attaining the age of eighteen years.

Explanation – This clause applies whether the marriage was solemnized before or after the commencement of the Marriage Law (Amendment) Act, 1976.

13-A. Alternate Relief in Divorce Proceedings – If any proceeding under this Act, on a petition for dissolution of marriage by a decree of divorce, except in so far as the petition is founded on the grounds mentioned in clauses (ii), (vi) and (vii) of sub-section (1) of Section 13, the court may, if it considers it just so to do having regard to the circumstances of the case, pass instead a decree for judicial separation.

13-B. Divorce by mutual consent –

(1) Subject to the provisions of this Act a petition for dissolution of marriage by a decree of divorce may be presented to the District Court by both the parties to a marriage together, whether such marriage was solemnized before or after the commencement of the Marriage Laws (Amendment) Act, 1976, on the ground that they have been living separately for a period of one year or more, that they have not been able to live together and that they have mutually agreed that the marriage should be dissolved.

(2) On the motion of both the parties made earlier than six months after the date of the presentation of the petition referred to in sub-section (1) and not later than eighteen months after the said date, if the petition is not withdrawn in the mean time, the Court shall, on being satisfied, after hearing the parties and after making such inquiry as it thinks fit, that a marriage has been solemnized and that the averments in the petition are true, pass a decree of divorce declaring the marriage to be dissolved with effect from the date of the decree.

14. No petition for divorce to be presented within one year of marriage –

(1) Notwithstanding anything contained in this Act, it shall not be competent for any Court to entertain any petition for

dissolution of marriage by a decree of divorce, unless at the date of the presentation of the petition one year has elapsed since the date of the marriage:

Provided that the court may, upon application made to it in accordance with such rules as may be made by the High Court in that behalf, allow a petition to be presented before one year has elapsed since the date of the marriage on the ground that the case is one of exceptional hardship to the petitioner or of exceptional depravity on the part of the respondent, but, if it appears to the court at the hearing of the petition that petitioner obtained leave to present the petition by any misrepresentation or concealment of the nature of the case, the court may, if it pronounces a decree, do so subject to the condition that the decree shall not have effect until after the expiry of one year from the date of the marriage or may dismiss the petition without prejudice to any petition which may be brought after the expiration of the said one year upon the same or substantially the same facts as those alleged in support of the petition so dismissed.

(2) In disposing of any application under this section for leave to present a petition for divorce before the expiration of one year from the date of the marriage, the court shall have regard to the interests of any children of the marriage and to the question whether there is a reasonable probability of a reconciliation between the parties before the expiration of the said one year.

15. Divorced persons. When may marry again – When a marriage has been dissolved by a decree of divorce and either there is no right of appeal against the decree or, if there is such a right of appeal, the time for appealing has expired without an appeal having been presented, or an appeal has been presented but has been dismissed, it shall be lawful for either party to the marriage to marry again.

16. Legitimacy of children of void and voidable marriages –

(1) Notwithstanding that a marriage is null and void under Section 11, any child of such marriage who would have been legitimate if the marriage had been valid, shall be legitimate, whether such a child is born before or after the commencement of the Marriage Laws (Amendment) Act, 1976, and whether or not a decree of nullity is granted in respect of the marriage under this Act and whether or not the marriage is held to be void otherwise than on a petition under this Act.

(2) Where a decree of nullity is granted in respect of a voidable marriage under Section 12, any child begotten or conceived before the decree is made, who would have been the legitimate child of the parties to the marriage if at the date of the decree it had been dissolved instead of being annulled, shall be deemed to be their legitimate child notwithstanding the decree of nullity.

(3) Nothing contained in sub-section (1) or sub-section (2) shall be construed as conferring upon any child of a marriage which is null and void or which is annulled by a decree of nullity under Section 12, any rights in or to the property of any person, other than the parents, in any case, where, but for the passing of this Act, such child would have been incapable of possessing or acquiring any such rights by reason of his not being the legitimate child of his parents.

17. Punishment of Bigamy – Any marriage between two Hindus solemnized after the commencement of this Act is void if at the date of such marriage either party had a husband or wife living; and the provisions of Sections 494 and 495 of the Indian Penal Code (45 of 1860) shall apply accordingly.

18. Punishment for contravention of certain other conditions for a Hindu marriage – Every person who procures a marriage of himself or herself or to be solemnized under this Act in contravention of the conditions specified in clauses (iii), (iv), and (v) of Section 5 shall be punishable –

(a) in the case of a contravention of the condition specified in clause (iii) of Section 5, with simple imprisonment which may extend to fifteen days, or with fine which may extend to one thousand rupees, or with both;
(b) in the case of a contravention of the condition specified in clause (iv) or clause (v) of Section 5, with simple imprisonment which may extend to one month, or with fine which may extend to one thousand rupees, or with both;
(c) Clause (c) omitted by Act 2 of 1978.

Jurisdiction and Procedure

19. Court to which petition shall be presented – Every petition under this Act shall be presented to the District Court within the local limits of whose ordinary original civil jurisdiction:

(i) the marriage was solemnized, or
(ii) the respondent, at the time of the presentation of the petition, resides, or
(iii) the parties to the marriage last resided together, or
(iv) the petitioner is residing at the time of the presentation of the petition, in a case where the respondent is at that time, residing outside the territories to which this Act extends, or has not been heard of as being alive for a period of seven years or more by those persons who would naturally have heard of him if he were alive.

20. Contents and verification of Petitions –

(1) Every petition presented under this Act shall state as distinctly as the nature of the case permits the facts on which the claims to relief is founded and, except in a petition under Section 11, shall also state that there is no collusion between the petitioner and the other party to the marriage.
(2) The statements contained in every petition under this Act shall be verified by the petitioner or some other competent person in the manner required by law for the verification of plaints, and may, at the hearing, be referred to as evidence.

21. Application of Act 5 of 1908 – Subject to the other provisions contained in this Act and to such rules as the High Court may make in this behalf all proceedings under this Act shall be regulated, as far as may be, by the Code of Civil Procedure, 1908.

21-A. Power to transfer petitions in certain cases –

(1) Where –
    (a) a petition under this Act has been presented to a District Court having jurisdiction by a party to marriage praying for a decree for a judicial separation under Section 10 or for a decree of divorce under Section 13; and
    (b) another petition under this Act has been presented thereafter by the other party to the marriage praying for a decree for judicial separation under Section 10 or for a decree of divorce under Section 13 on any ground, whether in the same District Court or in a different District Court, in the same State or in a different State,

    the petitions shall be dealt with as specified in sub-section (2).
(2) In a case where sub-section (1) applies, –
    (a) if the petitions are presented to the same District Court, both the petitions shall be tried and heard together by that District Court;
    (b) if the petition are presented to different District Courts, the petition presented later shall be transferred to the District Court in which the earlier petition was presented and both the petitions shall be heard and disposed of together by the district court in which the earlier petition was presented.

(3) In a case where clause (b) of sub-section (2) applies, the court or the Government, as the case may be, competent under the Code of Civil Procedure, 5 of 1908 to transfer any suit or proceeding from this District Court in which the later petition has been presented to the district court in which the earlier petition is pending, shall exercise its powers to transfer such later petition as if it had been empowered so to do under the said Code.

21-B. Special provision relating to trial and disposal of petitions under the Act –

(1) The trial of a petition under this Act, shall, so far as is practicable consistently with the interests of justice in respect of the trial, be continued from day to day until its conclusion unless the Court finds the adjournment of the trial beyond the following day to be necessary for reasons to be recorded.
(2) Every petition under this Act shall be tried as expeditiously as possible, and endeavour shall be made to conclude the trial within six months from the date of service of notice of the petition on the respondent.
(3) Every appeal under this Act shall be heard as expeditiously as possible, and endeavour shall be made to conclude the hearing within three months from the date of service of notice of appeal on the respondent.

21.-C. Documentary evidence – Notwithstanding anything in any enactment to the contrary, no document shall be inadmissible in evidence in any proceeding at the trial of a petition under this Act on the ground that it is not duly stamped or registered.

22. Proceedings to be in camera and may not be printed or published –

(1) Every proceedings under this Act shall be conducted in camera and it shall not be lawful for any person to print or publish any matter in relation to any such proceeding except a judgment of the High Court or of the Supreme Court printed or published with the previous permission of the Court.
(2) If any person prints or publishes any matter in contravention of the provisions contained in sub-section (1), he shall be punishable with fine which may extend to one thousand rupees.

23. Decree in proceedings –

(1) In any proceeding under this Act, whether defended or not, if the Court is satisfied that –
 (a) any of the grounds for granting relief exists and the petitioner except in cases where the relief is sought by him on the grounds specified in sub-clause (a), sub-clause (b) and sub-clause (c) of clause (ii) of Section 5 is not any way taking advantage of his or her own wrong or disability for the purpose of such relief, and
 (b) where the ground of the petition is the ground specified in clause (i) of sub-section (1) of Section 13, the petitioner has not in any manner been accessory to or connived at or condoned the act or acts complained of, or where the ground or the petition is cruelty the petitioner has not in any manner condoned the cruelty, and
 (bb) when a divorce is sought on the ground of mutual consent, such consent has not been obtained by force, fraud or undue influence, and
 (c) the petition not being a petition presented under section 11 is not presented or prosecuted in collusion with the respondent, and
 (d) there has not been any unnecessary or improper delay in instituting the proceeding, and
 (e) there is no other legal ground why relief should not be granted, then, and in such a case, but not otherwise, the court shall decree such relief accordingly.

(2) Before proceeding to grant any relief under this Act, it shall be the duty of the Court in the first instance, in every case where it is possible so to do consistently with the nature and circumstances of the case, to make every endeavour to bring about a reconciliation between the parties:

Provided that nothing contained in this sub-section shall apply to any proceeding wherein relief is sought on any of the grounds specified in clause (ii), clause (iii), clause (iv), clause (v), clause (vi) or clause (vii), of sub-section (1) of Section 13.

(3) For the purpose of aiding the Court in bringing about such reconciliation, the court may, if the parties so desire or if the Court thinks it just and proper so to do adjourn the proceedings for a reasonable period not exceeding fifteen days and refer the matter to any person named by the parties in this behalf or to any person nominated by the Court if the parties fail to name any person, with directions to report to the Court as to whether reconciliation can be and has been effected and the court shall in disposing of the proceeding have due regard to the report.

(4) In every case where a marriage is dissolved by a decree of divorce, the court passing the decree shall give a copy thereof free of cost to each of the parties.

23-A. Relief for respondent in divorce and other proceedings – In any proceedings for divorce or judicial separation or restitution of conjugal rights, the respondent may not only oppose the relief sought on the ground of petitioner's adultery, cruelty or desertion, but also make a counter-claim for any relief under this Act on that ground; and if the petitioner's adultery, cruelty or desertion is proved, the Court may give to the respondent any relief under this Act to which he or she would have been entitled if he or she had presented a petition seeking such relief on that ground.

24. Maintenance pendente lite and expenses of proceedings – Where in any proceeding under this Act it appears to the Court that either the wife or the husband, as the case may be, has no independent income sufficient for her or his support and the necessary expenses of the proceeding, it may, on the application of the wife or the husband, order the respondent to pay the petitioner the expenses of the proceeding such sum as, having regard to the petitioner's own income and the income of the respondent, it may seem to the Court to be reasonable.

25. Permanent alimony and maintenance –

(1) Any court exercising jurisdiction under this Act may, at the time of passing any decree or at any time subsequent thereto, on application made to it for the purposes by either the wife or the husband, as the case may be, order that the respondent shall pay to the applicant for her or his maintenance and support such gross sum or such monthly or periodical sum for a term not exceeding the life of the applicant as, having regard to the respondent's own income and other property of the applicant, the conduct of the parties and other circumstances of the case, it may seem to the Court to be just, and any such payment may be secured, if necessary, by a charge on the immoveable property of the respondent.

(2) If the Court is satisfied that there is a change in the circumstances of either party at any time after it has made an order under sub-section (1), it may at the instance of either party, vary, modify or rescind any such order in such manner as the court may deem just.

(3) If the Court is satisfied that the party in whose favour an order has been made under this Section has re-married or, if such party is the wife, that she has not remained chaste or if such party is the husband, that he has had sexual intercourse with any woman outside wedlock, it may at the instance of the other party vary, modify or rescind any such order in such manner as the court may deem just.

26. Custody of children – In any proceeding under this Act, the Court may, from time to time, pass such interim orders and make such provisions in the decree as it may deem just and proper with respect to the custody, maintenance and education of minor children, consistently with their wishes, wherever possible, and may, after the decree, upon application by petition for the purpose, make from time to time, all such orders and provisions with respect to the custody, maintenance and education of such children as might have been made by such decree or interim orders in case the proceedings for obtaining such decree were still pending, and the Court may also from time to time revoke, suspend or vary any such orders and provisions previously made.

27. Disposal of property – In any proceeding under this Act, the Court may make such provisions in the decree as it deems just and proper with respect to any property presented at or about the time of marriage, which may belong jointly to both the husband and the wife.

28. Appeals from decrees and orders –

(1) All decrees made by Court in any proceeding under this Act shall, subject to the provisions of sub-section (3), be appealable as decrees of the Court made in the exercise of its original civil jurisdiction and every such appeal shall lie to the Court to which appeals ordinarily lie from the decisions of the Court given in the exercise of its original civil jurisdiction.
(2) Orders made by the Court in any proceedings under this Act, under Section 25 or Section 26 shall, subject to the provisions of sub-section (3), be appealable if they are not interim orders and every such appeal shall lie to the Court to which appeals ordinarily lie from the decisions of the Court given in exercise of its original civil jurisdiction.
(3) There shall be no appeal under this section on subject of costs only.
(4) Every appeal under this section shall be preferred within a period of thirty days from the date of the decree or order.

28(A) Enforcement of decrees and orders – All decrees and orders made by the Court in any proceeding under this Act, shall be enforced in the like manner as the decrees and orders of the Court made in the exercise of its original civil jurisdiction for the time being enforced.

29. Savings –

(1) A marriage solemnized between Hindus before the commencement of this Act, which is otherwise valid, shall not be deemed to be invalid or ever to have been invalid by reason only of the fact that the parties thereto belonged to the same gotra or pravara or belonged to different religion, castes or sub-divisions of the same caste.
(2) Nothing contained in this Act shall be deemed to affect any right recognized by custom or conferred by any special enactment to obtain the dissolution of a Hindu Marriage, whether solemnized before or after the commencement of this Act.
(3) Nothing contained in this Act shall affect any proceeding under any law for the time being in force for declaring any marriage to be null and void or for annulling or dissolving any marriage or for judicial, separation pending at the commencement of this Act, and any such proceeding may be continued and determined as if this Act had not been passed.
(4) Nothing contained in this Act shall be deemed to effect the provisions contained in the Special Marriage Act, 1954 (43 of 1954), with respect to marriages between Hindus solemnized under that Act, whether before or after the commencement of this Act.

30. Repeals – (Repealed by the Repealing and Amendment Act, 1960 (58 of 1960), Sec. 2 and the First Schedule.)

Chapter 14

Kancha Ilaiah's *Why I Am Not a Hindu: A Sudra Critique of Hindutva Philosophy, Culture, and Political Economy*

Ilaiah is a social activist of the so-called Scheduled and Backward castes. Professor and head of the department of political science at Osmania University in India, Ilaiah has worked extensively against the *varṇa*, class, system in Hinduism and has labored for civil liberties and for the Dalitbaujans, who are, according to Ilaiah the "people and castes who form the exploited and suppressed majority" in India.[1] Ilaiah's writings address the discrimination that he faced growing up as a member of the Kuruma Golla caste, a caste of sheep-grazers. He challenges his readers to confront the significant cultural differences between his world and the *brāhmaṇa*-centric one that is put forth by many as archetypal Hinduism. He argues that it is incorrect to subsume the beliefs and practices of Dalitbaujans under the rubric of "Hindu." This is especially true, he argues, given that the Dalitbaujans were, and continue to be, oppressed under Hindu hegemony.

There are two selections here, "Introduction," and "Childhood Formations." The former frames his thinking and writing in the larger political context. In it he implored his readers to open their minds up to this new, provocative, and liberating perspective. In "Childhood Formations," Ilaiah offers readers an insight into the Dalitbaujan worldview in which he was raised and contrasts it with the dominant *brāhmaṇa* one.

Note

1 Kancha Ilaiah, *Why I Am Not a Hindu: A Sudra Critique of Hindutva Philosophy, Culture, and Political Economy.* Calcutta: Samya, 2005, p. ix.

Further reading

Bayly, Susan, *Caste, Society and Politics in India from the Eighteenth Century to the Modern Age.* Cambridge: Cambridge University Press, 1999.
Ganguly, Debjani, *Caste, Colonialism and Counter-modernity: Notes on a Postcolonial Hermeneutics of Caste.* London: Routledge, 2005.
Ilaiah, Kancha, "Towards the Dalitization of the Nation" in P. Chatterjee (ed.), *Wages of Freedom: Fifty Years of the Indian Nation-State.* Delhi: Oxford University Press, 1998.
Shah, Ghanshyam (ed.), *Dalit Identity and Politics.* New Delhi: Sage Publications, 2001.

Why I Am Not a Hindu

Introduction

I was born in a small South Indian Telangana village in the early fifties and grew up in the sixties. Our village had undergone all the turbulence of the freedom movement as they were part of a historical struggle known as the Telangana Armed Struggle. Perhaps as part of the first generation that was born and brought up in post-colonial India, an account of my childhood experiences would also be a narrative of the cultural contradictions that we are undergoing. Village India has not changed radically from my childhood days to the present. If there are any changes, the changes are marginal. Urban India is only an extension of village India. There is a cultural continuum between village India and urban India.

Suddenly, since about 1990 the word 'Hindutva' has begun to echo in our ears, day in and day out, as if everyone in India who is not a Muslim, a Christian or a Sikh is a Hindu. Suddenly I am being told that I am a Hindu. I am also told that my parents, relatives and the caste in which we were born and brought up are Hindu. This totally baffles me. In fact, the whole cultural milieu of the urban middle class – the newspapers that I read, the T.V. that I see – keeps assaulting me, morning and evening, forcing me to declare that I am a Hindu. Otherwise I am socially castigated and my environment is vitiated. Having been born in a Kurumaa (shepherd caste) family, I do not know how I can relate to the Hindu culture that is being projected through all kinds of advertising agencies. The government and the state themselves have become big advertising agencies. Moreover the Sangh Parivar harasses us every day by calling us Hindus. In fact, the very sight of its saffron-tilak culture is a harassment to us.

The question before me now is not whether I must treat Muslims or Christians or Sikhs as enemies, as the Hindutva school wants me to do. The question is What do we, the lower Sudras and Ati-Sudras (whom I also call Dalitbahujans), have to do with Hinduism or with Hindutva itself? I, indeed not only I, but all of us, the Dalitsbahujans of India, have never heard the word 'Hindu' – not as a word, nor as the name of a culture, nor as the name of a religion in our early childhood days. We heard about *Turukoollu* (Muslims), we heard about *Kirastaanapoollu* (Christians), we heard about *Baapanocllu* (Brahmins) and *Koomatoollu* (Baniyas) spoken of as people who were different from us. Among these four categories, the most different were the Baapanoollu and the Koomatoollu. There are at least some aspects of life common to us and the Turukoollu and Kirastaanapoollu. We all eat meat, we all touch each other. With the Turukoollu, we shared several other cultural relations. We both celebrated the *Peerila* festival. Many Turukoollu came with us to the fields. The only people with whom we had no relations, whatsoever, were the Baapanoollu and the Koomatoollu. But today we are suddenly being told that we have a common religious and cultural relationship with the Baapanoollu and the Koomatoollu. This is not merely surprising; it is shocking.

Experience As Framework

It is for this reason that I thought I should examine the socio-economic and cultural differences between us and the Brahmins, the Kshatriyas and the Baniyas. The socio-cultural differences would be better understood if we set them in the context of the different stages of our lives – childhood, family life, market relations, power relations, the Gods and Goddesses that we respect, death, and so on.

Excerpts from Kancha Ilaiah, *Why I Am Not a Hindu: A Sudra Critique of Hindutva Philosophy, Culture, and Political Economy.* Calcutta: Samya, 2005.

Narratives of personal experiences are the best contexts in which to compare and contrast these social forms. Personal experience brings out reality in a striking way. This method of examining socio-cultural and economic history is central to the social sciences; significantly, the method of narrating and deconstructing experiences has been used by feminists. Further, Indian Dalitbahujan thinkers like Mahatma Phule, Ambedkar and Periyar Ramasamy Naicker have also used this method. Instead of depending on Western methods, Phule, Ambedkar and Periyar spoke and wrote on the day–day experiences of the Dalitbahujan castes. I would argue that this is the only possible and indeed the most authentic way in which the deconstruction and reconstruction of history can take place.

Certainly there are problems in contrasting our own experiences, with the experiences of the 'others' – the Brahmins and the Baniyas. This becomes more problematic in a society like ours in which the Dalitbahujan castes and the Hindu castes (Brahmins, Baniyas, Kshatriyas and neo-Kshatriyas) may live in one village, but the Hindu 'upper' caste culture is completely closed to the Dalitbahujan castes. In this respect I am exceptionally fortunate because after I joined Osmania University I made many friends – particularly feminists – who came from Brahmin families. I had long discussions with many of them. My association with the Dalit and civil rights movements helped me understand both the cultures in some depth. I have, therefore, tried to analyse, critique and problematize many popular notions in this small book. Let me make it clear, however, that I am not writing this book to convince suspicious brahminical minds; I am writing this book for all those who have open minds. My request to Brahmin, Baniya and Neo-Kshatriya intellectuals is this: For about three thousand years you people learnt only how to teach and what to teach others – the Dalitbahujans. Now in your own interest and in the interest of this great country you must learn to listen and to read what we have to say. A people who refuse to listen to new questions and learn new answers will perish and not prosper.

CHAPTER I

Childhood Formations

Why I am not a Hindu

I was not born a Hindu for the simple reason that my parents did not know that they were Hindus. This does not mean that I was born as a Muslim, a Christian, a Buddhist, a Sikh or a Parsee. My illiterate parents, who lived in a remote South Indian village, did not know that they belonged to any religion at all. People belong to a religion only when they know that they are part of the people who worship that God, when they go to those temples and take part in the rituals and festivals of that religion. My parents had only one identity and that was their caste: they were Kurumaas. Their festivals were local, their Gods and Goddesses were local, and sometimes these were even specific to one village. No centralized religious symbols existed for them. This does not mean they were tribals. My ancestors took to life on the plains about 500 years ago. They were integrated into the village economy, paid taxes to the village panchayat or to the state administration in whichever form the administration required. As long as they were shepherds, they paid the tax in the form of *pullara* (levy for sheep-breeding). In the years before I was born, they shifted the occupation from sheep-breeding to agriculture and paid land rent to the local landlord and to the tehesil office. Even in my childhood I remember my parents paying taxes both for sheep-breeding and for cultivating the land. But they never paid a religion tax, something which all feudal religions normally demand. Not only that, they never went to a temple in which they could meet villagers belonging to all castes. In fact, there was no temple where all the village people could meet on a regular basis.

This does not mean that my family alone was excluded from the religious process because it was a family that could be ignored or neglected. Not so. For two generations my ancestors had been the caste heads. My mother and her mother-in-law (that is, my grandmother) were members of a leading family of the Kurumaa caste. In the village economy, Kurumaas, Gollaas, Goudaas, Kaapus, Shalaas, Chakaalies, Mangalies and Maadigaas, formed the majority in terms of numbers. The entire village economy was governed by the daily operations of these castes.

Cultural Differences Between the Hindus and US

Let me now narrate how my childhood experiences were shaped. The social structure in which I first became conscious of the world around me was a Kurumaa social structure. My playmates, friends, and of course relatives, all belonged to the Kurumaa caste. Occasionally the friendship circle extended to Goudaa boys and Kaapu boys. We were friends because we were all part of the cattle-breeding youth. We took the cattle to the field and then began playing *chirragone* (our cricket), *gooleelu* (a game with marbles), *dongaata* (a hide-and-seek game), and so on. Surprisingly, whenever a Goudaa friend came to my house he would eat with us, but sit slightly apart; when we went to Kaapu homes their parents would give us food but make us sit a little distance away. While eating we were not supposed to touch each other. But later we could play together and drink together from the rivers and streams. If we had carried our mid-day food to the cattle field, we sometimes attempted to touch each other's food, but suddenly the rules that our parents had fixed would make their appearance: we would speak insultingly of each other's castes and revert to eating separately. Within moments, however, we were together again.

Agriculture being a collective activity of the village, the cows, bulls and buffaloes were commonly owned as property of many castes. This was perhaps a meeting ground for the village economy. Thus when we went along with cattle, social life on the cattle ground became an inter-caste affair. But as we grew up, this life we had in common and the shared consciousness began splitting even in terms of production relations. I and my Kurumaa friends withdrew from common cattle-tending activities and were trained in sheep-breeding, which is a specific occupation of Kurumaas and Gollaas alone. At the same time, my Goudaa friends were drawn into their toddy-tapping and Kaapu friends into plough-driving.

The Caste Training of Boys

Each one of us was supposed to pick up the language of our particular caste. I was introduced to the specific language of sheep and sheep-rearing tasks. I was taught the different names of the sheep – *bolli gorre, pulla gorre, nalla gorre*, and so on. I learnt about the diseases that the sheep were afflicted with, how a delivery should be 'midwifed', how young ones should be handled, which was the best green grass for rearing the sheep. Goats required special treatment as they were to be fed with tree leaves (goats do not eat grass). We learnt what herbal medicines should be applied when sheep and goats are attacked by diseases. If the diseases were nerve-based ones, we learnt how to touch the sheep with a hot iron rod at the relevant place. One of the most difficult and expert tasks was shearing the wool from the sheep's body. The scissors had to be handled with such care that they cut close but did not cut the skin of the sheep. All this was part of the expertise of a sheep-rearer, and we were carefully educated in all these tasks.

The Caste Training of Girls

How were the girls being educated or brought up? Whether they were my sisters or others, the pattern of training was the same. The elder girls were taught, even as they turned three, how to handle a younger brother or sister. Holding a three-month-old baby requires skill and care, more so when the arms are those of a three-year-old girl. This was the most important help that the mother needed when she left home for sheep-related activities or agrarian work, early in the morning. Mothers would also teach them how to powder chillies, husk the paddy, sweep the home and clean the eating bowls.

Besides this, a Kurumaa woman teaches her daughter how to separate the wool from the thorns that stick to it and to prepare it for thread-making (*taadu wadakadam*). All these tasks are extremely skilled. By the age of twelve or thirteen (by the time she has reached puberty) a Kurumaa girl is supposed to know the basics of cooking. She begins with lighting the hearth and learning to handle it. A Kurumaa hearth consists of three stones with an extension on one side. On this extension stands a pot, known as a *vothu*, on which water is kept boiling. It requires a special skill not to upset or crack the vothu while cooking on the main hearth. Kurumaa girls also learn how to manage the *kuraadu* which is an important part of Kurumaa cooking (as it is of all other Dalitbahujan castes). A Kurumaa kuraadu consists of *ganji* (starch), drained from cooked rice and then left to ferment slightly until it gives out a mild sour smell. While cooking rice or *jawar*, the kuraadu is invariably used as the liquid (*yesaru*). Kuraadu is considered good for health, in addition, it drives away evil spirits from the food. Every girl is initiated into these skills at an early age. First of all, handling pots that are vulnerable to breaking requires care and cultivated skill. The only activity that was not taught to our girls which an urban girl might have to learn today was washing clothes. This is because washing was the washerman/woman's task. A girl born in a Chakaali (washerman) family learns all these activities in addition to learning how to wash various kinds of clothes.

The girls of these families are also taught, at a young age, how to seed the furrow by carefully dropping seed after seed. They are taught how to weed and even out extra growth in the crop; they learn how to plant with bent backs, moving backwards in the muddy land. Quite a lot of explanation by the adults go into the teaching of these activities to the young ones. Invariably there are experts in each activity who acquire a name for themselves. Young people are proud to emulate such experts.

Sexual Mores

Sexual behaviour and mores are also taught as part of family and peer group life. A girl listens to older women talking to each other in groups about 'disciplined' women and 'indisciplined' women; their sexual life-styles, their relations with husbands and others. A father does not hesitate to talk in front of his children about his approach to life or his relations with other women. More important than the father's is the mother's approach towards the children. A Dalitbahujan mother trains her children as a hen trains the chickens. She takes the children along with her to the fields, and sets them very small tasks in the field. While walking to the fields she often shares her problems with the children, particularly with the girls. It is not unconventional for her to talk to them about every aspect of her life.

If any Dalitbahujan woman has a relationship with a man who is not her husband, the relationship does not remain a secret. The entire *waada* discusses it. Even the children of that family come to know about it. Particularly when the father and mother quarrel, every aspect of life becomes public. No quarrel hides inside the house. For the children the house is a place of pleasure and of pain but it is all in the open. Male children learn about women and about sex in the company of their friends, in the cattle-rearing grounds or sheep-feeding fields. All kind of sexual trials take place in the fields. The 'bad' and 'good' of life are learnt at quite an early stage. Each one of these practices are discussed in terms of its morality and immorality. But this morality and immorality is not based on a divine order or divine edict. It is discussed in terms of the harmony of the families.

Caste Language

Caste language is structured by its own grammar. It is a flexible and alert grammar, designed for production-based communication. Though it has developed without the help of writing, it is no less sophisticated than 'standard' brahminical Telugu. Children's experience of language begins with fixing the names of things – birds, animals, trees, insects, everything that is around them. Every tree, every insect, every living and non-living being bears a name. Many of these things do not have words for them in 'standard' brahminical language. Brahminical language does not understand our ways of making-up new names. These names are not taught through the written word but are orally repeated in communication that is use-based.

Each caste is rooted in its productive process and its language is structured around that production. The Kurumaas have their own language as do the Lambadaas, the Erukalaas or the Koyaas. The Kurumaas not only know about the sheep, goats, trees, plants, and so on, they know the names of every instrument used in wool-making and blanket-weaving. A Goudaa knows the names of a whole range of instruments, skills and activities that are required for toddy-tapping. The specialization that one acquires in communicating these caste occupational tasks is as much or more sophisticated than that possessed by a Brahmin who utters the several names of his Gods while reciting a mantra. What is ironical is that the recitation of several names of one God or many Gods is construed as wisdom, whereas knowing the language of production and the names of productive tools is not recognized as knowledge. The Brahmins have defined knowledge in their own image. But the fact still remains that each caste has built a treasure house of its own knowledge and its own vocabulary. Each caste has built its own special consciousness. As individuals we acquire a consciousness of ourselves, our environment, our production and procreation. This consciousness has nothing to do with organized religion. Further, language here is a social instrument of communication and of the expression of that particular consciousness.

Our Gods and Consciousness

What further separated a Hindu from us was the nature of the consciousness of the other world, the divine and the spiritual. For children from our castes, *Jeja* (the concept of God) is introduced in the form of the moon. As children grow up, they also get acquainted with Pochamma, Polimeramma, Kattamaisamma, Kaatamaraju, Potaraju and other deities. Among Dalitbahujans, there is no concept of a temple in a definite place or form: Goddesses and Gods live in all forms and in all shapes and in different places. Every Dalitbahujan child learns at an early age about these Goddesses and Gods. The children are part of the caste congregations that take place during festivals such as Bonaalu, Chinna Panduga, Pedda Panduga, and so on. Every Dalitbahujan child learns at an early age that smallpox comes because Pochamma is angry. The rains are late because Polimeramma is angry. The village tank gets filled or does not get filled depending on the sympathies of Kattamaisamma. Crops are stolen by thieves because Potaraju is angry. For Kurumaas whether sheep and goats will prosper depends on the attitude of Beerappa, a caste-specific God.

Thus there are common village Dalitbahujan Gods and Goddesses and caste-specific Gods and Goddesses. Of course, for us the spirit exists, the *atma* (soul) exists, dead people come back to re-live in our own surroundings in the form of ghosts if they have not been fed well while they were alive. But there is no *swarga* (heaven) and there is no *naraka* (hell). All the dead live together somewhere in the skies. This consciousness has not yet taken the shape of an organized religion. The Dalitbahujan spirit in its essence is a non-Hindu spirit because the Hindu patriarchal Gods do not exist among us at all.

We knew nothing of Brahma, Vishnu or Eswara until we entered school. When we first heard about these figures they were as strange to us as Allah or Jehova or Jesus were. Even the name of Buddha, about whom we later learnt of as a mobilizer of

Dalitbahujans against brahminical ritualism, was not known to us.

The language that a Brahmin, Baniya or Kshatriya child learns to speak, all the social relationships that these children were supposed to be picking up as part of Hindu culture, were also alien to us. I have later learnt and observed that a Brahmin child is not taught to go to the field, or to look after the cattle or crops, but is supposed to go to school at an early age. Many of my Brahmin friends have told me that a traditional Brahmin father never touches his children. Child-rearing is essentially a wife's burden. Washing a child is seen as an unclean activity and hence it is left to the woman. While the mother looks after the child, does the so-called upper caste father help in the kitchen? No. The kitchen too is a dirty place which he should not enter. Thus the brahminical notion of purity and pollution operates even at home. In contrast to our skill-based vocabulary they learn words like Veda, *Ramayana, Mahabharatha*, Purana, and so on. At an early age they hear names like Brahma, Vishnu, Rama, Krishna, Lakshmi, Saraswathi, Sita and Savithri. Their children are told the stories of these Gods' heroism (mostly killing) and the Goddesses' femininity. Vishnu, for example, is shown to be reclining on a serpent, with Lakshmi at his feet, pressing them.

Even a Brahmin family might talk about Pochamma, Maisamma or Ellamma, but not with the same respect as they would about Brahma, Vishnu, Maheswara. For them Pochamma and Maisamma are 'Sudra' Goddesses and supposed to be powerful but in bad, negative ways. A Pochamma according to them does not demand the respect that Lakshmi or Saraswathi do, because Lakshmi and Saraswathi are supposed to be ideal wives of ideal husbands, whereas no one knows who Pochamma's husband is, any more than they can name Maisamma's husband. This is the reason why even if a Brahmin invokes the name of Pochamma when there is smallpox in his house, it is only in a derogatory way. No Brahmin or Baniya child bears the name of Pochamma, Maisamma or Ellamma. Whereas in our families Pochamma, Maisamma and Ellamma are revered names and we name our children after these Goddesses. In Dalitbahujan families Pochamma and Maisamma are Goddesses revered in their own capacity. It does not strike an average Dalitbahujan consciousness that these Goddesses do not have husbands and hence need to be spoken of derogatorily. This is because there are many widows in our villages who are highly respected, whose stature is based on their skills at work and their approach towards fellow human beings. I remember many young widows in my village who were the team leaders of agrarian operations as they were the most respected persons.

Between the people and Pochamma there is no priest. In fact there is no need of a priest at all in the worship of our Gods and Goddesses. Even as children we used to appeal to her to be kind to us so that we would not fall prey to smallpox or fever. As children we never thought that these Gods and Goddesses did not understand our language or that we needed a priest to talk to God in Sanskrit. Like our parents, who appealed to these Gods and Goddesses in our own language, we too appealed to them in our native tongues. We related ourselves to these Goddesses in a variety of ways.

A Hindu family is hierarchical. Girls must obey boys, children must obey elders. Sex and age are two determining and measuring rods of the status within the family. Children are trained not to get involved in production-related tasks, which Brahmins condemn as 'Sudra' tasks. Similarly their friendship with Dalitbahujan children is censured. 'Upper' castes speak of Dalitbahujans as 'ugly'. 'Sudra' is an abusive word; 'Chandala' is a much more abusive word. 'Upper' caste children are taught to live differently from Dalitbahujan children, just as they are taught to despise and dismiss them. Hindu inhumanism becomes part of their early formation; hating others – the Dalitbahujans – is a part of their consciousness.

Discussion of sexual behaviour is a taboo in Hindu families. Mothers are not supposed to talk to daughters about their sexual experiences. The father's atrocities against the mother cannot be discussed in Brahmin or Baniya families. But this is not so in our families. The father abuses the mother right in front of the children and the mother will pay back in the same coin then and there. The children are a witness to all that. In Hindu families the father can abuse the mother, but the mother is not supposed to retort. A wife is supposed to put up with all the atrocities that a husband commits against her; the more a wife puts up with the husband's atrocities the more she is appreciated. In addition, brahminical 'upper' castes teach their children about the need for *madi* (wearing a wet cloth on one's body to remain 'pure' while cooking). The cooking of food must take place according to ritual modes. Each girl is taught to cook according to the tastes of the male members. A dozen curries must be cooked as part of the Brahmin *bhojanam*. Every girl is supposed to know that every Brahmin male's good eating is equivalent to God's good eating. If there are poor Brahmins and even if they can only afford a few items, those items must be prepared in terms of their relation to God. In these families God and men are equated in many respects. But in our families the situation is very different.

Maadigaas and Hindus

Let us turn to the Maadigaas, whom the Hindutva school claims as part of their religion. My village used to have about 40 Maadigaa families who lived adjacent to the locality of the Goudaas. These two castes had no relations of touching with each other. In my village, I do not recall ever having had a childhood Maadigaa friend. The Maadigaa boys who were younger than me were *jeetaas* (farm servants). Their family and cultural relations were very similar to ours. But what was different was that from childhood they were taught to be always fearfully obedient, addressing the young and the old of the so-called upper castes as *ayya baanchan*. While they were jeetas, at the age of five, they were supposed to look after the cattle and the buffaloes and watch the crops. Their childhood was much tougher than ours. But in certain areas they were far more skilled and intelligent. They knew how to skin dead cattle, convert the skin into soft and smooth leather and transform the leather into farm instruments and shoes. Their skill in playing the *dappu* (a special percussion instrument) was far beyond that of any one of us. Maadigaa boys and girls were taught, right from childhood, and as a matter of their daily survival, to be humble before the landlord, Brahmin and Koomati.

The same is true of the Chakaali and Mangali children. At home they live as equals, eating, drinking and smoking together. They are equals from childhood onwards. The father and the mother teach children these things as part of their education. Equality and morality are not two different entities for parents and children. They teach the children that 'they must shiver and shake before the "upper" caste master'. This is not because the Maadigaa, Chakaali and Mangali parents have great respect or real love for the 'upper' caste landlord, the Brahmin or the Baniya, but because there is always the fear of losing their jobs. They will say, 'My son, be careful with that bastard, pretend to be very obedient, otherwise that rascal will hit us in our stomachs.' The child pretends to be obedient as Gandhi pretended to be poor. But a pretence that starts at an early age becomes part of a person's behaviour during a lifetime. Fear of the 'upper' caste *dora* is gradually internalized. Every Dalitbahujan family that teaches children about equality at home also teaches them about hierarchical life in society for the simple reason that otherwise terrible atrocities may follow. Except for the fact that they are made untouchables, except for their appalling economic conditions, the Maadigaas are absolutely like the Kurumaas, the Goudaas and others. There is less religiosity among them than in any other castes. If the Kurumaas, Goudaas, Kapuus and Shalaas have seven or eight Goddesses and Gods, the Maadigaas have one or two. They play the dappu for every occasion, but in a total participatory way they celebrate only the festival of Ellamma who is their *kuladevataa* (caste Goddess). For them even hell and heaven do not exist. Each day, earning the food for that day is at the heart of their life struggle. A day without food is hell and a day with food, heaven.

Among all these castes what was unknown was reading the book, going to the temple, chanting prayers or doing the *sandhyaavandanam* (evening worship). The Bhagavad Gita is said to be a Hindu religious text. But that book was not supposed to enter our homes. Not only that, the Hindu religion and its Brahmin wisdom prohibited literacy to all of us. Till modern education and Ambedkar's theory of reservation created a small educated section among these castes, letter-learning was literally prohibited. This was a sure way of not letting the religious text enter our lives. In addition even the idol or *murthy*-based, priest or pujari-centred temple was prohibited to the young, the adult and the old from the Dalitbahujan castes. Today, though some 'lower' castes are allowed into temples they can never relate to that God or Goddess.

School Education

As the first generation in Dalitbahujan history to see a slate and a pencil, we jumped straight out of the jungle into school. Even there, what was there in common between the Hindus and us? The Brahmin-Baniya children are the privileged. They are better dressed and better fed. Though they are born in the same village, the children enter the school with different cultures. Our eating habits are not the same. For all Dalitbahujans good food means meat and fish. We enjoy it, we relish it. For Brahmin-Baniya boys and girls even a discussion about meat and fish makes them feel like vomiting. For Maadigaas and Muslims beef is an item to be relished; though for us it was prohibited, we never hated it as the Brahmin-Baniyas did. These differences are not the differences of individual tastes, they are differences created as part of our upbringing.

Our school teacher's attitude to each one of us depended on his own caste background. If he was a Brahmin he hated us and told us to our faces that it was because of the evil time – because of *kaliyuga*, that he was being forced to teach 'Sudras' like us. In his view we were good for nothing. That 'wise' teacher used to think of us as coming from *suudari* families (families of field hands). Working in the field in his view was dirty and unaesthetic. According to him only mad people would work in dirty, muddy fields. Today we realize it was good that we were muddy. We realize that mud is the birthplace of food and of the working people's ideas.

But who, according to the teachers, were the great ones? The children who came from Brahmin, Baniya and of course the 'upper' caste landlord families. These were the 'great' ones. Because they did not do dirty farm work, their faces were cleanly washed, their clothes were cleaner, their hair carefully oiled and combed. They came to school wearing chappals, whereas those who feed cattle and those who make chappals from the skin of the cattle do not have chappals to wear. These were the reasons why we were ignorant, ugly and unclean. It is not merely the teacher, even 'upper' caste school children think about Dalitbahujan children that way.

As we were growing up, stepping into higher classes, the text-books taught us stories which we had never heard in our families. The stories of Rama and Krishna, poems from the Puranas, the names of two epics called *Ramayana* and *Mahabharatha* occurred repeatedly. Right from early school up to college, our Telugu textbooks were packed with these Hindu stories. For Brahmin-Baniya students these were their childhood stories, very familiar not only in the story form but in the form of the Gods that they worshipped. Whenever they went to temples with their parents they saw the images of these *devataas*. The boys bore the names of these Gods; the girls the names of the Goddesses. I distinctly remember how alien all these names appeared to me. Many of the names were not known in my village. The name of Kalidasa was as alien to us as the name of Shakespeare. The only difference was that one appeared in Telugu textbooks while the other appeared in English textbooks. Perhaps for the Brahmin-Baniya students the situation was different. The language of textbooks was not the one that our communities spoke. Even the basic words were different. Textbook Telugu was Brahmin Telugu, whereas we were used to a production-based communicative Telugu. In a word, our alienation from the Telugu textbook was more or less the same as it was from the English textbook in terms of language and content. It is not merely a difference of dialect; there is difference in the very language itself.

To date I have not come across a Telugu textbook which is written in this production-based, communicative language. I have not come across a lesson on Pochamma, Potaraju, Kattamaisamma, Kaatamaraju or Beerappa. This is not because these Gods and Goddesses do not have narratives associated with them. Without such narratives they would never have survived for thousands of years among the people. If we listen to Dalitbahujan story-tellers telling these stories, they keep us spellbound. The simple reason is that no writer – and the majority of writers happen to be Brahmins – thought that these stories could be written down so that they could go into school and college textbooks. In their view the very names of our Goddesses and Gods are not worth mentioning.

No mainstream Telugu poet ever thought that going down to the people's culture means talking about these Goddesses and Gods too. No poet thought that what people talk about, discuss and communicate with each other every day makes poetry. Even poets and writers who were born in these Hindu families and later turned Communist, atheist or rationalist, they too never picked up the contents of our daily lives as their subjects. Ironically even the names of those revolutionary leaders sounded alien to us. For them, Yellaiah, Pullaiah, Buchaiah, Buchamma, Lachamma were names of the Other. And the Other need never become the subject of their writings or the centre of their narratives.

The purohits praised the Puranas and the Communist and rationalist writers wrote critiques of these Puranas. But nobody thought that we too have a soul and that that soul needs to be talked about. Nobody thought that there are Pochamma, Maisamma and Potaraju who need to be talked about too. Even the Communists and rationalists spoke and wrote in the language of the purohit himself. Their culture was basically Sanskritized; we were not part of that culture. For good or ill, no one talked about us. They never realized that our language is also a language, that it is understood by one and all in our communities; not to forget the fact that these communities are not small in number; they are made up of lakhs and crores whereas the Hindu 'upper' castes are few in number. If our parents had been conscious about the conspiracy of this silent violence, they would have simply inhaled all the Hindus as *nasham* (like they usually inhale tobacco powder). What was arrested and what was stifled was that consciousness. The consciousness of 'us' and of 'our' culture was never allowed to exercise our minds.

Childhood formations are important for a person – female or male – to become a full human being. But our childhoods were mutilated by constant abuse and by silence, and by a stunning silence at that. There was the conspiracy to suppress the formation of our consciousness. For hundreds of generations the violent stoppage of the entry of the written word into our homes and our lives nipped our consciousness in the very bud. Even after schools were opened to us because of independence or *swaraj*, a word which even today I fail to understand, the school teacher was against us, the textbook language was against us. Our homes have one culture and the schools have another culture. If our culture was Dalitbahujan, the culture of the school was Hindu. The gap between the two was enormous. There was no way in which one resembled the other. In fact these two cultures were poles apart.

What difference did it make to us whether we had an English textbook that talked about Milton's *Paradise Lost or Paradise Regained*, or Shakespeare's *Othello* or *Macbeth* or Wordsworth's poetry about nature in England, or a Telugu textbook which talked about Kalidasa's *Meghasandesham*, Bommera Potanna's *Bhagavatam*, or Nannaya and Tikkana's *Mahabharatham* except the fact that one textbook is written with twenty-six letters and the other in fifty-six letters? We do not share the contents of either; we do not find our lives reflected in their narratives. We cannot locate our family settings in them. In none of these books do we find words that are familiar to us. Without the help of a dictionary neither makes any sense to us. How does it make any difference to us whether it is Greek and Latin that are written in Roman letters or Sanskrit that is written in Telugu?

Right from school 'their' male children talked about 'their' initiation into the Hindu religion through the *upanayana*. From the day after the upanayana a white thread hangs around their bodies, and from then on they are known as twice-born, thus more pure and superior, whereas we always remain once-born. When we first heard about the upanayana, we too desired to wear such a thread. It is a different thing that many of us would have later thrown that thread into muddy waters as Basava did at the early age of twelve. But the fact is that at the age of seven or eight, if there had been an occasion when we became the focal point of the house and a priest came to initiate us into religion, we would have gained confidence. Not only that, when we learnt that in the Brahmin, Baniya and other 'upper' caste families, initiation into writing takes place at the age of four and that it is also a festive occasion, how much we resented it!

In the olden days, after such initiation, the so-called upper castes used to send their sons to *gurukulas* (brahminical schools). Now they send them to English-medium convent schools; the very schools that were hated by the same Hindus during the freedom struggle. Even in the 1990s Hindutva ideologues condemn such schools as 'anti-Hindutva' schools – of course, only to send their children into the same schools promptly after the upanayana. The Hindus condemn English, yet they send their children to English-medium schools. We have not yet acquired the consciousness to condemn the complete domination of Telugu-medium schools by the Hindu scriptures. Having had no alternative we send our children to schools that teach only the Puranas, or the epics in every textbook. This is a paradox, and we live with many such paradoxes.

When we were told that Hindu girls and boys were married even when they were children, we thought of these practices as familiar since child marriage was also part of our lives. But when we read in the textbooks that the girls whose husbands died must remain widows and have their heads shaved; that they were to be clad only in white, we found it strange. In our families, girls whose in-laws did not look after them well, got divorced very easily and within days second husbands were found for them. While marriages take place at home and are celebrated with one type of meal and drink, divorces also take place with food and drink. Seeking divorce from an irresponsible husband is as much a sanctioned social act as performing marriages. In my childhood, when I read about Savithri struggling against the death of her husband, because otherwise she would become a widow, I was very happy that our women do not have to struggle like her.

Similarly, when we read that Hindu women ought to die along with their dead husbands I was extremely happy that our women do not have to die like that. I was so glad that we do not belong to such a religion because if suddenly my father were to die my mother would not have to die also. If she so desired she could get me a stepfather. What about history textbooks and Telugu textbooks that told us story after story about women who committed *sati* but there was not a single lesson about our women who still lived after their husbands' deaths, who worked, brought up their children and got them married? There was not a single lesson about women who found it difficult to get a divorce and had to struggle hard to make that divorce actually take place. There was not a single lesson which talked about the parents who had to struggle hard to get their daughter married three times or four times because husband after husband turned out to be a bad person. Not a single textbook gave us moral lessons that there were brave parents who never wanted to let down their daughters. The textbook morality was different from our living morality.

In all these stories and lessons we read about ideal men and women and of cultures that were very different from ours. In the Hindu texts, a knowledgeable man was one who knows the Vedas, a courageous person was one who kills enemies – even if the enemies are friends and relatives. In the *Ramayana* and the *Mahabharatha*, knowledge and courage were defined in these terms. But in our real life a knowledgeable person is one who has knowledge of social functions – one who knows about sheep-breeding, agriculture, rope making; one who can diagnose the nature of the diseases of animals and human beings. A courageous person is one who can fight tigers, lions, snakes, wild bulls; who can travel deep into forests, swim the rivers and find the missing goats and sheep.

Hindu Ideals and Our Ideals

In Brahmin *waadas* and families, narratives about heroes and heroines do not exist within a human context. This is because Brahmin life is alienated from the kind of socioeconomic environment in which a real hero or a heroine can be constructed. Their social settings are the reading of *slokaas* or mantras with proficiency. The greatest achievement is learning the whole of the *Ramayana* or the *Mahabharatha* or the Bhagvad Gita by heart. Womanhood is discussed in terms of devotion to the husband and cooking with purity and pollution in mind. In fact brahminical culture eulogizes negative heroes and negative heroines. For example, Krishna who encourages one to kill one's own relatives is a hero. Arjuna who killed his relatives is a hero. In these narratives acquiring private property (the whole of the *Mahabharatha* is constructed around land becoming the private property of minorities, who are not involved in production) is idealized.

In 'Sudra' waadas it is just the opposite. There are a number of real-life situations from which ideal heroes and heroines emerge. Their daily working interaction with nature provides the scope for their formation. One who kills relatives, for whatever reason, and one who commits crimes, for whatever reason, becomes a crook. One who encourages killing is not a God but a devil worth condemning. A Pochamma did not become our heroine because she killed somebody, a Kattamaisamma did not become our heroine because she killed somebody; a Beerappa did not become our hero because he killed somebody. They became our heroines and heroes because they saved us from diseases, or from hunger, and so on. Hindu morality is just the opposite of our living morality. Take another example. An ideal woman in a Hindu text is one who does not eat and drink in the presence of older women and men of all ages. A woman is not supposed to smoke and drink even if the man is a chain-smoker and the worst drunkard. But in our homes no one talks badly about a woman who smokes or has a drink. All our women drink toddy or liquor along with our men. Our women smoke *chuttaas* (cigars made with leaves and tobacco) at home and in the fields. They try to be at least notionally equal to men in all respects.

Those who say that all of us are Hindus must tell us which morality is Hindu morality? Which values do they want to uphold as right values? The 'upper' caste Hindu unequal and inhuman cultural values or our cultural values? What is the ideal of society today? What shall we teach the children of today? Shall we teach them what has been taught by the Hindus or what the Dalitbahujan masses of this country want to learn? Who makes an ideal teacher?

Who becomes a good hero? One who produces varieties of crops, one who faces lions and tigers or one who kills the relatives and friends, simply because what 'upper' castes think is *dharma* and what others think is *adharma*? Where do we begin and where do we end? We must begin by creating our history and we must end by changing this very social fabric.

The Brahmin-Baniyas think that their non-productive ritualistic life is great and the Dalit-bahujan non-ritualistic working life is mean. This philosophical make-up moulds the child population of these two communities differently. The Brahmin-Baniya 'upper' caste children think that they are the greater race, and that they are better bred. All this was proclaimed so consistently that it went into our psyches as if it might be true. Thus Brahminism consolidated its own socio-cultural position in society. Since our parents have been denied education, which alone could have enabled them to assess their own position realistically, whatever social status the Brahmin, parading as an *ayyagaaru*, assigned to our parents, they passed on to us. Right from childhood, in spite of the fact that we had such great skills, we remained diffident. Once Brahminism had unnerved human beings who were so much mightier and powerful, the diffidence was passed on from generation to generation. The whole lot of us – the whole Dalitbahujan population – were made to see things upside down.

Brahmin-Baniya temples were not only far from us, but the Gods sitting and sleeping in those temples were basically set against us. There were Brahmin-Baniya houses within our villages, but the very same houses built up a culture inimical to ours. The Brahmin-Baniyas walked over the corpses of our culture. They were the gluttons while our parents were the poor starving people – producing everything for the Other's comfort. Their children were the most unskilled gluttons, whereas our children were the contributors to the national economy itself. Their notion of life was unworthy of life itself, but they repeatedly told our parents that we were the most useless people. Having gone through all these stages of life, having acquired the education that enabled us to see a wider world, when we reflect upon our childhood and its processes it is nothing but anger and anguish which keep burning in our hearts.

Chapter 15

Hindutva: Vinayak Damodar Savarkar and the Rise of Hindu Nationalism

> *Hindu Dharma of all shades and schools, lives and grows and has its being in the atmosphere of Hindu culture, and the Dharma of a Hindu being so completely identified with the land of the Hindus, this land to him is not only a Pitribhu but a Punyabhu, not only a fatherland but a holyland.*[1]

For Vinayak Damodar Savarkar (1833–1966), one of the most influential Hindu nationalists, being a Hindu meant orienting oneself towards India. With the goal of making India a Hindu, and not secular, state, Savarkar, born a Maharastran *brāhmaṇa*, sought to reclaim a holy land that he felt had been adulterated by Muslims and Christians and that they were not part of what he called Hindutva, Hindu-ness. Savarkar believed that Hindutva was a culture, and not merely a religion, that encompassed Jainism, Buddhism, Lingayats, and other traditions not typically categorized as Hindu. Savarkar identified the essence of Hindutva to be *sanskriti*, or concerning the Sanskrit language, and to be identifying with the Indian subcontinent. Additionally, he believed that these groups as well as the *varṇas*, shared a genetic stock whose origins could be found in the Aryans. Hindutva identity was thus both cultural and ethnic.

Savarkar had an adventurous life that took him to England in 1906 to become a barrister.[2] There he joined with others who had a revolutionary nationalist agenda and founded the Free India Society. He became politically active and, after his brother Babarao was arrested in India for his own political activity, Savarkar became even more radicalized. At this time he also met Gandhi, with whom he disagreed about the strategies to achieve independence. Savarkar sought violent means while, Gandhi, of course, did not. Gandhi's *Hind Swaraj* was written in response to trouble brought upon Savarkar and his cohort's violence.[3] After being arrested in 1910 for purportedly terrorist activities (Savarkar was an alleged gun smuggler), Savarkar was jailed for 14 years and released in 1924. It was during this time that his revolutionary drive to free India from the rule of the British morphed into Hindu nationalism. During his incarceration, Savarkar wrote his most influential work, *Hindutva: Who Is a*

Hindu?, a treatise that has achieved, and continues to achieve, foundational status for other extreme Hindu nationalists. In this text, published in 1923, Savarkar outlines his ideology of *Hindutva*. Sarvarkar's imaginative and controversial retelling of history was founded on a nostalgia for an unadulterated and pure India, excised of those who neither fit into the Hindutva culture nor were part of the Hindutva racial lineage. The group, moreover, that was least likely to fit this invented and idealized identity were Muslims and Christians, and Savarkar strove in his writings and activities to eliminate them from the Indian landscape. Violence, of course, was a legitimate strategy to achieve this goal. Savarkar subsequently played an important role in the Hindu Nationalist movement and eventually became the president of the Hindu-Mahā-Sabhā in 1937, a pre-independence right-wing Hindu political party.[4]

Savarkar's theories and imaginative retellings of history are part of a complex methodological challenge that revolves around defining the term Hinduism (or in Savarkar's case, Hindutva), and deriving its essential components.[5] Many passages in *Hindutva* are attempts at unifying ideas and peoples, all with the idea of achieving a Hindu India. The ideology espoused in Savarkar's text has been the axis for the Rāṣṭriya Svayam Sevak Saṅgh (RSS) (founded in 1925), the Viśva Hindu Pariṣad (VHP) (founded in 1964), and the Bharatīya Janata Party (BJP), India's Hindu nationalist political party (founded in 1951). In this text one finds passages retelling India's history, redefining Hindutva and Hinduism, as well as proposing that India become a Hindu nation.

Notes

1 Vinayak Damodar Savarkar, *Hindutva: Who Is a Hindu?* Bombay: Veer Savarkar Prakashan, 1923, p. 111.

2 Chetan Bhat, *Hindu Nationalism: Origins, Ideologies and Modern Myths.* Oxford: Berg, 2001, p. 81.

3 Bhat, *Hindu Nationalism*, p. 83.

4 Gavin Flood, *An Introduction to Hinduism.* Cambridge: Cambridge University Press, 1999, pp. 262–3.

5 For an overview of the attempts to define Hinduism, see Brian K. Pennington, *Was Hinduism Invented? Britons, Indians, and the Colonial Construction of Religion.* New York: Oxford University Press, 2005; and Heinrich von Stietencron, "Hinduism: On the Proper Use of a Deceptive Term" in G. Sontheimer and H. Kulke (eds.), *Hinduism Reconsidered.* Delhi: Manohar, 2001, pp. 32–53.

Further reading

Bhat, Chetan, *Hindu Nationalism: Origins, Ideologies and Modern Myths.* Oxford: Berg, 2001.

Flood, Gavin, *An Introduction to Hinduism.* Cambridge: Cambridge University Press, 1999.

Jaffrelot, Christophe, *The Hindu Nationalist Movement in India.* New York: Columbia University Press, 1996.

Ludden, David (ed.), *Making India Hindu.* Oxford: Oxford University Press, 2005.

Pennington, Brian K., *Was Hinduism Invented? Britons, Indians, and the Colonial Construction of Religion*. New York: Oxford University Press, 2005.
Ram-Prasad, C., "Contemporary Political Hinduism" in G. Flood (ed.), *A Blackwell Companion to Hinduism*. Oxford: Blackwell Publishing, 2003.
Sharma, Jyotirmaya, *Hindutva: Exploring the Idea of Hindu Nationalism*. Delhi: Penguin Books India, 2003.
Van der Veer, Peter, *Religious Nationalism: Hindus and Muslims in India*. Berkeley, CA: University of California Press, 1994.
von Stietencron, Heinrich, "Hinduism: On the Proper Use of a Deceptive Term" in G. Sontheimer and H. Kulke (eds.), *Hinduism Reconsidered*. Delhi: Manohar, 2001, pp. 32–53.
Zavos, John, *The Emergence of Hindu Nationalism in India*. Oxford: Oxford University Press, 2000.

Hindutva

Who is a Hindu?

The words Hindutva and Hinduism both of them being derived from the word Hindu, must necessarily be understood to refer to the whole of the Hindu people. Any definition of Hinduism that leaves out any important section of our people and forces them either to play false to their convictions or to go outside the pale of Hindutva stands self-condemned. Hinduism means the system of religious beliefs found common amongst the Hindu people. And the only way to find out what those religious beliefs of the Hindus are, i. e., what constitutes Hinduism, you must first define a Hindu. But forgetting this chief implication of the word, Hinduism which clearly presupposes an independent conception of a Hindu many people go about to determine the essential of Hinduism and finding none so satisfactory as to include, without overlapping all our Hindu communities, come to the desperate conclusion – which does not satisfy them either – that therefore those communities are not Hindus at all; not because the definition they had framed is open to the fault of exclusion but because those communities do not subject themselves to the required tenets which these gentlemen have thought it fit to lable as 'Hinduism'. This way of answering the question 'who is a Hindu' is really preposterous and has given rise to so much of bitterness amongst some of our brethren of Avaidik school of thought, the Sikh, the Jain, the Devsamaji and even our patriotic and progressive Aryasamajis.

'Who is a Hindu?' – he who is subject to the tenets of Hinduism. Very well. What is Hinduism? – those tenets to which the Hindus are subjected. This is very nearly arguing in a circle and can never lead to a satisfactory solution. Many of our friends who have been on this wrong track have come back to tell us 'there are no such people as Hindus at all!' If some Indian, as gifted as that Englishman who first coined the word Hinduism, coins a parallel word 'Englishism' and proceeds to find out the underlying unity of beliefs amongst the English people, gets disgusted with thousands of sects and societies from Jews to the Jacobins, from Trinity to Utility, and comes out to announce that 'there are no such people as the English at all,' he would not make himself more ridiculous than those who declare in cold print 'there is nothing as a Hindu people.' Any one who wants to see what a confusion of thought prevails on the point and how the failure to analyse separately the two terms Hindutva and Hinduism renders that confusion worst confounded may do well to go through the booklet 'Essentials of Hinduism' published by the enterprising 'Natesan and Co.'

Hinduism means the 'ism' of the Hindu; and as the word Hindu has been derived from the word Sindhu, the Indus, meaning primarily all the people who reside in the land that extends from Sindhu to Sindhu, Hinduism must necessarily mean the religion or the religions that are peculiar and native to this land and these people. If we are unable to reduce the different tenets and beliefs to a single system of religion then the only way would be to cease to maintain that Hinduism is a system and to say that it is a set of systems consistent with, or if you like, contradictory or even conflicting with, each other. But in no case can you advance this your failure to determine the meaning of Hinduism as a ground to doubt the existence of the Hindu nation itself, or worse still to commit a sacrilege in hurting the feelings of our Avaidik brethren and Vaidik Hindu brethren alike, by relegating any of them to the Non-Hindu pale.

The limits of this essay do not permit us to determine the nature or the essentials of

---

Excerpts from V. D. Savarkar, *Hindutva*. Bombay: S. S. Savarkar, 1969.

Hinduism or to try to discuss it at any great length. As we have shown above the enquiry into what is Hinduism can only begin after the question 'who is a Hindu?' is rightly answered determining the essentials of Hindutva; and as it is only with these essentials of Hindutva, which enable us to know who is a Hindu, that this our present enquiry is concerned, the discussion of Hinduism falls necessarily outside of our scope. We have to take cognizance of it only so far as it trespasses on the field of our special charge. Hinduism is a word that properly speaking should be applied to all the religious beliefs that the different communities of the Hindu people hold. But it is generally applied to that system of religion which the majority of the Hindu people follow. It is natural that a religion or a country or community should derive its name from the characteristic feature which is common to an overwhelming majority that constitutes or contributes to it. It is also convenient for easy reference or parlance. But a convenient term that is not only delusive but harmful and positively misleading should not any longer be allowed to blind our judgement. The majority of the Hindus subscribes to that system of religion which could fitly be described by the attribute that constitutes its special feature, as told by Shruti, Smriti and Puranas or Sanatan Dharma. They would not object if it even be called Vaidik Dharma. But besides these there are other Hindus who reject either partly or wholly, the authority – some of the Puranas, some of the Smritis and some of the Shrutis themselves. But if you identify the religion of the Hindus with the religion of the majority only and call it orthodox Hinduism, then the different heterodox communities being Hindus themselves rightly resent this usurpation of Hindutva by the majority as well as their unjustifiable exclusion. The religion of the minorities also requires a name. But if you call the so-called orthodox religion alone as Hinduism then naturally it follows that the religion of the so-called heterodox is not Hinduism. The next most fatal step being that, therefore, those sections are not Hindus at all!! But this inference seems as staggering even to those who had unwillingly given whole-hearted support to the premises which have made it logically inevitable that while hating to own it they hardly know to avoid arriving at it. And thus we find that while millions of our Sikhs, Jains, Lingayats, several Samajis and others would deeply resent to be told that they – whose fathers' fathers up to the tenth generation had the blood of Hindus in their veins – had suddenly ceased to be Hindu! – yet a section amongst them takes it most emphatically for granted that they had been faced with a choice that either they should consent to be a party to those customs and beliefs which they had in their puritanic or progressive zeal rejected as superstitions, or they should cease to belong to that race to which their forefathers belonged.

All this bitterness is mostly due to the wrong use of the word, Hinduism, to denote the religion of the majority only. Either the word should be restored to its proper significance to denote the religions of all Hindus or if you fail to do that it should be dropped altogether. The religion of the majority of the Hindus could be best denoted by the ancient accepted appellation, the Sanatan dharma or the Shruti-smriti-puranokta Dharma[1] or the Vaidik Dharma; while the religion of the remaining Hindus would continue to be denoted by their respective and accepted names Sikha Dharma or Arya Dharma or Jain Dharma or Buddha Dharma. Whenever the necessity of denoting these Dharmas as a whole arises then alone we may be justified in denoting them by the generic term Hindu Dharma or Hinduism. Thus there would be no loss either in clearness, or in conciseness but on the other hand a gain both in precision and unambiguity which by removing the cause of suspicion in our minor communities and resentment in the major one would once more unite us all Hindus under our ancient banner representing a common race and a common civilization.

The earliest records that we have got of the religious beliefs of any Indian community – not to speak of mankind itself – are the Vedas. The Vedic nation of the Saptasindhus was sub-divided into many a tribe and class. But although the majority then held a faith that we for simplicity call Vedic religion, yet it was not contributed to by an important minority of the Sindhus themselves. The Panees, the Dasas, the Vratyas[2] and many others from time to time seem to have either seceded from or never belonged to the orthodox church and yet racially and nationally they were conscious of being a people by themselves. There was such a thing as Vedic religion, but it could not even be identified with Sindhu Dharma; for the latter term, had it been coined, would have naturally meant the set of religions prevailing in Saptasindhu, othodox as well as heterodox. By a process of elimination and assimilation the race of the Sindhus at last grew into the race of Hindus, and the land of the Sindhus i. e. Sindhustan, into the land of the Hindus i. e. Hindusthan. While their orthodox and the heterodox schools of religions have, – having tested much, dared much and known much, – having subjected to the most searching examination possible till then, all that lay between the grandest and the tiniest, from the atom to the Atman – from the Paramanu to the Parabrahma, – having sounded the deepest secrets of thoughts and having soared to the highest altitudes of ecstasy, – given birth to a synthesis that sympathizes with all aspirants towards truth from the monist to the atheist. Truth was its goal, realization its method. It is neither Vedic nor non-Vedic, it is both. It is the veritable science of religion applied. This is Hindudharma – the conclusion of the conclusions arrived at by harmonizing the detailed experience of all the schools of religious thought-Vaidik, Sanatani, Jain, Baudda, Sikha or Devasamaji. Each one and every one of those systems or sects which are the direct descendants and developments of the religious beliefs Vaidik and non-Vaidik, that obtained in the land of the Saptasindhus or in the other unrecorded communities in other parts of India in the Vedic period, belongs to and is an integral part of Hindudharma.

Therefore the Vaidik or the Sanatan Dharma itself is merely a sect of Hinduism or Hindu Dharma, however overwhelming be the majority that contributes to its tenets. It was a definition of this Sanatan Dharma which the late Lokamanya Tilak framed in the famous verse.

‘प्रामाण्यबुद्धिर्वेदेषु साधनानामनेकता।
उपास्यानामनियम एतद्धर्मस्य लक्षणम्।।’

Belief in the Vedas, many means, no strict rule for worship – these are the features of the Hindu religion.

In a learned article that he had contributed to the Chitramaya jagat which bears the mark of his deep erudition and insight Lokmanya in an attempt to develop this more or less negative definition into a positive one, had clearly suggested that he had an eye not on Hindutva as such but only on what was popularly called Hindudharma, and had also admitted that it could hardly include in its sweep the Aryasamajis and other sects which nevertheless are racially and nationally Hindus of Hindus. That definition, excellent so far as it goes, is in fact not a definition of Hindudharma, much less of Hindutva but of Sanatan Dharma – the Shruti-Smriti-puranokta[3] sect, which being the most popular of all sects of Hindu Dharma was naturally but loosely mistaken for Hindu Dharma itself.

Thus Hindu Dharma being etymologically as well as actually and in its religious aspects only, (for Dharma is not merely religion) the religion of the Hindus, it necessarily partakes of all the essentials that characterize a Hindu. We have found that the first important essential qualification of a Hindu is that to him the land that extends from Sindhu to Sindhu is the Fatherland, (Pitribhu) the Motherland (Matribhu) the land of his patriarchs and forefathers. The system or set of religions which we call Hindu Dharma – Vaidik and Non-Vaidik – is as truly the offspring of this soil as the men whose thoughts they are or who ‘saw’ the Truth revealed in them. To Hindu Dharma with all its sects and systems this land, Sindhusthan, is the land of its revelation, the land of its birth on this human plane. As the Ganges, though flowing from the lotus feet of Vishnu himself, is even to the most orthodox devotee and mystic so far as human plane is concerned the daughter of the Himalayas, even so, this land is the birth-place – the Matribhu (motherland) and Pitribhu (fatherland) – of that Tatvajnana (philosophy) which in its religious aspect is signified as Hindu Dharma. The second most important essential of Hindutva is that a Hindu is a descendant of Hindu parents, claims to have the blood of the ancient Sindhu and the race that sprang from them in his veins. This also is true of the different schools of religion of the Hindus; for they too being either founded by or revealed to the Hindu sages, and seers are the moral and cultural and spiritual descendants and development of the Thought of Saptasindhus through the process of assimilation and elimination, as we are of their seed. Not only is Hindu Dharma the growth of the natural environments and of the thought of the Indus, but also of the Sanskriti or culture of the Hindus. The environmental frames in which its scenes, whether of the Vaidik period or of Bauddha, Jain or any extremely modern ones of Chaitanya, Chakradhar, Basava, Nanak, Dayananda or Raja Rammohan, are set, the technical terms and the language that furnished expression to its highest revelation and ecstasies, its mythology and its philosophy, the conceptions it controverted and the conceptions it adopted, have the indelible stamp of Hindu culture, of Hindu Sanskriti, impressed upon them. Hindu Dharma of all shades and schools, lives and grows and has its being in the atmosphere of Hindu culture, and the Dharma of a Hindu being so completely identified with the land of the Hindus, this land to him is not only a Pitribhu but a Punyabhu, not only a fatherland but a holyland

Yes, this Bharatbhumi, this Sindusthan, this land of ours that stretches from Sindhu to Sindhu is our Punyabhumi, for it was in this land that the Founders of our faith and the Seers to whom 'Veda' the Knowledge was revealed, from Vaidik seers to Dayananda, from Jina to Mahavir, from Buddha to Nagasen, from Nanak to Govind, from Banda to Basava, from Chakradhar to Chaitanya, from Ramdas to Rammohan, our Gurus and Godmen were born and bred. The very dust of its paths echoes the footfalls of our Prophets and Gurus. Sacred are its rivers, hallowed its groves, for it was either on their moonlit ghats or under their eventide long shadows, that the deepest problems of life, of man, soul and God, of Brahma and Maya, were debated and discussed by a Buddha or a Shankar. Ah! every hill and dell is instinct with memories of a Kapil or a Vyas, Shankar or Ramdas. Here Bhagirath rules, there Kurukshetra lies. Here Ramchandra made his first halt of an exile, there Janaki saw the golden deer and fondly pressed her lover to kill it. Here the divine Cowherd played on his flute that made every heart in Gokul dance in harmony as if in a hypnotized sleep. Here is Bodhi Vriksha, here the deer-park, here Mahaveer entered Nirvana. Here stood crowds of worshippers amongst whom Nanak sat and sang the Arati 'the sun & the moon are the lights in the plate of the sky![4] Here Gopichand the king took on vows of Gopichand the Jogi and with a bowl in his hand knocked at his sister's door for a handful of alms! Here the son of Bandabahadur was hacked to pieces before the eyes of his father and the young bleeding heart of the son thrust in the father's mouth for the fault of dying as a Hindu! Every stone here has a story of martyrdom to tell! Every inch of thy soil, O Mother! has been a sacrificial ground! Not only 'where the Krishnasar is found' but from Kasmir to Sinhar it is 'Land of sacrifice,' sanctified with a Jnana Yajna or an Atmaajna (self-sacrifice) so to every Hindu, from the Santal to the Sadhu this Bharata bhumi this Sindhusthan is at once a Pitribhu and a Punyabhu – fatherland and a holy land.

That is why in the case of some of our Mohammedan or Christian countrymen who had originally been forcibly converted to a non-Hindu religion and who consequently have inherited along with Hindus, a common Fatherland and a greater part of the wealth of a common culture – language, law, customs, folklore and history – are not and cannot be recognized as Hindus. For though Hindusthan to them is Fatherland as to any other Hindu yet it is not to them a Holyland too. Their holyland is far off in Arabia or Palestine. Their mythology and Godmen, ideas and heroes are not the children of this soil. Consequently their names and their outlook smack of a foreign origin. Their love is divided. Nay, if some of them be really believing what they profess to do, then there can be no choice – they must, to a man, set their Holyland above their Fatherland in their love and allegiance. That is but natural. We are not condemning nor are we lamenting. We are simply telling facts as they stand. We have tried to determine the essentials of Hindutva and in doing so we have discovered that the Bohras and such other Mohammedan or Christian communities possess all the essential qualifications of Hindutva but one and that is that they do not look upon India as their Holyland.

It is not a question of embracing any doctrine propounding any new theory of the interpretation of God, Soul and Man, for we honestly believe that the Hindu Thought – we are not speaking of any religion which is dogma – has exhausted the very possibilities of human speculation as to the nature of the Unknown – if not the Unknowable, or the nature of the relation between *that* and *thou*. Are you a monist – a monotheist – a pantheist – an atheist – an agnostic? Here is ample room, O soul! whatever thou art, to love and grow to thy fullest height and satisfaction in this Temple of temples, that stands on no personal foundation but on the broad and deep and strong foundation of Truth. Why goest then to fill thy little pitcher to wells far off, when thou standest on the banks of the crystal-streamed Ganges herself? Does not the blood in your veins, O brother, of our common forefathers cry aloud with the recollections of the dear old scenes and ties from which they were so cruelly snatched away at the point of the sword? Then come ye back to the fold of your brothers and sisters who with arms extended are standing at the open gate to welcome you – their long lost kith and kin. Where can you find more freedom of worship than in this land where a Charvak could preach atheism from the steps of the temple of Mahakal – more freedom of social organization than in the Hindu society where from the Patnas of Orissa to the Pandits of Benares, from the Santalas to the Sadhus, each can develop a distinct social type of polity or organize a new one? Verily whatever, could be found in the world is found here too. And if anything is not found here it could be found nowhere.[5] Ye, who by race, by blood, by culture, by nationality possess almost all the essentials of Hindutva and had been forcibly snatched out of our ancestral home by the hand of violence – ye, have only to render whole-hearted love to our common Mother and recognize her not only as Fatherland (Pitribhu) but even as a Holyland (punyabhu); and ye would be most welcome to the Hindu fold.

This is a choice which our countrymen and our old kith and kin, the Bohras, Khojas, Memons and other Mohammedan and Christian communities are free to make – a choice again which must be a choice of love. But as long as they are not minded thus, so long they cannot be recognized as Hindus. We are, it must be remembered, trying to analyse and determine the essentials of Hindutva as that word is actually understood to signify and would not be justified in straining it in its application to suit any pre-conceived notions or party convenience.

A Hindu, therefore, to sum up the conclusions arrived at, is he who looks upon the land that extends from Sindu to Sindu – from the Indus to the Seas, as the land of his forefathers – his Fatherland (Pitribhu), who inherits the blood of that race whose first discernible source could be traced to the Vedic Saptasindhus and which on its onward march, assimilating much that was incorporated and ennobling much that was assimilated, has come to be known as the Hindu people, who has inherited and claims as his own the culture of that race as expressed chiefly in their common classical language Sanskrit and represented by a common history, a common literature, art and architecture, law and jurisprudence, rites and rituals, ceremonies and sacraments, fairs and festivals; and who above all, addresses this land, this Sindhusthan as his Holyland (Punyabhu), as the land of his prophets and seers, of his godmen and gurus, the land of piety and pilgrimage. These are the essentials of Hindutva – a common nation (Rashtra), a common race (Jati) and a common civilization (Sanskriti). All these essentials could best be summed up by stating in brief that he is a Hindu to whom Sindhusthan is not only a Pitribhu but also a Punyabhu. For the first two essentials of Hindutva – nation and Jati – are clearly denoted and connoted by the word Pitrubhu while the third essential of Sanskriti is pre-eminently implied by the word Punyabhu, as it is precisely Sanskriti including sanskaras i.e. rites and rituals, ceremonies and sacraments, that makes a land a Holyland. To make the definition more handy, we may be allowed to compress it in a couplet: –

A Sindu Sindhu paryanta, Yasya Bharatbhumika

Pitribhuh Punyabhushchaiva sa vai Hinduriti smritah

आसिंधुसिंधुपर्यंता यस्य भारतभूमिका।
पितृभू: पुण्यभूश्चैव स वै हिंदुरिति स्मृतः॥

Hindus in Sindh

The rough analysis to which the conception of Hindutva was subjected in the foregoing pages has enabled us to frame a working definition embodying or rather indicating the salient essentials of it. It now remains to see how far this general definition can stand a detailed examination that could be best conducted by testing a few typical and some of the most different cases which have in fact made the necessity of a definition so badly felt. While developing it we have tried at each step to free it, so far as it is possible to do so in the case of so comprehensive and elusive a generalization as that, from the defect of being too wide. If we find in testing a few typical cases in the light of this definition that they all fit in well then we may be sure that it is free from the opposite defect of being too narrow. We have seen that it is not open to Ativyapti,[6] it remains to be seen whether it is not open to Avyapti [7] also.

The geographical divisions that obtain amongst the Hindus would, at a glance, be seen to harmonize well with the spirit of our definition. The fundamental basis of it is the land from Sindhu to Sindhu, and although many of our brethren, and especially those who had been the most undoubted descendants of the ancient Sindhus and who besides are the very people that to this day have never changed the ancient name either of their land or of their race, and are called to-day as five thousand years ago, Sindhi, the children of Sindhudesha, inhabit the other bank of the Indus; yet, as in the mention of a river the mention of both its banks is implied as a matter of course so that part of Sindh which constitutes the western bank of the Indus is a natural part of Sindhusthan and is covered by our definition. Secondly, accessories to the mainland are always known by the name of the latter. And thirdly, our Hindu people on that side of the Sindhu had throughout history looked upon this land of Bharatvarsha as their real Pitribhu as well as Punyabhu. They had never been guilty of matricide in attempting to set up the patch they inhabit as their only Pitribhu or only Punyabhu. On the other hand their Banaras and Kailas and Gangotri are our Banaras and Kailas and Gangotri. From the Vedic time they are a part integral of Bharatvarsha, Sindhushivisauveers are mentioned in Ramayan and Mahabharat as the rightful constituents of the great Hindu confederacy and commonwealth. They belong to our Rashtra, to our Jati and to our Sanskriti. Therefore they are Hindus and their case is well-covered by our definition.

But even if one rejects the contention that the ownership of a river does employ, unless otherwise stated, the ownership of both its banks yet the definition remains as sound as ever and applies to our Sindhi brethren on other grounds. For apart from the special case of our Sindhi brethren that inhabit the other side of the Indus, there are hundreds of thousands of Hindus who have settled in all parts of the world. A time may come when these our Hindu colonists, who even to-day are the dominating factor in trade, numbers, capacity and intellect in their respective lands, may come to own a whole country and form a separate state. But will this simple fact of residence in lands other than Hindusthan render one a non-Hindu? Certainly not; for the first essential of Hindutva is not that a man must not reside in lands outside India, but that wherever he or his descendants may happen to be he must recognize Sindhusthan as the land of his forefathers. Nay more; it is not a question of recognition either. If his ancestors came from India as Hindus he cannot help recognizing India as his Pitribhu. So this definition of Hindutva is compatible with any conceivable expansion of our Hindu people. Let our colonists continue unabated their labours of founding a Greater India, a Mahabharat to the best of their capacities and contribute all that is best in our civilization to the upbuilding of humanity. Let them enrich the people that inhabit the earth from Pole to Pole with their virtues and let them in return enrich their own country and race by imbibing all that is healthy and true wherever found. Hindutva does not clip the wings of the Himalayan eagles but only adds to their urge. So long as ye, O Hindus! look upon Hindusthan as the land of your forefathers and as the land of your prophets, and cherish the priceless heritage of their culture and their blood, so long nothing can stand in the way of your desire to expand. The only geographical limits of Hindutva are the limits of our earth!

So far as the racial aspect of our definition is concerned we cannot think of any exception that can seriously challenge its validity. Just as in England we find Iberians, Kelts, Angles, Saxons, Danes, Normans now fused, in spite of the racial restrictions on intermarriages, into one nation, so the ancient racial distinctions of Aryans, Kolarians, Dravidians and others even if they had ever been keen, can no longer be recognized. We have dealt with the point as exhaustively as necessary in the foregoing pages and pointed out that the Anulom and Pratilom systems recognized in our law-books bear indisputable testimony to the fact that a fusion sufficient to keep the flow of common blood through our body politic vigorous and fresh was even then an accomplished fact. Nature again broke the barriers where custom refused to pull them down in time. Bheemsen was neither the first nor the last of Aryans to make love to a Hidimba, nor the Brahmin lady the mother of Vyadhakarma, to whom we have referred already, was the only Aryan girl that took a fancy to a Vyadha youth. Out of a dozen Bhils or Kolis or even Santals, a youth or a girl may at times be picked up and dropped in a city school without any fear of being recognized as such either by a physical or by a moral test. The race that is born of the fusion, which on the whole is a healthy one, because gradual, of the Aryans, Kolarians, Dravidians and all those of our ancestors, whose blood we as a race inherit, is rightly called neither an Aryan, nor Kolarian, nor Dravidian – but the Hindu race; that is, that People who live as children of a common motherland, adoring a common holyland – the land that lies between the Sindhus. Therefore the Santals, Kolis, Bhils Panchamas, Namashudras and all other such tribes and classes are Hindus. This Sindhusthan is as emphatically, if not more emphatically, the land of their forefathers as of those of the so-called Aryans; they inherit the Hindu blood and the Hindu culture; and even those of them who have not as yet come fully under the influence of any orthodox Hindu sect, do still worship deities and saints and follow a religion however primitive, are still purely attached to this land, which therefore to them is not only a Fatherland but a Holyland.

There would have been no serious objection raised against the cultural aspect of Hindutva too, but for the unfortunate misunderstanding that owes its origin to the confusing similarity between the two terms Hindutva and Hinduism. We have tried already to draw a clear line of demarcation between the two conceptions and protested against the wrong use of the word Hinduism to denote the Sanatan Dharma alone. Hindutva is not identical with Hindu Dharma; nor is Hindu Dharma identical with Hinduism. This twofold mistake that identifies Hindutva with Hindu Dharma and both with Sanatani sect is justly resented by our non-Sanatani sects or religious systems and goads a small section of people amongst them – not to explode this mistaken notion, but unfortunately to commit another grave and suicidal mistake in the opposite direction and disown their Hindutva itself. We hope that our definition will leave no ground for any such bitterness of feelings on either side and based on truth as it is, would be acknowledged by all the fair-minded people throughout our Hindu society. But as in the general treatment of this question we could not take any notice of any special case we shall do so now. Let us first take the case of our Sikh brotherhood. No one could be so silly as to contest the statement that Sindusthan, Asindhu Sindhu Paryanta yasya Bharatbhumika,[8] is their Fatherland – the land that ever since the first extant records of the Vedic Period has been the land where their forefathers lived and loved and worshipped and prayed. Secondly, they most undoubtedly inherit the Hindu blood in their veins as much as any one in Madras or Bengal does Nay more, while we Hindus in Maharashtra or Bengal inherit the blood of the Aryans as well as of those other ancient people who inhabited this land, the Sikhs are the almost direct descendants of those ancient Sindhus and can claim to have drunk their being at the very fountain of this Ganges of our Hindu life before she had descended down to the plains, Thirdly, they have contributed to and therefore are the rightful co-partners in our Hindu culture, For Saraswati was a river in the Punjab before she became the Deified Image of Learning and Art. To this day, do millions of Hindus throughout Hindusthan join in the enchanted chorus with which the Sindhus, your forefathers, oh Sikhs, paid the tribute of a grateful people to, and extolled the glories of the River on whose banks the first seeds of our culture and civilization were sown and catching their Rigvedic accents sing 'Ambitame, Naditame, Devitame Saraswati;[9] the Vedas are theirs as they are ours, if not as a revelation yet as revered work that sings of the first giant struggles of man to tap the sources of nature. The first giant struggle of Light against the forces of darkness and ignorance, that had stolen and kept imprisoned the spirited waters and refused to allow the rays of Illumination touch man and rouse the soul in him. The story of the Sikhs, like any one of us must begin with the Vedas, pass on through the palaces of Ayodhya, witness the battlefield of Lanka, help Lahu to lay the foundation of Lahore and watch prince Sidhartha leave the confines of Kapilavastu and enter the caves to find some way out to lighten the sorrows of man. The Sikhs along with us bewail the fall of Prithviraj, share the fate of a conquered people and suffer together as Hindus. Millions of Sikh udasis, Nirmalas, the Gahangambhirs and the Sindhi. Sikhs adore the Sanskrit language not only as the language of their ancestors but as the sacred language of their land. While the rest cannot but own it as the tongue of their forefathers and as the Mother of Gurumukhi and Punjabi, which yet in its infancy is still sucking the milk of life at its breast. Lastly the land Asindhu Sindhuparyanta is not only the Pitribhu also the Punyabhu to the Sikhs. The land spread from the river, Sindhu, to the seas is not only the fatherland but also the holyland to the Sikhs. Guru Nanak and Guru Govind, Shri Banda and Ramsing were born and bred in Hindusthan; the lakes of Hindusthan are the lakes of nectar (Amritsar) and of freedom – (Muktasar); the land of Hindusthan is the land of prophets and prayer – Gurudvar and Gurughar. Really if any community in India is

Hindu beyond cavil or criticism it is our Sikh brotherhood in the Punjab, being almost the autochthonous dwellers of the Saptsindhu land and the direct descendants of the Sindhu or Hindu people. The Sikh of to-day is the Hindu of yesterday and the Hindu of to-day may be the Sikh of tomorrow. The change of a dress, or a custom, or a detail of daily life cannot change the blood or the seed, nor can efface and blot out history itself.

To the millions of our Sikh brethren their Hindutva is self-evident. The Sahajdhari, udasi, Nirmal, Gahangambhir and the Sindhi Sikhs are proud of being Hindus by race and by nationality. As their Gurus themselves had been the children of Hindus they would fail to understand if not resent any such attempt to class them as Non-Hindus. The Gurugrantha is read by the Sanatanis as well as by the Sikhs as a sacred work; both of them have fairs and festivals in common. The Sikhs of the Tatkhalsa sect also so far as the bulk of their population is concerned, are equally attached to their racial appellation and live amongst Hindus as Hindus. It cannot be but shocking to them to be told that they had suddenly ceased to be Hindus. Our racial Unity is so unchallenged and complete that inter-marriages are quite common amongst the Sikhs and Sanatanis.

The fact is that the protest that is at times raised by some leaders of our Sikh brotherhood against their being classed as Hindus would never have been heard if the term Hinduism was not allowed to get identical with Sanatanism. This confusion of ideas and the vagueness of expression resulting therefrom, are at the root of this fatal tendency that mars at times the cordial relations existing between our sister Hindu communities. We have tried to make it clear that Hindutva is not to be determined by any theological tests. Yet we must repeat it once more that the Sikhs are free to reject any or all things they dislike as superstitions in Sanatandharma, even the binding authority of the Vedas as a revelation. They thereby may cease to be Sanatanis, but cannot cease to be Hindus. Sikhs are Hindus in the sense of our definition of Hindutva and not in any religious sense whatever. Religiously they are Sikhs as Jains are Jains, Lingayats are Lingayats, Vaishnavas are Vaishnavas; but all of us racially and nationally and culturally are a polity and a people, one and indivisible, most fitly and from times immemorial called Hindus. No other word can express our racial oneness – not even Bharatiya can do that for reasons dealt with in the forgoing pages. Bharatiya indicates an Indian and expresses a larger generalization but cannot express racial unity of us Hindus. We are Sikhs, and Hindus and Bharatiyas. We are all three put together and none exclusively.

Another reason besides this fear of being identified with the followers of Sanatanpanth which added to the zeal of some of our Sikh brothers and made them insist on getting classed separately as non-Hindus, was a political one. This is not the place of entering into merits or demerits of special representation. The Sikhs were naturally anxious to guard the special interests of their community and if the Mohammedans could enjoy the privilege of a special and communal representation, we do not understand why any other important minority in India should not claim similar concession. But we feel that, that claim should not have been backed up by our Sikh brothers by an untenable and suicidal plea of being non-Hindus. Sikhs, to guard their own interests could have pressed for and succeeded in securing special and communal representation on the ground of being an important minority as our non-Brahmins and other communities have done without renouncing their birthright of Hindutva. Our Sikh brotherhood is certainly not a less important community than the Mohammedans – in fact to us Hindus they are more important than any non-Hindu community in India. The harm that a special and communal representation does is never so great as the harm done by the attitude of racial aloofness. Let the Sikhs, the Jains, the Lingayats, the non-Brahmins and even, for the matter of that, Brahmins press and fight for the right of special and communal representation, if they honestly look upon it as indispensable for their communal growth. For their growth is the growth of the whole Hindu-society. Even in ancient times our four main castes enjoyed a kind of special representation on communal basis in our councils of State as well as in local bodies. They could do that without refusing to get fused into the larger whole and incorporated into the wider generalization of Hindutva, let the Sikhs be classed as Sikhs religiously, but as Hindus racially and culturally.

The brave people placed their heads by hundreds under the executioner's axe rather than disown their Guru.[10] Will they disown their seed, forswear their fathers and sell their birthright for a mess of pottage? God forbid! Let our minorities remember that if strength lies in union, then in Hindutva lies the firmest and yet the dearest bond that can effect a real, lasting and powerful union of our people. You may fancy that it pays you to remain aloof for the passing hour, but it would do incalculable harm to this our ancient race and civilization as a whole – and especially to yourselves. Your interests are indissolubly bound with the interests of your other Hindu brethren. Whenever in the future as in the past a foreigner raises a sword against the Hindu civilization it is sure to strike you as deadly as any other Hindu community. Whenever in future as in the past the Hindus as a people come to their own and under a Shivaji or a Ranjit, a Ramchandra or a Dharma, an Ashoka or an Amoghwarsha feeling the quickening touch of life and activity mount the pinnacles of glory and greatness – that day would shed its lustre on you as well as on any other members of our Hindu commonwealth. So, brothers, be not lured by the immediate gains, partly or otherwise, nor be duped by misreadings and misinterpretations of history. I was once told by one who posing as a Granthi was nevertheless convicted for committing a dacoity in the house of a Brahmin to whom he owed money and whom he consequently murdered, that the Sikhs were not Hindus and that they could incur no guilt by killing a Brahmin as the sons of Govindsing were betrayed by a Brahmin cook. Fortunately there was another Sikh gentleman and a real Granthi and was recognized as such by all learned Sikhs who immediately contradicted and cornered him by several examples of Matidas and others, who had sheltered the Guru and proved true to the Sikhs even unto martyrdom. Was not Shivaji betrayed by his kith and kin and his grandson again by a Pisal who too was a Hindu? But did Shivaji or his nation disown their race and cease to be Hindus? Many of the Sikhs have acted treacherously first at the time of desertion of the heroic Banda, then again at the time of the last war of the Khalsa forces with the English. Guru Govindsing himself was deserted by a number of Sikhs in the very thick of the fight and it was this act of treacherous cowardice of these Sikhs which by forcing our lion-hearted Guru to try a desperate sortie gave occasion to that cursed Brahmin wretch to betray his two sons, If, therefore, for the crime of the latter we cease to be Hindus, then for the crime of the former we ought to cease to be Sikhs too!

This minority of the Hindus as well as the major communities of them did not fall from the skies as separate creations. They are an organic growth that has its roots embedded deep in a common land and in a common culture. You cannot pick up a lamb and by tying a Kachchha and Kripan[11] on it, make a lion of it! If the Guru succeeded in forming a band of martyrs and warriors he could do so because the race that produced him as well as that band was capable of being moulded thus. The lion's seed alone can breed lions. The flower cannot say 'I bloom and smell: surely I came out of the stalk alone – I have nothing to do with the roots!' No more can we deny our seed or our blood. As soon as you point at a Sikh who was true to his Guru you have automatically pointed at a Hindu who was true to the Guru for before being a Sikh he was, and yet continues to be a Hindu. So long as our Sikh brethren are true to Sikhism they must of necessity continue to be Hindus for so long must this land, this Bharatbhumika from Sindhu to the seas, remain their Fatherland and their Holyland. It is by ceasing to be Sikhs alone that they may, perhaps, cease to be Hindus.

We have dealt at some length with this special case of our Sikh brotherhood as all those arguments and remarks would automatically test all similar cases of our other non-Vaidik sects and religions in the light of our definition. The Devsamajis for example are agnostics but Hindutva has little to do with agnosticism, or for the matter of that, atheism. The Devsamajis look on this land as the land of their forefathers, their fatherland as well as their Holyland and are therefore Hindus. Of course, it is superfluous, after all this to refer to our Aryasamaj. All the essentials of Hindutva hold good in their case so eminently that they are Hindus. We, in fact, are unable to hit upon any case that can lay our definition open to the charge of exclusiveness.

In one case alone it seems to offer some real difficulty. Is, for example, Sister Nivedita a Hindu? If ever an exception proves the rule it does so here. Our patriotic and noble-minded sister had adopted our land from Sindu to the seas as her Fatherland. She truly loved it as such, and had our nation been free, we would have been the first to bestow the right of citizenship on such loving souls. So the first essential may, to some extent, be said to hold good in her case. The second essential of common blood of Hindu parentage must, nevertheless and necessarily, be absent in such cases as these. The sacrament of marriage with a Hindu which really fuses and is universally admitted to do so, two beings into one may be said to remove this disqualification. But although this second essential failed, either way to hold good in her case, the third important qualification of Hindutva did entitle her to be recognized as a Hindu. For she had adopted our culture and come to adore our land as her Holyland. She *felt*, she was a Hindu and that is, apart from all technicalities, the real and the most important test. But we must not forget that we have to determine the essentials of Hindutva in the sense in which the word is actually used by an overwhelming majority of people. And therefore we must say that any convert of non-Hindu parentage to Hindutva can be a Hindu, if *bona fide*, he or she adopts our land as his or her country and marries a Hindu, thus coming to love our land as a real Fatherland, and adopts our culture and thus adores our land as the Punyabhu. The children of such a union as that would, other things being equal, be most emphatically Hindus. We are not authorized to go further.

But by coming to believe into the tenets of any sects of the Hindus a foreign convert may be recognized as a Sanatani, or a Sikh, or a Jain; and as these religions being founded by or revealed to Hindus, go by the name of Hindudharma the convert too, may be religiously called a Hindu. But it must be understood that a religious or cultural convert possesses only one of the three essentials of Hindutva and it is owing to this disqualification that people generally do not recognize as a Hindu any one and every one who subscribes to the religious beliefs of our race. So deep our feeling of gratitude is towards a Sister Nivedita or an Annie Besant for the services they rendered to the cause of our Motherland and our culture, so soft-hearted and sensitive to the touch of love as a race we Hindus are, that Sister Nivedita or a person like her who so completely identifies his or her being with the Being of our people, is almost unconsciously received in the Hindu fold. But it should be done as an exception to the rule. The rule itself must neither be too rigid nor too elastic. The several tests to which we have subjected our definition of Hindutva have, we believe, proved that it satisfies both these requirements and involves neither Avyapti nor Ativyapti; neither contraction nor expansion of the exact connotation.

Unique Natural Blessings to Hindusthan

So far we have not allowed any considerations of utility to prejudice our inquiry. But having come to its end it will not be out of place to see how far the attributes, which we found to be the essentials of Hindutva, contribute towards the strength, cohesion, and progress of our people. Do these essentials constitute a foundation so broad, so deep, so strong that basing upon it the Hindu people can build a future which can face and repel the attacks of all the adverse winds that blow; or does the Hindu race stand on feet of clay?

Some of the ancient nations raised huge walls so as to convert a whole country into a fortified castle. To-day their walls are trodden to dust or are but scarcely discernible by a few scattered mounds here and there; while the people they were meant to protect are not discernible at all. Our ancient neighbours, the Chinese, laboured from generation to generation and raised a rampart, embracing the limits of an empire, so wide, so high, so strong, a wonder of the human world. That too, as all human wonders must, sank under its own weight. But behold the ramparts of Nature! Have they not, these Himalayas, been standing there as one whose desires are satisfied – so they seemed to the Vedic bard – so they seem to us to-day. These are *our* ramparts that have converted this vast continent into a cosy castle.

You take up buckets and fill your trenches with water and call it a moat. Behold, Varuna himself, with his one hand pushing continents aside, fills the gap by pouring seas on seas with the other! This Indian ocean with its bays and gulfs, is *our* moat.

These are our frontier lines bringing within our reach the advantages of an island as well as an insular country.

She is the richly endowed, daughter of God – this our Motherland. Her rivers are deep and perennial. Her land is yielding to plough and her fields loaded with golden harvests. Her necessaries of life are few and a genial nature yields them all almost for the asking. Rich in her fauna, rich in her flora, she knows she owes it all to the immediate source of light and heat – the sun. She covets not the icy lands; blessed be they and their frozen latitudes. If heat is at times 'enervating' here, cold is at times benumbing there. If cold induces manual labour, heat removes much of its very necessity. She takes more delight in quenched thirst than in the parched throat. Those who have not, let them delight in exerting to have. But those who have – may be allowed to derive pleasure from the very fact of having. Father Thames is free to work at feverish speed, wrapped in his icy sheets. She loves to visit her ghats and watch her boats gliding down the Ganges on her moonlit waters. With the plough, the peacocks, and lotus, the elephant and the Gita, she is willing to forego, if that must be, whatever advantage the colder latitudes enjoy. She knows she cannot have all her own way. Her gardens are green and shady, her granaries well-stocked, her waters crystal, her flowers scented, her fruits juicy and her herbs healing. Her brush is dipped in the colours of Dawn and her flute resonant with the music of Gokul. Verily Hind is the richly endowed daughter of God.

Neither the English nor the French with the exception of the Chinese and perhaps the Americans, no people are gifted with a land that can equal in natural strength and richness the land of Sindusthan. A country, a common home is the first important essential of a stable strong nationality; and as of all countries in the world our country can hardly be surpassed by any in its capacity to afford a soil so specially fitted for the growth of a great nation; we Hindus whose very first article of faith is the love we bear to the common Fatherland, have in that love the strongest talismanic tie that can bind close and keep a nation on firm and enthuse and enable it to accomplish things greater than ever.

The second essential of Hindutva puts the estimate of our latent powers of national cohesion and greatness yet higher. No country in the world with the exception of China again, is peopled by a race so homogeneous, yet so ancient and yet so strong both numerically and vitally. The Americans too, whom we found equally fortunate with us so far as excellent geographical basis of nationality is concerned, are decidedly left behind. Mohammedans are no race nor are the Christians.

They are a religious unit, yet neither a racial nor a national one. But we Hindus, if possible, are all the three put together, and live under our ancient and common roof. The numerical strength of our race is an asset that cannot be too highly prized.

And culture? The English and the Americans feel they are kith and kin because they possess a Shakespeare in common. But not only Kalidas or a Bhasa but, Oh Hindus! ye possess a Ramayan and Mahabharat in common – and the Vedas! One of the national songs the American children are taught to sing attempts to rouse their sense of eternal self-importance by pointing out to the hundred years twice told that stand behind their history. The Hindu counts his years not by centuries but by cycles – the Yuga and the Kalpa and amazed asks

रघुपतेः क्व गतोत्तरकोशला ।
यदुपतेः क्व गता मथुरापुरी !!

The Uttra Kosala of Raghupathi is nowhere to be seen, nor is Shri Krishna's city of Mathura.

He does not attempt to rouse the sense of self-importance so much as the sense of proportion which is Truth. And that has perhaps made him last longer than Ramses and Nebuchadnezzar. If a people that had no past has no future, then a people that had produced an unending galaxy of heroes and hero-worshippers and who are conscious of having fought with and vanquished the forces whose might struck Greece and Rome, the Pharaohs and the Incas, dead, have in their history a guarantee of their future greatness more assuring than any other people on earth yet possess.

But besides culture the tie of common holyland has at times proved stronger than the chains of a Motherland. Look at the Mohammedans. Mecca to them is a sterner reality than Delhi or Agra. Some of them do not make any secret of being bound to sacrifice all India if that be to the glory of Islam or could save the city of their prophet. Look at the Jews; neither centuries of prosperity nor sense of gratitude for the shelter they found, can make them more attached or even equally attached to the several countries they inhabit. Their love is, and must necessarily be divided between the land of their birth and the land of their Prophets. If the Zionists' dreams are ever realized – if Palestine becomes a Jewish State and it will gladden us almost as much as our Jewish friends – they, like the Mohammedans would naturally set the interests of their Holyland above those of their Motherland in America and Europe and in case of war between their adopted country and the Jewish State, would naturally sympathize with the latter, if indeed they do not bodily go over to it. History is too full of examples of such desertions to cite particulars. The crusades again, attest to the wonderful influence that a common holyland exercises over peoples widely separated in race, nationality and language, to bind and hold them together.

The ideal conditions, therefore, under which a nation can attain perfect solidarity and cohesion would, other things being equal, be found in the case of those people who inhabit the land they adore, the land of whose forefathers is also the land of their Gods and Angels, of Seers and Prophets; the scenes of whose history are also the scenes of their mythology.

The Hindus are about the only people who are blessed with these ideal conditions that are at the same time incentive to national solidarity, cohesion and greatness. Not even the Chinese are blessed thus. Only Arabia and Palestine, if ever the Jews can succeed in founding their state there, can be said to possess this unique advantage. But Arabia is incomparably poorer in the natural, cultural, historical, and numerical essentials of a great people; and even if the dreams of the Zionists are ever realized into a Palestine State still they too must be equally lacking in these.

England, France, Germany, Italy, Turkey proper, Persia, Japan, Afganistan, Egypt of to-day (for the old descendants of 'Punto' and their Egypt is dead long since), and other African states, Mexico, Peru, Chile (not to mention states and nations lesser than all these), though racially more or less homogeneous are yet less advantageously situated than we are in geographical, cultural, historical and numerical essentials, besides lacking the unique gift of a sanctified Motherland. Of the remaining nations, Russia in Europe, and United states in America, though geographically equally well-gifted with us, are yet poorer, in almost every other requisite of nationality. China alone of the present comity of nations is almost as richly gifted with the geographical, racial, cultural essentials as the Hindus are. Only in the possession of a common, a sacred and a perfect language, the Sanskrit, and a sanctified Motherland, we are so far as the essentials that contribute to national solidarity are concerned more fortunate.

Thus the actual essentials of Hindutva are, as this running sketch reveals, also the ideal essentials of nationality. If we would, we could build on this foundation of Hindutva a future greater than what any other people on earth can dream of, greater even than our own past; provided we are able to utilize our opportunities. For let our people remember that great combinations are the order of the day. The league of Nations, the alliances of powers Pan-Islamism, Pan-Slavism, Pan-Ethiopism, all little beings are seeking to get themselves incorporated into greater wholes, so as to be better-fitted for the struggle for existence and power. Those who are not naturally and historically blessed with numerical or geographical or racial advantages are seeking to share them with others. Woe to those who have them already as their birth-right and know them not; or worse, despise them! The nations of the world are desperately trying to find a place in this or that combination for aggression – can any one of you, Oh Hindus! whether Jain or Samaji or Sanatani or Sikh or any other subsection afford to cut yourselves off or fall out and destroy the ancient, the natural and the organic combination that already exists? – a combination that is bound not by any scraps of paper nor by the ties of exigencies alone, but by the ties of blood, birth and culture? Strengthen them if you can: pull down the barriers that have survived their utility, of castes and customs, of sects and sections: What of interdining? – but intermarriages between provinces and provinces, castes and castes, be encouraged where they do not exist. But where they already exist as between the Sikhs and Sanatanies, Jains and Vaishnayas, Lingayats and Non-Lingayats – suicidal be the hand that tries to cut the nuptial tie. Let the minorities remember they would be cutting the very branch on which they stand. Strengthen every tie that binds you to the main organism, whether of blood or language or common Motherland. Let this ancient and noble stream of Hindu blood flow from vein to vein, from Attock to Cuttack till at last the Hindu people get fused and welded into an indivisible whole, till our race gets consolidated and strong sharp as steel.

Just cast a glance at the past, then at the present: Pan-Islamism in Asia, the political Leagues in Europe, the Pan-Ethiopic movement in Africa and America – and then see, O Hindus, if your future is not entirely bound up with the future of India and the future of India is bound up in the last resort, with Hindu strength. We are trying our best, as we ought to do, to develop the consciousness of and a sense of attachment to the greater whole, whereby Hindus, Mohammedans, Parsis, Christians and Jews would feel as Indians first and every other thing afterwards. But whatever progress India may have made to that goal one thing remains almost axiomatically true – not only in India but everywhere in the world – that a nation requires a foundation to stand upon and the essence of the life of a nation is the life of that portion of its citizens whose interests and history and aspirations are most closely bound up with the land and who thus provide the real foundation to the structure of their national state. Take the case of Turkey. The young Turks after the revolution had to open their Parliament and military institutions to Armenians and Christians on a non-religious and secular basis. But when the war with Servia came the Christians and Armenians first wavered and then many a regiment consisting of them went bodily over to the Servians, who politically and racially and religiously were more closely bound up with them. Take the case of America; when the German war broke out she suddenly had to face the danger of desertions of her German citizens; while the Negro citizens there sympathize more with their brethren in Africa than with their white countrymen. American State, in the last resort, must stand or fall with the fortunes of its Anglo-Saxon constituents. So with the Hindus, they being the people, whose past, present and future are most closely bound with the soil of Hindusthan as Pitribhu, as Punyabhu, they constitute the foundation, the bedrock, the reserved forces of the Indian state. Therefore even from the point of Indian nationality, must ye, O Hindus, consolidate and strengthen Hindu nationality; not to give wanton offence to any of our non-Hindu compatriots, in fact to any one in the world but in just and urgent defence of our race and land; to render it impossible for others to betray her or to subject her to unprovoked attack by any of those 'Pan-isms' that are struggling forth from continent to continent. As long as other communities in India or in the world are not respectively planning India first or mankind first, but all are busy in organizing offensive and defensive alliances and combinations on entirely narrow racial or religious or national basis, so long, at least, so long O Hindus, strengthen if you can those subtle bonds that like nerve threads bind you in one organic social being. Those of you who in a fit suicidal try to cut off the most vital of those ties and dare to disown the name Hindu will find to their cost that in doing so they have cut themselves off from the very source of our racial life and strength.

The presence of only a few of these essentials of nationality which we have found to constitute Hindutva enabled little nations like Spain or Portugal to get themselves lionized in the world. But when all of those ideal conditions obtain here what is there in the human world that the Hindus cannot accomplish?

Thirty crores of people, with India for their basis of operation, for their Fatherland and for their Holyland with such a history behind them, bound together by ties of a common blood and common culture can dictate their terms to the whole world. A day will come when mankind will have to face the force.

Equally certain it is that whenever the Hindus come to hold such a position whence they could dictate terms to the whole world – those terms cannot be very different from the terms which Gita dictates or the Buddha lays down. A Hindu is most intensely so, when he ceases to be Hindu; and with a Shankar claims the whole earth for a Benares 'Waranasi Medini!' or with a Tukaram exclaims

'आमुचा स्वदेश । भुवनत्रयामध्यें वास ।'

'my country! Oh brothers, 'the limits of the Universe – there the frontiers of my country lie?'

Chapter 16

The Constitution of India

On November 26, 1949 the Constitution of India was passed by the Constituent Assembly of India and was instituted two months later on January 26, 1950. Work on it begin 3 years earlier after India obtained independence from the British on August 15, 1947. One of the greatest challenges faced by its authors was how to embrace the principles of a liberal democracy, given the long history of social inequality in Hinduism. The members of the Constituent Assembly were a group of leaders who were appointed by provincial assemblies, which were, in turn, elected by the people of India. Members like Dr B. R. Ambedkar, who was born as an untouchable and was regarded as the chief architect of the Constitution, sought ways to promote social change in India.

Many of these changes pertained to the long history of discrimination in India manifested in the *varṇa* system in Hinduism. Assembly members desired both to do away with the inequalities of the so-called "caste system" and to institute reparations for those who had been wronged. Many laws were also designed to protect women and children whose rights had only begun to be addressed in the institution of British laws.

These changes are evident in several passages included here. Articles 14–16 concerned the broad principles of equality while Article 17 abolished "untouchability." Yet Articles 19 and 25–28 centered on freedom of religion, and this, of course, includes segments of Hinduism that upheld the centrality of *varṇa*, class. Articles 29, 30, 46, 341–342, and 366 are focused on the rights of minority communities, in particular (in Article 46) the rights of the so-called "Scheduled Castes" and "Scheduled Tribes." The communities are moreover defined in Articles 341 and 342. The "Anglo-Indian," whose status was made even more complicated after 1947 was also defined in Article 366.

Further reading

Ambedkar, B. R., *States and Minorities: What Are Their Rights and How to Secure Them in the Constitution of Free India*. Hyderabad [India]: Baba Saheb Dr. Ambedkar Memorial Society, 1970.

Baird, Robert D. (ed.), *Religion and Law in Independent India*. New Delhi: Manohar, 2005.

Derrett, J. Duncan, *Religion and the State in India*. New York: The Free Press, 1968.

Galanter, Marc, *Competing Equalities: Law and the Backward Classes in India*. Delhi; New York: Oxford University Press, 1991.

Government of India, *Report on the Backward Castes Commission* (Comp. B. P. Mandal). Shmla: Manager Government of India Press, 1984.

Larson, Gerald, *India's Agony over Religion*. Albany, NY: SUNY Press, 1995.

Mahajan, Gurpreet, *Identities and Rights: Aspects of Liberal Democracy in India*. New York: Oxford University Press, 1998.

Saksena, K. P., *Human Rights and the Constitution: Vision and the Reality.* New Delhi: Gyan Publishing House, 2003.

Shabbir, Mohammad (ed.), *Ambedkar on Law, Constitution, and Social Justice*. Jaipur: Rawat Publications, 2005.

Smith, Donald Eugene, *India as a Secular State*. Princeton, NJ: Princeton University Press, 1963.

Smith, Donald Eugene (ed.), *South Asian Politics and Religion*. Princeton, NJ: Princeton University Press, 1963.

Verma, G. P., *Caste Reservation in India: Law and the Constitution*. Allahabad: Chugh, 1980.

Constitution of India

[. . .]

Right to Equality

14. Equality before law – The State shall not deny to any person equality before the law or the equal protection of the laws within the territory of India.

15. Prohibition of discrimination on grounds of religion, race, caste, sex or place of birth –

(1) The State shall not discriminate against any citizen on grounds only of religion, race, caste, sex, place of birth or any of them.

(2) No citizen shall, on grounds only of religion, race, caste, sex, place of birth or any of them, be subject to any disability, liability, restriction or condition with regard to –

- (*a*) access to shops, public restaurants, hotels and places of public entertainment; or
- (*b*) the use of wells, tanks, bathing ghats, roads and places of public resort maintained wholly or partly out of State funds or dedicated to the use of the general public.

(3) Nothing in this article shall prevent the State from making any special provision for women and children.

[(4) Nothing in this article or in clause (2) of Article 29 shall prevent the State from making any special provision for the advancement of any socially and educationally backward classes of citizens or for the Scheduled Castes and the Scheduled Tribes.]

[(5) Nothing in this article or in sub-clause (*g*) of clause (1) of Article 19 shall prevent the State from making any special provision, by law, for the advancement of any socially and educationally backward classes of citizens or for the Scheduled Castes or the Scheduled Tribes insofar as such special provisions relate to their admission to educational institutions including private educational institutions, whether aided or unaided by the State, other than the minority educational institutions referred to in clause (1) of Article 30.]

16. Equality of opportunity in matters of public employment –

(1) There shall be equality of opportunity for all citizens in matters relating to employment or appointment to any office under the State.

(2) No citizen shall, on grounds only of religion, race, caste, sex, descent, place of birth, residence or any of them, be ineligible for, or discriminated against in respect of, any employment or office under the State.

(3) Nothing in this article shall prevent Parliament from making any law prescribing, in regard to a class or classes of employment or appointment to an office under the Government of, or any local or other authority within, a State or Union territory, any requirement as to residence within that State or Union territory prior to such employment or appointment.

(4) Nothing in this article shall prevent the State from making any provision for the reservation of appointments or posts in favour of any backward class of citizens which, in the opinion of the State, is not adequately represented in the services under the State.

(4A) Nothing in this article shall prevent the State from making any provision for the reservation in matters of promotion, with consequential seniority, to any class or classes of posts in the services under the State in favour of the Scheduled Castes and the Scheduled Tribes which, in the opinion of the State, are not adequately represented in the services under the State.

(4B) Nothing in this article shall prevent the State from considering any unfilled vacancies of a year which are reserved for being filled up in that year in accordance with any provision for reservation made under clause (4) or clause (4A) as a separate class of vacancies to be filled up in

Excerpts from The Constitution of India.

any succeeding year or years and such class of vacancies shall not be considered together with the vacancies of the year in which they are being filled up for determining the ceiling of fifty per cent. reservation on total number of vacancies of that year.

(5) Nothing in this article shall affect the operation of any law which provides that the incumbent of an office in connection with the affairs of any religious or denominational institution or any member of the governing body thereof shall be a person professing a particular religion or belonging to a particular denomination.

17. Abolition of Untouchability – "Untouchability" is abolished and its practice in any form is forebidden. The enforcement of any disability rising out of "Untouchability" shall be an offence punishable in accordance with law.

[...]

Right to Freedom

19. Protection of certain rights regarding freedom of speech, etc –

(1) All citizens shall have the right –

(a) to freedom of speech and expression;

(b) to assemble peaceably and without arms;

(c) to form associations or unions;

(d) to move freely throughout the territory of India;

(e) to reside and settle in any part of the territory of India; and

* * * * *

(g) to practise any profession, or to carry on any occupation, trade or business.

(2) Nothing in sub-clause (a) of clause (1) shall affect the operation of any existing law, or prevent the State from making any law, in so far as such law imposes reasonable restrictions on the exercise of the right conferred by the said sub-clause in the interests of the sovereignty and integrity of India, the security of the State, friendly relations with foreign States, public order, decency or morality, or in relation to contempt of court, defamation or incitement to an offence.

(3) Nothing in sub-clause (b) of the said clause shall affect the operation of any existing law in so far as it imposes, or prevent the State from making any law imposing, in the interests of the sovereignty and integrity of India or public order, reasonable restrictions on the exercise of the right conferred by the said sub-clause.

(4) Nothing in sub-clause (c) of the said clause shall affect the operation of any existing law in so far as it imposes, or prevent the State from making any law imposing, in the interests of the sovereignty and integrity of India or public order or morality, reasonable restrictions on the exercise of the right conferred by the said sub-clause.

(5) Nothing in sub-clauses (d) and (e) of the said clause shall affect the operation of any existing law in so far as it imposes, or prevent the State from making any law imposing, reasonable restrictions on the exercise of any of the rights conferred by the said sub-clauses either in the interests of the general public or for the protection of the interests of any Scheduled Tribe.

(6) Nothing in sub-clause (g) of the said clause shall affect the operation of any existing law in so far as it imposes, or prevent the State from making any law imposing, in the interests of the general public, reasonable restrictions on the exercise of the right conferred by the said sub-clause, and, in particular, nothing in the said sub-clause shall affect the operation of any existing law in so far as it relates to, or prevent the State from making any law relating to, –

(i) the professional or technical qualifications necessary for practising any profession or carrying on any occupation, trade or business, or

(ii) the carrying on by the State, or by a corporation owned or controlled by the State, of any trade, business, industry or service, whether to the exclusion, complete or partial, of citizens or otherwise.

[...]

Right to Freedom of Religion

25. Freedom of conscience and free profession, practice and propagation of religion –

(1) Subject to public order, morality and health and to the other provisions of this Part, all persons are equally entitled to freedom of conscience and the right freely to profess, practise and propagate religion.
(2) Nothing in this article shall affect the operation of any existing law or prevent the State from making any law –

(a) regulating or restricting any economic, financial, political or other secular activity which may be associated with religious practice;
(b) providing for social welfare and reform or the throwing open of Hindu religious institutions of a public character to all classes and sections of Hindus.

Explanation I – The wearing and carrying of kirpans shall be deemed to be included in the profession of the Sikh religion.

Explanation II – In sub-clause (b) of clause (2), the reference to Hindus shall be construed as including a reference to persons professing the Sikh, Jaina or Buddhist religion, and the reference to Hindu religious institutions shall be construed accordingly.

26. Freedom to manage religious affairs – Subject to public order, morality and health, every religious denomination or any section thereof shall have the right –

(a) to establish and maintain institutions for religious and charitable purposes;
(b) to manage its own affairs in matters of religion;
(c) to own and acquire movable and immovable property; and
(d) to administer such property in accordance with law.

27. Freedom as to payment of taxes for promotion of any particular religion – No person shall be compelled to pay any taxes, the proceeds of which are specifically appropriated in payment of expenses for the promotion or maintenance of any particular religion or religious denomination.

28. Freedom as to attendance at religious instruction or religious worship in certain educational institutions –

(1) No religious instruction shall be provided in any educational institution wholly maintained out of State funds.
(2) Nothing in clause (1) shall apply to an educational institution which is administered by the State but has been established under any endowment or trust which requires that religious instruction shall be imparted in such institution.
(3) No person attending any educational institution recognised by the State or receiving aid out of State funds shall be required to take part in any religious instruction that may be imparted in such institution or to attend any religious worship that may be conducted in such institution or in any premises attached thereto unless such person or, if such person is a minor, his guardian has given his consent thereto.

Cultural and Educational Rights

29. Protection of interests of minorities –

(1) Any section of the citizens residing in the territory of India or any part thereof having a distinct language, script or culture of its own shall have the right to conserve the same.
(2) No citizen shall be denied admission into any educational institution maintained by the State or receiving aid out of State funds on grounds only of religion, race, caste, language or any of them.

30. Right of minorities to establish and administer educational institutions –

(1) All minorities, whether based on religion or language, shall have the right to establish

and administer educational institutions of their choice.

(1A) In making any law providing for the compulsory acquisition of any property of any educational institution established and administered by a minority, referred to in clause (1), the State shall ensure that the amount fixed by or determined under such law for the acquisition of such property is such as would not restrict or abrogate the right guaranteed under that clause.

(2) The State shall not, in granting aid to educational institutions, discriminate against any educational institution on the ground that it is under the management of a minority, whether based on religion or language.

[...]

46. Promotion of educational and economic interests of Scheduled Castes, Scheduled Tribes and other weaker sections – The State shall promote with special care the educational and economic interests of the weaker sections of the people, and, in particular, of the Scheduled Castes and the Scheduled Tribes, and shall protect them from social injustice and all forms of exploitation.

[...]

341. Scheduled Castes –

(1) The President may with respect to any State or Union territory, and where it is a State, after consultation with the Governor thereof, by public notification, specify the castes, races or tribes or parts of or groups within castes, races or tribes which shall for the purposes of this Constitution be deemed to be Scheduled Castes in relation to that State or Union territory, as the case may be.

(2) Parliament may by law include in or exclude from the list of Scheduled Castes specified in a notification issued under clause (1) any caste, race or tribe or part of or group within any caste, race or tribe, but save as aforesaid a notification issued under the said clause shall not be varied by any subsequent notification.

342. Scheduled Tribes –

(1) The President may with respect to any State or Union territory, and where it is a State, after consultation with the Governor thereof, by public notification, specify the tribes or tribal communities or part of or groups within tribes or tribal communities which shall for the purposes of this Constitution be deemed to be Scheduled Tribes in relation to that State or Union territory, as the case may be.

(2) Parliament may by law include in or exclude from the list of Scheduled Tribes specified in a notification issued under clause (1) any tribe or tribal community or part of or group within any tribe or tribal community, but save as aforesaid a notification issued under the said clause shall not be varied by any subsequent notification.

[...]

366. Definitions – In this Constitution, unless the context otherwise requires, the following expressions have the meanings hereby respectively assigned to them, that is to say–

(2) "an Anglo-Indian" means a person whose father or any of whose other male progenitors in the male line is or was of European descent but who is domiciled within the territory of India and is or was born within such territory of parents habitually resident therein and not established there for temporary purposes only;

(3) "article" means an article of this Constitution;

[...]

(24) "Scheduled Castes" means such castes, races or tribes or parts of or groups within such castes, races or tribes as are deemed under article 341 to be Scheduled Castes for the purposes of this Constitution;

(25) "Scheduled Tribes" means such tribes or tribal communities or parts of or groups within such tribes or tribal communities as are deemed under article 342 to be Scheduled Tribes for the purposes of this Constitution;

[...]

Index